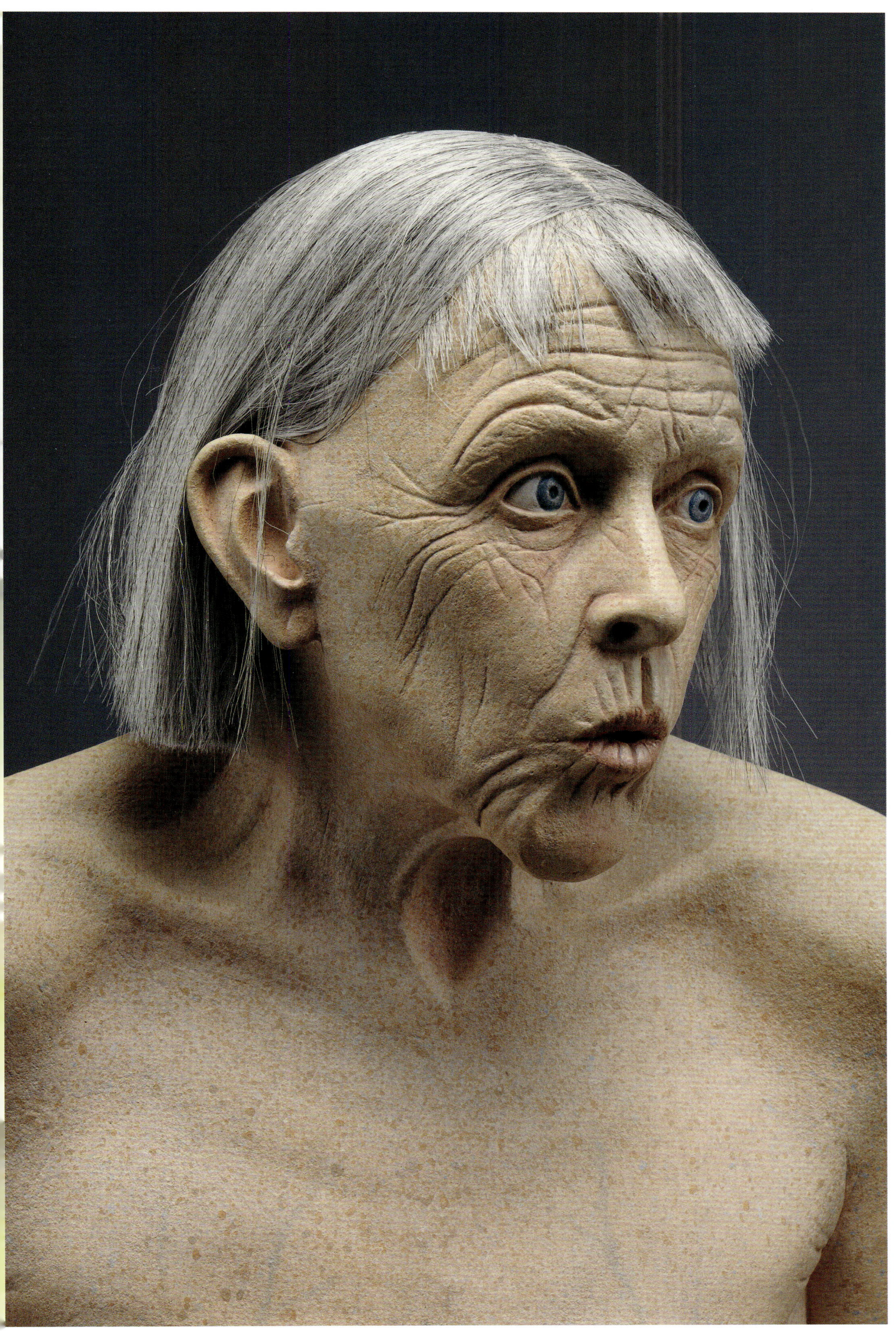

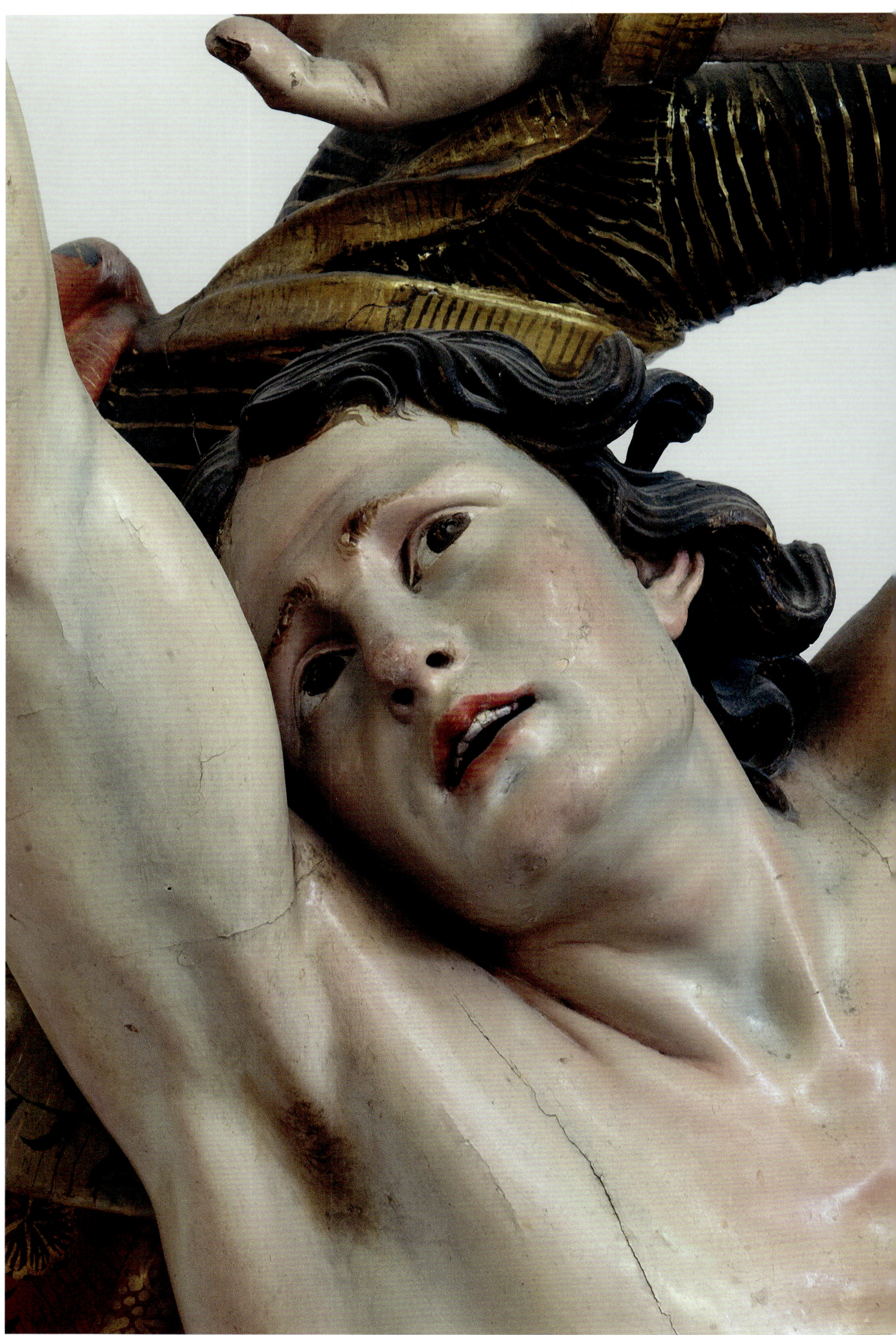

LIKE LIFE

SCULPTURE, COLOR, AND THE BODY

LUKE SYSON, SHEENA WAGSTAFF,
EMERSON BOWYER, AND BRINDA KUMAR
WITH CONTRIBUTIONS BY
BHARTI KHER, JEFF KOONS, ALISON SAAR,
HILLEL SCHWARTZ, MARINA WARNER, AND FRED WILSON

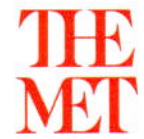

THE METROPOLITAN MUSEUM OF ART, NEW YORK
DISTRIBUTED BY YALE UNIVERSITY PRESS,
NEW HAVEN AND LONDON

This catalogue is published in conjunction with
"Like Life: Sculpture, Color, and the Body (1300–Now),"
on view at The Metropolitan Museum of Art, New York,
from March 21 through July 22, 2018.

The exhibition is supported in part by the
Jane and Robert Carroll Fund.
The catalogue is made possible by the
Mary C. and James W. Fosburgh Publications Fund.

PUBLISHED BY THE METROPOLITAN MUSEUM OF ART,
NEW YORK

Mark Polizzotti, Publisher and Editor in Chief
Gwen Roginsky, Associate Publisher and General
Manager of Publications
Peter Antony, Chief Production Manager
Michael Sittenfeld, Senior Managing Editor

Edited by Kamilah Foreman with Elizabeth Franzen,
Elizabeth C. Gordon, Marcie Muscat, and Elisa Urbanelli
Designed by Catherine Mills
Production by Christopher Zichello
Bibliography edited by Penny Jones
Image acquisitions and permissions by Elizabeth De Mase

Photographs of works in The Metropolitan Museum of
Art's collection are by Joseph Coscia, Jr., Juan Trujillo,
Peter Zeray, Paul H. Lachenauer, and Anna-Marie Kellen,
Imaging Department, The Metropolitan Museum of Art,
unless otherwise noted.
Additional photography credits appear on page 299.

Typeset in Benton Sans and Dante
Printed on 150 gsm Perigord
Separations by Professional Graphics, Inc., Rockford, Illinois
Printed and bound by Conti Tipocolor S.p.A., Florence

Front cover, top to bottom: Johan Gregor van der
Schardt, *Self-Portrait*, ca. 1573 (cat. 26, detail); Charles Ray,
Aluminum Girl, 2003 (cat. 5, detail); Reza Aramesh, *Action
105: An Israeli soldier points his gun at the Palestinian youth
asked to strip down as he stands at a military checkpoint along
the separation barrier at the entrance of Bethlehem, March
2006*, 2017 (cat. 45, detail). Back cover, top to bottom:
Mary Sibande, *Rubber Soul, Monument of Aspiration*, 2011
(cat. 79, detail); John Gibson, *The Tinted Venus*, ca. 1851–56
(cat. 8, detail); Ignaz Günther, *Christ at the Column*,
1754 (cat. 99, detail).

Page I: Tip Toland, *The Whistlers*, 2005 (cat. 27, detail).
Page II: Anton Maria Maragliano, *Saint Sebastian*, 1700
(cat. 105, detail). Page 75, top to bottom: Domenico
Poggini, *Bacchus*, 1554 (cat. 2, detail); Charles Ray,
Aluminum Girl, 2003 (cat. 5, detail); John Gibson, *The
Tinted Venus*, ca. 1851–56 (cat. 8, detail). Page 99, top to
bottom: George Segal, *Meyer Schapiro*, 1977 (cat. 29,
detail); Johan Gregor van der Schardt, *Self-Portrait*,
ca. 1573 (cat. 26, detail); attributed to Sri Ram Pal, *Raj
Kissen Mitter*, ca. 1840 (cat. 34, detail). Page 135, top to
bottom: Juan Martínez Montañés, *Saint John the Baptist*,
ca. 1620–30 (cat. 48, detail); John De Andrea, *Self-Portrait
with Sculpture*, 1980 (cat. 37, detail); Reza Aramesh, *Action
105: An Israeli soldier points his gun at the Palestinian youth
asked to strip down as he stands at a military checkpoint along
the separation barrier at the entrance of Bethlehem, March
2006*, 2017 (cat. 45, detail). Page 161, top to bottom:
Yayoi Kusama, *Phallic Girl*, 1967 (cat. 60, detail); Bertel
Thorvaldsen, *Lay Figure*, before 1806 (cat. 56, detail);
Corpus with Movable Arms, 1500–1510 (cat. 55, detail). Page
187, top to bottom: Mary Sibande, *Rubber Soul, Monument
of Aspiration*, 2011 (cat. 79, detail); Edgar Degas, cast by
A. A. Hébrard Foundry, Paris, *The Little Fourteen-Year-Old
Dancer*, ca. 1880, cast 1922 (cat. 68, detail); Nero Alberti,
Saint Roch, 1528 (cat. 70, detail). Page 211: Greer Lankton,
Rachel, 1986 (cat. 102, detail); Robert Gober, *Untitled*, 1990
(cat. 87, detail); Ignaz Günther, *Christ at the Column*, 1754
(cat. 99, detail). Page 253, top to bottom: Paul McCarthy,
Paul Dreaming, Vertical, Horizontal, 2005/12 (cat. 114, detail);
Alison Saar, *Strange Fruit*, 1995 (cat. 110, detail); Fontana
Workshop, *Anatomical Venus*, 1780–85 (cat. 115, detail)

The Metropolitan Museum of Art
1000 Fifth Avenue
New York, New York 10028
metmuseum.org

Distributed by
Yale University Press, New Haven and London
yalebooks.com/art
yalebooks.co.uk

Cataloguing-in-Publication Data is available
from the Library of Congress.
ISBN 978-1-58839-644-0

Since the dawn of history, humans have created three-dimensional renderings of the body, and for centuries artists strove for realism, often creating works of stunning verisimilitude. *Like Life: Sculpture, Color, and the Body* focuses on sculptures from the fourteenth century to the present, juxtaposing objects from different eras to test our preconceptions about the human form, the canon of Western art, and our understanding of ourselves. Of particular interest is the role of color in these objects, which for many artists heightened the realism of their work while enhancing its religious, cultural, or personal meaning.

Artists have also been keenly aware of how the presence or absence of color in figurative sculpture can unsettle and disarm observers. The often-uncanny quality of figurative sculpture forces us to wonder about how we imagine ourselves and others, and to think deeply about our common humanity. In considering such matters, *Like Life* presents a range of surprising and little-seen works by artists from El Greco, Anna Morandi Manzolini, Jean-Léon Gérôme, and Edgar Degas to Louise Bourgeois, Meret Oppenheim, Isa Genzken, Kiki Smith, and Yinka Shonibare MBE.

As an exploration of diverse aesthetic traditions from a variety of countries and time periods, *Like Life* fulfills several goals of our program at The Met Breuer in considering contemporary art in a larger historical and cultural context. Fittingly, this volume and the exhibition that it accompanies are the result of a fruitful collaboration between the Department of European Sculpture and Decorative Arts and the Department of Modern and Contemporary Art. I wish to thank Luke Syson, Iris and B. Gerald Cantor Chairman, European Sculpture and Decorative Arts; Sheena Wagstaff, Leonard A. Lauder Chairman, Modern and Contemporary Art; Brinda Kumar, Assistant Curator, Modern and Contemporary Art; Elyse Nelson, Research Associate, European Sculpture and Decorative Arts; and, at the Art Institute of Chicago, Emerson Bowyer, Searle Associate Curator of European Painting and Sculpture, for spearheading this project and opening our eyes to new ways of interpreting figurative sculpture.

We would like to express our appreciation to the Jane and Robert Carroll Fund, which helped to make the exhibition possible, and to the Mary C. and James W. Fosburgh Publications Fund, for its generous support of this catalogue.

To see the austerely monochromatic figure of Domenico Poggini's *Bacchus* (1554), the vivid colors of Pedro de Mena's *Ecce Homo* (ca. 1674–85), the disquieting presence of Alison Saar's *Strange Fruit* (1995), and the viscera of Marc Quinn's hematologic self-portrait (1999) is to be reminded of the power of art. As *Like Life* urges us to consider the relation between representation and reality, it also prompts self-reflection and a painstaking consideration of human nature.

DANIEL H. WEISS
President and CEO
The Metropolitan Museum of Art

ACKNOWLEDGMENTS

A publication and exhibition spanning many centuries and regions, *Like Life: Sculpture, Color, and the Body* is the result of years of collaboration across a number of institutions worldwide and departments at The Metropolitan Museum of Art. Our debts of gratitude accumulated along the way are correspondingly significant.

To begin, we wish to acknowledge the essential role played by Elyse Nelson, Research Associate, European Sculpture and Decorative Arts, who tirelessly contributed to the catalogue and logistical development of the show. Thomas P. Campbell, former director and CEO, and Jennifer R. Russell, former associate director, provided early support for an ambitious exhibition that would necessitate a productive collaboration between the Departments of European Sculpture and Decorative Arts and Modern and Contemporary Art. Throughout the making of this show, members of these departments provided incomparable insights and abiding support: from European Sculpture and Decorative Arts, Denise Allen, Kristen Hudson, Tommaso Mozzati, Erin E. Pick, Melinda Watt, and Denny Stone along with her team, Juan Stacey and Sam Winks; and from Modern and Contemporary Art, Ian Alteveer, Cynthia Hazen Polsky and Leon Polsky Curator of Contemporary Art Kelly Baum, Estrellita B. Brodsky Curator of Latin American Art Iria Candela, Leonard A. Lauder Curator of Modern Art Stephanie D'Alessandro, Clare Davies, Randall Griffey, Cynthia Iavarone and her team, Rebecca R. Kusovitsky, Christian Alexander Larsen, Sally K. McBride, Pari Stave, and Jacques and Natasha Gelman Curator Sabine Rewald. Our colleagues Paul and Jill Ruddock Senior Curator Barbara D. Boehm, Melanie Holcomb, and Michel David-Weill Curator in Charge C. Griffith Mann in Medieval Art and The Cloisters allowed a group of important sculptures within their permanent displays to travel to The Met Breuer. Our warmest thanks go as well to the members of other lending departments: our former colleague Carlos A. Picón and Seán Hemingway, Greek and Roman Art; Joyce Frank Menschel Curator in Charge Jeff L. Rosenheim and Beth Saunders, Photographs; Lawrence A. Fleischman Curator in Charge Sylvia Yount, Marica F. Vilcek Curator of American Decorative Arts Amelia Peck, and Marica F. Vilcek Curator of American Paintings and Sculpture Thayer Tolles, The American Wing; Sherman Fairchild Conservator in Charge Marjorie Shelley and Kraig Smith, Paper Conservation; and John Pope-Hennessy Chairman Keith Christiansen, European Paintings. In addition, Met curators James A. Doyle, Florence and Herbert Irving Curator of the Arts of South and Southeast Asia John Guy, Ronda Kasl, Ceil and Michael E. Pulitzer Curator in Charge Alisa LaGamma, Andrall E. Pearson Curator Joanne Pillsbury, and Brooke Russell Astor Curator of Chinese Art Zhixin Jason Sun shared their expertise and guidance throughout the research and planning phases. It was a pleasure and a privilege to work with our catalogue authors Hillel Schwartz and Marina Warner along with artists Bharti Kher, Jeff Koons, Alison Saar, and Fred Wilson, who have enriched this volume with their thoughtful interpretations of this complex material. We are deeply grateful for the Jane and Robert Carroll Fund, which provided essential support for the show, and for the Mary C. and James W. Fosburgh Publications Fund, which made this striking publication possible.

Collectors, scholars, and curators have in every case responded to queries and requests to lend with generosity and interest; their contributions are the lifeblood of the exhibition, while their questions, comments, and expertise have informed the project on every level. The names of the lenders may be found on pages XI–XII of this publication. We appreciate the time and behind-the-scenes efforts of countless collection managers, registrars, and art handlers, whose work is crucial to the successful realization of such special exhibitions. We are grateful to Coco Alcala, Maximiliano Araujo, Laurent Barrenechea, Maria Brucato, Mark Castro, Jorge Coll, Gabriella Gattobigio, Rachel Graham, Tom Henry, Daniel Aquino Lara, Alexandra Leckerling, Luca Leoncini, Marco Locchi, Anne Matheron, Johann Melchor, Thierry Morel, Gladys Elizabeth Palala, Claudia Quentin, Ana María Urruela de Quezada, Laurent Roturier, Raffaela Violini, Patricia Wengraf, and Alison Wright for their assistance with loans from the various churches, private collections, foundations, and institutions.

Among the many individuals who have assisted in the loan process at institutions are those with whom we have had extensive communication.

In North America: Christopher Bedford (Baltimore Museum of Art); Simone Wicha and Veronica Roberts (Blanton Museum of Art); Joanne Heyler (Broad Art Foundation); Salvador Salort-Pons, Alan Darr, Jill Shaw, and Michelle Smith (Detroit Institute of Arts); Mark A. Roglán and Anne Lenhart (Meadows Museum); Michele Marinelli and Jeremie Ryder (Morris Museum); Patrick Charpenel and Rocío Aranda-Alvarado (El Museo del Barrio); Sara Gabriela Baz Sánchez, Ariadna Patiño Guadarrama, and Ana Leticia García Rodríguez (Museo Nacional de Arte); Glenn D. Lowry and Ann Temkin (Museum of Modern Art); Earl A. Powell III, C. D. Dickerson III, Shannon Schuler, and Lisa MacDougall (National Gallery of Art); Marc Mayer (National Gallery of Canada); Julián Zugazagoitia and Leesa Fanning (Nelson-Atkins Museum of Art); Dan L. Monroe, Karina H. Corrigan, and Carla Galfano (Peabody Essex Museum); Steven High (John and Mable Ringling Museum of Art); Brian P. Kennedy and Halona Norton-Westbrook (Toledo Museum of Art); Thomas J. Loughman, Linda Roth, Mary Busick, and Paige Culbert (Wadsworth Atheneum Museum of Art); and Noah Khoshbin (Watermill Center Collection).

In Europe and the Middle East: Gunnar B. Kvaran (Astrup Fearnley Collection); Elisa Minchielli (Chiesa di Santa Croce); Christine Germain-Donnat and Romane Sarfati (Cité de la Céramique); Rosemary Harden (Fashion Museum Bath); Mario Guderzo (Fondazione Canova); Astrid Welter (Fondazione Prada); Eran Neuman and Neta Peretz (Israel Museum); Chris Gebel, Ingrid-Sibylle Hoffmann, Cornelia Ewigleben, and Olaf Siart (Landesmuseum Württemberg); Anna Domingo, Claire Treacy, and Simon Casey (Madame Tussauds); Daniel Birnbaum and Kristina von Knorring (Moderna Museet); Catherine Chevillot, Audrey d'Hendecourt, and Diane Tytgat (Musée Rodin); Antonio Falcone (Museo della Civiltà Romana); Marina Rovelli and Valeria Cafà (Museo Correr); María Bolaños and Ana Pérez (Museo Nacional de Escultura); Miguel Falomir Faus and Gracia Sánchez (Museo Nacional del Prado); Paola D'Agostino, Ilaria Ciseri, and Andrea Staderini (Museo Nazionale del Bargello); Gianni Iacovelli and Gaspare Baggieri (Museo Storico Nazionale dell'Arte Sanitaria); Alfred Weidinger and Jan Nicolaisen (Museum der Bildenden Künste); Matteo Capurro (Oratorio della Santissima Trinità); Giovanna Residori, Annalisa Managlia, and Cristina Nisi (Museo di Palazzo Poggi); Taco Dibbits, Frits Scholten, and Eefje van der Weijden (Rijksmuseum); Andreas Spillmann, Peter Wyer, Mylène Ruoss, and Maya Jucker (Schweizerisches Nationalmuseum); Benedek Varga and Balázs Lencz (Semmelweis Orvostörténeti Múzeum); Roland Enke and Stephan Koja (Staatliche Kunstsammlungen Dresden); Udo Kittelmann and Joachim Jäger (Staatliche Museen zu Berlin); Annette Johansen (Thorvaldsens Museum); Jayne Dunn, Alexandra Broekema, and Subhadra Das (University College London); Caroline Ducourau and Hélène Palouzié (Université de Montpellier); and Sandra Penketh, Godfrey Burke, Anne Fahy, and Janette Moran (Walker Art Gallery).

Considerable conservation work was undertaken at The Met in preparation for the exhibition by Linda Borsch, Giulia Chiostrini, Marijn Manuels, Sarah Scaturro, and Jack Soultanian, Jr., while Lucretia Kargère-Basco, Sherman Fairchild Conservator in Charge of Photograph Conservation Nora W. Kennedy, Rachel Mustalish, Shawn Digney-Peer, Sherman Fairchild Conservator in Charge of Objects Conservation Lisa Pilosi, and Kendra Roth offered valuable guidance on loans and installation. Glenn O. Petersen in The Costume Institute constructed a new tutu for Edgar Degas's *The Little Fourteen-Year-Old Dancer* on this occasion. We would also like to acknowledge the extensive conservation expertise that Lyndsey Bracken of Patina Art has shared with us.

Every detail in the making of this volume was overseen to the highest standards of production and design by our colleagues in the Publications and Editorial Department: Mark Polizzotti, Gwen Roginsky, Peter Antony, and Michael Sittenfeld. Kamilah Foreman carefully and sensitively edited the text with the assistance of Elizabeth Franzen, Elizabeth C. Gordon, Marcie Muscat, and Elisa Urbanelli; proofreaders Richard Gallin, Tanya Heinrich, and Richard Slovak; and bibliographer Penny Jones. Anne Rebecca Blood, who provided excellent counsel, and Sophia Bruneau facilitated the review process. This striking publication has been thoughtfully designed by Catherine Mills, with typesetting assistance by Tina Henderson, and at The Met, augmented by the production skill of Christopher Zichello and the tenacity of Elizabeth De Mase in securing images and permissions. Exceptional photographs of Met works were taken by Joseph Coscia, Jr., Juan Trujillo, Peter Zeray, Paul H. Lachenauer, Anna-Marie Kellen, and other members of Barbara J. Bridgers's team in the Imaging Department.

Special thanks are owed to Daniel H. Weiss, President and CEO, and Jeanette O'Keefe in the Office of the President. Quincy Houghton, Deputy Director for Exhibitions, was a supportive steward of the project, as was Carrie Rebora Barratt, Deputy Director for Collections and Administration. Sharon H. Cott, Martha Deese, Sophie Golub, Amy Desmond Lamberti, and Nicole Sussmane were instrumental in helping us prepare loan letters and exhibition-related documentation. Michael Langley, Brian Oliver Butterfield, Anna Rieger, and Daniel Koppich, under Emile Molin's direction, created an impeccable and imaginative design of the exhibition and graphics. The multivalent themes of the show were made accessible to a wide audience through various educational, digital, audio, and Live Arts programs. Many colleagues developed these initiatives, including Sandra Jackson-Dumont, Frederick P. and Sandra P. Rose Chairman of Education; Maricelle Robles; Marianna Siciliano; Limor Tomer; Elizabeth Perkins; Nina Diamond; Skyla Choi; Austin Fisher; Paul Caro; and Robin Schwalb. Kenneth Weine, Ann M. Bailis, Alexandra Kozlakowski, and Micol Spinazzi in Communications and Marketing extensively promoted the project to the public. Katy Uravitch managed every aspect of the exhibition's logistics, liaising between the numerous departments involved with ease. We thank her as well as Allison E. Barone, The Met Breuer's registrar under Aileen Chuk, Chief Registrar; Patrick John Paine, Robin C. Madray; and Tempris Small. We are also grateful to Taylor Miller and Deborah Gul Haffner in Construction and Facilities for their advice. In Development, Clyde B. Jones III, Jason Herrick, John Wielk, and Elizabeth A. Burke secured the necessary funds for the exhibition and publication.

LUKE SYSON
Iris and B. Gerald Cantor Chairman
European Sculpture and Decorative Arts
The Metropolitan Museum of Art

EMERSON BOWYER
Searle Associate Curator of
European Painting and Sculpture
Art Institute of Chicago

SHEENA WAGSTAFF
Leonard A. Lauder Chairman
Modern and Contemporary Art
The Metropolitan Museum of Art

BRINDA KUMAR
Assistant Curator
Modern and Contemporary Art
The Metropolitan Museum of Art

MUSEUMS AND PUBLIC INSTITUTIONS

Art Institute of Chicago
Astrup Fearnley Collection, Oslo
Baltimore Museum of Art
Bâtiment Historique de la Faculté de
    Médecine, Université de Montpellier
Blanton Museum of Art, University of
    Texas at Austin
Broad Art Foundation, Los Angeles
Chiesa di Santa Croce, Umbertide
Cité de la Céramique, Sèvres and Limoges
Detroit Institute of Arts
El Museo del Barrio, New York
Fashion Museum Bath
Fondazione Canova, Gipsoteca e Museo
    Antonio Canova, Possagno
Gemäldegalerie Alte Meister, Staatliche
    Kunstsammlungen Dresden
Glenstone Museum, Potomac, Maryland
Israel Museum, Jeruslaem
Landesmuseum Württemberg, Stuttgart
Madame Tussauds, London
Meadows Museum, Southern Methodist
    University, Dallas
Moderna Museet, Stockholm
Morris Museum, Morristown, New Jersey
Musée Rodin, Paris
Museo Correr, Musei Civici di Venezia, Venice
Museo Nacional de Arte, Instituto Nacional de
    Bellas Artes, Mexico City
Museo Nacional de Escultura, Valladolid
Museo Nacional del Prado, Madrid
Museo Nazionale del Bargello, Florence

Museo Storico Nazionale dell'Arte Sanitaria,
    Rome
Museum der Bildenden Künste, Leipzig
Museum of Modern Art, New York
National Gallery of Art, Washington, D.C.
National Gallery of Canada, Ottawa
Nelson-Atkins Museum of Art,
    Kansas City, Missouri
Neue Nationalgalerie, Staatliche Museen
    zu Berlin, Nationalgalerie
Oratorio della Santissima Trinità, Rapallo
Peabody Essex Museum, Salem,
    Massachusetts
Rijksmuseum, Amsterdam
John and Mable Ringling Museum of Art,
    State Art Museum of Florida, Florida State
    University, Sarasota
Schweizerisches Nationalmuseum, Zurich
Semmelweis Orvostörténeti Múzeum,
    Budapest
Sistema Museale di Ateneo—Museo di
    Palazzo Poggi, Alma Mater Studiorum,
    Università di Bologna
Thorvaldsens Museum, Copenhagen
Toledo Museum of Art, Ohio
University College London
Wadsworth Atheneum Museum of Art,
    Hartford, Connecticut
Walker Art Gallery, National Museums
    Liverpool
Watermill Center Collection, Water Mill,
    New York

LIKE LIFE

EMBODIED HISTORIES

SHEENA WAGSTAFF

> It is undeniable that from man, as from a perfect model,
> statues and pieces of sculpture...were first derived.
> GIORGIO VASARI
>
> The image of the human body remains the most directly comprehen-
> sible emblem. Across national traditions and limitations of education
> and language, the recognition of the attitudes, physiognomy, and
> gestic action of the body produces a space permanently open to
> philosophical plastic reflection.
> JEFF WALL

Like Life: Sculpture, Color, and the Body seizes on the unexpected consequences of the glorification of freestanding, white classical marble statuary—idealized and abstracted, mythic and heroic—as the epitome of fine art sculpture during the European Renaissance. The presumption of the original whiteness of Greek and Roman classical sculpture was, in fact, a misidentification: these white marble sculptures had originally been polychromed. This perception, which defined the Western artistic canon as it was created and sanctioned during the Renaissance, persisted well into the nineteenth century and notably inspired the eschewal of practices that could be seen as too real, especially the use of color to heighten the verisimilitude of the three-dimensionally rendered human figure. Yet realism has existed across cultures and time (from Egyptian funerary arts to Kamakura sculptures in Japan), often hand in hand with polychromy or other chromatic means.

In European aesthetics, however, the historical elevation of the monochromatic ideal makes a focus on figurative sculpture at the intersection of realism and color the starting point for us to reconsider a primary understanding of sculpture. Over time, this dominant Western aesthetic was refracted in myriad ways through artistic practices in and beyond Europe. Indeed, throughout art history, one increasingly encounters objects that manifest a shift in this perception: from the Renaissance onward, while certain modes of representation and the ideal (and idea) of mono-chromatic purity were perpetuated via the unquestioned primacy of white marble statuary, parallel practices remained. They were often seen in regional courtly and liturgical traditions or in the scientific, ethnographic, popular, or decorative-arts realms, where the potency of color and realistic depiction remained significant even as those objects were rarely considered fine art. The critical and public response to these challenges to the canon shifted significantly over a long period of time, notably from the nineteenth century, through the advent of modernism, alongside the development of new fields of art-historical inquiry and the breakdown of teleological art-historical discourse in the late twentieth century. One aim of this book is to question existing narratives of sculpture, foregrounding objects that both engage with the histories of classicism and contend with chromatic figuration: sculptural bodies rendered to evoke a sense of literal presence, like life.

For nearly half a century until 2016—when The Met publicly signaled a broader interpretation of the art-historical canon—the museum was identified with a distinctive letter *M* logo, adapted from the 1509 book *Divina proportione* by Italian mathematician Luca Pacioli. Modeled on Leonardo da Vinci's famous *Vitruvian Man*, which itself was based on the correlation of ideal human proportions with geometry described by the ancient Roman architect Vitruvius, the logo was rooted in ideas that saw the Renaissance of classical antiquity as the apotheosis of the canon and featured at its core an ideally proportioned man, who existed perceptually at the center of the world (figs. 1–3).

This sensibility, rooted in cultural classicism, was espoused by many Western museums, especially those that claim universalist ambitions in their encyclopedic scope, consciously endorsing the seminal thesis of Jacob Burckhardt's *The Civilization of the Renaissance in Italy* (1860). Burckhardt traced the cultural patterns of transition back to the early Renaissance, which had rediscovered classical principles and awakened the modern spirit in a new society that birthed the self-conscious individual, a human being who saw himself in the center of his own cosmos. This phenomenal cultural paradigm was visually epitomized by Leonardo, Michelangelo, and their contemporaries such as Domenico Poggini, all of whom dominated the definition of civilization for the next three hundred years. The fact that this new dawn of modernity was based on an illusion—the presumed whiteness of ancient sculpture—is as shocking a revelation as the tendentious definition of what constitutes a civilization. Burckhardt identified the source of the Italian Renaissance in the evolution of numerous microstates as a politically expedient means to resist the centralized control of both the church and the state. "In them," he argues, "for the first time we detect the modern political spirit of Europe, surrendered freely to its own instincts, often displaying the worst features of an unbridled egotism, outraging every right, and killing every germ of a healthier culture."[1] One could argue that such an "egotism" also

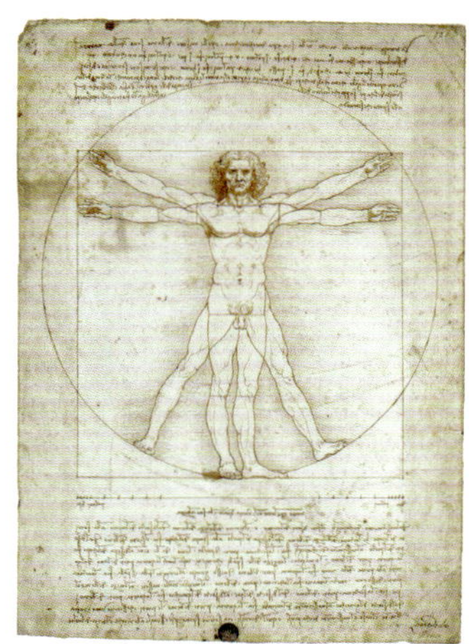

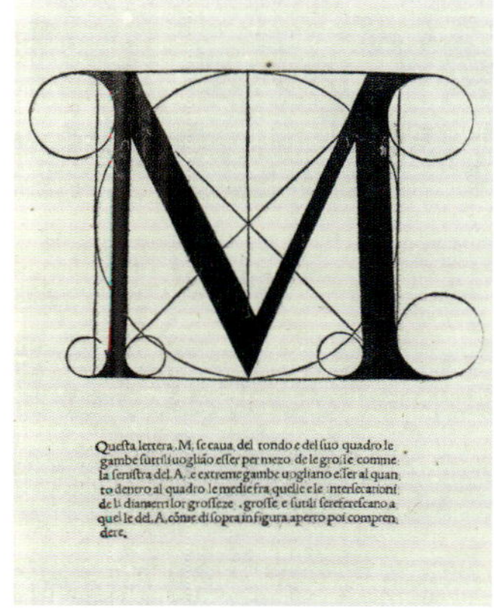

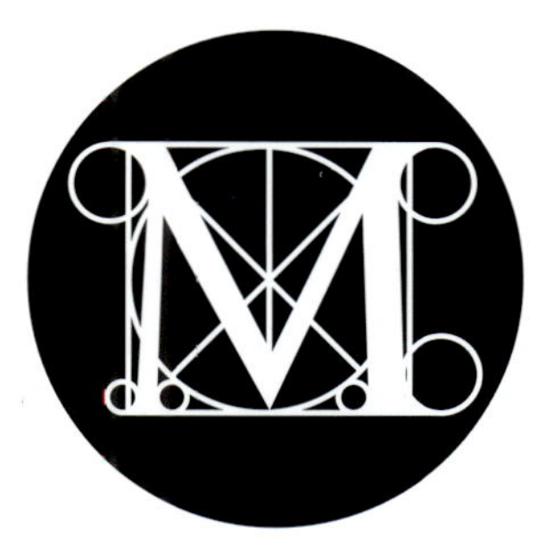

Fig. 1 Leonardo da Vinci. *Vitruvian Man*, ca. 1490. Pen and ink on paper, 13 ½ × 10 in. (34.4 × 25.5 cm). Galleria dell'Accademia, Venice

Fig. 2 Fra Luca Pacioli. Folio from *Divina proportione*, June 1, 1509. Woodcut illustration, 11 5/16 × 7 ⅞ in. (28.7 × 20 cm). The Metropolitan Museum of Art, New York, Rogers Fund, 1919 (19.50)

Fig. 3 The Metropolitan Museum of Art logo, 1971–2016

pervaded European art and culture to the exclusion of other cultures worldwide. Unsurprisingly, non-Western sculpture—often colored and displaying realism to varying degrees and for myriad cultural and social ends—was rarely considered fine art until the twentieth century, and then in often-problematic ways. Color could thus be construed as ideological, folded into racially motivated justifications for colonization, while the elevation of whiteness perpetuated through Western aesthetics and civilization above all others reached its apogee in the mid-nineteenth century, when European countries were at the height of their colonial power.

In the same period, a controversy erupted around John Gibson's *The Tinted Venus* (ca. 1851–56, cat. 8) that provoked a hiatus in its probing of the layered meanings of color and the evocation of fleshly (white) realism. As art historian Michael Hatt notes:

> [Color] connotes false consciousness, a deceptive and opaque surface that hides truth.
>
> What becomes apparent here is the idea that whiteness is not only the colour of form, but also signifies at what one might call a meta-representational level: the whiteness of sculpture signifies a culture that can understand what whiteness signifies. In other words, the presence of uncoloured sculpture will only be found in a civilization which can conceptualize the metaphysical rather than the literal, the rational rather than the bodily, the Christian rather than the pagan; a civilization that can understand the world, like sculpture itself, as made of thoughts as well as things.
>
> . . . What makes whiteness such a powerful political category is its flexibility, and the easy possibility of ideological revision in the light of historical or social change.[2]

Notwithstanding the Gibson dispute, the aesthetic and ideological potency of whiteness (including as a sculptural ideal) remained pervasive. Concurrently, the museum evolved as a public institution in the nineteenth century, with the enshrinement of fine-art canons of sculpture and painting premised on these aesthetic norms, which found new expression in galleries devoted to the unfolding of a timeless, unchanging, universal story of art. Historically, encyclopedic museums served as public repositories of private collections created though a European or Western sensibility within an emerging art market, while also incorporating artifacts amassed through international trade, exploration, and colonialism.[3] At the same time, encyclopedic institutions and the canon that they have long upheld have come to provide fertile ground for subsequent generations of artists and scholars to find and articulate new ways to consider how both art and collections can expand and represent multiple narratives that decenter or reevaluate earlier presuppositions. What questions can one critically and productively ask within the museum? How far can one propose a self-reflective assessment of the history of the Western museum and its constitutive role in the history of art? How far can an exhibition as a proposition contribute to the ongoing reassessment of the canon by expanding art history and widening cultural understandings? How far can sculptures across time keep company with one another? How can objects be promiscuous?

Like Life juxtaposes sculptures that compare formal concerns shared by artists throughout time and contrasts their distinctive understandings of humanity: for instance, both a copy of a marble figure of Hermes (A.D. 1st or 2nd century, cat. 1) attributed to Polykleitos and Duane Hanson's *Housepainter I* (1984/88, cat. 15) deploy the stance of the classical contrapposto, but to triumphal and quotidian effect, respectively. Each theme within this publication delineates the tactical use of color across centuries as artists negotiate realism toward differing ends, from the furor surrounding Gibson's *The Tinted Venus* to the provocative, historically nuanced meanings of Jeff Koons's *Michael Jackson and Bubbles* (1988, cat. 14). Another group of works explores the production of likenesses, images of people made real through casting, polychromy, and the incorporation of bodily matter, with the result that the reliquary bust of Saint Juliana (ca. 1376, cat. 20) and the frozen-blood self-portrait of artist Marc Quinn (1991, cat. 21) find unexpected affinities in form and meaning. Conversely, images such as Charles-Henri-Joseph Cordier's ethnographic sculptures (cats. 30, 33) and Rigoberto Torres's community portraits (cats. 31–32) might present apparent similarities but in fact diverge more fundamentally in their sympathies toward—and in the agency of—their subjects. The pleasures and perils of the lifelikeness of sculpture yielded the myth of Pygmalion most famously in the titillating painting by Jean-Léon Gérôme (ca. 1890, cat. 36) and finds its more modern analogue in Pablo Picasso's *Vollard Suite* (1930–37, cat. 39). In many folios of the sculptor in the studio, Picasso explicitly addresses the issues of the mirroring of the sculpture and model, setting up an ambiguity between animate and inanimate presence as well as the erotic charge of desire between model and sculpture (in the presence of the sculptor), with frequent references to classical statuary and, of course, to Galatea herself.

Concomitantly, realistically colored figurative sculpture bears an inescapable artificiality; a range of proxy bodies, from the artist's stuffed lay figure to mannequins, refers to such replicants. Yet, it was precisely the combination of the proximity to and distance from the genuinely human that renders such ersatz figures as potent objects of erotic fantasy and experimentation as well as sites for examining identity and bodily integrity—from Hans Bellmer's endlessly pliable *poupées* (dolls, cats. 62–64) to the proliferation of suggestive appendages on Yayoi Kusama's *Phallic Girl* (1967, cat. 60). The lay figure and mannequin, too, are linked to clothing and thus contrast with the classicized nude, and it is in the layering of this second skin that a figure's identity is further constructed and made socially visible and sometimes culturally locatable. Identity, however, is not a stable construct and is subject to remixing, particularly at the hand of the artist: in *Girl Ballerina* (2007, cat. 69) Yinka Shonibare MBE has transformed the tutu of Edgar Degas's *The Little Fourteen-Year-Old Dancer* (ca. 1880, cat. 68); Isa Genzken has used garments from her wardrobe to clothe a mannequin and create an alter ego (2013, cat. 76). Indeed, the permanence and durability of sculpture are interrogated by the presentation of works that evince the real mortality and frailty of the body, from the pathos of the brutalized body of the *Nellingen Crucifix* (1430–35, cat. 90) and the literal and spiritual transfiguration in Lucio Fontana's *Crocifisso* (see cat. 91) to sculptural bodies laid out on beds or daises, suggestive of a liminal state between life and death or, in their verisimilitude, of the transitional space between life and art.

The special exhibition, or the temporary display of objects in a museum setting as a form of institutional critique, was adopted by Fred Wilson in his seminal exhibition "Mining the Museum" (1992), which brought together historic artifacts to reveal uncomfortable truths about contemporary times.[4] Through his assumed role as a "Foucauldian archaeologist" who has systematically "unearth[ed] objects that reveal hidden histories, and more importantly, the internal . . . ideological paradigms of . . . museum collections," Wilson not only recovered a repressed history but also provoked the viewer toward a meditation on the past and a difficult reflection on the present.[5]

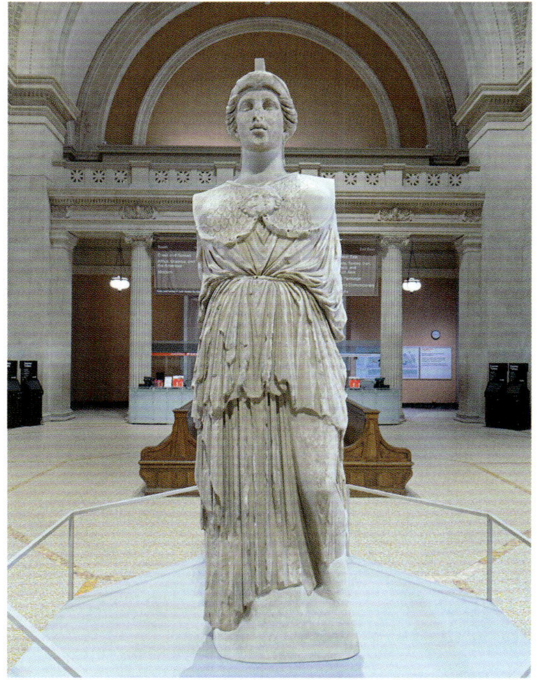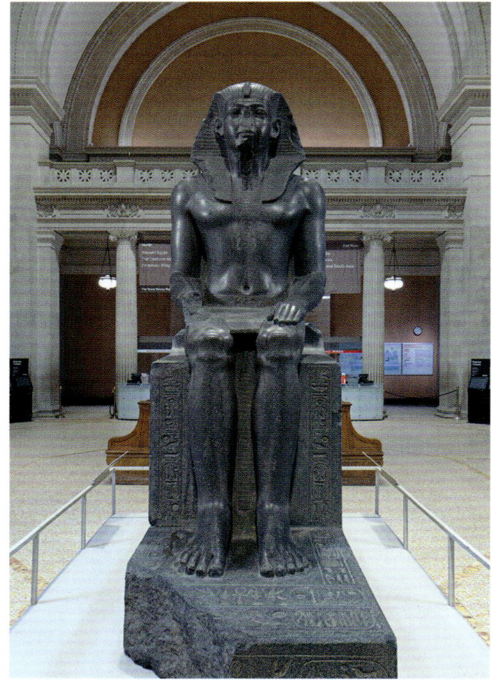

Fig. 4 A. *Statue of Athena Parthenos*, ca. 170 B.C. Marble, H. 14 ft. 11 ¹⁵/₁₆ in. (457 cm), W. 51 ³/₁₆ in. (130 cm), D. 37 in. (94 cm).
Greek. Antikensammlung, Staatliche Museen zu Berlin. B. *Seated Statue of Amenemhat II*, ca. 1919–1885 B.C. Granodiorite,
H. 10 ft. 6 in. (320 cm), W. 43 ½ in. (110.5 cm), D. 82 ⁵/₁₆ in. (209 cm). Egyptian. Aegyptisches Museum, Berlin. Installation view,
The Great Hall, The Metropolitan Museum of Art, New York, 2017

Central to Wilson's project is the historical construction and consideration of blackness in art.[6] These aims reoccur in *The Mete of the Muse* (2006, cat. 3), a juxtaposition of two female figures, one white, one black. Based on plaster reproductions but now cast in bronze and painted to emulate what some viewers might assume to be their original colors, the figures have a charged contemporary resonance. The white sculpture is a well-known depiction of a Venus / Aphrodite figure—a popular Greco-Roman type represented in many museum collections and also sold as Arcadian garden ornaments in horticultural centers; its black counterpart is a reproduction of an eighteenth-century Egyptian representation of the goddess Nephthys in the collection of the Musée du Louvre, Paris.[7] Not only do Wilson's copies of copies constituting *The Mete of the Muse* speak to the persistence of an image passed from century to century, but they also attest to the ubiquity and longevity of certain types of art, or "muses," exemplars whose position in the canon is reinscribed time and again through art-history books, museum tours, posters, postcards, and the internet. The "mete" refers to both the ethical justice of how a muse is determined and how the boundaries or limits of that definition can nonetheless broaden.

From the frontal and hieratic stance of the Egyptian figure on the left to the lyrical contrapposto of the Neoclassical figure on the right, the work contrasts color, form, movement, and ultimately a different set of aesthetic principles and ideals. The presentation of the white figure next to the black (or vice versa) establishes a binary, two poles, two directions to take. This pairing brings to mind a similar scenario in The Met's Great Hall (fig. 4), where between 2016 and 2021 visitors entering the museum encounter on one side the colossal white marble *Statue of Athena Parthenos* (ca. 170 B.C.) and on the other the equally monumental *Seated Statue of Amenemhat II* (ca. 1919–1885 B.C.) hewn in black granodiorite. Signifiers of entire civilizations, each stands as a monumental sentinel to the galleries beyond, offering visitors the choice between Greek and Roman or Egyptian art. While such a division dates back to nineteenth-century museological taxonomies of art and cultures,[8] according to Wilson, "they distinctly represented Africa and Europe, however their color and countenances were different, one to another."[9]

For Wilson, as an African American artist, the fact that color can be read ideologically is inarguable. He has explained, "Placing [the objects in *The Mete of the Muse*] together heightened their differing 'personalities.' Finding the exact distance apart was the most important creative act I could do. It often is, in my work. The subtle relationship is created by objects' adjacencies. I can safely say, juxtaposition is the strongest component in my art.... For me, simple shifts in the relationship of objects can change meaning demonstrably."[10] Wilson's intervention thus links a marginalized aesthetics of blackness with a proposition—implied by the real and conceptual space between the figures—to make good the work's central void through a reckoning with an alternative history of art that decenters Renaissance Europe as well as what has been narrowly inscribed as fine art.

Trade, especially through colonization, has introduced other means to destabilize, and arguably broaden, the canon. For as cultural historian Dipesh Chakrabarty argues, it was through colonialism that Enlightenment humanism (and by extension Western aesthetics) became accessible to, and which had the potential to be co-opted by, agents at the margins, both within and outside Europe. Accordingly, it was translated and transformed in profound ways: "Provincializing Europe is not a project of rejecting or discarding European thought.... Provincializing Europe becomes the task of exploring how this [European] thought—which is now everybody's heritage and which affect[s] us all—may be renewed from and for the margins.... Of course, the margins are as plural and diverse as the centers."[11]

For Bharti Kher, born to Indian parents in the United Kingdom before moving to New Delhi as an adult, this movement from the so-called center to the periphery literally and metaphorically enables a significant shift in her perspective and the possibilities for her art. Kher's *Mother* (2016, cat. 6) is at first a straightforward body cast of an elderly female figure on a modeling stool and trolley, itself a gesture toward the studio practice of drawing from life as established in European art pedagogy. Cast in plaster and conveying every last ridge and fall of her subject's wrinkled and sagging flesh, the work through its material connects to a long history of casting dating back to the ancient Egyptians. Kher's touch is tender and intimate yet dispassionately methodical. Although solemnly seated on a stool in a hieratic pose that can seem archetypal, this likeness is intensely personal and specific while arguably indistinguishable in form from *Six Women* (2013–15, fig. 5), a series of similarly rendered women, each of whose occupation is a sex worker. This ambiguity and broad gesture of humanity is of interest to Kher, and, indeed, only the title gives each sculpture's particularity away.[12] Yet, it is the confluence of identity and familial relationship that endowed the former work with a different set of undertones when it was first installed in the Freud Museum, London, to assess the meaning of "mother," and point to the fraught cultural background of India, where Kher lives and works.[13]

Kher's *Mother* is in a line of feminist responses to male representations of the female body, including the nude and contrasts starkly with Hiram Powers's *California* (1850–55, cat. 4), Gérôme's *The Ball Player* (1901, cat. 38), or John De Andrea's *Self-Portrait with Sculpture* (1980, cat. 37). In further consideration of the female body and sculpture, Kiki Smith's *Untitled (Self Portrait)* (1996, fig. 6) depicts the artist sitting in a similar pose as Kher's *Mother,* with coveralls pulled down to expose

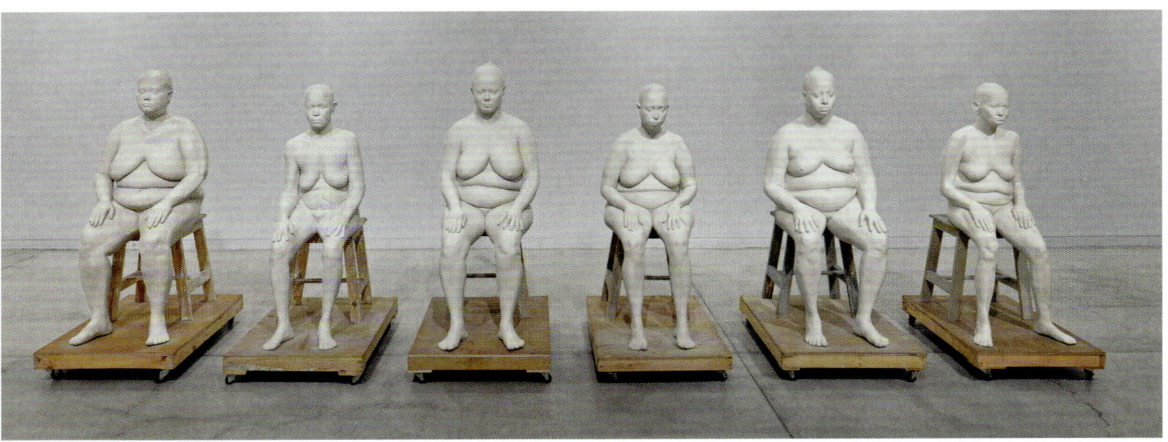

Fig. 5 Bharti Kher. *Six Women*, 2013–15. Plaster of Paris, wood, and metal, each: H. 48 ⅜ in. (123 cm). W. 24 in. (61 cm), D. 37 ⅝ in. (95.5 cm). Courtesy of the artist and Hauser & Wirth

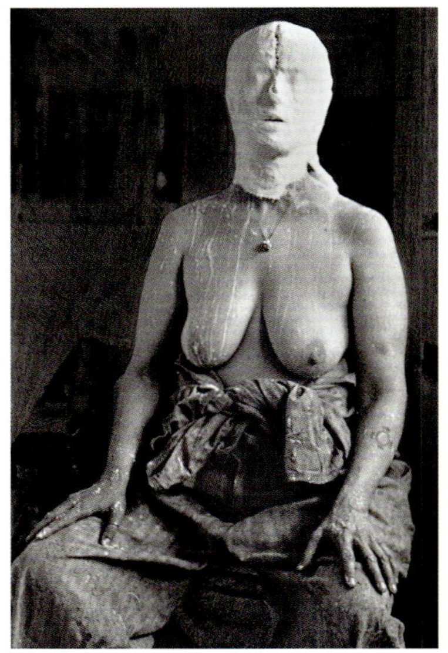

Fig. 6 Kiki Smith. *Untitled (Self Portrait)*, 1996. Gelatin silver print, 8 ⅞ x 6 in. (22.6 x 15.2 cm). Rhode Island School of Design Museum, Providence, Gift of Glenn Gissler

her breasts but with her head masked in a plaster mold, suggesting a transitional state in the sculpture-making process. The work confronts the viewer with the female sculptor as both creator and (unidealized) subject—in direct riposte to Gérôme's *Pygmalion and Galatea*. Kher's and Smith's works are *real* bodies, with the passing of time registering directly on the surface of the skin—the soft plaster seeping into the crevices, gradually hardening, and circumscribing the contours of the transforming flesh—reminding us that the body itself is a contingent site.

A body cast of a young woman was the first state of Charles Ray's *Aluminum Girl* (2003, cat. 5), which reveals the artist's personal response to classicist rhetoric and its implied ideals. Ray describes *Aluminum Girl* as "an attempt to develop [his] interest in figurative sculpture, to move away from the idealized forms."[14] Modeled on a friend of the artist's, the figure manifests Ray's intent to create an unfolding of sculptural events on its surface; the nakedness of the girl is heightened by the conspicuous depiction of her labia, suggesting both a vulnerability and a carnality at odds with the dispassionate demeanor of the standing figure. This intervention is reminiscent of a gesture found in Ray's *Male Mannequin* (1990, cat. 61), in which the figure bears pendant genitals, which were modeled on the artist's own and by Ray's admission serve as a tribute to the kouroi (statues of youths from ancient Greece) that he greatly admires (fig. 7).[15]

An acute observer of ancient art, Ray has a unique perspective on time, navigating it fluidly, to the extent that he sees "great archaic and classic sculptures as contemporary."[16] Perusing *Aluminum Girl*, the viewer is almost choreographed to engage closely with the work's process of creation by following the fluid line of the surface to be slowed by the detailed pitted aureoles of the nipples, or the figure's genitals. The overall form oscillates between realism and stylization, the smooth surface belying a meticulously labored process that combines both technical prowess and handcrafted modeling. Ray disrupts the temporal register in which classical form traditionally exists (that is, universally evident and eternal) through a "tangled interrelation of ratio and affect, historical past and present, precise calibration and individual idiosyncrasy."[17] In so doing, he creates figures that exist in a specific moment, but just as easily slip out of it: they register presence and simultaneously slide into the uncanny, what Sigmund Freud described as familiar yet estranged.[18]

This palpable unsettling presence—the simultaneous embrace and disruption of the real, literal body—was of abiding interest to the Surrealists in the early twentieth century. For them, the human figure was agitated in ways that confuse signs of familiarity and otherness, presence and absence, and which ultimately question humanity's relationship via the human body to reality. By taking a miniature plaster souvenir of the *Venus de Milo* (3rd–1st century B.C.), a timeless paragon of classical sculpture, in *Les Menottes de Cuivre* (*The Copper Handcuffs*, 1936, cat. 7), René Magritte tethered it to the present through his variegated use of colored paint. In a letter to poet André Breton, Magritte commented, "Here, the head is white, the body is flesh-coloured, the drapery is blue. . . . In my opinion this gives the Venus new and unexpected life."[19] Breton's response to Magritte, in proposing a title for the piece, noted that the advantage of naming it "The Copper Handcuffs" was that "it gives an additional colour to the object, but not arbitrarily, since copper is the metal corresponding to Venus."[20] In essence, it epitomizes the playful subversion of classicism in which the Surrealists reveled. These composite works prevent an immediate recognition of objects and the body through the combination of discordant elements, resulting in hybrid creatures. Both Salvador Dalí's *apparitions d'êtres-objets* (phantom object beings, see fig. 68) and Wilhelm Freddie's *objets-mannequins* (cat. 66) used the mannequin,

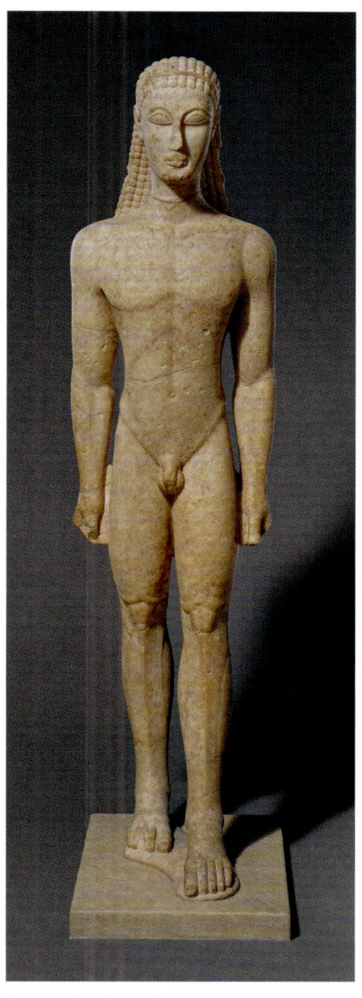

Fig. 7 *Marble Statue of a Kouros (Youth)*, ca. 590–580 B.C. Naxian marble, H. without plinth 76 ⅝ in. (194.6 cm), W. 20 ⁵⁄₁₆ in. (51.6 cm), D. 24 ⅞ in. (63.2 cm). Greek. The Metropolitan Museum of Art, New York, Fletcher Fund, 1932 (32.11.1)

itself a proxy for the human body, in combination with motley elements to disrupt the body and make it strange. Likewise, John Outterbridge used assemblage to explore figuration in his Ethnic Heritage series (1978–82, cat. 92) as well. The often-fragmentary, doll-like *Broken Dance* figures are complex amalgams of found metal, fabric, recycled wood, and leather that "[break] down the barriers created by both the art world's use of traditional materials and society's tolerance of exclusionary policies."[21] While Outterbridge's politics naturally differentiate his works from those of the Surrealists, they nevertheless share an interest in a practice in which "the materials bring with them their own history that calls to the viewer, who may or may not be aware of it, and the familiar becomes unfamiliar through the reworking of objects. . . . The works are imbued with an unfamiliarity that derives from their construction process and influences."[22]

At the core of the Surrealist project was art that drew on the psychological effect of estrangement, as addressed by Freud, whose notion of the uncanny, or *Unheimlich*, became the focus of a highly influential eponymous exhibition in 1993 by artist Mike Kelley (fig. 8). Running counter to the avant-garde rejection of hyperreal mimesis that dominated post–World War II art, he observed that "historically, literalness has been considered the enemy of art."[23] Kelley's presentation of a

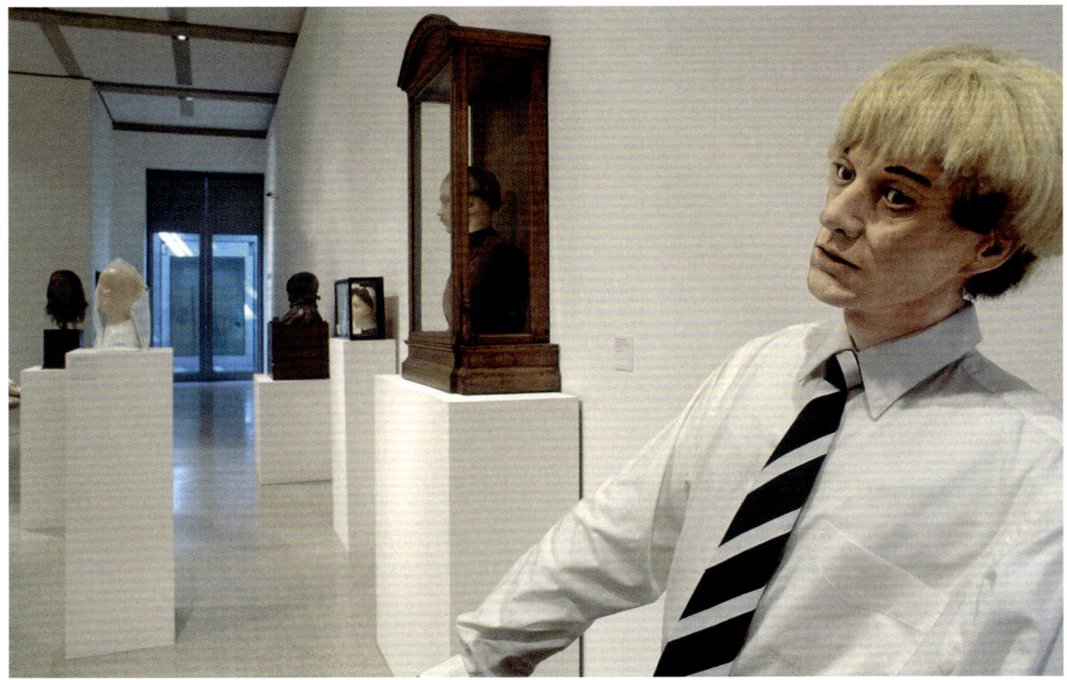

Fig. 8 Installation view, "Mike Kelley: The Uncanny," Museum Moderner Kunst Stiftung Ludwig Wien, Vienna, 2004

highly personal, eclectic collection of so-called art and nonart objects that included polychrome sculpture, mannequins, anatomical models, wax figures, and taxidermied animals revealed that the enduring, comforting, familiar, and disturbing coexist within the real.[24] In particular, the psychological effects of doubling in Kelley's project underscore the continued, at times morbid and fetishistic, fascination with the representation of the body in abject semblance. "Mike Kelley: The Uncanny" (1993/2004) and "The Human Factor: The Figure in Contemporary Sculpture" (2014) were notable exhibitions that seriously addressed the question of figuration, especially as an underexamined strand in the history of twentieth-century sculpture. "The figure is not the *raison d'etre* . . . so much as a rhetorical point of departure. It is engaged not to affirm our existing notions of subjectivity and identity, but as a means of looking askance. . . . Far from invoking some universalised aspect of humanity, the sculpted figure is treated . . . as a network of multiple and contradictory meanings."[25]

Yet, the endurance of the idealized figure in sculpture over the centuries demonstrates the aesthetic and sensual powers of realism, up until the dawn of the twentieth century. However, during the 1920s and 1930s, the classicized white sculptured body became the leitmotif of the ideal body-citizen of totalitarian regimes, notably in Germany, Russia, and Italy. (White) figurative statuary became a means to reinscribe a social and racial ideology at the heart of nation-building in Germany, while the prescription of Socialist Realism in Soviet Russia stood as a counterpoint to "the avant-garde movements [that] understood that industrialized modernity destroyed the social bases for such a notion of the human image, and that . . . promotion of the traditional ideal of statuary would be in the service of a deceptive ideology of 'unity,' the unity of the power-state. Thus, statuary, either nude or uniformed, collapsed as a legitimate sculptural form."[26]

For artists in the West, this co-option of sculpture by the state led to a gradual turn away from the idealized classical figure toward abstraction and expressionism, as well as a conscious fragmentation, often inflected via implied violence inflicted on the integrity of the human body as a consequence of the horrors of World War I. The post–World War II period saw a further rejection of the sculpted figure within the avant-garde, in which "the figure generally has been conspicuous by its absence."[27] Increasingly, sculpture entailed an understanding of nonfigurative "sculpture in the expanded field," from Minimalism and Land art to installations, performances, and other socially engaged practices.[28]

It was not until the 1960s that artists such as Marcel Duchamp (*Étant donnés*, 1946–66, fig. 27) as well Edward Kienholz and Duane Hanson, and later John Ahearn and Rigoberto Torres, found renewed possibilities in figurative sculpture. In his theatrical tableaux that approximate quotidian scenes, Kienholz's subjects, hapless members of society cast in literal renditions, bring into focus the failures of capitalism and those who, by virtue of their social status, are unable to partake in the American dream. Surrounded by their possessions (often the commodities seem to subsume the subjects), these figures are in unremarkable settings, in which viewers encounter not only the social reality depicted but also confront their own voyeurism, as in *Woman Washing with Scrutator with Parrot Affixed Also* (1983, cat. 80).

The elemental mimesis of realistic polychrome sculpture and its affective immediacy were essential to Hanson's interest in picturing working-class American life, enabling him to explore socially and politically charged issues, including poverty and racism. The hyperrealism of Hanson's work inspires in the viewer both empathy and discomfort, familiarity and surprise. Casting figures from life, he would occasionally use the same cast to create different sculptures. Joe Lance, a construction worker, became the model for *Housepainter I* and a series of subsequent sculptures: *Custodian*, *Windowwasher* (fig. 10) and *Housepainter II* (all 1984). In so doing, Hanson not only reflected on the individual's real or imagined transposable roles, for instance the multiple low-paying jobs that Lance may have held, but also the viewer's inability to distinguish individuals beyond their social status, as judged by their uniform, accessories, or title, but also, significantly, their race. This invisibility and (mannequin-like) interchangeability of the black body, especially in an art setting, is also reflected on in Wilson's *Guarded View* (1991, fig. 11). Hanson chose to position his protagonist in a pose reminiscent of the *Doryphoros* of Polykleitos (fig. 9), linking his figure to classical statuary, but the resultant sculpture remains ambiguously heroic (and ironically could be read as a comment on Socialist Realism during the Cold War)—laboring yet abject.

Mary Sibande at once embraces hyperrealism to consider the indentured body, specifically the history of female servitude in South Africa, where her mother and grandmother were maids. Where Hanson's figures are steadfastly committed to the real, Sibande's vignettes hover between reality and fantasy. Adopting a semiautobiographical alter ego named Sophie who appears in the artist's sculptural and photographic works, Sibande uses costume to create a more complex identity. In *Rubber Soul, Monument of Aspiration* (2011, cat. 79), Sophie appears in a khaki-colored uniform, and in a composite system of visual signifiers, the artist addresses issues of race, class, and power in postapartheid South Africa. Her black figure wears a luxurious Victorian gown, the type of dress that a white (landowner) mistress would have worn, but now covered by an apron: it reads as an exotic uniform, complicating an elevated status with the notion of subordination. Her dynamic leap onto a pedestal endows this sculpture with further meaning. Sibande visibly destabilizes the norms of sculptural balance, presenting a provocative counterpoint to the figures one might typically find on a pedestal: Sophie is neither nude, white, nameless, idealized, standing, nor mythic but is rather a powerful presence on her own terms.

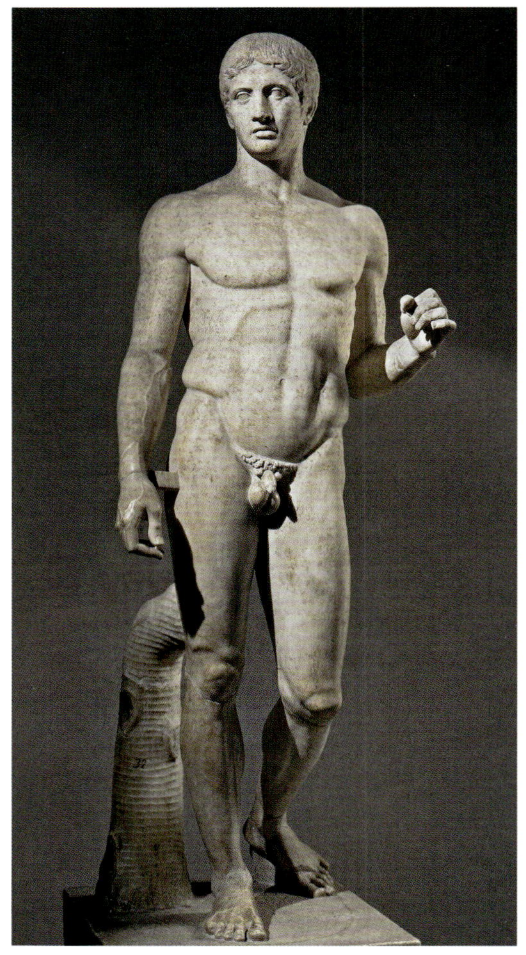

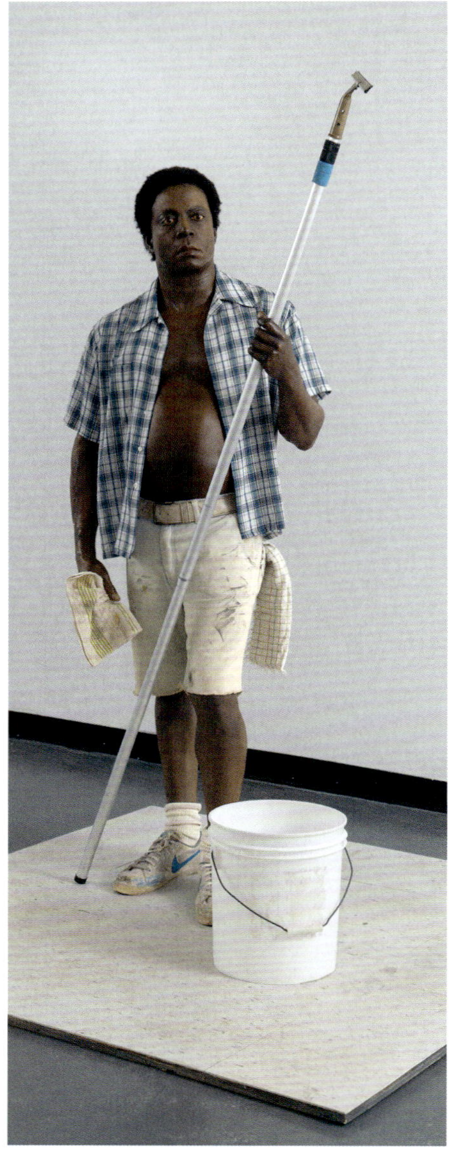

Fig. 9 Copy of work attributed to Polykleitos. *Doryphoros*, before A.D. 79
from a 440 B.C. original. Marble, H. 79 ½ in. (202 cm). Museo Archeologico
Nazionale, Naples

Fig. 10 Duane Hanson. *Windowwasher*, 1984. Polychromed bronze,
mixed media, and accessories. Collection of Dick Anderson,
Overland Park, Kansas

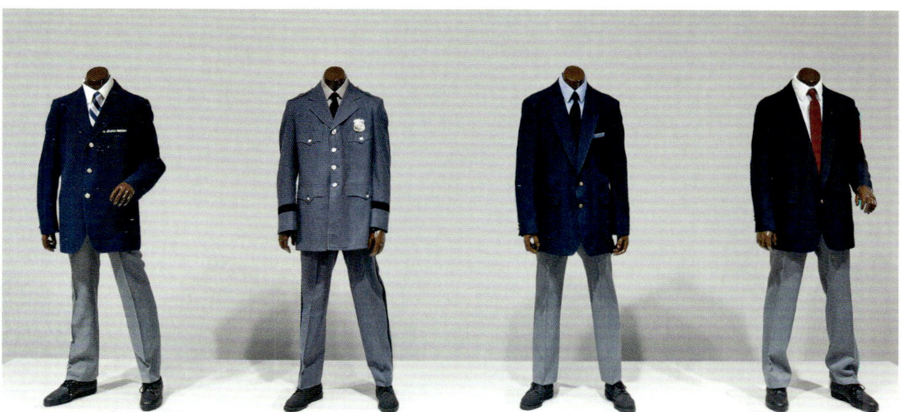

Fig. 11 Fred Wilson. *Guarded View*, 1991. Wood, paint, steel, and fabric, dimensions variable. Whitney Museum of American Art, New York, Gift of the Peter Norton Family Foundation

The traditional categories of fine art (that is, sculpture and painting), art history as a discipline, and museums themselves are all related to the European Enlightenment; historic objects assembled within museums remain connected to this lineage. At the same time, cultural institutions have evolved from repositories for the collection and study of the visual culture of Western civilizations toward places that seek to engage with art across all times and cultures and to question the process by which history is inscribed, which includes the art of the present time. The dominance of Western narratives of art and aesthetics has been—and continues to be—interrogated and disrupted.

The way that we view the past is necessarily colored by present-day realities. By focusing on a specific trajectory of chromatic and figurative sculptures that closely resemble human beings, *Like Life* undertakes a consciously anachronistic, thematic approach to the material, juxtaposing objects from contrasting periods, even as those objects carry within them divergent histories. While certain works share similarities, it is their differences that are most instructive. Time is not flattened but instead made dynamic. Neither the exhibition nor this volume purports to be a comprehensive or chronological survey of figuration in sculpture. Nor is it designed to chart a new history. Rather, this synthetic presentation will hopefully stimulate visual and conceptual conversations that span surprising arcs of history and geography. In so doing, new spaces—within the museum, beyond the canon—can be found for self-reflection, where we can refresh our readings of sculpture, color, the body, and ourselves.

POLYCHROME AND ITS DISCONTENTS

A HISTORY

LUKE SYSON

In winter 2008–9, a person standing at the top of the spiral of New York's Solomon R. Guggenheim Museum, one of the world's great temples to art, would have spied Maurizio Cattelan's Pinocchio floating far below in the waters of the clean, modernist fountain, polluting its pristine whiteness with his bright Disney hues (fig. 12). That we instinctively believed the figure was dead stems directly from the deeply built-in conviction that he was once alive. We know, almost without knowing, that Pinocchio was thrice brought to life: first in Carlo Collodi's 1881 children's story; then, within that captivating fiction, by the craftsmanship and love of a childless wood-carver; and, finally, in 1940, when he was resurrected for a vast audience by America's cuddly Uncle Walt. Now another artist has remade, brought to life, and apparently killed his puppet-son, turning him back into an inanimate toy, a corpse whose limbs float cruciform as though he has drowned. The title, *Daddy, Daddy* (2008), brashly alludes to the story of Christ, another child given life, then sacrificed by his creator-father, a mischievous paraphrase of the Savior's last, despairing cry on the Cross: "My God, my God, why hast thou forsaken me?"[1]

The Italian artist's new Pinocchio gleefully exploits a series of paradoxes that have long confused the making and viewing of naturalistically colored figurative sculpture in the Western tradition, giving this category its profoundly equivocal status. This work contains them all: alive / dead, artificial / natural, religious / profane, material / magic, statue / doll, object / viewer, elevated / accessible (or more simply, high / low), serious / entertaining, loved / loathed, and, in conjunction with Frank Lloyd Wright's fountain, colored / white. Some binaries are intrinsic to the genre. Others evolved gradually but powerfully over six centuries. All, however, challenge any possibility of a unified notion of art. Not least because he was born and raised in a Catholic country, Cattelan knows all about the fraught European history of polychromy, and he tapped into the

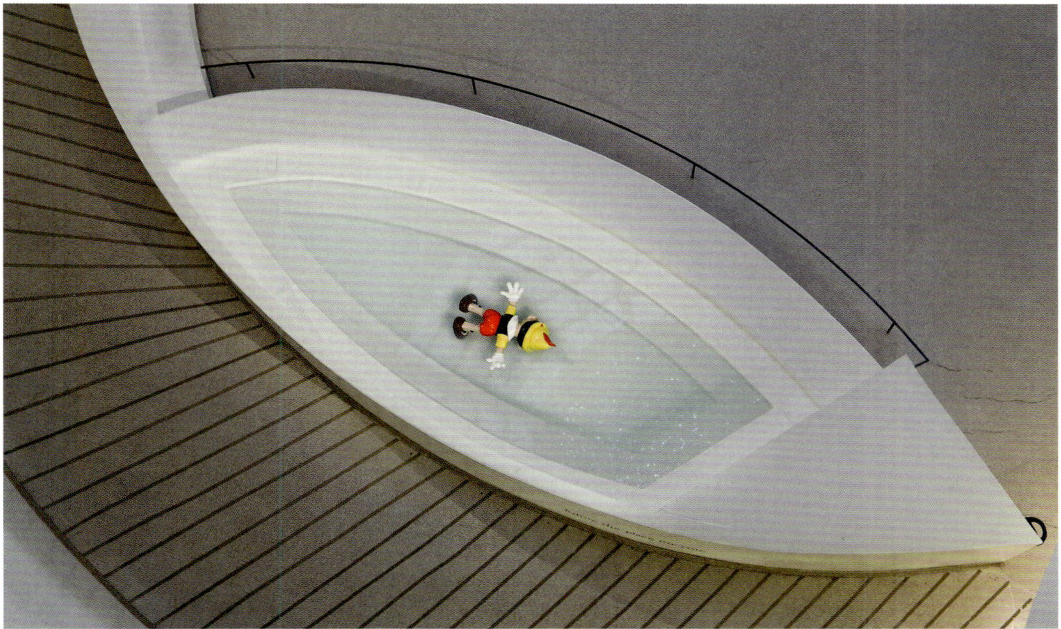

Fig. 12 Maurizio Cattelan. *Daddy, Daddy*, 2008. Polyurethane resin, paint, and steel. H. 14 ¾ in. (37.5 cm),
W. 38 ½ in. (97.8 cm). D. 34 ½ in. (87.6 cm). Solomon R. Guggenheim Museum, New York, Anonymous gift, 2012

long condemnation of not just the application of colored paints to the surfaces of carved or
modeled statuary—to use the strict definition of "polychrome"—but also those sculptures that
use colored media to imitate flesh and skin.[2] To understand more about the absolutist thinking
that lies behind which works we are taught to identify as "art," what has been traditionally—often
rashly—excluded, and what these views mean for today's thinking and making of sculpture, both
colored and monochrome, we should know that history better.

Many of these tensions have been present for more than six centuries, from about the
moment when the vividly modeled and naturalistically colored portrait bust of the Florentine
politician and diplomat Niccolò da Uzzano (1430s, cat. 17) was fashioned. The current debate about
the attribution of this piece clearly indicates their ongoing impact. Made from painted terracotta,
the work's surface appears soft, fleshy, and skinlike. Niccolò vigorously turns his head, the sinews
in his neck fiercely stretched, his eyebrows slightly knitted, and his eyes raised piously to the
heavens. Partly because of its brilliant animation, but especially because of the human conviction
of the piece, from the early twentieth century the portrait was (perhaps incorrectly) thought to be
cast from life or adapted from a death mask.[3] In the mid-sixteenth century, artist and art historian
Giorgio Vasari had associated these impressed effigies with the wax votive portraits, all lost,
that once populated the Florentine church of Santissima Annunziata, conflating the making of
waxworks and the taking of face and head casts from sitters, whether alive or recently deceased.[4]
For both categories, direct contact with a real body was believed to transfer an element of life, of
the essence of the person, into the resulting image. Thus, the bust of Niccolò might be lumped
together with works considered more as acts of faith than as works of art, executed, moreover,
using a sculptural method that could be reckoned worryingly primitive or pseudomagical.

Worrying not least because this portrait comes from exactly the moment when the glorious revival of what was then assumed to be pristine white marble and gleaming bronze sculpture in high-minded emulation of ancient Greece and Rome had just gotten under way. It was long believed that the bust was executed by Donatello, always considered the sculptural trailblazer-in-chief of the Renaissance recovery of ancient aesthetic values. However, the forceful realism of this head has recently been considered to fit rather uncomfortably into what was becoming a dominant concept of high (or distanced) art. Consequently, another opinion now prevails. A leading scholar of Italian sculpture, Francesco Caglioti, has pronounced that "no work securely attributed to this master reveals such a detailed, meticulous, and self-contained interest in the changing particulars of individual appearance, which for Donatello was always only a starting point, one that had to be elevated to a more universal meaning. . . . There would have been no need to inconvenience Donatello with such a menial and mechanical task."[5] Instead, Caglioti revisited an old attribution of the bust to Desiderio da Settignano and, still unsatisfied, pushed the piece farther down the attributional ladder; "in the light of the use of the old death mask," he classified it as a workshop production.[6]

COLOR, THE ENEMY OF ART

It would in fact have been entirely characteristic of Donatello, as earthy as he was elevated, to have questioned this idealizing notion of art just as it was being formulated. When a commission demanded it, his work reveals a profound interest in the specificity of individual appearance, and this was a likeness after all. Therefore, Caglioti's unease is more reflective of the negative attitudes toward polychrome sculpture that had been baked into elite art criticism a little less than a century after the portrait bust was made. "The power and virtue of the sculptor lie in the effects of the chisel, and if some clumsy oaf in this field uses colors, it denies the very nature of that art," fulminated Vasari's contemporary Vincenzo Borghini.[7] Arguing that the application of paint would conceal the inspired artistry of the sculptor, he was in the vanguard of an army of critics who would formulate an entire arsenal of chromophobic attack.[8]

By the time Borghini was writing, it was widely agreed that a work of art should *be about* rather than just *be*. High art should imitate and improve upon the works of nature so as to render visible precisely what cannot be seen in daily life. Artists therefore needed to find ways of creating a distance between their works and the beholder to provide the intellectual space for sustained philosophical or theological meditation. The idea was all-important. At the highest level, this position responds to Plato's fourth-century B.C. philosophical attack on mimetic art in *The Republic*. What we see on earth, he thought, is merely the meager reflection of the perfect idea of everything that exists only in the supreme creator's mind. The more accurate the copying of an observed reality, the further it moves away from the idea. Centuries later, the application of naturalistic color to a form already too imitatively three-dimensional came to be viewed as an almost emblematic transgression. From the Renaissance onward, it was regularly suggested that an artist can get closer than nature itself to perfection by idealizing or abstracting the world, giving rise to art deliberately separated from quotidian experience.[9] These works were supposed to be difficult to understand, and their meanings are expressed using visual languages that the cognoscenti had first to invent, then learn. The art that resulted is now considered the canon of Western sculpture. Furthermore, this hierarchy was made bulletproof by its persistent reiteration; it was agreed from the Renaissance to the later nineteenth century, and indeed afterward, that for sculpture, so worryingly concrete, to approach perfection, it must be monochrome, preferably a pure, ideologically charged white. Critics over six centuries have been consistently suspicious of color.[10] The eminent Victorian Walter Pater pondered the philosophy of his great predecessor, German art theorist Johann Joachim Winckelmann, for whom classical marble sculpture possessed a "white light purged from the angry blood-like stains of action and passion, [which] reveals not what is accidental in man, but the god, as opposed to man's restless movement."[11]

To promote this concept of high art, strenuous efforts have been made by the church and academy to suppress or dismiss alternative, more accessible modes of expression—including, par excellence, realistic polychrome sculpture. The astonishing verisimilitude of such works and, accordingly, the ingenuity of their makers could be applauded, but in general, critics have condemned the categories of sculpture in which the imitation of us—the viewers—is powerful enough to convince us that some form of life inheres. Central to this substantial, sustained bombardment is the anxious recognition that these works communicate more directly, and across a broader social spectrum, than the high art these critics championed. Polychrome sculpture must perforce be judged too easy and too popular to be good art, high art, or even art at all.

The artists who created such works were thus regularly denigrated or ignored, and the large audiences for polychrome sculpture were also conveniently condemned as superstitious, stupid, or downright vulgar. By employing a kind of circular prejudice, the works they respond to could then be dismissed as what would come to be called kitsch. Since these artists did not generally define their aims in writing, this flood of elite opprobrium is extraordinarily helpful in that it identifies the essential ingredients of what might be termed an "anticanon." Though these complaints probably do not correlate precisely with the ambitions of the works they berate, the standard objections tend to focus on exactly those things that make such sculptures so compelling, memorable, and dangerously accessible. Indeed, what these critical brickbats actually achieved is the bestowal of a problematic status for realistic polychrome sculpture that has become extremely useful for a number of artists today, working at a time when questioning what has long been aesthetically ordained is—sometimes and very carefully—encouraged.

Proof of this detrimental popularity is found in the long association of colored sculpture with theater, mystery plays, processions, fairgrounds, and other places and rituals for wide public participation. It is implied that when a sculpture is lifelike enough to attract a crowd, its realism constitutes a hurdle to the contemplation of more metaphysical meanings, a form of attention assumed to be beyond most viewers. The immediacy of a work of art has been positioned to denote a dearth of significance. Curator Ruba Katrib's analysis of the hyperrealist works of American contemporary artist Duane Hanson (cats. 15, 35) sums up this position: "Building up his sculptures piece by piece until they become legible as contemporary subjects, he removed the distancing effects found in most sculptural representations of the human body. . . . They are too close to real, eliminating the space required for interpretation."[12] It is clear that realistic polychrome sculpture can still be judged too "literal," a pejorative term in much establishment art criticism.

It cannot be denied that realistic polychrome sculpture is supremely literal. Our first sight of such pieces more closely resembles an encounter with a fellow human being than with what has been defined as a work of art. That is precisely the point. They occupy an Everyman's zone between life and art. Sculptures were designed to provoke visceral, emotional, and empathetic reactions—pain, pity, shock, and arousal, sometimes all at once—a range of responses that neither church nor academy nor any other elite institution could easily control. Many writers would have us believe that such sculptures' affect can be strong enough to make us fall, quite improperly, in love (or lust) and that we can even bring the works to life through our ardor. An instance of this theme played out in real life, when the great nineteenth-century American sculptor Augustus Saint-Gaudens was asked by Charles Gould, a grieving widower, to remake one of his series of white marble busts of his long-dead wife, Louise Adele (Dickerson) Gould, in subtly colored wax, the better to bring her back to life (cats. 40–41).[13] No wonder naturalistic religious sculptures of the beautiful protagonists of Christian stories were regularly condemned as idols, charged with the love of their viewers, who vested them with powers that neither the human nor the inanimate should possess. This unapologetically theatrical art form ("theatrical" is another long-standing term of critical abuse) requires an engaged audience, and for the pieces to function, they demand that the highly involved protagonist becomes a sort of cocreator.[14] These sculptures are theatrical in another sense, too; they perform for their audiences rather as actors do. In religious sculpture, particularly representations of Christ's Passion, bodily realism is often heightened by large, but not necessarily emotionally inaccurate, gesture and by agonized facial expression.[15] We are meant to *feel* these pieces.

At the same time as it is condemned for being too real, sculpture that takes semblance as its starting point can be damned by a connection "with sham, counterfeit, forgery, fraudulence, deceit, cheating, trickery," to quote psychoanalyst Janine Chasseguet-Smirgel.[16] If it is agreed that the more idealized or abstracted the work of art, the more truthful it is, when surface appearances are too precisely imitated, the opposite must be true: the work is all surface, nothing more than an enormous lie. This message lies behind the many stories of frustrated love for the animatedly inanimate. Well before the love-dolls Coppelia or Olympia, antiheroines of the nineteenth-century stage, fashioned—sometimes mechanical, always illusory—figures of a beloved appeared in love stories like the twelfth-century romances *Floris and Blanchefleur* (ca. 1150), where a statue moves and speaks, and Thomas de Bretagne's tale of Tristan (ca. 1170), with its robotic copy of the beautiful Isolde.[17] Even without worrying about Plato, nothing could be more artificial than an artist's dissimulating appearance of reality. One tremendous irony of this genre is that the more thrillingly alive a replicant appears, the more profoundly its deadness resonates. The more we are conscious that a sculpture cannot do the things real people do that make them human—think, believe, love, and return love—the more one can condemn the work as lacking heart, mind, and soul. There was only one thoughtful solution. The frisson of being fooled into believing that a sculpture is alive could be turned into entertainment. Such a work might indeed be soulless, but that phenomenon becomes the point. A sculpture can look too much like life precisely so it will evoke death, dreams, and nightmares.

The visual and material tactics for making affective or illusory polychrome sculpture have remained remarkably consistent for over six hundred years and notably differ from those of the sculptural mainstream. First and foremost is the accurate sculpting of the body, followed by its naturalistic coloring, which in the medieval and early modern periods was usually executed by

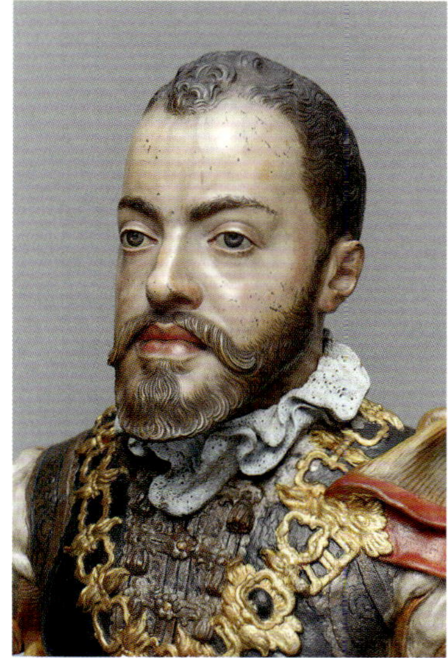

Fig. 13 Pompeo Leoni. *King Philip II of Spain*, ca. 1580, lower part of the bust executed by Balthasar Ferdinand Moll, 1753 (detail). Head: painted silver; bust: painted terracotta, H. 24 3/16 in. (61.5 cm), W. 17 1/8 in. (43.5 cm), D. 11 7/16 in. (29 cm). Kunsthistorisches Museum, Vienna

a painter in another guild. The significance of this process of coloring, of making the sculptures bloom, is made especially clear in Spanish. In the last part of his 1649 treatise on painting, the Sevillian practitioner Francisco Pacheco gives an account of *encarnación* (making flesh), a technique for applying flesh tones to sculpture.[18] This transformation of materials into (apparently) living flesh, however, began to concern those patrons who were becoming aware of modern critical and theological objections to color. In 1579 the Madrid-based Milanese sculptor Pompeo Leoni, for instance, was asked to execute the bronze votive portraits of Philip II and his consort for the capilla mayor at the royal residence El Escorial, with faces and hands that were to be *encarnado*, or "fleshed."[19] These would have looked very much like the lifesize, colored silver portrait head of the king in Vienna (fig. 13), but Philip changed his mind and, bowing to new ideas, chose instead a lavishly gilded monochrome.

On occasion, valuable materials like colored marbles were used to make polychrome sculpture. Pierre Le Gros the Younger's use of colored stone in *The Death of Saint Stanislas Kostka* (1703, fig. 14), for example, makes the piece more affecting and properly adheres to ancient precedent.[20] In its day it was both endowed with cult properties for worshippers and recognized as an accomplished work of art. This latter judgment was possible because it only semiconvinces as a real human being. Greater verisimilitude generally called for different, cheaper

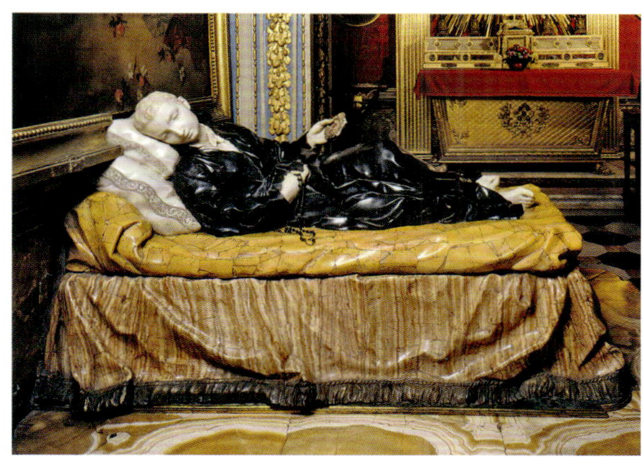

Fig. 14 Pierre Le Gros the Younger. *The Death of Saint Stanislas Kostka*, 1703. Black touchstone, Sicilian jasper, yellow marble, Carrara marble, and gilt bronze. Sant'Andrea al Quirinale, Rome

media. For the apologists of high art, the frequent use of rags, straw, horsehair, papier-mâché and plaster, wood and clay, and especially wax—all commonplace in comparison to elevated marble or bronze—provided another target. Many of these materials had organic or long-established metaphorical associations with human flesh because they can grow and decay, are soft and malleable when worked, or can be suffused with color. Sculptors understood them as a conventional means of convincing viewers that these sculptures were somehow inhabited, that they had personality or spirit. However, the works could all too easily be accused of material impoverishment.

Even when dismissed by an elite, the making of polychrome sculpture was never completely abandoned, and popular impulse has almost always successfully combated elite prescription. Only rarely intended for palaces or art galleries, these works were long spurned by curators and collectors alike. Even so, they could still be seen in places of worship (chiefly in Catholic countries), ornamenting grand dinner tables, embellishing ships' prows, displayed in industrial exhibitions or shop windows, and paraded through the streets. The lack of reverence on the part of the viewers in these nonart contexts has meant their responses were difficult to regulate, another problem that concerned secular and ecclesiastical authorities and their critical apologists. Cheap, disruptive, entertaining, egalitarian, extremely available, polychrome sculpture was and remains an art for the people, an art moreover concerned primarily with ordinary human experience and emotion. Establishment opposition has, if anything, only increased its power.

RELIGION AND REGULATION

Opposition began early. For Christians all over Western Europe, such works had provoked anxiety for a century or more before the Reformation divided the Church. Animated by faith, the corporeal relics of the saints had long been agreed to have sacred powers. The medieval reliquary cases that contained them, though made by human hand, were therefore occupied by exactly the materials that made these holy figures eternally—and miraculously—alive. To reinforce this notion, reliquary cases were frequently given the appearance of life, shaped like the body parts they contained (an arm for an arm bone, a head for the skull) and sometimes also painted with a surface material made to look like skin (cat. 20). Thus following a circular logic, the most literal method for making a figure "incarnate" became the incorporation of real body parts, whether internal (bones, teeth, dried blood, or mummified soft organs) or external (hair); this was a method that might carry across to the making of portrait sculpture. From the late fifteenth century, however, the veneration of bodily relics was much disparaged by religious reformers, wary of fraud and aware that body fragments, especially hair, could also be attached to witches' poppets, those rudimentarily sculpted stand-ins for the targets of black magic. For many, faith had moved too close to superstition.

The problems of realism only increased, when, about this time and with the best of devotional intentions, religious works of art, not least polychrome sculptures, were specifically created to appeal to the laity, to save souls beyond the gates of convents and monasteries. What became standard reasons for Christian image making were regularly adduced, replete with well-known references to the teachings of Saints Gregory, Bernard, and Bonaventure: reaching and teaching the illiterate, for example, and making memorable the holy figure as well as, more importantly, what she or he stood for.[21] As the people's art, such sculptures had to be more than just recognizably human to be persuasive; they had to establish emotional connections between the viewer and the protagonist represented. Viewers were to become witnesses.

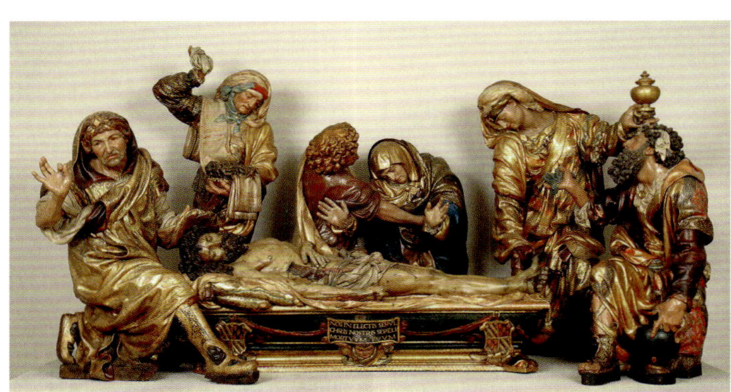

Fig. 15 Juan de Juni. *The Entombment of Christ*, 1541–44. Polychromed wood, approximately lifesize, overall dimensions variable. Museo Nacional de Escultura, Valladolid

Greater piety would be inspired by not just seeing, but also sympathetically feeling the work of art. According to the thirteenth-century theologian now known as the Pseudo-Bede, the devout should focus on Christ's torment, "as if you were actually present at the very time when he suffered. And in grieving you should regard yourself as if you had our Lord suffering before your very

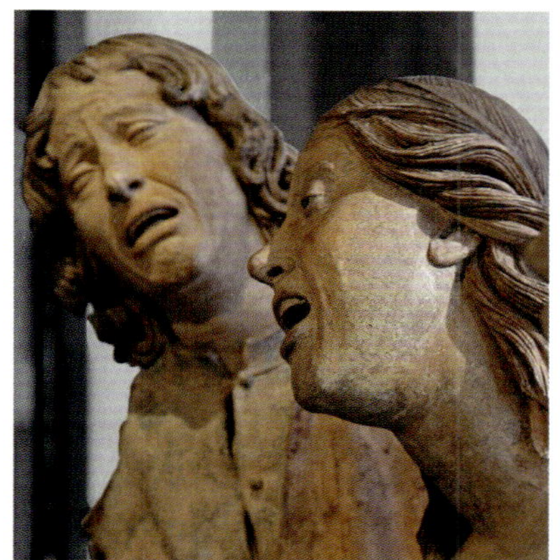

Fig. 16 Guido Mazzoni. *Saint John the Evangelist* and *Magdalene* (detail) from *Lamentation*, ca. 1485–89. Terracotta with traces of polychromy, approximately lifesize. Musei Civici, Padova

eyes, and that he was present to receive your prayers."[22] The Franciscans, in particular, promoted the compassionate precepts of the *imitatio Christi* (Imitation of Christ), the understanding of the humanity and suffering of Christ through both experience and emulation.[23] And in much fourteenth-century German mystical literature, especially writing aimed at and concerned with the visions of women, was the expectation that any spectator could become a visionary.[24]

The lay devout were quick to take realistic, human-size polychrome sculpture to heart, and sculptors became vivid storytellers, brilliant at conveying the pain of a penitent saint mortifying his flesh, for example. They learned how to represent the extremes of emotion and sensation: ecstasy, sorrow, and pain. Sculpted Lamentation and Pietà groups became wildly popular (fig. 15). Screaming, gaping mouths; flailing arms; and agitated draperies—paroxysms of grief in their own right—are dominant features of quattrocento, Northern Italian painted clay sculpture, most remarkably by Niccolò dell'Arca and Guido Mazzoni (fig. 16).[25] Many of these figure groups were given naturalistic settings and turned into tableaux with landscapes painted on the walls around them. Women, in particular, were invited to consider the crucial role of the Virgin by looking at especially empathic images celebrating her loving relationship with her infant, an experience many viewers may have shared. One anonymous German sculptor working for the parish church at Ebern at the end of the fifteenth century would extend that notion of the common experience of women when he represented with exquisite tenderness the exhaustion of Saint Anne after giving birth to her daughter Mary (ca. 1480, cat. 116). The reality of the mother is enhanced not just by the beautiful rendered skin tones in paint, but by the all-important act of touch. She touches both herself and her little girl, establishing the crucial emotional connection between the protagonists, and with

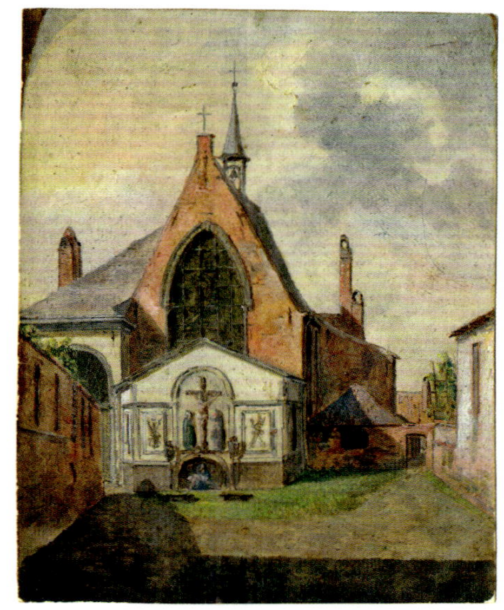

Fig. 17 *View of the Beguinage Church of Poortakker in Ghent with Calvary and Pietà*, first half of the 19th century. Oil on paper. Netherlandish. Atlas Goetghebuer, Stadsarchief, Ghent

us, and helping us understand her better as a living creature with senses of her own. Such compellingly naturalistic sculptures were commissioned by lay communities all over Europe. Many Pietàs were made, for example, to foster the faith of the Beguines, groups of semireligious women in the Netherlands. By the early nineteenth century but probably much earlier, the Beguines of Ghent had sited a large polychrome Pietà group outside their church at street level, with a sculpted crucifix and the mourning figures of John and Mary in a niche above (fig. 17).[26] Thus the people of the town daily witnessed the Passion of Christ. They lived with it. They absorbed it into their lives.

The Church authorities, however, were forced early on to wrestle with a precarious conundrum: on the one hand, to make the divine emotionally compelling, the figures should be rendered especially human, a grimly effective tactic when the piece depicted pain or suffering. On the other hand, the main protagonists of the Christian story had to be more than just recognizably the same sort of people as the viewers; they needed to be humanly but also inhumanly, or extrahumanly, beautiful. Flesh coloring thus made the perfect bared breast of the nursing Virgin Mary or the naked bodies of Christ, the Magdalene, or Saint Sebastian (cat. 44) potentially, and perilously, desirable. In conveying their spiritual essence too powerfully, too concretely, too seductively, these figures might come to be worshipped with an idolatrous conviction by ignorant masses—as they were thought of—unable to comprehend that the images were supposed to convey only the idea of a holy figure. Moreover, sculptures that the faithful were persuaded had moved or smiled, bled or wept, provided dangerous proof of the potential power of the image, especially when artistic realism had played a part. The Dutch reformer-scholar Desiderius Erasmus fiercely ridiculed this kind of response in *The Praise of Folly* (1509): his main character, Folly herself, denounces the use of images since they would distract from the idea of her: "I [am not] yet so foolish as to require Statues or painted Images, which do often obstruct my Worship, since among the stupid and gross multitude those Figures are worship't for the Saints themselves."[27]

There were some precocious attempts at regulation. One of the many articles of the 1418 Synod of Saint Wenceslas declared: "Church images can be kept in the church, but only if they are not superfluous in number and not wantonly or falsely adorned in such a way as to seduce the eyes of communicants from respect for the Lord's body, or as to distract the mind, or as otherwise to be an impediment."[28] These instructions were heeded only half-heartedly, and a more radical solution was tried at the end of the fifteenth century: the polychromy that by then had become expected might profitably be eliminated. Between 1490 and 1492, German artist Tilman Riemenschneider carved what is thought to have been the first unpainted lindenwood altarpiece for the town church of Münnerstadt.[29] By leaving it monochrome, the sculptor had found a new way to create the appropriate devotional distance for the devout viewer. Another unpainted retable (altarpiece), commissioned for Bamberg in 1523, was carved by another superbly gifted German sculptor, Veit Stoss. It came with instructions: "Let no Prior lightly have it painted with colours: every master skilled in the art will tell him why."[30] While the Church approved these decisions, congregations resisted this absence of color, and by popular demand Riemenschneider's Münnerstadt altarpiece was polychromed in 1503–4, ironically enough, by Stoss himself.[31] In a similar episode of a popular repudiation of the monochrome, a white marble Saint John the Baptist with two saintly companions by the workshop of Venice-based sculptor Pietro Lombardo was set up on the high altar of the Cappella Colleoni in Bergamo. The brilliant whiteness of the sculptures so upset a local bookseller, Paolo di Acquate, that one night in June 1491, shortly after the altarpiece was installed, he broke into the chapel to (dis)color the figure of the Baptist, breaking one of its fingers in the process.[32]

In newly Protestant territories, the complete snuffing out of the power of sculpted images, especially those invested with miraculous powers, required public debunking. In February 1538, for instance, the Rood of Grace, a miraculous crucifix from the Abbey of Boxley, was carried to the Maidstone marketplace in southeastern England, "and there shewed openlye to the people the craft of movinge the eyes and lipps."[33] In the later sixteenth century and throughout the seventeenth century, the Catholic powers, however, fully understood the wide appeal of realistic sacred imagery, not least polychrome sculpture, as they urgently sought to bolster the popularity of the Church during the Counter-Reformation. Indeed, they could hardly ignore painted sculpture, so fundamental was it for the widespread practice of the faith. In 1636, for example, the Italian city of Genoa saw the conversion of a ship's figurehead, rescued from the sea by a pair of unlettered sailors, into the Madonna della Fortuna.[34] The priest of the maritime parish San Vittore dei Marinari allowed it to be set up in his church, though he squeamishly absented himself from the dedication ceremony. Healing miracles and exorcisms were quickly and eagerly reported. After failing to shut down this proletarian cult by closing the church and walling up the Madonna herself, the Genoese church authorities chose instead to sanction this new devotion but give it a respectable face by ensuring it was taken up by members of the city's social and political elite.[35]

This kind of balancing act between the compelling and the dangerously out-of-control lay behind the religious tenets put forth by the Council of Trent (1545–63), organized to achieve reconciliation but also to counter Protestant doctrine. At its final session (December 3, 1563), it was agreed "that the images of Christ, of the Virgin Mother of God, and of the other saints, are to be had and retained, particularly in temples, and that due honour and veneration are to be given to them, not that any divinity, or virtue, is believed to be in them, on account of which they are to be worshipped; or that anything is to be asked of them; or, that reposed trust is to be in images, as was of old done by the Gentiles who placed their hope in idols; but because the honour which is shown them is referred to the prototypes which those images represent."[36] For that to be certain, "in the invocation of saints, the veneration of relics, and the sacred use of images, every superstition shall be removed, all filthy lucre be abolished; finally, all lasciviousness be avoided; in such wise that figures shall not be painted or adorned with a beauty exciting to lust."[37]

The sculpted representation of holy pain and suffering might therefore become even rawer and more affecting, as can be seen in the many carved and painted wood figures made in Spain, its colonies, and parts of Italy. Naturalistic detail became more intense, with the incorporation of bone teeth, glass eyes, and weeping resin tears, combined with the painting of trickling blood and livid bruises. Thanks to long-standing art-historical prejudice, we are only now understanding the individual approaches of Spain's post-Tridentine sculptors. Some, like those of Gregorio Fernández (cat. 111) or Pedro de Mena (cat. 96), have been studied reasonably well, while those of others, especially artists working into the eighteenth century, remain obscure. It has recently been established, for example, that La Roldana (Luisa Roldán) made her profoundly affecting, jewel-like Entombment group (1700–1701, cat. 97) for Philip V of Spain, to welcome him to the throne and to ensure her continued role as sculptor to the king.[38] Her observation of the passions of the main protagonists and of the almost casual participation of the laborers waiting to place the lid on Christ's tomb strikingly combines high drama and the reality of daily existence. However, we know very little of how this and her other small-scale tableaux were used, either devotionally or artistically. The career of her contemporary Juan Alonso Villabrille y Ron, also based in Madrid, is so far only briefly sketched out. His emotional realism at its most extreme is profoundly and deliberately disturbing. His signed half-length sculpture *Saint Paul the Hermit* (ca. 1715, cat. 103) conveys the physical suffering and spiritual purity of the saint, an exemplar for Catholic penitents bent on mortification of the flesh. Paul's legend states that he lived in the desert for over a hundred years, fed and clothed only by a palm tree and a raven. Villabrille's embodiment hovers in a place between senility and ecstasy.[39] Many such sculptures, including those containing large groups of figures, were borne on carts or were carried on the shoulders of the faithful in processions staged for the edification of enormous crowds (fig. 18). These acts of devotion were sometimes made possible by the use of especially lightweight materials.

This period was also marked by an increasing anxiety about the long-established practice of dressing sculpted figures in real clothing. Sometimes the practice was simply intended to increase a sculpture's credibility; unlike carved draperies, textiles move freely with the breeze. On other occasions, however, the beauty and richness of the clothing had been understood as ostentatious signals of the honor and reverence paid to the sculpted holy figure—a form, it was feared, of idolatry. Thus, the third provincial council of 1585, held in Mexico City, affirmed the edicts of the Council of Trent but with a new emphasis: "It is most advisable that there be nothing profane or indecent in the images that could impede or temper the devotion of the faithful. . . . Painted images are preferred, but if they are sculpted, their robes also should be. . . . There shall be no need to dress them; excepting, however, the ones of this kind with their special dress, that presently exist."[40] In 1600, the Synod of Gerona in Spain similarly declared, "Images of the saints are not to be dressed in profane garments, establishing that henceforth they . . . be carved so that they do not need clothing for their adornment."[41]

These edicts were only partially observed, and in 1690, for example, a Mexican cleric ordered a figure's sculpted draperies to be cut away so it could be dressed.[42] As late as 1771, the fourth Mexican provincial council was still trying, rather feebly, to enforce the ban prohibiting the

> making [of] images with just the face and hands and dressing the rest of the body with worldly adornments of necklaces, chokers, bracelets and other items not in keeping with the modesty of the Most Holy Mary and the Virgin saints, images that continue to be taken out of the church and carried to private homes to dress them according to their own idea, when all of this is childishness that diminishes the respect laypersons should have for images, which are not esteemed when they are dressed over cardboard or wooden armatures.[43]

Just as the Church sought to regulate yet exploit popular impulse, artists working in this terrain continued their attempts to lift the artistic status of their works, according to a now firmly established hierarchy, while ensuring that the devotional power of their sculptures was undiminished. Theological and aesthetic compromises rather than refutations, their solutions were subtler than those tried earlier by Riemenschneider and Stoss. They might take self-conscious account of the sculptural languages of the antique, Michelangelo, or other masters, while still "fleshing" their figures. A Saint John the Baptist (ca. 1620–30, cat. 48) by Juan Martínez Montañés, now in The Met, was acclaimed early on a masterpiece. The Seville-based sculptor mitigated the obligatory naturalism of the polychrome surface—which may well have been painted by Pacheco himself (he was a frequent collaborator)—by giving the saint a Herculean muscularity.[44] By this means, he makes the saint heroic and otherworldly in a strong departure from the standard emaciate, while at the same time declaring both his authorship and the figure's "madeness." In Genoa the dazzlingly talented Anton Maria Maragliano carved a heartrending Saint Sebastian for the Confraternità dei Disciplinanti in nearby Rapallo (1700, cat. 105), basing the figure and the entire composition of tree, cloak, and discarded weaponry on a white marble group by the renowned French sculptor Pierre Puget. But in this part of Italy, the power of polychrome religious sculpture held sway, and Maragliano's 1700 contract stipulates that the work should be "colorita in color di carne [flesh-colored]."[45] The painter responsible was Corrado Torre, a specialist in polychromy. Costume and armor were carved in wood as was the figure; this sculpture was neither dressed nor adorned in a way deemed inappropriate by Church authorities, though it would continue to be used in procession well into the twentieth century.[46]

The partial elimination of color was another solution, favored by the Church on at least one fascinating occasion. In 1590, the authorities were called to deal with another disruptive incident when, on the night of Holy Thursday, a crucifix in Igualada (near Barcelona) was seen miraculously to bleed. After a thorough investigation, leading to another attempt to close down a new popular cult, it was decided to lighten the polychromy, so "now it is white as if just made by a master artist."[47] This telling phrase says much about the Church's hope that evident artistry would reduce superstition. To ensure that religious statuary was both theologically acceptable and popularly affective, major sculptors in Germany therefore worked out a way of reducing naturalistic color without eradicating it. Ignaz Günther's *Christ at the Column* (1754, cat. 99) was intended to elevate subtly the people's

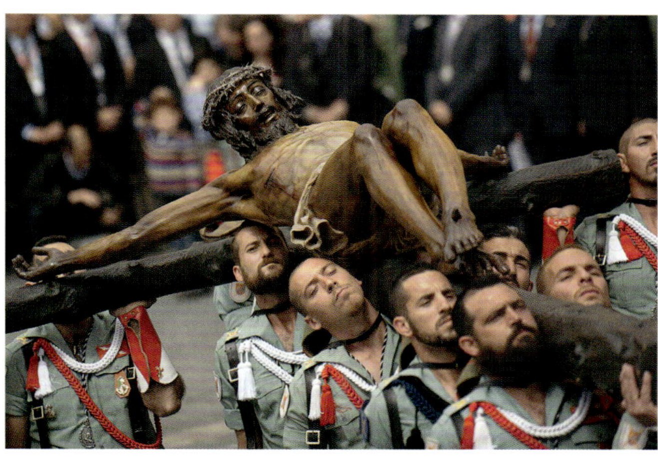

Fig. 18   Members of the Spanish Legion carrying a *Dead Christ* to the Church of Santo Domingo de Guzmán during a Holy Week procession, Málaga, Spain, April 17, 2014

faith in an existing miraculous sculpture, while deriving its authority from the piece from which it originated. As the story goes, in 1730, Father Magnus Straub and Brother Lukas Schweiger in Steingaden had pieced together a flagellated Christ from parts of different existing wood sculptures, a work that would be carried in procession on Good Friday. His wounds were too gory for the faithful public, and after its debut this Frankenstein Christ stood forgotten in the attic of the monastery inn. The innkeeper's cousin, Maria Lory, rescued the figure and took it to her farm in Wies, where it was venerated by her whole family. In June 1738 it is said that Lory found tears on the statue's cheeks.[48] There is an alternative account from 1779: "In the spring of 1733, in Steingaden's walled garden, preparations were under way for the next day's Good Friday procession. All sculptures and objects to be carried were assembled and reviewed. As it happened, "a disrespectful [*unehrerbietig*] fifteen-year-old monastery student tugged on the flagellated Jesus' beard. Suddenly the 'lifeless' statue moved in such a way that the chains attached to its hands and feet made such a terrible noise that the perpetrator [*Frevler*] fell to the ground."[49] This coming-alive was much more threatening.

Whatever the precise nature of the miracle, pilgrims flocked to Wies, and as was normal in the making of devotional imagery, the miraculous sculpture was copied several times, not least by Günther's sculptor father. The image and the pilgrimage became so important that the abbot of Steingaden built the grandiose Wieskirche, a church dedicated in 1754, the same year Günther signed his sculpture, signaling its status as an authored work. As he would going forward, Günther not only gave the figure a tremendous artistic elegance (this is a deliberately un-upsetting Flagellation), but he also toned down the polychromy, choosing muted pastels to remind viewers they were looking at a representation, not a living body. His sculpture thus borrowed the human and spiritual presence of the miraculous Wieskirche Christ while introducing an artifice that would remind viewers that transcendence depended on the spiritual exercise of looking beyond the real.

After the Reformation, Protestant objections to polychrome sculpture were emblematic of a much larger rejection of Catholic practice, a doctrinaire distaste that lingers in Western thinking on art today. Polychrome was a Catholic thing, and all the more so if the figures were wax. In 1672, the diarist John Evelyn, writing in tense times, connected the display of wax figures to what he viewed as attempts to restore Catholicism to Britain:

> [I] went to see the fopperies of the Papists at Somerset house and York house, where now the French Ambassador had caused to be represented our Blessed Saviour at the Pascal Supper, with his Disciples, in figures and puppets made as big as the life, of wax work, curiously clad, and sitting round a large table, the roome nobly hung and shining with innumerable Lamps and Candles, this exposed, to all the world, all the Citty came to see; such liberty had the Roman Catholics at this time obtained.[50]

Perhaps Evelyn was right to be worried. This display was seemingly an act of provocation, designed to have a broad impact. Many in that period, as well as before and since then, believed that wax, a natural material with transformative potential, was endowed with supernatural properties, and the use of wax was often connected to the fashioning of witches' poppets. The doomed, deluded Duchess of Malfi, the eponymous heroine of John Webster's macabre play first performed in 1613, expressed that belief. She was forced to look at wax figures of her husband and children, portrayed as if dead. Believing her loved ones had really departed, she avows, "It wastes me more / Than were't my picture, fashion'd out of wax, / Stuck with a magical needle and then buried / In some foul dunghill."[51]

In the early modern period, however, with superstition or belief still effective weapons of propaganda, waxworks were created by the political elite for popular consumption. Until the execution in 1649 of the imprudent Charles I made it impossible to continue the practice, the full-length, crowned, and gowned effigies of the English kings and queens were paraded recumbent on the lids of their coffins so as to encourage the crowds to pray for their immortal souls. Initially fashioned from wood or leather, by the end of the sixteenth century the figures were made from wax, perhaps following Italian fashion.[52] In Florence, three clothed wax effigies of Lorenzo de' Medici by Orsino Benintendi had been carefully situated in different locations in or near the city, one placed at SS. Annunziata, another wearing the overcoat in which *il Magnifico* had revealed himself, complete with bandaged neck, to the citizenry after surviving the assassination attempt that had killed his brother in 1478.[53] Such sculptures were not cheap. Various prices are recorded for making wax effigies for SS. Annunziata, but it is known that Isabella d'Este, Marchioness of Mantua and an avid art collector, paid twenty-five gold coins in 1507 for the "image of a realistic portrait" by Filippo Benintendi, a member of the next generation of the family of Florentine effigy makers.[54] Filippo negotiated its prestigious location within the church with the friars. Prices for waxworks remained consistently high over time. In 1702, for example, Frances Stuart, Duchess of Richmond and the former mistress of King Charles II, paid one Mrs. Goldsmith an enormous £260 to fashion her funeral figure (and even had her own parrot stuffed to go with it).[55] The sculpture took nearly a year to make.

So powerful was the belief that these figures contained the essence of the person depicted that, once those represented were considered enemies, their votive effigies could be symbolically killed (just as Cattelan would murder his Pinocchio). In 1527, for example, after the invasion of Italy by the troops of Holy Roman Emperor Charles V, the figures of the Medici Popes Leo X and Clement VII were attacked in Florence; a contemporary commentator called it an "assassination."[56] From the point of view of the art establishment, with its need to promote the individuality of artists, waxworks became problematic for precisely this reason; that sort of reaction to and treatment of waxworks by their beholders demonstrates the extent to which viewers might remain so oblivious to the "madeness" of these sculptures that they could forget they were responding to authored works of art. Our empathetic response to these objects somehow overpowers any agency the artists might claim. A snippet of gossip about Lady Godolphin, daughter of the Duchess of Marlborough, makes just this point. She was said to have loved playwright William Congreve so dearly that she found his death quite intolerable: "her husband endured the relationship and following the death of Congreve, mourned by himself also, he allowed his wife to place a wax figure of the writer at the table every day as an invited guest and to take the same to her bedroom at night."[57] Who was this love-sculpture by? Tellingly, art historians have no idea. The low standing and current anonymity of many of these artists have reinforced the sense that an encounter with their works is almost unmediated. Like the grieving Lady Godolphin, we the viewers are granted higher status in the emotional and creative exchange around the work than the makers.

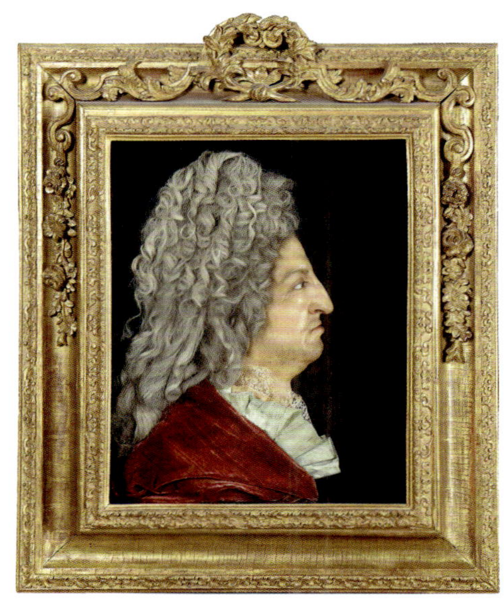

Fig. 19 Antoine Benoist. *Louis XIV*, ca. 1705. Pigmented beeswax, painted glass enamel eye, human hair, white lace, silk, velvet, pins, nails, and gilded wood frame, H. 33 9/16 in. (85.3 cm), W. 27 15/16 in. (71 cm), D. 4 3/4 in. (12 cm). Musée National des Châteaux de Versailles et de Trianon

As a result, these specialist sculptors were often denigrated in their own day and usually quickly forgotten. Indeed, history provides just one superstar among waxwork makers: Antoine Benoist, a knighted member of the Académie Royale de Peinture et de Sculpture. Louis XIV gave him the title of "the king's painter and his only sculptor of colored wax" and sat for him an astounding seven times.[58] Benoist must be the author of the single surviving lifesize wax profile of the king, a remarkable unsigned but unforgettable object created about 1705, replete with real hair, pockmarks, and a five-o'clock shadow (fig. 19). Encouraged by Louis, he also made wax effigies of French courtiers and other celebrities that were frequently dressed in the clothes they had donated for the purpose. The monarch and his entourage, Madame de Sévigné and the like, admired waxworks of the extravagantly garbed ambassadors of Algeria, Morocco, Russia, and Siam in a lavish public display at the rue des Saints-Pères, Paris, called *Le Cercle*. Some subjects had donated their own clothes, and costuming a portrait in its subject's own garments, a kind of contact relic after all, was a way of enveloping and energizing a sculpture with its own life force.

The virtues of this waxwork display, proclaimed by the poet Martin Baraton, enable a classic sequence of approval, celebrating the features that critics, for the most part, deplored:

Even this celebrated sculptor was rather quickly consigned to oblivion, a fate he shared with most of his fellow specialists. Vasari certainly felt the need to tell his readers how to identify the works by the best of all quattrocento waxwork makers, so obscure had he become just a century later: "With regard to wax images, in the…church of the Servi [SS. Annunziata], all models bearing a capital O on the bottom with an R and a cross on top were made by the hand of Orsino [Benintendi], all of a remarkable beauty which has rarely been equaled by others."[60]

Even an elite sculptor might be punished in print for dabbling in polychromy. The seventeenth-century Florentine artist and art historian Filippo Baldinucci gave a revealingly patronizing account of what he saw as a rather silly sideline to the principal efforts of his famous contemporary, the bronze sculptor Pietro Tacca, author of one of the grandest equestrian monuments in Florence. Tacca "amused himself by making figures from colored wax, among which he made the life-sized head and bust of the Grand Duke Cosimo II, from life, with eyelashes, real beard and hair and such eyes of glass as to seem almost his own. The whole figure gave no look of being false but seemed to be alive."[61] After Cosimo's death, his mother, Christine of Lorraine, responded to Tacca's portrait in a way that complimented the sculptor's verisimilitude, but treated it more as a substitute for her dead child than as the product of a great artist's talent: "Before entering the house of Tacca to view his work, [she] requested that the figure of her son be removed as her poor heart could not bear the sight of her dear deceased son, who seemed to have returned to life in the semblance of a mute statue."[62]

If making such works could taint elite practitioners, the standing of waxwork makers was not enhanced by the fact that from the late seventeenth century onward, many were women. Beyond Madame Tussaud, now remembered as more a show woman or brand than significant artist, many other women operated successfully in this arena, and a handful achieved a certain celebrity in their lifetimes. For example, the eighteenth-century Bolognese Anna Morandi Manzolini, an anatomical wax modeler who was trained by her husband, became fantastically famous, receiving invitations from Catherine the Great in Saint Petersburg and the Royal Society, London (cat. 23). After her husband's death, Pope Benedict XIV paid her a salary "to relieve her in her domestic situation and allow her to proceed with renewed courage in the exertion of her studies."[63] The funeral effigy of the hero of Trafalgar, Horatio Nelson, was executed for Westminster Abbey by Catherine Andras, who was permitted to show her wax portraits at the Royal Academy, London.[64] These names are only emerging from long obscurity, and in general female waxwork makers were marginalized even as they conquered commercially. The Neapolitan nun Caterina de Julianis was little known beyond her community of religious devotees.[65] Active in the late eighteenth century, Marie Marguerite Bihéron, daughter of a Parisian apothecary, created what were dismissed as "sad imitations of cadavers."[66] In London was a slew of women waxwork makers, commercially successful but aesthetically ignored:

Mrs. Mills, Mrs. Clark, Mrs. Bullock, and the American Patience Wright.[67] Mary Salmon is known to have executed a self-portrait dandling her baby on her lap that could be seen at her London wax museum. In another context and age, this piece might be interpreted as a statement on motherhood, artistry, and different kinds of female creation and procreation. As women in the eighteenth century were generally praised for their skills and manual dexterity but not their innate artistic talent, Salmon was casually trivialized in her own era. In 1763, twenty-three years after her death, James Boswell wrote in the *London Journal*: "This afternoon I went and saw Mrs Salmon's famous wax-work in Fleet Street. It is excellent in its kind, and amused me very well for a quarter of an hour."[68] No more than fifteen minutes should be wasted, he clearly thought, on what was merely a diversion.

Moreover, the making of waxworks was a practice that crossed class and economic boundaries, a factor that was a problem in and of itself. Wax ex-votos—heads, legs, arms, organs, and even the genitalia that so intrigued Enlightenment antiquarian Richard Payne Knight—were for centuries cast from cheaper, standardized molds and not necessarily colored (cat. 86).[69] Their personalization came about largely through acts of devotional presentation and supplication. As early as the second half of the fourteenth century, the Florentine Franco Sacchetti condemned what he thought had become a dangerously widespread practice. He wrote a novella satirizing the manufacture and deluded dedication of such votive offerings (including, absurdly, the image of a lost cat): "These ex-votos and similar things are offered every day and they are more a form of idolatry than of Christian faith.... [God] wants our hearts and our minds; he doesn't go searching for images of wax....[I]t would seem that many traps, with which it looks as though one would go to paradise, more often will lead to hell."[70]

NIGHTMARES IN WAX

Superstition and artistic anonymity were thus major impediments to the acceptance of realistic polychrome waxworks. Another was the slippage between elite patronage, serious devotional practice, and popular entertainment. As early as 1511, a list was drawn up of all the effigies of famous people in Santissima Annunziata, which had become a tourist attraction providing ample opportunity to gawp at celebrities.[71] The situation was not only distressingly democratic, but a worrying fascination with the gruesome had also emerged. Guidebook author Francesco Bocchi was intrigued by the effigies with attributes that referred to their donors' miraculous deliverances from extreme peril. Writing in 1592, Bocchi described the image of a man saved from public execution in Florence as "the portrait [*ritratto*] of his horrible experience" and went on to observe, a little clinically, that "the way of cutting off the heads in public executions, as seen in this image, is very different from that which is used in many places."[72] From early on, death, execution, and assassination—all things grisly—were key to the appeal of wax portraits. When Michel Bourdin exhibited in 1611 a wax bust of Henri IV of France, the king had only just been murdered. This occasion may have been the first time an audience was asked to pay for the pleasure of viewing a wax figure, one moreover who they knew was both alive (in the sculpture) and dead (in reality).[73]

By about 1700, anatomical wax models provided another kind of substitute body and introduced an additional layer to the continuing association of wax and flesh, as well as to the medium's capacity to blur the distinction between life and death. They also serve as another example of how works of art created with serious intent could become too popular for their own good. Some of the first such models were tableaux of medical misery, wax representations of massed plague sufferers by Giulio Gaetano Zumbo, grandly entitled *The Triumph of Time* and *The Plague* (both before 1700). In 1929 Zumbo's biographer, Giuseppe Carobbi, twisted himself in knots, simultaneously admiring and deploring the sculptor's depiction of the effects of syphilis: "It is a beautiful piece of large dimensions . . . possibly the most important of Zumbo's works although the subject matter is particularly gruesome and disgusting *for its excessive realism.*"[74] Shocking they may have been, but that was the aim. Images such as these became highly popular; we are all aware that these controlled sensations of disgust provoke a particular brand of pleasure.

Most anatomical models were intended as permanent alternatives to the dissected cadaver, and models of women were especially useful for teaching obstetrics, previously the domain of the midwife, not the doctor (cat. 115). They fed what had already become a craze for human anatomy. For some time, European universities had sold tickets to the public to witness dissections of human corpses, and one may surmise that the popularity of these anatomical performances was fueled not just by a disinterested spirit of scientific inquiry but rather more by a collective desire to satisfy morbid curiosity, to face the fear of death.[75] In 1775 the extraordinary museum La Specola, made to contain the vast collection of models assembled by the Medici family, opened in Florence.[76] Specialists and the public alike flocked to see its displays, but such spectacles were at first treated as a proper entertainment for the better-off and better-educated. The intended demographic is indicated by their steep ticket prices. When in 1727 and 1730 surgeon Guillaume Desnoues, former partner of the great Zumbo, showed his anatomical models in Britain—his second exhibition was held at a chemist's shop on the corner of Pall Mall and the Haymarket—the entry fee was a sizable five shillings.[77]

Quite soon, however, these exhibitions had moved down the economic and social ladder, and critics had the excuse they needed to declare them of merely prurient interest. When, in 1825, a "Florentine" anatomical Venus was displayed in London, the *Literary Gazette* knew exactly what was happening: "Under the pretense of imparting anatomical knowledge, this filthy French figure, the property of one Monsieur Esnaut, is exhibited. It is a large, disgusting Doll, the alvus of which being taken off like a pot-lid, shows the internal parts, heart, liver, lungs, kidneys and as remotely from anatomical precision or utility as any of the sixpenny wooden dolls which you may buy at Bartholomew fair. . . . The thing is a silly imposture, and as indecent as it is wretched."[78] By the end of the nineteenth century, advertisements shamelessly stressed the sensational aspects of their displays. For example, a handbill for J. W. Reimer's Anatomical and Ethnological Museum, London, boasted "500 Magnificent Preparations in Wax." The sought-after audience was clear: "For Gentlemen only . . . No person will be admitted under 18 years."[79] The cost of admission was now a very affordable sixpence.

Against this background of peepshow science, the French critic Champfleury, later such a champion of artistic realism, wrote his critique of waxworks, published in 1852. Employing a tone as lurid as some of the waxworks he attacked, he compared the sculptures to corpses in a morgue that had been cut up by murderers and reassembled by morticians. He described the wax museum's awful appeal: "One is deeply disturbed on entering into the halls, thoughts go to crime, to assassinations. The sight can be compared to that of a morgue or a slaughter-house. . . . No longer concerned with biblical figures or kings and emperors, our wax museums had become a sort of court gazette held standing up, life-sized, in coloured gowns. It represented the consecration of crime."[80] For him, such displays were even capable of "corrupting and inducive of evil behavior."[81] He described a wax tableau of members of the Spanish court gathered by candlelight: "I have never seen any sight so gruesome. The people seem to have been fed on poison for a whole month."[82] The spiritual charge that remained in such works had been turned on its head; the waxwork was no longer the perpetually alive representation of the dead, no longer a person's spiritual proxy, but instead their combined realism and artificiality became, for Champfleury, a nasty reminder of the inevitable death of the viewer.

THAT'S ENTERTAINMENT

If, by the eighteenth century, statuary signaled its significance by avoiding color, polychromy became associated with objects all too easily classed as frivolities, even when carved or modeled by major talents. Seventeenth-century Venetian sculptor Andrea Brustolon, the pupil of a pupil of Gian Lorenzo Bernini, carved what are probably the most celebrated pieces of dark wood furniture that depict Africans in roles that are literally support-ing (fig. 20).[83] His pieces bolstered a tradition of blackamoor furniture, which usually lacked the excuse of his brilliant carving. In this way, non-Europeans, especially Africans, were made doubly into possessions. The application of color to such sculpted images became a way of emphasizing the exoticism of the peoples represented, a means by which their otherness was stressed. White heroes were to be carved from white marble. At the time, the critique was not that this genre was offensive, but that it was furniture, rather than serious statuary. These objects are now classed with the decorative arts; polychrome sculpture had fallen victim to yet another hierarchy, not least when such objects came to be made for a mass market. Here indeed are the origins of the notion of kitsch. American artist Mike Kelley's definition is useful: "Kitsch, outwardly characterized by gaudy colors, is a cheap and false version of the true, made for and consumed by the underclasses."[84] It is also sometimes a cheap term of abuse for a work of art the elite views as lacking gravitas. Colored ceramic sculpture had also hiccuped its way into existence in the sixteenth century with an equally dubious group of maiolica busts of "Moors" and elderly, ugly women, essentially images of exotic people and society's human jokes.[85] This interlocking of color and the Other for the purpose of giving what for their consumers was an uncomplicated pleasure continued into the eighteenth century when multicolored porcelain figures were placed in front of diners with the desserts. The table suddenly danced with Harlequins, while beggars acted coun-terpoint to the feasting. More than just theatrical, the practice derived from popular and profane theater. The sculptors employed at Europe's leading porcelain manufacturers were a highly skilled group—Johann Joachim Kändler at Meissen (cat. 13), Giuseppe Gricci in Naples and Spain, Franz Anton Bustelli in Berlin, and Joseph Willems in Chelsea—but they were called on to create models that would then be molded to make multiples (a de facto cheapening of the statue) and colored

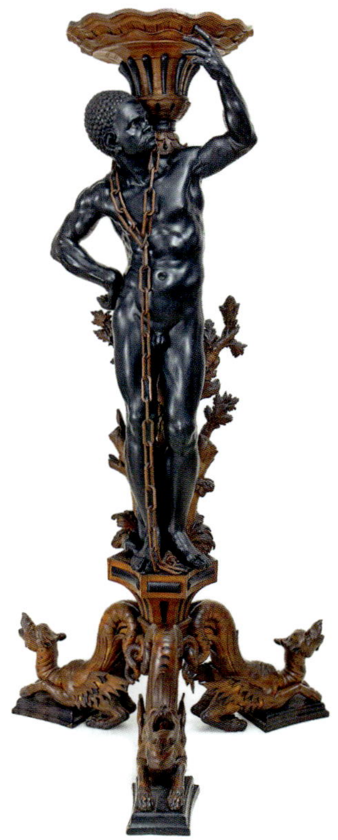

Fig. 20 Andrea Brustolon. *Pedestal with figure of an "Ethiopian,"* ca. 1700. Carved and patinated ebony and boxwood, H. 47 ¼ in. (120 cm), W. 23 ⅝ in. (60 cm), D. 20 ⅞ in. (53 cm). Ca' Rezzonico, Venice

by artisans who often worked beyond the creators' control.[86] Their huge success at an elite level ensured a trickle-down into less refined markets, and by the beginning of the nineteenth century, the application of color, initially rather restrained, became positively garish. Figurines were made in bulk at the Staffordshire potteries, daubed with gaudy colors, and dubbed "image toys" or "chimney ornaments."[87] After the 1851 Great Exhibition in London, a number of potteries manufactured enormous majolica sculptures of cheery cupids, blousy goddesses, exotic peacocks, and, once again, numerous blackamoors.[88] This was art that was not, in theory at least, owned by the cultural elite.

The popularity of such works was a red rag to the critics, who judged them vulgar, and the putative origins in science or faith offered no protection against such a sentiment. Automata, for example, mechanically animated figures that were often lifesize, were first inspired by scientific efforts to imitate life and, for a short time, were the serious playthings of the seriously rich. They enjoyed huge prestige in seventeenth-century Europe, especially in France, with celebrated examples performing in grand palaces and great gardens, including the pleasure park at Hesdin, made for Philippe, Duke of Artois, that was populated by a host of mechanical musicians and their brethren, and the grottoes at Saint-Germain-en-Laye, which contained mechanical figures created for Henry IV of France by the Francini brothers.[89] The vogue for these marvelous creations reached its peak in the eighteenth century, when Voltaire felt moved to praise:

> The audacious [Jacques de] Vaucanson, rival of Prometheus
> Imitating Nature's action, seemed to use
> Heavenly fire to kindle life in animate matter.[90]

Their subject matter was usually similar to porcelain and pottery figures; figures of gods and goddesses were featured, but the makers of mechanical sculpture mainly fashioned exotics, entertainers, and lowlife subjects that could not be taken for high art. Mechanical statuary suffered a comparable trajectory to that of colored ceramics when its ever more widespread enjoyment precipitated a decline in its critical esteem. In 1647 mechanical—and wax—figures were described for the first time at London's Bartholomew Fair, where teeming masses could not only enjoy the portraits of rulers, politicians, and writers but also grotesques, freaks, and famous criminals. By the end of the eighteenth century, the fair and its automata could be seen as a metaphor for the febrile falseness of the city itself. Poet William Wordsworth listed the exhibits at Bartholomew Fair in *The Prelude* of 1799–1805:

> The Bust that speaks and moves its goggling eyes,
> The Wax-work, Clock-work, all the marvellous craft
> Of modern Merlins, Wild Beasts, Puppet-shows,
> All out-o'-the-way, far-fetched, perverted things,
> All freaks of nature, all Promethean thoughts
> Of man, his dullness, madness, and their feats
> All jumbled up together, to compose
> A Parliament of Monsters. Tents and Booths
> Meanwhile, as if the whole were one vast mill,
> Are vomiting, receiving on all sides,
> Men, Women, three-years' Children, Babes in arms.[91]

By the mid- to late nineteenth century, the enormous popularity of French automata at the Expositions Universelles was considered proof that even the elite could behave like fools:

"Among the collection of toys on exhibition at the entrance to Class 46 are to be seen Senators, deputies and *conseille[u]rs d'état* in official dress paying their respects, like simple mortals with none of the heavy responsibilities of state, to shiny cardboard dolls no less sparkling than their own embroidered uniforms."[92] That the simple appeal of such works could be a social leveler was occasionally acceptable but more often judged threatening to the societal—and by extension, artistic—order. The same commentator exclaimed of the 1867 exposition in Paris: "Lord! but it's amusing to see people enjoying themselves! If you too wish to enjoy this spectacle, come to the Universal Exhibition at the hour when the greatest number of people are there, and...you will observe, face to face, just how far the naivety of the most intelligent people on this earth may go."[93] The making of these pieces was a serious commercial proposition and Paris the center of production. When one of the city's specialist sculptors, Alexandre-Nicolas Théroude, executed his *Flute Player* (ca. 1869–77, cat. 52), he was tapping into a market not just for objects that would be exhibited publicly but which also would be sold for home entertainment. Thanks to his collaboration with organ maker Pierre-Ernest Kelsen, the flutist plays four tunes. Represented as a richly dressed up but barefoot African youth, Théroude's musician is a technologically embellished example of the blackamoor tradition that was central to both the furnishing of the home and musical entertainment in the West. The piece therefore embodies a history of visual and actual subjugation that now makes us feel deeply and rightly uncomfortable. However, it is important to recognize that this dominant feature in the history of European and North American polychrome sculpture is perhaps another factor that causes us to flinch in our examination of the genre.

The mid-eighteenth-century English fad for painted lead garden sculpture, with its similar subject matter, would also provide critics and satirists with grist for their mills. The lead sculpture of John Cheere was implicitly condemned, for instance, by Regency engraver, painter, and devout Neoclassicist John Thomas Smith, who dismissed them as "cast in lead as large as life and frequently painted with an intention to resemble nature. They consisted of Punch, Harlequin, Columbine and other pantomimical characters; mowers whetting their scythes, haymakers resting on their rakes, gamekeepers in the act of shooting and Roman soldiers with firelocks, but above all that of an African, kneeling with a sundial on his head."[94] Several poets of the 1750s and 1760s used the "squabby Cupids" and "clumsy Graces" made in workshops located north of Piccadilly as ammunition for their attacks on the estates bought—emphatically not inherited—by City financiers, merchants, and tradesmen.[95] Too imitative of the real and insufficiently elevated in their subject matter, these objects were not to be taken seriously, and they were owned by the wrong people. Small surprise then that very little in this category survives today.

Eighteenth-century British dramatist Richard Cumberland invented an occasion when, during a visit to Sir Theodore and Lady Thimble, a particularly idiotic visitor mistook "a leaden statue on a pair of scates [*sic*], painted in a blue and gold coat, with a red waistcoat" made at Hyde Park Corner, for his host.[96] That this guest was bamboozled was sufficient evidence that he could not be a person of quality. Though such works were purchased by aristocrats, they were primarily associated in literature with this arriviste social group. This critical judgment deliberately confused the subjects represented, the class of object, and those viewing, that is, the arriviste middling classes, the gawping lower classes, and what were regarded as primitive foreigners.

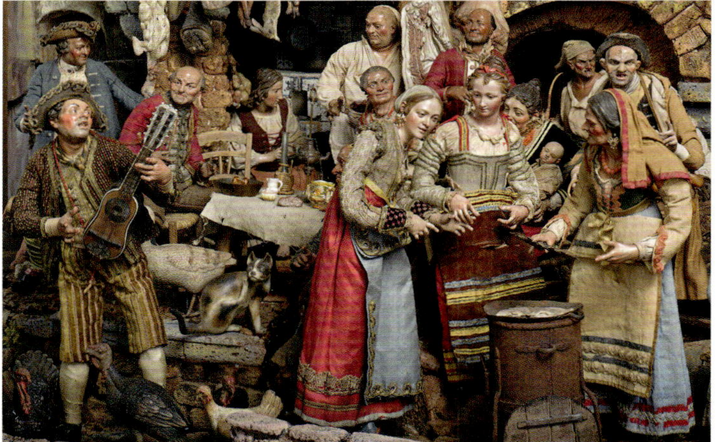

Fig. 21 *Neapolitan Crèche*, mid-18th century (detail). Polychromed terracotta, fabrics, leather, paper, glass, string, straw, basket fibers, cork, wire, hemp, papier-mâché, twigs, moss with watercolor and gouache, alabaster, marble, gold, silver, pearl, coral, ivory, bone, iron, silver, lead, string, other metals, raw clay, ceramic, wax, leather, and wood. H. 14 ft. 1 5⁄16 in. (430 cm), W. 15 ft. 3 1⁄16 in. (465 cm), D. 55 1⁄8 in. (140 cm). Art Institute of Chicago, Restricted gifts of Mr. and Mrs. James N. Bay; Linda and Vincent Buonanno and Family; Charles H. and Mary F. Worcester Collection and Eloise W. Martin Legacy funds; and Mrs. Robert O. Leavitt

An ostensibly religious context did nothing to help. In 1752 Luigi Vanvitelli, the Dutch-born, Rome-trained architect of signal austerity, wrote to his brother from the royal palace at Caserta—"I have been to Naples, where I saw the Cribs. For all their clumsiness in other things, the Neapolitans are particularly skilful at creating these childish works"—an observation that damns with faint praise.[97] The collection and arrangement of figures carved from wood and dressed with real textiles had begun as a childish pastime for aristocrats, not least the royal family, and thus there arose a corrosive whiff of amateurism. Pietro D'Onofrij in 1789 recorded King Carlo's pleasure in watching Queen Maria Amalia sewing little costumes for the shepherds while he could be found "in the idle hours of the day, with his royal hands, moulding and baking little bricks and arranging *sòveri* [the bark of cork-oak used to fashion scenery] shaping the stable, designing the background, putting the statuettes in their places."[98] Royal they may have been, but they had turned the making of art into a distraction, a way of killing time.

The protagonists were now familiar types. Exotics could be seen in the retinues of the Magi, and the scenes teem with peddlers and peasants. During the last quarter of the eighteenth century, as a response to the newly burgeoning discipline of ethnography, labels were placed inside the chest sections of statuettes identifying the figurines as a "woman of Genzano" or a "peasant of Comino."[99] Because of the presence of these characters and because they were later to become such a prominent part of the Neapolitan Christmas, the audience for these crèches (fig. 21) is almost always assumed to be a popular one, an extra blow to their reputation.

TAKING COLOR SERIOUSLY

From the Renaissance on, popularity itself had become the single most significant impediment to critical success, even when the efforts made to introduce color counted as serious. The nineteenth-century French sculptor Charles-Henri-Joseph Cordier saw himself as a pioneer of anthropology. He made a sequence of sculptures of the women and men of North and West Africa, China, and elsewhere that he hoped would break down the hierarchy between Europeans and people from other parts of the globe (cats. 30, 33). "Beauty is not," he declared, "the province of a privileged race."[100] But early modern anthropology had already gravitated toward pseudoscientific spectacle, attitudes that informed the public exhibition of foreign peoples in Europe throughout the nineteenth century. At Reimer's Anatomical and Ethnological Museum, "Amongst the Wonders of the 'Gallery of All Nations'" were exhibited "the well-known AZTEC LILLIPUTIANS."[101] When members of the Société d'Anthropologie, Cordier among them, studied the Nubians, Sami,

Argentinian gauchos, and others exhibited at the Jardin d'Acclimatation that opened in the Bois de Boulogne in 1859, their curiosity, once again, was often substantially voyeuristic.[102]

Writer Théophile Gautier praised Cordier for the intelligent modernity of his artistic ambitions, but for most commentators there was a ferocious failure to understand his means or motives. After seeing Cordier's sculpted heads of a Chinese couple, critic Claude Vignon grumbled:

> But what is less art, and what appears supremely out of place at the Salon of 1852, are these busts done in the manner of characters on Chinese screens [i.e. chinoiserie porcelain]. Sculpture may bend a bit to accommodate fantasy, but not to this degree. We will absolutely not determine whether or not the Chinese are more or less authentic, or whether they are well or poorly executed. To appreciate these would be to accept them as works of art, and this we will never do.[103]

Journalist and writer Hector de Callias liked *The Jewish Woman of Algiers* (1862, cat. 30) well enough but still determined that Cordier's sculptural method would not "arrive at Phidias" but would instead remain too reminiscent of waxworks by the Swiss Philippe Curtius (fig. 22, cat. 113) or his famous niece Madame Tussaud.[104] Cordier's sculptures failed to sell, and he essentially gave up this high-minded endeavor. At his stand at the Exposition Universelle of 1867, he showed anthropomorphic torchères, sculpted Indian women who, once again, had been turned into furniture. Sadly, they were a spectacular commercial success.[105] Both this subject matter and colored sculpture as a category ensured that the works' voyeuristic reception would sully his elevated intent.

A similar situation arose when, about 1800, it became more widely known that the ancients had applied color to their marble sculptures. Greek and Roman sculptures had been excavated with traces of pigment on them, which for the first time were not scrubbed off. As a result, in 1851 George Scharf, an English illustrator and future director of the National Portrait Gallery, London, tried to find a way for color to penetrate the pale, hallowed halls of idealizing sculpture: "Hitherto no distinction has been drawn between the *real* and *ideal* in this branch: a shiny painted figure, and a great wax doll with real silk or velvet, real lace, and real glittering trinkets, are equally objectionable; but a sober, harmonious, well-balanced application of colour and metal to sculpture is likely to meet with a very different result."[106]

Pursuing this very end, Charles Garnier boasted when describing his sculptures for the staircase of Paris Opéra: "I am proud to think that I am going to revive on a grand scale the polychrome sculpture that the Romans sometimes used on their busts."[107] But, as Cordier found, the critical assumptions that greeted such works were just too strong. In 1855 Pierre-Charles Simart's chryselephantine reproduction of Phidias's *Athena Parthenos* was relegated to the section of the Exposition Universelle devoted to "industrial products."[108] It was in this same spirit of Neoclassical correctness that John Gibson made his celebrated marble *The Tinted Venus* (ca. 1851–56, cat. 8), but his efforts,

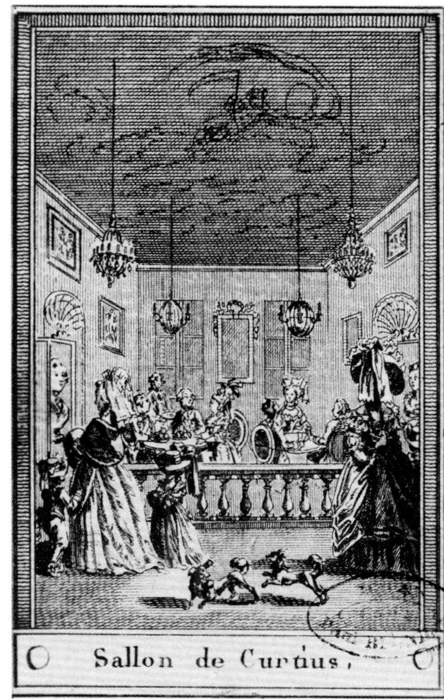

Fig. 22 *Salon de Curtius*, ca. 1786. Engraving, 3 9/16 × 2 1/8 in. (9 × 5.4 cm). French. Cabinet des Estampes, Bibliothèque Nationale de France, Paris

too, fell flat. He had colored the flesh "like warm ivory" in "a fashion unprecedented in modern times" and exhibited his colored ideal at the 1862 International Exhibition, London.[109] It could not have helped that he had clearly fallen in love with his own creation, exclaiming: "Here is a little nearer approach to life—it is therefore more impressive—yes—yes indeed she seems an ethereal being with her blue eyes fixed upon me! At moments I forgot that I was gazing at my own production; there I sat before her, long and often. How was I ever to part with her!"[110] This erotic charge and the self-conscious reenactment of the Pygmalion legend gave the critics their cue. One saw her as "a naked, impudent English woman . . . but in no respect a Venus."[111]

While some praise was directed at these sculptures and also at the naturalistically proportioned shop mannequins declared to be "modern," it was not enough to protect Edgar Degas's *The Little Fourteen-Year-Old Dancer* (ca. 1880, cat. 68) from an equally appalled response, one surely anticipated, if not courted, by the artist himself.[112] Another route to acceptance was needed, one that made a virtue of precisely those features that for many rendered the sculptures perverse. A productive clue could be found in Marquis de Sade's *Juliette, or Vice Amply Rewarded* (1797), that scandalous blend of cruelty, desire, and death. De Sade had given an account of the "fearful truth" of Zumbo's plague tableaux: "So powerful is the impression produced by this masterpiece, that even as you gaze at it your other senses are played upon; moans audible, you wrinkle your nose as if you could detect the evil odors of mortality."[113]

This "fearful truth" turned into an asset the conditioned state of anxiety induced by the confusion in these works between life and death. German psychiatrist Ernst Jentsch, whom Sigmund Freud, no less, cited in "The Uncanny" (1919), located this new notion in our "doubts" as to "whether an apparently animate being is really alive; or, conversely, whether a lifeless object might not in fact be animate."[114] This paradox was exploited by a generation of fin-de-siècle sculptors, the Belgian Fernand Khnopff and the German Max Klinger (cat. 47), among others. This period saw the creation of fetishized, mostly female figures that hover between the animate and the inanimate, the supremely natural, the inauthentic and the frighteningly artificial, the alluring and the terrible, and, now something that could be openly explored, the living and the dead. These artists set out to explore the seductive space between the imitation of life and the acknowledgment of artifice. Working just after the period when Italian terracotta sculpture and German wood carving had been stripped of color to satisfy the art market, they looked again at Renaissance portrait and reliquary busts, as well as polychrome sculpture from the ancient world, to create images of women who double as sirens, as Medusas, dangerous and powerful but emotionally hollow. Painted ladies abound—Bellonas, Cassandras, Salomes—and the Pygmalion myth was now adduced in a Freudian context.[115] The impact of Freud's theories is all too evident in the mannequin art of the Surrealists, culminating in the extraordinary display by Salvador Dalí and his peers at the 1938 Surrealist exhibition.[116] Founded on an already unlovely view of women and the female body, these works grew ever more misogynist into the twentieth century. Rather as the ideal of the Madonna had been rendered incarnate by the sculptors of the late Middle Ages, the Surrealists in the first half of the twentieth century gave concrete reality to erotic dreams and sexual nightmares. Their figures were now deliberately soulless, and German artist Hans Bellmer could celebrate the fact that "an object that is identical with itself is without reality."[117]

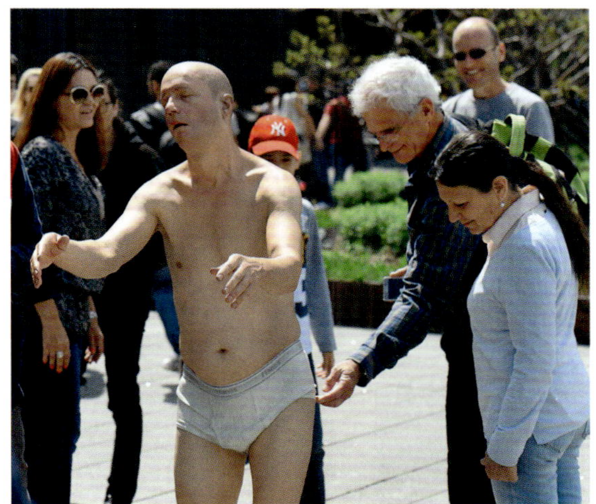

Fig. 23 Tony Matelli. *Sleepwalker*, 2014. Painted bronze, lifesize. Installation view, High Line, New York, 2016

RECENTLY AND NOW

During the second half of the twentieth century, democratizing rhetoric notwithstanding, the notion of art was still defined largely by elite prescription, concerns that still have something in common with the rules for art laid down in the Renaissance. The art world does not typically embrace works that communicate straightforwardly to ordinary people about themselves. Thus, the rejection of popular, realistic, colored sculpture remained a given in many quarters, with a particular objection to hyperrealist works. Influential Italian author Umberto Eco, for example, in his acutely snobbish *Travels in Hyperreality* (1975), sneered at what he saw as a vulgar, peculiarly American obsession with refabrications of the real, a line of attack many in the sixteenth or eighteenth century would have applauded and which indeed emerges from that elite European tradition.[118] Continuities can be found on both sides. Creating his taxonomy of ordinary people, Duane Hanson used many of the same tactics as historical waxwork makers, including casting from faces and figures from life and persuading his subjects to donate their own clothes. His tactics were still found artistically, even morally, impoverished, and the Canadian writer and artist Douglas Coupland has linked the poignant loneliness of Hanson's figures to the sculptor's own critical isolation:

> Hanson created hyperrealist figurative work at a moment in art history when to be sculpturally figurative was academically anathema. His work was enormously popular with the public and this also made him critically suspect, a fact of which he was well aware. To be underrated because of transient political vogues left Hanson without a full sense of artistic community, and this feeling of isolation is in evidence in his work, particularly in the solo figures created in the last two decades of his life.[119]

Tony Matelli's *Sleepwalker* (2014, fig. 23) might be interpreted rather similarly. Wearing just a remarkably dismal pair of white briefs, this Everyman, sunk into middle age and far from idealized, is sculpted with extreme realism. Represented somewhere between waking and sleep, he is physically, extraordinarily present but, with his eyes closed, quite oblivious to being viewed. He becomes our dream, our nightmare of near-naked public humiliation. Stumbling his way, as if to his own Gethsemane, intriguing amused crowds on New York's High Line, the figure embodies the outsider, exposed and mocked. Is he an embodiment of Matelli himself, enjoyed by the wrong people, in a public space rather than an art gallery, living with us as the Beguines' Christ lived and died surrounded by the people of Ghent?

Despite, or because of, public acclaim, Matelli and his *Sleepwalker* are still not invited into the temple of art. Critic Sean O'Hagan wrote of the popular success of Australian hyperrealist sculptor Ron Mueck's *Dead Dad* (1996–97) at the provocative 1997 exhibition at the Royal Academy—"Mueck had gatecrashed the *Sensation* party and stolen the show"—and his verbs are telling.[120] Mueck, too, creates profoundly accessible meditations on the fundamental but everyday ingredients of human existence: birth, death, and sleep, as well as race. The only meditative distance he provides is through radical shifts in scale from the lifesize that both accentuate and destabilize his

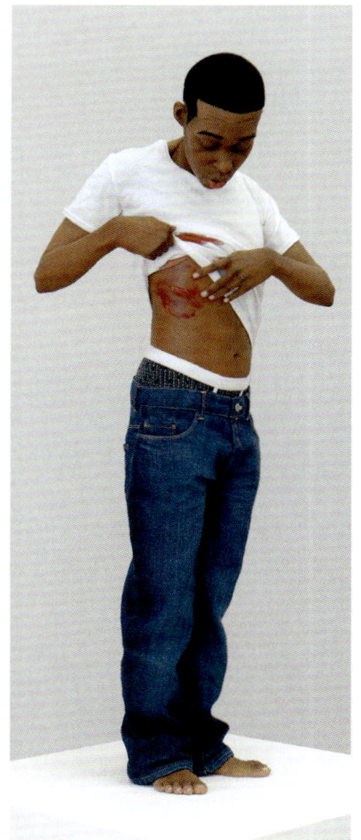

Fig. 24 Ron Mueck. *Youth*, 2009. Mixed media, H. 25 9/16 in. (65 cm), W. 11 in. (28 cm), D. 6 ¼ in. (16 cm); plinth: H. 42 ⅛ in. (107 cm), W. 15 ¾ in. (40 cm), D. 15 ¾ in. (40 cm). Courtesy the artist and Hauser & Wirth

extreme reality. Like many artists discussed here, he was trained outside the academy, as a model maker in the film world. Commissioned to make a work for his mother-in-law, painter Paula Rego—notably, a figure of Pinocchio—he became the serious entertainer we know today. Among the range of references that give his works their pathos, religious sculpture seems to resonate particularly. *Youth* (2009, fig. 24), for instance, depicts a miniaturized young Afro-Caribbean man lifting his T-shirt to reveal, both to himself and the viewer, that he has been wounded in his side.[121] He resembles a polychrome sculpture of the resurrected Christ. The diminutive figure of Mueck's dead dad lies on the floor like the Christ of the Lamentation; he has made a new kind of Pietà. In a similar vein, his *Old Woman In Bed* (2000, cat. 117) has the slack-jawed pathos of Villabrille's *Saint Paul the Hermit*, curled in a fetal position, sleeping her way to death. Her cheap, crisply clean sheets and blanket are as resonant as Christ's shroud.

O'Hagan saw Mueck's presence in "Sensation" as disruptive, and he was right. The whole exhibition set out to shock but in the process created a new conceptual norm into which Mueck fits somewhat awkwardly. This, too, can be made into a positive, when critics and curators allow. The desire to disrupt has now become a primary motive in the making of polychrome sculpture, used to upset both the assumptions of the art world and the sacred cows of society at large. By melding realism with a particularly sexualized Surrealism, sculptors like Paul McCarthy or the Chapman brothers have come to typify the boisterous antibourgeois artist. Arguably, however, the resulting works can occasionally become the excuse for the inexcusable.

With characteristic nerve, curator Norman Rosenthal has recently championed British Pop artist Allen Jones, author of a series of sculptures of women (fig. 25) posed to turn them into chairs, hat stands, and coffee tables (with something of the same denigrating character as the furniture carved by Brustolon). Jones, claims Rosenthal, "made a speciality of life-size mannequin figures, dressed in their impossibly kinky costumes, as though he is deliberately railing against all those purist feminist imperatives that our age wants to define with political correctness, and that makes Minimalist abstraction so much easier for our society to absorb."[122]

Many remain unconvinced by both such sculptures and the excuses made for them, and the critical terms of disquiet should, by now, be entirely familiar. Jed Perl recently attacked the sculptures of Jeff Koons by calling them soulless.[123] The angry exchange between Edward Kienholz and his critics can be thought of as exemplary. Almost entirely self-taught, Kienholz was another sculptor who redeployed many material and visual practices from

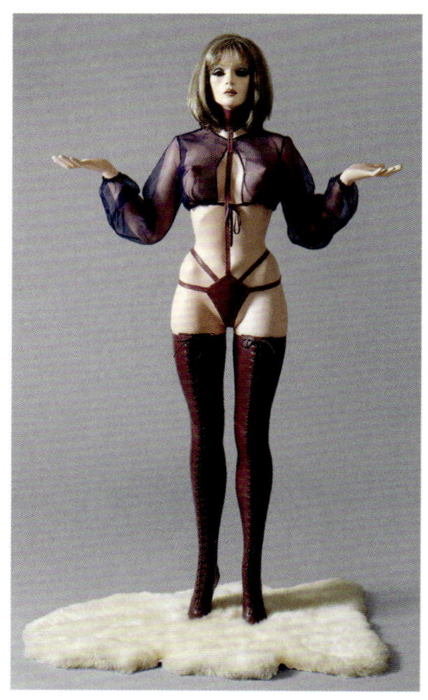

Fig. 25 Allen Jones. *Hat Stand*, 1969. Fiberglass, paint, resin, mixed media, and tailor-made accessories, H. 72 7/16 in. (184 cm), W. 42 15/16 in. (109 cm), D. 11 1/16 in. (28 cm). Courtesy of the artist

the past, another whose works are full of allusions to Catholic art. *John Doe* (1959), for example, contains several clear references to reliquaries. He has a cross where his heart might be, and a mechanism that connects it to his detachable, sometimes erect phallus.[124] There is a play here on the familiar theme of sacred desire. By arranging groups of figures in tableaux, using rags and other found objects, and casting from life, Kienholz annexed a popular language for sculpture to make us go on thinking about sex, death, and their interconnection. He revels in provoking our shared, shamed, excited voyeurism. *Back Seat Dodge '38* (1964) draws on the prurient thrills of Madame Tussauds's Chamber of Horrors.[125] The lovers in the back seat of this commonplace automobile appear to be frozen at their moment of death: sexual congress as a crime scene. Of the many skeptical critics, Hal Foster and his *équipe*, writing in *Art Since 1900* (2004), are perhaps the most hostile. Their angry, direct tone seems to take its cue from the works themselves, and using an all-too-familiar terminology, they complain that Kienholz tries too hard: "force-feeding the beholder with a heavy, unmistakable, unidimensional message." They continue, "like any advertisement, his works are one-liners pounded into the beholder's head with a skull-crashing baseball bat."[126]

Unwittingly, these critics appear to have surrendered to their visceral reaction, and in so doing, they actually get the point. Kienholz ensured that his polychrome sculpture had its glorious, absurdist revenge. He began collaborating with his wife, Nancy Reddin Kienholz, in 1972, and their work *The Art Show* (1963–77, fig. 26) took the critics on. In it, nineteen figures, made from life casts of well-known critics, friends, collectors, and other personalities, chatter, eye one another, and scrutinize the art on the walls. In place of mouths are air-conditioning vents that blow hot air when the beholder presses a button. At the same time, a tape recorder is activated, and the dignitaries can be heard uttering "pompous fatuous remarks."[127]

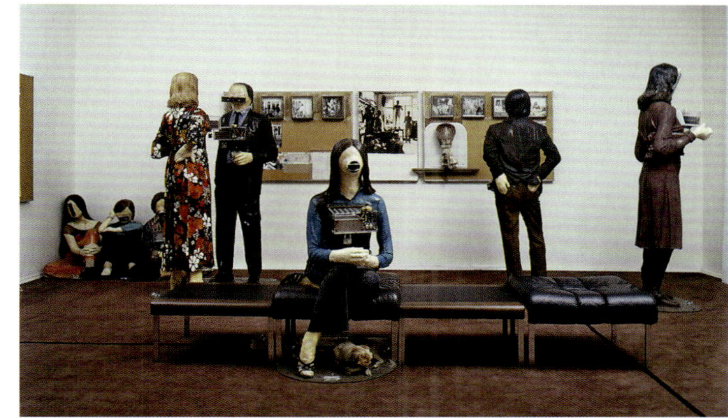

Fig. 26 Edward Kienholz and Nancy Reddin Kienholz. *The Art Show*, 1963–77 (detail). Mixed media

Perhaps unsurprisingly, Marcel Duchamp approved Edward Kienholz's sculpture: "Marvelously vulgar artist. Marvelously vulgar. I like that work."[128] Duchamp had always regarded audience response as key to the meaning of his works and in a 1964 interview with critic Calvin Tomkins declared: "If there's no onlooker there's no art. . . . It's a little game between the onlooker and the artist. Like roulette, or like a drug. . . . So the magic part of it—I don't believe in it anymore, I'm afraid I'm an agnostic in art, so to speak. I don't believe in it with all the trimmings, the mystic trimming and the reverence trimming and so forth."[129]

Duchamp's stance resulted in the very opposite of the elevated art of the ideal and the abstract that had been promoted for so long. In the last decades of his life, he had come to be seen as the highly serious (and retired) prankster of the art world, but he played out this statement in his last, surreptitious work of art, *Étant donnés* (1946–66, fig. 27).[130] Art historians and critics have found its meaning elusive, but perhaps if considered as the product of the long, popular history

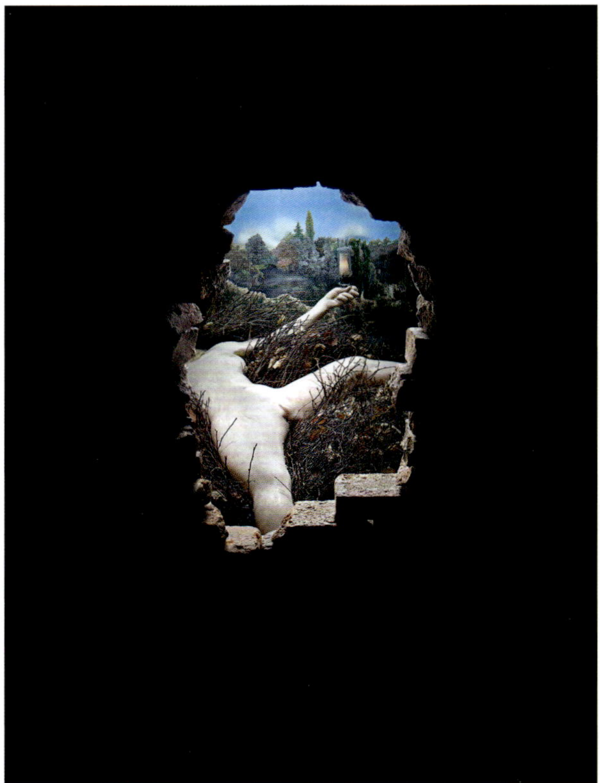

Fig. 27 Marcel Duchamp. *Étant donnés: 1° la chute d'eau, 2° le gaz d'éclairage…* *(Given: 1. The Waterfall, 2. The Illuminating Gas…)*, 1946–66. Wood door, iron nails, bricks, stucco, velvet, parchment over an armature of lead, steel, brass, synthetic putties and adhesives, aluminum sheet, welded steel-wire screen, and wood; pegboard, hair, oil paint, plastic, steel binder clips, plastic clothespins, twigs, leaves, glass, plywood, brass piano hinge, nails, screws, cotton, collotype prints, acrylic varnish, chalk, graphite, paper, cardboard, tape, pen ink, electric light fixtures, gas lamp (Bec Auer type), foam rubber, cork, electric motor, cookie tin, and linoleum. H. 95 in. (242.6 cm), W. 70 in. (177.8 cm), D. 49 in. (124.5 cm). Philadelphia Museum of Art, Gift of the Cassandra Foundation, 1969

of sculptural polychromy and the opinions of its detractors, the work might be understood as possessing a meaning that is in some ways human and uncomplicated. He has made another adult peepshow, a new tableau, occupied by a desired and possibly dangerous woman. One at a time, visitors are invited to look through peepholes pierced through a battered wood door, specially imported from Spain (giving the work a subtle flavor of Spanish religious sculpture), a method of viewer interaction that turns him—it seems to be a "him"—into a physically distanced but sexually involved voyeur. We see an array of found objects and the part-painted, part-photographed landscape that provides the setting for a prone, naked female figure, sculpted, colored, and adorned with real hair. Her face is invisible, but her legs are spread wide to expose her labia. The main model for this woman, Maria Martins, the Brazilian sculptor and Duchamp's mistress from 1946 to 1951, was subjected to multiple life casts. The woman raises a gas lamp like a libertine Lady Liberty, and her arm was provided by Duchamp's American second wife, Alexina (Teeny) Sattler. Duchamp has created a composite beloved, a proxy lover, a crafted ideal (or anti-ideal) of the female body with echoes of both Pygmalion's Galatea and Oskar Kokoschka's Alma Mahler doll (see fig. 64, cat. 58). This mannequin-woman is understood as sexually available, and deeply disturbingly, we are led to think she may also be a corpse, murdered and abandoned in scrubby urban woodland. These are familiar resonances. Understanding that Duchamp made his own tinted, anatomical Venus in the kind of tableau setting favored for Lamentation groups or Madame Tussauds's historical performances strips this piece of too many mystical, metaphorical trimmings. This kind of viscerally direct, psychologically fundamental experience of sex and death is made with its audience in mind, which adherence to this tradition can provide.

This piece baffled the artist's first generation of disciples on its unveiling in 1969 but has had a huge impact on later practitioners.[131] Because Duchamp (despite his best efforts?) was long ago admitted into the high-art fold, the best works of those conceptually indebted to him are now deemed artistically significant. He paved the way for a new wave of polychrome figurative sculptures—a strand of making and a visual language that have proved especially powerful in the United States; in that, at least, Eco was right. It is still a people's art. In recent years, the unruly populism of polychrome sculpture has been harnessed to turn the form into an oppositional force within the art world, an agent of a semiofficial resistance. The casting of faces and figures from life has become

acceptable. Artists have reem-
braced the traditional materials,
such as wax and textiles, of the
polychrome sculpture of the
past, and to this materiality of
an earlier era, they have added
other modern, equally modest
media, like rubber, plastics, and
fiberglass. The past few years
have also witnessed a revival in
the making of sinister, soulless
automata. The desire to shock,
disrupt, and explore themes of
sex, death, and violence long

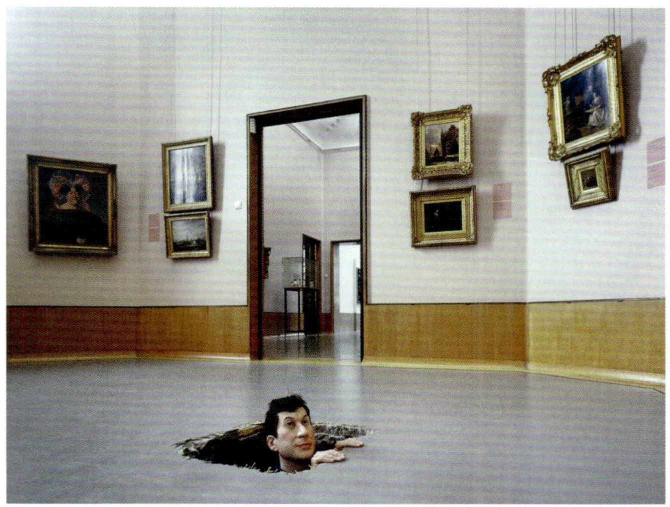

Fig. 28 Maurizio Cattelan. *Untitled*, 2001. Wax, pigment, human hair, fabric, and polyester,
H. 59 ¹⁄₁₆ in. (150 cm), W. 23 ⁵⁄₈ in. (60 cm), D. 15 ¾ in. (40 cm). Museum Boijmans Van
Beuningen, Rotterdam

implicit in polychrome sculpture is being taken to new explicit extremes. Some artists take a
more conciliatory approach. As his commentary in this volume shows, Koons sets out to unite
the human and the exalted by bridging the gap between objects others would dismiss as kitsch—
sculptures made from glossy porcelain or carved wood saints—and those always classed as high
art. He has also celebrated figures, like Michael Jackson (cat. 14), who are perceived as residing
in a heroic or imaginative realm above our messy quotidian world. Buster Keaton, melancholy,
put-upon, human yet remote in his movie silence, is even turned into a twentieth-century Christ
entering Jerusalem (cat. 53).[132] Cattelan explores the same territory and tensions. He has taken
Duchamp's place as an esteemed court jester; luckily, he has a clown's face. In 2002 he used it when
he represented himself breaking into the Museum Boijmans Van Beuningen, Rotterdam, tearing
a hole in the floor of a revered but remote gallery of old masters (fig. 28) through which his alter
ego, the foolish interloper, emerges.[133] In this now-permanent installation, the disruptive presence
forever resides with this polite row of pictures, serious but much less vivid, from the past. There
is a challenge here, but also an acknowledgment that high and low art can coexist.

    Although its huge capacity to disturb, disrupt, and annoy remains intact, this art form,
now legitimately visceral and seriously entertaining, has begun to be revisited. After the initial
emotional impact that derives from these works—so literal, so theatrical—and sometimes in
response to those first sensations, our readings can become more layered and complex. At other
times our gut reaction is more than enough. Either way, the meanings of these works continue to
rest largely in audience reaction. They become more complicated when we choose to explore that
response. Dealing as they do with mortality, gender and sexuality, and race—essential issues for
all of us—this art operates in social spaces using a mode that may not be mysterious or elevated
but is certainly popular, even populist. Works from the past fifty years or so are more than just
the result of six centuries of creation and opposition; they are objects that teach us to think again
about the aims and ambitions of the polychrome sculptures of the past. Through learning this
history, we may even revalue the notion of popular entertainment in art, ponder the implications
of the easy emotional response, and move past the tyranny of good taste.

NO DEAD MATTER

MARINA WARNER

What fine chisel
Could ever yet cut breath?
WILLIAM SHAKESPEARE

There is no dead matter.… Lifelessness is only a disguise behind which hide unknown forms of life. The range of these forms is infinite and their shades and nuances limitless.
BRUNO SCHULZ

IN THE BEGINNING

Foundation myths about the origin of the world ascribe the power to create living beings to the gods, and yet the metaphors to evoke this power depend on ideas about human skills, about art and making—sculpture and pottery. The prophet Isaiah, when he entreats God for mercy, uses this imagery: "But now, O Lord, thou art our father; we are the clay, and thou our potter; and we all are the work of thy hand."[1] In Genesis, Adam is made of clay, as his name in Hebrew implies, and in the first telling of the creation story, woman is made at the same time: "So God created man in his own image, in the image of God created he him; male and female created he them" (fig. 29). The narrative goes on to describe how God animates his creation: he "breathed into his nostrils a breath of life; and man became a living soul."[2] In Islamic tradition, creation follows similar lines—*adim* means the surface of the earth—and Allah so delights in the perfection of the humans he has made that he commands the angels to worship Adam and Eve; alone among them, Satan protests, saying that he is far superior to the mere earth of human beings, as he is composed of the higher elements, air and fire (fig. 30).[3]

In classical myth, the Titan Prometheus molds a figure of the first man out of mud and then brings him to life (fig. 31), and the Olympians create the first woman in the form of a beautiful "manufactured maiden";[4] she is an eidolon, an illusion or phantom, and they then ensoul her, adorn her, and call her Pandora, meaning all-gifted (fig. 32, cat. 10).[5] Pandora's story is told with variations by the Greek poet Hesiod in the eighth century B.C., and he explicitly draws an analogy with art: she is made in "the image of a girl."[6] In his epic poem *Theogony*, the Olympians Athena and Hephaestus, both closely associated with manufacturing skills (weaving, forging), undertake the making of the "modest virgin";[7] in Hesiod's other pastoral epic, *Works and Days*, Aphrodite, goddess of love, joins in to bring Pandora to perfection. She is a wonder, a fabricated figure endowed with consciousness. Like a miraculous statue in a Catholic cult, she is arrayed like a bride, with a belt, "golden necklaces," and on her head "the Seasons wove spring flowers into a crown."[8] But, as in the story of Eve, Pandora is destined to be fatal to humanity and to provide an explanation for the presence of evil in the world: while Eve offers the forbidden fruit to Adam, Pandora opens the forbidden box, causing all the woes of the world fly out. In *Theogony*, Hesiod calls her a *kalon kakon*, literally "the beautiful evil"—*kakon* being a neuter word that yokes oxymoronically with "beautiful" and produces one of those detonations in a text that continues to reverberate centuries later.[9]

The Greek poet's attitude toward Pandora radiates far beyond his own personal misogyny: his narratives foreshadow the turbulent feelings that continue to swirl around beautiful artifices and artistic simulacra, and depict the desire or other idolatrous passions they incite, including sacrilege. Both classical and biblical stories of creation thus associate the making of viable human forms with godlike prerogatives, and both first mothers prefigure the erotic appeal of women and art. Because graven images are forbidden by the second commandment in the Bible, and are therefore identified as idolatry, the question of representation has long remained a sensitive point of debate in Judeo-Christian thought. Hubristic, blasphemous risks cling to the makers of lifelike illusions; nudity and beauty send out contradictory signals to those viewing them. Interestingly, although the Qur'an does not include an explicit prohibition, orthodox believers hold that Allah alone has the power—and the right—to generate life, and so lifelike images are also condemned in Islam; statues and three-dimensional simulacra are particularly singled out as sinful (in the *Arabian Nights*, talking, moving idols are an eerie feature of an indicted, pagan world of the infidel jinni).

When Hesiod goes on to tell the Greek story of the fall initiated by Pandora's opening of the forbidden box, he calls her a *dolos*, a trick or trap—the same word he uses when Zeus orders the gods

to put in
Sly manners, and the morals of a bitch[10]

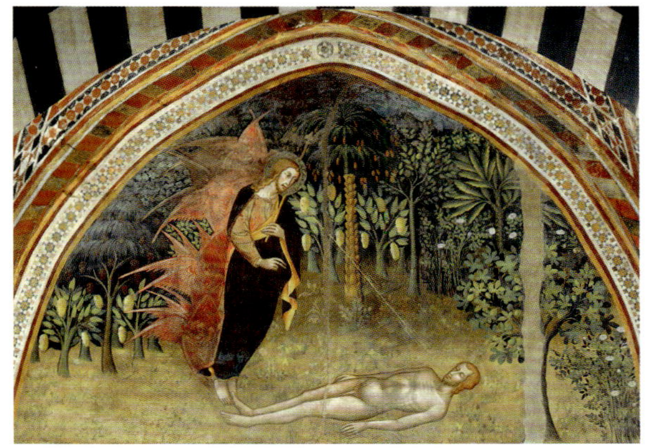

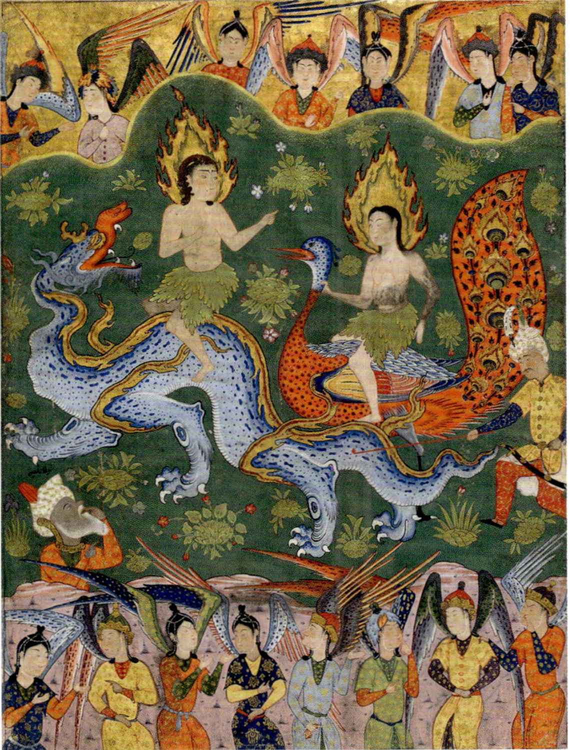

Fig. 29 Bartolo di Fredi. *The Creation of Man*, 1356. Fresco. Church of the Collegiata, San Gimignano

Fig. 30 *Adam and Eve in Paradise, Adam on a Dragon, Eve on a Peacock*, folio from the Falnameh (Book of Omens), mid-1550s. Opaque watercolor, ink, and gold on paper, 23 ½ × 17 ¹¹/₁₆ in. (59.7 × 44.9 cm). Arthur M. Sackler Gallery, Smithsonian Institution, Washington, D.C., Purchase – Smithsonian Unrestricted Trust Funds, Smithsonian Collections Acquisition Program, and Dr. Arthur M. Sackler

The poet then declares: "The deep and total trap was now complete."[11]

Dolos is also applied by Homer to the net of fine mesh that Hephaestus makes to catch Aphrodite and her lover, Ares, and hold them up for ridicule in front of all the other male immortals.[12] It recurs to describe the Trojan horse made by Epeius, with the help of Athena, one of the principal goddesses involved in lavishing gifts on Pandora.[13] Pandora is made like a work of the highest technical art, and she seduces through the trickery of the arts that her artist-creators, gods and goddesses, bestowed upon her. As classicist Froma I. Zeitlin comments, "Fashioned at the orders of Zeus…the female is the first imitation, who, replying to the first deception, embodies now for all time the principle of deception. She imitates both divine and bestial traits, endowed by the gods with an exterior of wondrous beauty and adornment that conceals the thievish and greedy nature of her interior. Artefact and artifice herself, Pandora installs the woman as *eidolon* in the frame of human culture, equipped by her 'unnatural' nature to delight and deceive."[14] Zeitlin implies the problematic nature of the association with art and artistry that freights sculptural lifelikeness with ambiguity and danger. The definition of woman partakes of the definition of art: both are beautiful and exercise fascination on the male (the prevalent angle of view for these ancient texts). Hesiod, in his spleen, declares woman's charms counterfeit in the same way as Plato later warned against the illusion of images.

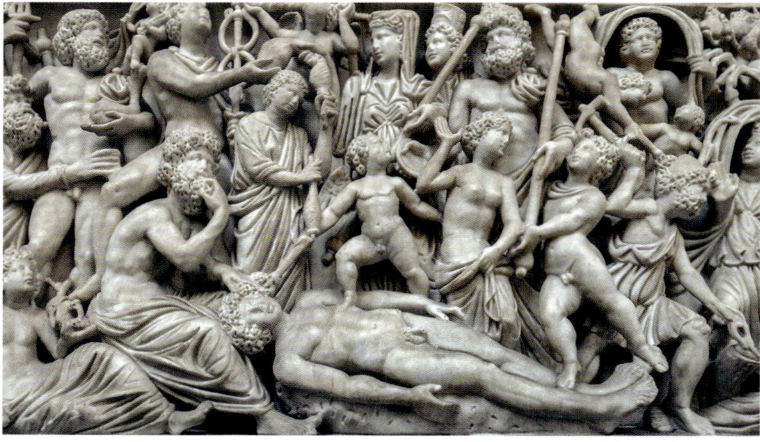

Fig. 31 *Sarcophagus Featuring the Legend of Prometheus Creating the First Man*, A.D. 4th century. Marble, H. 42 ½ in. (108 cm), W. 100 ¹³⁄₁₆ in. (256 cm), D. 36 ³⁄₁₆ in. (92 cm). Roman. Museo Archeologico Nazionale, Naples

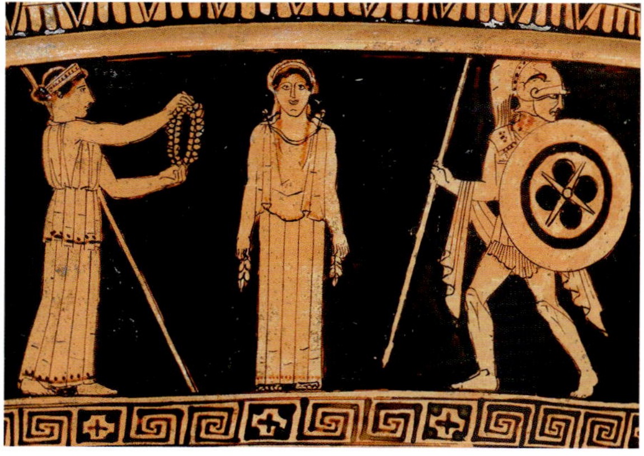

Fig. 32 *Calyx Krater Featuring the Creation of Pandora*, 5th century B.C. Painted terracotta, H. 19 ⁵⁄₁₆ in. (49 cm), Diam. 19 ¹¹⁄₁₆ in. (50 cm). Greek. British Museum, London

Even though centuries separate us from the ancient Greeks, we still share in their *iconodulia*—the worship of images (*dulia* meaning "adoration" in Greek)—through the long legacy of the classical revival. The worship of beauty, especially the physical beauty of the human body, inspired in the fourth century B.C. a type of idealized realism that held sway over the Renaissance, especially influencing Neo-Platonism in Florence, and this psychological and emotional principle continues to underlie the pursuit of lifelikeness. The higher the artistry involved, the more efficacious the artifact and the more powerful the spell it casts. Of course, such displays of mastery intensify response, but the implications of this extend far beyond the museum or the connoisseur's cabinet.

The social functions of art are exciting greater interest among those who make it alongside those who study it today; anthropologically minded thinkers, such as art historian Aby Warburg and, more recently, Alfred Gell, an anthropologist by profession, have profoundly shaped contemporary approaches.[15] After his travels in Arizona and New Mexico in the 1890s, Warburg connected the arts of the Renaissance, especially pageants and processions, with the culture of the Pueblo Indians, and advocated attending to the social functions of dance, music, narrative, and art. Gell, who had done fieldwork in the Pacific, takes Warburg's insights in a yet more radical direction, and proposed that art and aesthetics are not primarily an expression of the higher beauty and truth but of social relations, operating as a form of collective action to ensure the safety and status of the group.[16] Seen from this perspective, fine art and its exhibitions become showcases of values, such as beauty, but also of perceived virtue, power, security, wealth, and other dynamics in the community, including dangers: the force that radiates from supreme artistry can be harnessed to repel as well as attract. In the case of Medusa, her vividly rendered monstrous head was emblazoned on armor and doorways to ward off harm.

MEDUSA

Myths about generating life from inert clay, mud, or marble form one large and fruitful family on the great tree of metamorphoses; in counterpoise stands another large group of stories, which reverse the process and relate how living beings—humans, animals, plants—are turned to stone.

Medusa is one of the Gorgons, three beautiful sisters in Greek myth, but she was afflicted with snakes for hair after she refused the attentions of Poseidon, who also gave her the fatal power of literally petrifying anyone who looked at her. Perseus kills her, after deflecting her gaze with a mirror that Athena has given him. The goddess takes Medusa's severed head to wear on her aegis, rendering herself more terrible to her enemies. In the Renaissance, the snaky, screaming head continued to act as a powerful symbol of death-dealing force. The Grand Duke Cosimo I de' Medici commissioned Benvenuto Cellini to make a sculpture of Perseus holding Medusa's bleeding head high in trophy as he tramples her mangled body. The statue (1545–54), which still stands in the Loggia dei Lanzi in Florence, constitutes the duke's response to Michelangelo's *David* (1501–4), a prince's supreme justice overtaking Republican virtue. Interestingly, the Gorgon's head also appears on the shield of a Saracen effigy, a carved figure commissioned as a target for the jousting at the Grand Duke Francesco I de' Medici's wedding celebration in 1579 (cat. 57); in these festive circumstances, the horror of the beheaded Gorgon, while heightening the ferocity of the sculpture, adds a touch of grisly entertainment.

Paradoxically, Medusa's terrible curse makes her an agent of art, especially of sculpture, and many artists have responded to her affinity with the genre, rendering her with exceptional, lurid veracity.[17] Those subject to Medusa's gaze effectively become statues, as when Perseus interrupts the orgiastic riot of the Lapiths and the Centaurs and, averting his own eyes, brandishes the head of Medusa at his assailants and turns them to stone. In the early eighteenth century, Italian painter Sebastiano Ricci depicted the turbulent scene, in a painting in the J. Paul Getty Museum, Los Angeles, where the Gorgon's victims are frozen into poses that allude to classical marble sculptures (fig. 33).[18] Translation into imperishable matter can also announce art's victory over mortal decay.

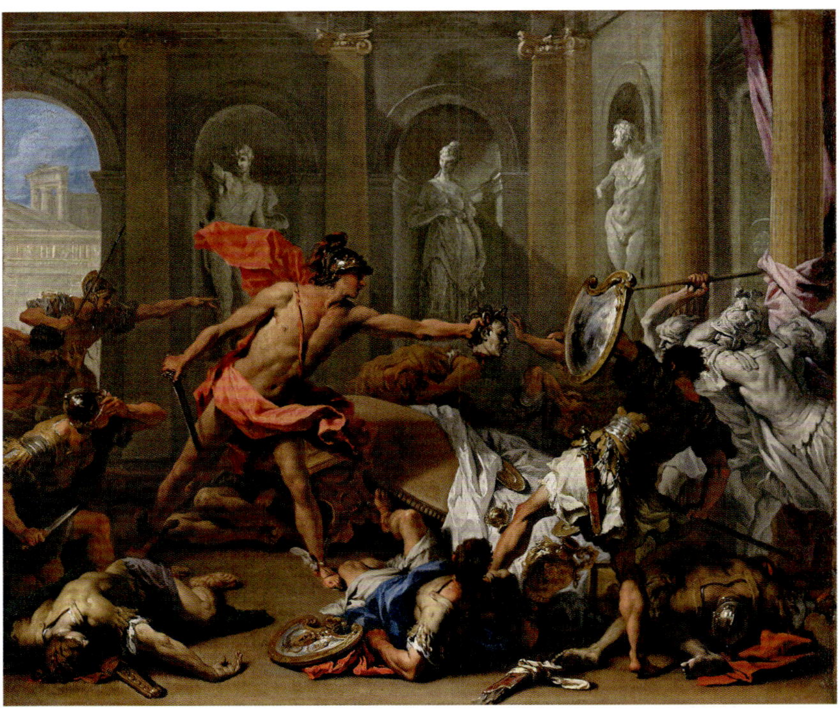

Fig. 33 Sebastiano Ricci. *Perseus Confronting Phineus with the Head of Medusa*, ca. 1705–10. Oil on canvas, 25 ¼ × 30 ⅜ in. (64.1 × 77.2 cm). J. Paul Getty Museum, Los Angeles

The Roman poet Ovid was intent on securing eternal fame through his work (the last word of the *Metamorphoses* is *vivam*, meaning "I shall live"), and several times in the poem from the first century A.D. he reaches for metaphors of timeless petrification, playing them in a bright key to express the abiding, transformative powers of art—and, above all, *his* art. Narcissus gazing at his reflection in the pool, Andromeda clinging to the rock from which Perseus will deliver her, are among the dramatis personae likened to beautiful statues.[19] In this aesthetic appreciation of sculpture, Ovid mirrors Greek encomia to heroes and heroines. In the fifth-century B.C. Greek tragedian Euripides's *Hecuba*, when the herald gives a long, ekphrastic, and horrifying account of the death of Polyxena, who has been sacrificed to keep the ghost of Achilles company in the Underworld, he compares her to a marble statue as she bares her throat to the executioner's sword.[20]

The Medusa effect announces mortification: to be turned to stone is to be turned into a thing that is not lifelike but deathlike, drained of animation. Ever since Sigmund Freud formulated his castration theory and used her severed head as an image of the mother's genitals, its terror has been primarily associated with sexuality and the figurative death of impotence. The bristling head, he explained, symbolizes the mother's lack of a penis; when glimpsed by her son, her private parts stiffen him with fear that the same misfortune might overtake him.[21] Freud's startling analysis has been much discussed and rightly contested, but it can be useful in thinking about the complex responses that lifelikeness in sculpture arouse: attraction and repulsion, the desire to touch and the desire to flee, the pull of the beautiful form and the shudder before a corpse. The entirely stilled Medusa-struck image shares with saints' effigies or waxworks the uncanny state of suspension between life and not life; it is an object endowed with the power of "animacy," to use the term introduced by Gell in his book *Art and Agency* (1998) and subsequent essays.[22] Gell usefully distinguished "animation," the illusion of vitality conveyed through motion, as in a puppet, robot, or automaton, from "animacy," the quality of radiating live energy, as in a devotional relic. Animacy refers to artifacts that the onlooker experiences as active, when we know they are not animate. Gell gives the example of a camera: "Devotees believe for instance that the idol in whose eyes they gaze also looks at them, just as one can say, and see, that a camera looks at something without claiming at the same time that it is alive."[23] He is interested in the reasons for the inert artifact's continuing fascination when a made thing—a work of art and artifice—is *not* mistaken for something real but still radiates power to affect reality.

The magnetism around a sacred/profane thing plays a crucial role in some of the stories of the *Arabian Nights*, in which many inert objects are magically charged with influence over future outcomes. "The Tale of the City of Brass" reveals the enthralling mixture of dread and wonder that an elaborate, costumed effigy of a dead personage can produce on the reader, while inside the story the dramatis personae who dare to desecrate the precious ambiguous artifact meet their fate.[24] The city was once the capital of a great and ancient civilization, raised and adorned by human skills and trades, overflowing with luxury and plenty. But when the group of travelers finds it at last, buried under drifts of sand in the desert, everything and everyone inside has been suspended in time, exactly as they were aeons ago. The petrified city brings to the mind's eye a Sleeping Beauty castle that is also a Platonist nightmare, a civilization entirely made up of illusions and artifice, where everything is dead, though it gives the impression of life. When they reach the city's heart, they enter a resplendent decorated pavilion and find, lying in the center, the young queen arrayed in pearls and red gold; she is "no more than an artfully preserved shell. Her eyes were removed after death and given a backing of quicksilver before being put back in place. As they gleam, it seems as though the eyelashes are moving. . . . They appear to be twinkling to those who look at her, while, in fact, she is dead."[25] The queen is the ultimate illusory artifact, the mummy of Tadmurah, Princess of the Amalekites. Around her bed, inscriptions tell the city's story in her own words: after seven years of drought and famine, they struggled by every means to find sustenance, but failed. Another plaque urges wayfarers who have reached her to take the city's wealth but warns "do not touch anything that has been placed on [her] body to cover [her] nakedness and to equip [her] on [her] journey from this world."[26] But Talib the treasure hunter is greedy and loots the corpse. The automata that stand guard over her—one white slave, one black, one armed with a club, and one with a saber—strike him to the ground and cut off his head. The uncanny status of the imperishable corpse transmits its uncanny powers to these statues guarding her—artificial life imagined in a fairy tale a long time ago. This "city of brass" offers a mirror image of a culture's ambitions and a catastrophic warning to the story's characters and readers.

BE STONE NO MORE

One of the stories that Ovid tells has become a famous allegory of love and the processes of art. In his long narrative poem of myths and transformation, the *Metamorphoses*, he stages the god Orpheus telling us how the sculptor Pygmalion carves a statue "with marvelous art" and

> gave it greater beauty
> Than any girl could have
>
> . . .
>
> The image seemed
> That of a virgin, truly, almost living,
> And willing, save that modesty prevented,
> To take on movement.[27]

Pygmalion uses ivory, the material conventionally used to depict the flesh of goddesses in antique sculpture. Such works would be later imitated in polychrome busts, such as Max Klinger's *New Salome* (1893–1903, cat. 47), while the practice of rendering skin colors in colored marbles continued with the portrait busts sculpted by Charles-Henri-Joseph Cordier (*La Capresse des Colonies*, 1861, cat. 33, and *The Jewish Woman of Algiers*, 1862, cat. 30) and by other Orientalists traveling in the French colonial empire.[28]

Pygmalion treats the statue as if it were real, lavishing it with jewels, fondling and kissing it, and finally "takes her to bed...calls her *Darling, My darling love!*"[29] Even Ovid's supreme wordsmithery does not quite avoid a note of absurdity. The sculptor's prime motive, the poet tells us from the start, is misogynist cynicism and despair. He deems all women no better than prostitutes and spurns them in favor of his own creation, and so, at a festival of Venus that takes place soon after this, he begs the goddess:

> I pray my wife may be—
> (He almost said, *My ivory girl*, but dared not)—
> One like my ivory girl.[30]

His prayers are granted (Venus being cruel and capricious in Ovid's poem, and no friend to her sex): when he returns to bed that night, he "felt the ivory soften / Under his fingers." Ovid now opens up the implicit analogy with artists' procedure:

> Imagine beeswax from Mount Hymettus, softening under
> the rays of the sun; imagine it moulded by human thumbs
> into hundreds of different shapes, each touch contributing value.[31]

Pygmalion is amazed: "Yes, she was living flesh!" Gradually, after more caresses,

> She felt his kisses, and blushed;
> then timidly raised her eyes to the light and saw her lover
> against the sky. The goddess graced the union she'd granted.[32]

Ovid does not name her; later writers called her Galatea, after one of the nymphs, and George Bernard Shaw names her Eliza Doolittle in his play *Pygmalion* (1913).[32] The statue mediates between the world of image making and the creation of life. When she steps out of illusion and into reality, through her creator's desire and the goddess's powers, she fulfills a long-held, deeply rooted aesthetic ideal that artists can, and should, "ape" nature, as William Shakespeare writes in *The Winter's Tale* (1623).[34] But the desired conflation of image and reality is never unambiguous. It inspires recognizable feelings of disturbance in the viewer, raised by the success of a counterfeit, uncanny semblance of life.

In his late romance *The Winter's Tale*, Shakespeare revisits Ovid, one of his recurring sources, passionately reworking, and in several ways transforming, the emotional balance of the Pygmalion story. The likeness of the wronged Queen Hermione is revealed, enshrined like a votive statue behind a curtain. It is, we are told, "a piece many years in doing and now newly performed by that rare Italian master Giulio Romano, who, had he himself eternity and could put breath into his work, would beguile nature of her custom, so perfectly he is her ape. He so near to Hermione hath done Hermione that they say one would speak to her and stand in hope of answer."[35]

Setting aside Shakespeare's seeming confusion about the artist—who was a painter but, as far as we know, did not make polychrome sculpture—the scene is uncanny and places the audience in a state of anticipatory uncertainty: Are we looking at a real woman or at an illusion, an eidolon like Pandora and the phantom surrogate of Helen of Troy? When the family friend Paulina draws back the curtain on the statue, the King of Sicilia, Leontes, is struck dumb with wonder, and exclaims:

> Her natural posture.
> Chide me, dear stone, that I may say indeed
> Thou art Hermione. [36]

Shakespeare, besides taking a cue from Ovid, was also inspired by miracle stories about statues coming to life and claiming a bridegroom or a sinner for their own, and he spliced these widespread legends from Catholic folklore with elements from the recently banned cult of images, so-called Papist rituals that had been suppressed under the Protestant reforms of Henry VIII and his successors. [37]

At the vision of the statue, Perdita, Hermione's daughter, kneels and asks her blessing, like a votary before a statue of Madonna, adding, to preempt criticism in front of a Reformation audience, "and do not say 'tis superstition." Likewise, in a transport of hope, Leontes also proclaims his determination to touch and kiss the statue:

> There is an air comes from her. What fine chisel
> Could ever yet cut breath? Let no man mock me,
> For I will kiss her. [38]

Paulina prevents him from approaching:

> Good my lord, forbear.
> The ruddiness upon her lip is wet;
> You'll mar it if you kiss it, stain your own
> With oily painting. Shall I draw the curtain? [39]

In a reversal of the outcome in Ovid, Leontes bitterly repents his previous actions and is cured of his misogynist fury. However, Shakespeare adds a subtle, perceptive, and gently humorous touch: Hermione is not represented as an enduringly ideal, youthful love object, sovereign to time, but is instead a bit more "wrinkled" than when her husband last saw her. Paulina explains the artist is so skilled he has shown her "as she lived now." [40] Then, seeing Leontes's repentance, Paulina promises to conjure more "amazement" and make the statue move. She calls out for music and then gives the command:

> 'Tis time; descend; be stone no more; approach;
> Strike all that look upon with marvel—come.

The polychrome statue comes to life, and Hermione steps down and into Leontes's embrace: "O! she's warm!" he exclaims.

> If this be magic, let it be an art
> Lawful as eating. [41]

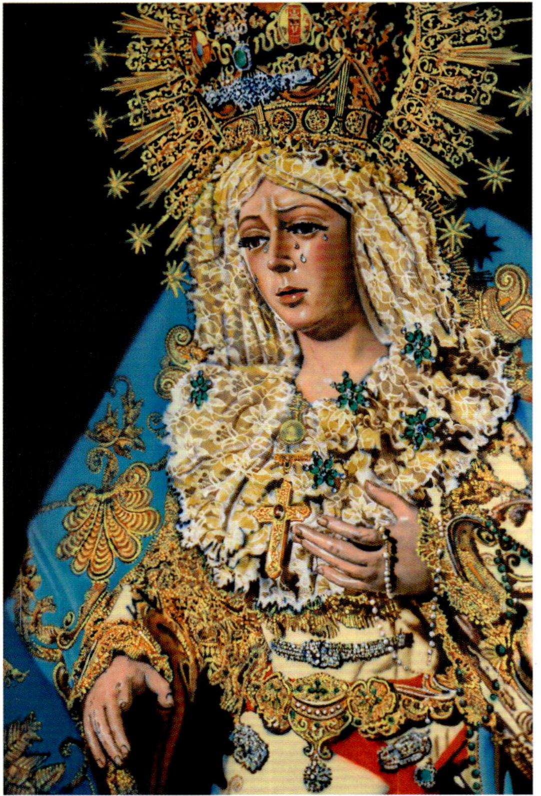

Fig. 34 Audrey Flack. *Macarena of Miracles*, 1971. Oil on canvas, 66 × 46 in. (167.5 × 116.7 cm). The Metropolitan Museum of Art, New York, Gift of Paul F. Walter, 1979 (1979.556)

Hermione's resurrection remains ambiguous: Is it a miracle, reimagined by Shakespeare as Ovidian metamorphosis? Or has Hermione truly been hidden away by Paulina, for sixteen years, for her safety? Directors have chosen both approaches, but whichever way the scene is played, the moment when the statue moves, when the illusion ceases and Hermione crosses the boundary into reality, works an instance of exceptionally powerful wonder in theater.

SHINING ILLUSION

The Greeks called lifelikeness in art *enargeia*, and they held it as the highest ideal, achieved by the supreme skills of the artist.[42] As art historian Caroline van Eck discusses in her study *Art, Agency, and Living Presence* (2015), the word comes from *argès*, meaning "shining." Pandora, Eve, Galatea, and Hermione possess it to such a degree they overcome their status as artifacts and come to life. In Latin, *enargeia* was rendered by the much weaker *illustratio* or *evidentia*, and Van Eck continues to explain that the counterpart of this property of *enargeia* is *energeia*, a term not etymologically related, in spite of its close resemblance, which means "actuality" or "motion" (as in energy). The illusion of animate, sentient beings achieved by works of human artifice derives from both properties and renders them compelling and disturbing. Pedro de Mena's *Mater Dolorosa* convinces the onlooker that she is weeping, the *Housepainter I* (1984/88, cat. 15) by Duane Hanson inspires a double take, and the artist in Rigoberto Torres's sculpture *Shorty Working in the C&R Statuary Corp.* (1985, cat. 31) establishes two levels of aesthetic make-believe: the polychrome figure seems persuasive at a higher degree of intensity than the white—plaster of Paris? marble?—religious statuette he is making. Such destabilizing effects were characterized by Freud for later generations as *Unheimlich*, or uncanny, though they have a long history before his analysis. Achilles's marvelous shield in the *Iliad* is intricately wrought to give a protocinematic illusion of movement and even sound.[43] Over nearly two hundred lines, Homer dramatically animates a bright, kinetic illusion wrought by divine artistry; his extended ekphrasis brings to the mind's eye of the reader or listener a moving picture, as the words become image-flesh, to adopt twentieth-century French philosopher Maurice Merleau-Ponty's resonant concept.[44]

The ideal of supreme, incarnate lifelikeness generated numerous legends about artists' powers to imitate or even surpass nature: the famous fifth-century B.C. Greek sculptor Myron, it was said, was so skilled that calves lowed at his cow, and one died for want of nourishment from her bronze teat.[45] Pliny of first-century A.D. Rome offers another exemplum, about Zeuxis, who painted a bunch of grapes so faithfully that birds flew in to peck at them. He admitted to being outshone, however, when his rival, Parrhasius, painted an image of a curtain, which Zeuxis asked

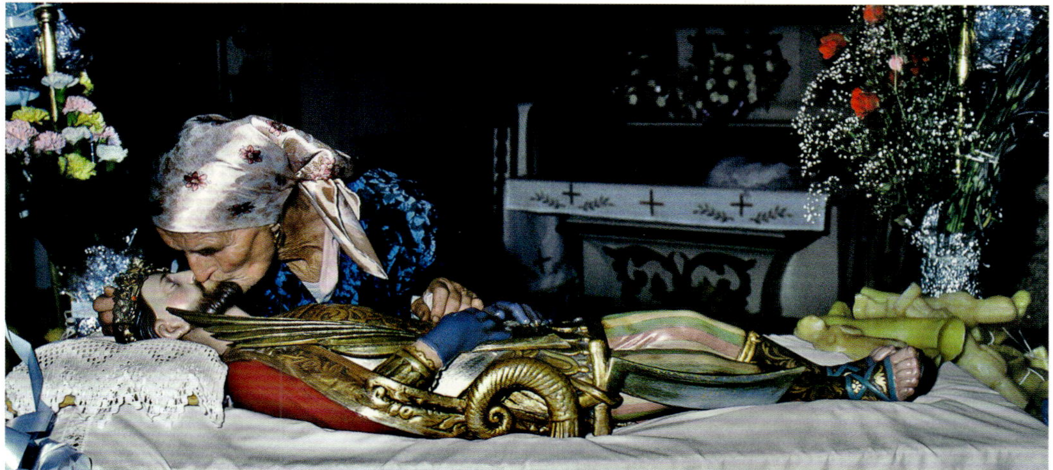

Fig. 35 Cristina García Rodero. *Woman Kisses San Campio de Lonxe, Figuiero (Pontevedra)*, 1989

to be drawn so he could see the picture.[46] The hallucinatory sense of a larger-than-life presence of so many artworks in *Like Life* bears out this quality of brilliancy and dazzle achieved by the supersaturation of exact sensory information.

The Power of Images is the title of David Freedberg's 1989 study, a book that shook up art-historical pieties about art for art's sake and argued passionately that art has designs on the minds of its audience and achieves its ends through arousing a range of passionate emotions, from pity, as in the case of a Pietà group, painted or sculpted, to desire, as in the case of reclining naked Venuses or the sprawling Barberini faun.[47] Freedberg swept away with some vehemence the idea that art could be held aloof from the subjective life of the individual spectator or the collective life of the community of viewers, whether a congregation or procession, a city guild or an institution. The identity of the group can be embodied in a work of art, sometimes literally, as in the embalmed, fully clothed effigy of Jeremy Bentham (1832, cat. 22) on display in University College London, which was a very early nondenominational place of higher education in Britain. Bentham specified this unusual form of burial in his will, to proclaim his positivist rejection of a world beyond this one. Yet this modern mummy is still thoroughly uncanny. As Freedberg discusses, the means to charge an image with the desired power—to be affecting and effective—depends on engaging the full sensorium of the onlooker, overcoming the inherent limitations of the artifact (stillness, muteness, flatness) and present tactile possibilities that offer affordances for the devotee to enflesh the illusion.

Adornment is central to ritual and a prime way of glorifying and consecrating; ingenious and lavish accretions magnify the object of the decoration—a person, a statue, or an icon—enhancing the power of its presence and infusing it with magical efficacy. The difference between a painting of the Madonna by Fra Angelico or Leonardo, and a miraculous icon of the Virgin, such as her cult statues in Seville or Guadalupe, lies in the layers of ornament the statues have accrued: these totems of the nation and the people, these objects of millions of pilgrims' hopes and prayers, are richly dressed in jewels and velvet, their luxurious apparel changed according to the liturgical calendar; they are often made up, with false eyelashes and hair; they are covered in offerings of flowers and, sometimes, money. La Macarena in Seville has tears of crystal falling down her painted cheeks (see fig. 34). Russian Orthodox icons are richly paneled all over, with only the Madonna's face and that of her child's peeping out from jewel-studded silver and gold. The need to adorn stretches beyond the sacred icon to the chapel where it stands: the greater the sunbursts of gold, silver, jewels, and flowers around these images, the greater their thaumaturgic powers. The luxury, color, and plenitude are intrinsic to aesthetics if the images are to be active and efficacious for the worshippers who throng and wait their turn to touch or kiss a sacred icon or statue of the crucified Christ, or to lift a child to make contact with an image of the Madonna, as in the photographs taken by Cristina García Rodero in contemporary Spain (fig. 35).[48] The tourists who queue for long hours outside Madame Tussauds's want to have a photograph taken with a wax effigy of Beyoncé, and they take delight in shuddering at tableaux of gruesome murders in the Chamber of Horrors in proportion to the intensity of the illusion.

IDOLS

After monarchs died, their lifesize effigies were made as lifelike as possible, robed and arrayed in the symbols of their state and then carried in procession to follow the bier: the mortal coil lay in the coffin and would be consigned to earth, but the essence of divine kingship would live on in the mantled and bejeweled statue. However, while such simulacra of sacred ritual and devotion lost their aura during the Enlightenment, a species of secular statuary was gaining intense popularity and even adoration: the waxwork. Waxworks began explicitly as surrogates for the actual presence of the hero or sacred personage—or monster—such as monarchs, celebrities, and malefactors. For those subjects who could not make the journey to Versailles to see the king and queen and the royal children having lunch in public, as was the custom, they could visit the tableau vivant of the scene—accurate in every appearance from the table setting to their costumes, hair dressing, and gestures—which the ceroplast, or wax modeler, Philippe Curtius set up in his Cabinet de Cire on the Boulevard du Temple (fig. 22). Ever since Madame Tussaud left revolutionary France and began touring her collection of sculptures around England in 1802, waxworks have continued to grow in appeal as artifacts for public exhibition and entertainment.

Curtius was Madame Tussaud's uncle (though the exact relation may have been different), and he taught her the art of ceroplasty. He began his career as an artist of medical models, exact and detailed anatomical and physiological studies for medical students to examine; these wax figures acted as substitutes for cadavers themselves, which were very difficult to obtain, surrounded by legal, religious, and psychological taboos. The methods that the wax casters and sculptors applied are not fully understood, but they involve complex preserving and embalming techniques. In Bologna, Florence, and Padua, where the practice reached the height of accurate replication, wax sculptures consisted of direct casts of organs, musculature, veins, and nervature, incorporated actual elements of the subjects' bodies, such as bones, hair, and clothing, and were dressed in jewels and clothes that belonged to the deceased. The anatomical models were laid on silk or velvet cushions, with their drapery parted to reveal obstetric data, their wigs lifted to show the brains: these eerie "Venuses" of anatomical cabinets (cat. 115) were destined to become figures such as the *Sleeping Beauty* (1765, cat. 113) in Madame Tussauds's collection. Their display coincides with the rise in popularity of Gothic romance. Jane Austen mocked such tropes in *Northanger*

Abbey (1817), while Mary Shelley created its most magnificent mythic figure, the creature made by Dr. Frankenstein, in which she compacted the horror, dismay, and fear felt at the procurement of corpses for science.

This new disregard for the integrity of the body after death gradually sharpened the value of its integrity and liveliness in life. At the same time as the medical sculptors were perfecting their techniques, portraitists in Italy, Germany, and the Netherlands were scrutinizing the features of individuals for their particularities. It is significant that trust in the revelations of outward portraiture grew and still continues: as Duncan remarks in *Macbeth*, "There's no art to find the mind's construction in the face."[49] Skills that made it possible to anatomize the corpse without compunction, to dissect and then cast in wax the nerves which give expression to a person's face, or lay bare the convolutions of the brain, also

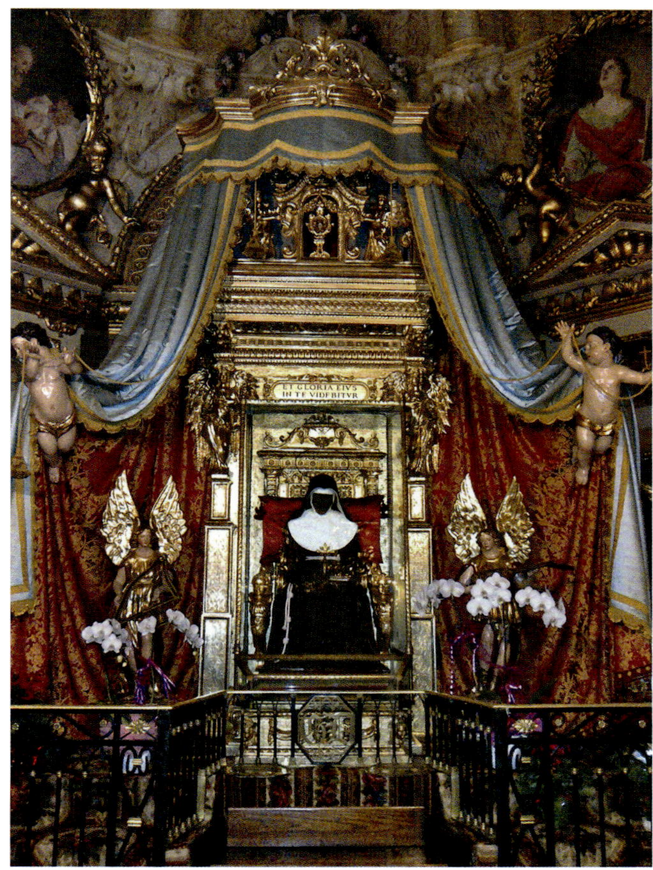

Fig. 36 Mummified effigy of Saint Catherine of Bologna, Church of Corpus Domini, Bologna

made it possible to create an illusion of suspended time or of immortality in the images of the once-living individual, especially the polychrome bust. This forensic intensity spurred the ambitions of new practitioners in physiognomy, phrenology, and, eventually, portrait photography.

When the biological sciences of the Enlightenment converge with the quest to grasp the secret of life, we find a new emphasis on the face as the repository of individuality. The immortal soul may flee once life has ceased, but that which made the person himself or herself remains behind in the flesh, in the image that the body has become. Artists strove to produce increasingly accurate likenesses in polychrome media so that an image, and especially a portrait, could preserve, in the memory of the living, the subject's particular mien. Anatomical models, secular waxworks, and portrait statues cast from life reprise elements from the spectacular presentation of saints' bodies in Catholic cult, and the rituals that attend them and their relics. A medieval girl such as Saint Fina in San Gimignano; the mummy of Saint Catherine in Bologna, sitting up on the altar in her habit with her possessions around her (fig. 36); or even the corpse of a modern visionary, such as Saint Bernadette of Lourdes, are displayed as they looked in life. The person has been miraculously preserved (or so it is held by believers), her flesh sovereign to mortal disintegration. It is more likely that such corpses have been embalmed and painted—in the case of the virgin martyr Saint Victoria in the church of Santa Maria della Vittoria, in Rome, one can see her finger bones through the wax integument that has cracked and is falling off. Effigies such as

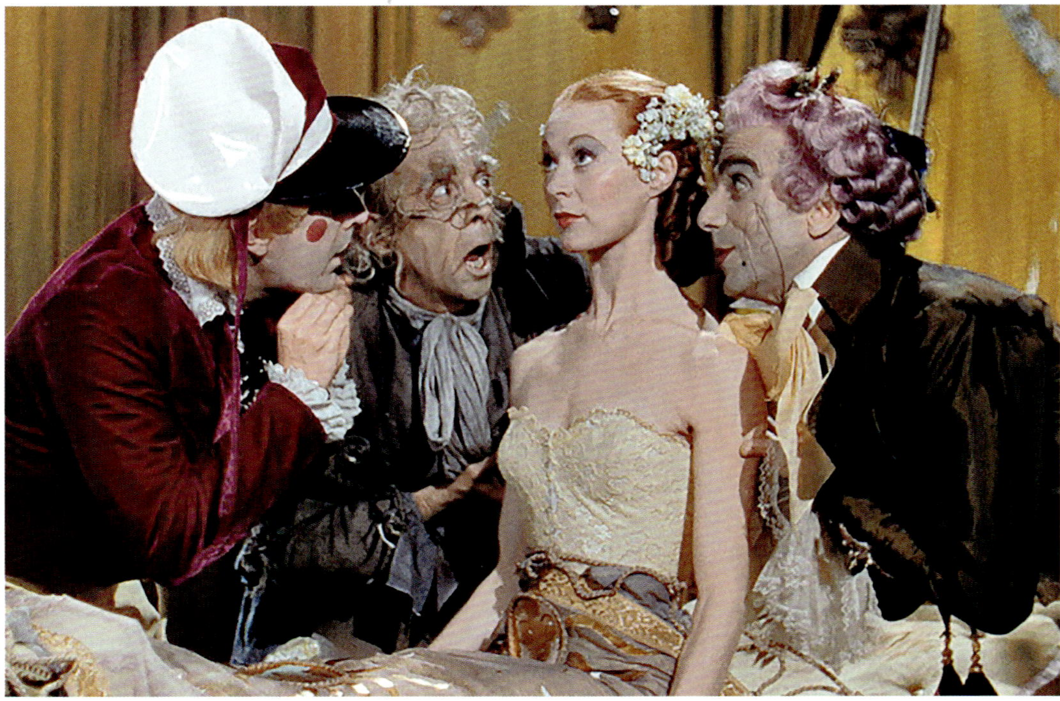

Fig. 37   The doll Olympia in Michael Powell and Emeric Pressburger's film *The Tales of Hoffmann* (1951)

Catherine's or Bernadette's attempt proleptically to fix their subjects in a Medusan timeless eternity. In "L'immagine immemoriale" (1986), the Italian philosopher Giorgio Agamben notes that the word "likeness" shares the same root as the German word for "corpse" (*Leiche*) and connects it with a classical concept of the eternal image: in the afterlife, our phantom selves will resemble us unerringly and completely.[50]

These forms of sculptural artifact share many affinities in their fabrication and display, and the technical virtuosity that aims at lifelikeness. However, more can be learned about such works if we attend to the unsettling responses they stir in us, the spectators. A saint's preserved body or a waxwork film star inspires the shiver of the uncanny because these figures belong to a larger category of artifact—the idol—and they prompt all the powerful, polemical reactions, thoughts, and emotions that the term "idol" still produces. The sites they occupy today often straddle an uncertain boundary between the sacred and the profane, and this indeterminacy is key to their incarnation in the contemporary art gallery and museum. Questions about idols and idolatry lie at the core of the "iconoclashes" of our time, to use contemporary French philosopher Bruno Latour's resonant term.[51] "Iconoclash" admits that *iconophilia*, or the love of images, is struck from the same coin as iconoclasm, the urge to deface and destroy them. Relics arouse feelings of intimate connection with the departed saint, prophet, or hero—Madame Tussaud included such indexical souvenirs in her collections from the very start, such as Napoleon's cloak and even the blade of the guillotine. When the Protestant reformers during Oliver Cromwell's rule (1653–58) scratched out the eyes of the Virgin Mary or the devil, took a hammer to the face of Christ, or exhumed and scattered the bones of Saint Frideswide at Oxford, they recognized the power of images and actively rebelled against it. (There is a story—perhaps apocryphal—that Salvador Dalí once challenged fellow Surrealist André Breton to piss in a baptismal font: "No, I won't," Breton responded. "I'm not a believer.")

The Surrealists adopted transgressiveness as a fundamental principle and a means to revolution, and the weight of the past continues to inspire artists to iconoclastic blasphemy against their own practice. The conversation with ideals and beliefs, conventions and myths, calls for artists to disfigure and deface their predecessors' and even exemplars' creations. Surrealist works, such as Hans Bellmer's series of disarticulated *poupées* (dolls, cats. 82–84), and the Chapman brothers' cartoon graffiti over Goya prints and their perverse child monsters, blatantly glory in their own acts of blasphemy and destruction. In Jeff Koons's spin on the idols of contemporary fame, as in *Michael Jackson and Bubbles* (1988, cat. 14), is the artist in earnest? Is he adding to the sacred aura or mocking the idol and the fans who idolize him? Yinka Shonibare MBE transforms Edgar Degas's *The Little Fourteen-Year-Old Dancer* (ca. 1880, cat. 68) when he dresses her in African prints and turns her into a gun-toting postimperialist rebel (2007, cat. 69). In her new incarnation, this beloved icon of modern art overturns the conditions that determined her first, subjugated appearance. By contrast, Bharti Kher invests *Mother* (2016, cat. 6) with determined, quiet resistance to the classical aesthetic canon. Kiki Smith revitalizes the sacred energy of such figures as Eve, Lilith, and even the tempter Satan, to whom she gives her own features, in the series of drawings called *Play* (1994). In full consciousness of the weight of myths about Eve, Pandora, and Galatea, female artists including Smith, Louise Bourgeois, and Yayoi Kusama have set out to reoccupy these figures and often disfigure them: Kusama turns phallologocentrism against itself in a ferocious spirit of playful iconoclasm with *Phallic Girl* (1967, cat. 60).

THING-SOUL

Charles Baudelaire, in an essay from 1853, remembers how he was absorbed in his childhood toys, and how their stubborn refusal to be fully, humanly alive provoked a rage of frustration in him. The French poet calls toys "cette statuaire singulière" (this singular statuary), and reflects on children's anger toward their playthings.[52] They shake them, he writes, hurl them to the ground, and often break them, asking, "But *where is its soul?* This moment marks the beginnings of stupor and melancholy."[53]

Baudelaire's memories about his encounters with toys' uncanny life are echoed by the German poet Rainer Maria Rilke in "Some Reflections on Dolls" (1914), written more than half a century later.[54] Rilke emphasizes that play is a process of animation—of the doll and through the doll. But he, too, broods on his memories of trying to feed, coddle, and *animate* his toys. He made his doll into "a confidant, a confederate, like a dog, not, however, receptive and forgetful like a dog...taken into cots, dragged into the heavy folds of illnesses." Then he adds the crucial phrase, that "they lay there...allowing themselves to *be dreamed.*" His reminiscences end in tenderness, even rhapsodic nostalgia, with a prayer, a prose-poem. Rilke hymns: "O doll-soul, not made by God, you soul, asked for capriciously from some thoughtless fairy, thing-soul breathed forth by an idol with mighty effort."[55]

In the tale "The Sand-Man" (1817), German Romantic E. T. A. Hoffmann imagines a terrible fate arising when a young man, the student Nathaniel, mistakes a singing doll, Olympia, for a real flesh-and-blood girl and falls passionately in love with her (fig. 37). Freud analyzes the story in his celebrated essay on the *Unheimlich*, or the uncanny, in which he does not accept the earlier analysis of Ernst Jentsch, that the uncanny results from the threshold state between animate and inanimate.[56] His remarkable misreading of Hoffmann's tale diagnoses the locale of the uncanny instead in the return of the familiar, and the creepy sensation or déjà vu that is aroused when a profound, buried experience returns. However, unlike Nathaniel, who is entirely deluded, the poet who played with dolls remained conscious of their ambiguity, as do most viewers when they come across a simulacrum in a church, art gallery, or waxworks museum. We know that the artifacts are not alive, yet we still feel a profound frisson, not necessarily because a particular memory returns, but because the fundamental compass bearings on reality are thrown off by the depth of the illusion.

The arrival of digital media—especially photography, with its qualities of presence-in-absence—and the possibilities of manipulation the new technologies offer have heightened contemporary encounters with the uncanny and intensified conspiratorial affinities between imaginative acts of artists and representations of reality. Imaginative make-believe remains central to the work of artists in every medium—literary and artistic—while play itself, according to psychoanalysts D. W. Winnicott, Marion Milner, and Melanie Klein, has a necessary role in the formation of the inner psyche and its relations to reality.[57] However, lifelike simulacra, especially when lifesize, do carry a special charge of equivocal eroticism, drawing viewers into the intimate private fantasies of their makers. In 1918 the German artist Oskar Kokoschka commissioned a life-size replica of Alma Mahler, whom he loved and who left him. He gave a professional doll maker, Hermione Moos, detailed instructions, down to the last tuft, couched in the language of forensic wax modeling: "Please make it possible," he wrote, "for the touch to enjoy these parts where fat or muscles suddenly give way to sinews, and where the bone penetrates to the surface, like the shin-bone." He wanted especially to reenact his passion through touch: "Often hands and finger tips see more than eyes."[58] The images of the result, photographed and painted by the obsessed artist (fig. 64), produce in us now shudders of queasy disgust or disbelieving laughter, but the figure also resembles a giant example of a child's favorite soft toy or comfort rag, a "transitional object," in that most useful phrase of Winnicott's. Ultimately, the poor, grotesque doll ended up trashed in the back garden, just as in one of Cindy Sherman's mise-en-scènes, or like one of those soft toys dustmen impale on the squalid prow of their grinding garbage trucks.

The boys and girls made out of plaster and photographed by Morton Bartlett, a Boston loner who died in 1992, are scale replicas of real children, all faithful to dress, anatomy, expression, and gesture. Bartlett called his creations from the 1950s "sweethearts," but the boys look like him at the age of eight, when both his parents died.[59] Photographing his effigies, Bartlett used atmospheric lighting to render the fall of shadow on a sleeping child's face or the tears springing from a girl's eyes. In 1963 he published the images in *Yankee Magazine*, and they must have looked less creepy in that context, for he seems to have excited no protests. After this, Bartlett never went back to what he called his "hobby." He had, however, understood something about the modern uncanny, that is, its heightened relationship to photography and cinema, and his work foreshadows the uncanny verisimilitude that state-of-the-art resins, vinyls, and digital reproductive techniques have made possible.

A photographed doll is a copy of a copy, and as such it can ratchet up the effect of lifelikeness, which, when it reaches supersaturation, tips the simulacrum into the uncanny valley, where it no longer convinces as real and instead becomes a memento mori.[60] The unsettling ambiguities that both Baudelaire and Rilke experienced in their childhood games cling to artworks that give their subjects the look of life: such illusions raise troubling questions about life and death, semblance and reality.

Contemporary vernacular sculptures of individuals—unnamed, ordinary folk pursuing routine tasks or undergoing ordinary human experience—by Edward Kienholz and Nancy Reddin Kienholz (cat. 80) and John Ahearn (cat. 28) tap the resources of sacred energy found in the tradition of effigy, icon, and eidolon. Their resulting stature, presence, and dignity demand attention to the interiority of these figures, the disposable precariat who do not always engage our interest; the modes of *enargeia*—polychrome simulacra—endow them with active power to rouse within us passions of sympathy, pity, horror, and desire.

When we are astonished and deceived today by artists' persuasive skills of imitation and reproduction, the experience reverberates down the dark and backward abysm of time, where illusory images were exhibited to exalt their subjects, often consecrating them as holy. The several hundred years covered by the current show reveal the long, deep connections that still exist between us and ancient rituals, which attributed power to the human form as artifact. Dazzling simulations seduce the onlooker into close attention and awe. But they never cease to provoke perturbation. The lifelike yet inanimate artifact confronts its spectators with the quiddity and mystery of life itself. Playing with this power of images, artists have dared to take us to this debatable land, and we still respond viscerally, with shudders and anxiety, tingling with amazement.

DOUBLE OR NOTHING

HILLEL SCHWARTZ

While we share the planet with a dozen other species that recognize themselves in mirrors, we are the only ones who seek out our reflections, the only ones who eight thousand years ago rubbed obsidian smooth to find our faces staring back at us.[1]

While earth-moving species galore build towering, tunneled, or funneled homes of mud, stalk, and stone, we alone forge doubles of our bodies. Chimps and gorillas passionate for paint become abstract expressionists; male bowerbirds, as many-splendored are the seductions of their bowers, never craft busts of their intended.[2]

While species everywhere court, catch, and kill with the help of colors astonishing or invisible to human eyes, no others have colonized and enslaved to possess the sources from which colors are extracted.[3] Mineral, vegetable, insectile, or crustacean, the colors that we compound and apply to our bodies, semblances, and structures may fade away; so far as cultures go, colors are neither ephemeral nor accidental nor inconsequential.

Yet figures rounded and colored suffer a double jeopardy. While the substance and sensuality of the body have had glaringly few partisans among Western thinkers, color was even harder pressed. Since Democritus, color has been blanched of value, belittled as illusion.[4] Crucial though colors are to political and religious ritual, to tactics of war and commerce, their omnipresence has often been resented, their powers of persuasion repudiated, unlike pre-Columbian Aztecs, for example, or the Anangu of present-day South Australia, both with cultures intensely alive to a cosmos structured by color.[5] Europeans have had no truck with color as a force that gives the world its shape.[6]

While Western artists have known since the fifteenth century that Greco-Roman sculpture was painted in bright polychrome, they celebrated instead the putatively natural stone of those classical works from which the reds, blacks, blues, and yellows had worn away, clean of the masquerade of added color, the pettiness of paint.[7] As regards *la peinture* itself, which unites color and drawing, the latter must have the upper hand—so claimed a French critic in 1870—lest color be its downfall, "just as Eve was the downfall of humanity." Thus declared Charles Blanc, who despite his surname surely appreciated the allure of color, authority as he was on jewelry and the oeuvre of Rembrandt.[8] But sculpture was a world apart, wrote the American sculptor Lorado Taft in 1908, exulting in "this chaste, austere art of ours—this venerable art with its suggestion of eternity."[9] Color was to truth (so went the old philosophical trope) as cosmetics were to inner beauty—a cloak, deceptive and fleeting.[10]

In the run of Western art theory, such "chromophobia" has been less a color blindness than a blind rage at color, an aesthetic panic at the riot of hues discernible within our visible spectrum, that strait of electromagnetic waves between 0.00038 and 0.00076 millimeters.[11] Typically sighted humans can distinguish at least two million colors across a mere 0.00038 millimeters (380 nanometers) of light stimuli. Joseph Lovibond's Tintometer, patented in 1886 to assure a consistent color in "medium daylight" for the beers from his family's Salisbury brewery, had nine million possible permutations; new estimates of the number of differentiable colors soar beyond sixteen million.[12] So many we are almost speechless: while the photoreceptive cones of our retinas begin to tell apart those millions and relay their impulses to the optical cortex for further analysis, no language has more than a few thousand color-specific terms. Ian Paterson begins *A Dictionary of Colour* by confessing that "any attempt to define any particular colour merely by means of words is doomed to failure."[13] We look instead for cultural metaphors that put us in mind, say, of the blue of George Segal's painted plaster cast of the art historian *Meyer Schapiro* (1977, cat. 29), a polyvalent blue wrinkled across so many planes that it must be the fatigued denim of the working classes for whom Schapiro tirelessly fought, tintometered with that approaching-storm blue of the Romanesque surfaces he studied lifelong.[14]

True, seeing color is as probabilistic as color words are allusive. The third of our brain devoted to consolidating vision acts like a corps of statisticians, averaging hues and saturations as reported by a population of some 4,600,000 cones or, in dim light, levels of brightness reported by some 92,000,000 retinal rods.[15] By algorithm and asymptote, our gray matter arrives at the colors and shapes of this blue-green planet.

True, too, color is metameric. We find the same blue-green arising from spectrally dissimilar stimuli. Since our eyes cannot separate out the strands (technically, the "spectral profile") of incoming light, different profiles yield matching colors.[16] Bluntly put, we are assured of no exclusive correlation between a color we think to see and its source. Our polychromatic world consists of sets of metamers and maybes.

Yet, despite ontological skepticism and optical surprises, we manage to negotiate color.[17] We manage because we have—each of us uniquely, and together, culturally—a history with color. Whatever the quanta of light scattered or reflected, we come to a consensus about the quotidian work of colors, their range of meanings, their positions in our cosmologies, our economies of metals and spices (where color is crucial to valuation, quality, age, uniqueness), our diagnostic systems. Harsh, hurtful, bruised black and blue in the red heat of argument, a consensus may collapse. But cultural anthropologists and historians of rhetoric assure us that where there be bodies in play, there be colors at work, making vivid what we desire or despise. We are all, necessarily, bodies *in* color.[18]

The 127 works of art in *Like Life: Sculpture, Color, and the Body* deserve therefore to be viewed through the lenses of the history of light, eyesight, colors, and the body as well as its reconfigurations. Were the exhibition less broad and bold, such an approach would have less warrant. Where Charles-Henri-Joseph Cordier's *The Jewish Woman of Algiers* (1862, cat. 30) jostles with Reza Aramesh's *Action 105* (2017, cat. 45), there is warrant aplenty.

What happened over the last eight hundred years to light, sight, colors, bodies, and figural sculpture?

Light became more manipulable in the privacy of a home or laboratory while more unpredictable in public. Reliant initially on sunlight, firelight, rushlight, candlelight, and oil lamps, the West moved on to gas lamps, incandescent bulbs, carbon arc floodlights, fluorescing tubes, ultraviolet (tanning) and infrared (scanning) lights, lasers, halogen bulbs, and LEDs. At each transition, middling and upper classes had more qualities of light at their command, more lumens at their disposal, but at every public turn the glare and color balance of light would fluctuate more wildly, day and night—especially as highly reflective surfaces spread across domestic and urban environments in the form of mirrors and cut glass, silver plating and foils, and plate-glass windows. "We are violently enamoured of gas and of glass," wrote Edgar Allan Poe in 1840, but the glare and "the rage for *glitter*" did not abate. Brilliance became more indiscriminate, with glass-skinned buildings, vehicles of steel and chrome, and then—with reds and blues flashing toward accidents, white strobes bolted above emergency exits—more threatening.[19]

The first of the newer light sources emerged during the last decades of the Northern Hemisphere's Little Ice Age, three or more centuries (at least 1550–1840) of lower average temperatures and more persistent cloud cover, under which gradually arose a yearning for plentiful light.[20] That yearning, met by the open skies of landscape painting, by luminous Baroque interiors, by the expansion of street lighting and the popularity of sky-blue dress, was met in the 1800s by power companies whose gas (later, electric) lighting systems relied on technologies that would paradoxically darken the land and smog the atmosphere. The rise of "artificial light," which enabled 24-7 factory schedules, inspired counterinsurgencies of mountain climbing, sunbathing, and sunrooms suffused with natural light. Yet the light under which billions today work and play comes not from the sun or full-spectrum lamps. It comes from computer monitors, mobile phones, and color televisions whose internal phosphors emit light with a blue component so strong that it disrupts patterns of sleep already disturbed by two centuries of night shifts.[21]

Bleary-eyed, sight itself has been losing ground among the senses regardless of calls for visual thinking, as in digital mapping and the "spatial humanities."[22] If dazzled by modern circuses of light, sight has been challenged since the first use of magnifying glasses and eyeglasses during the 1200s. Once native vision—that is, the eyes we are born with—must be assisted or corrected, the clear authority of sight is at risk. To the extent that our native visual powers were subsequently amplified by optical prosthetics (telescopes, microscopes, endoscopes, x-rays, CAT scans) or restored by ophthalmic interventions (prescription lenses for astigmatism, surgery for cataracts, prostaglandin drops for glaucoma, cryotherapy for retinal detachment), to a similar extent those native powers would appear vulnerable and inadequate.

Worse, the healthier we got and the longer our life expectancy, the more our eyes failed us with regard to needlework, distance vision, night vision, and color vision. As the oils of old master paintings lose vibrancy over the years and dry to a spurious, mottled golden glow, so with age do the macular pigments and lenses of our eyes thicken, letting through less light, particularly less blue (short-wavelength) light, biasing our vision toward the yellow end of the spectrum.[23] Worst, while we have a way to go to understand the specifics of color vision loss, experimental psychologists and optical physicists since the 1880s have shown us how completely eyes young or old are tricked by deftly paralleled lines, adjacent color solids, and checkerboard hues on cubes.[24]

Contingent as they are on juxtapositions of hues, colors themselves have become more various and accessible. After oils were brushed over egg tempera in thirteenth-century paintings, the West embarked on an expansion of its material palette that went hand in fist with imperial conquest, sweeping up the cochineal reds of Central and South America, the indigo of India and the West Indies, the malachite green of central Africa.[25] Over time a few synthetic pigments were produced: antimony yellow (Naples yellow), Prussian blue. When alchemical closets became cabinets of chemical "elements," other synthetics became feasible: cobalt blue, chrome yellow, Schweinfurt green. But only when coal was transmuted into gas/light and English chemist William Perkin in London chanced on a process to extract dyes from the coal-tar byproducts of gasworks did the color palette go berserk or (depending on one's politics in the 1860s) democratic. Now there would be such bold, cheap hues as mauve, magenta, and fuchsia. Derived from copper shavings dissolved in arsenic, the popular Schweinfurt green became toxic when its arsenic evaporated off the walls of parlors; lead-based house paints, on store shelves until the 1980s, were equally toxic over the long run. Yet how enlightened and egalitarian must have seemed the miracles of modern chemistry when schoolchildren had finger paints at their fingertips, then large boxes of crayons and a multitude of felt-tip markers; when hobbyists and set designers could avail themselves of quick-drying acrylics and UV-sensitive paints that glowed under black light; when contractors could order buckets of custom-tinted latex wall paints (the pink on the roller of Duane Hanson's *Housepainter 1*, 1984/88, cat. 15); when dressmakers could dye last year's elephant's-breath gray into this year's crushed-strawberry red; when aircraft companies and teenagers had their choice of spray cans of a hundred hues, matte or glossy.[26]

Aside from decals on space probes and color-bonded plastics, few of the new color media, snapshots included, were meant to last a lifetime. The newest color media—digital paintings, 3-D printing, holograms, volumetric color-forming pixels—are they any less fugitive?[27] Ephemerality continues to haunt color, in arts fine and applied. While fashion editors today collude in backstories to ignite each season's dominant shade, Sokari Douglas Camp's *Material Salsa* (2011, cat. 75) reminds us that fashion has long been drawn to textiles, jewelry, and hair weaves that confound the boundaries between natural and synthetic, temporary or permanent, local or global.[28] Given our polymerized world of transient substrates, unfaithful adhesives, and temperamental binders, the majority of colors in our built and prêt-à-porter environments (as in self-taught art, visionary art, or performance art) are fated to vanish sooner than later . . . as are some of the most resplendent of other species, trapped in shrinking ecological niches.

Across eight hundred years of environmental encroachment, human bodies have inched toward greater height and girth, benefiting from readier access to protein, higher overall caloric intake, and effective sanitation. Bodies also became more regular in feature as leprosy, erysipelas, smallpox, and tertiary syphilis were driven off the chart of endemic infectious diseases. Features have been further evened out under the rollers of mass-mediated photo-manipulated "good-looking" faces and campaigns for the straightening of teeth and repair of cleft lips, double chins, crow's-feet. Finally, as life spans lengthened, bodies became more composite, benefiting from advances in the safe surgical replacement of aging knees, hips, hearts, and kidneys, and seamless attachments of prosthetic arms, hands, legs, and feet. If not more composite, then more engineered: while the earth's colors, carried by dust, ash, and pollen, were adsorbed by the skins of laborers who pick

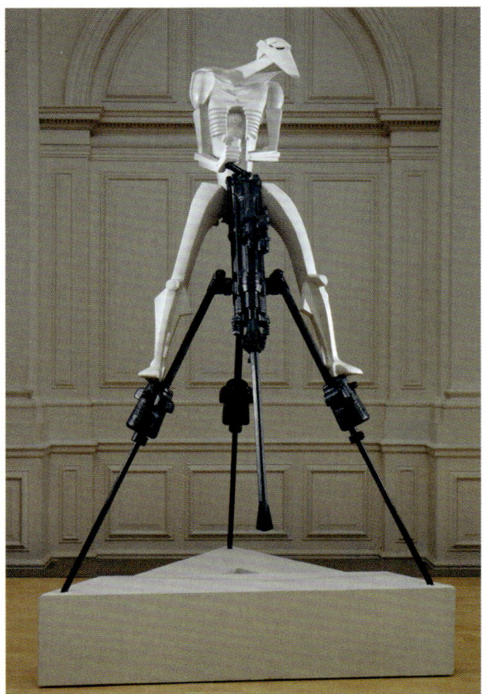

Fig. 38 Sir Jacob Epstein. *Rock Drill*, ca. 1913–15, reconstructed 1973–74. Polyester resin, metal, and wood, H. 80 11/16 in. (205 cm). Birmingham Museums and Art Gallery, U.K.

our crops and lay our foundations, the wealthy could demand plastic surgery for egregious noses, ears, lips, bellies, breasts, butts, genitals. Inside and out, Western adults scarcely resemble what their counterparts by class, age, or gender would have seen in the mirror or morgue during the 1200s, 1500s, 1800s.[29]

Having radically reconstructed our bodies to keep pace with a world in apparently furious motion, we should not be surprised that sculpture moved off its pedestals and altars and out of alcoves hallowed or princely. By the mid-1800s figural sculpture had become as free-floating, and frequently as kinetic and anxious, as those sculptors who could no longer count on patronage or a series of private and public commissions. The consequences for bodies in color were sharp, for sculptors would now be in the dark as to where a finished piece would be positioned, in what streams of light, beside which other sculptures, prints, or hanging plants. Absent the anchorage of a fated place, sculptures had to be invested with sufficient dynamism to appear at ease under any light, across any space. Sculpture was newly nomadic.[30]

The itineracy to which their pieces were destined would prompt many sculptors to abandon classical marble and idealized proportions. Abandoning such numbed fantasies as American artist Hiram Powers's *California* (1850–55, cat. 4), which turned a cold marble shoulder to Native Americans, Spaniards, Mexicans, and the ethnic medleys of Gold Rush camps, they left themselves open to workaday bodies resilient despite fatigue and sagging flesh (Bharti Kher's *Mother*, 2016, cat. 6). Reversing the dramatic arc of French artist Jean-Léon Gérôme's (and Ovid's) *Pygmalion and Galatea* (ca. 1890, cat. 36), a sculptor's supreme ambition might not be the ecstatic release of bodies from prisons of stone but the capture in silicone rubber of an *Old Woman In Bed* (2000, cat. 117), huddled under Australian artist Ron Mueck's coverlet of polyurethane foam. Is she too old, too exhausted to dream of rising to meet her maker—or her engineer-prince (Swiss waxwork maker Philippe Curtius's *Sleeping Beauty*, 1765, cat. 113)? The future would seem to belong rather to bodies that are congeries of found objects and repurposed mechanisms, beginning perhaps with the two forms of British artist Sir Jacob Epstein's "armed, sinister figure of to-day and to-morrow," *Rock Drill* (ca. 1913–15, fig. 38), which he transmuted during World War I from a gangly robotic humanoid steadied by the spine of an actual drill to a one-drill-armed bronze torso harboring a dark metal embryo. If sixty years later American artist John Outterbridge sutured a figure of leather, cloth, and stainless steel athwart a wood box of 105-round ammunition as if machine-gun nests were at once our birthplace and prosthetic future (*Broken Dance, Ethnic Heritage Series*, ca. 1978–82, cat. 92), then American artist Bruce Wood's *Rosie the Rocketeer* (2015, fig. 39) dreams of a pastoral aeronautics where the future is already old hat and horse bridles, dressed to the steam-punk nines for implausible flight.[31]

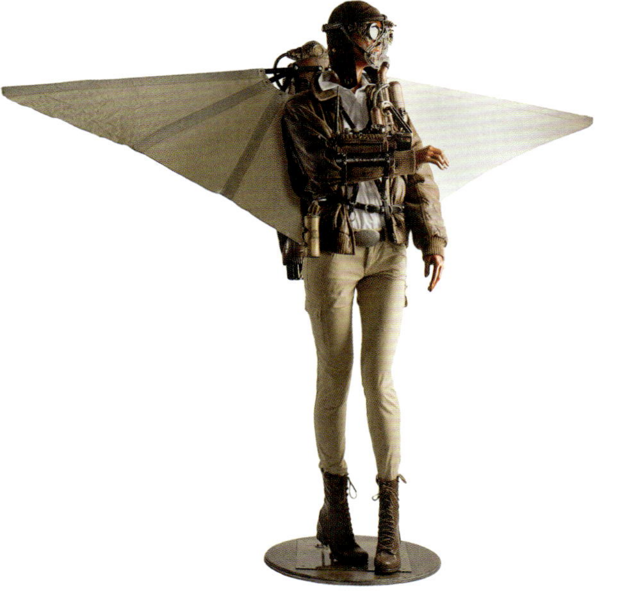
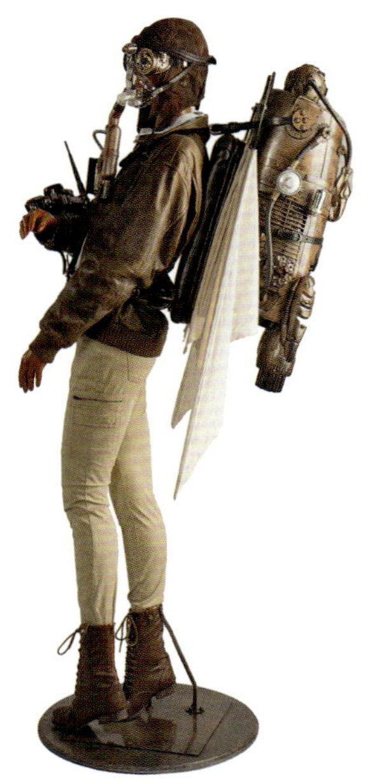

Fig. 39 Bruce Wood. *Rosie the Rocketeer*, 2015. Fiberglass, humidifier, Nerf guns, water shutoffs, gas valve, steam valve, flex hose, plastic tubing, plastic toy parts, used horse bridles, PVS pipe, air gage, TV remote, toy gun, squirt gun parts, clock gears, scrap plastic, clock gears, and canvas and meta rods, wings outspread: H. 73 in. (185.4 cm), W. 89 in. (226.1 cm), D. 29 in. (73.7 cm). Courtesy of the artist

I rush to contradict myself. Since Upper Paleolithic times, people could be found creating nomadic sculptures. These we call fetishes, household idols, tutelary spirits, or plain old figurines. Small and sometimes painted, they bespoke deities, elders, ancestors—or simply playpals.[32] Soon there would be children's dolls, and wood oarsmen laid into tombs for afterworld travels. Such realms of the figurine are no quibble from antiquity. Figurines circulated as votive objects throughout Latin Christendom (less fragile than Lucio Fontana's terracotta *Crocifisso* (see cat. 91), and as shamanic tools or apotropaic media throughout lands with competing gods. Produced by the thousands in eighteenth-century porcelain factories (see *The Judgment of Paris*, ca. 1762, cat. 13) or cast in bronze editions in nineteenth-century foundries, figurines were a handy solution to the footloose economics of nomadic art. With us still (*Shorty Working in the C&R Statuary Corp.*, 1985, cat. 31), they stand articulated in art studios as lay figures with a tradition of abuse by artists such as Hans Bellmer, Paul Huot, Yayoi Kusama, and Bertel Thorvaldsen. They stand bound within the cellophane windows of action-figure boxes. They perch on mantels as mementos of cruises, shrines, or museum shops. Age-old, ubiquitous, diverse, they have been runaway models for lifesize figures in wicker, wire, driftwood, plastic, or the clay and straw of Sri Ram Pal's *Raj Kissen Mitter* (ca. 1840, cat. 34), the foam core and polystyrene of Oliver Herring's *Patrick* (2004, cat. 95), the polyester resin of Hanson's *Housewife* (1969–70, cat. 35).

How people relate to miniatures remains mysterious.[33] Considering that adults are bizarre giants to the infants they once were, our reactions to simulacra supersize, one-size-fits-all, or travel size are as perplexed by passages of time as by changes in size. In the presence of two floors of three-dimensional bodies meant to be recognizably human despite absurd or subtle manipulations of scale, despite a lack of functional internal organs, despite colors laid on too monochromatically across expanses of skin that should be pored, wrinkled, spotted, veined, and unevenly translucent to underlayers of arterial exchange (excepting Marc Quinn's blood-made *Self*, 1991, cat. 21), we need to ask what we are doing here.[34] All of us.

All of us—curators, readers, visitors, critics, semblances—inhabit a world whose economies profit by making the similar seem remarkable, the identical authoritative; whose sciences promote

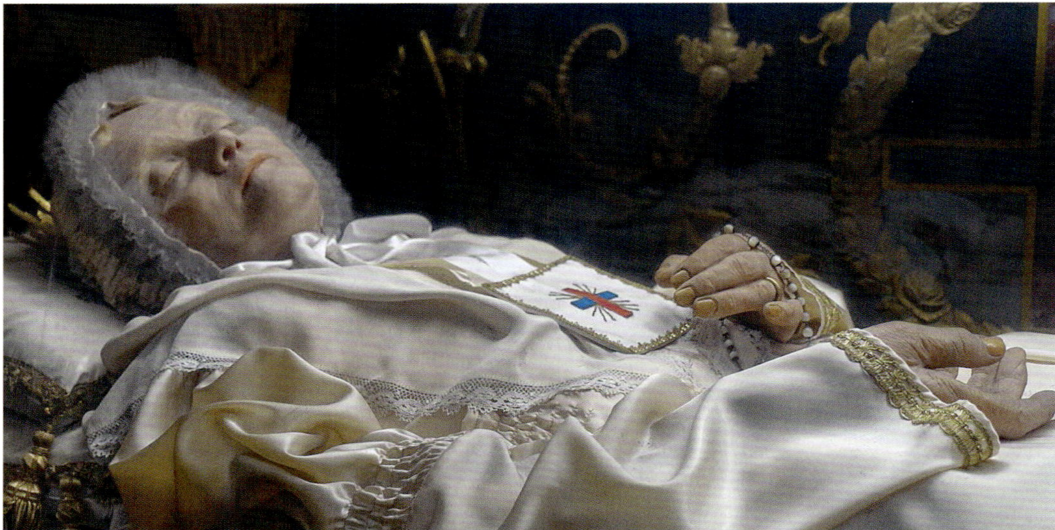

Fig. 40 Blessed Anna Maria Taigi, Church of San Crisogono, Rome

replication as the avenue toward discovery and proof; whose ethics of the unique and authentic run at right angles to desires for community.[35] Have we come here therefore because we expect our semblances, like companionable twins, to disclose remarkable things about us? Because we expect them to drive us, like doppelgängers preempting our careers, toward insights into individuality and integrity? Because we expect them, like automata and robots in the history of technology and more flexible androids in science fiction, to confirm our suspicions about humanity in general? Because we expect them to surprise us, like evil twins, with what we pretend never to have known but deep down must needs confess? Or because, like mute ghosts, we expect from them nothing more than to shiver us out of our skins—a thrilling terror from which we escape back into our humdrum bodies with inordinate pleasure?

None of the above, in so far as none hinges on the plenitude of color, on color as generative and genitive, shaping and possessing our familiars. The import of this volume is not to amaze us with the fact that our bodies are by nature colorful (who knew?), or that painting our bodies and simulacra goes back to the Neanderthals, but to explore how colors realistic, surreal, or superreal incorporate our doubles, *body them forth*, ennobled, environed, enlivened, or envenomed.[36]

Colors ennoble by imparting or sustaining majesty, heroism, sanctity. Paints ground from precious metals or rare pigments may do this as may jewels or death-defying cosmetics. In the transit from death to public immortality, many a body of a king, queen, general, revolutionary, or saint has been polychromatically translated from corpse into replica. Through reliquaries (*Reliquary Bust of Saint Juliana*, ca. 1376, cat. 20), through embalming (reenacted in Maurizio Cattelan's *Now*, 2004, cat. 112), through death masks and effigies (*Funeral Effigy of Doge Alvise III Mocenigo(?)*, 1732, cat. 16), and at last through artful conversions of dessicated flesh into colored wax or painted plaster, the bodies of notables become their own doubles. Catholic saints are doomed to undergo these conversions, for their bodies' incorruptibility is proof of sanctity. How strange the lifted hand and rounded fingers of the body of Blessed Anna Maria Taigi (fig. 40): to

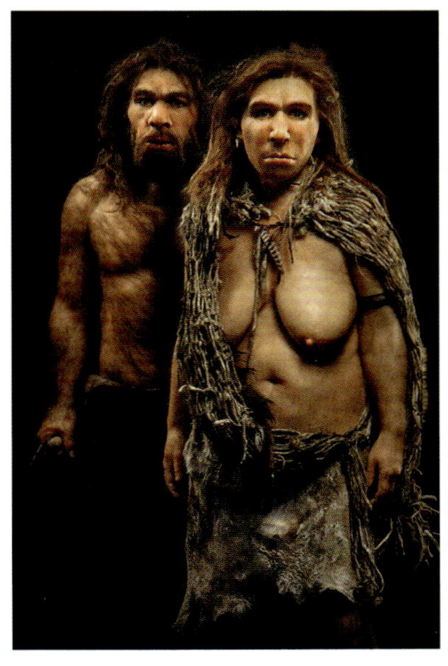

Fig. 41 Elisabeth Daynés. Reconstruction of Neanderthal couple, Saint-Césaire, France

Fig. 42 Diorama of Neanderthal family outside the Devil's Tower rock shelter at Gibraltar, near the Mediterranean Sea, created in the 1920s and still on view during the 1950s, Field Museum, Chicago

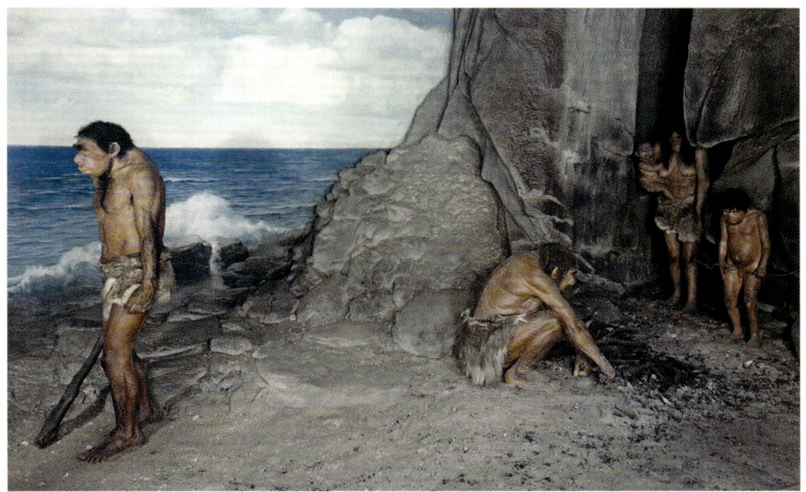

be extolled for a life of humility, honesty, and gifts of healing, then postmortem to participate in an unending impersonation of oneself.[37]

Colors environ by situating bodies so as to appear either indigenous or triumphantly secure. Call the first the art of camouflage, the second the art of staging. Figures that are chromatically integrated with their settings instruct us about design, ecology, and efficiency (Thomas Southward Smith and Jacques Talrich's *Auto-Icon of Jeremy Bentham*, 1832, cat. 22) or, when oddly incongruous, about complicity (Goshka Macuga's *To the Son of Man Who Ate the Scroll*, 2016, cat. 51). Body doubles in nude scenes and political doubles at assemblies teach us how bodies can be manipulated to assure reputation, safety, allure. Take a hint from Neanderthals in museum dioramas. They began as lifesize but recessive slouching figures, indistinct from cavescapes; as paleologists unearthed their achievements and recalibrated their crania, Neanderthals gained color and bright complexions, coming to seem, if not a triumphant species, at least secure (as well they were, for more millennia than *Homo sapiens*, figs. 41–42).[38]

Colors enliven by bringing to light those inner motions we call sorrow, desire, despair, animus, love: color as upwelling emotion. When worshippers during the thirteenth century lifted their eyes away from the Judgment toward the Passion, away from Eve's sinfulness toward Mary's warmth, sculptors looked to the body's own palette to express the intrinsic humanity of Jesus as/and Mother.[39] Since the Fourth Lateran Council of 1215, Western sculptors have used colors to enliven figures sacred and secular through transubstantial acts: not wounds but acts of bleeding; not loss but acts of grief (La Roldana's *The Entombment of Christ*, 1700–1701, cat. 97; Francesco di Giorgio Martini's *Lamentation of Christ*, 1476–77); not love but arousal and frustration (Oskar Kokoschka's *Self-Portrait with Doll* [*Mann mit Puppe*], ca. 1922, cat. 58). Wax anatomical figures lie inert because their luscious colors are not intended to make them actors (not even the Fontana Workshop's *Anatomical Venus*, 1780–85, cat. 115); painted to be splendidly coherent, they remain specimens, bodies to be seen, not watched. Dolls, especially baby dolls and sex dolls, have better odds at life because their colors enjoin them to interact.

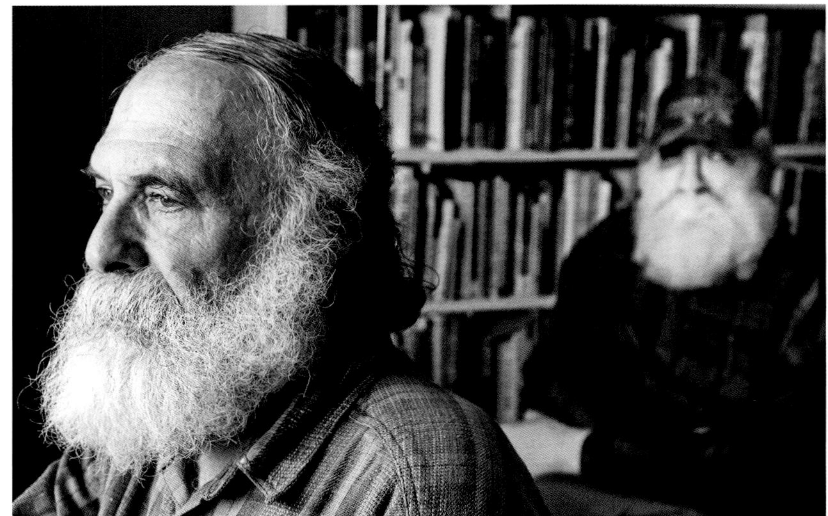

Colors envenom by sardonic contrast: Yinka Shonibare MBE's *Girl Ballerina* (2007, cat. 69), feet in fourth position, holding a pistol behind a tutu that has blossomed into evening wear. Colors envenom by poisoning the atmosphere: gaudy scarecrows in cornfields. They envenom by blistering the skins of disaster-dummies with acid burns.[40] They envenom by doubling back on doubles in regressions as taunting (Paul Delvaux's *Pygmalion*, 1939) as they may be multiple (Elmgreen & Dragset's *The Experiment*, 2012, cat. 71).

I myself have a doppelgänger (fig. 43). He has jointed legs too insubstantial to hold him up, an unbreathing chest, unfeeling fingers; still, I write *he*, not *it*. Created by the artist Donna Sasso, he sits in a corner of my study in his gray baseball cap, blue plaid shirt, and green khakis, holding a book. There is nothing saintly or majestic about him, though he appears to age less swiftly than I. If he has been envenomed, it is to caution me against taking myself too seriously. He is so well environed that some days I forget he is there, but I will miss his company when he is gone, all the same.

From earliest doll-play, mirror-gaze, and fondling of figurines to the fashioning of twins of identical size fleshed out in cotton, clay, birch, or polyvinyl, our doubles make us who we think we are. In more than one sense, they constitute us. Bodies. Color. It's double or nothing.

MATERIAL HISTORIES

MAKING *MOTHER* AND *FATHER*

The body is a container—of viscera, heart, guts, and sexual organs, but also of emotions and force. Before making *Mother* (2016, cat. 6), I had shown my mother *Six Women* (2013–15, fig. 5) and asked, "What if I were to cast you and put you in between these six women? Who would know who you are?" I wanted to investigate how we *look* at the body, at the female form. How important is it for the viewer to know that the six women are sex workers and that the other woman who's here, who sits in the middle of them—which is not even the same work—is my mother. What does it mean?

There's a truth that the self is multiple, which is the reality of many women's lives. It's akin to role-playing, and there's quite a lot of that in my work. Specifically, in *Mother*: the way that she sits calls the work into a dialogue with the history of the mother and child. The mother is always young, and more often than not, the child is always a boy, especially in religious art. Even in Hindu mythology, there would always be the goddess with the son, the male child.

For me, the idea was to invert it and say, "This is the mother, and she's mine." She's also older. I wanted to engage the body of the older woman politically and compassionately. Some people were quite surprised and asked, "Wow, your mother agrees that you cast her? How was that experience?" I think because she believes in me, she believes in my work. She felt that I was trying to speak about motherhood, femininity, and the idea that perhaps women are tired of being revered as virgin goddesses. There's no heroism in my piece. I'm not making her bigger than she is. She sits on that stool. She's made from the first cast of the plaster that holds her essence. It's quite simple actually—and not.

In making *Father* (2016, fig. 44), a sculptural portrait of my father that anticipates *Mother* through its pose, color, and wheeled platform, I was trying to go inside him. I already know my mother because I have lived inside her, but what would it be like to be inside him? I made both a positive cast and a negative of the positive. I did the outside casting to play with this duality of inside and outside, positive and negative, to see what happens inside the body. Through the large cavity I made that begins in his chest and exits out his back, I could now go inside. The hole,

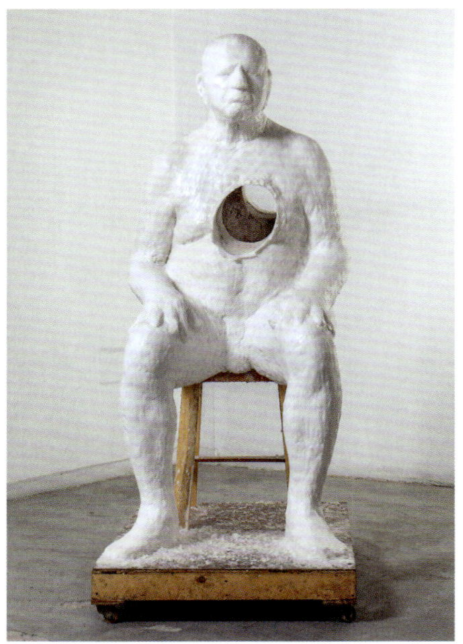

Fig. 44 Bharti Kher. *Father*, 2016. Wax, wood, and plaster of Paris, H. 58 ¼ in. (148 cm), W. 27 ½ in. (70 cm), D. 37 in. (94 cm). Courtesy of the artist and Hauser & Wirth

near the heart, was created just two months before he had heart surgery. Whatever was excavated has made room from the inside, to exit to the outside, as if it were healing. You make a space, you heal, and then it can become a receptacle that metaphorically holds something else like light.

When I ask myself why I'm casting, a process I've practiced for close to fifteen years, I think of the oppositions and forces in the positive and the negative, not as polarities, but as frictions that galvanize the body. Without that grist of casting, the essence of the body, the smell of the skin, the heat of the plaster that goes into the body and impregnates the skin, taking something away with it—a lot of figures would become static. I almost need the connection to a living, breathing body, or I have to find another way to animate the work, animate the material. It's almost like a myth, where the creator would make a clay figure and then blow breath into it to bring it to life (fig. 29).

EMBODIED MEMORY

If you're going to use your own work as a vehicle for metaphor, then in the life of these works, the outside skin serves as a function to cover, to maintain the integrity of the body as well as the soul. There's also the question of how you absorb the memory of another person through your skin. Do you carry those memories inside your body? Does doing so make you a bit more of them or less of yourself? We all have bodies, and our bodies are containers for energy, for actions. How do changes affect coverings? If you wait and watch all things animate and inanimate, they will reveal themselves to you, especially when you make art.

WAXING FRAGILITY

I chose to coat *Father* in wax, which is a material that I started using in the past year or so. Physically, it is one of very few materials that always goes back to its original form. It has zero transformation, no matter how much you try to alter it. It's like mercury. René Descartes wrote in his *Meditations on First Philosophy* (1641) an analogy that asked how two things can have different properties yet still be the same. The theory felt related conceptually to my bindi work, to the idea of the masculine and feminine, the bodies of hybrids and containers, insides and outsides. I loved wax because it has this kind of narrative, this sensuality of impermanence. It is quite fragile and speaks for itself.

With *Father*, wax became a transformer. As an artist, there is the maker in me that wants to make marble look like wood or like folds of skin, as they did in the sixteenth century. Since I simply cannot do that, I have to conjure up other ways to be transformative and make a material be what it is not. I covered the outside of my father as a way to go inside him. What I am saying in some way is, "I melt you." I'm melting, softening, going inside the material and you.

There is a fragile and beautiful moment when you either hold on to an image or lose it; hold a sculpture or lose it. All of us artists, from way back, perhaps from when we put our first handprints on a cave wall, were trying to capture this thing called the human spirit. Like a will-o'-the-wisp, it's a hard thing to catch. You think you have it, and it slips out from the side of your studio and out the door. I am constantly trying to catch it, using materials to do so, like an alchemist. I am trying to create the manifestations of different things, to find this enigmatic stone I've been searching for. It's probably in my pocket, and I don't know it's there.

CAPTURING THE EPHEMERAL

All artists try to slip into this other axis and hold things you can't see or even hold. For me, it started when my art teacher said, "We're going to do a drawing exercise, and you're going to draw this table and chair, and on the chair is a bowl of fruit." We all drew it, and he responded, "No, wrong, wrong. What are you really drawing about? I want you to draw *everything*." I started to understand that he wanted us to draw the negative space and everything around the table to describe it. And I think that is how I still approach all of my work and the human body, that is, by not approaching the body. I approach it from everything that is around the body, to catch the spirit of that body. Sometimes that could be through the skin, which I cover to release the body; I'll make a hole in it to forgive the body; or I cut off bits to allow it to become something else. I am trying to understand negation and its power to describe presence, which is why I do lots of positive-negative casting and recasting. It's a way to know things.

MATERIAL WISDOM ALISON SAAR

EARLY INFLUENCES

In some ways my work is a marriage between the influences of my mother, Betye Saar, and my father, Richard Saar. My father was classically trained, and so I was constantly fed images of Michelangelo, Leonardo, and classical sculpture. As a conservator, he worked on Assyrian and kouros figures, and I saw them when I was quite young. My mother, of course, was look-ing at the occult and the arts of Africa, India, and Mexico. She had all these books about art and spirit. I put the two together. *Strange Fruit* (1995, cat. 110) reflects African and non-Western cultures, but the body is very much informed by Western traditions, from the Renaissance and even pre-Renaissance.

I am a self-taught sculptor; I haven't really received any formal train-ing in it. Up until maybe the last two months of my graduate work, I was just doing 2-D work. Then my father gave me some chisels, and I got a four-by-four-inch piece of wood and created my first carving. It was very much like a puppet, a doll. That really early work was, and later ones since then continue to be, informed by my study of non-Western art, specifically that of Africa and of self-taught African American artists. You can see in *Strange Fruit* a reflection of Kongo Nkisi figures (fig. 45). She has these objects embedded in her belly and in some ways becomes a reliquary. The body is this exterior, and there are windows to the interior, to the soul or

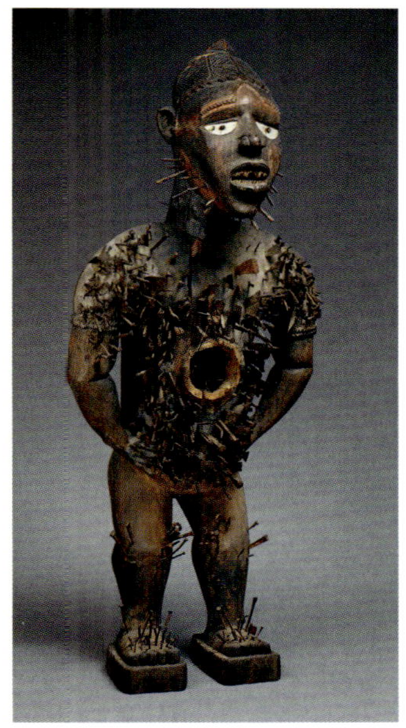

Fig. 45 *Power Figure* (Nkisi N'Kondi: Mangaaka), 19th century. Wood, iron, resin, ceramic, plant fiber, textile, and pigment. H. 46 ½ in. (118 cm), W. 19 ½ in. (49.5 cm), D. 15 ½ in. (39.4 cm). Kongo peoples; Yombe group. The Metropolitan Museum of Art, New York, Purchase, Lila Acheson Wallace, Drs. Daniel and Marian Malcolm, Laura G. and James J. Ross, Jeffrey B. Soref, The Robert T. Wall Family, Dr. and Mrs. Sidney G. Clyman, and Steven Kossak Gifts, 2008 (2008.30)

the ideas within. Inside, I think, are a rose and a fig leaf, which play off the figure of Eve. There are other little objects in the crook of her arm.

HISTORY ENDURES

Her skin is made of ceiling tin, and its baroque patterning here becomes a form of scarification or keloiding, again looking back to African culture and customs. But it also becomes a form of armor. At its base, this rusted material creates an impermeable surface to protect her. All the tin I used came from New York tenements. Most of it dates as far back as the 1890s but had remained in these tenements until the 1980s and 1990s, when I was finding the stuff on the street and dragging it back to the studio. I love the idea of a material having a specific wisdom or history. This tin witnessed people being born, dying, having sex, throwing parties. I hope that by coating, covering, skinning, or cladding these figures with it, the material brings its history to the figure, too.

It is a similar thing in the museum, where many pieces are no longer in their place of origin but are still empowered by history. Spiritual objects may lose something if they are no longer among devotees, but they don't lose their history. I see some similarities with relics, which are often just fragments. People respond and enliven these fragments of dead things and imbue them with spirit, giving them continued life. The objects embedded in *Strange Fruit* really talk about who she is, what she's experienced in her past, and what her future is. They're impacted in there with mud and different materials that cement them to her. The doorknob, which is a kind of keyhole, refers to the voyeurism of other cultures. Looking at art history, say Paul Gauguin's *Eve* figures (cat. 49), World's Fairs, or Saartjie Baartman, there is this idea of bringing the "savage" world to the West, to be looked at. The keyhole represents a very colonial, imperialist way to peer into this figure and her history as an outsider.

BODIES OF COLOR

Strange Fruit also speaks to the depiction of women of color, specifically to the sudden embrace of black and brown bodies in the 1980s. It felt very colonial, as if outsiders were claiming the bodies of others, and so I made the work. The title of the piece is, of course, the title of Billie Holiday's song about lynching. But for me, it really talks about how these women are still reduced to objects, strange fruit, exotic fruit. It's an inversion of a lynching: she is not hung by her neck, but she is still being hung. The idea is how the media and the general public think of these women as something to be plucked and consumed. It isn't necessarily a death of the body but more a psychological death. She is alive but in a strange limbo where she is not free to be herself.

In terms of this propensity for people to regard the black body as something that can be used and consumed by anyone, artists of color are authoring and putting these images out there that have a derogatory history. The question is whether that is enough to enable the piece to transcend that initial intention. Ultimately, viewers are in control and can take it wherever they want to take it. I hope putting these images out there, and information about my intentions, will lead viewers to think beyond whatever racist or bigoted ideas they may carry, even unconsciously. As artists, we aspire to create work that elicits discussion. There are risks: it is totally possible that the piece could be misinterpreted. That's why it's art and not illustration.

I've been coming to The Met for a long time, starting from when I was a student, when I was behind the scenes, seeing plaster casts and not knowing at the time that they were different from what was on display, and then as an educator. It made me think about the variety of ways that art can exist. The reverence was still there, but the works took on an approachability that let me think about them more broadly. Similarly, being able to see works from different departments, not necessarily next to each other, but somewhat tangential to each other, has been very influential on what I've ended up doing.

COPIES AND CONTEXT

My work *The Mete of the Muse* (2006, cat. 3) presents two found objects. The European figure would have been a garden ornament. The Egyptian figure is, from what I gather, a copy of a copy at the Musée du Louvre, Paris. I am always interested in copies, as they take on their own histories as they proceed though time. They change. Many things that I produce seem historical but have in fact assumed other meanings as they move along throughout history. I am not reproducing historical objects specific to what they were. Rather, it's about how they are seen in our time and all the meanings they have accumulated along the way.

BEYOND BLACK AND WHITE

It was a funny thing to use black and white in this work, because I don't think of things in such a simplistic way. However, they were like that, and I'm always thinking about the signifiers of objects that people assign meaning to in our world. Here one could come up with different meanings of black and white—European and non-European, or African and Asian—and I expect people to see the work from their own perspective. But if you assign one as European, the other as non-European, what does that say about their relationship or about who they are? I found that possibility really fascinating and wanted to leave it there. I'm not suggesting anything in particular; I want people to tease out and think about how they view the relationship between the two figures. Of course, I have my own view, too.

NEW SETTING, NEW MEANING

Ubiquitous items that are banal, ordinary, or fake can hold my interest for as long as ones that are perfect or in a museum. They hold just as much interest for me because of their meaning within a culture and how they can mean something else entirely, or nothing at all, in another. A lot of that is about myself, in that my family moved every five years. I found myself as a young man in various environments, becoming a chameleon, with people seeing me in a certain way wherever I went. They saw me as what they knew, or not at all, which relates to my history and identity as an artist of color.

RACIAL INVISIBILITY

As a young man it was just a given: one grew accustomed to not seeing oneself on television or anyplace, certainly not in museums. That realization of my invisibility had a lot to do with how I saw myself. Even looking back at my drawings as a child, it is shocking, because I remember seeing what was depicted and feeling that it was me, but it certainly was not. The world was different then—unquestioning. Thinking about race in the mainstream was a much later phenomenon. In art school, it also was never brought up. In fact, at graduation the head of the school said to me, "Do you want to be part of the black art world or the white art world?" I had just assumed that there was only one art world. The rude awakening was coming to New York after that and seeing what the real situation was. Becoming a museum educator made me much more aware of what was not being represented.

When we look at sculptures of human bodies, we are looking for ourselves and our emotions in them. We are completely hardwired for that. I've made works about the so-called blackamoors (fig. 20), particularly for the Venice Biennale (2003, fig. 46), because their image is omnipresent in Venice, like "black collectibles" in the United States and other places. They are usually in service, in one way or another. A decorative art object is supposed to just sit there; you're not supposed to really think too hard about it. But I like working with such common items that are not considered high art, because they authentically represent a culture, good or bad. Here they also represent a prejudice.

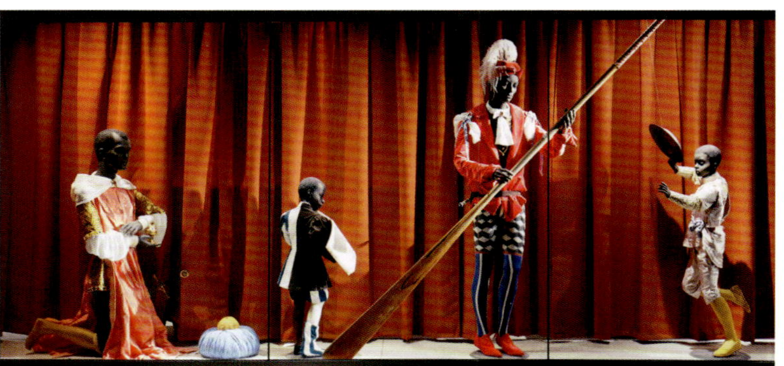

Fig. 46   Fred Wilson. *Sacre Conversazione* from the installation *Speak of Me as I Am*, 2003 (detail). Cast-resin mannequins, acrylic paint, handmade fabric, metal, and various objects, dimensions variable. Installation view, U.S. Pavilion, Venice Biennale, 2003

These are images that are supposed to be me, but are not me. However, there is something in them that I am supposed to be. I do not shy away from the stereotype of mammies, pappies, and blackamoors, but if I am going to use them, I have a responsibility either to expose their histories or find the humanity within them. Obviously, people will see what they want to see. I can only take these things very seriously and try to put all my feelings into them so that I either empower these objects in a way that they were not or lay bare their subtext.

DEMOCRATIZING MATERIAL JEFF KOONS

One of my fondest childhood memories is of this little ashtray that my grandparents had. It was about six inches long and shaped like a woman lying on a couch. Her legs were up in the air, and you could move them back and forth. I was mesmerized by this movement. My awe and wonderment equaled what anybody could feel for a work of art. When I recently walked through The Met, I felt that same awe and wonderment. That ashtray performed on the same level as a Pergamon head in the Greek and Roman galleries. My work tries to embrace that feeling and remove all judgments and hierarchies. It's about becoming and embracing our experiences and our past, instead of disempowering ourselves. My work seeks to remove guilt and shame.

I see porcelain as a democratized material. It's the material of Marcel Duchamp's urinal *Fountain* (1917), so it has that sort of connotation, but then it also has all the cultural refinement of something coming from the king's kitchen, of a society trying to make the best things it can to preserve. I love that about porcelain. It has a beautiful sexual tension.

CONTEMPORARY GODS

With *Michael Jackson and Bubbles* (1988, cat. 14), the absolute main idea was a Christ-like figure, a Pietà. I was thinking directly of Michelangelo's sculpture. Michael Jackson was godlike, and I felt like I had to have a figure with a little bit of spiritual authority. That way, people could feel secure enough to let go and embrace banality, to embrace their own cultural history. The monkey is also important. I love how the monkey has been used in art. The way its eyes are painted here references Egyptian art (figs. 51–52), as does the application of gold, tying it to the pharaohs and King Tutankhamun.

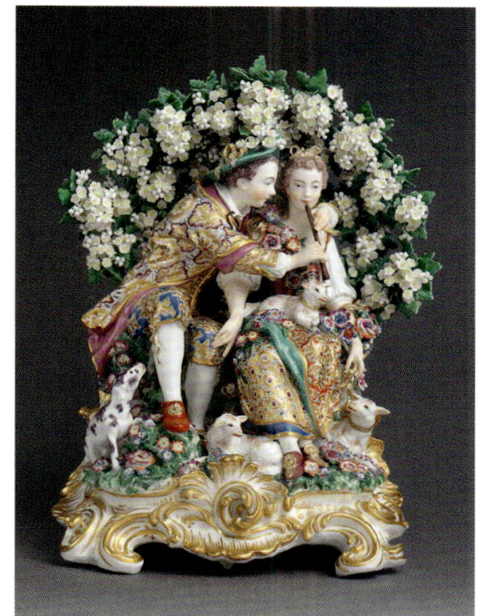

Fig. 47 Chelsea Porcelain Manufactory, modeled by Joseph Willems, after two engravings by François Boucher. *The Music Lesson*, ca. 1765. Soft-paste porcelain, H. 15 ⅜ in. (39.1 cm), W. 12 ¼ in. (31.1 cm), D. 8 ¾ in. (22.2 cm). The Metropolitan Museum of Art, New York, Gift of Irwin Untermyer, 1964 (64.101.519)

I think of somebody like David Bowie and of this spectacle of a rock show being larger than life. Someone can really end up getting lost in that idea. The individuals watching feel they're not as great as the thing they're identifying with. They would like to become it, to touch it. Color and light—that's the spectacle, the show.

MYTHOLOGICAL FUTURES

All the porcelain artisans for the Banality series (1988) came from just outside Milan, in Bassano del Grappa and Val Gardena. I chose them based on the work they had already done. I was definitely referring back to mythology and various classical figures, and the Italians understood that. They would say, "It's difficult, but let me think about it." The artisan I chose to make *Michael Jackson and Bubbles* had made these beautiful Venus figures coming out of conch shells whose interiors were all gold.

In my work, I collect images that I like and continue to look at porcelain from Meissen, Samson, and Staffordshire, to the kind of work from the Chelsea Porcelain Manufactory seen at The Met (fig. 47). The works range from mythic nudes to lots of animals to lovers. To me, they deal with being human but also aim toward something metaphysical. The surface reflects right here, right now because it completely catches the viewer. But then, the viewer is able to travel through time, through gradual renderings of time—sunrise, sunset, the sky. You can take these images and costumes from the past and tie them to the way we look at mythology or other things that take us back. One feels the here and now; one feels the past; and then one feels one's own possibility, which is a way of putting a foot in the future.

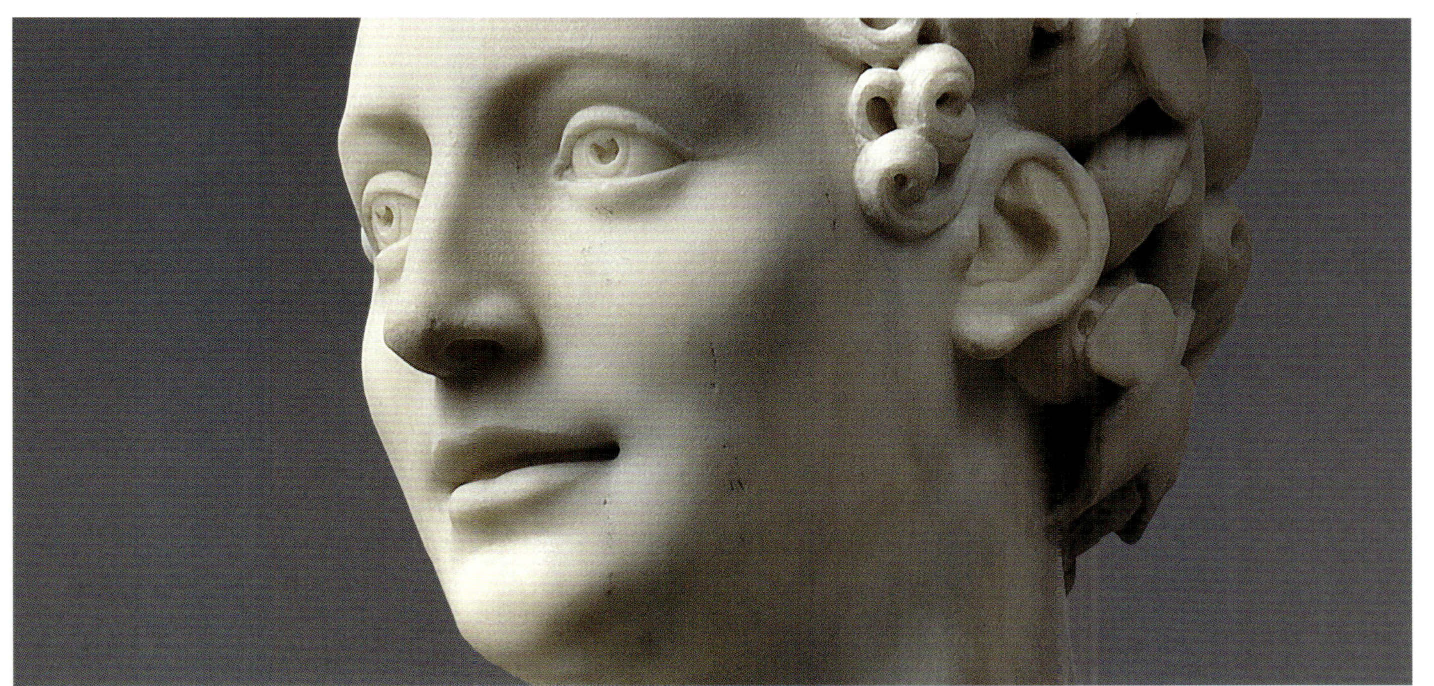

THE
PRESUMPTION
OF WHITE

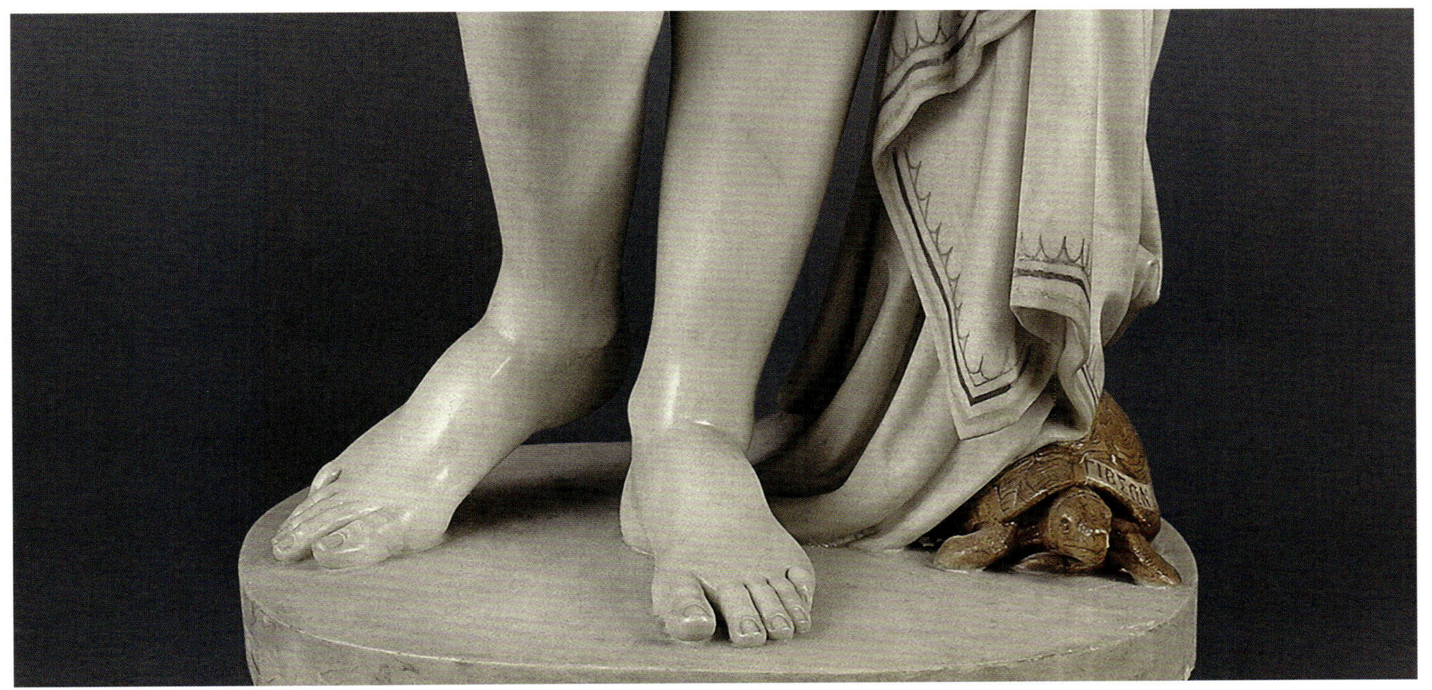

THE PRESUMPTION OF WHITE

EMERSON BOWYER

Georg Wilhelm Friedrich Hegel did not like it when statues looked back at him. The sculpted eye, the German philosopher argued, "should not protrude or, as it were, project itself into the external world."[1] It should be more absent than present, a blank—even blind—orb hovering in the recesses of carved stone. By contrast, the eye that looked back denoted a sculpture too entangled in the material world, a sculpture that misguidedly claimed the particularity and temporality of a living individual. Sight, with all its messy embodiedness, belonged to the observer of statues, not the objects of that vision.[2] For Hegel, the withdrawal of the eye characterized the best sculptures, namely, those preserved from Greek and Roman antiquity (fig. 48).[3] This trait is echoed in works by many of the greatest sculptors of his lifetime, such as Antonio Canova. It contributes to the distant and rarified air of the Italian sculptor's *Ideal Head (Erato?)* (ca. 1812), as opposed to the more immediately engaging portraits by his older French contemporary Jean Antoine Houdon, with their hollowed irises and floating, three-dimensional pupils cunningly carved to catch the light (fig. 49). The point for Hegel is that the sculpted body should inhabit a realm physically and intellectually removed from the quotidian world, a realm confined to the space plotted out by its pedestal. Above all, this conception of sculpture required the absence of naturalistic color—a bleaching of all the myriad and changeable hues of real, living bodies. It sought, one could argue, the transcendence of whiteness.

Writing in the heady heyday of modern aesthetics, Hegel believed that sculpture, more than any other art form, trafficked in the ideal. This principle, strictly codified by Neoclassical theorists in the late eighteenth and early nineteenth centuries, cast a long shadow and, to some extent, retains authority even today. Sculpture, Hegel summarized, is "always concerned solely with the abstraction of form and must therefore on the one hand abandon what is strictly natural in the body, i.e. what hints at merely natural functions, while on the other hand it may not proceed to particularize the most external details."[4] This was a fine line to tread: sculpted bodies should not reproduce the frail and fleshly figures of the real world, yet they should be recognizably human. For the eighteenth-century British academician Sir Joshua Reynolds, the natural body was but a starting point. "Imitation," he counseled, "is the means, and not the end, of art.... The sculptor employs the representation of the thing itself; but still as a means to a higher end,—as a gradual ascent always advancing towards faultless form and perfect beauty."[5]

Since the Renaissance, it was widely believed that such perfection was manifest in ancient Greek sculpture. Consider a marble first- or second-century A.D. Roman copy of a mid-fifth-century B.C. Greek statue of Hermes (cat. 1). This perfectly proportioned male nude is all clarity and unity. One can identify flesh, but only in a general sense—as a series of smooth and regular planes. The body is fully self-contained; at rest, certainly, but with the suggestion of possible movement. Retrieved from the earth after centuries of obscurity, statues such as these provided models for ambitious sculptors of the Renaissance. Italian sculptor Domenico Poggini's *Bacchus* (1554, cat. 2), for instance, carefully emulates the antique, albeit with a slightly giddy earnestness. The *Hermes* and other canonical compositions created chains of replication that continued through the nineteenth century with works such as American sculptor Hiram Powers's *Fisher Boy* (1841–44, fig. 50), which the sculptor affectionately described as "a kind of Apollino."[6]

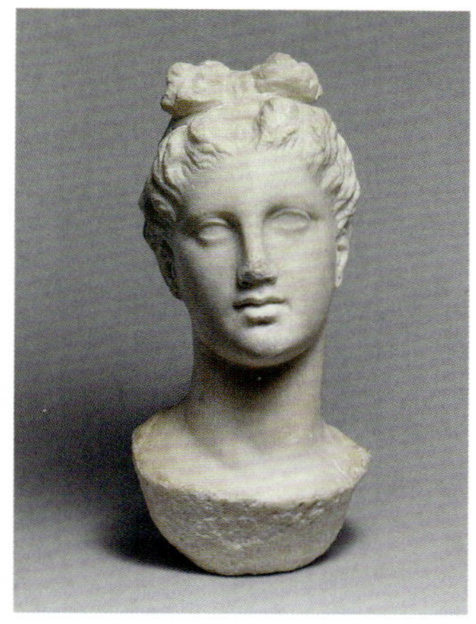

Fig. 48 *Marble Head of a Young Woman from a Funerary Statue*, late 4th century B.C. Marble, H. 16 in. (40.6 cm), W. 7 ½ in. (19.1 cm), D. 8 in. (20.3 cm). Greek. The Metropolitan Museum of Art, New York, Bequest of Walter C. Baker, 1971 (1972.118.112)

Fig. 49 Jean Antoine Houdon. *Denis Diderot*, 1773. Marble, with socle: H. 21 in. (53.3 cm), W. 10 in. (25.4 cm), D. 6 ½ in. (16.5 cm); base: W. 6 in. (15.2 cm), D. 6 in. (15.2 cm). The Metropolitan Museum of Art, New York, Gift of Mr. and Mrs. Charles Wrightsman, 1974 (1974.291)

Fig. 50 Hiram Powers *Fisher Boy*, 1841–44, carved 1857. Marble, H. 57 ½ in. (146.1 cm), W. 19 in. (48.3 cm), D. 16 in. (40.6 cm). The Metropolitan Museum of Art, New York, Bequest of Hamilton Fish, 1894 (94.9.1)

By the early twentieth century, the long-held preference for the Greek ideal over the real was contested. German artist Georg Scholz's *Female Nude with Plaster Bust* (1927), for example, presents two women: on the one hand, a bleached, sightless and disembodied ancient bust; on the other, a warm-blooded woman, her gaze directed out beyond the edge of the composition. This young flapper exists in the here and now, her pliant flesh cushioned for comfort. Her embeddedness in the real is only heightened by an up-to-date *Bubikopf* (bob) hairstyle and stockings that encase her legs—the trappings of ephemeral fashion. She is no longer simply the raw matter from which a more perfect figure is produced. Instead, she shares the table with the classical bust, overwhelming it with her materiality. Tellingly, there is evidence that Scholz originally titled the painting "The Old and New Venus."[7] By contrast, Bharti Kher's *Mother* (2016, cat. 6) blurs conventional distinctions between the ideal and the real, the general and the particular. Cast from life, the sculpture reproduces with uncanny exactitude the external form of the artist's own mother: the plaster records every wrinkle, protuberance, and fold of flesh. Yet, at the same time, there is something distinctly unearthly about this solemn and composed figure, a sense that she transcends prosaic detail to represent a broader notion of motherhood. This generality is heightened by the sculpture's lack of naturalistic coloration, which recalls the European tradition of idealized white marble statuary.

For Hegel and his allies, sculpture was pure form, unpolluted by painters' illusory tricks. This conception was inherited from the Renaissance, a period during which newly rediscovered antique statuary was found to be uncolored, or cleaned and polished until it appeared so. The long history of the *paragone*—the comparison between sculpture and painting—placed color firmly in the camp of painting. For supporters of sculpture, its virtues consisted of

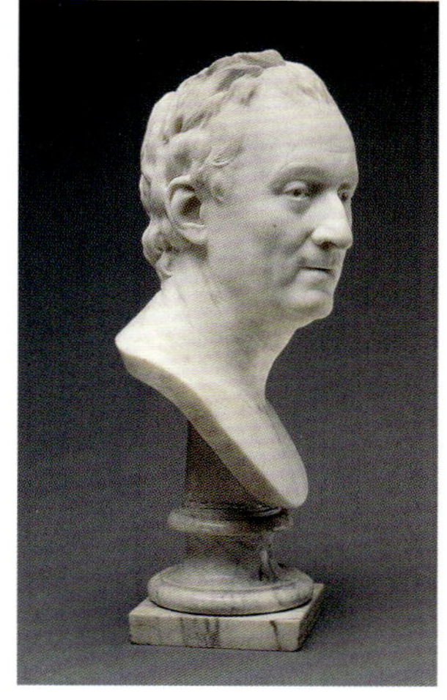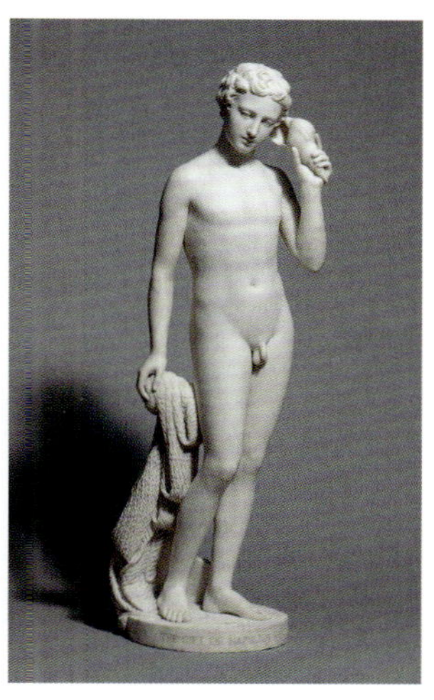

tangible, durable materiality and an emphasis on contour. Sixteenth-century Italian artist Benvenuto Cellini, for example, criticized painting as "nothing more than the reflection in a fountain of a tree, a man, or some other thing. The difference between painting and sculpture is immense; it is like the difference between a shadow and the thing that cast it."[8] Color, as an additive property, distracted the viewer from sculpture's essence. "On the whole," wrote Hegel, "a sculpture is uniformly coloured, hewn from white marble and not from something variously coloured; it also has metals at command as material, this original matter, self-identical, undifferentiated, a so-to-say congealed light without opposition and without the harmony of different colours."[9] Despite his reference to metals—bronze, especially—white marble excited him most: "Marble in its soft purity, whiteness, absence of color, and the delicacy of its sheen harmonizes in the most direct way with the aim of sculpture."[10] White marble encapsulated this quality of congealed light. Hegel was well versed in Johann Wolfgang von Goethe's contemporary research on color and color perception. "Pure water," wrote Goethe, "crystallised to snow appears white, for the transparence of the

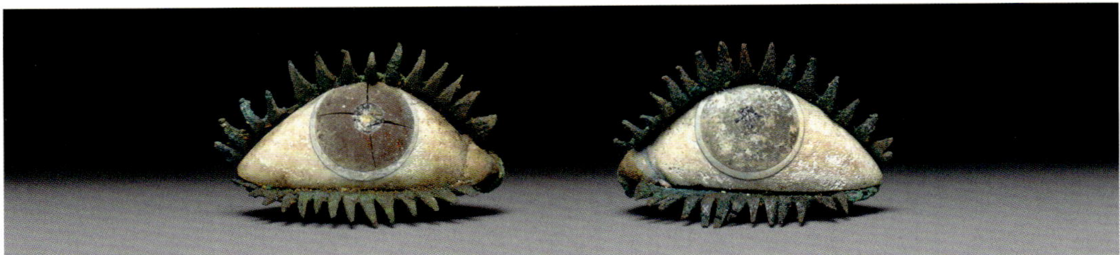

Fig. 51 *Pair of Eyes*, 5th century B.C. or later. Bronze, marble, frit, quartz, and obsidian, H. 1 ½ in. (3.8 cm), W. 2 in. (5.1 cm), D. 2 in. (5.1 cm). Greek. The Metropolitan Museum of Art, New York, Purchase, Mr. and Mrs. Lewis B. Cullman Gift and Norbert Schimmel Bequest, 1991 (1991.11.3a, b)

separate parts makes no transparent whole.... The accidentally opaque state of a pure transparent substance might be called white."[11] In other words, white marble was contentless: a disinterested medium for visual representation.

Of course, in cultural terms, whiteness is suffused with meaning. The supposed synchronicity of ideal bodies and whiteness is inseparable from racial discourse in the West. The historical privileging of light (European) skin tones lurks beneath seemingly innocuous statements by art historians and theorists such as the pioneering eighteenth-century scholar Johann Joachim Winckelmann.[12] "Since white is the color that reflects the most rays of light," he wrote in 1764, "and thus is most easily perceived, a beautiful body will be all the more beautiful the whiter it is."[13] The bleaching of color afforded by white marble, combined with the deployment of the ideal classical form, displaced racial difference in a way that was comfortable for Western audiences. Take, for example, Powers's allegorical representation of the state of California or, as the artist described her, the "Goddess of Gold" (1850–55, cat. 4). Early in its production, Powers explained the work as follows:

> I am now making a statue of "La Dorado" or California—an Indian figure crowned with pearls and precious stones. A kirtle surrounds her waist, and falls with a feather fringe down to just above the knees. The kirtle is ornamented with Indian embroidery, with tracings of gold, and her sandals are tied with golden strings. At her side stands an inverted Cornucopia, from which is issuing at her feet lumps and grains of native gold, to which she points with her left hand, which holds the divining rod. With her right hand she conceals behind her a cluster of thorns. She stands in an undecided posture—making it doubtful whether she intends to advance or retire—while her expression is mystical. The gold about the figure must be represented, of course, by color as well as form. She is to be the genius of California.[14]

The completed work bears little resemblance to this description. Nearly all elements that would have been considered exotic—whether colored materials or the (perceived) accoutrements of Native American culture—have been excised. Now represented by a classicizing white nude, *California* does not readily depict

a non-European body. In fact, when the artist had difficulty securing an American buyer for the sculpture, he did not hesitate to suggest to potential British patrons that the statue be renamed "Australia."[15]

Through a simple act of juxtaposition in *The Mete of the Muse* (2006, cat. 3), American artist Fred Wilson exposes the stereotypical racial associations of black and white, and their superimposition on to modern histories of art and aesthetics. The work consists of two painted bronze figures: one, a hieratic ancient Egyptian figure; the other, a livelier Greek nude. In Wilson's binary pair, Western classicism is white, and non-Western, nonclassical sculpture is black. The "mete" of the work's title is multivalent, referring simultaneously to meeting, measurement, and boundaries. While the objects speak of difference, confrontation, and relative values, the subtlety of Wilson's composition consists in their shared space. Gathered together on a single plinth, the artist activates the negative space between the statues: a space for creative dialogue and exchange.

Unfortunately for Hegel and his Neoclassical contemporaries, by the late eighteenth century archaeological evidence of colored (polychrome) sculpture among the ancient Greeks was omnipresent. The philosopher was even forced to admit that the illustrious ancients had both painted and inserted precious stones in the eyes of their statues (fig. 51).[16] But he dismissed such practices as merely the residual traditions of a more primitive stage in Greek culture or ones dictated by the religious imperative to adorn representations of the gods. In Denis Diderot's *Encyclopédie* (1751), the eighteenth-century French sculptor Etienne Maurice Falconet issued a more scathing response: "The sheen of gilt, the sudden clash of discordant colors of different marbles might dazzle a populace attracted by tawdry glitter. The man of taste will be disgusted.... Remaining within its prescribed framework, sculpture will lose none of its advantages, which would certainly be the case if it should use the techniques of painting. Each of these arts has its own means of imitating nature: color is not that of sculpture."[17]

What might Falconet have thought of American artist Jeff Koons's gaudy yet sepulchral *Michael*

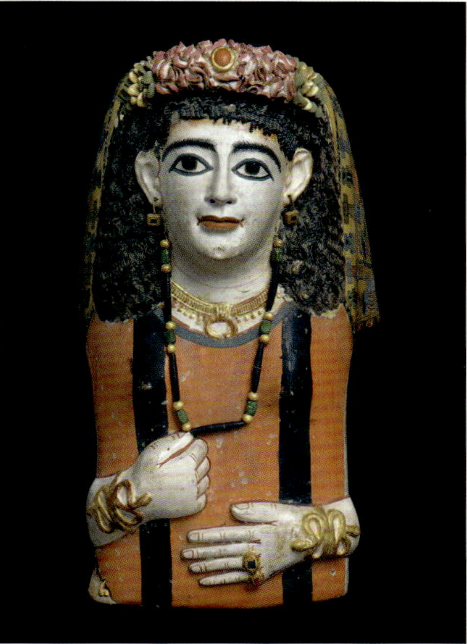

Fig. 52 *Mummy Mask*, A.D. 60–70. Cartonnage, plaster, paint, and plant fibers, H. 20 ⅞ in. (53 cm), W. 24 ¹³/₁₆ in. (63 cm), D. 13 in. (33 cm). Egyptian. The Metropolitan Museum of Art, New York, Rogers Fund, 1919 (19.2.6)

Fig. 53 Antonio Canova. *Hebe*, 1800–1805. Marble, H. 62 ³/₁₆ in. (158 cm), W. 29 ⅛ in. (74 cm), D. 32 ⁵/₁₆ in. (82 cm). State Hermitage Museum, Saint Petersburg

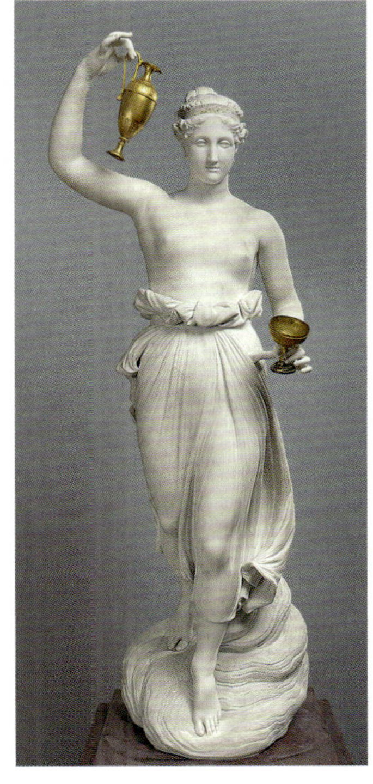

Jackson and Bubbles (1988, cat. 14)? Although posed like a reclining Roman river god, Jackson's gleaming ceramic body is gilded and colored, referencing the less exalted genre of painted porcelain figurines—for example, the frothy confection *The Judgment of Paris* (ca. 1762, cat. 13), whose design is attributed to German artist Johann Joachim Kändler. Jackson's rouged cheeks, vermilion lips, and thickly outlined eyes are closer to Egyptian mummy masks (fig. 52) than to Falconet's Greek ideal. In fact, the paint is applied in such a manner as to suggest the application of makeup. Cosmetics have long been associated with artifice and, by implication, feminine deception. In eighteenth-century art theory and criticism, maquillage was often invoked—disparagingly—as the equivalent of painting, or vice versa. For example, in his satirical *Dictionnaire critique* (1768), Louis-Antoine de Caraccioli wrote the following: "*To Paint:* There is no one more skilled in the art of painting than a coquettish woman. She makes up her hair, eyebrows, cheeks, and sometimes her breast, in such a way as to give an air of truth to that which is nothing but lies and paint."[18] To paint the sculpted body, then, is to disguise, embrace the superficial and the illusory, or be preoccupied with ornament over essence.

Despite long-standing hostility to polychromy, even the staunchly Neoclassical artist Canova experimented with the technique. When a version of his marble *Hebe* (1800–1805, fig. 53) was displayed at the Paris Salon of 1808, one critic was dismayed to find the statue adorned with gilt bronze accoutrements, its flesh "impregnated with a preparation of sulphur and wax," and the troubling indication that its cheeks and lips were rouged.[19] Canova, the critic asserted, was flirting with barbarism. Although all trace of the statue's polychromy has disappeared, color does remain on a small plaster model for the artist's colossal *Creugas* (1795–96, cat. 11). With a peach-toned body, straw-yellow hair, and dabs of red on his cheeks and lips, this rendition of the famed Greek boxer has none of the distant monumentality of the finished marble. The plaster's oddly schematic, pretty coloration seems to underscore its comparatively diminutive size, providing it with an almost doll-like appearance.

British artist John Gibson's *The Tinted Venus* (ca. 1851–56, cat. 8), one of the earliest and most controversial nineteenth-century polychrome statues, emerged from the artist's belief that the Greeks were entirely correct to have colored their sculpture. "The moderns," he argued, "being less refined than the Greeks in matters of art, are from long and stupid custom reconciled to the white statue."[20] Instead, he tinted the flesh of his Venus an ivory color, the eyes blue, the hair blond. "'Here,'" he exclaimed, "'is a little nearer approach to life—it is therefore more impressive—yes—yes indeed she seems an ethereal being with her eyes fixed on me!'"[21] For one critic, however, those eyes belonged not to the goddess of love, but rather "a naked, impudent Englishwoman."[22] For another, it lacked "an essential quality in sculpture, chastity." Instead, the statue seemed to be nothing more than a lifesize variant of the mildly titillating painted porcelain figurines sold to middle-class consumers on the streets of Paris.[23]

René Magritte's statuette *Les Menottes de Cuivre* (*The Copper Handcuffs*, 1936, cat. 7) intentionally references the commerce in female bodies. The sculpture is a plaster reduction of the *Venus de Milo* (3rd–1st centuries B.C.)—the kind of cheap souvenir available

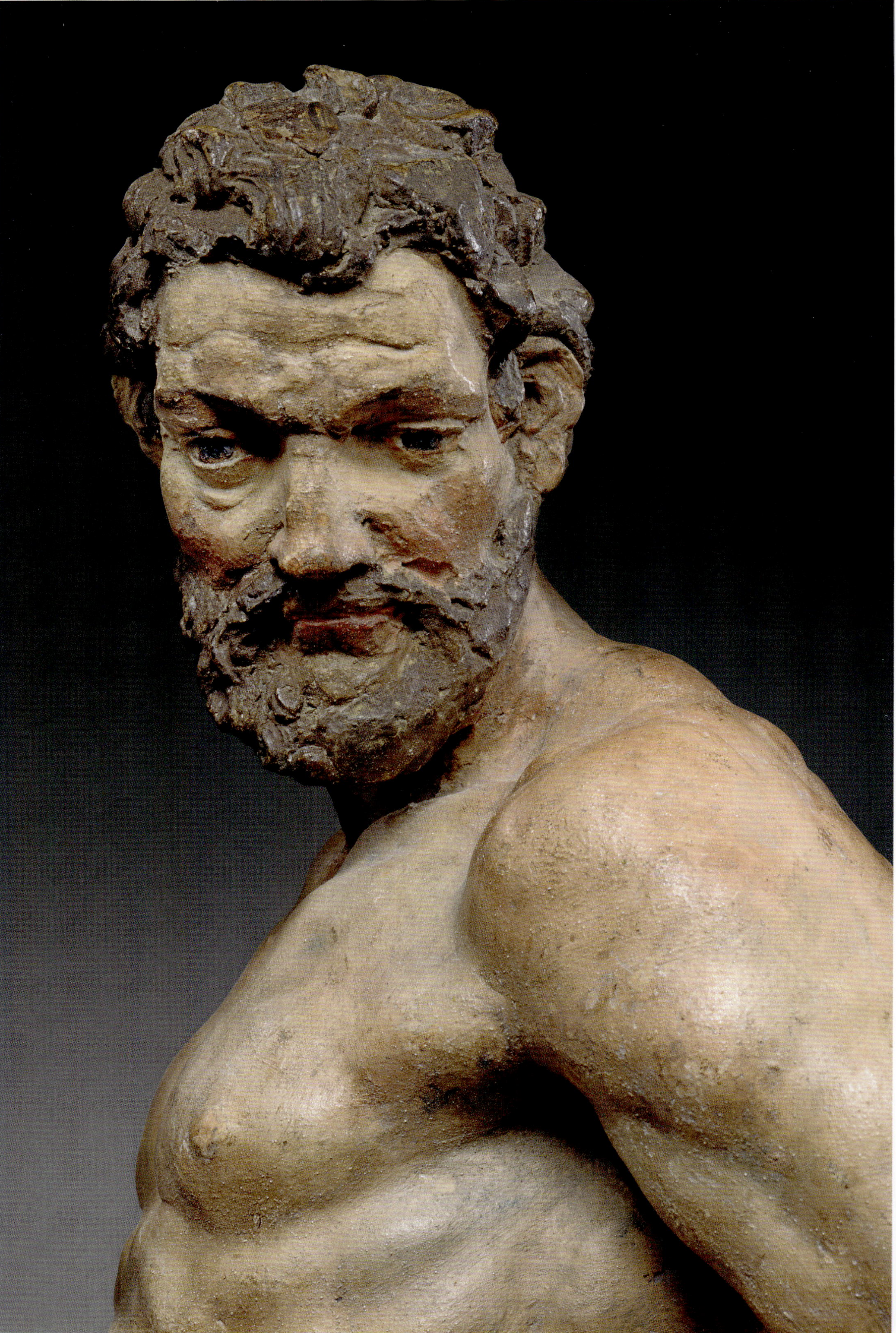

at museum shops. Painted in blocks of unmodulated and opaque color, the work is more akin to painting by numbers or industrial production than Gibson's delicate tinting. It is at once an archaeological reconstruction and a crude defacement. Magritte also managed to playfully reverse the shock of Gibson's colored statue: now, it is precisely the absence of color on the head of his Venus that affronts.

The extreme naturalism of Netherlandish sculptor Willem Danielsz van Tetrode's painted *Hercules* (ca. 1545–60, cat. 12), by contrast, hits one like a punch to the gut. All the carnal density of a living, naked body—that which is offset by white marble—here returns to sculpted form. The whiff of eroticism that accompanies such virile, earthy figures as Tetrode's can be, even today, unnerving. For the predictably prudish Victorian sculptor Richard Westmacott, it was entirely unacceptable, even immoral. "A male statue," he wrote in 1859, "such for instance as the [ancient Roman] Farnese Hercules…if presented to public exhibition in flesh tints…would not for a moment be tolerated. Would any father willingly take the females of his family into a gallery so peopled?"[24] Thankfully for Westmacott, it is doubtful that Tetrode's *Hercules* was designed for broad public consumption. The figure's small size suggests the intention for a selective, intimate viewership, probably within the private *studiolo* of an enlightened collector. This must also be the case with El Greco's pair of painted statuettes *Epimetheus* and *Pandora* (1600–1610, cat. 10). Like the *Hercules*, these figures present unabashed nakedness, their articulated and realistic genitals made all the more visceral by the addition of painted pubic hair. Fully incarnate, *Epimetheus* and *Pandora* carry with them all the potential for procreation—in fact, during the Renaissance this mythical couple was considered the pagan equivalent of Adam and Eve.

This emphasis on procreation necessarily references time—the body that reproduces is also one that ages and dies—and the naturalistic coloring of statues interrupts the timelessness of idealized sculpted form. Here, for example, is the Romantic sculptor Pierre Jean David d'Angers: "Marble, by its whiteness, has something pure, celestial. Colors are terrestrial. We carry the imprint of destruction imprinted on our features. By contrast, sculpture bears the image of eternity. The more brilliant the colors of a flower, the less it lasts."[25]

Color, then, is itself a vanitas symbol, a reminder of the brevity of life and the inevitable degradation of the body, an idea made literal in German artist Michel Erhart's *Allegory of Transience* (ca. 1470/80). Carved from a single block of wood, the sculpture depicts three conjoined figures: a youthful couple and an aged woman. To circle the sculpture is to enact the unstoppable unfurling of time. The polychromy that imparts the blush of vitality to the young woman, posed after the Venuses of antiquity, also heightens the sagging decrepitude of the old crone, her mottled skin punctuated by painted flies that await the imminent decomposition of her body.

American artist Frank Benson's *Human Statue* (2005, cat. 9) presents another, wittier meditation on sculpture, color, and time. His nude male, posed atop a white pedestal like Michelangelo's *David* (1501–4) and yet cast from a living model, has two distinct layers of color: first, various tones to imitate human skin, and second, an uneven, smeared application of silver paint. Even as it suggests the canonical statues of antiquity, such lofty models are contaminated by reference to the ephemeral pleasures of the low-brow entertainment industry. The depicted figure is a performer, one of those "living sculptures" found on tourist-packed street corners. Here, the viewer tumbles into dizzying mise-en-abyme, confronted by a statue imitating a man who imitates a statue. The pedestal is no longer the marker of permanence, but rather a stagelike space from which the statue/performer will descend when his audience has finally dispersed. With this clever provocation, Benson undermines all that Hegel had sought to codify. Any distinction between the ideal and the real, truth and artifice is made hopelessly ambiguous by this sculpted tableau vivant. The ideal and the real, he seems to suggest, are simply parts to be played in the theater of appearances. The presumption of white, so powerfully expressed and enforced by Hegel and others, has often obscured an entirely different history and genealogy of sculpture. From Tetrode to Koons, artists have pursued an understanding of figural sculpture that investigates the real rather than the ideal, and color has provided a key tactic in their work. The application of color to sculptural representations of the human form raises important questions concerning the boundaries of artistic media, the value and parameters of imitation, as well as the cultural and political significance of the body as a colored entity. Rather than being removed from the quotidian realm, many of these colored sculptures are immersed in the world, and therein lies their continuing power and fascination.

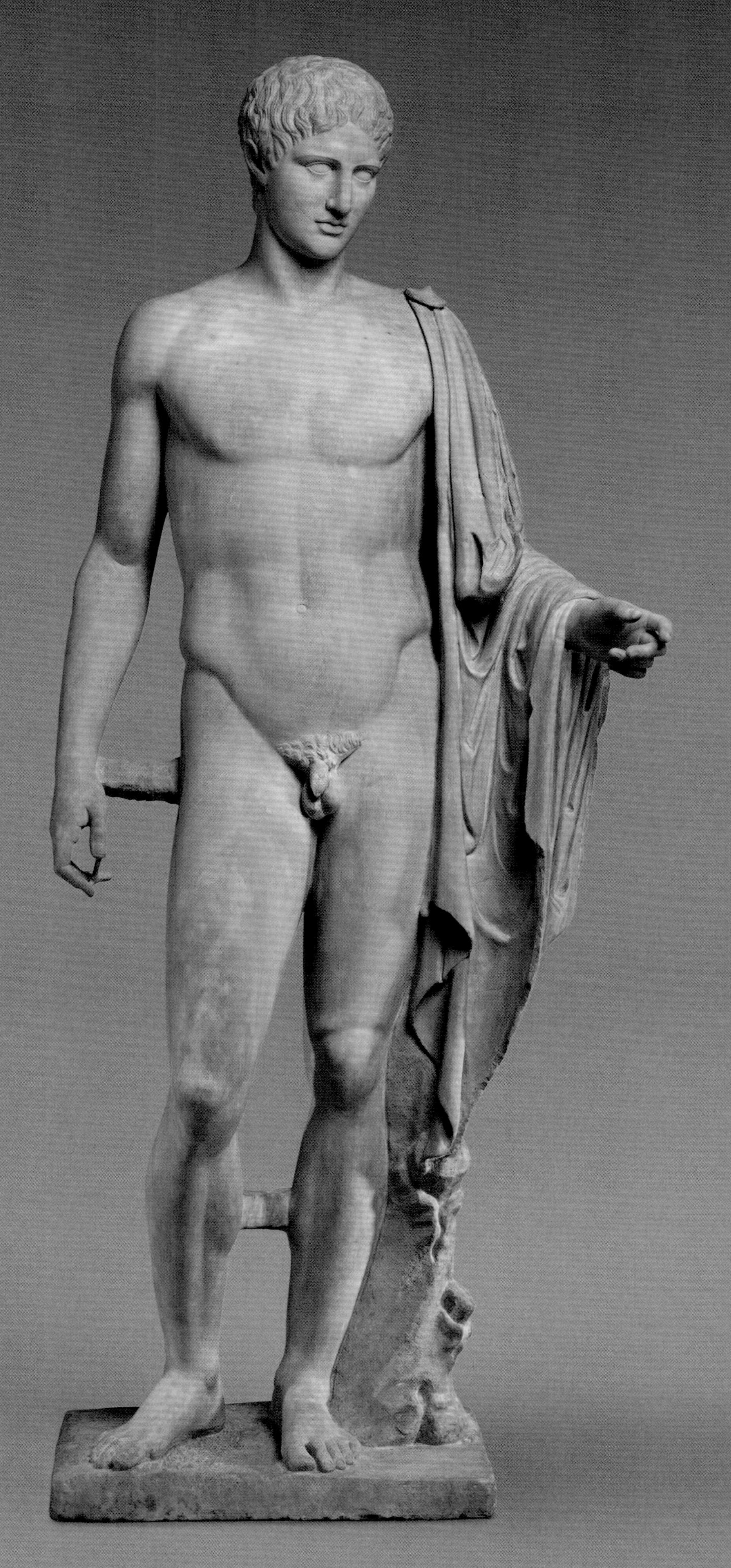

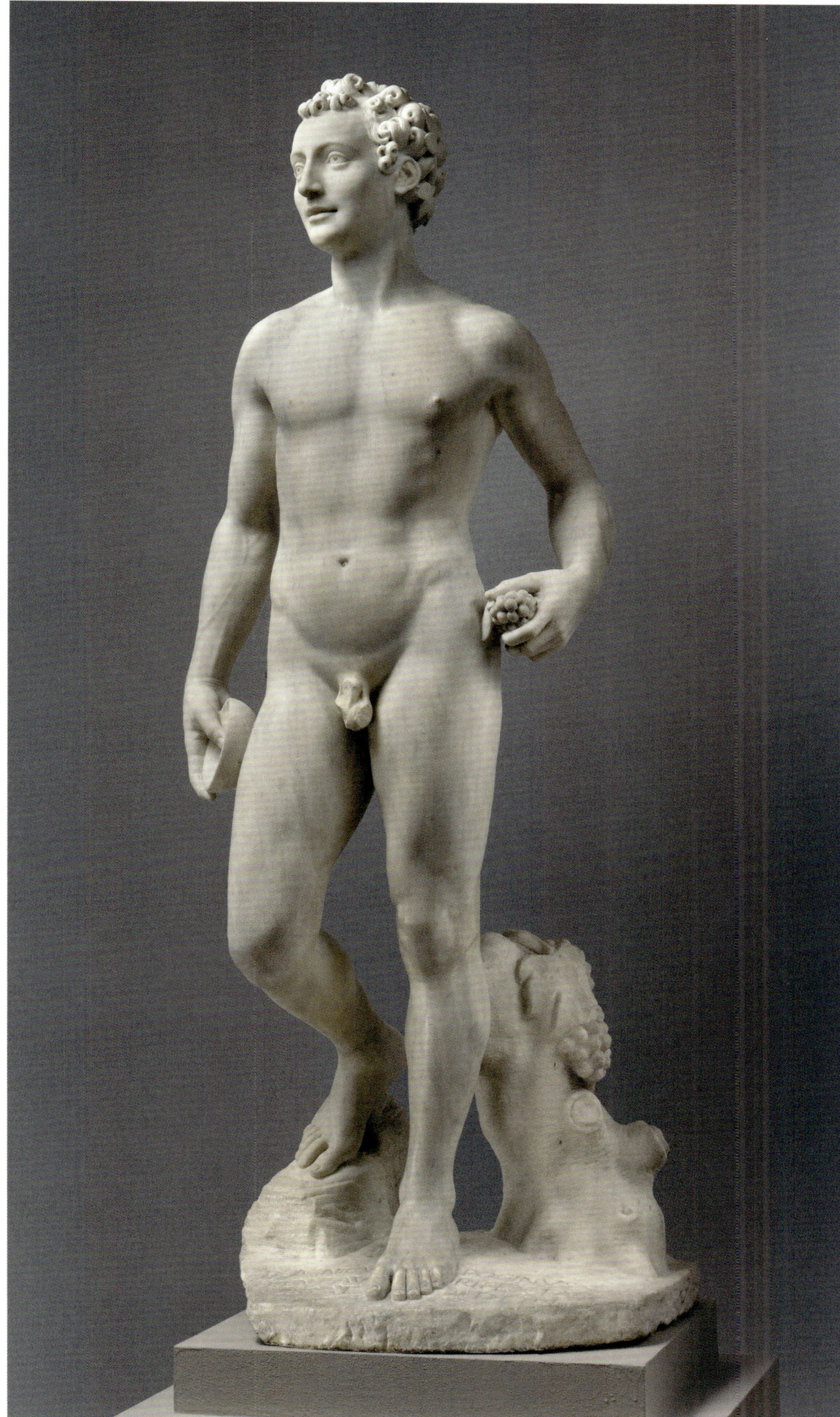

1. Copy of work attributed to Polykleitos. *Hermes*, A.D. 1st or 2nd century. Pentelic marble, H. 71 ¼ in. (181 cm), W. 29 ½ in. (74.9 cm), D. 23 ½ in. (59.7 cm). Roman. The Metropolitan Museum of Art, New York, Gift of The Hearst Foundation, 1956 (56.234.15)

2. Domenico Poggini. *Bacchus*, 1554. Marble, H. 54 in. (137.2 cm), W. 21 in. (53.3 cm), D. 18 in. (45.7 cm). The Metropolitan Museum of Art, New York, Bequest of George Blumenthal, 1941 (41.190.269)

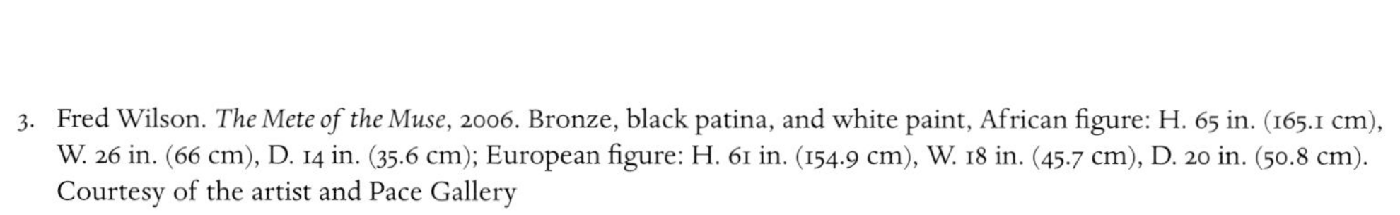

3. Fred Wilson. *The Mete of the Muse*, 2006. Bronze, black patina, and white paint, African figure: H. 65 in. (165.1 cm), W. 26 in. (66 cm), D. 14 in. (35.6 cm); European figure: H. 61 in. (154.9 cm), W. 18 in. (45.7 cm), D. 20 in. (50.8 cm). Courtesy of the artist and Pace Gallery

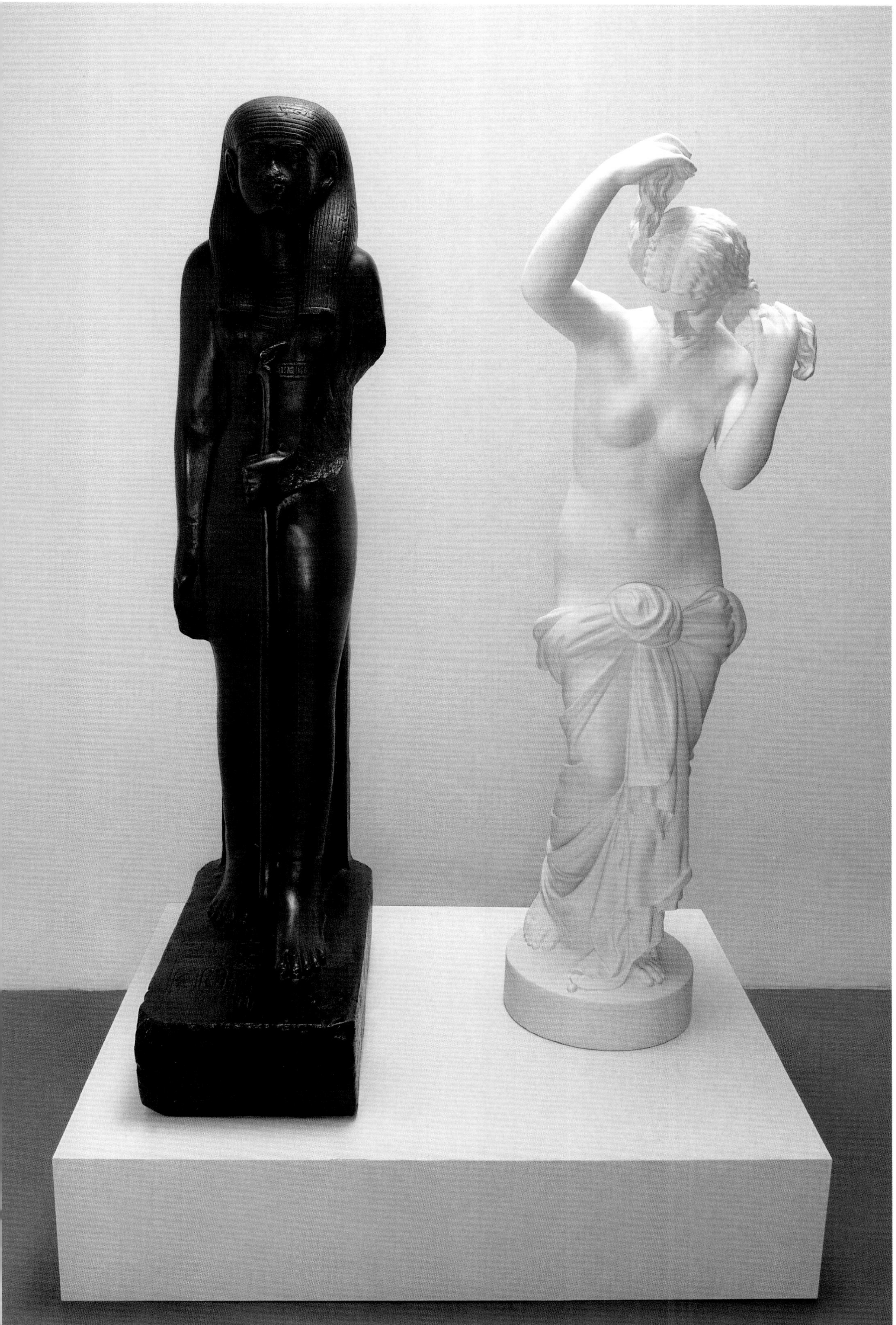

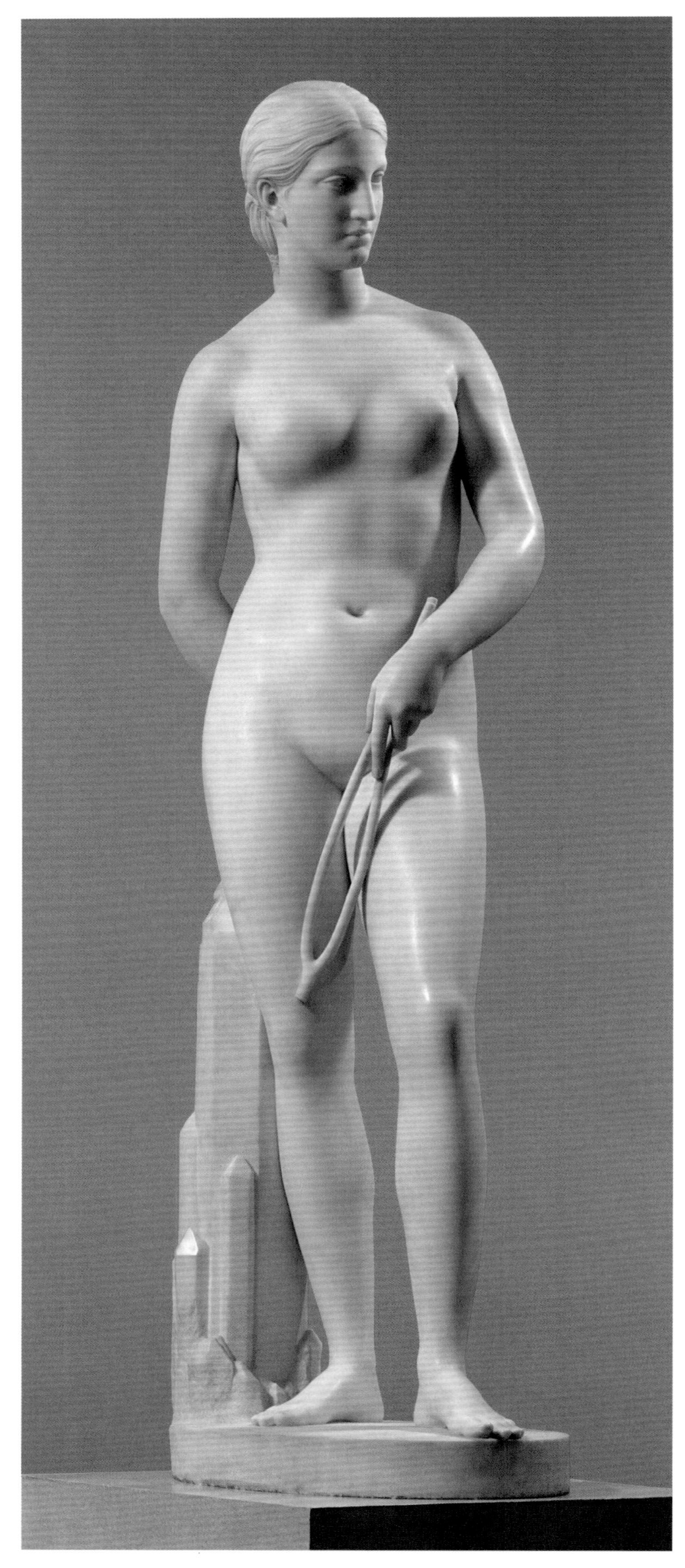

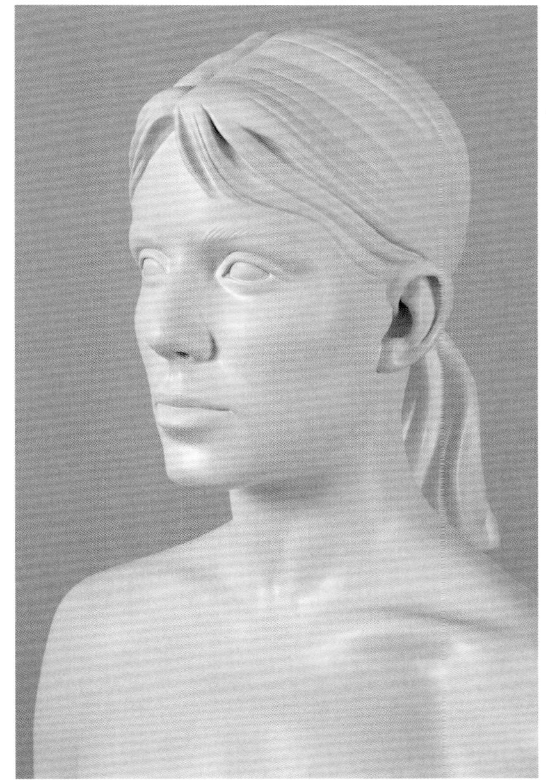

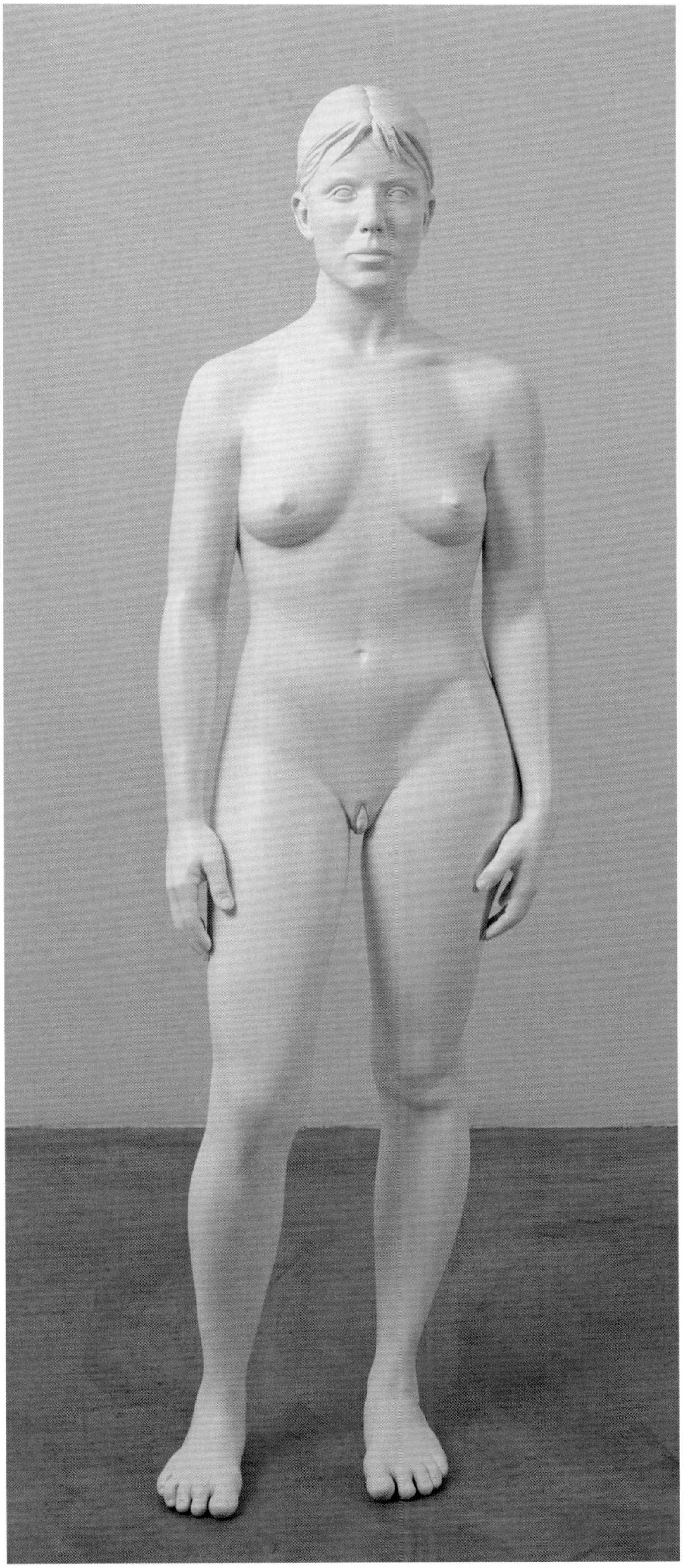

4. Hiram Powers. *California*, 1850–55, carved 1858. Marble, H. 71 in. (180.3 cm), W. 18 ¼ in. (46.4 cm), D. 24 ¾ in. (62.9 cm). The Metropolitan Museum of Art, New York, Gift of William Backhouse Astor, 1872 (72.3)

5. Charles Ray. *Aluminum Girl*, 2003. Aluminum and paint, H. 62 ⅝ in. (159 cm), W. 18 ½ in. (47 cm), D. 11 ⁷⁄₁₆ in. (29 cm). Astrup Fearnley Collection, Oslo

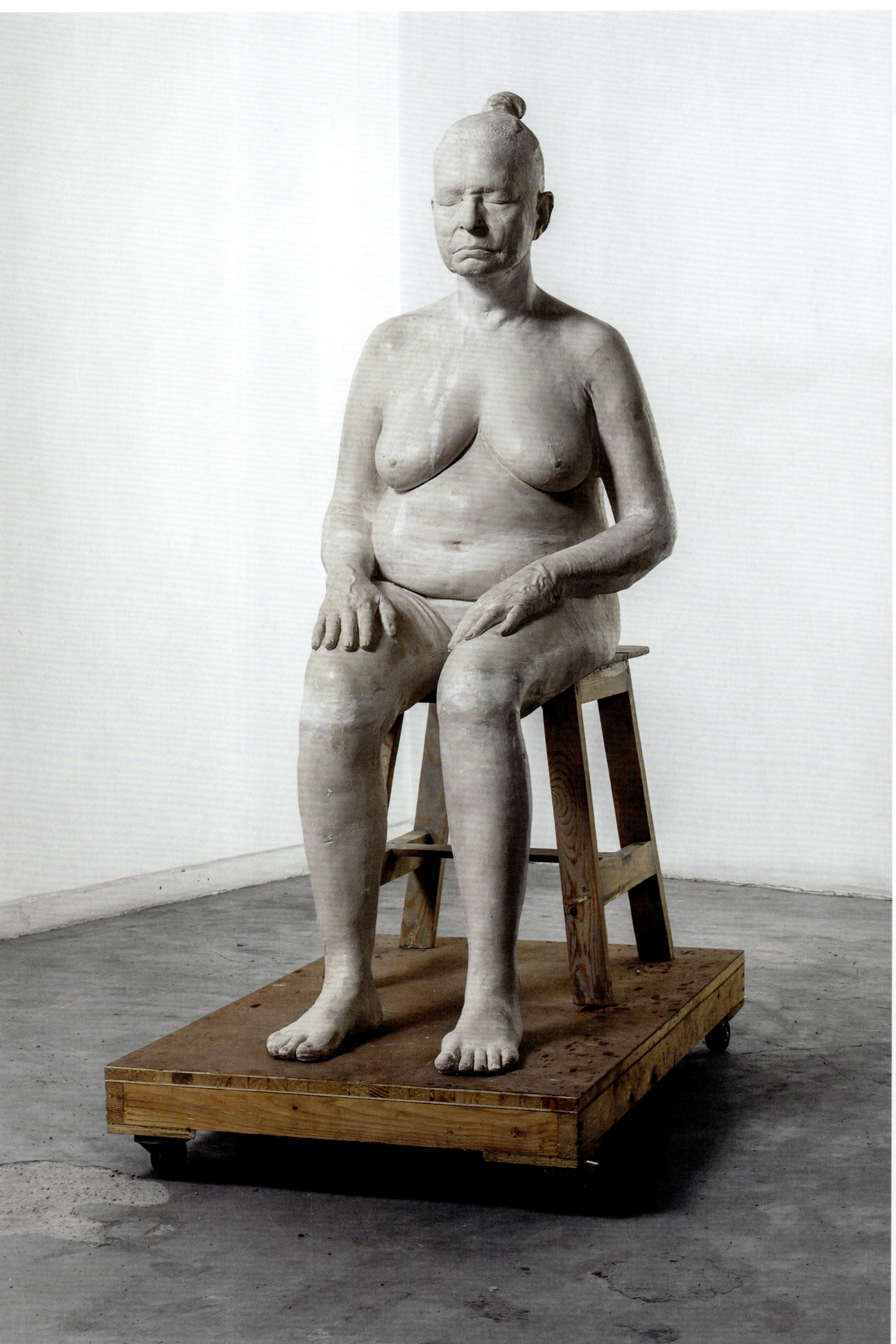

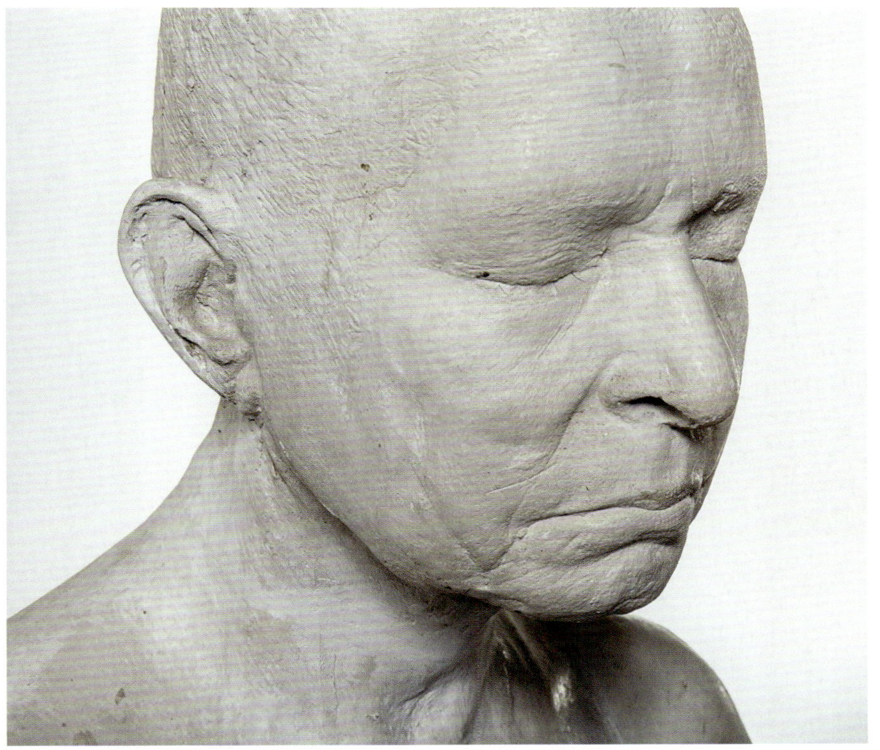

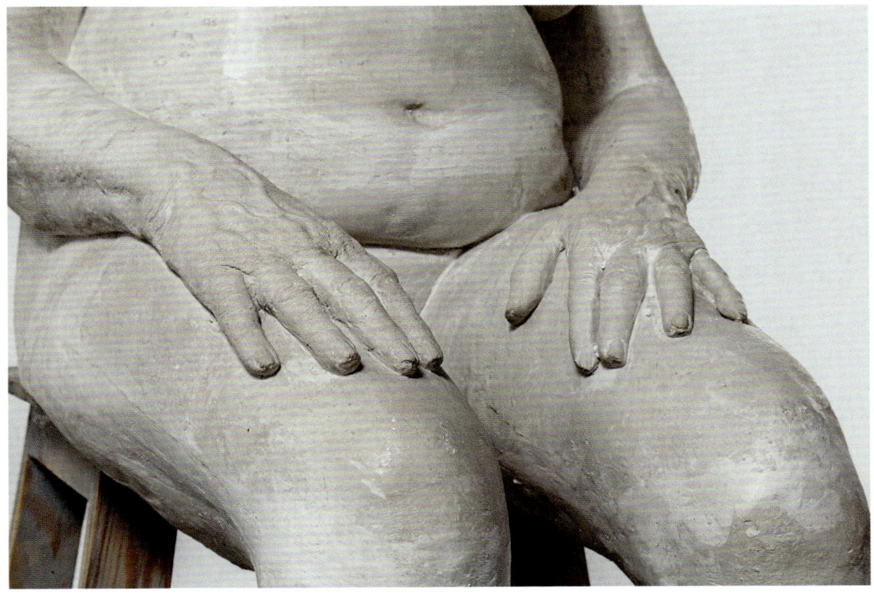

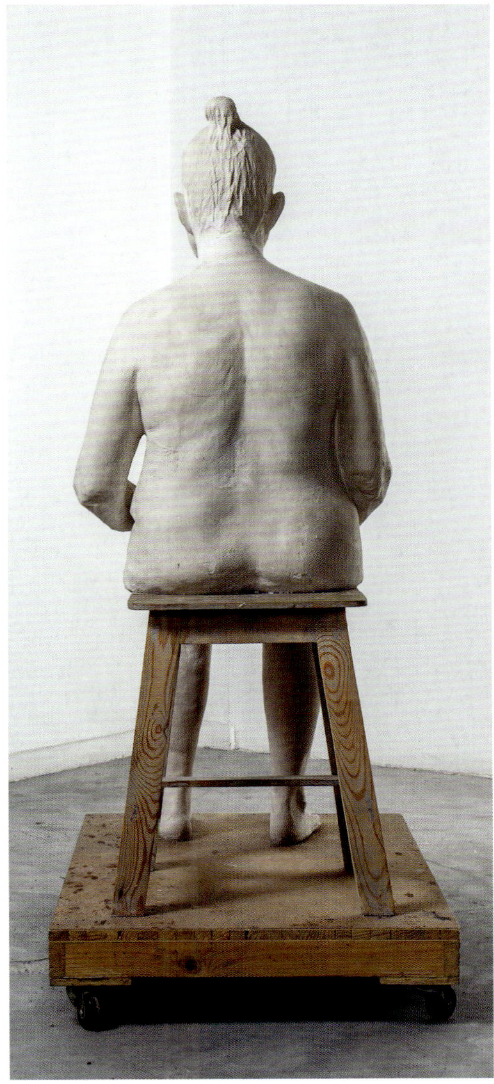

6. Bharti Kher. *Mother*, 2016. Plaster of Paris and wood, H. 55 ⅛ in. (140 cm),
   W. 24 ¹³⁄₁₆ in. (63 cm), D. 37 ¹³⁄₁₆ in. (96 cm). Courtesy of the artist and
   Hauser & Wirth

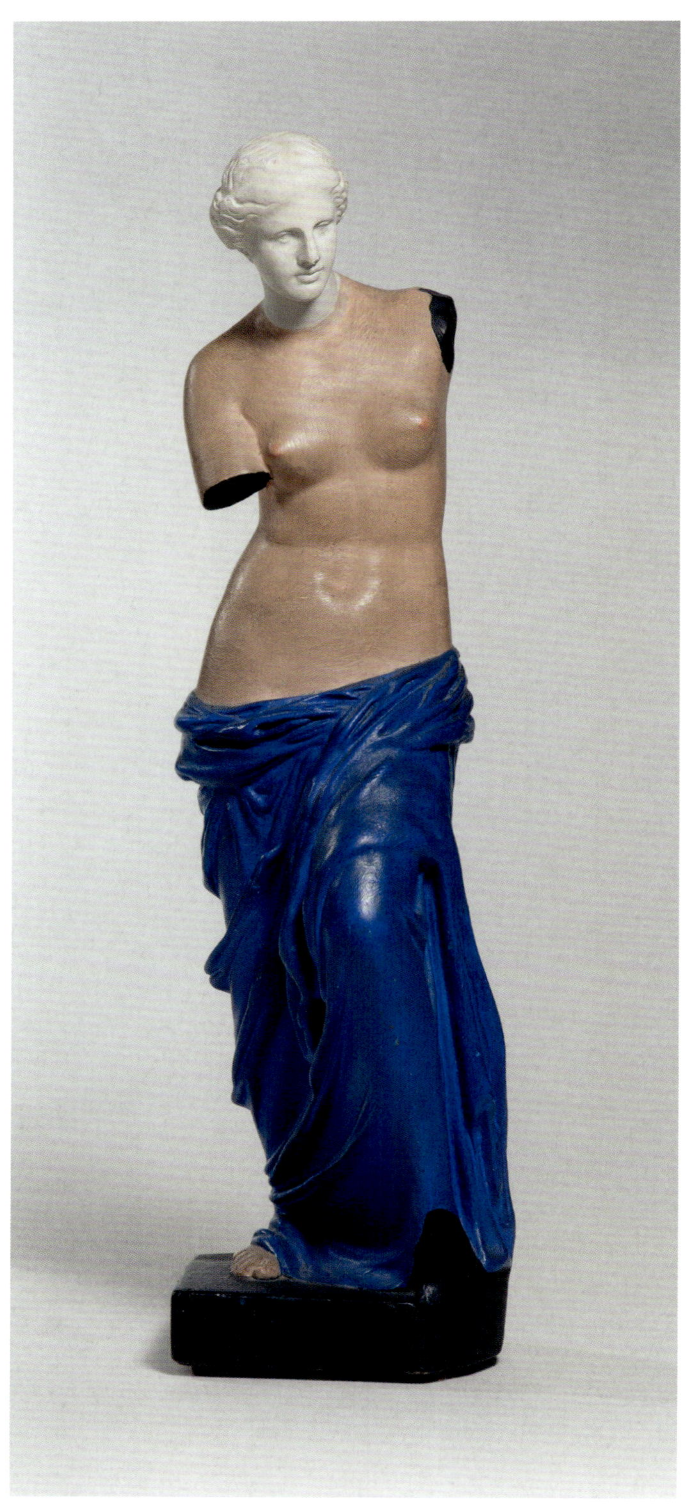

7. René Magritte. *Les Menottes de Cuivre* (*The Copper Handcuffs*), 1936. Oil on plaster miniature of the *Venus de Milo*,
H. 14 9/16 in. (37 cm), W. 4 9/16 in. (11.5 cm), D. 4 5/16 in. (11 cm). Private collection

8. John Gibson. *The Tinted Venus*, ca. 1851–56. Tinted marble, H. 69 5/16 in. (176 cm), W. 25 9/16 in. (65 cm), D. 17 11/16 in.
(45 cm); base: W. 20 1/16 in. (51 cm), D. 17 5/16 in. (44 cm). Walker Art Gallery, National Museums Liverpool

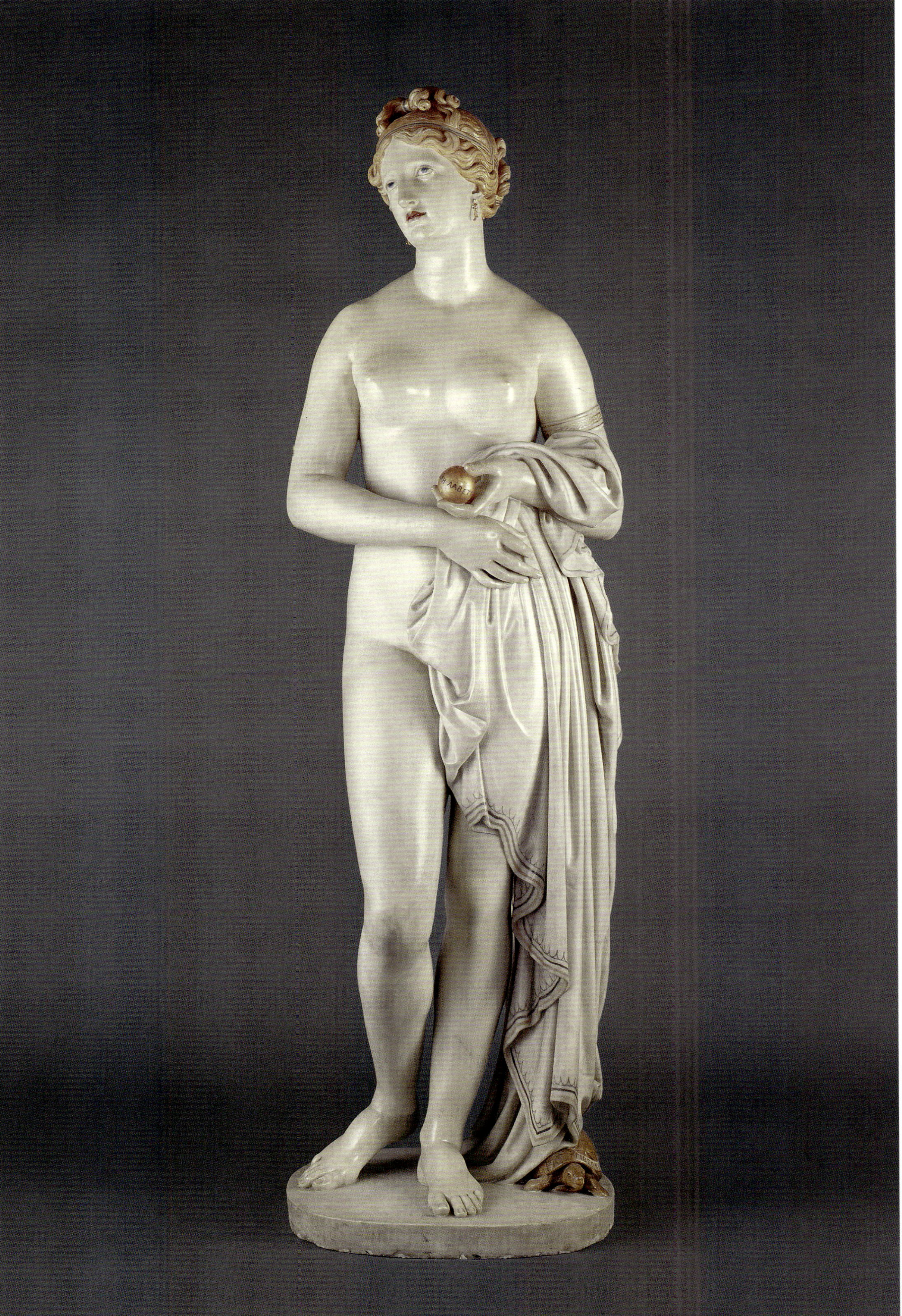

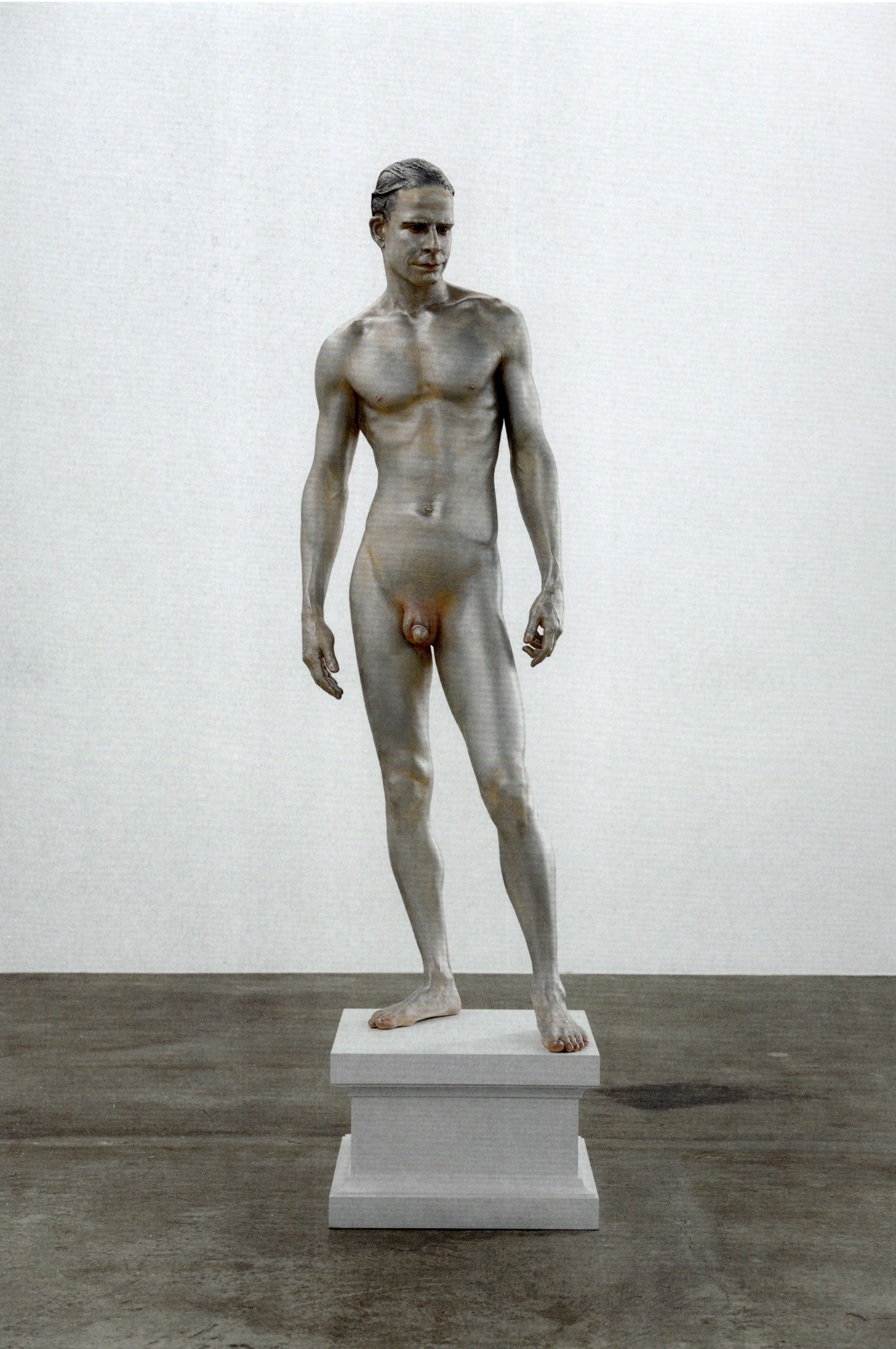

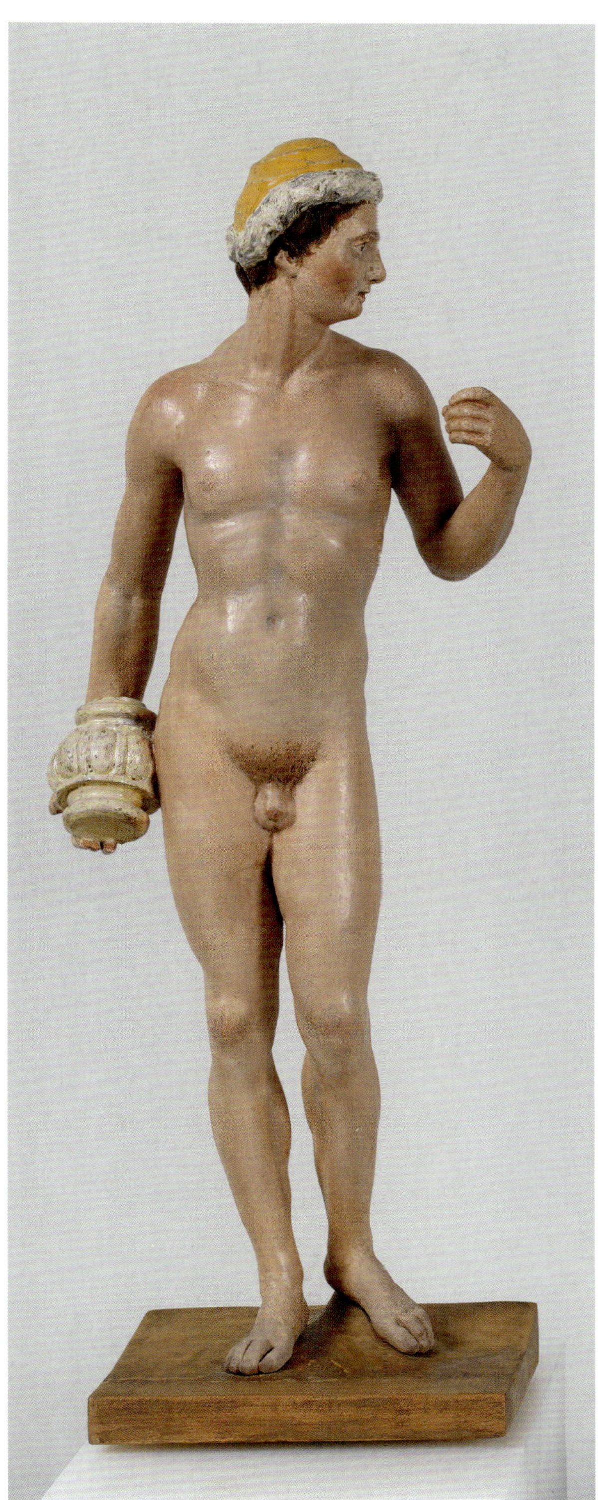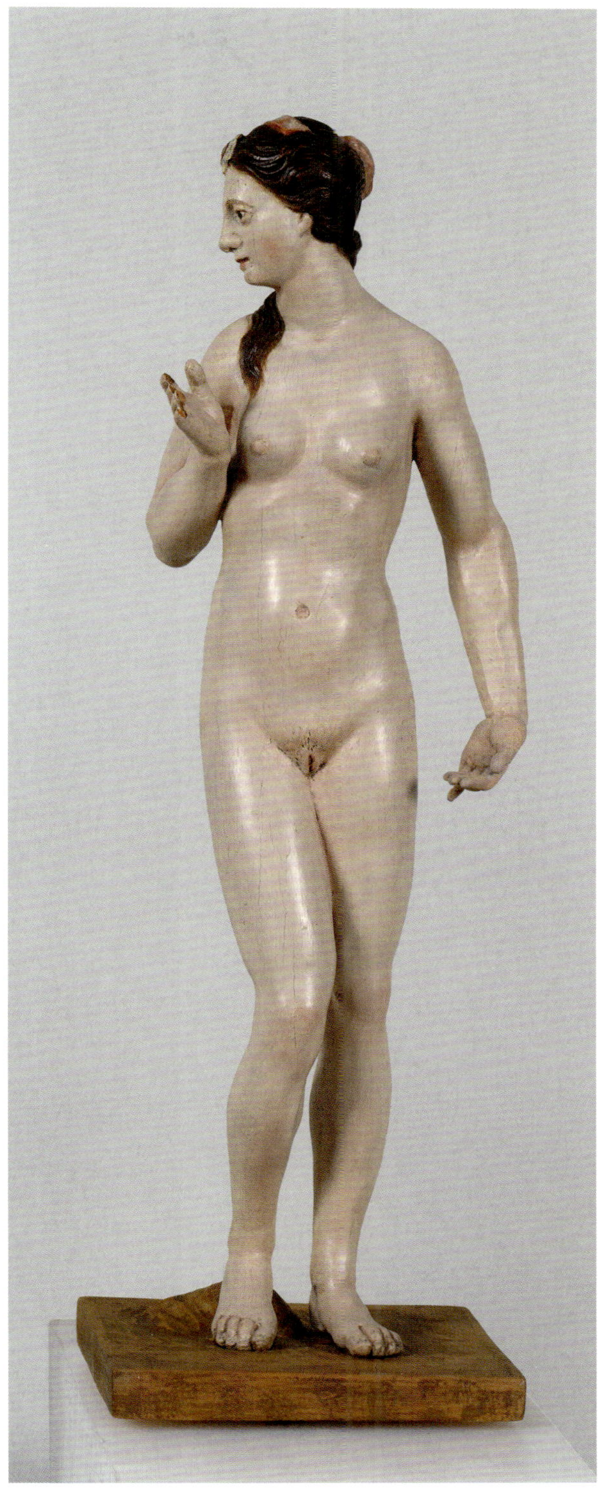

9. Frank Benson. *Human Statue*, 2005. Fiberglass, medium-density fiberboard, acrylic, and oil paint,
    H. 68 ⅛ in. (173 cm), W. 19 ¹¹⁄₁₆ in. (50 cm), D. 11 ¹³⁄₁₆ in. (30 cm). Astrup Fearnley Collection, Oslo

10. El Greco (Doménikos Theotokópoulos). *Epimetheus* and *Pandora*, 1600–1610. Polychromed wood,
    Epimetheus: H. 17 ⁵⁄₁₆ in. (44 cm); *Pandora*: H. 16 ¹⁵⁄₁₆ in. (43 cm). Museo Nacional del Prado, Madrid

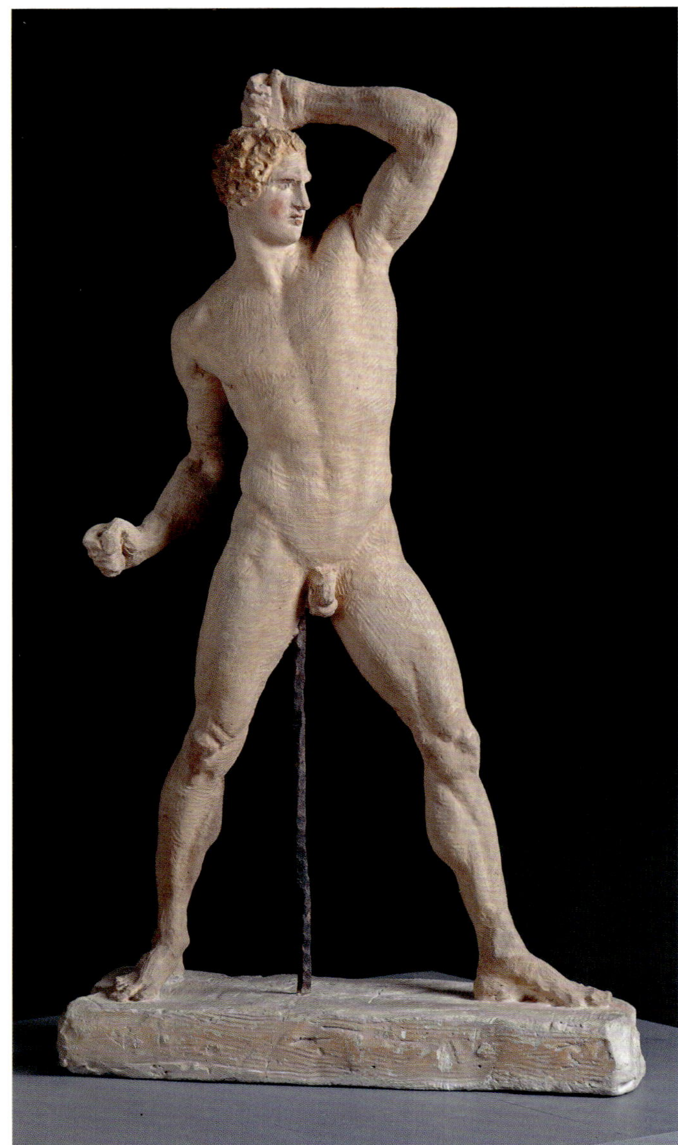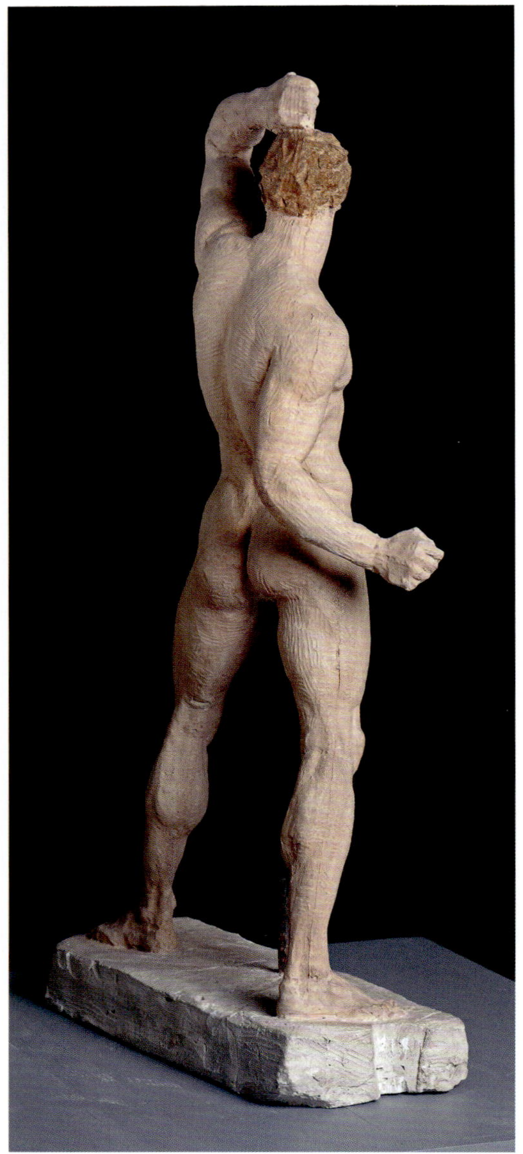

11. Antonio Canova. *Creugas*, 1795–96. Plaster and paint, H. 32 ⁵⁄₁₆ in. (82 cm), W. 18 ⅞ in. (48 cm), D. 7 ½ in. (19 cm). Fondazione Canova, Gipsoteca e Museo Antonio Canova, Possagno

12. Willem Danielsz van Tetrode. *Hercules*, ca. 1545–60. Terracotta and paint, H. 18 ½ in. (47 cm), W. 8 ¹¹⁄₁₆ in. (22 cm), D. 5 ⅞ in. (15 cm). Quentin Foundation, London

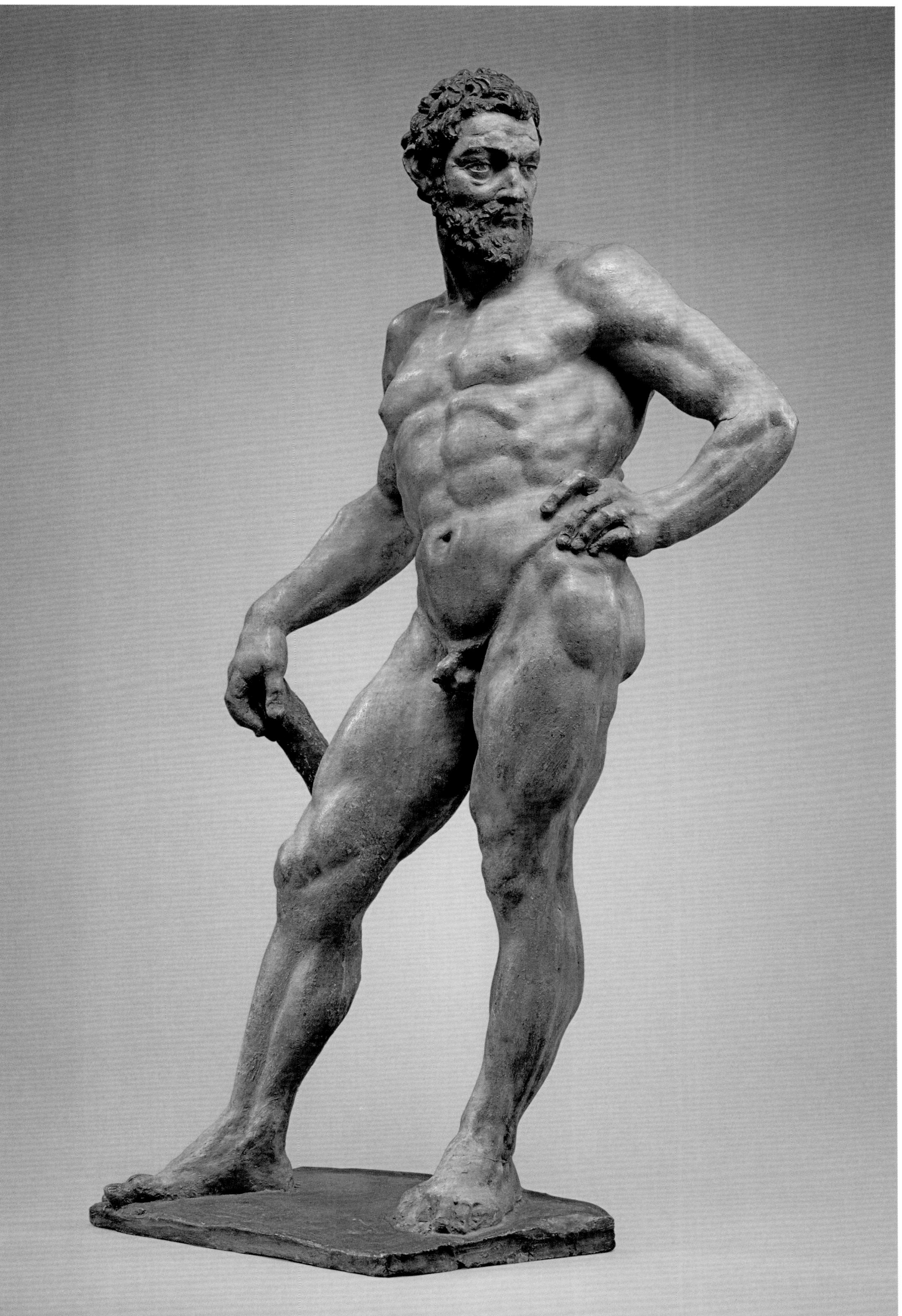

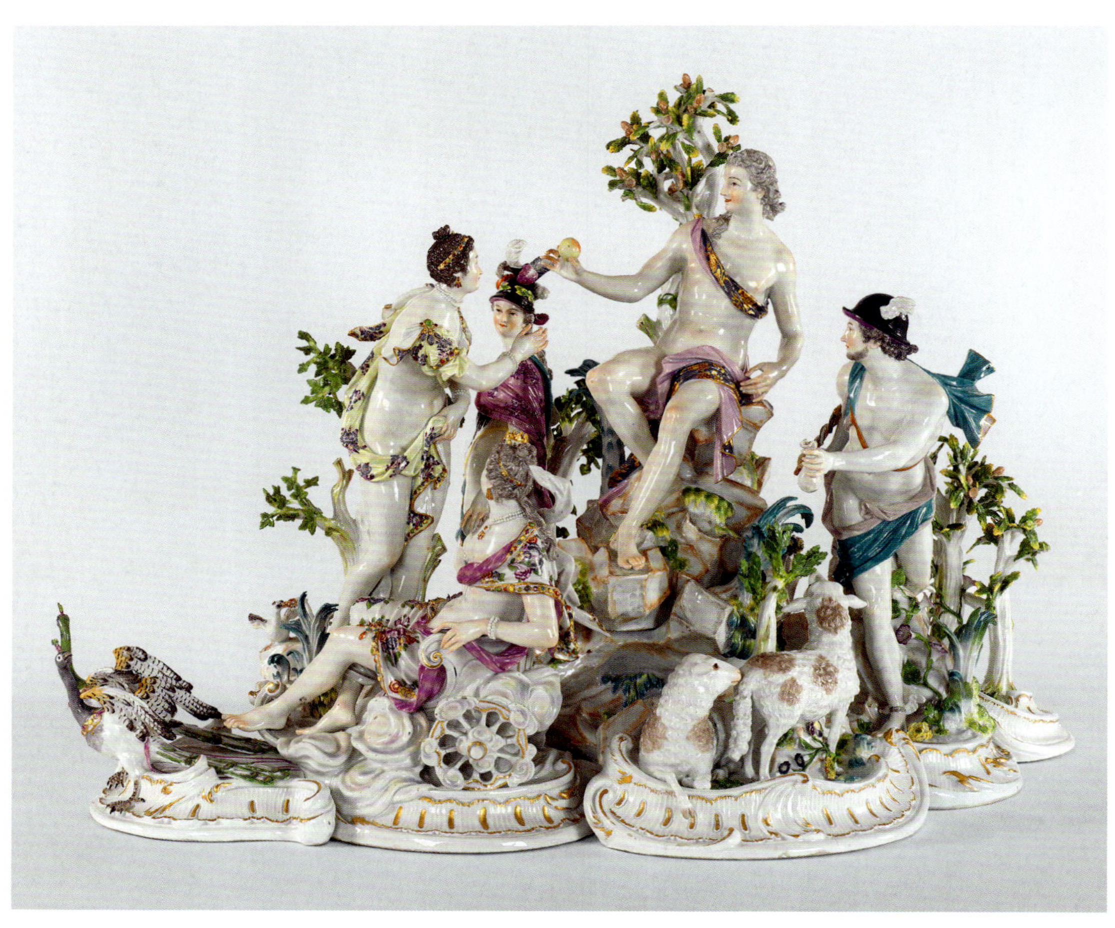

13. Meissen Manufactory, design attributed to Johann Joachim Kändler. *The Judgment of Paris*, ca. 1762. Hard-paste porcelain, H. 23 ⅟₁₆ in. (58.5 cm), W. 26 in. (66.1 cm), D. 33 ⅟₁₆ in. (83.9 cm). Wadsworth Atheneum Museum of Art, Hartford, Connecticut, Gift of J. Pierpont Morgan

14. Jeff Koons. *Michael Jackson and Bubbles*, 1988. Ceramic, glaze, and paint, H. 42 in. (106.7 cm), W. 70 ½ in. (179.1 cm), D. 32 ½ in. (82.6 cm). Astrup Fearnley Collection, Oslo

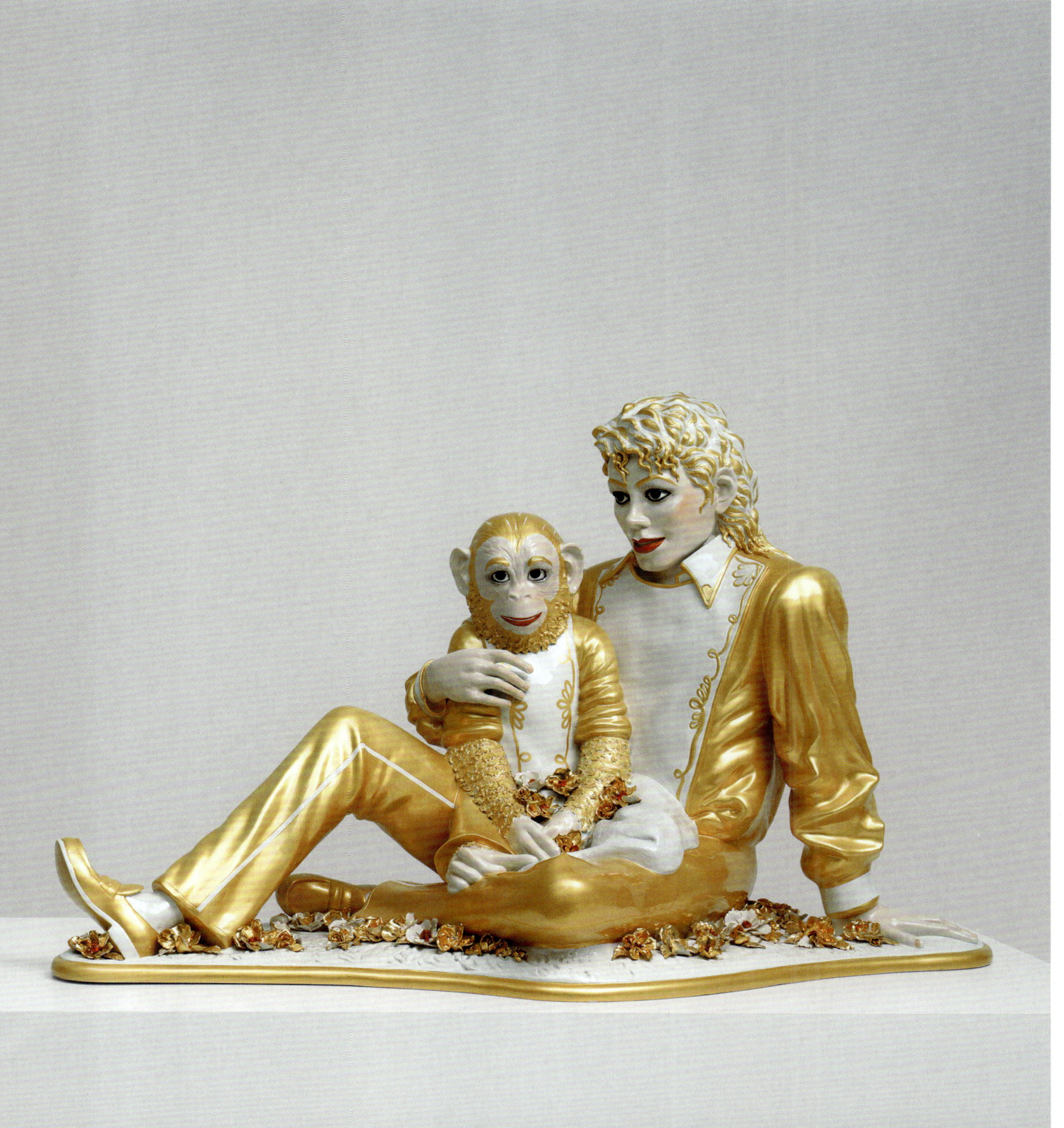

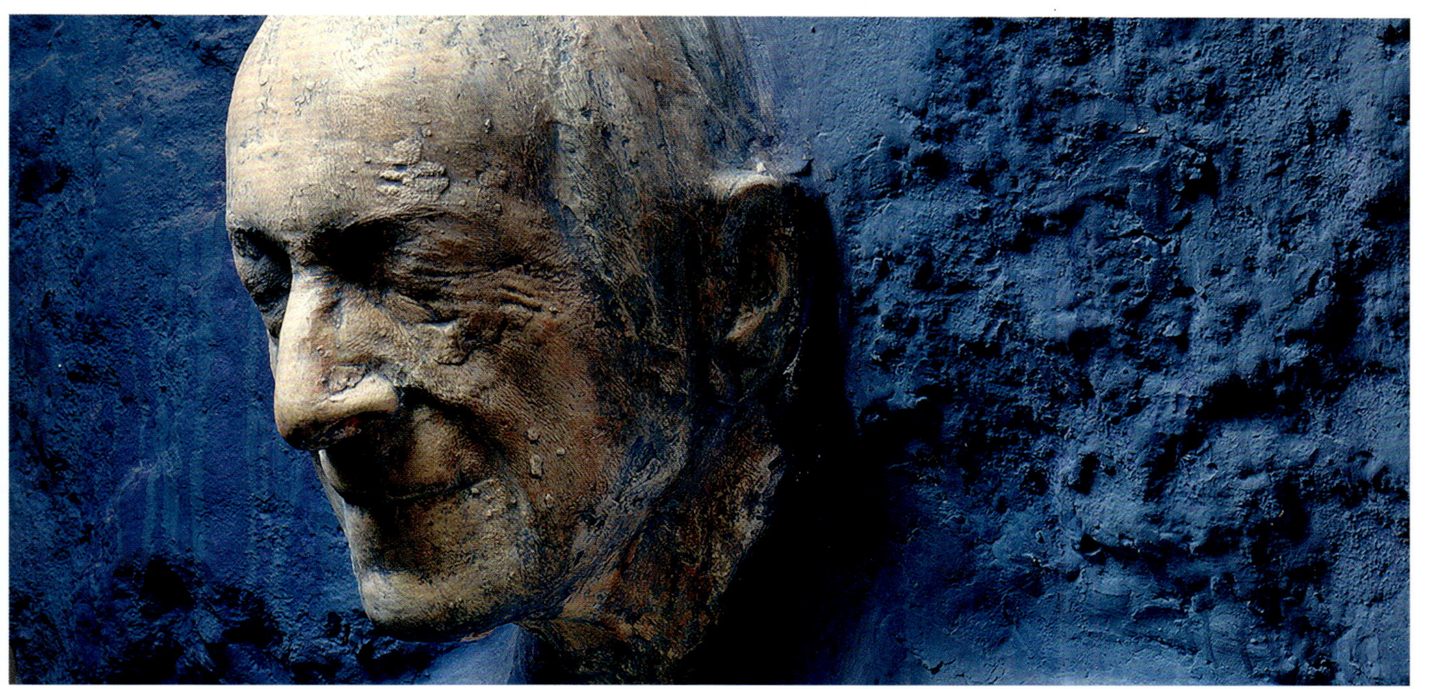

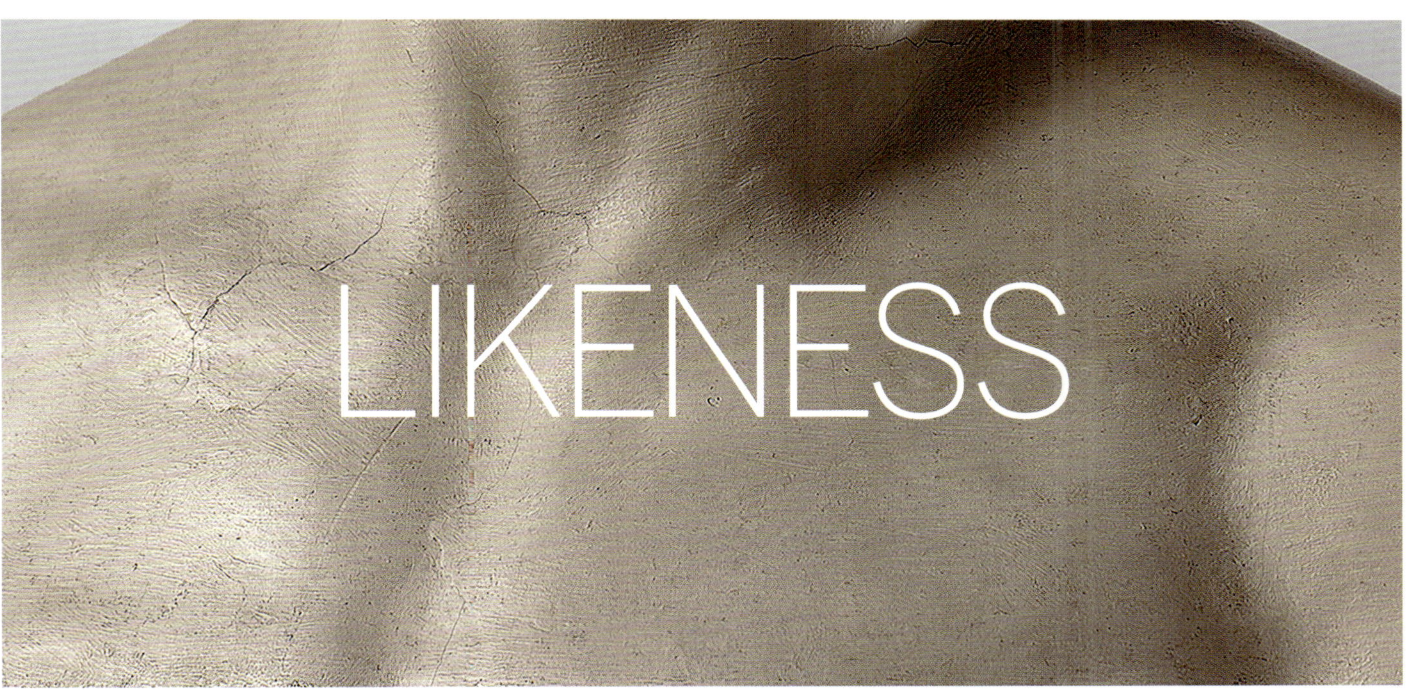
LIKENESS

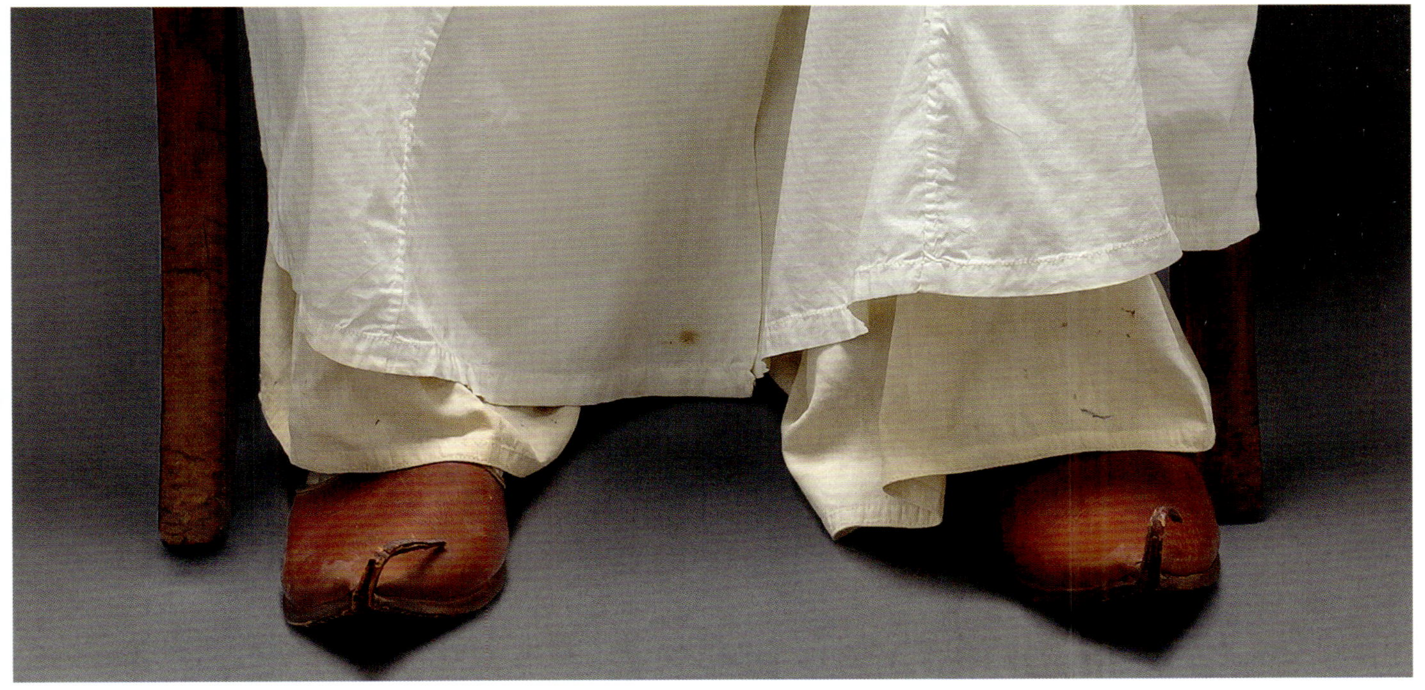

LIKENESS

BRINDA KUMAR

The propensity to reproduce the likeness of human beings has flourished across cultures and throughout history, from fourteenth-century B.C. Egypt and second-century Gandhara in India to thirteenth-century Japan, even as the methods and motivations in achieving verisimilitude vary. To narrate the story of realistic portraiture in Europe, a specific strand of art history draws a through line between naturalistic representation in classical antiquity and its so-called rebirth during the Renaissance, particularly the early fifteenth-century "adoption of intensely illusionistic, closely observed facial likeness, including idiosyncrasies and imperfections."[1] Yet, realism is always inflected by prevailing artistic imperatives, and its presence or absence no more indicates ability as much as it responds to larger aesthetic and cultural priorities.[2]

The posthumous polychrome terracotta bust of the politician Niccolò da Uzzano (1430s, cat. 17) is one of the most celebrated early portrait busts from the Florentine Renaissance. The work has been variously attributed to Desiderio da Settignano and the more illustrious Donatello, who is rightly credited with bringing about a "new wave of verism and moral and spiritual humanity . . . into the soul of the art of sculpture."[3] It was once believed to represent the ancient Roman philosopher Cicero, on account of the style of his robes; the sartorial feature is more consistent with the vogue for antiquarianism and an interest in Roman portrait busts. The portrait is also thought to be a composite of a likeness taken from a death mask and other figural elements.[4] The work is also one of a few surviving early Renaissance busts with its original polychromy, and its carefully applied layers of paint enhance the realism of the modeled surfaces.[5] In this instance the application of pigments serves not just to emulate the real, but also to enliven and reanimate. After all, the figure may be partly based on a death mask, and the stiffness of the features wrought by rigor mortis notwithstanding, the subject is seemingly once again infused with life color through the sculpture's painted details. The virtuosity of the composition, seen in the casting, modeling, and polychromy, makes this work a high watermark in Florentine Renaissance realism.

Departing remarkably from the painted terracotta portrait busts that were widespread in Europe by the sixteenth century is the self-portrait bust by the Netherlandish artist Johan Gregor van der Schardt (ca. 1573, cat. 26). One of the earliest sculptural self-portraits, this "nude bust, with features that suggest a nature both assured and nervously questing," evinces an enhanced confidence in the status of the artist.[6] Curator Frits Scholten has argued that the artist's decision to portray himself radically extended the genre of portrait busts and demonstrated Van der Schardt's expertise as a sculptor as well as his sophisticated understanding of the cultural context in which his work circulated, from his strategic position within systems of patronage to his intelligent navigation of current aesthetic debates.[7] The portrait was created at half-size, suggesting that it was made through modeling by looking in a mirror, rather than the more expedient technique of life casting, thereby indicating the artist's virtuosity. He completed the work through painting the surface in delicate tones, "accentuated by a playful detail: the balding back of the sculptor's head."[8] The illusionism of Van der Schardt's self-portrait remains startling and anticipates by several centuries the hyperrealism of twentieth- and twenty-first-century artists like Duane Hanson, Maurizio Cattelan, and Ron Mueck.[9]

The self-portrait as a mode of self-fashioning is also seen in an extraordinary work by Anna Morandi

Manzolini (ca. 1755, cat. 23), the eighteenth-century Bolognese anatomist and anatomical wax modeler. In contrast to the languorous anatomical nudes that her male contemporaries produced, often highlighting sex organs and female reproductive systems, Morandi's self-portrait bears no hint of titillation. Serious and sober, she is an unidealized middle-age figure who gazes steadily and confidently into the distance. The "woman is no longer the docile anatomical object of discovery, the vacant-eyed cadaver, at the center of the thronging theater, splayed and rent by the master anatomist. Rather . . . she is herself the master anatomist who directs her own knowing gaze on and inside the parts of the body she uncovers."[10] Although she began investigating human anatomy and producing anatomical wax models with her husband Giovanni Manzolini, she continued their profession long after his sudden death in 1755.[11] She took an especial interest in the brain, the sensory organs, and male genitalia, with the former as the object of inquiry in her self-portrait. Morandi presented herself as carefully coiffed and richly attired in a pink gown with pearl necklaces and bracelets and cuts a stately figure. Once likely holding anatomy instruments, the elegantly rendered fingers hover knowingly above a human head whose skull has been partially removed and cranial flap pulled back to reveal the brain matter below.

The eighteenth century was the heyday for wax modeling in Europe. While the properties of the material to capture fine details and emulate the sensual qualities of skin had long been recognized, this period saw a preponderance of ceroplastic figuration from the anatomical models that the Fontana workshop in Florence (cat. 115) and the Manzolinis specialized in to religious figures and wax portraits. The role of the funeral effigy in the last rites of sovereigns was known from the fourteenth century in England and onward across Europe.[12] Although the actual body would have been interred soon after death in a more private event, ceremonial processions and prolonged mourning rituals necessitated the creation of proxy bodies for a double funeral. These bodies could simply be "a shapeless mass essentially qualified by robes and insignias."[13] Of greater importance was the visibility and recognizability of the face, often achieved by making death casts that captured the physiognomic details of the deceased and were then cast in wax. Resultant works, such as the *Funeral Effigy of the Doge Alvise III Mocenigo(?)* (1732, cat. 16), show remarkable buccal details such as lines and stubble around the mouth,

but the face is articulated only to the extent that it would have been seen beneath the sovereign's vestments. The Bolognese sculptor Angelo Piò is best known for processional images and stucco and terracotta reliefs of religious and allegorical scenes, but he also worked on similar subjects in wax. He deftly used the material to render highly realistic details, such as the furrowed brow and slightly agape mouth with visible teeth in *Portrait of a Monk* (18th century, cat. 25).[14] Focus on the details is heightened by Piò's integration of real hair into the figure's bearded visage and the shrouding of the figure under dark hooded robes.

In the eighteenth century, when portrait sculpture was approaching its height in Europe, a mode of realistic polychrome sculpture was emerging in India as well. In Bengal, the Maharaja Krishnachandra Roy of Nadia, who reigned from 1728 to 1783, had supported the production of unfired clay sculptures of the Great Goddess for worship and subsequent immersion in the sacred Ganges River—a tradition that continues today through the annual Durga Puja festival. These sculptures were made by potter-sculptors from Krishnanagar, a small town fifty miles upriver from Calcutta (Kolkata). The British East India Company made the rapidly changing, increasingly cosmopolitan, late eighteenth-century city of Calcutta its trading hub and later capital, from which the company would ultimately control the rest of the subcontinent. In this early moment of contact, however, cultural exchange was more vibrant and fluid. British artists would visit and record their experiences, while officers and administrators employed native artists to record in a naturalistic style, now known as Company School paintings, the flora, fauna, and people of the new context in which they found themselves (fig. 54).[15] At the same time, trade with Europe and America enriched Bengali merchants, who were in turn adopting and engaging with European aesthetics and technology, including having their portraits made by English painters and later reproduced in daguerreotypes as well.[16]

The realism and subject matter of Company School paintings were soon adapted by the Krishnanagar sculptors, and the earliest surviving example of the resultant unfired clay sculptures made their way to America via these new trade networks. In 1823 an American captain named James B. Briggs presented six lifesize clay sculptures "by a distinguished native artist of Calcutta," representing individuals of different occupations, to the East India Marine Society (EIMS, now the Peabody Essex Museum), Salem,

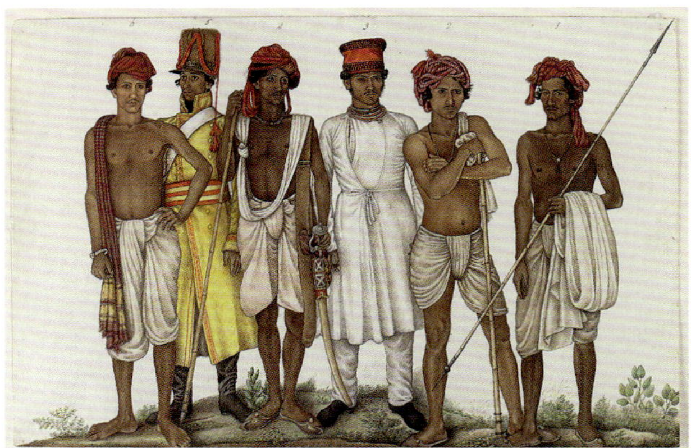

Fig. 54 Attributed to the family of Ghulam Ali Khan. *Six Recruits*, folio from the Fraser Album, 1815–16. Watercolor, ink, and gold on Whatman paper (watermarked 1814), 9 15/16 × 15 1/2 in. (25.3 × 39.4 cm). Arthur M. Sackler Gallery, Smithsonian Institution, Washington, D.C.

Massachusetts.[17] While the figures were naturalistically rendered and modeled from life, the identity of the models was never preserved, as the sculptures were intended to serve as types rather than individuals whose social roles and positions were distinguishable by race, physiognomy, marks, clothing, and accessories. By the mid-nineteenth century three additional lifesize sculptures entered the EIMS collection, ones more readily identifiable as portraits. Although made in the same process of unfired clay and realistically depicted, they nevertheless denote three different Calcutta merchants with close business ties to the East India merchants in Boston.[18] Two are attributable to Sri Ram Pal, at the time the most renowned potter-sculptor working in this mode. In his portrait *Raj Kissen Mitter* (ca. 1840, cat. 34), the merchant was originally seated on a Western-style chair and "dressed in proper Bengali style," complete with hookah. In their public display at the East India Marine Society Museum, the three portraits were seen as "an amusing and educational representation of Bengali society for Americans to enjoy."[19] Yet, here the portraits, intended as presentations of specific individuals, slip into the representation of types. Tellingly the artists who made such sculptures would find new patronage in the nineteenth century at various world's fairs, where they would win awards for their careful renderings of ethnographic models.[20]

If the Krishnanagar portraits are unwittingly rendered as types through the ethnographic lens of nineteenth-century visual culture, during the late twentieth century American artist Duane Hanson self-consciously deployed an ethnographic mode in his photorealistic sculptures that nevertheless subtly critiqued the social reality of the subjects and the contexts of their display. "He draws his types from the world of the ordinary, but the degree of ordinariness is carefully selected (with several significant exceptions) so as to be *out* of the ordinary in the context in which his works are likely to be seen. The pensive hard-hat worker, self-absorbed patience player and footsore, laden-down shopper are not likely frequenters of galleries, museums or art collections, or at least not in the costumes which determine their social roles, as the artist shows them."[21] Being cast from life, painted realistically, and dressed in actual clothes, the works on the one hand are three-dimensional facsimiles of real people, yet Hanson identified his figures not by their names but by their occupation or profession, such as *Housepainter I* (1984/88, cat. 15) or *Housewife* (1969–70, cat. 35). "The subject matter that I like best deals with the familiar lower-class and middle-class Americans of today," wrote Hanson. "For me, the resignation, emptiness, and loneliness of their existence captures the true reality of life for these people. As a realist I'm not interested in the ideal human form, but rather a face or body which has suffered, like some weather worn landscape, the erosion of time. In portraying this aspect of life I want to achieve a certain tough realism, which speaks of the fascinating idiosyncrasies of our time."[22] Hanson's singling out of moments of drudgery and despair was not done with condescension toward his subjects, but rather hints more ominously at a systemic social malaise brought about by gendered, racial, and economic frictions that exist beyond the individual, and in which the viewer, too, becomes implicated; the uncanniness of the encounter with Hanson's figures is simultaneously familiar and distancing, thus engendering the viewer's complicity in the figure's alienation. In other words, as author and artist Douglas Coupland has pointed out, Hanson's figures have come to represent "archetypes" rather than "stereotypes."[23] Rendered with sympathy and sharp understanding of their social context, they mark a historical moment and experience rather than merely record specific people and roles.

Where Hanson's work illustrates a kind of ethnographic move in sculpture, the genre of ethnographic sculpture itself has its roots in nineteenth-century Europe and America, when it stood at the intersection of art, particularly portraiture, and anthropology in that era's visualization of theories of race. "Ethnographic sculptures were often produced for anthropological study collections or museum exhibits for public instruction. The museum models included a range of three-dimensional objects: facial masks, portrait busts, and full-length figures, made through carving in stone,

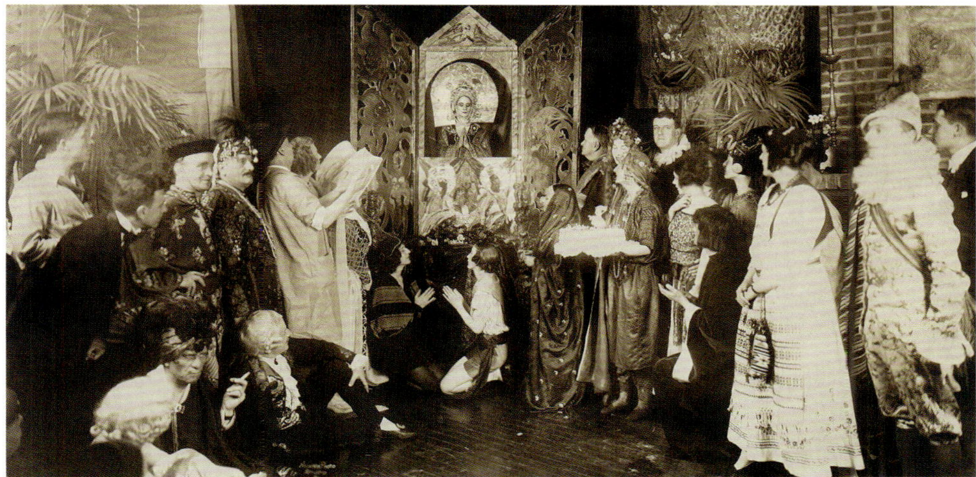

Fig. 55 Group tableau with Anna Pavlova posing as a Byzantine Madonna at her birthday party,
Malvina Cornell Hoffman's studio, 157 East Thirty-Fifth Street, New York, 1924

modeling in clay, or through a direct casting process."[24] French artist Charles-Henri-Joseph Cordier epitomized the ethnographic sculptor, notably producing a series of polychromed representations of black colonial subjects under a French government commission in the mid-nineteenth century. After traveling to North Africa, his task was to represent racial "types" by synthesizing multiple features into a single ideal or "ensemble type,"[25] resulting in the production of "ethnic, racial and cultural generalizations of the sometimes interchangeable titles attached to his sculptures."[26] *La Capresse des Colonies* (1861, cat. 33) was also known as *La Négresse des Colonies*, while male and female types were often paired together.[27] In hindsight, given the prevailing understanding of racial difference, the idealized realism of Cordier's busts was premised on the artist-ethnographer's "white gaze" as an "objective" tool and determinant of beauty.[28] Motivations and approach aside, the works themselves occupy a more complicated position: Cordier's radical use of colored materials (enameled bronze with vibrantly patterned Algerian onyx) challenged the Neoclassical preference for marble, even as he espoused traditionalism in his eschewal of more indexical methods of casting from life.[29] Furthermore, while the works were made through creative assemblage and do not represent a specific individual, by following conventions of portraiture and through their extreme detail, they demonstrate a "specificity [that] seems not to signal a (stereo)type, but an individual, recognizable and legible to those who would have known her."[30] Ironically, Cordier's busts seem portraitlike, even as they were intended to be ethnographic types. The

reverse held true for one of the last notable efforts at ethnographic sculptures, created by Malvina Cornell Hoffman, in the figures she created for the 1933 exhibition "The Races of Mankind" at the Field Museum, Chicago. Although initially celebrated, in the postwar era the long-running display came to represent a misguided approach to ethnographic representation of racial difference and was removed from public view by 1969.[31] In 2016 the figures were once again displayed in a special exhibition whose self-reflexivity is evident in its title "Looking at Ourselves: Rethinking the Sculptures of Malvina Hoffman." The reclamation of the identities of individual models, including their names, became an important and meaningful gesture in the twenty-first-century reinstallation of the sculptures.[32]

Hoffman had been a leading, early twentieth-century American sculptor, who trained under Auguste Rodin in Paris. In the 1910s after having seen Anna Pavlova perform onstage in London, Hoffman developed a close friendship with the ballerina and subsequently created a number of sculptures and reliefs of the famous dancer performing energetic and lyrical movements. In 1924 Hoffman hosted an elaborate costume party at her Sniffen Court studio in New York for Pavlova's birthday. The Russian American stage designer Boris Anisfeld created an elaborate frame modeled on a Russian icon, and at midnight the niche opened and revealed Pavlova, eyes closed, bedecked with a jeweled headdress, and presented as a Byzantine Madonna. After remaining still, a moment captured in a photograph of the evening's revelries (fig. 55), the "icon" came to life as the dancer opened her eyes and smiled.[33] Hoffman would memorialize the event in a series of sculptures, including the *Mask of Anna Pavlova* (1924, cat. 19), modeled in tinted wax to mimic flesh. Art historian Janis Connor has observed, "It is remarkable that, in the end, Hoffman chose to represent only the visage of this supreme symbol of physicality, a face in a stylized setting.... The vision of Pavlova as a Byzantine Madonna, with all its eccentricity and period oddness, suggests the literally worshipful feelings of the artist for her subject."[34] For Hoffman in this instance, the portrait became a site for an extremely personal and symbolic interpretation of a particular friendship.

Artists often make portraits of friends, intimates, and patrons, works that encapsulate specific relationships and sometimes include idiosyncratic elements to personalize the moment of creation or the character of the subject. In an archaizing gesture not dissimilar to that of Hoffman in her mask of Pavlova, the French sculptor Antoine-Emile Bourdelle incorporated Greco-Egyptian (A.D. first–third century) funerary styles in the framing of his portrait of the American lawyer Stephen Millett's wife, Irene (fig. 56). The subtle tinting of the work suggests that it was intended for execution in *pâte de verre*, the same medium that Rodin used in his *Mask of Hanako, Type E* (1911, cat. 18). *Pâte de verre* is a casting process in which ground glass is placed in a mold and fired. When used to create figures and faces, the resultant forms are translucent with realistic coloring and exude lifelike qualities. An ancient Egyptian process, it was revived in the late nineteenth century and popularized by artists such as Rodin and Bourdelle. Rodin used it in his late experimental works, including this portrait mask of the Japanese stage actress Ohta Hisa known as Hanako, whom Rodin had encountered during the 1906 Exposition Coloniale in Marseilles. Rodin was especially drawn to the manner in which the actress's face conveyed her character's complex emotions when performing ritual suicide, or hara-kiri. Rodin produced several versions of Hanako's portrait, conveying multiple states in the process toward the subject's realization of impending death. The countenance, known as *Type E*, showed "Hanako's lips hanging open; her

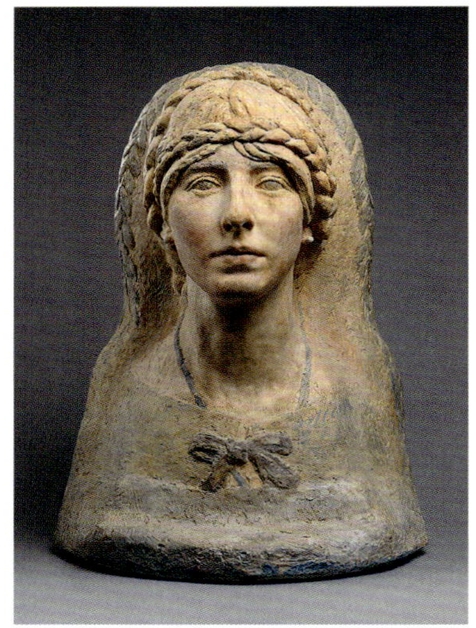

Fig. 56 Antoine-Emile Bourdelle. *Irene Millett*, 1917. Original plaster, tinted and polychromed. H. 20 ½ in. (52.1 cm), W. 15 ¾ in. (40 cm), D. 10 ¾ in. (27.3 cm). The Metropolitan Museum of Art, New York, Gift of Stephen C. Millett, 1966 (66.42)

eyelids droop heavily and her eyes are glazed over, unseeingly directed towards some distant and unfathomable void. A stillness hangs over this face, as though all agony, all horror, had in mid-gasp come to a sudden end."[35] This version was chosen for subsequent translation into *pâte de verre*, whose properties imbue the work with disturbing eeriness; the translucency of the medium seemingly freezes the moment of the ebbing of the lifeblood. A more literal freezing of subject or self can be seen in British artist Marc Quinn's series Self (1991–present, cat. 21), in which the artist has used his own blood as the medium in which his head is cast through refrigeration. The material fragility of the work becomes a metaphor for the ephemerality of life itself.

Quinn, like the American artist Paul Thek (cat. 94), also references the form and concept of the reliquary. Historically reliquary busts of saints were found across Europe from the ninth century through the Renaissance.[36] Busts were the preferred form to hold skull relics and were most often modeled in precious metals as well as adorned with gems to suggest the "expected luminosity of a heavenly being."[37] The shimmering busts were awe-inspiring and intended to communicate the supraworldly nature of these figures. Yet artists occasionally chose to draw attention to the mortal aspects of these figures in order to indicate "the saints' status as intercessors: inhabitants of heaven, yet still recognizably human."[38] The *Reliquary Bust of Saint Juliana* (ca. 1376, cat. 20) was commissioned by the abbess Gabriella Bontempi of Perugia to hold a fragment of the skull of the saint. Created out of copper, such a reliquary would have been the work of skilled Sienese goldsmiths; however, in this instance the metallic substructure of the face and shoulders was softened by the application of a layer of gesso, which was then painted in tones that articulate the delicate features of a young woman with fair skin, rosy lips, and gentle brown eyes. Although not individualized or recognizable in the way Renaissance portrait busts would be in subsequent centuries, when its human features and connection to the actual relic are considered in tandem, the reliquary could be considered a true likeness of the particular saint.

Whereas the Christian relic was an object of focused devotion in the European Middle Ages, the preservation of skeletal remains in the *Auto-Icon of Jeremy Bentham* (1832, cat. 22) represented a distinctly atheistic outlook, one product of the Age of Enlightenment. The English philosopher Jeremy Bentham was deeply committed to the theory of utilitarianism, and he specifically instructed in his will that his body be dissected after his death by his friend the British surgeon Thomas Southwood Smith, while his skeleton be preserved in the form of an "auto-icon." Bentham was known to have a sense of humor, and the term and manner of his memorialization were no doubt intended to poke fun at religion. After dissection Bentham's skeleton was padded with cotton wool, wood, straw, and hay, and was dressed in the philosopher's everyday clothes following detailed prescriptions of the manner in which the figure would be staged.[39] Bentham's head was intended to be desiccated through a Maori process of mummification and placed atop the auto-icon. The process did not work, and the head was replaced instead by a wax model made by Jacques Talrich. A French military surgeon, Talrich later became an anatomical wax modeler for the Faculté de Médecine in Paris and also worked for clients in London. His head of Bentham combines the conventions of portraiture and the acute realism achievable through wax modeling. With cane in hand, the philosopher in his old age bears jowly cheeks and is balding with wisps of disheveled gray hair. This hybrid figure sits in a case at the University College London—reading glasses beside him, blue eyes hooded beneath a wrinkled brow—and casts a steadfast gaze at generations of students who pass before him in amusement, curiosity, and wonder.

An interest in representing the body in fragile states of life has led the American artist Tip Toland to focus on the ungainly bodies of the very young and the old "to go after vulnerability. . . . That's where we find our humanity."[40] *The Whistlers* (2005, cat. 27), while not intended as a portrait, emerged from the realm of the personal and whimsical and references the conventions of Western classical sculpture.[41] The resulting almost-twinned figures—one of which came to resemble the artist's sister Phoebe, with whom she shares a close bond—of two elderly naked women face each other awkwardly. Truncated at the waist, the figure on the left purses her lips into an "O" and appears to be showing her companion how to whistle, her left hand slightly raised as if in tune with the rising note. The figure on the right mimics the expression and strains to follow, her left hand hovering as if to steady her in her effort. Just as in

the figure of Bharti Kher's *Mother* (2016, cat. 6), the aging female body is rendered tenderly and frankly, both in form and color. The hair has turned gray; the loosened skin covered in liver spots, wrinkles, and folds; the bluish veins protrude; the breasts sag and the body hunches over—all details articulated with poignancy and insight into the aging process, making this work a portrait and a self-portrait of a relationship.

The self-portrait as an externalization of self and site for self-reflection is also seen in a number of American artist Marisol's works from the early 1970s. Inspired by her visits to Venezuela she created a series of masklike objects that were cast from her face and integrated a range of elements, from bottles, cans, and keys to hair.[42] The latter sprouts enigmatically from a string of holes surrounding the artist's head, in a work titled *Veil* (1975, cat. 24). Hung from the wall in a manner akin to a votive such as the Latin American *milagro* or ex-voto, the face is mounted on a halolike plaque, consciously recalling Christian imagery, while at the same time subverting it with a deliberately banal epitaph scratched on to it: "MY NAME IS MARISOL I AM AN ARTIST I HAVE BEEN LIVING IN NEW YORK FOR TWENTY-FOUR YEARS MY STUDIO IS AT 795 BROADWAY MY FAMILY IS FROM VENEZUELA I LIKE THE WATER I SHOW MY WORK AT JANIS."

While Marisol continued to sculpt and often focused on portraiture, she more often worked in wood. Casting as an artistic process and the use of plaster as "the final material of the sculpture" was, however, the preferred medium of American artist George Segal.[43] While Segal's early works included mostly unidentifiable figures cast in rough white plaster, later works such as his portrait of the art historian Meyer Schapiro (1977, cat. 29) were produced by making a second casting from the interior of the original hardened plaster shell, reproducing sharp details of features and skin, and later painting them.[44] The artist's admiration for the renowned scholar is revealed in a sensitive bas-relief, in which the figure stands with his hands clasped, and as in Hoffman's portrait of Pavlova, Schapiro's eyes are closed in meditative contemplation. Through Segal's use of color, this otherwise sober portrait departs from tradition: the background and the body were painted in a brilliant blue, and even the face and hands, while painted naturalistically, were then glazed with a light wash of the same uniting azure tint.[45] In a recorded conversation between Segal and Schapiro, the art historian questioned the artist's choice of color in this particular work:

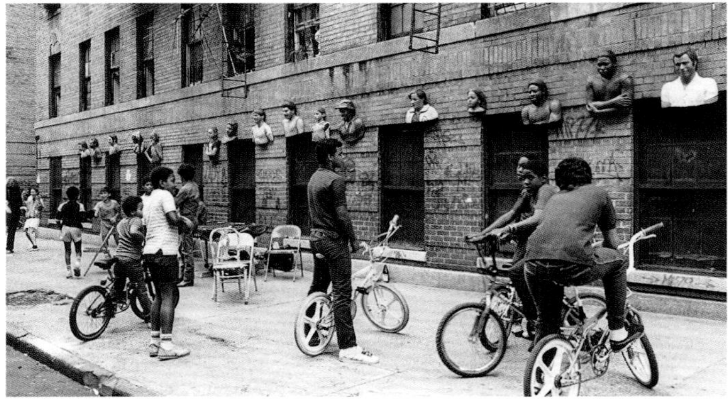
Fig. 57 Walton Avenue block party with kids hanging around casts of neighborhood figures hung on a building exterior, Bronx, New York, 1985

For Segal the choice of blue became a way of connecting the physical presence of an intellectual mentor with the theory of color—a conduit for fusing body and idea—moving one out of the realm of physicality and potentially into the symbolic.

For a sculptor like American artist John Ahearn, the use of color in his cast reliefs was more straightforwardly naturalistic though no less meaningful. In the late 1970s and early 1980s, Ahearn cast individuals in the South Bronx neighborhood in which he worked, a deliberate counterpoint to Manhattan's more established art neighborhoods downtown. In a highly participatory and public mode, Ahearn would collaborate with his subjects to come up with the poses in which they would be cast.[47] Engaging with the community and representing his subjects with

empathy as empowered individuals was important to Ahearn, particularly as he was aware of the circulation of his works in a remote and removed art world: "I work on a somewhat idealistic level with the sculpture. I consider that these sculptures will probably be seen in an alien environment, in an environment that is extremely hostile to the characters I am representing. So I feel that it makes sense for me to project, with them in mind, as strong and as forceful a presentation of them as I can put together, character that will be convincing. It is not that someone has to be hostile to confront hostility, but I think the characters have to come through with some kind of power or strength for them to survive in that kind of environment."[48] Ahearn's figures, children and adults alike, pose comfortably in their skin, sporting a favorite T-shirt, proudly displaying their tattoos, combing their hair, or simply standing and smiling with a hand lightly resting on their waist, as in *Bernice* (1981, cat. 28). Painted with robust acrylics, the colors of Ahearn's "community portraits" capture the vibrancy of dress and the diversity of skin tones of the multiethnic neighborhood in which he worked (fig. 57). Ahearn would often take Polaroids of his sitters in order to record their skin color; consequently the reliefs are mediated through the color range of the film.

A chance encounter with a Puerto Rican taxi driver led to Ahearn's meeting the man's cousin Rigoberto Torres, who would become Ahearn's assistant and collaborator (fig. 58). Torres and Ahearn shared a visual vocabulary, casting figures in plaster,

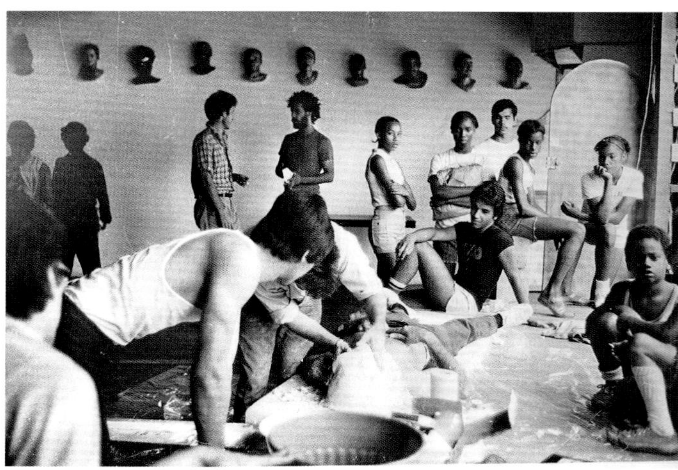
Fig. 58 Rigoberto Torres and John Ahearn casting at Fashion Moda. Artists Stefan Eins and Joe Lewis converse in the background, with neighborhood kids, South Bronx, 1979

even as they learned the process of fiberglass molding from Torres's uncle Raul Arce who ran Fábrica, a religious-statuary factory.[49] *Shorty Working in the C&R Statuary Corp.* (1985, cat. 31) demonstrates the kind of work done in his uncle's factory: as the eponymous Shorty details the traditional figure of the Virgin, the composition assumes a doubling role as a self-portrait of Torres the sculptor producing his own subject. In another kind of double portrait, *Raúl with Bust of Ruth Fernández* (1998, cat. 32), his uncle Raúl reverentially cradles and displays a portrait bust of the singer and celebrity Ruth Fernández, a hero in the Puerto Rican community and whose likeness would have been a popular product of the statuary factory. Both busts present strong visual contrasts between the artistic conventions and whiteness of the sculptures being created and the brown skin, tattooed arms, dark shirts, and mustached faces of the men who hold the works.

The shift toward highly realistic portrayals of individuals in the European context emerged from a specific conjunction of historic and cultural forces during the Renaissance. Yet even as realism was valorized, it was in this same context that the sculptural ideal, which gradually crystalized into the canon, largely eschewed polychromy as well as the process of casting from life.[50] Nevertheless, artists have employed these very means to amplify the realisms they sought. In time and especially in the wake of modernism, as artistic canons were challenged, artists found renewed possibilities in color, casting, and the production of likenesses. Whether through modeling, casting, or even imagination, the production of a likeness sets up a relationship among the subject, the artist, and eventually the viewer. This dialectical relationship is where the significance of identification and recognition emerges. Moreover, in the rendering of likeness, the personal, the peculiar, and the idiosyncratic qualities of a given work distinguish the individual from the type, the real from the ideal. On closer examination, however, these distinctions are in fact porous, and there has always been greater slippage, both intended and circumstantial, that has occurred between the categories.

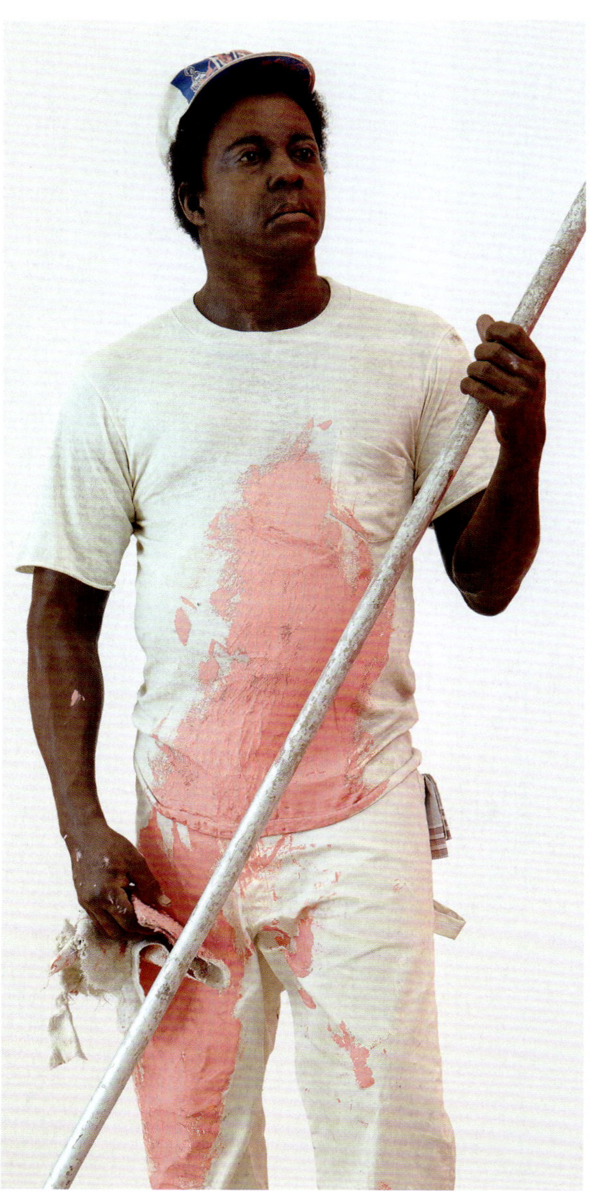

15. Duane Hanson. *Housepainter I*, 1984/88. Autobody
    filler, polychromed in oil, mixed media, and accessories,
    H. 70 ⅞ in. (180 cm), W. 25 ³⁄₁₆ in. (64 cm), D. 26 ¾ in.
    (68 cm). Catherine and John Madar Collection

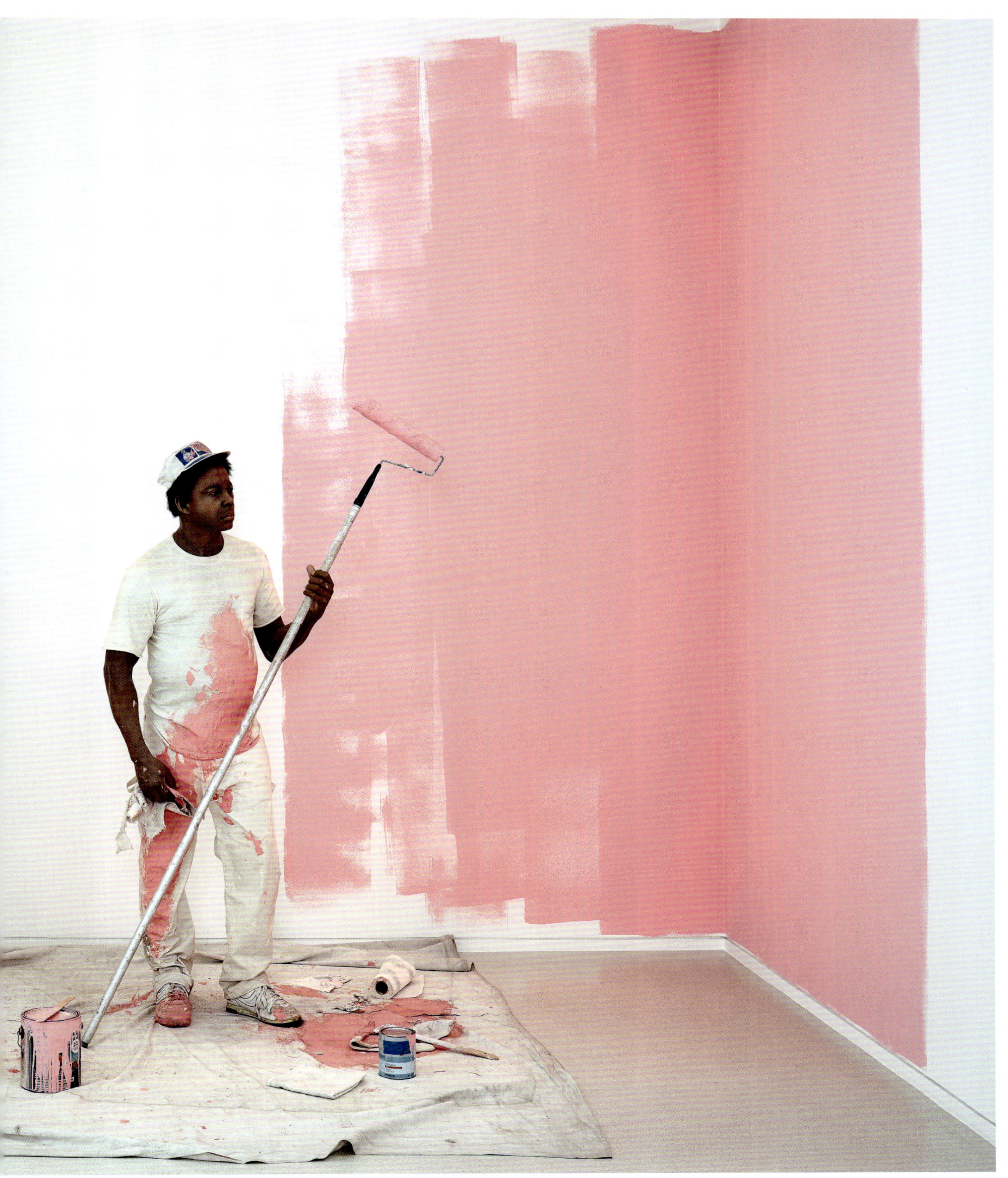

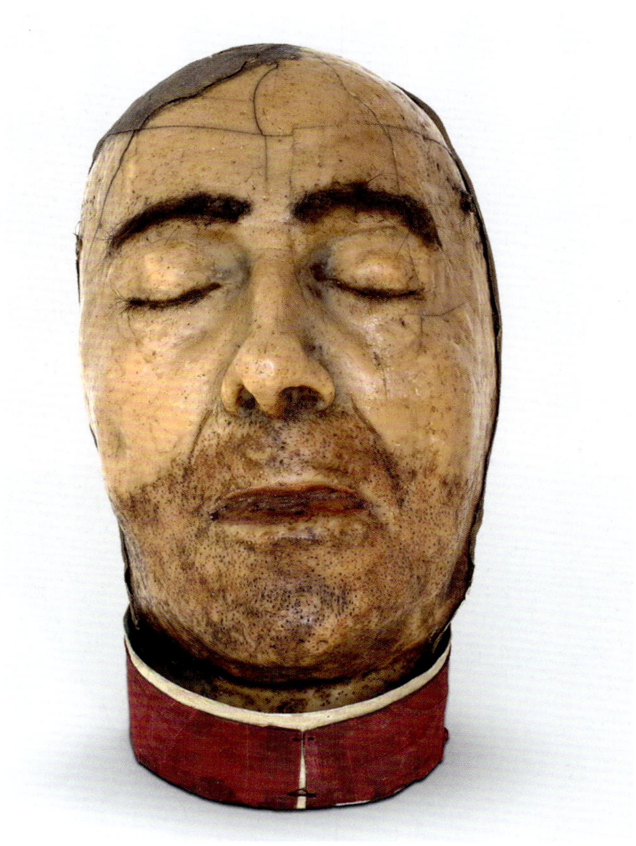

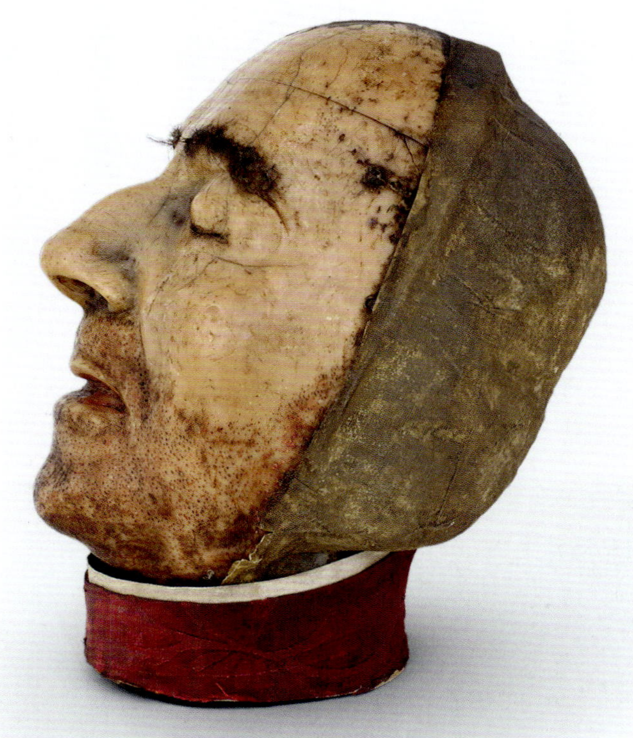

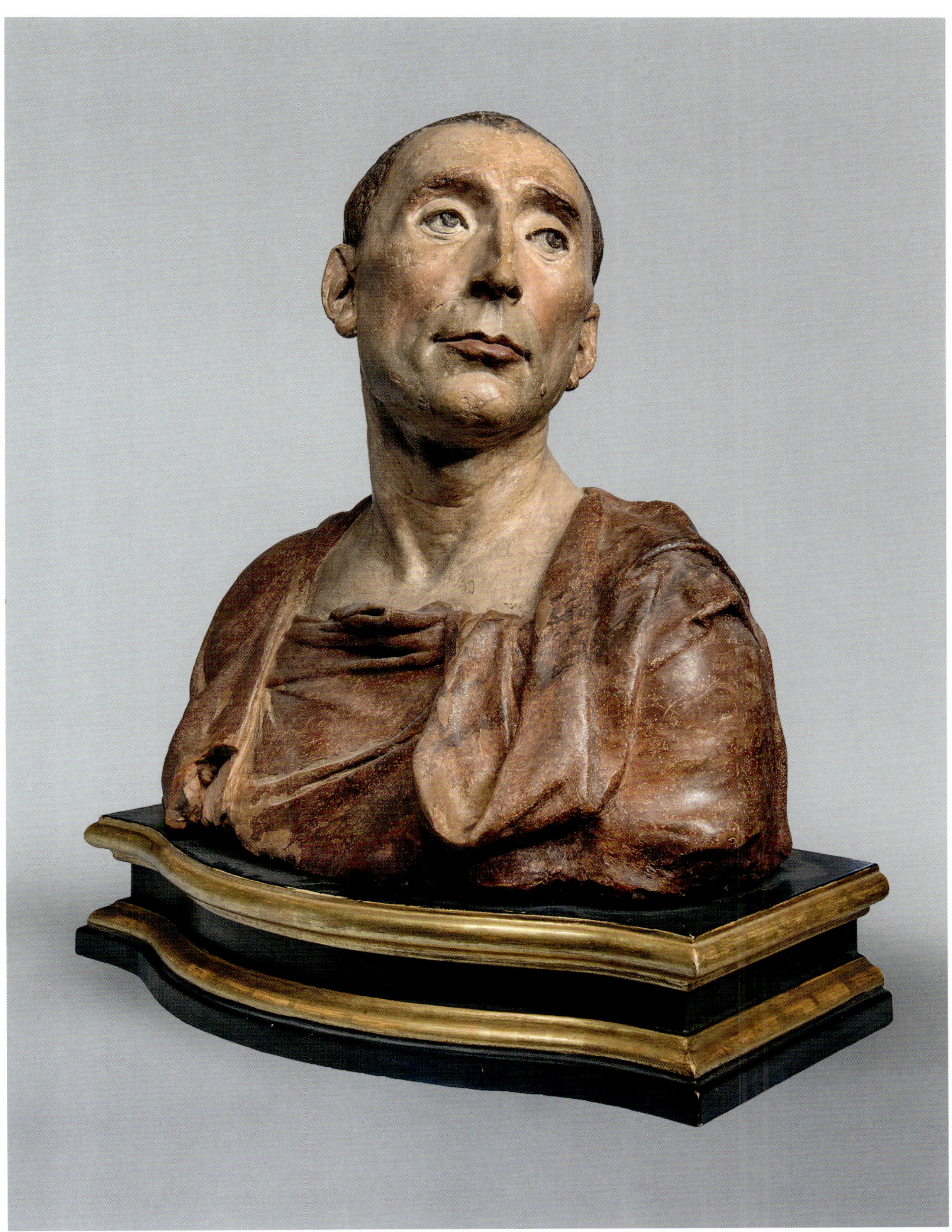

16. *Funeral Effigy of Doge Alvise III Mocenigo*(?), 1732. Polychromed wax and fabric, H. 10 ¼ in.
    (26 cm), W. 6 ⁵⁄₁₆ in. (16 cm), D. 9 ¹⁄₁₆ in. (23 cm). Venetian. Museo Correr, Musei Civici di
    Venezia, Venice

17. Donatello. *Bust of Niccolò da Uzzano*, 1430s. Polychromed terracotta, H. 18 ⅛ in. (46 cm),
    W. 17 ⁵⁄₁₆ in. (44 cm), D. 9 ⅝ in. (24.5 cm). Museo Nazionale del Bargello, Florence

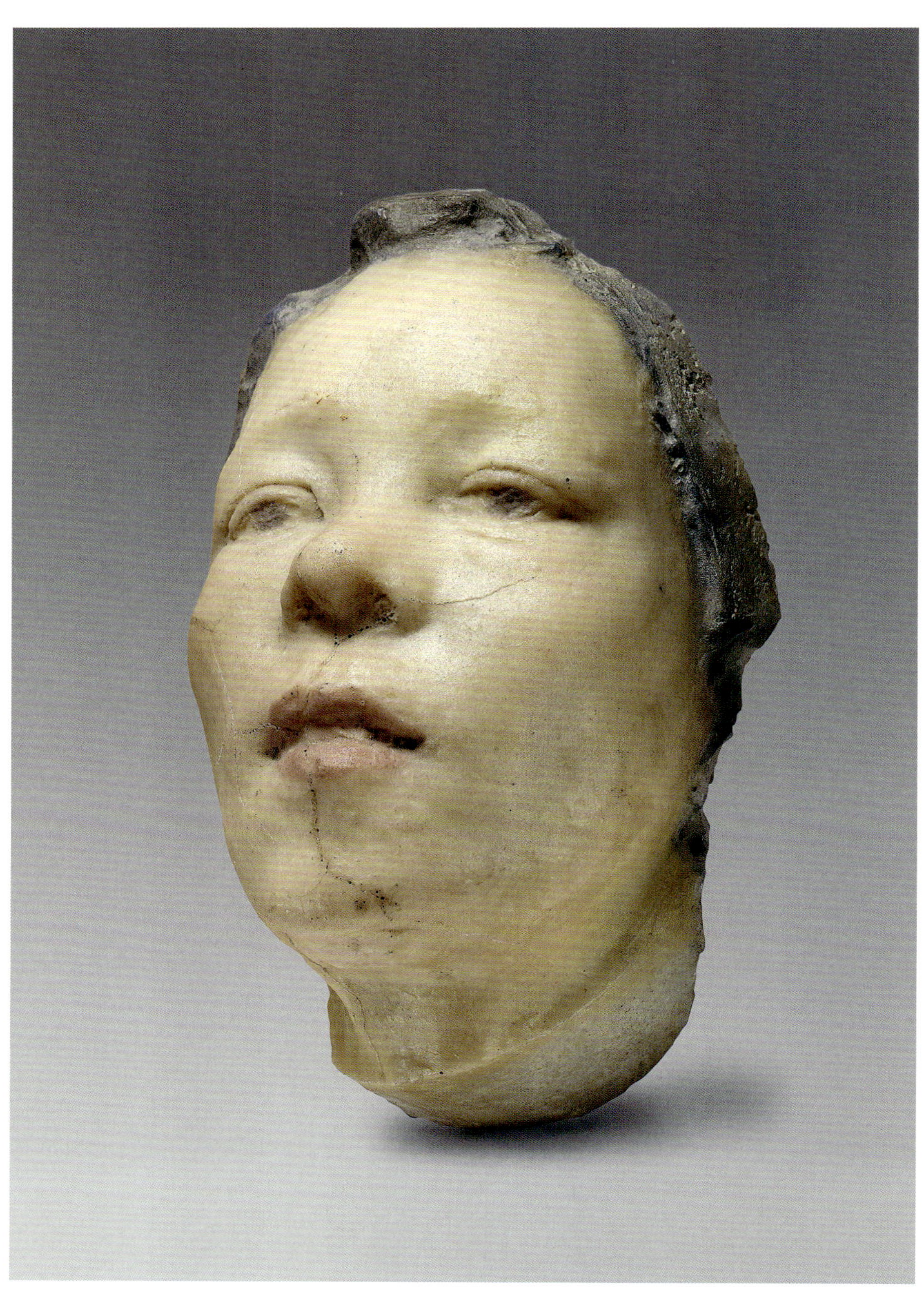

18. Auguste Rodin. *Mask of Hanako, Type E*, 1911. Pâte de verre, H. 8 ¾ in. (22.2 cm), W. 5 ½ in. (13.9 cm), D. 3 ¾ in. (9.5 cm). Musée Rodin, Paris

19. Malvina Cornell Hoffman. *Mask of Anna Pavlova*, 1924. Tinted wax, H. 16 in. (40.6 cm), W. 9 in. (22.9 cm), D. 7 in. (17.8 cm). The Metropolitan Museum of Art, New York, Gift of Mrs. L. Dean Holden, 1935 (35.107)

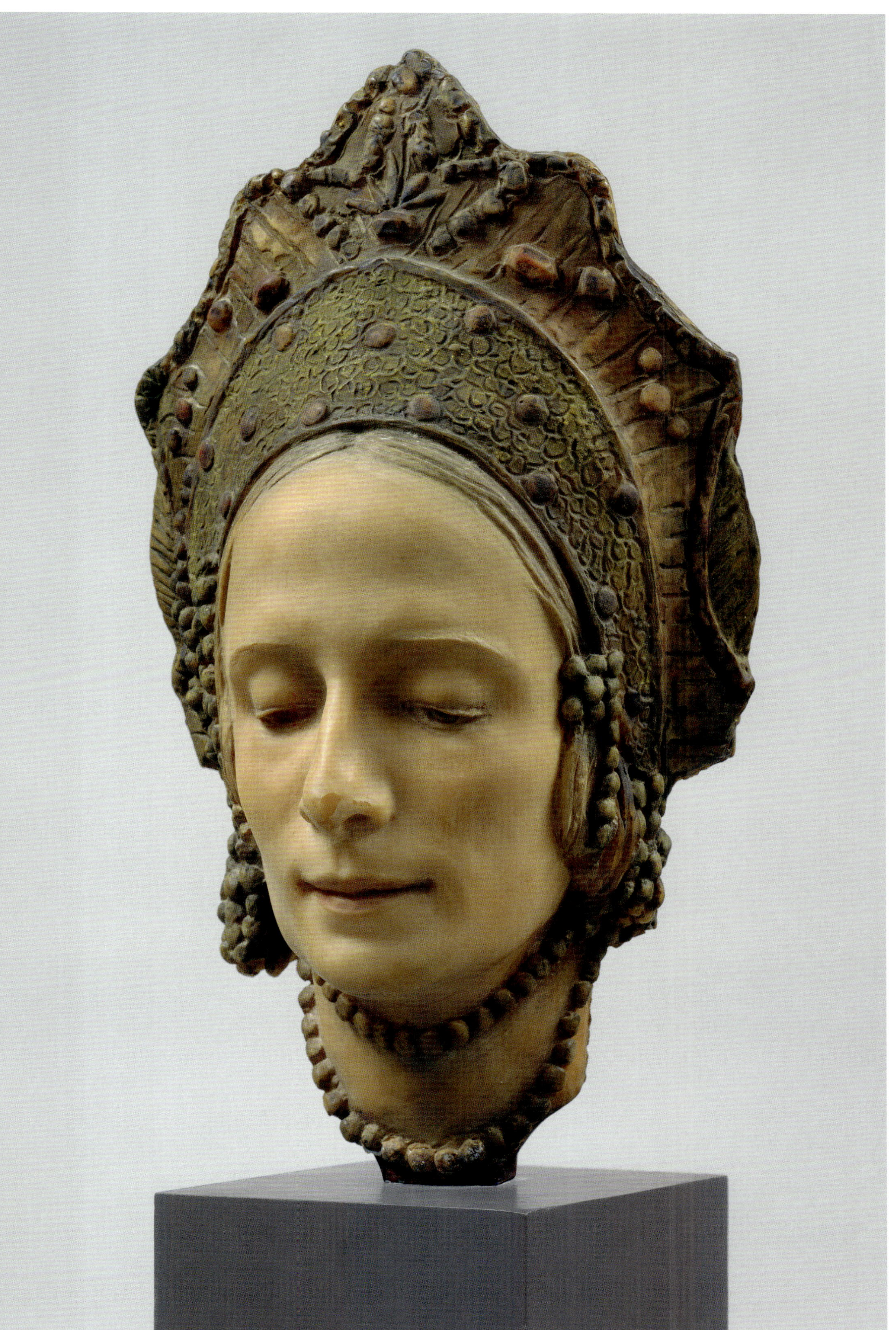

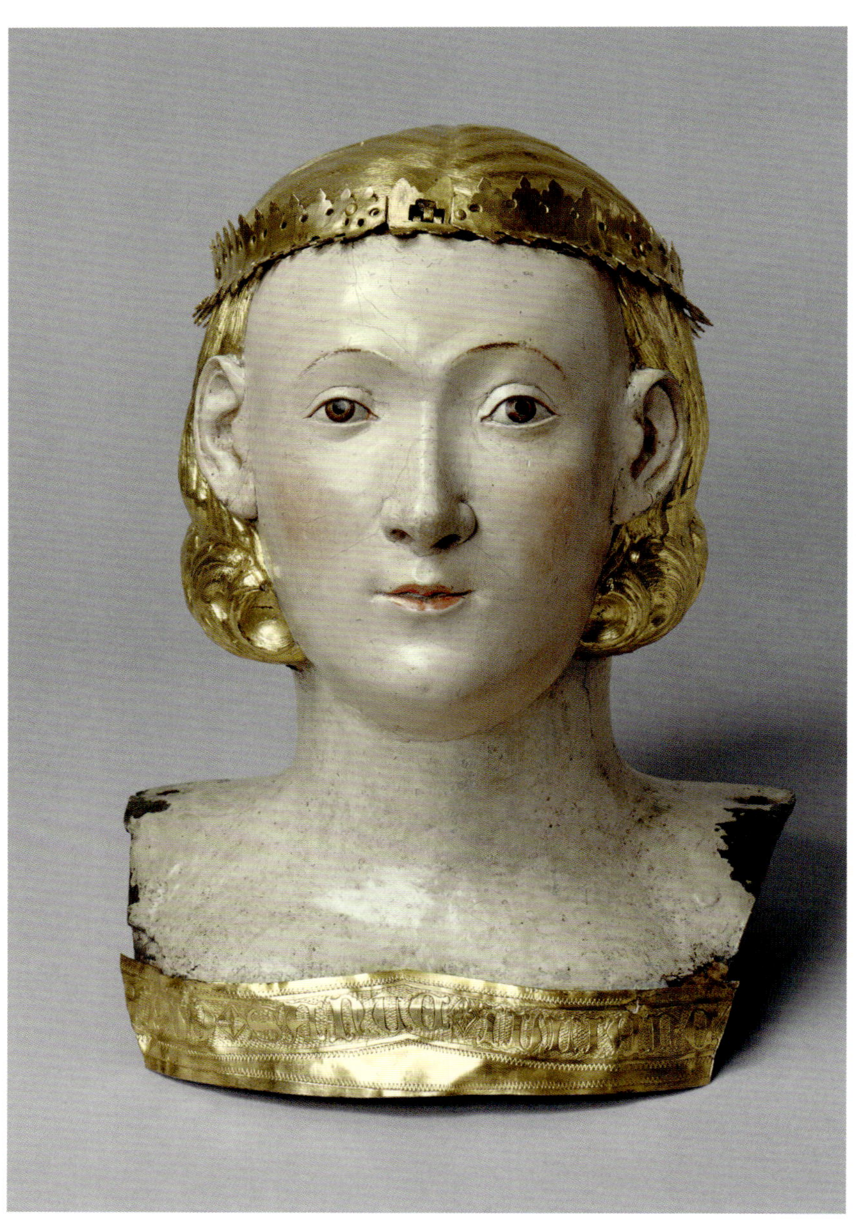

20. Circle of Giovanni di Bartolo. *Reliquary Bust of Saint Juliana*, ca. 1376. Copper, gilding, gesso, and tempera, H. 11 1/16 in. (28.1 cm), W. 9 in. (22.9 cm), D. 8 3/8 in. (21.3 cm). The Metropolitan Museum of Art, New York, The Cloisters Collection, 1961 (61.266)

21. Marc Quinn. *Self*, 1991. Blood, Perspex, stainless steel, and refrigeration equipment, H. 81 7/8 in. (208 cm), W. 24 13/16 in. (63 cm), D. 24 13/16 in. (63 cm). Private collection

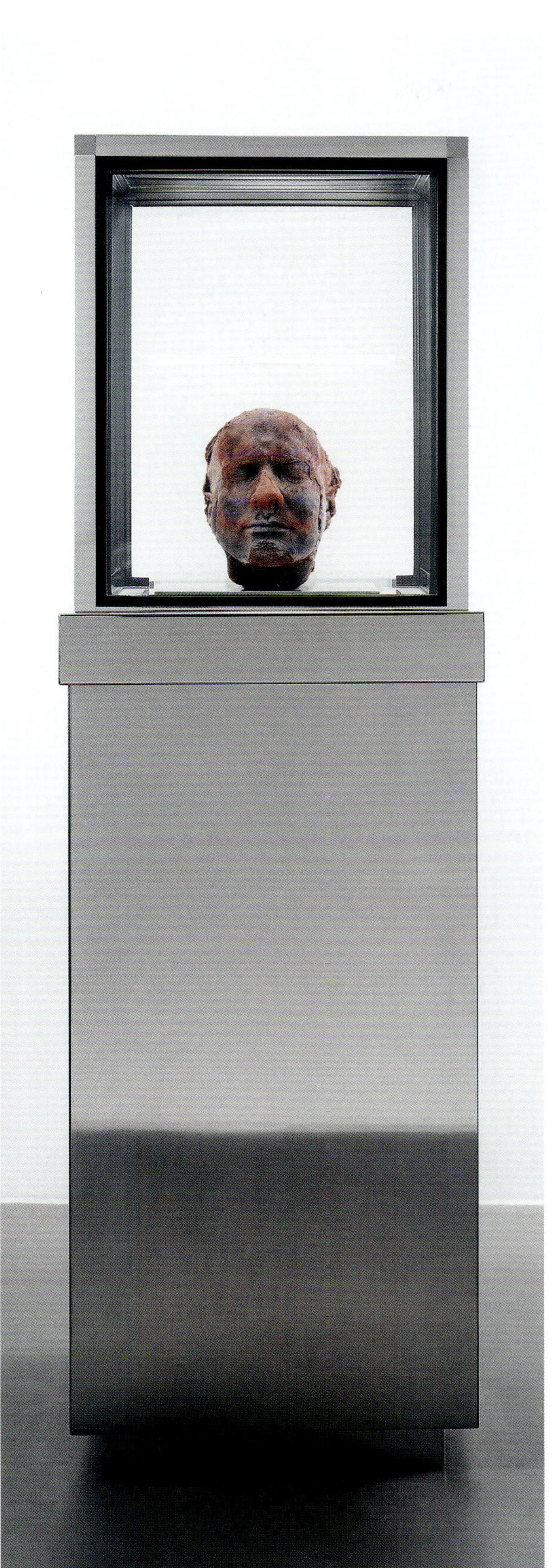

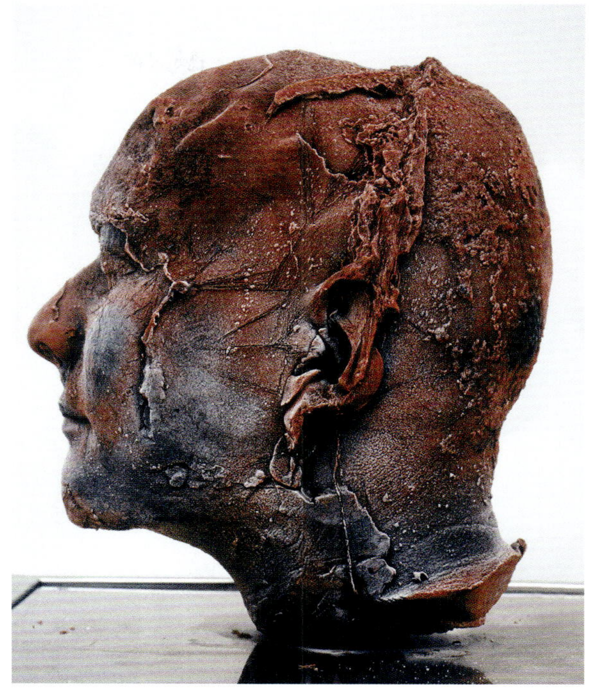

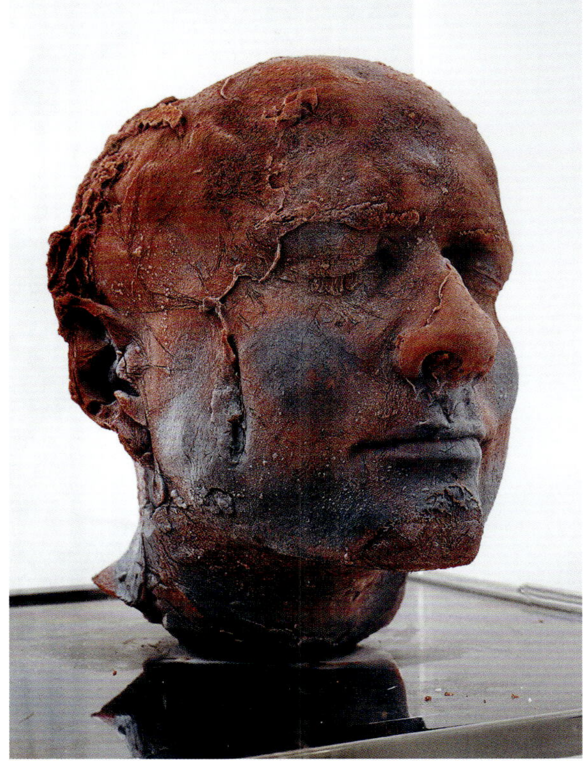

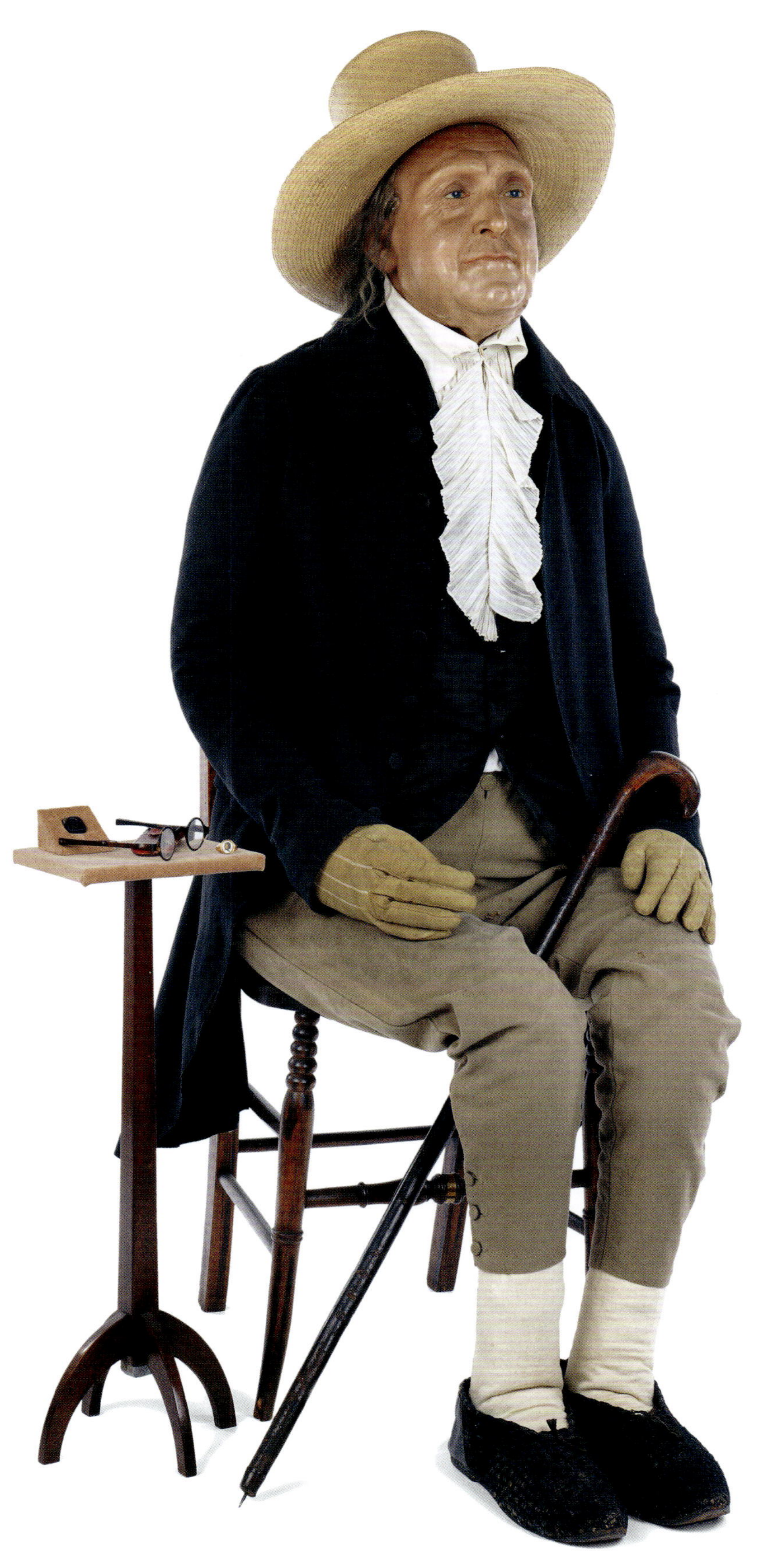

22. Thomas Southwood Smith and Jacques Talrich. *Auto-Icon of Jeremy Bentham*, 1832. Wax, human bones, human hair, wool, cotton and linen textiles, straw hat, glasses, wood walking stick, table, and chair, seated: H. 53 15/16 in. (137 cm), W. 24 7/16 in. (62 cm), D. 34 5/8 in. (88 cm). University College London

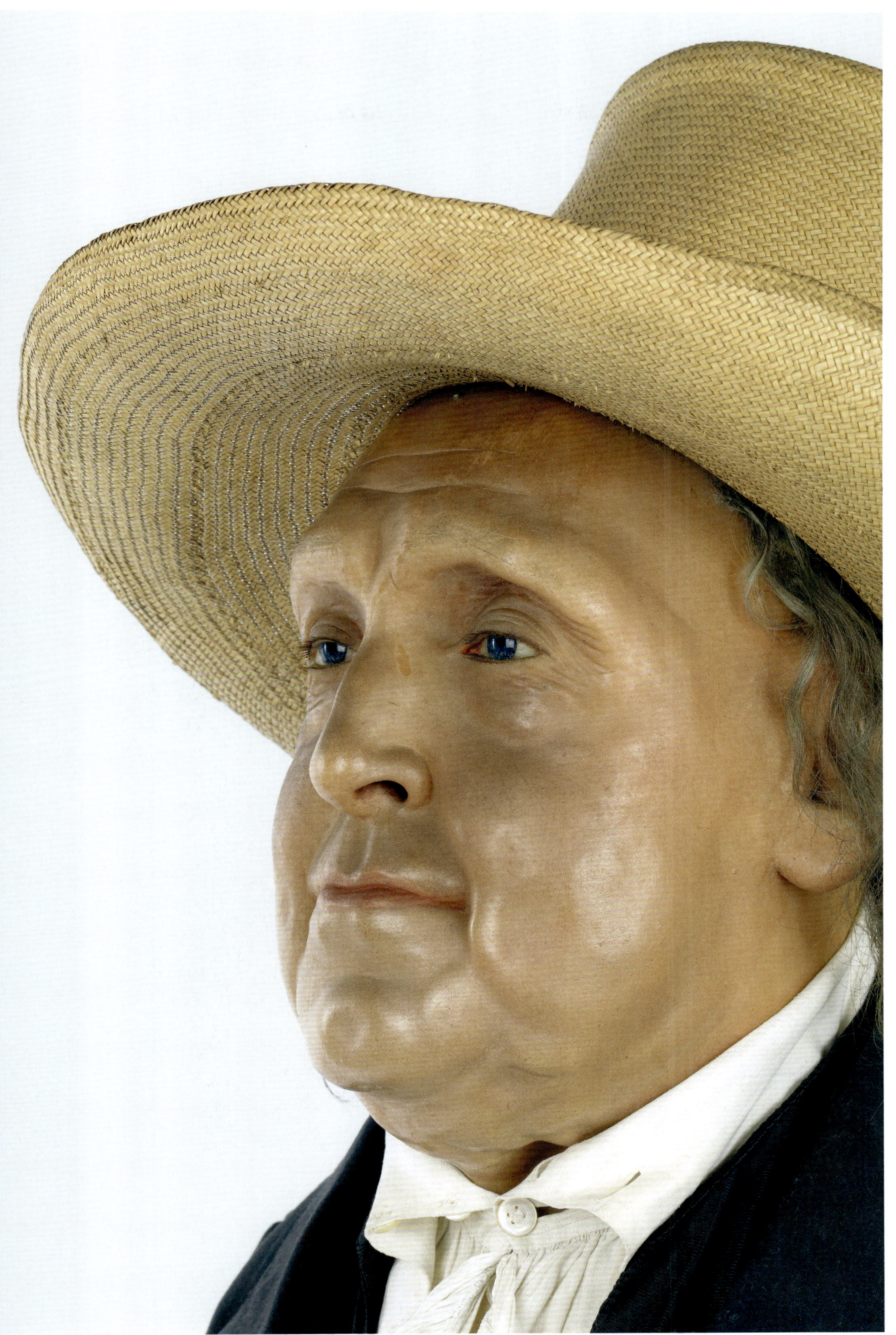

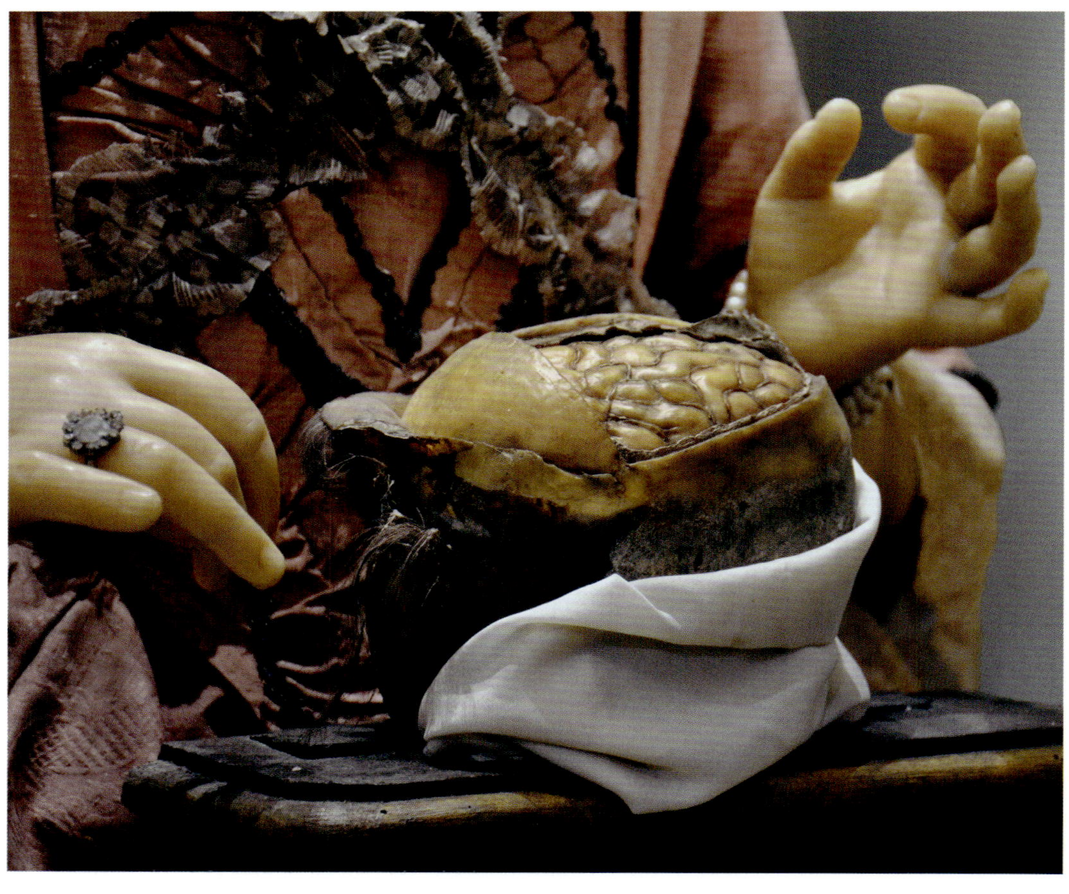

23. Anna Morandi Manzolini. *Self-Portrait*, ca. 1755. Wax, paint, silk, hair, pearls, metal, glass, and wood, H. 35 $^7/_{16}$ in. (90 cm), W. 32 $^5/_{16}$ in. (82 cm), D. 26 ¾ in. (68 cm). Sistema Museale di Ateneo—Museo di Palazzo Poggi, Alma Mater Studiorum, Università di Bologna

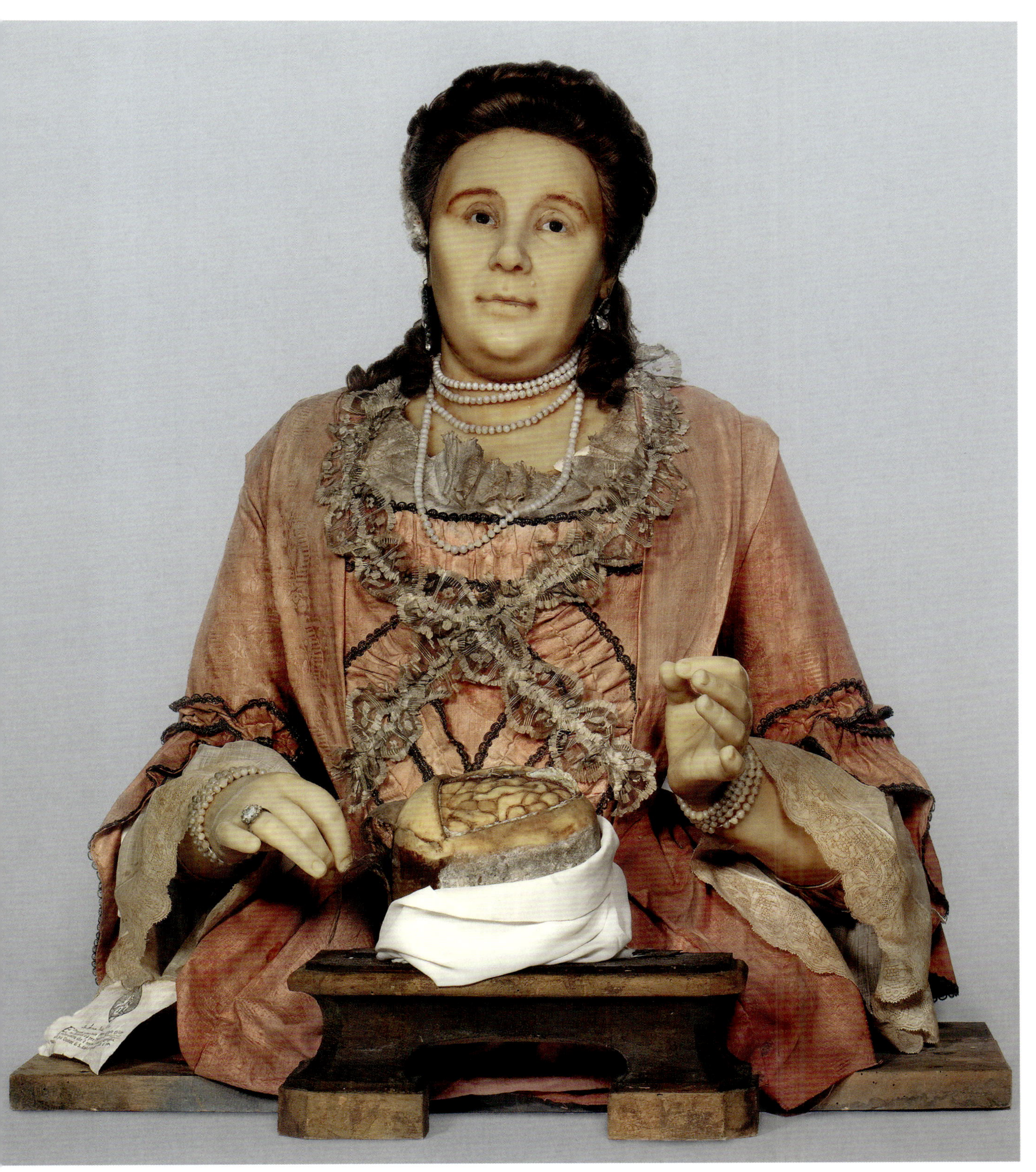

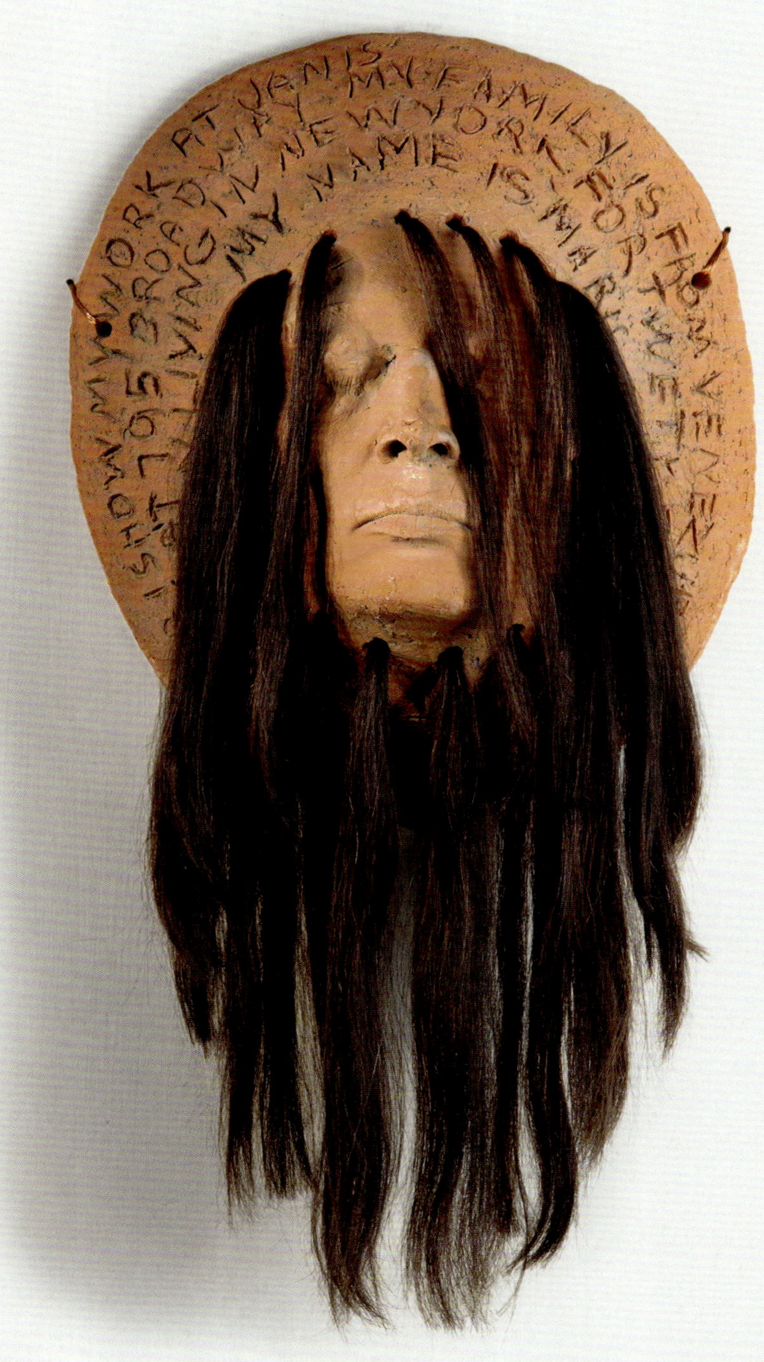

24. Marisol. *Veil*, 1975. Terracotta, rope, and hair, H. 20 ½ in. (52.1 cm), W. 11 in. (27.9 cm), D. 5 in. (12.7 cm). John and Mable Ringling Museum of Art, State Art Museum of Florida, Florida State University, Sarasota, Museum purchase, 1976

25. Angelo Piò. *Portrait of a Monk*, 18th century. Wax, hair, cloth, and glass, H. 31 ⅛ in. (79 cm), W. 28 ¾ in. (73 cm), D. 7 ⅞ in. (20 cm). Collection of Frances Beatty and Allen Adler, New York

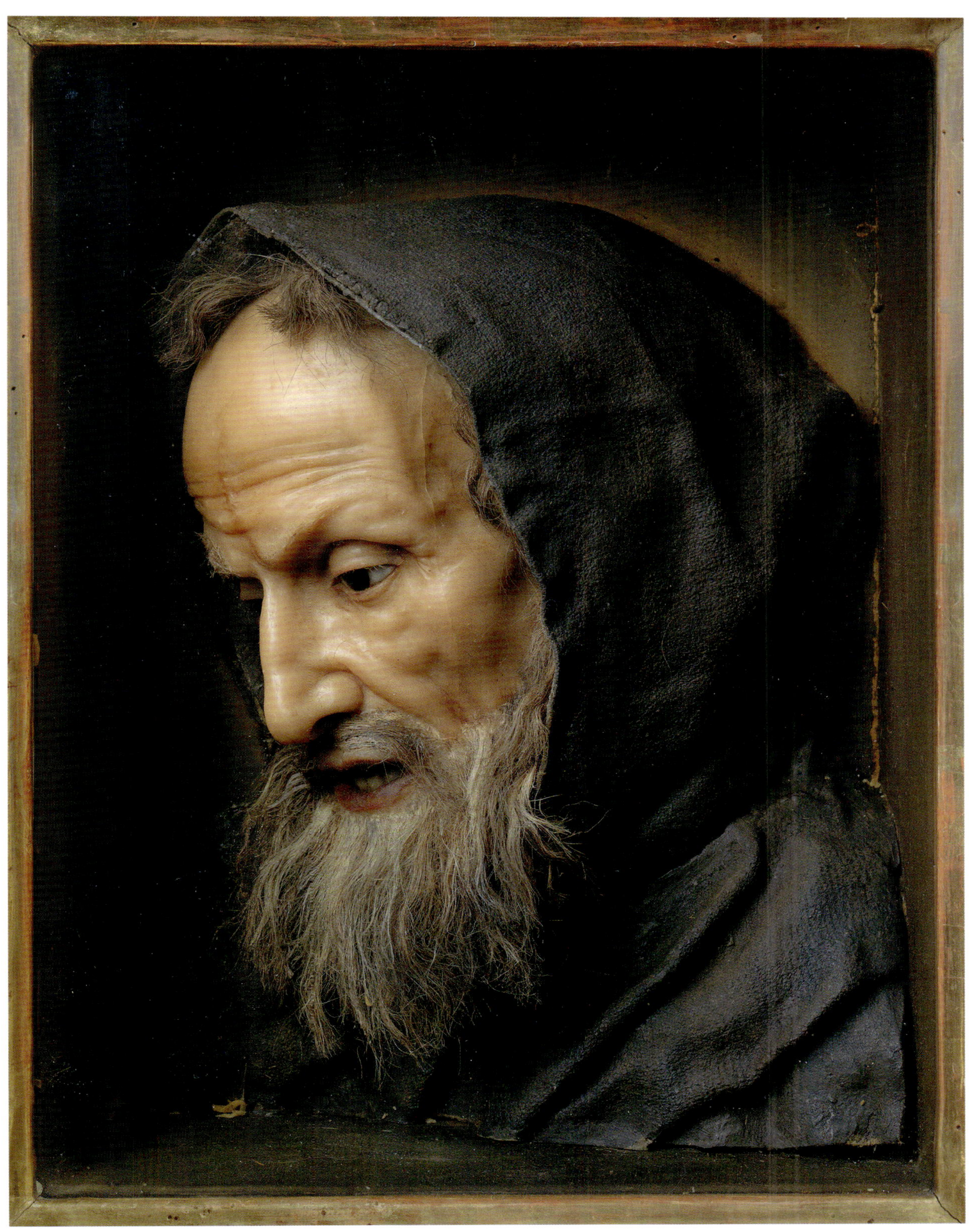

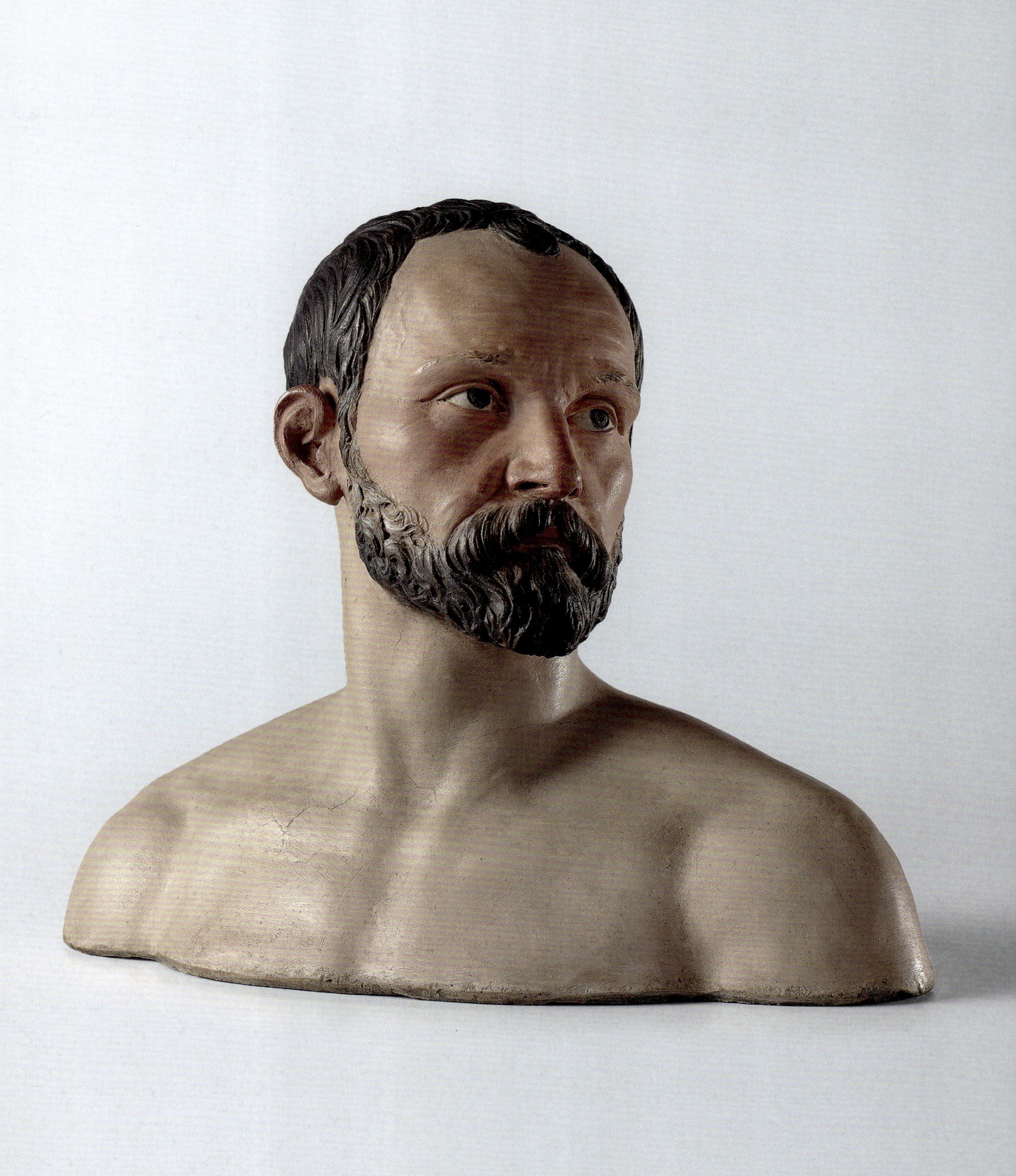

26. Johan Gregor van der Schardt. *Self-Portrait*, ca. 1573. Terracotta
and oil paint, H. 9 ⅟₁₆ in. (23 cm), W. 11 in. (28 cm), D. 5 ½ in.
(14 cm). Rijksmuseum, Amsterdam, Purchased with the support
of the Mondriaan Stichting, the BankGiro Loterij and the
Vereniging Rembrandt, with additional funding from the Prins
Bernhard Cultuurfonds

27. Tip Toland. *The Whistlers*, 2005. Stoneware, paint, pastel, and
synthetic hair, overall: H. 23 in. (58.4 cm), W. 50 in. (127 cm), D. 24 in.
(61 cm). The Metropolitan Museum of Art, New York, Gift of Dale
and Doug Anderson, 2011 (2011.591a, b)

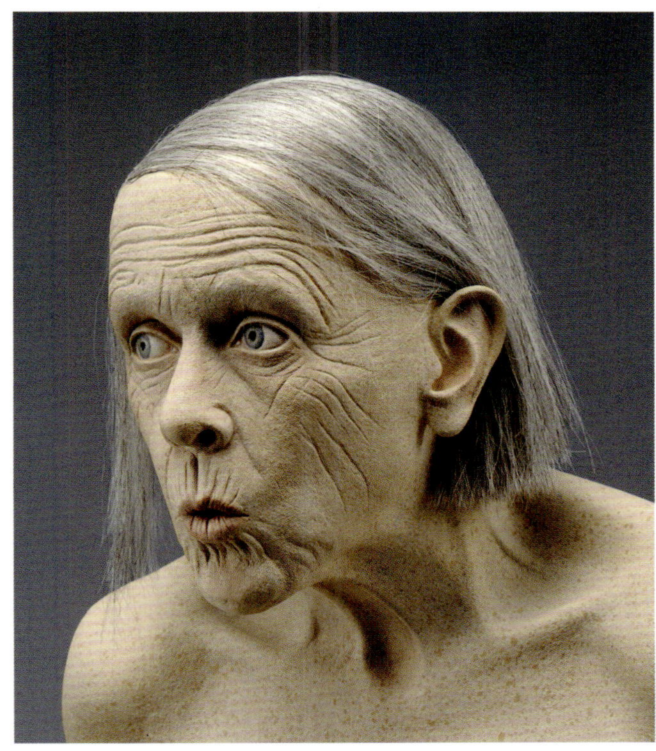

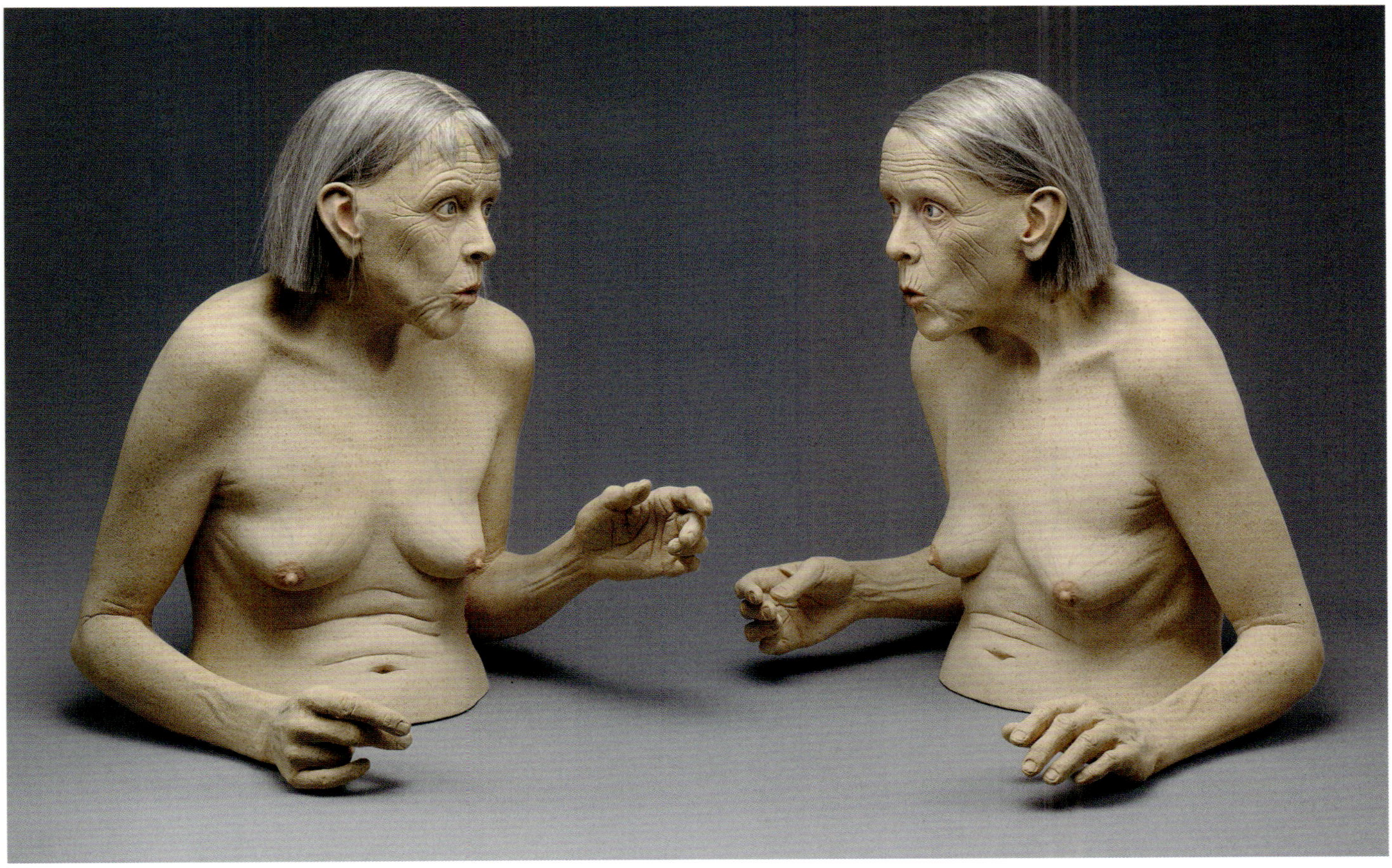

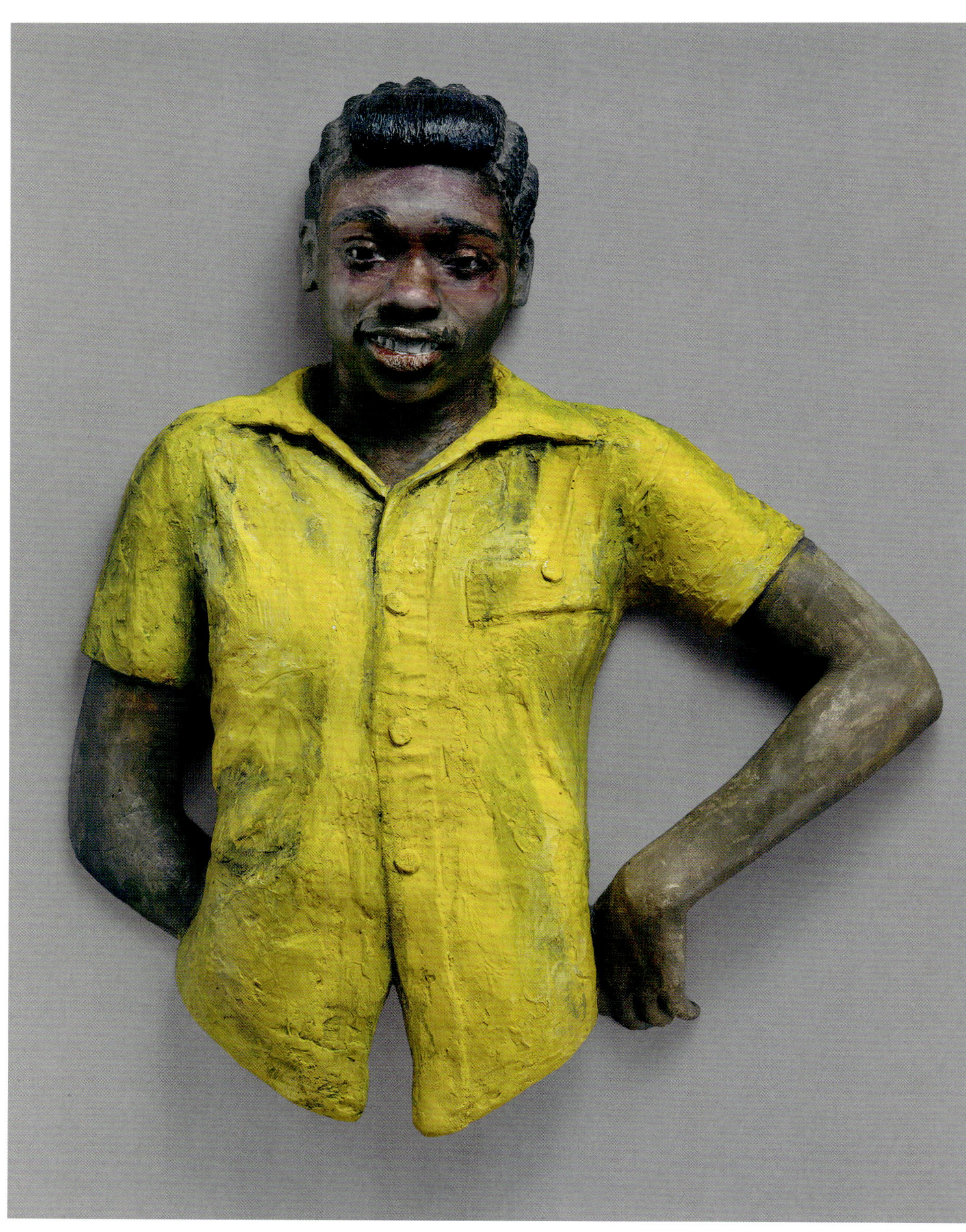

28. John Ahearn. *Bernice*, 1981. Plaster and paint, H. 28 ½ in. (72.4 cm), W. 27 in. (68.6 cm), D. 6 in. (15.2 cm). The Metropolitan Museum of Art, New York, Gift of Barbara and Eugene Schwartz, 1988 (1988.417.4)

29. George Segal. *Meyer Schapiro*, 1977. Plaster and paint, H. 37 ⅞ in. (96.2 cm), W. 26 in. (66 cm), D. 12 in. (30.5 cm). The Metropolitan Museum of Art, New York, Gift of Paul Jenkins, 1981 (1981.146)

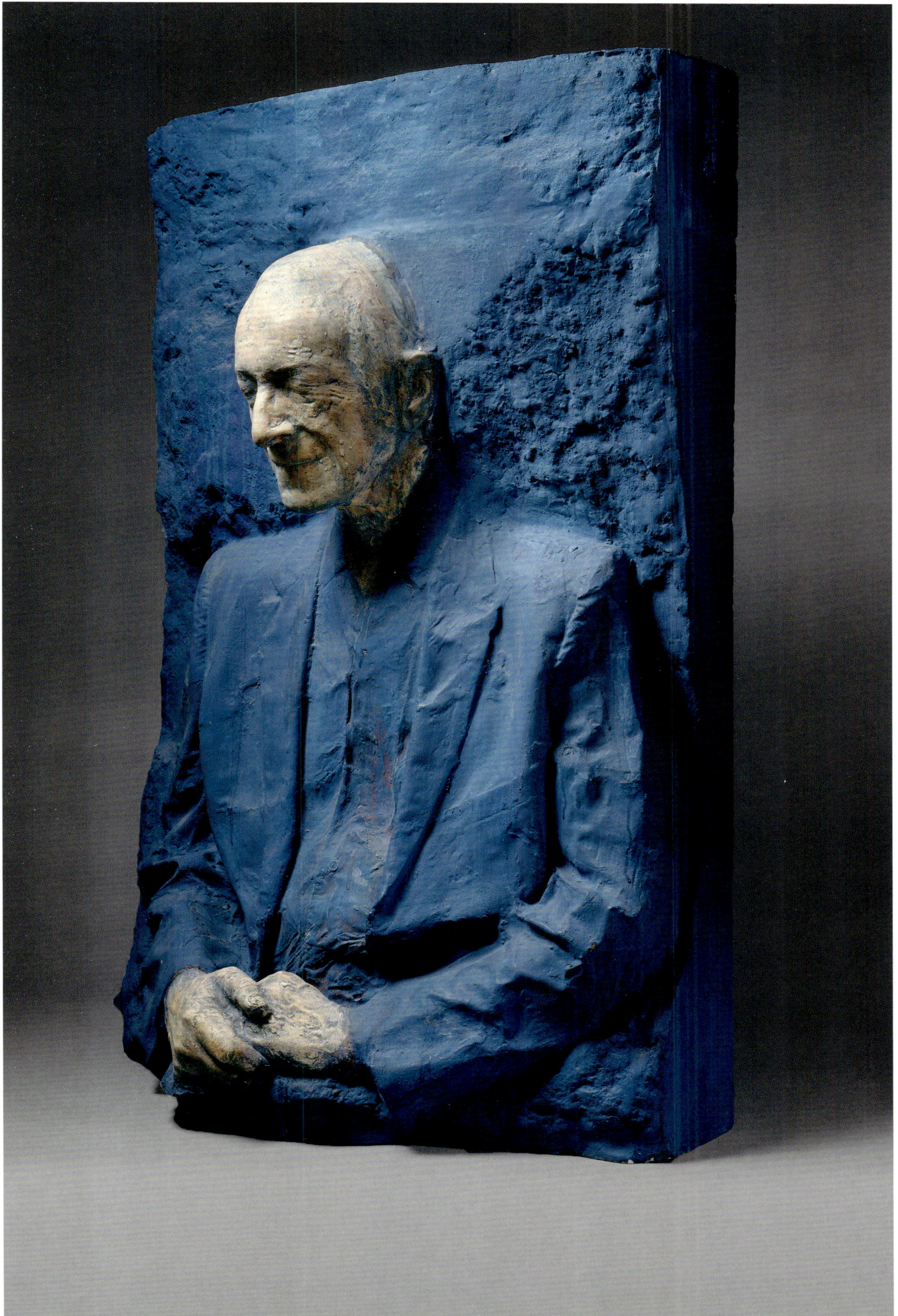

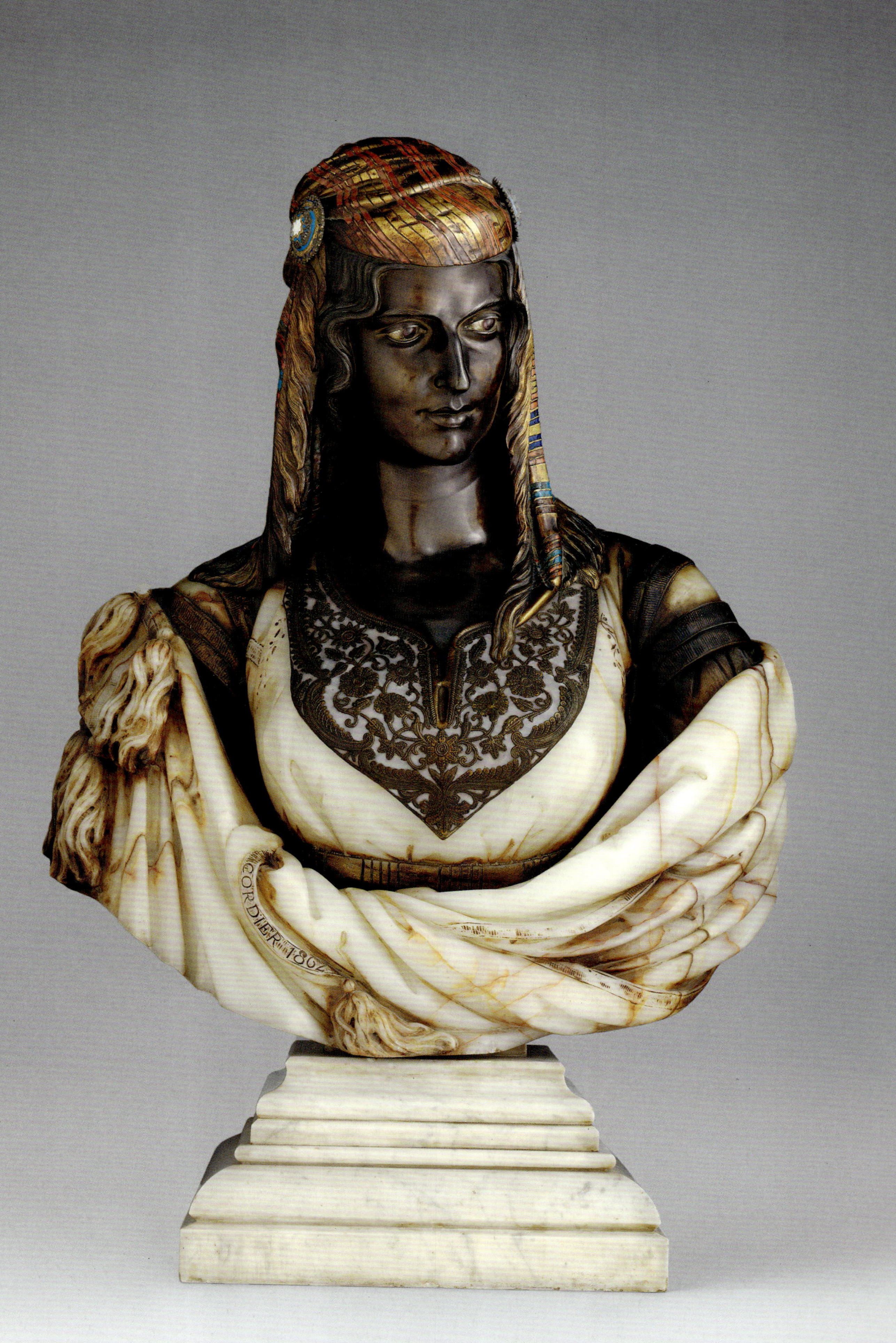

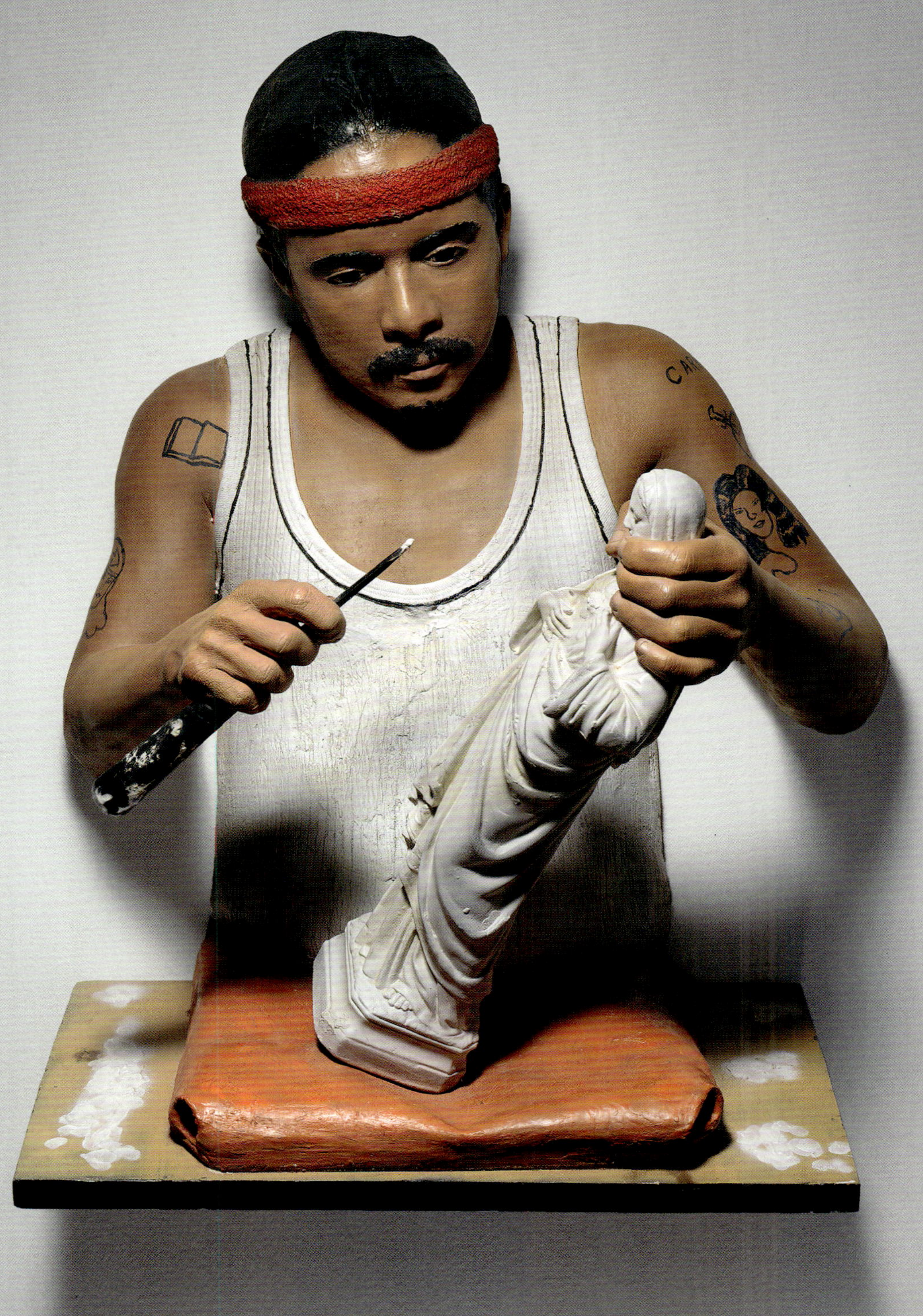

30. Charles-Henri-Joseph Cordier. *The Jewish Woman of Algiers*, 1862. Algerian onyx-marble, bronze, gilt bronze, enamel, amethyst, and white marble, with socle: H. 35 ½ in. (90.2 cm), W. 25 ¼ in. (64.1 cm), D. 13 ¾ in. (34.9 cm). The Metropolitan Museum of Art, New York, European Sculpture and Decorative Arts Fund, 2006 (2006.113a–c)

31. Rigoberto Torres. *Shorty Working in the C&R Statuary Corp.*, 1985. Acrylic on plaster, H. 29 in. (73.7 cm), W. 24 in. (61 cm), D. 11 ½ in. (29.2 cm). El Museo del Barrio, New York, Gift of John Ahearn, 2014

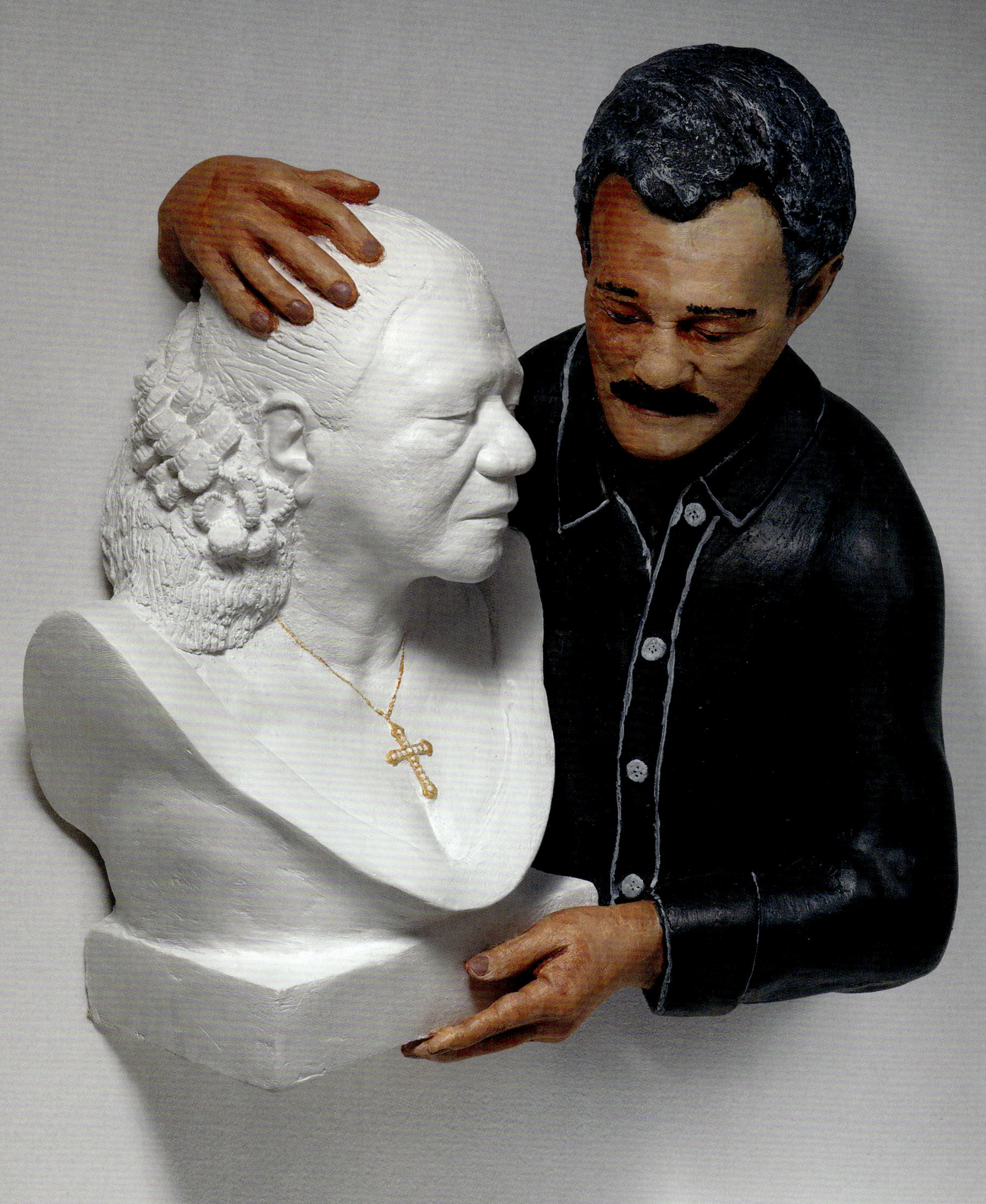

32. Rigoberto Torres. *Raúl with Bust of Ruth Fernández*, 1998. Acrylic on plaster, H. 28 in. (71.1 cm), W. 28 in. (71.1 cm), D. 12 in. (30.5 cm). El Museo del Barrio, New York, Gift of John Ahearn, 2014

33. Charles-Henri-Joseph Cordier. *La Capresse des Colonies*, 1861. Algerian onyx-marble, bronze, gilt bronze, enamel, and white marble, with socle: H. 37 ¾ in. (95.9 cm), W. 23 ¼ in. (59.1 cm), D. 12 ¼ in. (31.1 cm). The Metropolitan Museum of Art, New York, European Sculpture and Decorative Arts Fund, 2006 (2006.112a–c)

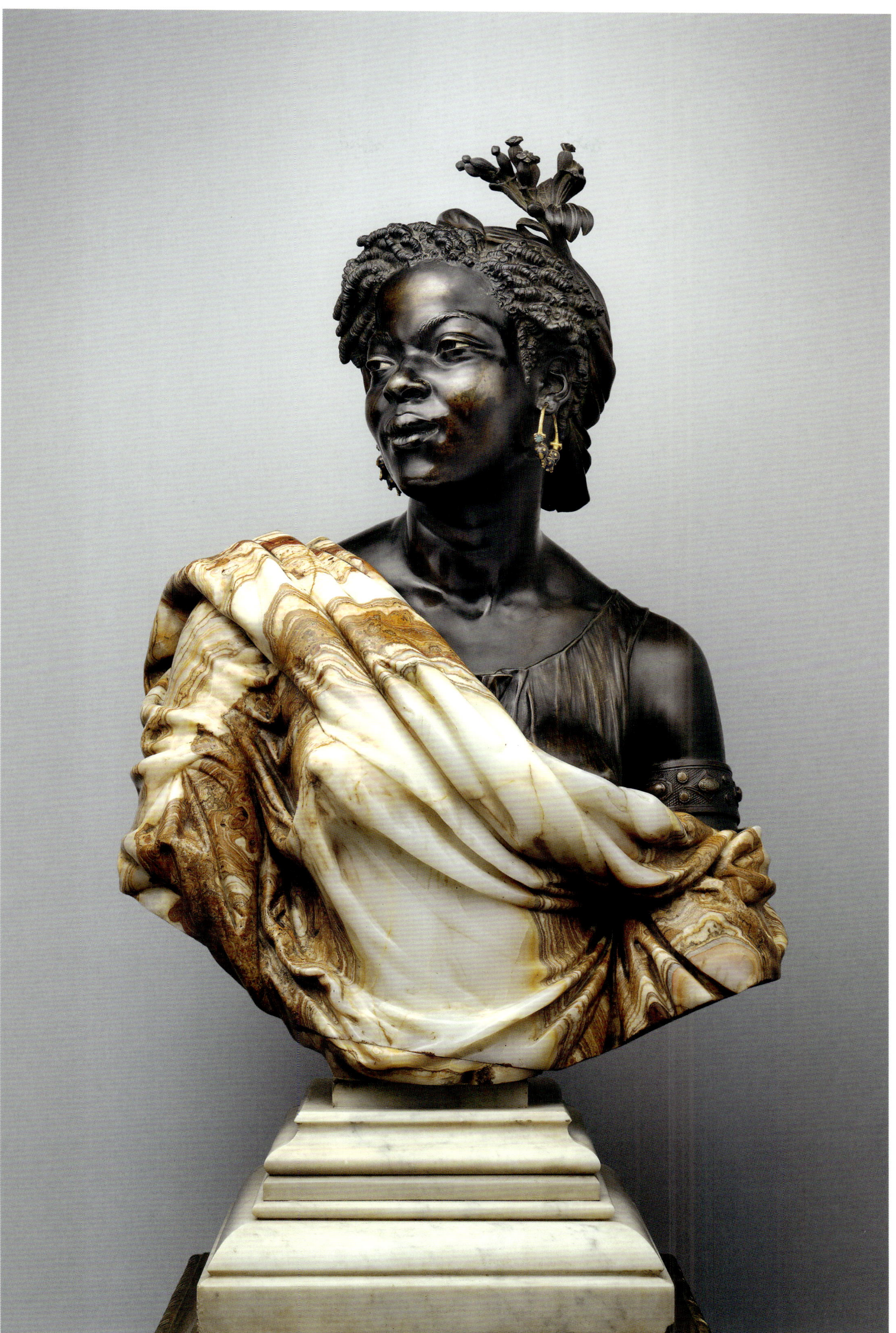

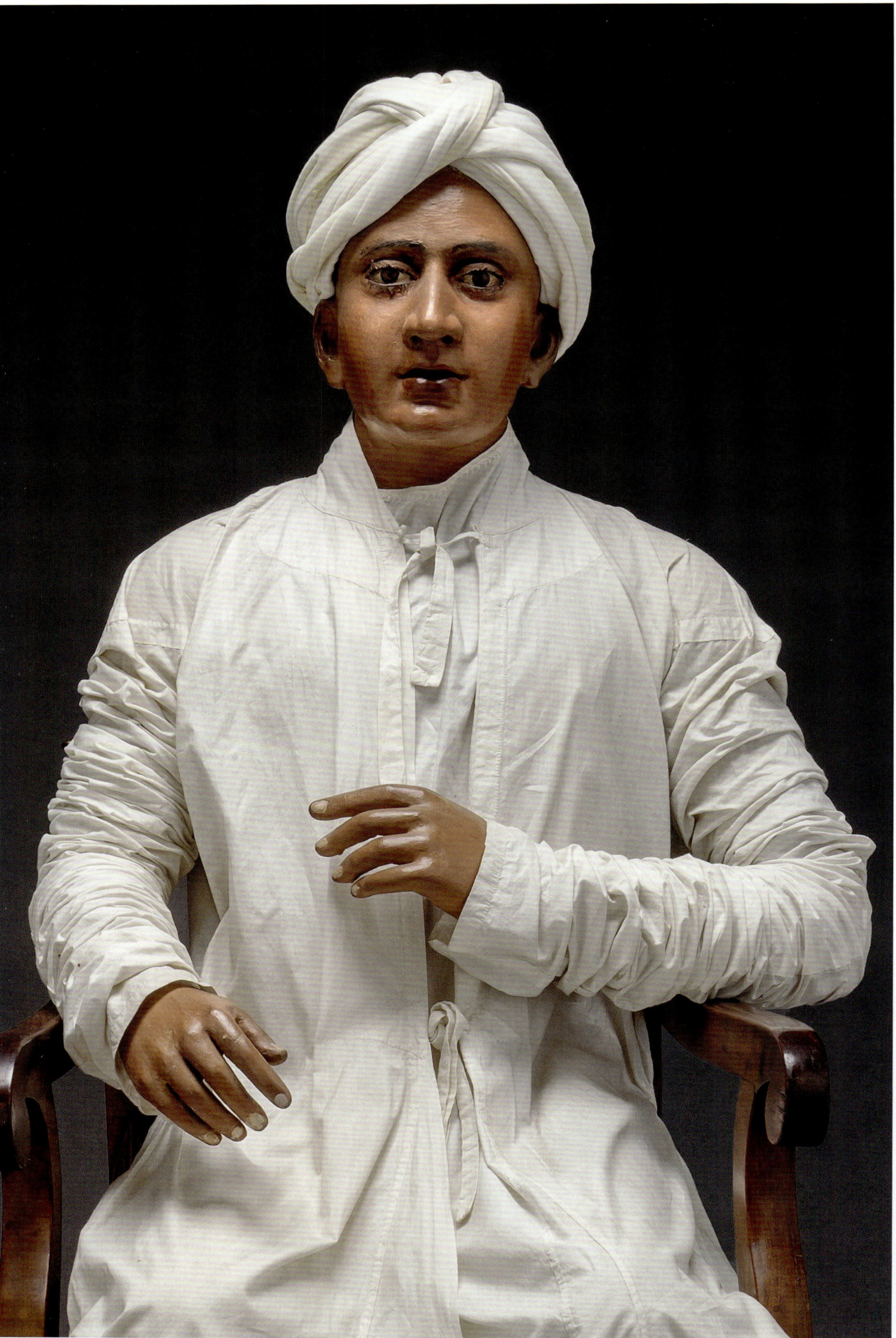

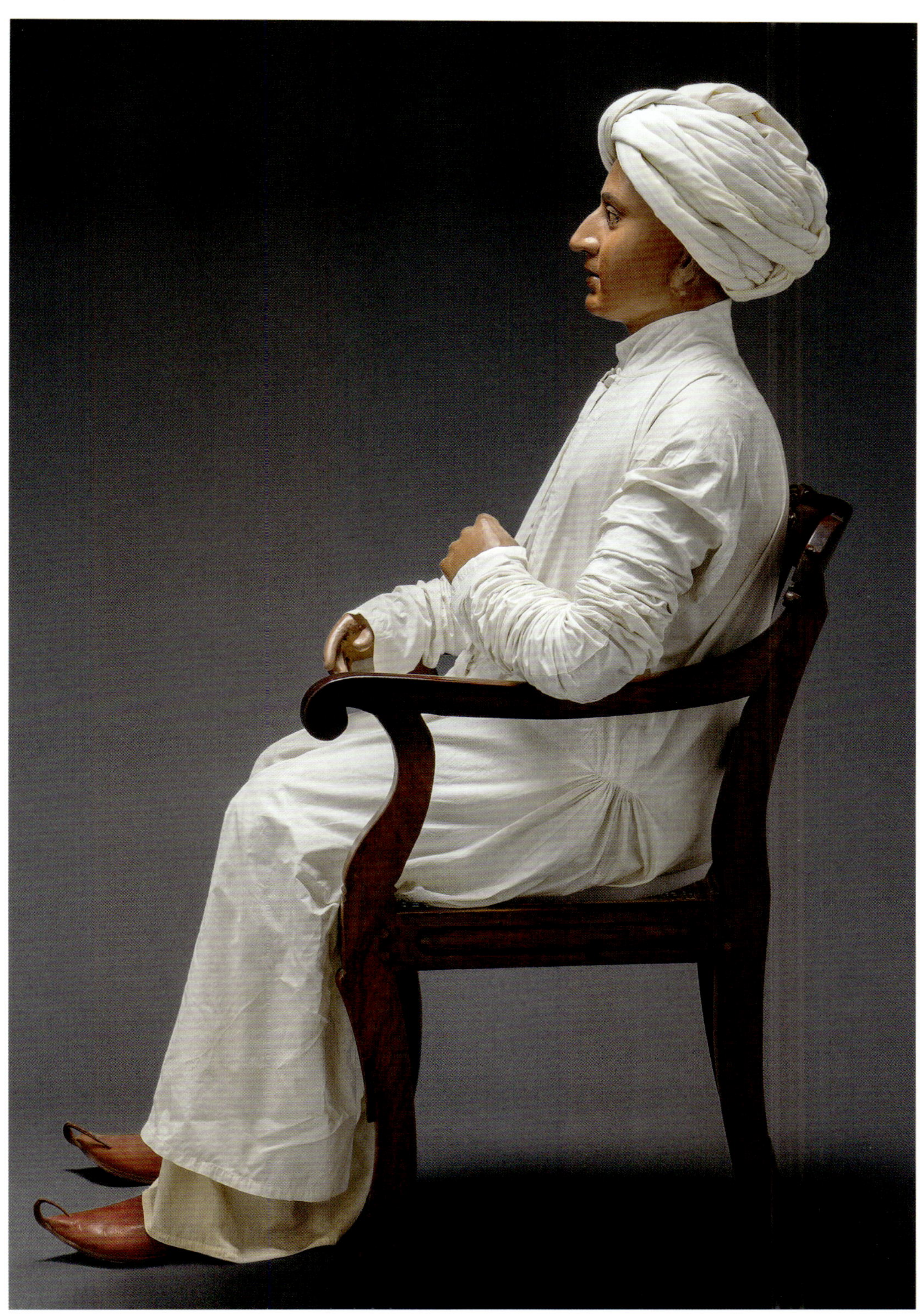

34. Attributed to Sri Ram Pal. *Raj Kissen Mitter*, ca. 1840. Unfired clay, pigments, cotton over bamboo, and straw, H. 48 in. (121.9 cm), W. 18 in. (45.7 cm), D. 29 in. (73.7 cm). Peabody Essex Museum, Salem, Massachusetts, Gift of John A. Parker, 1840

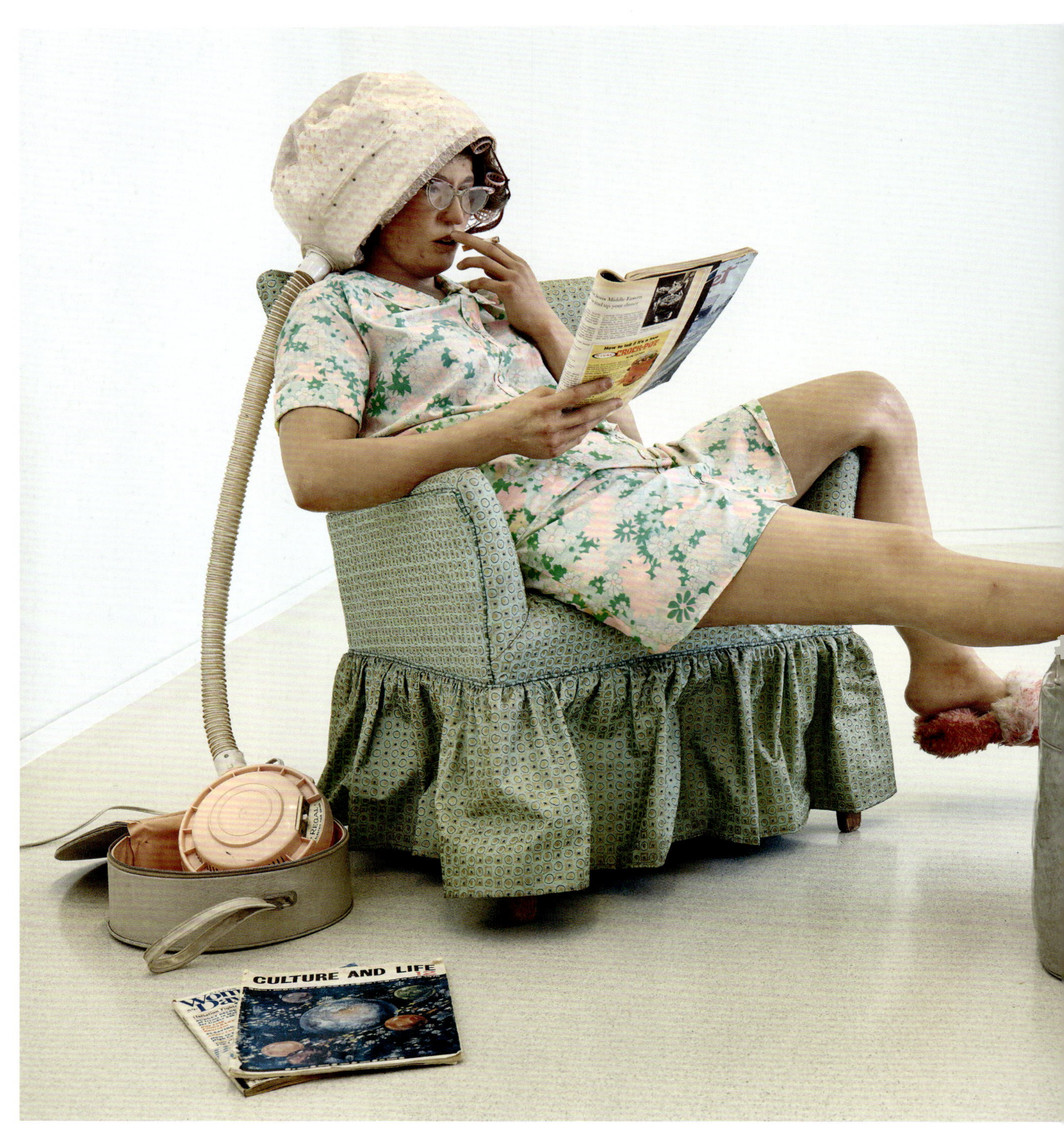

35. Duane Hanson. *Housewife*, 1969–70. Polyester, resin, fiberglass, oil, mixed media, and accessories, H. 44 in. (111.7 cm), W. 35 in. (88.9 cm), D. 61 in. (155 cm). Astrup Fearnley Collection, Oslo

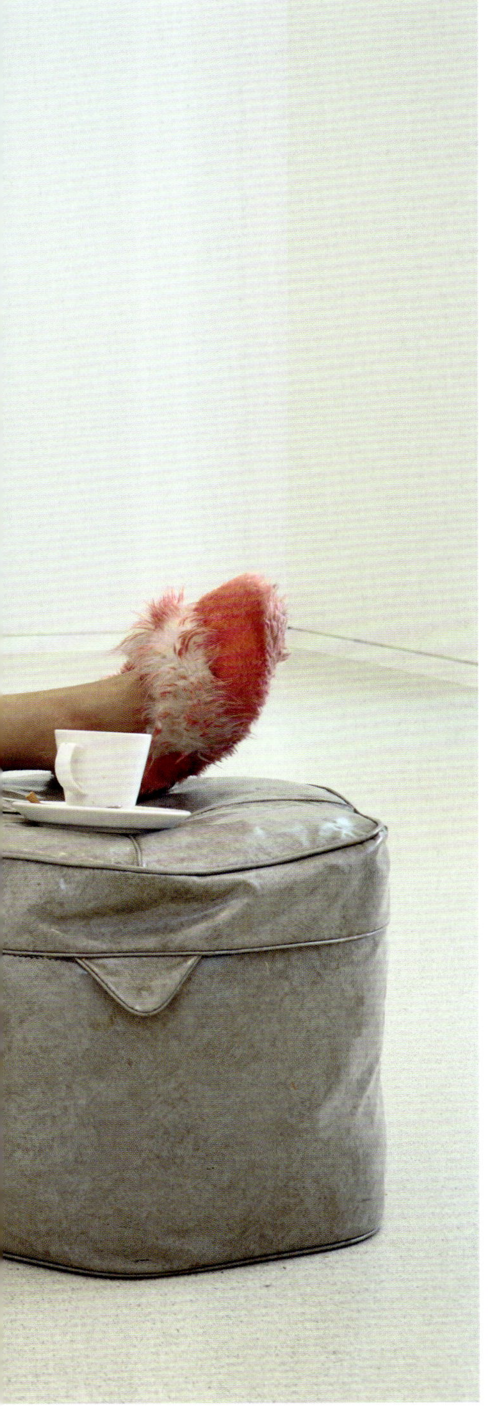

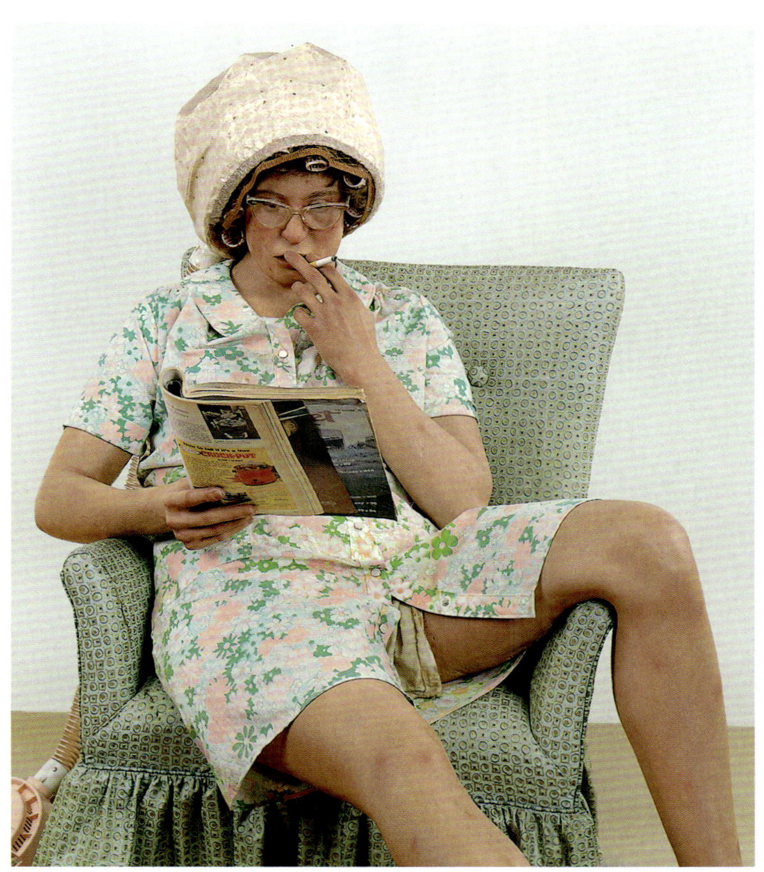

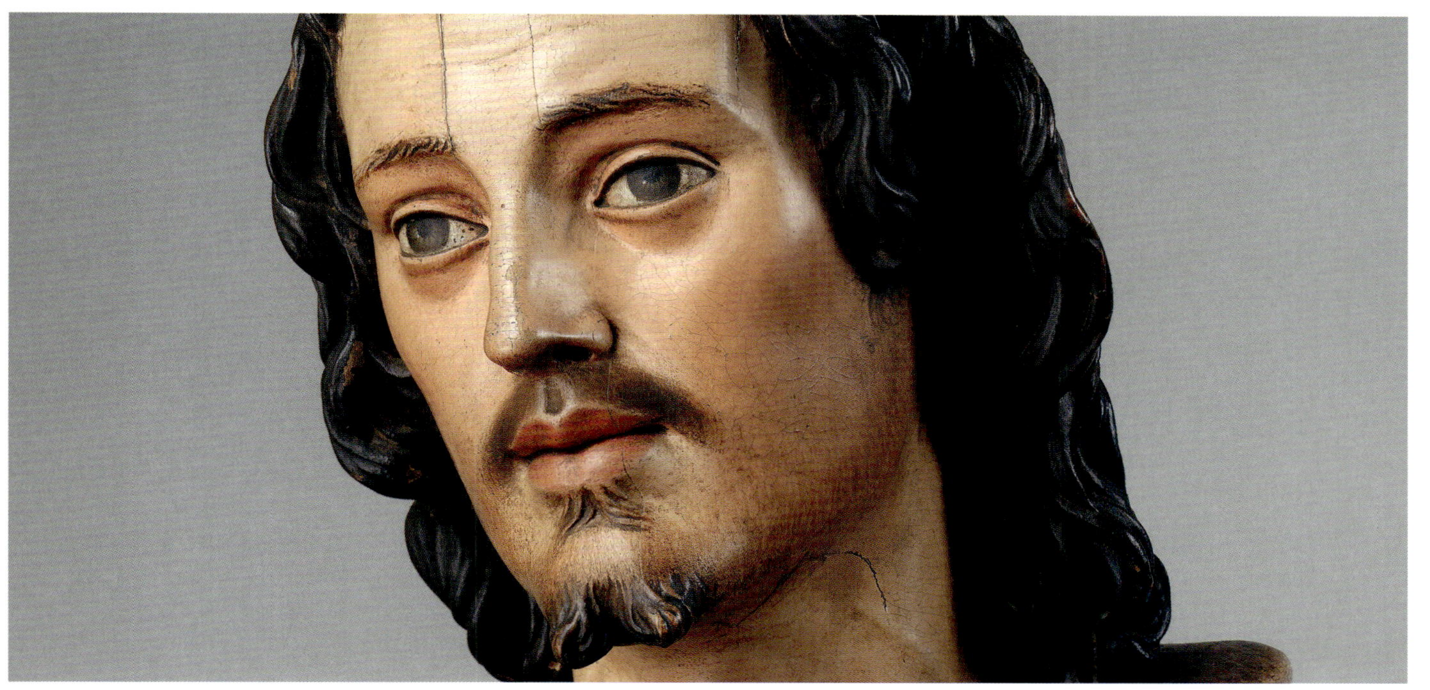

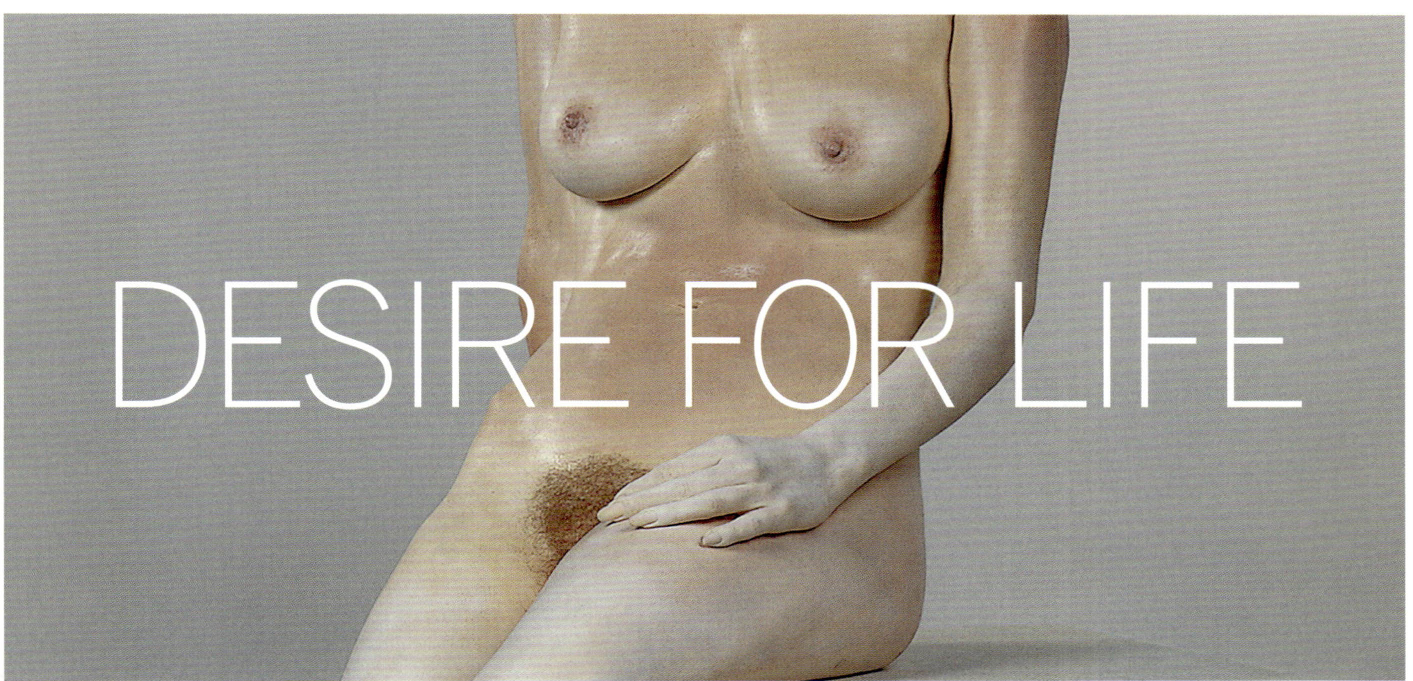
DESIRE FOR LIFE

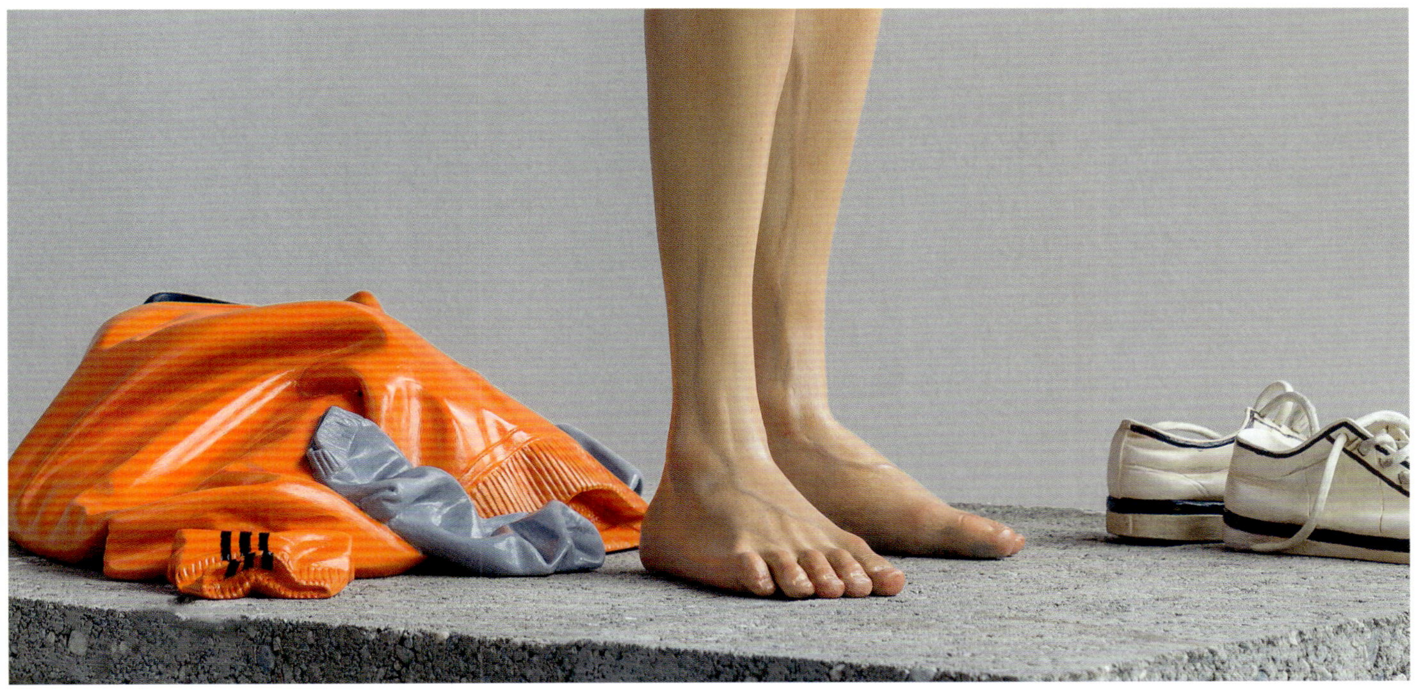

DESIRE FOR LIFE

EMERSON BOWYER

In 1986, American photographer Sheila Metzner produced a striking image for a Fendi fragrance advertisement (fig. 59). Simultaneously intimate and unsettlingly alien, it pictures a luxuriously clad model leaning in to kiss a marble bust. In contravention of museum propriety, fur and flesh press against stone, and in apparent contradiction of all rational behavior, a living person seeks the attention of an inanimate object. Statues are supposed to stand inert in space—senseless, bloodless things to be looked at but not touched. Here, however, a crafty camera angle suggests the impossible: a carved head has turned and lowered a little toward the model, awakening from its marmoreal slumber. The saturated colors of Metzner's print enhance the weathered surface of the marble, providing the impression of transformation toward flesh. Appropriately, the bust represents the Roman Emperor Hadrian's young lover Antinous in the guise of Bacchus. Yet the god is intoxicated not by wine but rather by the mysterious power of Fendi's pungent commodity, which has seemingly stirred a long-dormant desire for love and life.

Western culture is replete with tales of statues that come to life. In the Greco-Roman world, many believed that humankind began as inanimate sculpture. According to the ancient Greek writer Lucian, for example, it was the Titan Prometheus who created the first men and women from fistfuls of damp earth. "At a time when human beings did not exist," Lucian explained, "Prometheus conceived and fashioned them; he moulded and elaborated certain living things into agility and beauty; he was practically their creator, though [the goddess] Athene assisted by putting breath into the clay and bringing the models to life."[1] This myth is illustrated in a third-century Roman relief, where Prometheus sits at a sculptor's stand, having just completed one of a series of clay statues (fig. 60). At the left stands Athena, who imbues the sculptures with living souls.

Other versions cast Prometheus in the dual role of sculptor-enlivener: with fire stolen from the god Zeus, he awakened his creations.[2] Early Christian writers worked diligently to undermine the role of Prometheus as creator of humankind. The pagan story conflicted with the biblical teaching, which specifies that God "formed man of the slime of the earth and breathed into his face the breath of life; and man became a living soul." Prometheus, it was claimed, was merely the first mortal sculptor, the deficient imitator of God.[3] This effectively meant that he was the first creator of idols:

> And [Prometheus] indeed was the inventor of earthenware images. But posterity, following him, both carved them out of marble, and moulded them out of bronze; then in process of time ornament was added of gold and ivory, so that not only the likenesses, but also the gleam itself, might dazzle the eyes. Thus ensnared by beauty, and forgetful of true majesty, sensible beings considered that insensible objects, rational beings that irrational objects, living beings that lifeless objects, were to be worshipped and reverenced by them.[4]

For the Christian church, sculpture posed more problems than any other visual media. As anthropomorphic, thoroughly material objects, religious statues lent themselves more easily to imaginative, affective, and phenomenological relationships with worshippers.[5] This was useful, some argued, because the statues functioned as effective educational tools that made abstract theology tangible and relatable for the uneducated. The development of more naturalistic representations of saints and other holy figures—especially through polychromy—provided statues with heightened presence. The late Gothic German sculpture *Saint Barbara* (ca. 1490, cat. 43), for example, is carved in an elegant, asymmetrical pose that suggests bodily movement. Her painted flesh simulates a pale, Northern European complexion, touched by the blush of vitality, and her richly colored clothing is

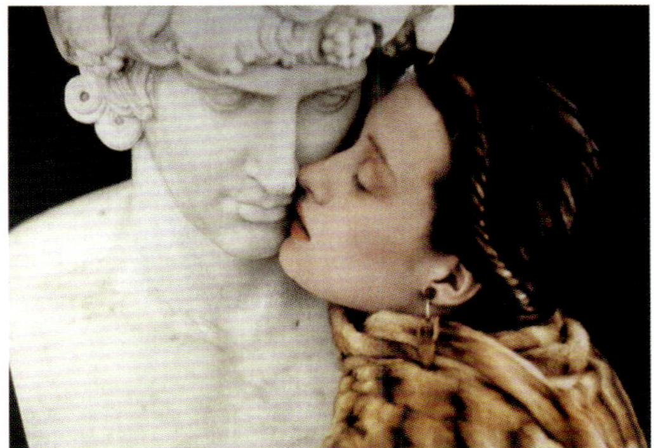

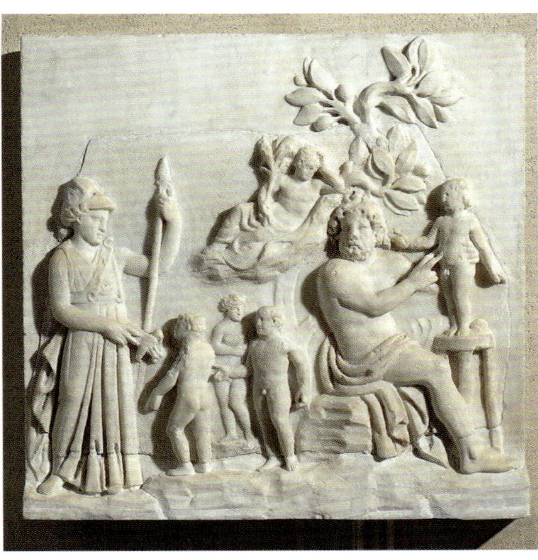

contemporary in design. These elements, combined with her three-dimensionality, concretize the appearance and personality of the saint.

Statuary also became a crucial focus for deeply empathic, emotional prayer, especially sculptures that depict the suffering Christ. Such works inspired new, ever-greater feats of realism in their desire to move the beholder. Perhaps the apogee of this trend is found in seventeenth-century Spanish sculpture. Gregorio Fernández's *Dead Christ* (1625–30, cat. 111) is a masterpiece of the genre. Here, shockingly, the viewer is confronted by the uncompromising reality of death. Laid out on a white sheet, with his head on an embroidered pillow, is a Christ whose life seems to have just been extinguished. Awkwardly posed, the angular limbs suggest a body that had twisted in torment. Blood streams from open wounds, as well as from his bruised and grazed knees. Furthering the body's extreme realism are eyes made from glass, and fingernails crafted from the horn of a bull. Still powerful today, this kind of sculpture could not help but provoke strong emotions from devout seventeenth-century worshippers, who were cast in the role of mourners. Here, paradoxically, the sculpture is "animated," but as a seemingly tangible, literal corpse. Italian artist Maurizio Cattelan's *Now* (2004, cat. 112) revisits this idea of hyperreal death. First exhibited in Paris at the Chapel of the Petits-Augustins in 2004, the sculpture is a lifesize wax effigy of U.S. President John F. Kennedy lying in a coffin. The very title of the work encapsulates the disconcerting actuality of the corpse and its hallucinatory immediacy.

However, statuary always retained a whiff of the archaic, of the demon-inhabited idols worshipped by pagan cults. Tales of statues that bled, wept, and performed other miraculous activities only deepened their association with magic and the supernatural. There was always the danger of worshippers confusing the statue with what it represented and projecting life on to the inanimate sculpted object. Mexican artist Ángel Zárraga y Argüelles's early twentieth-century *Votive Offering (Saint Sebastian)* (ca. 1910–12, cat. 46) seems to play with this problem. Pictured is a young woman kneeling in prayer before the saint. However, it is entirely ambiguous whether the object of her attention is a painted statue like Spanish artist Alonso Berruguete's mid-sixteenth-century *Saint Sebastian* (cat. 44), a literal living body, or a mystical vision.

To worship the statue rather than what is represented was the essence of idolatry—one of the great evils perceived by Reformation thinkers in sixteenth-century Europe. Working during that period, German artist Lucas Cranach the Younger illustrated a cautionary tale from the Old Testament: *The Idolatry of Solomon* (ca. 1537, cat. 42). Here, King Solomon is shown kneeling before a pagan idol introduced to him by one of his foreign wives. Rather pointedly, Cranach envisaged the idol as a polychrome statue, not unlike *Saint Barbara*. However, the statue is given a darker complexion to emphasize her exotic character. Dangerous, blasphemous feminine idols like the one worshipped by Solomon became the femmes fatales of fin-de-siècle Europe. At that time, many sculptors produced literal, three-dimensional idols that hovered ambiguously between life and death and, Medusa-like, stupefied men with their gazes, such as Paul Gauguin's *Eve* (1890, cat. 49) and Max Klinger's *New Salome* (1893–1903, cat. 47).

There are many historical accounts of the slippage between representation and real life, most often when statues are the focus of prolonged prayerful attention. In 1127, for example, Benedictine theologian Rupert of Deutz described an experience from his early life that was prompted by his worship before a sculpted crucifix on an altar:

> When I had most diligently gazed at it, I knew him to be the Lord Jesus himself, crucified and living, having his eyes open upon me....I was not satisfied unless I might seize him with my hands, and I might kiss affectionately the embraced one. But what could I do? He was too high on the altar for me to reach. But as he saw this thought or desire of mine, he, too, desired it for himself. I sensed indeed that he desired it, and at the nod of his will, the altar opened in the middle and received me running inside it. When I had quickly entered, I seized him...I held him, I embraced him, and I kissed him for a long while. I sensed how joyfully he received this gesture of love, since as he was being kissed he opened his mouth, that I might kiss him more deeply.[6]

While this strange and vivid account is typically described as a "vision," that word seems utterly incapable of encompassing Rupert's intense multisensory experience before the sculpture. It recalls the extraordinary painted statues of Christ with articulated limbs that populated churches throughout the medieval and Renaissance periods (*Corpus with Movable Arms*, 1500–1510, cat. 55). These figures could literally be detached from a cross, laid out horizontally among congregations, and buried in sepulchers. They were cleaned, caressed, and kissed by worshippers, and their movable limbs offered the possibility of active physical embrace.

Rupert's account is clear about the role of desire in the imaginative animation of statuary and of the frankly erotic elements of that desire. His narrative teeters on the edge of untrammeled sexual longing. The often beautiful, materially and visually available bodies of hypermimetic polychrome Madonnas, Christs, and Saint Sebastians always carried the possibility of illicit engagement. Berruguete's *Saint Sebastian*, for example, presents an Apollonian youth, nude except for a shimmering gilt loincloth (partly real fabric) that clings to his thighs. Flawless pink skin is marred only by the penetrative arrow wounds that appear to trickle blood in real time. The depiction of Saint Sebastian's twisting against the real rope binding him to the tree trunk makes it easy to imagine the potential for this body's animation within the flickering depths of a candlelit church.

This intersection of pain, desire, and lifelike statuary is echoed in Reza Aramesh's Action sculptures.

These polychrome limewood figures, like their Catholic predecessors, combine skillful carving with carefully painted surfaces, and even glass eyes to produce hypermimetic three-dimensional bodies. Aramesh's imagery is drawn from media coverage of international conflicts. Victims of war and political violence are excised from their immediate contexts and redisplayed as freestanding statues. *Action 105* (2017, cat. 45) presents a youth stripped down to his undergarments. With hands behind his back, he recalls images of the bound Christ, or of Christian martyrs, such as Saint Sebastian. A powerfully immediate evocation of fear and suffering, the figure is also, perhaps uncomfortably, an object of desire. Standing atop a concrete plinth, this less than lifesize, tabletop human invites possessive tactile and visual engagement.

Perhaps the ur-narrative of the desire for sculpture to become human is Ovid's saucy account of the Cypriot sculptor Pygmalion. Disgusted "by the numerous defects / of character Nature had given the feminine spirit," Pygmalion carves an ivory statue depicting his ideal woman, with which he falls in love.[7] The peculiar combination of artistic ability and Narcissus-like sexual desire for his own creation leads to confusion about the object's status: "Often he stretched forth a hand to touch his creation, / attempting to settle the issue—*was* it a body, / or was it—this he would not yet concede—a mere statue?"[8] The sculptor kisses and caresses his statue, presents it with a lover's gifts, adorns it with precious jewelry, and takes it to bed with him. During the festival of Venus, Pygmalion makes a sacrifice to the goddess, praying that she grant him a wife like his statue. Venus knows very well that he wants the statue itself as his wife and grants his unspoken wish:

> Once home, he went straight to the replica
>   of his sweetheart,
> threw himself down on the couch and repeatedly
>   kissed her;
> she seemed to grow warm and so he repeated the action,
>   kissing her lips and exciting her breasts with both hands.
> Aroused, the ivory softened and, losing its stiffness,
>   yielded, submitting to his caress as wax softens
>   when it is warmed by the sun, and handled by fingers,
>   takes on many forms, and by being used, becomes
>   useful.
> Amazed, he rejoices, then doubts, then fears he's
>   mistaken, while again and again he touches on what
>   he has prayed for.
> She is alive! And her veins leap under his fingers![9]

Beginning in the Renaissance, the story of Pygmalion gained notoriety as a metanarrative of

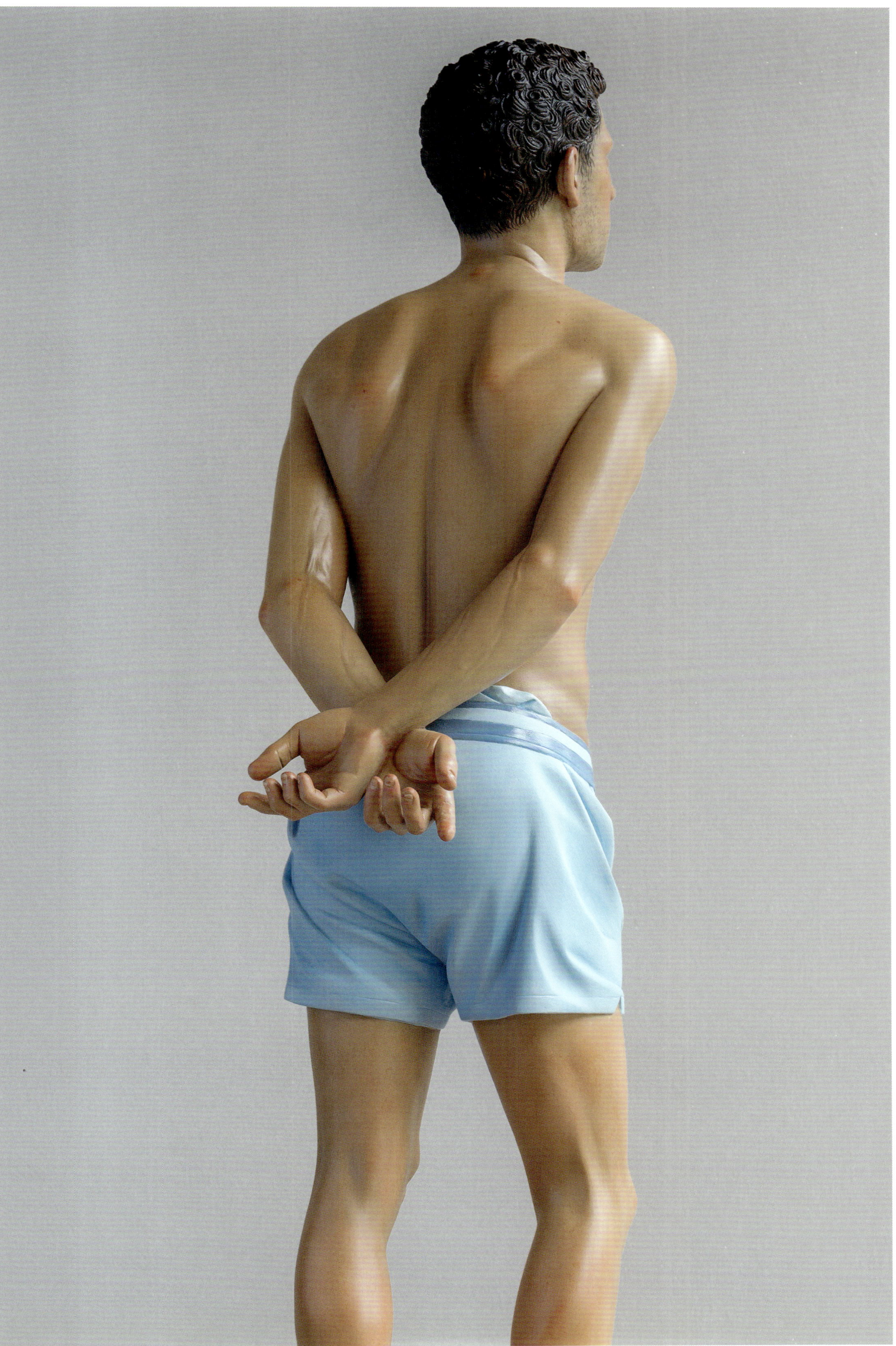

artistic creation.[10] By the nineteenth century, Venus's divine agency had been minimized, and Ovid's tale was understood more specifically as a celebration of a great sculptor's ability to create the illusion of life. Take, for example, French artist Jean-Léon Gérôme's *Pygmalion and Galatea* (ca. 1890, cat. 36), which pictures the moment of transformation in an almost shockingly indecorous manner. The object of the sculptor's desire has begun to mutate, the top half of her body moving to embrace him while she progressively shifts from white stone to rosy flesh. As in Ovid's story, the painting presents two interrelated or mutually supportive forms of touch—one by the creator (see the hammer abandoned in the foreground) and the other by the passionate lover. The spectral presence of a mischievous Cupid in the background only reinforces the fact that it is the libidinal (male) artist who creates life.

Gérôme's *Pygmalion and Galatea* is a kind of self-portrait, one that celebrates his sculptural prowess. However, for him it was ultimately the application of painted color that brought a sculpture to life. Perhaps the most visible proponent of polychromy in the late nineteenth century, Gérôme titled one of his pictures *Painting Breathes Life into Sculpture (Sculpturae Vitam Insufflat Pictura*, 1893).[11] This maxim is illustrated in a self-portrait of the artist painting his 1901 polychromed sculpture *The Ball Player* (cat. 38). Here, Gérôme seems to have played the role allotted to Venus in Ovid's tale, his paintbrush producing the wondrous metamorphosis from stone to flesh; to heighten the effect, the sculpture is positioned so that it appears the figure has awakened and turned to look down on the artist's progress. This scenario is repeated in American artist John De Andrea's hyperrealist *Self-Portrait with Sculpture* (1980, cat. 37). Having seemingly paused from his work, the sculptor gazes on his creation. Like Gérôme's *Galatea*, she is caught midtransformation, the bottom half of her figure as yet unpainted. De Andrea's figures are cast from life—it is the application of the painted surface that reanimates the figures. "I've always believed in the real thing," noted the artist with more than an echo of Gérôme, "if I could make it breathe I'd say I've done a good day's work."[12]

The notion of the breathing statue was literalized in the late eighteenth century with Swiss waxwork modeler Philippe Curtius's *Sleeping Beauty* (1765, cat. 113). Often considered the oldest waxwork composition in Madame Tussauds's London museum, the lifesize woman lies sprawled on a divan, deep in slumber. An ingenious internal clockwork mechanism (electrified since the early twentieth century) simulates the rise and fall of her sleeping chest. Combined with the extreme realism of tinted wax, a wig, and real clothing, the mechanized body seems poised on the thresholds between art and life, unconsciousness and awareness. Like Pygmalion's beloved statue, which he could not quite admit was mere stone, *Sleeping Beauty* is a passive object of desire, the forerunner of today's hyperreal sex dolls. "Such a sculpture," cultural historian Marina Warner has memorably described, "conveys a seductive vision of erotic, feminine catalepsy, which the peculiar translucence and slight sweatiness of the wax medium suit so creepily."[13]

With her clockwork chest, *Sleeping Beauty* also reflects the early modern fascination with mechanized bodies. Automata, or self-moving machines, had been produced as entertainment since antiquity. During the eighteenth century, however, they reached new heights of realism in their simulation of human bodies—both in their external appearance and in their internal mechanics. While remaining objects of pleasure, they also participated in Enlightenment debates concerning the relationship between living bodies and machines.[14] A progenitor of this discourse was René Descartes, the French philosopher who wrote that the human body is "nothing but a statue or machine made of earth," formed by God to resemble him as closely as possible.[15] For the eighteenth-century French philosopher Julien Offray de La Mettrie, the human body was essentially a self-winding clock, perpetually in motion. "Let us conclude boldly," he exclaimed, "that man is a machine."[16] This was tested by inventive clockmakers of the period, who created series of humanoid automata. These exquisitely finished objects simulated not merely the external appearance of the human body, but also its internal physiological processes. In the late 1730s, French inventor Jacques de Vaucanson, for example, produced a flute player whose "lungs" actually blew air via a varied embouchure into a real instrument, while spritely fingers played the notes.[17] Another well-known example is the Swiss watchmaker Henri Louis Jaquet-Droz's *The Draftsman* (1774, fig. 61), a young boy who sits at a table and produces drawings of landscapes and other subjects. *The Draftsman* and other similar automata raised the simultaneously thrilling and frightening possibility that human bodily processes, and even creativity itself, might be mechanized and artificially produced.

As new technologies developed during the nineteenth century, so too did (predominantly male)

fantasies of sculpture that comes to life. French
Symbolist writer Auguste Villiers de l'Isle-Adam's
infamous novel *The Future Eve* (1886) combined
recent electromagnetic and phonographic research
with the darker impulses of the Pygmalion myth.[18]
The author imagines a scenario where Thomas Alva
Edison invents the perfect robotic woman as a companion for his friend Lord Celian Ewald. In Pygma-
lionesque fashion, Ewald has become disgusted by
the supposed disparity between the beautiful body
and inferior mind of Alicia Clary, a singer whom
he loved. Named "Hadaly," the android is given the
outward appearance of the singer, while her internal physiognomy is rewired—replaced by electric
circuitry. Her intellect is reduced to the repetition
of phrases written by novelists and poets, which the
singer had read aloud and recorded on two golden
phonographs that function as Hadaly's lungs. With
her soft synthetic flesh, real clothing, and smooth
movements, the android is mistaken for its human
model by Ewald. The simulacrum triumphs. "Here
indeed," wrote one reviewer of the novel, "positive
science provides you with the means to possess,
at least physically, *the woman of your dreams.*"[19] Of
course, as Villiers's Edison warns Ewald, the android
is neither dead nor alive; untouched by the processes
of aging, she will outlive her mortal love.

In *To the Son of Man Who Ate the Scroll* (2016,
cat. 51), Goshka Macuga imagines the posthuman
world that Villiers's Edison hints at. At first glance,
the speaking and gesticulating android seems uncan-
nily lifelike. Closer inspection reveals exposed metal
elbow joints and other evidence of its underlying
mechanical apparatus. This artificial man sits like

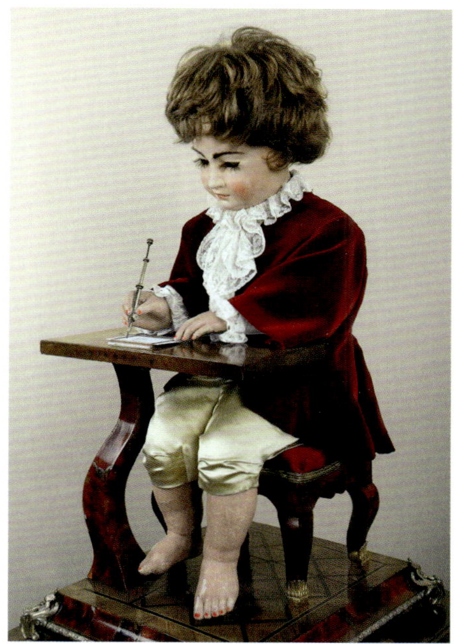

Fig. 61   Henri Louis Jaquet-Droz. *The Draftsman*, 1774.
H. 29 15/16 in. (76 cm), W. 15 11/16 in. (39.9 cm), D. 16 13/16 in.
(42.6 cm). Musée d'Art et d'Histoire, Neuchâtel

an ancient Greek philosopher, rehearsing a mono-
logue on life, death, and the cosmos. Like Villiers's
Hadaly, he is a recording or memory device, and his
oral utterances consist of famous speeches and writings from such disparate sources as the nineteenth-
century British author Mary Wollstonecraft Shelley
and the film *Blade Runner* (dir. Ridley Scott, 1982). *To
the Son of Man Who Ate the Scroll* provides an end of
sorts. Rather than evincing a desire for life, or a transformation from inanimate sculpture to the living
body, Macuga's android is resolutely nonhuman.
The successor to, or ghostly reminder of an extinct
humankind, it performs an elegy to human life.

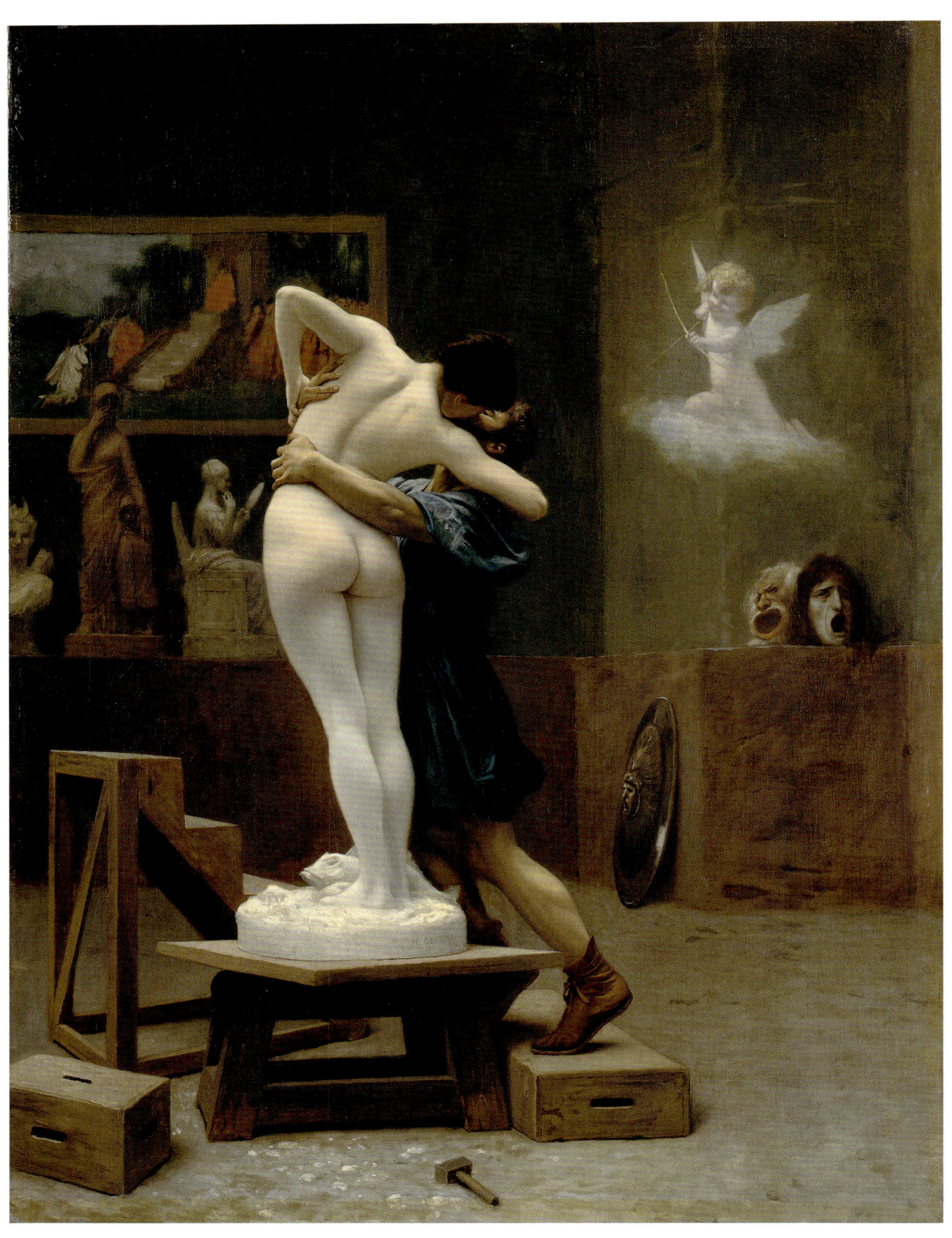

36. Jean-Léon Gérôme. *Pygmalion and Galatea*, ca. 1890. Oil on canvas, 35 × 27 in. (88.9 × 68.6 cm). The Metropolitan Museum of Art, New York, Gift of Louis C. Raegner, 1927 (27.200)

37. John De Andrea. *Self-Portrait with Sculpture*, 1980. Polyvinyl and oil paint, H. 62 in. (157.5 cm), W. 32 in. (81.3 cm), D. 62 in. (157.5 cm). Collection of Foster Goldstrom

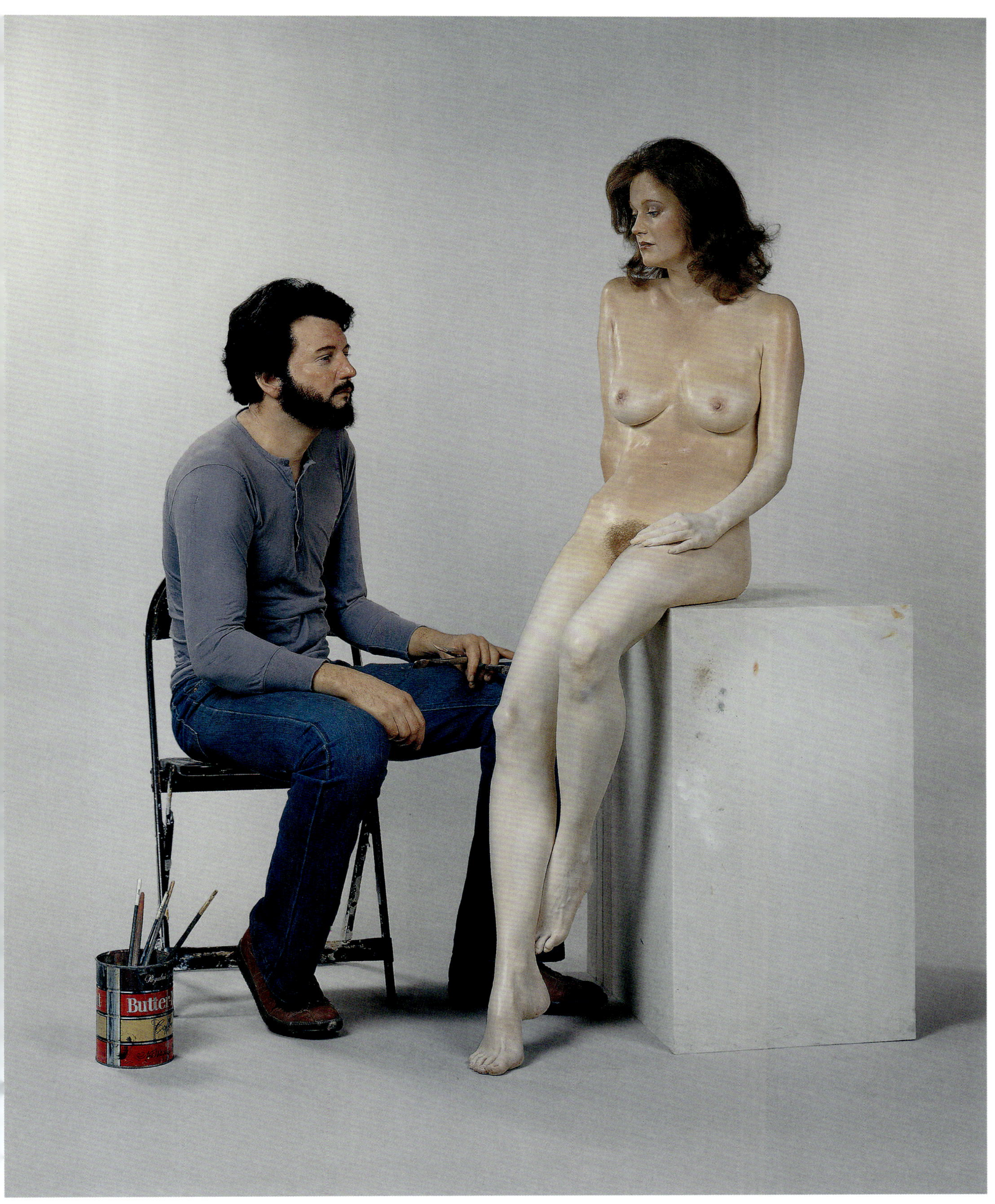

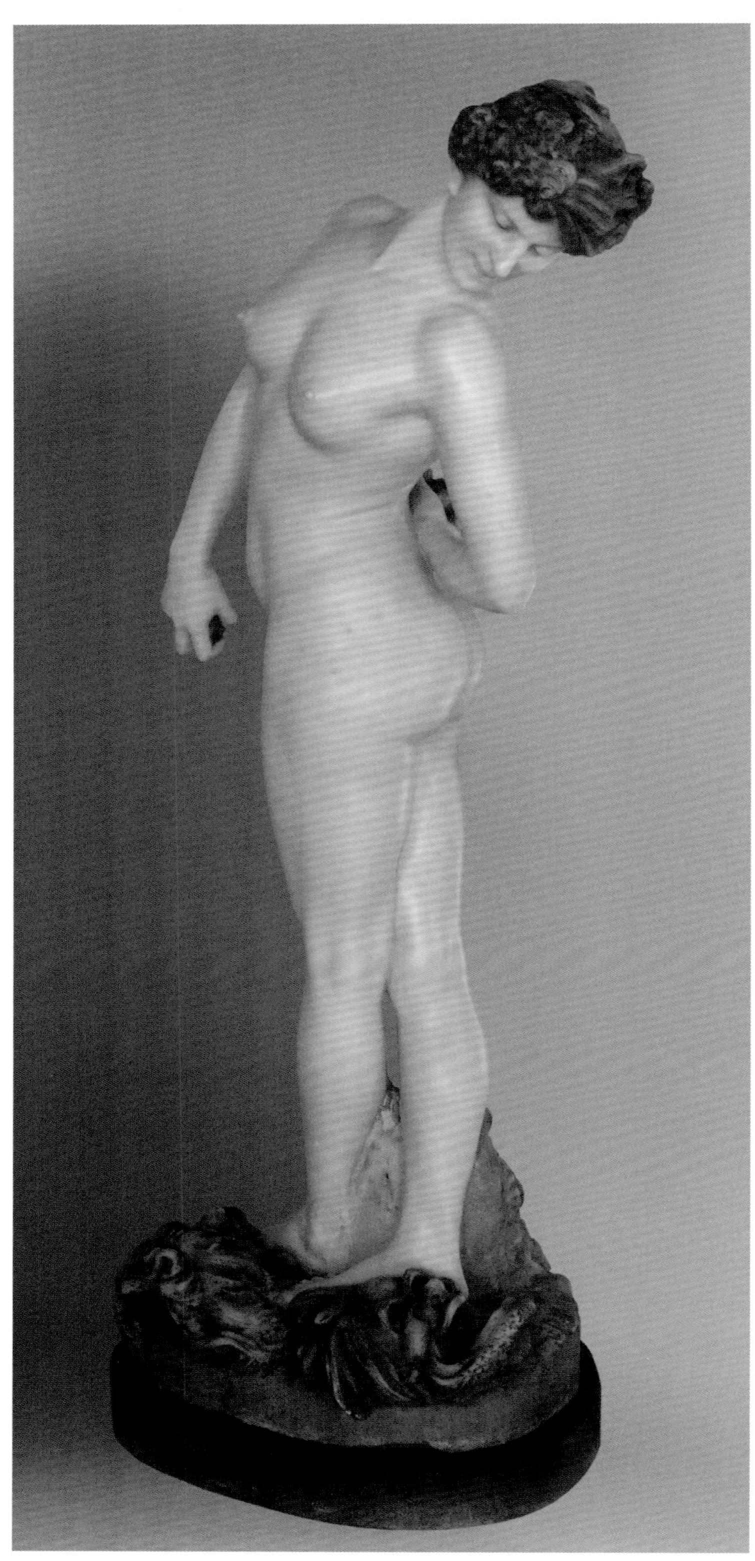

38. Jean-Léon Gérôme. *The Ball Player*, 1901. Polychromed marble, H. 65 ¾ in. (167 cm), W. 25 ½ in. (64.8 cm), D. 21 ½ in. (54.6 cm). Private collection

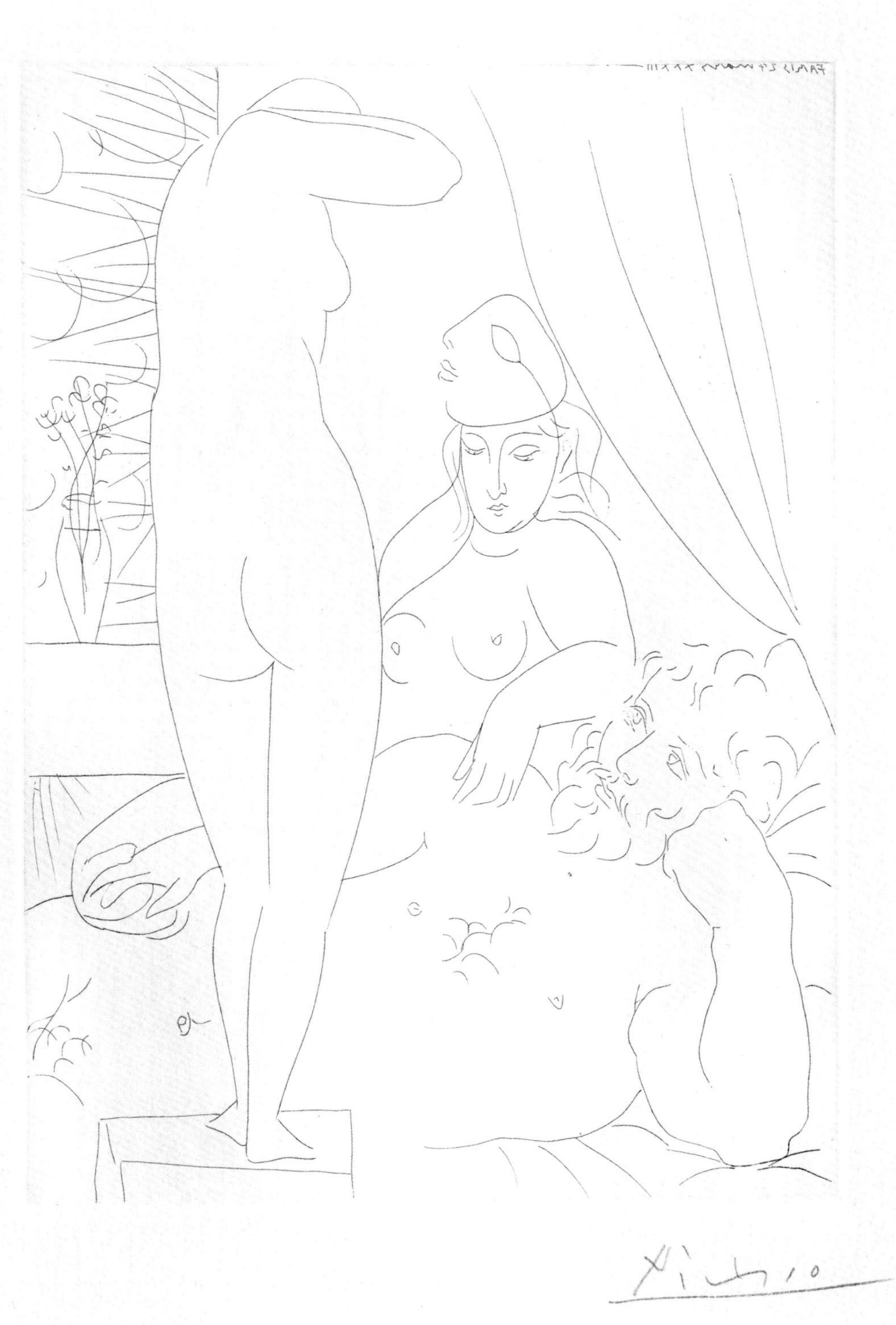

39. Pablo Picasso. Plates from the *Vollard Suite*. Etchings. Private collection
  A. *Reclining Sculptor and Model with Mask (Le Repos du Sculpteur et le Modèle au Masque)*,
plate 50, March 27, 1933. 10 ½ × 7 ⅝ in. (26.7 × 19.4 cm)

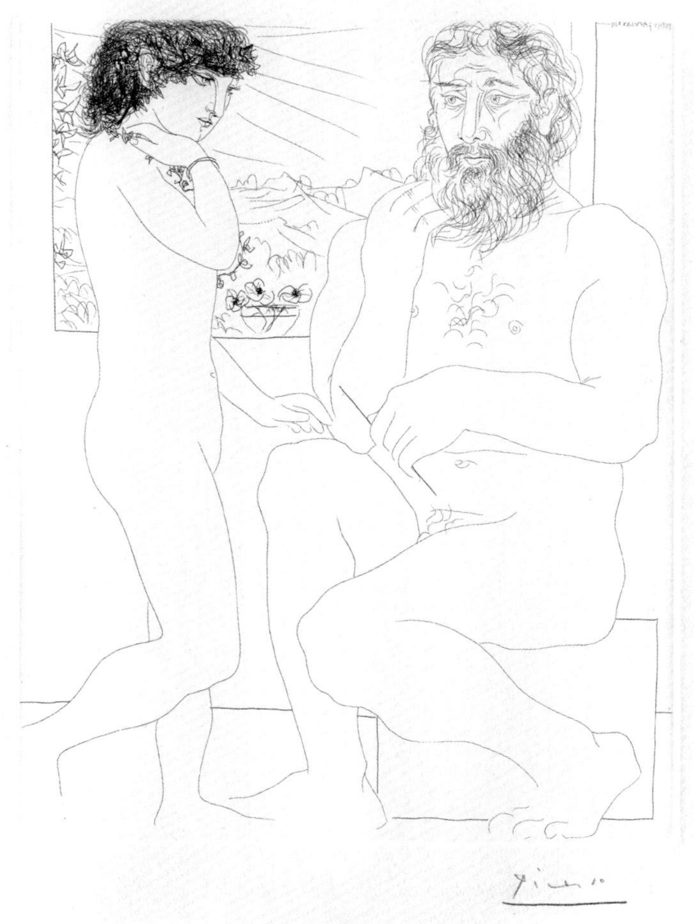

B.

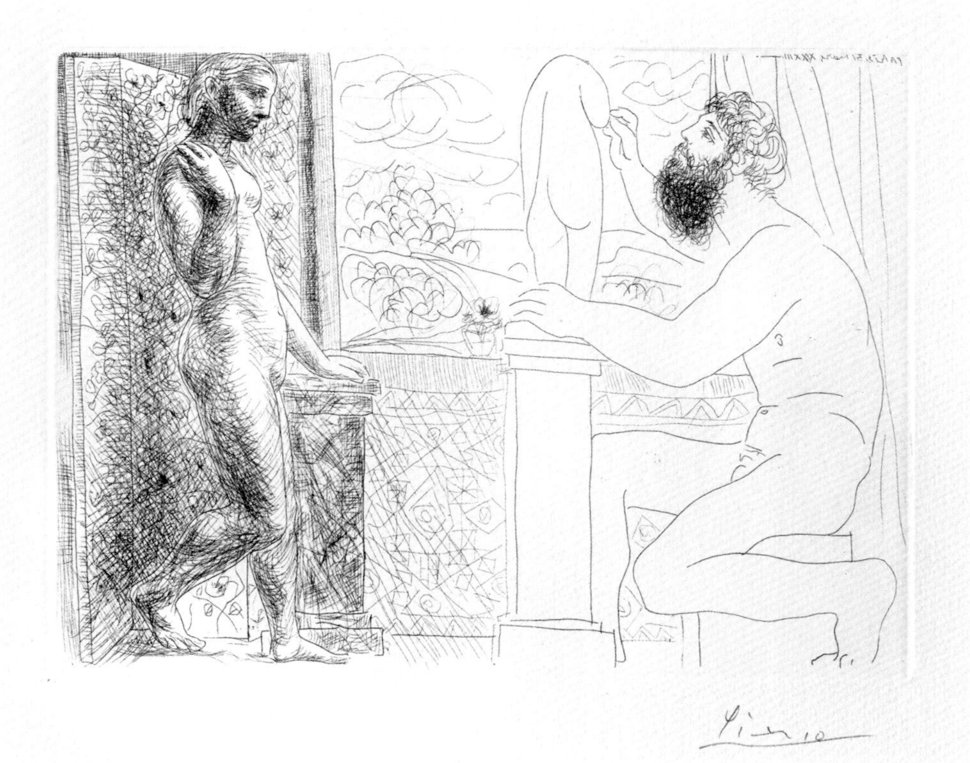

C.

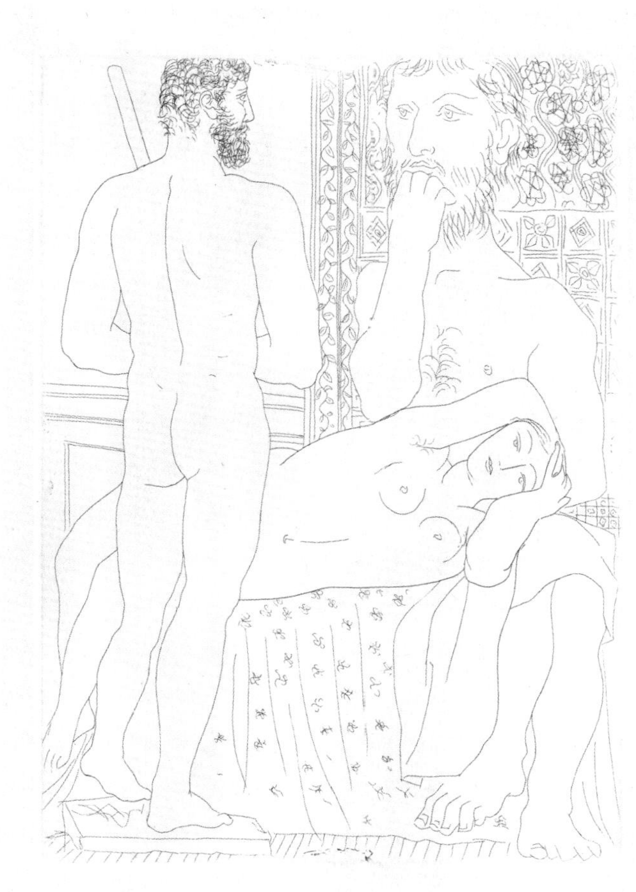

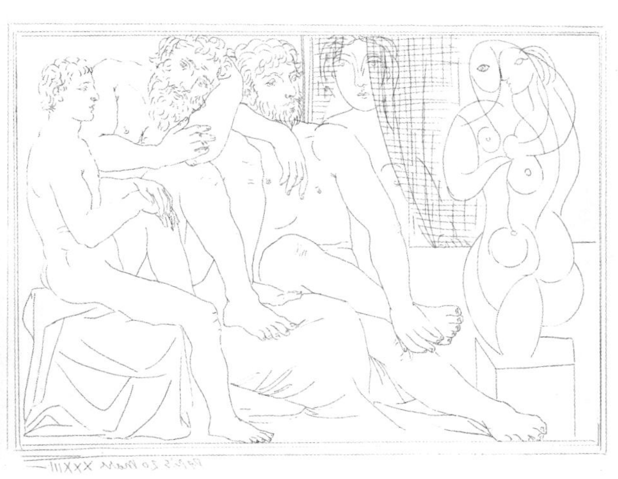

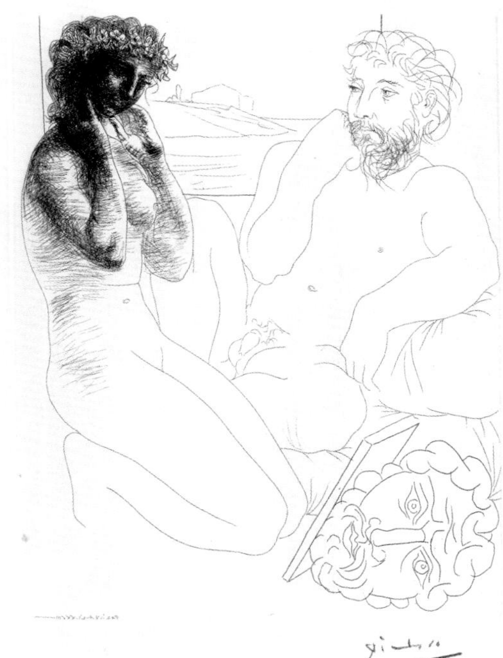

39. Pablo Picasso. Plates from the *Vollard Suite*. Etchings. Private collection

B. *Sculptor and Standing Model (Sculpteur et Modèle Debout)*, plate 68, April 7, 1933. 14 ⁷⁄₁₆ × 11 ¹¹⁄₁₆ in. (36.7 × 29.7 cm)

C. *Sculptor and His Model Before a Window (Sculpteur et Son Modèle Devant une Fenêtre)*, plate 59, March 31, 1933. 7 ¾ × 10 ⁹⁄₁₆ in. (19.7 × 26.8 cm)

D. *Sculptor, Reclining Model, and Sculpture (Sculpteur, Modèle Couché et Sculpture)*, plate 37, March 17, 1933. 10 ⁷⁄₁₆ × 7 ⅝ in. (26.5 × 19.4 cm)

E. *Sculptors, Models, and Sculpture (Sculpteurs, Modèles et Sculpture)*, plate 41, March 20, 1933. 7 ⅝ × 10 ⁷⁄₁₆ in. (19.4 × 26.5 cm)

F. *Sculptor and Kneeling Model (Sculpteur et Modèle Agenouillé)*, plate 69, April 8, 1933. 14 ⅜ × 11 ⅝ in. (36.5 × 29.5 cm)

D.

E.

F.

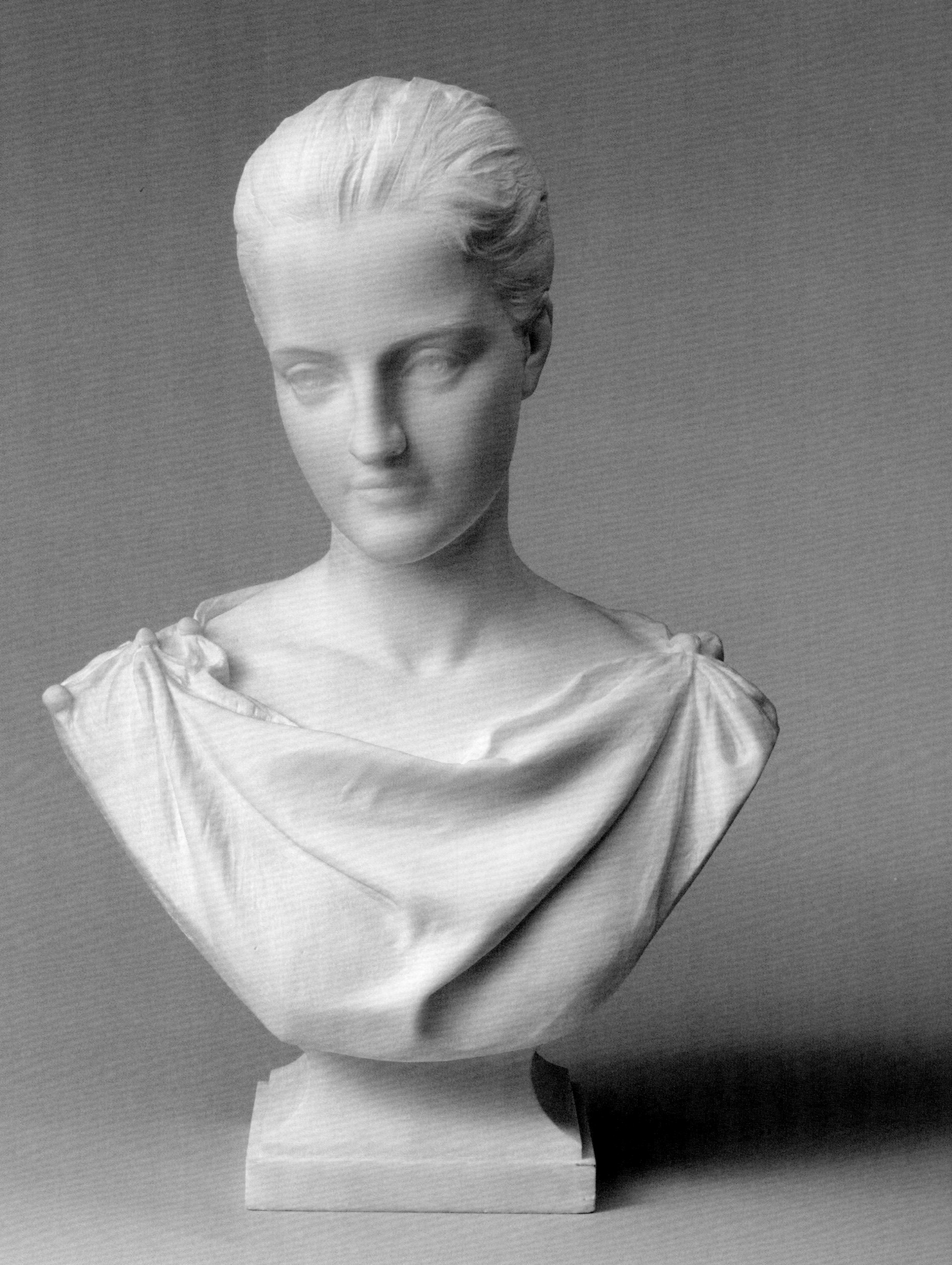

40. Augustus Saint-Gaudens. *Louise Adele Gould*, modeled 1894, carved 1895. Marble, H. 22 in. (55.9 cm), W. 15 ½ in. (39.4 cm), D. 10 in. (25.4 cm). The Metropolitan Museum of Art, New York, Gift of Charles W. Gould, 1915 (15.105.2)

41. Augustus Saint-Gaudens. *Louise Adele Gould*, after 1894. Pigmented wax, H. 14 ½ in. (36.8 cm), W. 17 in. (43.1 cm), D. 9 in. (22.8 cm). Collection of Jonathan and Ute Kagan

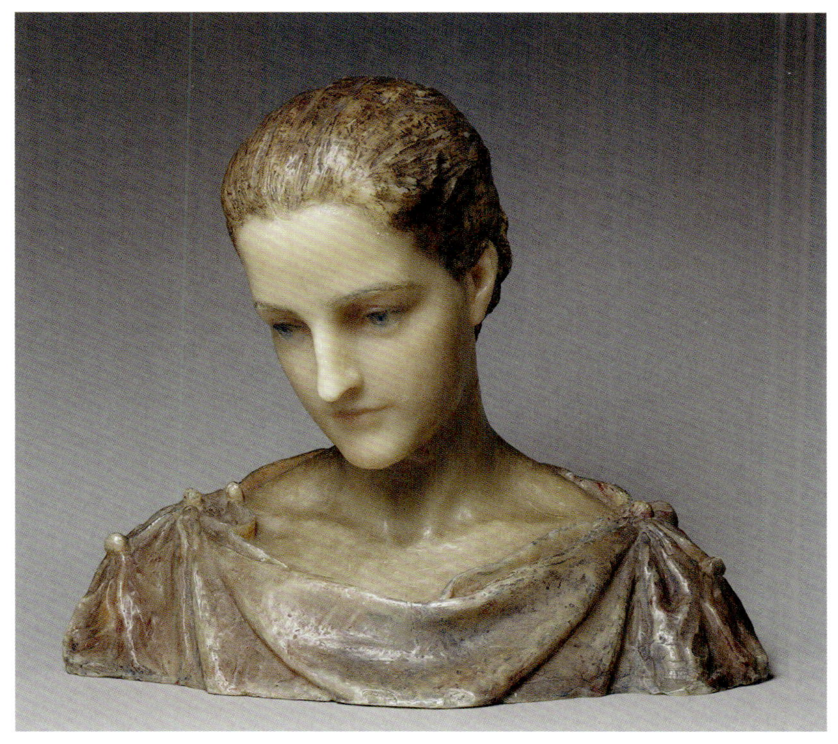

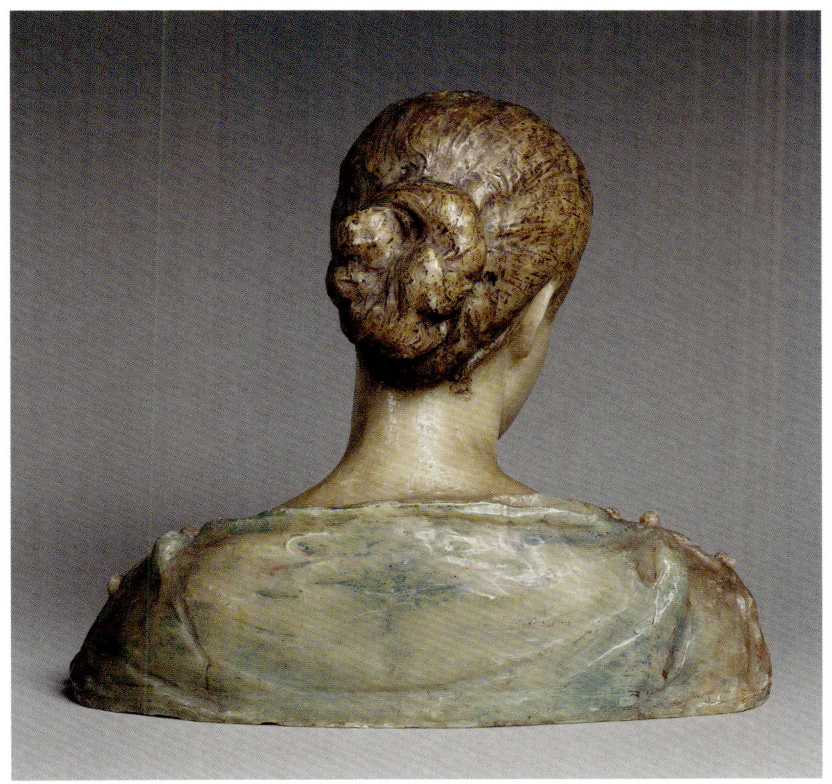

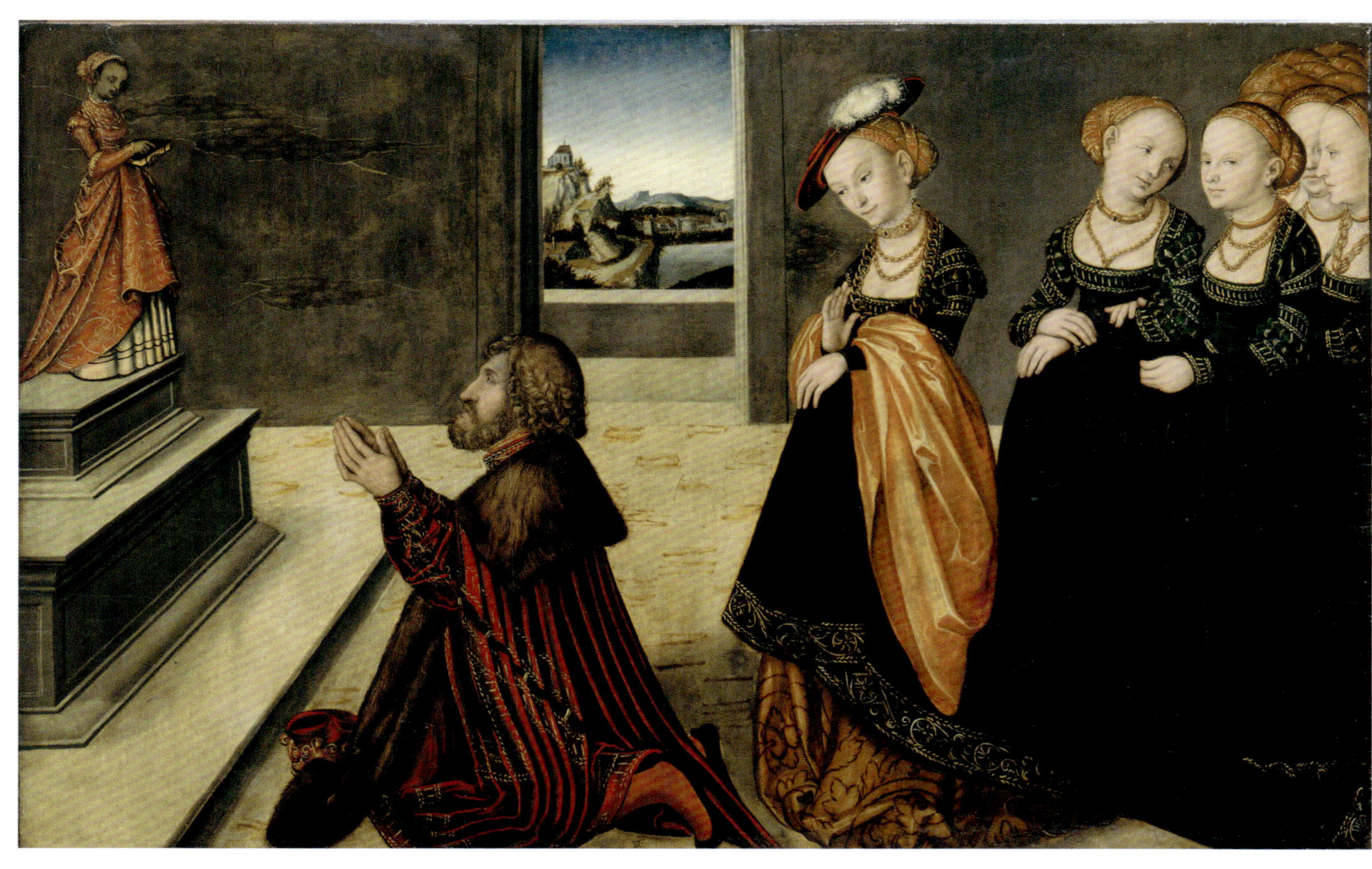

42. Lucas Cranach the Younger. *The Idolatry of Solomon*, ca. 1537. Oil on limewood, 47 ¹³⁄₁₆ × 29 ⅛ in. (121.5 × 74 cm). Gemäldegalerie Alte Meister, Staatliche Kunstsammlungen Dresden

43. *Saint Barbara*, ca. 1490. Limewood and paint, H. 50 ¼ in. (127.6 cm), W. 17 in. (43.2 cm), D. 13 ¼ in. (33.7 cm). Alsacian, probably Strasbourg. The Metropolitan Museum of Art, New York, The Cloisters Collection, 1955 (55.166)

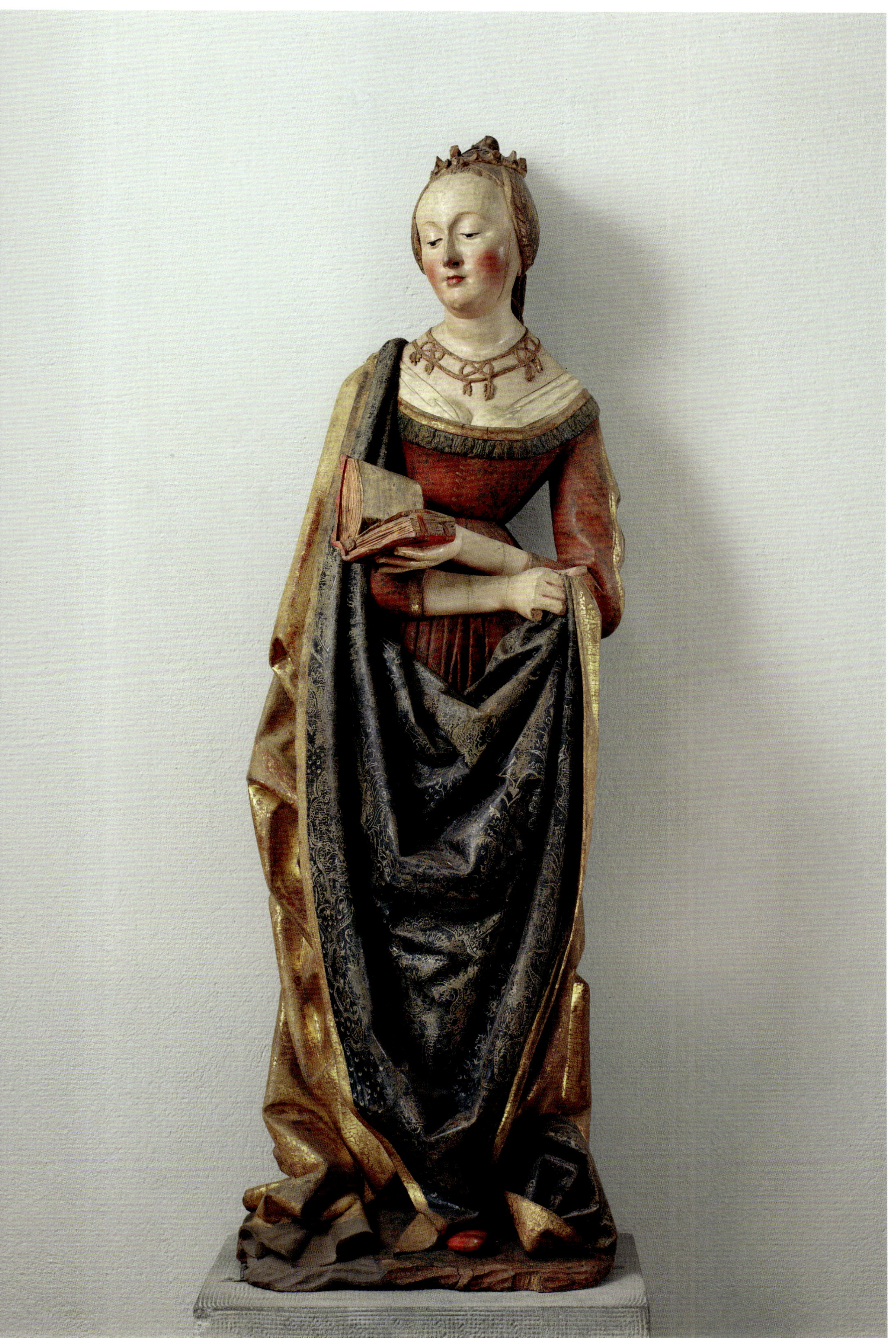

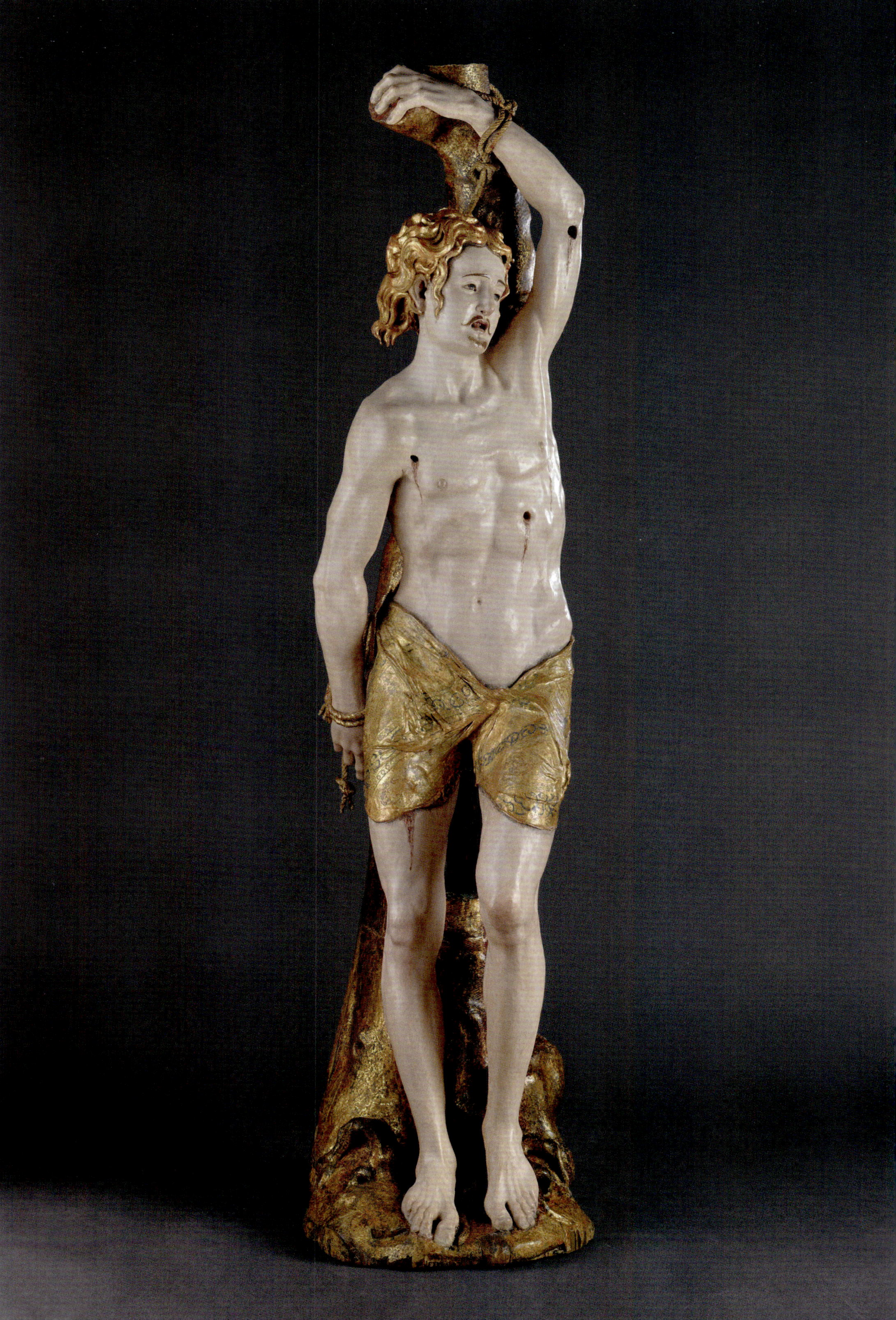

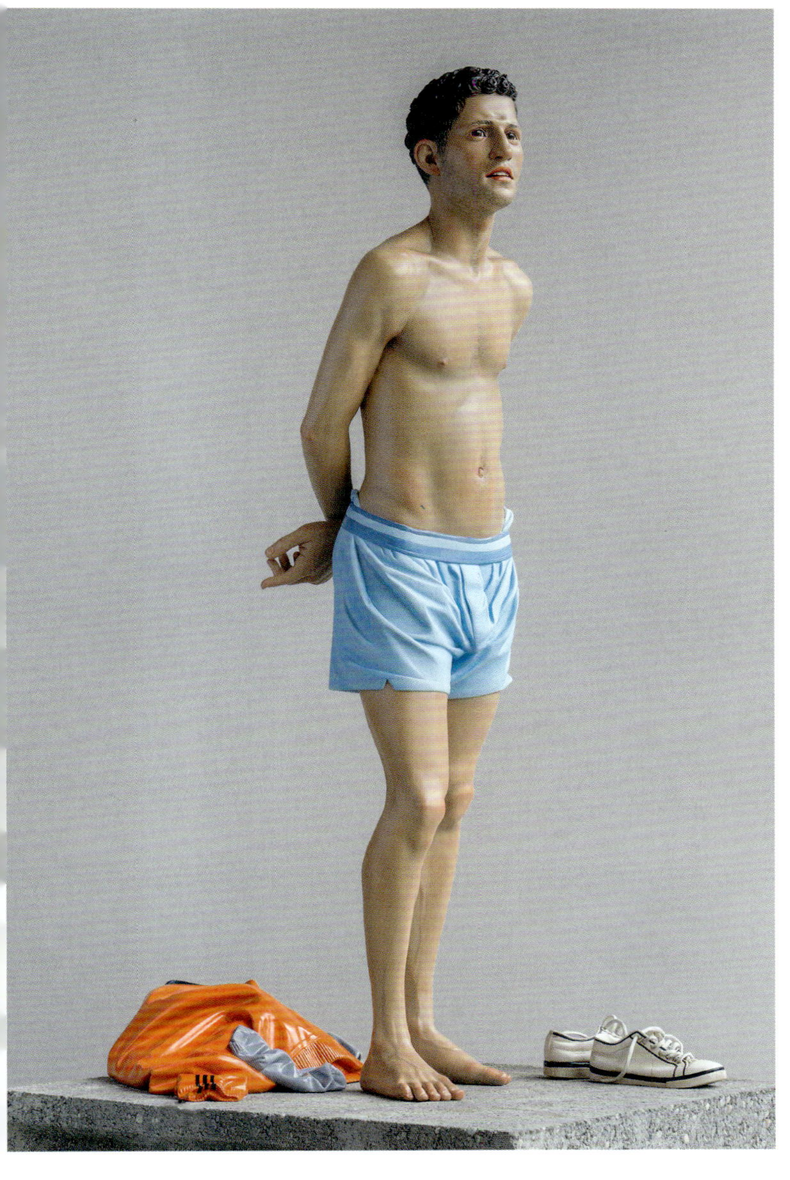

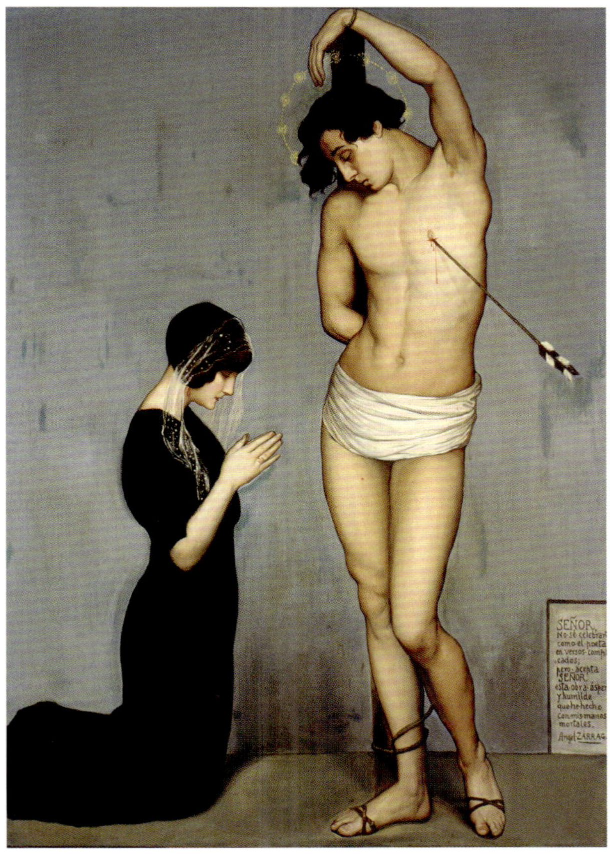

44. Alonso Berruguete. *Saint Sebastian*, mid-16th century. Polychromed wood and
parcel gilt, H. 64 ⁹⁄₁₆ in. (164 cm), W. 16 ⅛ in. (41 cm), D. 20 ¹⁄₁₆ in. (51 cm). Fondation
Palatine, courtesy Colnaghi, London

45. Reza Aramesh. *Action 105: An Israeli soldier points his gun at the Palestinian youth asked to
strip down as he stands at a military checkpoint along the separation barrier at the entrance of
Bethlehem, March 2006*, 2017 (detail). Hand-carved polychromed limewood, glass eyes,
and concrete plinth, H. 37 ³⁄₁₆ in. (94.5 cm), W. 8 ¼ in. (21 cm), D. 10 ¼ in. (26 cm);
plinth: 39 ⅜ in. (100 cm), W. 21 ⅝ in. (55 cm), D. 21 ⅝ in. (55 cm). Courtesy of the artist
and Leila Heller Gallery, New York and Dubai

46. Ángel Zárraga y Argüelles. *Votive Offering (Saint Sebastian)*, ca. 1910–12. Oil on canvas,
72 ¹³⁄₁₆ × 52 ¹⁵⁄₁₆ in. (185 × 134.5 cm). Museo Nacional de Arte, Instituto Nacional de
Bellas Artes, Mexico City

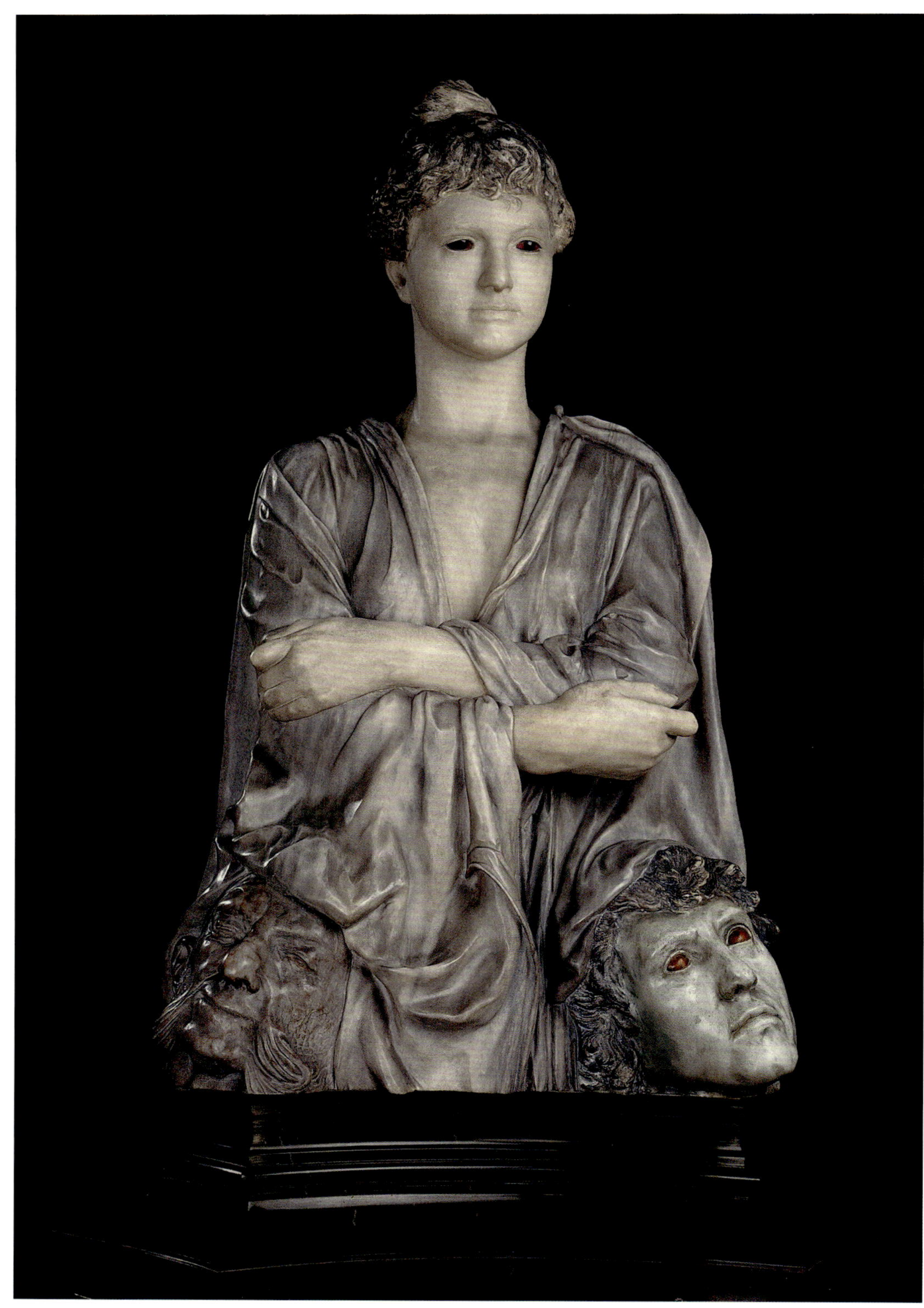

47. Max Klinger. *New Salome*, 1893–1903. Marble and paint, H. 34 ⅝ in. (88 cm), W. 21 ⅞ in. (55.5 cm), D. 17 ⅛ in. (43.5 cm); base H. 6 ⅝₁₆ in. (16 cm), W. 28 ¹⁵⁄₁₆ in. (73.5 cm), D. 22 ⁷⁄₁₆ in. (57 cm). Museum der Bildenden Künste, Leipzig

48. Juan Martínez Montañés. *Saint John the Baptist*, ca. 1620–30. Polychromed wood and gilding, H. 60 ⅝ in. (154 cm), W. 29 ⅝ in. (75.2 cm), D. 27 ⅝ in. (70.2 cm). The Metropolitan Museum of Art, New York, Purchase, Joseph Pulitzer Bequest, 1963 (63.40)

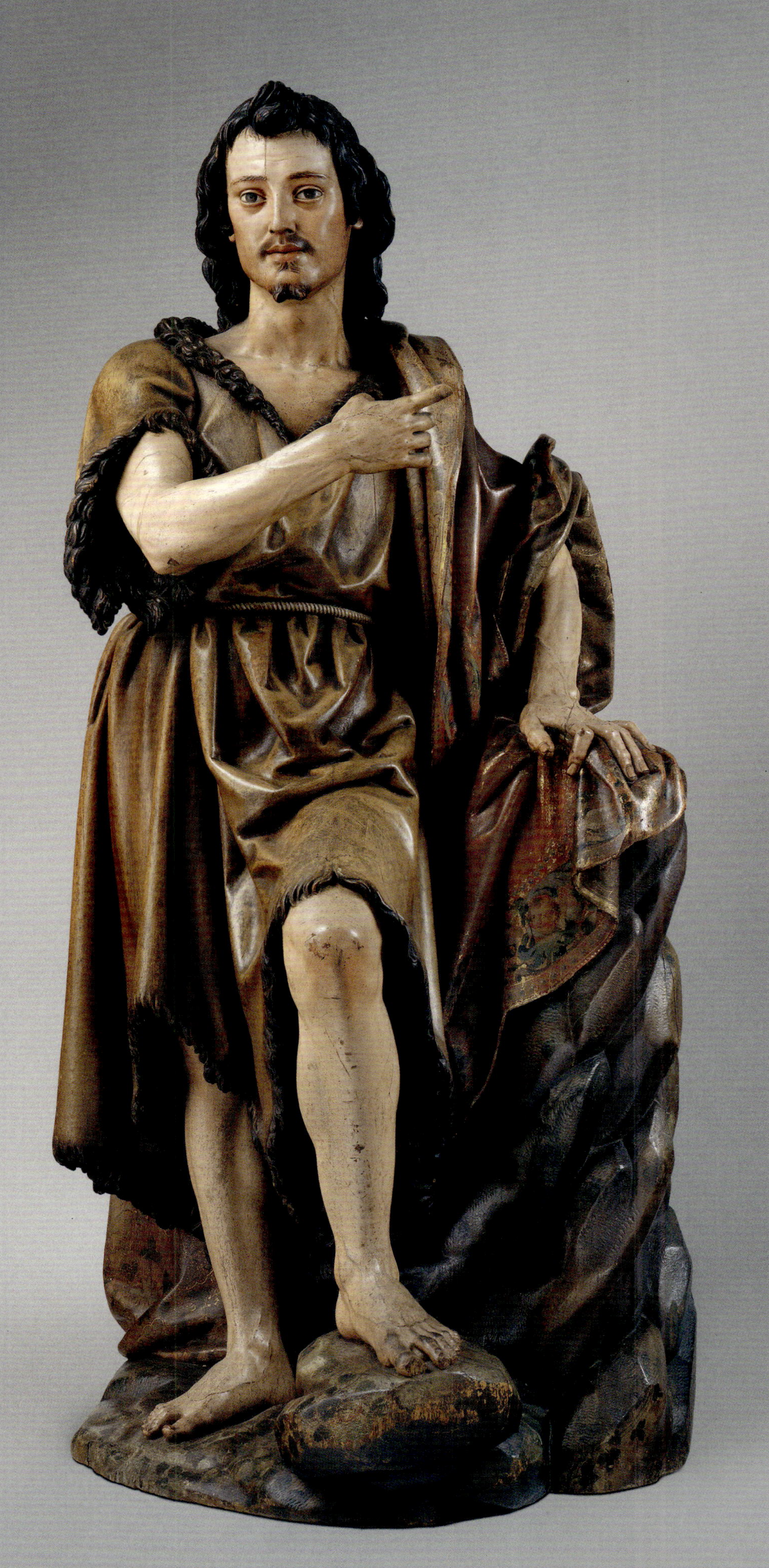

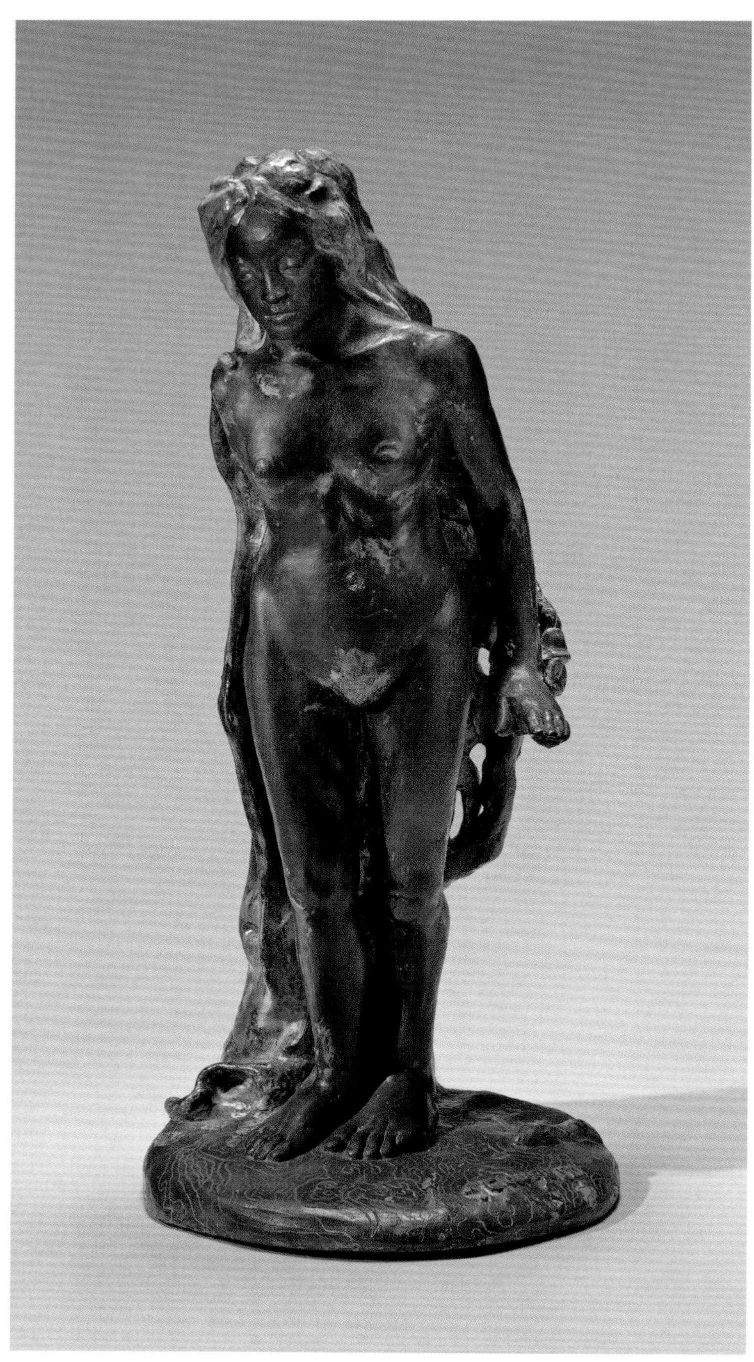

49. Paul Gauguin. *Eve*, 1890. Ceramic and glaze, H. 23 ⅞ in. (60.6 cm), W. 11 in. (27.9 cm), D. 10 ¾ in. (27.3 cm). National Gallery of Art, Washington, D.C., Ailsa Mellon Bruce Fund

50. Nancy Grossman. *Male Figure*, 1971. Leather and zippers on wood, H. 66 ¹⁵⁄₁₆ in. (170 cm), W. 27 ⁹⁄₁₆ in. (70 cm), D. 23 ⅝ in. (60 cm). Israel Museum, Jerusalem, Gift of Joseph H. Hazen, New York, to the American Friends of the Israel Museum

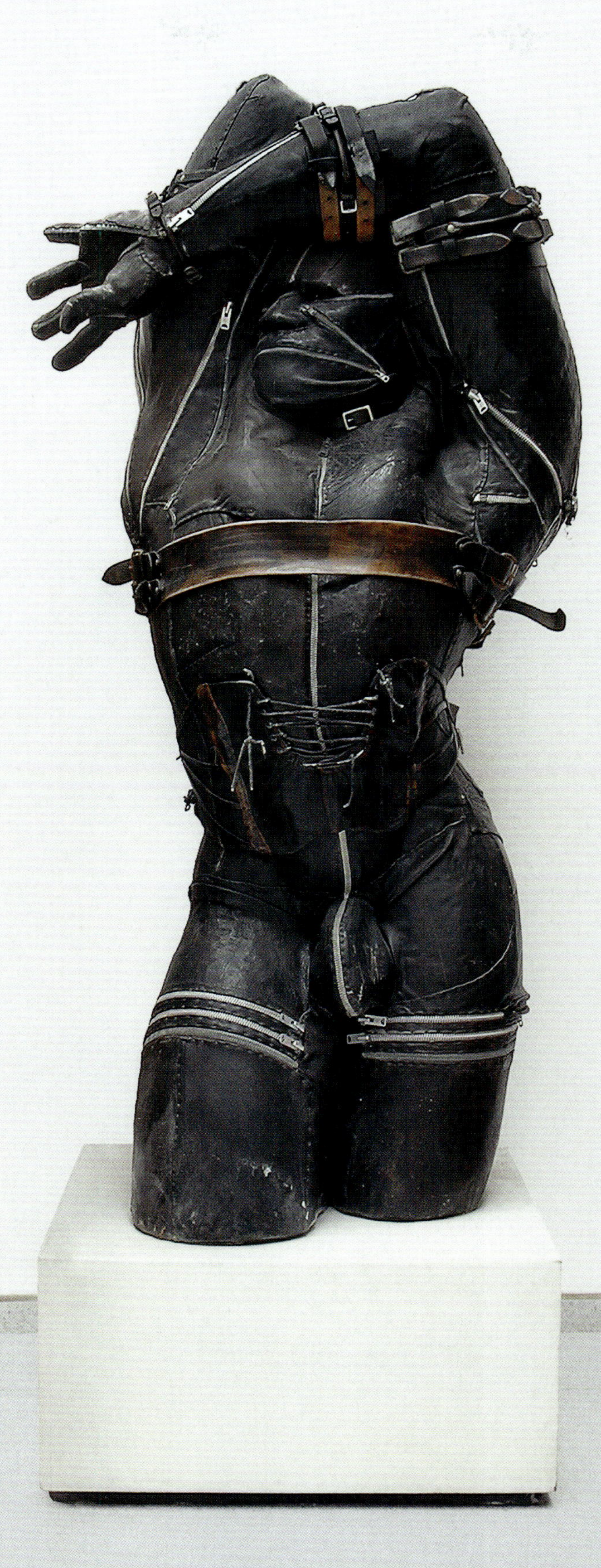

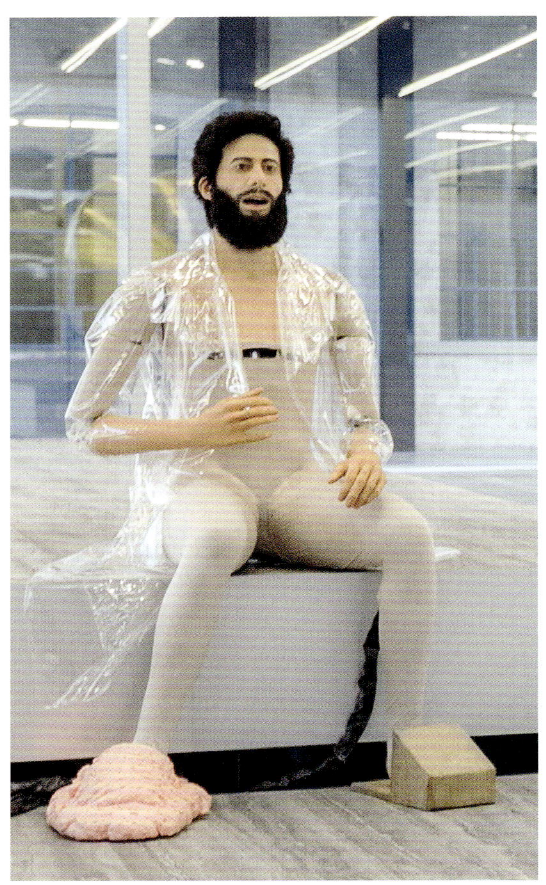

51. Goshka Macuga. *To the Son of Man Who Ate the Scroll*, 2016. Android, plastic coat, expandable foam shoe, and cardboard and linen shoe, seated: H. 55 ⅛ in. (140 cm), W. 19 ¹¹⁄₁₆ in. (50 cm), D. 33 ¹⁄₁₆ in. (84 cm), overall dimensions variable. Fondazione Prada, Milan and Venice

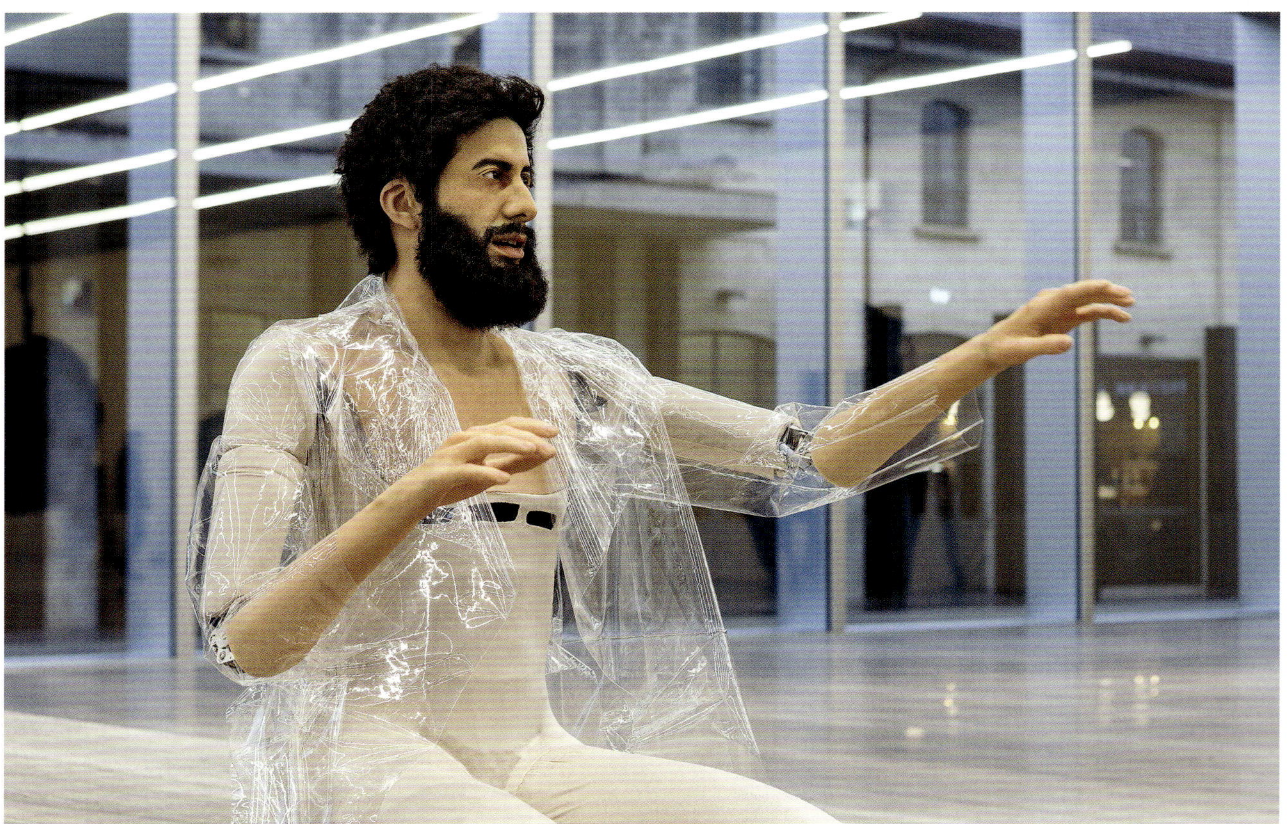

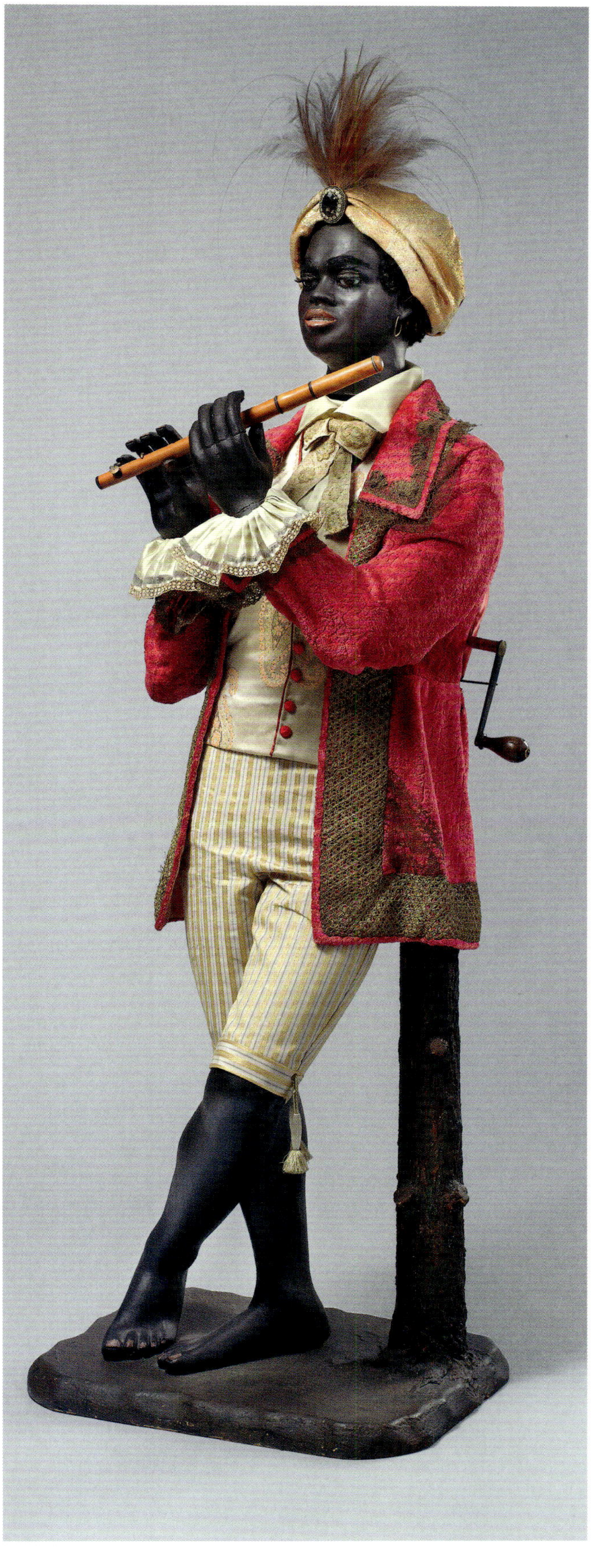

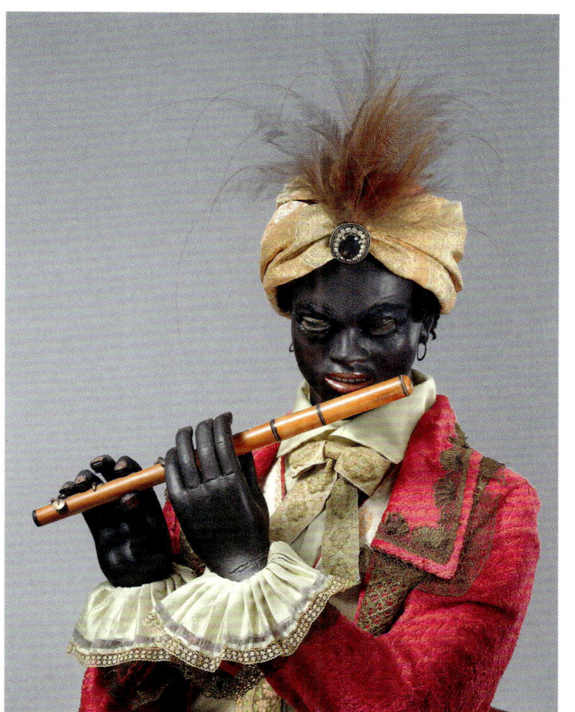

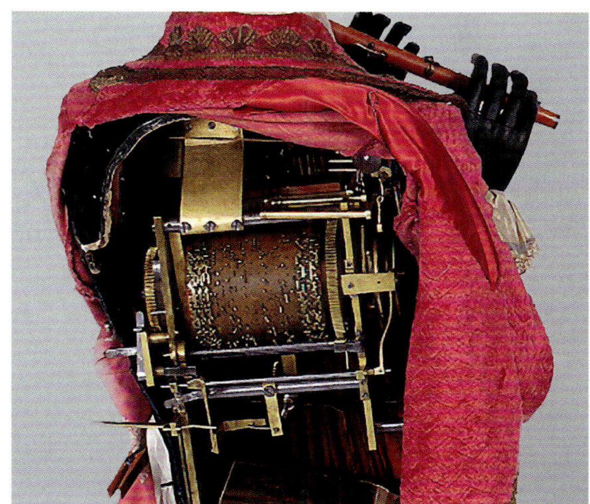

52. Alexandre-Nicolas Théroude. *Flute Player*, ca. 1869–77, costume 1970s. Textiles, European oak and pine, steel, iron, brass, papier-mâché, leather, glass, mohair, and oil paint, H. 60 in. (152.4 cm), W. 19 ½ in. (49.5 cm), D. 15 in. (38.1 cm). Murtogh D. Guinness Collection of Mechanical Musical Instruments and Automata, Morris Museum, Morristown, New Jersey

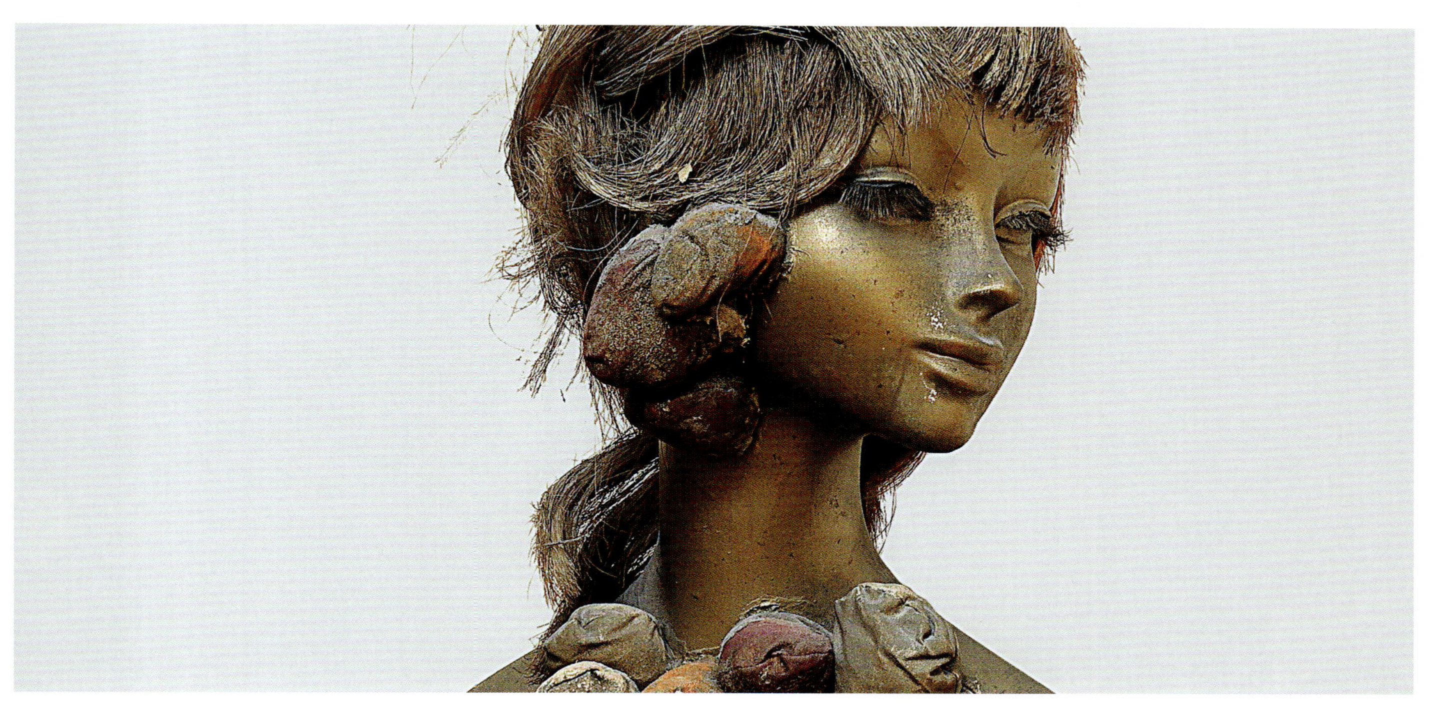

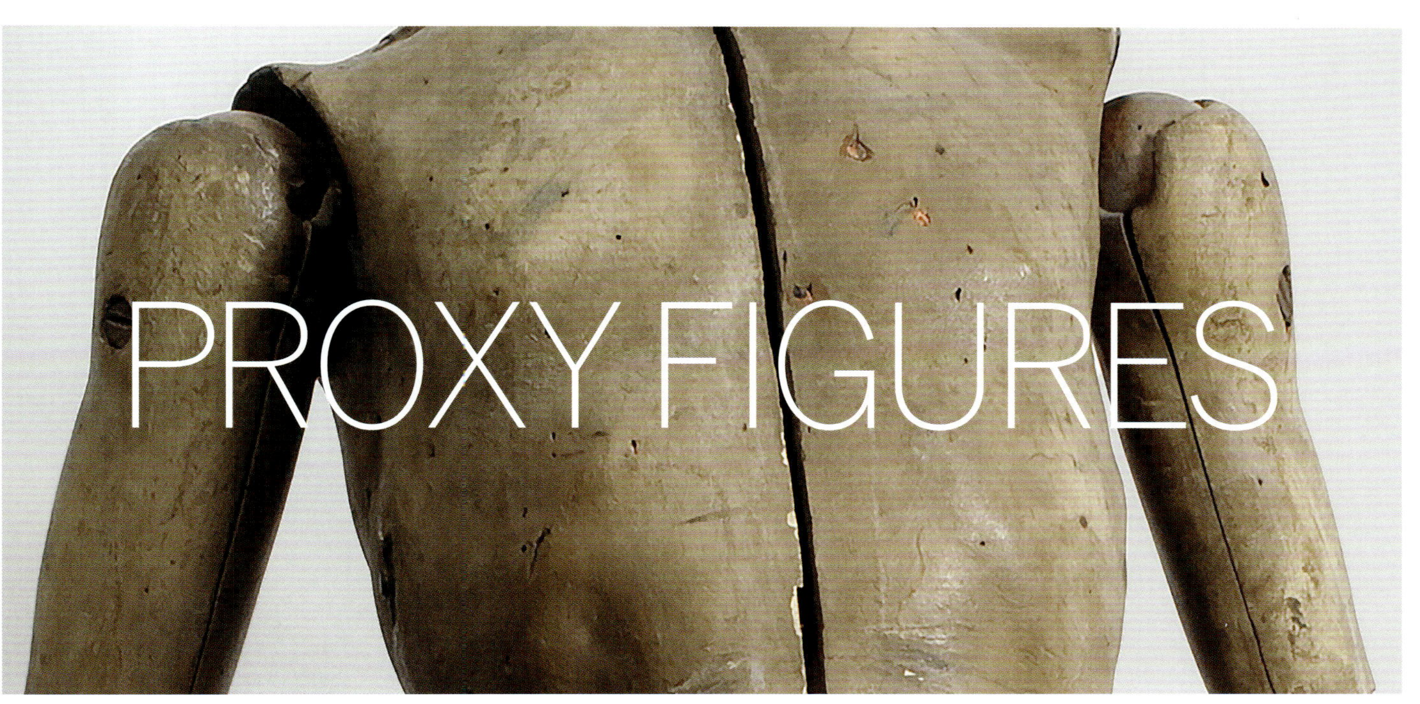

PROXY FIGURES

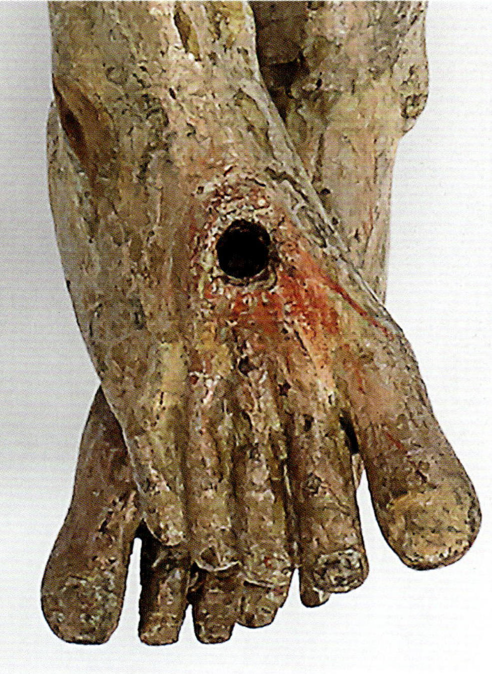

PROXY FIGURES

BRINDA KUMAR

Evidence of dolls, puppets, marionettes, and figurines—fashioned in the reflection of men, women, and children—date to ancient civilizations including the Egyptians, Minoans, Chinese, and Etruscans. These figures could stand in for humans themselves, for in spite of being "constructed, stylized and artificial," they were able to serve "as a powerful vehicle for conveying messages that would be too difficult, risky or explicit if handled by real bodies....[These] fake, substitute bodies...played a role in helping to reflect on the fluid ordering principles of social relations from politics to gender."[1] Often made from pliable, softer, and erodible materials, such as wood, wax, leather, wire, clay, and cloth, such figures have a much longer history of representing humans even though they rarely occupy museum sculpture galleries, where Neoclassical figurative sculpture, recognizably human yet not too real, maintained its status as an ideal art form in part owing to its emphasis on permanence. Rooted to a pedestal, hewn from hard, cool marble, the figures transcend the life-eroding trammels of time, stilled in perpetuity, literally and metaphorically petrified. By contrast, figures that have the ability to move or have articulate limbs that could simulate the flexibility of the human body, a key sign of liveliness, could be true proxies with ever-mutable functions to serve evolving societal and personal needs. This body of figures with articulated limbs and kinetic potential includes a motley range of objects from thirteenth-century crucifixes with movable arms, through artist lay figures and mannequins, to twentieth-century fetish dolls.

In central Europe in the late thirteenth century, the rites surrounding the Passion of Christ in medieval churches inspired a new kind of crucifixion figure. A sculpture of Christ with movable arms created a more realistic reenactment of the Descent from the Cross, for the arms could appear outspread while the figure hung from the cross, be used to lift the body off the cross, and finally lay folded alongside the body in a casket. The realism of such deposition figures often entails the concealment of the hinge mechanisms (as in the shoulder sockets of catalogue 55) with paint, parchment, or the addition of human hair and clothing.[2] In a crucifix with movable arms from the Schweizerisches Nationalmuseum, Zurich, a hole on the side of the head suggests that the figure once wore a wig and a crown of thorns. Although these elements are now lost and the paint has eroded, the figure retains a great deal of realistic wood-carved details from the leg musculature, protruding veins on the arms, and discernible ribs to the partially open eyes and mouth.[3] A string in its back enabled the head to droop while the figure hung from the cross and heightened the drama of the ebbing of the lifeblood as the head could gradually be moved. While these crucifixes are associated with other medieval movable sculptures encountered during Holy Week, such as the processional Resurrection figure and Palmesels, which depict Christ's entry into Jerusalem on a donkey (cat. 54), art historian Amy Powell has noted that the two kinds of figures created different effects:

> When the Palm Sunday ass was rolled through the streets of town and when the Resurrection figure was hoisted up...the fiction was that they were moving of their own accord or, at least, not by means of any human intervention....[They] were moved with the help of ropes, wheels, and pulleys, and from a distance great enough to dissociate the mover from the moved....By contrast, when the crucifix was taken down from the cross and its arms were laid by its sides, the fiction (and the fact) was that it had no volition whatsoever. Because the fact of the crucifix's stillness coincided with its fiction, it could be handled directly; in fact, it needed to

Therefore the limpness of the realistic and flexible arms underscores the crucifix's lifelessness, communicating a pathos vital to the rite. Conversely, the Palmesel's apparent autonomy of movement buoyed the wondrousness of the Christ figure brought to life.

The performative possibility of figures with articulate limbs when rendered at lifesize enabled them to function as true surrogates in both religious and other settings. In fourteenth-century England, for example, portable effigies were used in lieu of deceased monarchs in funeral processions whereas in medieval Italy a popular figure with movable arms was that of the jousting Saracen.[5] The Saracen would be placed in the center of a square or arena for a mounted horseman to charge the figure and attempt to hit it without in turn getting struck by the reactive momentum of the Saracen's weapon-wielding arm. Related to the Latin *Saraceno*, which appears in texts dating to the Middle Ages, the term "Saracen" was used to identify Eastern infidels, so-called enemies of Christianity and dangerous pagans. For these reasons, the Saracen was considered a formidable and worthwhile target, while his "otherness" was amplified by accentuated signs of racial and physiognomic difference. Architectural historian Medina Lasansky notes that extant Saracen jousting figures or those illustrated in paintings or tapestries "are consistently dark-skinned, dark-haired, stocky figures with menacing facial expressions. The wood Saracen made for the wedding of Medici Grand Duke Francesco I and Bianca Cappello in 1579 fits this description [cat. 57]. To add to its imposing demeanor, it carries a shield bearing the image of Medusa.... In the Renaissance, as during the [Italian Fascist] regime, the Joust of the Saracen enabled participants to playact cultural imperialism as Christian warriors overpowering the Eastern infidel."[6] The Joust of the Saracen, a tournament of games, eventually declined in popularity until its revival during the Fascist era in early twentieth-century Italy. Lasansky has argued that the festival reenactment of the joust in Arezzo, a popular sixteenth- and seventeenth-century tournament that returned in 1931, became a means to underscore Fascist hegemony, particularly given Italy's relationship with Ethiopia in the 1930s (fig. 62): "The image and meaning of the festival [were] carefully constructed in the popular press. While on the surface it appeared to be an entertaining event that animated a sense

of civic identity, it was simultaneously an advertisement for the regime's rhetoric of imperialism, virile strength, and racial superiority."[7]

If the crucifixes with movable arms and the jousting Saracens are kinetic sculptures that have a public visibility and purpose, related but more utilitarian flexible figures are the artist's lay figure and the dressmaker's mannequin.[8] Although they share a mechanical genealogy with the former, the latter types were intended to approximate the human form more generally rather than convey specific types or individuals. These proxy bodies functioned as tools to display the latest fashions, study drapery, or hold poses for longer periods than live models could. While the earliest mention of lay figures dates to Italian architect Filarete's *Treatise on Architecture* (1461–64), few examples survive from before the late eighteenth century, as the figures were used extensively in artists' studios and often passed down from master to apprentice.[9] Early figures had rudimentary

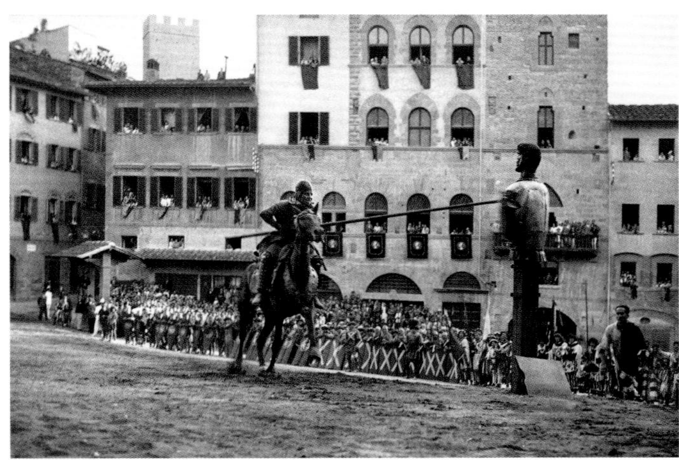

Fig. 62   Joust of the Saracen, Piazza Vasari, Arezzo, Italy, ca. 1935

mechanisms and limited flexibility; however, in time their production achieved a high degree of sophistication, aiming to achieve a "persuasive 'imitation of the human machine.'"[10] As human anatomy came to be better understood, the wood-and-metal armature of such lay figures increasingly resembled the skeleton and musculature of the human body, and the objects became capable of extremely naturalistic poses. Although generally associated with painters, lay figures were also a sculptor's tool, a fact borne out by the presence of one in the studio of Danish artist Bertel Thorvaldsen, one of the most famous Neoclassical sculptors of the late eighteenth and early nineteenth centuries (cat. 56). Said to be the work of Thorvaldsen's hand, the lifesize figure is a composite of carved sections of wood held together by metal hinges and screws. Although Thorvaldsen is best known for his production of marble sculptures, carving in wood was a skill he had perfected in childhood.[11] The muscles on the figure's arms and legs were subtly modeled, as was the chest, whose front comprises two sections of wood joined at the sternum. The waist and hips were made of different pieces, all of which allow the figure to twist and expand or contract into different poses and heights. While the hands and feet are now damaged, attention was clearly lavished on their articulation for maximal gestural effect.

Thorvaldsen's case was somewhat exceptional, for by the turn of the eighteenth into the nineteenth century, most artists seeking a lay figure would approach dedicated mannequin makers, with France becoming the leading center for such objects. Some makers attained a high degree of renown, including French artist Paul Huot, whose lay figures were sought after across Europe from London to Saint Petersburg and would often be passed down from generation to generation. His mannequins were so prized that a few examples have unusually survived (cat. 59). Unlike Thorvaldsen's lay figure, Huot's mannequins had a soft finish: while the metal-and-wood skeletal armature remained in place, the limbs and torso were molded with flax, held together by a skin constructed from a membrane of silk. Extant examples of Huot's mannequins suggest that he specialized in female figures, with small breasts and slender hips, while the delicately modeled head was typically made from papier-mâché and painted. The current figure has a band on its head where a wig could have once been affixed. The removable head could face different directions and rests on a cork stump that caps the figure's neck and on which Huot discreetly signed his work. The figure's pliable form allowed for its dressing with relative ease, and Huot's mannequins were known to have been furnished with a pamphlet of instructions.[12] The figure would have been mounted on a wood stand, and its internal mechanism could be accessed by keys via a series of holes in the silk above the joints. Today the figure, which was used in an artist's studio until it entered The Metropolitan Museum of Art's study collections, betrays signs of age, and its fabric skin is partially frayed and moth-eaten. Coincidentally, it resembles in form the mannequin in German artist Otto Dix's *Still Life in the Studio* (1924, fig. 63), albeit less menacing in its aspect.

With the beginnings of modernism and the move away from mimetic idealization, the mannequin figure as a technical tool diminished in usefulness for artists. Nevertheless, as a surrogate, such a proxy figure remained conceptually potent and still fueled the artistic imagination, less as an object to be dispassionately observed and studied, but more as a "quasi-subject" that seemed to possess a degree of animism and potential subjectivity.[13] It is in this context that Austrian artist Oskar Kokoschka's bespoke doll modeled on his former lover Alma Mahler and made by Hermione Moos was intended to function for the artist (fig. 64). Kokoschka implored Moos to "breathe into her [the Alma doll] such life that in the end, when you have finished the body, there is no spot which does not radiate feeling, to which you have not applied yourself to overcome by the most complex devices the dead material."[14] Yet the reality of the figure's nonexistent subjectivity (and Kokoschka's ultimate recognition of it) is amply evident in his series of paintings of the doll where its inevitable thingness, especially when juxtaposed next to the "live" body of the artist, is unavoidable (cat. 58).[15] The same holds true of the lay figure when seen next to the female model in Dix's painting. The figure's riddled skin and crumpled body droop limply in contrast to the glowing corpulence of the woman with a fearsome expression and flaring nostrils, her arm outstretched in a paroxysmal gesture. The headless mannequin embodies a palimpsest of meanings, from object to allegory:

> whether moth-eaten or bullet-riddled, [it] suggests decay and death. Given its strategic position between easel and model, in other words between the artist and his muse, it suggests the centrality of death in Dix's postwar aesthetic. But the dialectical relationship between model and dummy makes it evident that Dix also intends the work to be read as an allegory about the transience of life: in short, the traditional *vanitas* theme translated into the context of the twentieth century....Doubtless the dummy also refers to [Giorgio] de Chirico's mannikins, and to the doll Kokoschka had made in 1920 to symbolise his despair at the impossibility of genuine human relationships since the war.[16]

The devastations of World War I had thrown into disarray the preceding understanding of humanity. As proxies, the doll and mannequin came to be sites to consider both the promise and perils of the future of humankind. As art historian Hal Foster writes, "In Futurism, Constructivism, and the Bauhaus, these figures often appear sleek, almost perfect, so many avatars of a new (super)human to come; while in

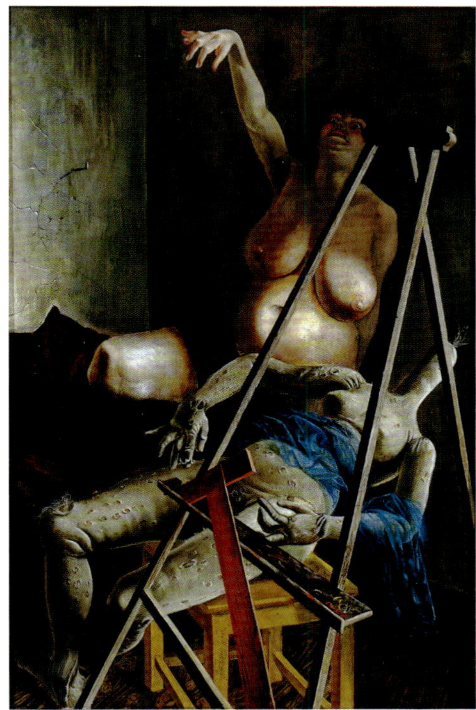

Fig. 63 Otto Dix. *Still Life in the Studio*, 1924. Oil and tempera on canvas, 57 ½ × 39 ⅜ in. (146 × 100 cm). Kunstmuseum Stuttgart

Dada, Surrealism, and Neue Sachlichkeit, they are usually broken and fragmentary, as if thrown together out of discordant parts."[17] The latter description can well refer to the series of dolls (French, *poupée*; German, *puppe*) made by German artist Hans Bellmer beginning in 1933. The doll became the consummate figure for Bellmer to explore erotics and engineering. His fixation on the female doll is said to have stemmed from both his introduction to a 1931–32 production of German-born French composer Jacques Offenbach's opera *The Tales of Hoffmann* (1877–80), in which the protagonist falls in love with an automaton, as well as his attraction to his cousin Ursula, who entered his life at about the same time. Bellmer's dolls were to have "anatomical possibilities" of both the sexual and the mechanical kind. Key to his approach was the distortion, manipulation, and control of the (female) body at the will of the (male) artist.[18] In Bellmer's words, "The body is like a phrase that invites us to disjoint it (to pull it apart), so that it can be recomposed through an infinite series of anagrams."[19] His pursuit of this ambition led him to create dolls with increasingly mutable body forms, particularly through his use of universal ball-and-socket joints, which gave his dolls greater flexibility. The permutations that the dolls could achieve and their subsequent staging in photographs, often hand-tinted to heighten their emotive quality, amplified the artist's and the viewer's voyeurism (cats. 63–64).[20] *La Demi-Poupée* (1972, cat. 62) was based on an unfinished drawing from

the 1930s and where some of Bellmer's other dolls relied on a doubling (of pelvises or sets of limbs), it has only one breast, one arm, and one leg that sports a white sock and girlish Mary Jane shoe.[21] In this version, Bellmer deployed an erotic pun in modeling the doll's head to unmistakably resemble that of a penis.

In the 1930s when Bellmer was making his first *poupées*, the Surrealists in Paris were exploring readymades, dolls, fetish objects, automata, and psychoanalytical investigations of the uncanny. Bellmer's experiments with his *poupées* were unsurprisingly a natural interest shared in Surrealist circles.[22] His photographs were exhibited in their exhibitions in London (1936), Japan (1937), and Paris (1938). The Paris exhibition was notable for its focus on the mannequin.[23] Termed *apparitions d'êtres-objets* (phantom object beings), these mannequins spoke of "the artists' engagement with the city of Paris, the spectacle of its shop windows and the shifting signification of the mannequin."[24]

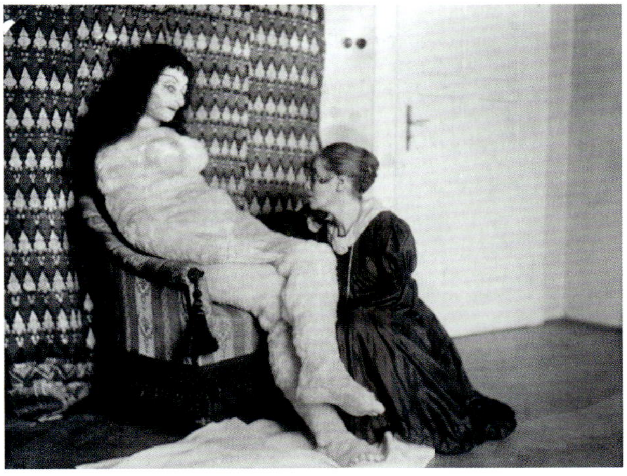

Fig. 64 Hermione Moos with the Alma Mahler doll, ca. 1919. Gelatin silver print. Private collection

As the nineteenth turned into the twentieth century, the artist's bespoke lay figure declined, but the period coincided with the greater visibility of commercially produced clothes mannequins, which served the need of a growing economy and evolving culture of fashion stores in European and American cities. Body forms were standardized and replicated to serve these once again public displays of proxy figures. In 1896 French artist Pierre Imans opened a workshop for mannequin making in Paris and became known for producing highly naturalistic figures modeled in wax, with glass or enamel eyes

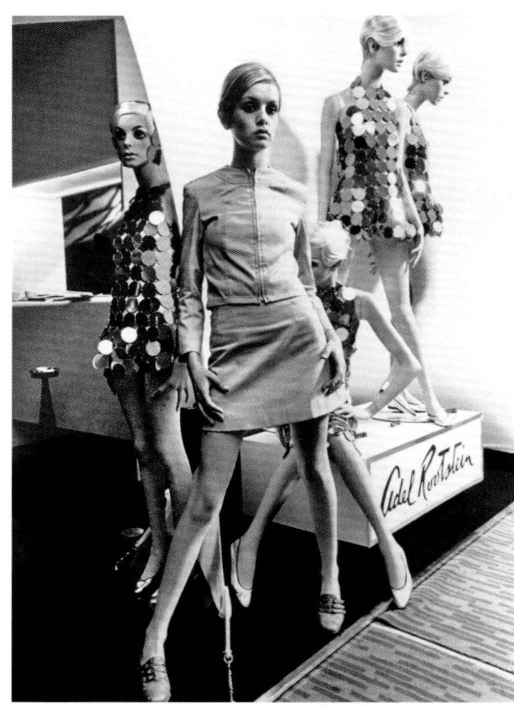

Fig. 65 Twiggy with her Rootstein mannequin, 1960s

and wigs of real hair.[25] The boundary between the real and the proxy was further blurred in Imans's strategy to give his mannequins names and his presentation of them as celebrities through portrait photographs in his marketing catalogues.[26] Imans's mannequins that resemble portrait busts, such as catalogue 65, would have been used by milliners or for the display of jewelry and a variety of coiffures. A later parallel to Imans's approach can be seen in the individualized mannequins of British artist Adel Rootstein, "who believed that mannequins 'should look like real people with real faces,'" although she would focus on creating likenesses of the glamorous, from the model Twiggy (fig. 65) to the film star Joan Collins.[27] More confronting was the realism of American artist Greer Lankton's doll-mannequin *Rachel* (1986, cat. 102), a papier-mâché three-quarter-length portrait of the artist's friend the performance artist Rachel Rosenthal. The emaciated figure of Rachel is now unclothed but once stood in the shop window of Einstein's, a boutique in New York's East Village, fitted in a black dress, wearing a flamboyant hat and dazzling jewelry, and a handbag slung over her outstretched arm (fig. 66). Striking, fierce, *Rachel* contrasts markedly with the alluring mannequins and portrait busts produced by the likes of Imans or even Rootstein.

While Imans's mannequin figures and busts had a highly refined quality, the Surrealists were more interested in the quotidian varieties of mannequins

that were by the 1920s and 1930s ubiquitous in Paris.[28] Nevertheless the ones borrowed for the "mannequin street," a row of sixteen mannequins that lined one side of the entrance corridor at the 1938 Surrealist exhibition, were chosen for their realism and range of hair colors and expressions.[29] The quintessential Surrealist object in the 1938 exhibition, the mannequin was manipulated, dressed, and accessorized in a variety of artistic interventions. The "dressing" took the form of a range of approaches, from French artist André Masson's *La Baillon Vert à Bouche de Pensée* (1938, see fig. 67), in which he famously gagged the mostly nude figure and then placed her head in a wicker cage, to Spanish artist Salvador Dalí's gloved and belted figure, whose otherwise nude body was covered with tiny spoons and a broken egg on her chest (fig. 68). Dalí's influence is evident in the work of Danish Surrealist Wilhelm Freddie. Deemed pornographic and frequently controversial, Freddie's *Sex-Paralysappeal* (1936, cat. 66), one of his "objets-mannequins," appeared in his 1937 solo exhibition "Træk Gaflen ud af Øjet på Sommerfuglen. Sex Surreal" (Pull the fork out of the eye of the butterfly. Sex surreal) in Copenhagen.[30] In it he transformed a standard portrait/mannequin bust into a Surrealist object in moves similar to those of Dalí and Masson by literally framing the head on three sides and adorning the figure with a rope necklace and dangling wine glasses. More explicitly he added the drawing of a penis that snaked along the left cheek, while in a Meret Oppenheimesque nod a gloved hand was nailed in place atop the orange-painted head.[31]

The Surrealist gesture of the unexpected juxtaposition of shapes, objects, and materials, especially in contexts related to the body to provoke the uncanny, would have an enduring impact and be revived in the 1960s. In Oppenheim's *Evening Dress with Bra-Strap Necklace* (*Abendkleid mit Büstenhalter-Collier*, 1968, cat. 67), the German-born Swiss artist combined a mannequin torso with disparate material of contradictory effect. The headless and limbless figure is at once reminiscent of antique statuary but is painted in mottled tones that approach the reptilian or even seem diseased; the "evening dress" is a truncated skirt of synthetic material of a vegetal print; the "bra-strap necklace" refers less to the soft intimacy of the supporting undergarment and is in fact a halter string of hard glass beads that is seemingly painfully affixed to the mannequin's nipples by garter clips.

The use of the mannequin by artists endured beyond the Surrealists' interventions. Its form and

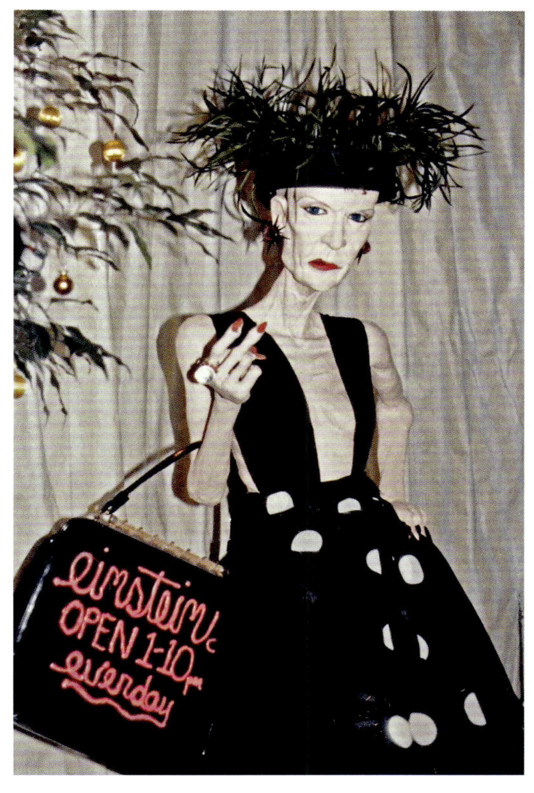

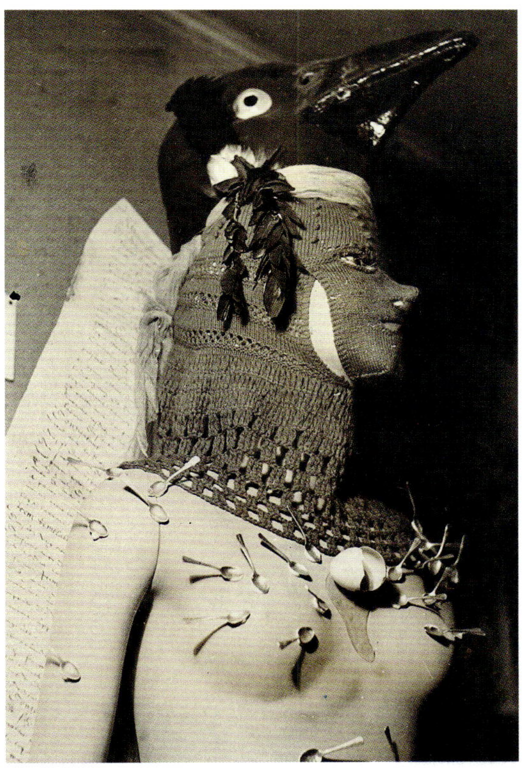

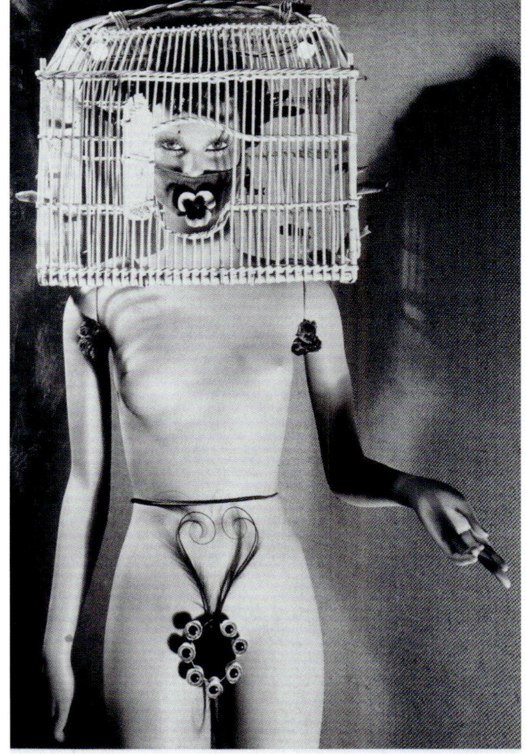

Clockwise from top left

Fig. 66   Greer Lankton's *Rachel* (1986) in the Christmas window display, Einstein's, New York, 1988

Fig. 67   Raoul Ubac. *Masson Mannequin*, 1938. Getty Research Institute, Los Angeles

Fig. 68   Gaston Paris. *Mannequin (Dalí)*, 1938. Gelatin silver print, 7 3/4 × 7 1/16 in. (19.7 × 18 cm). Cleveland Museum of Art. John L. Severance Fund

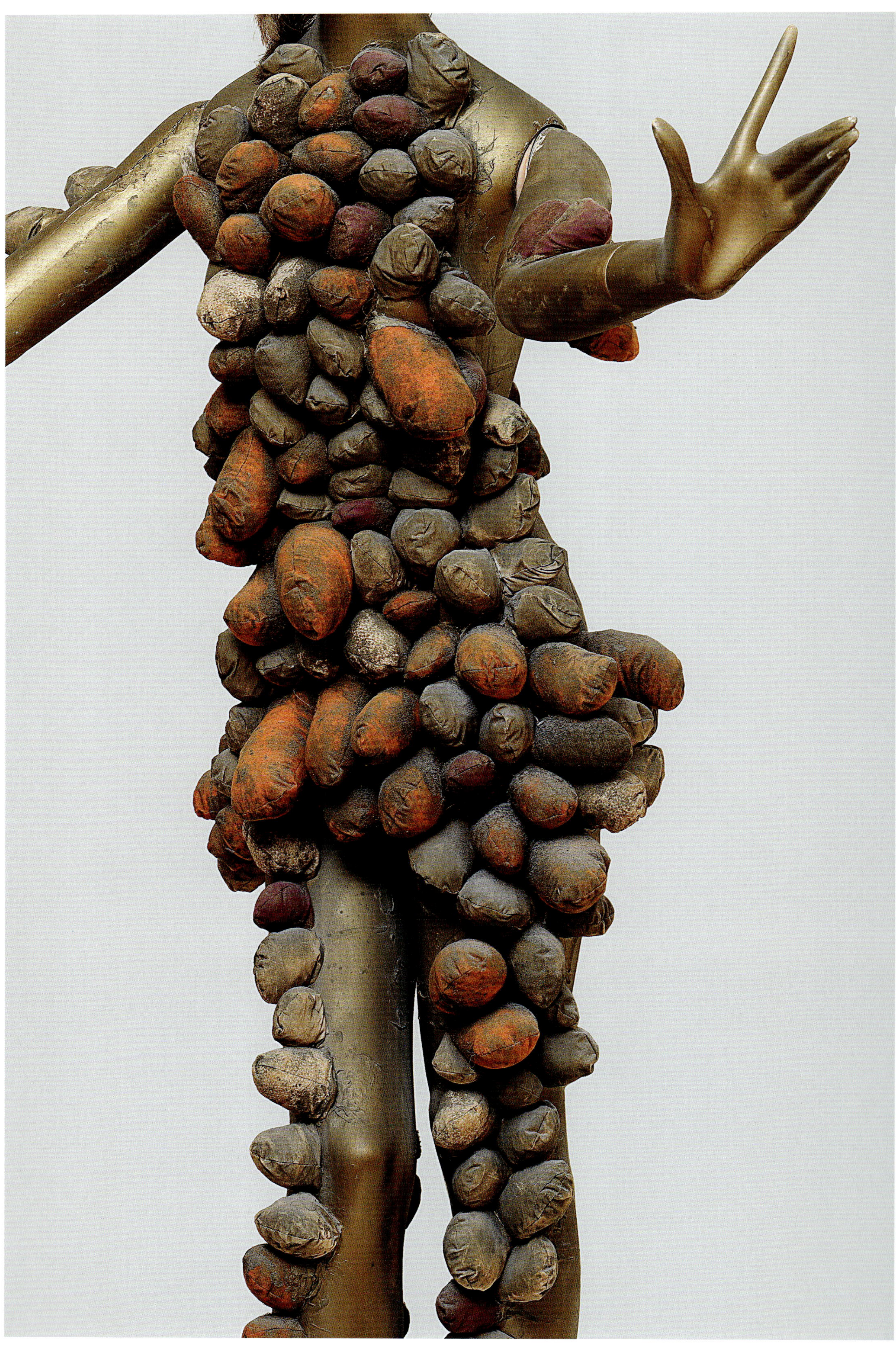

concept proved to be "malleable, multi-layered and absorptive.... This semantic versatility made it possible for the artist continually to renew and refresh his relationship with his inanimate partner."[32] While continuing to serve as a proxy for the human form, the mannequin's conceptual place for artists would change. While the (mostly male) Surrealists had explored the erotics of the (female) mannequin, often in allusive gestures that stemmed from voyeuristic and sadomasochistic desires, actual genitalia were rarely pictured (Bellmer's dolls and Freddie's graphic intervention were exceptions). Commercially produced mannequins, much like dolls of either gender, typically had unarticulated pubic areas that made them vaguely androgynous. In Charles Ray's *Male Mannequin* (1990, cat. 61), the American artist took a generic figure of masculine proportions and looks but emphatically registered his maleness through the conspicuous addition of genitalia. That the genitals have been cast from the artist's own body particularizes this otherwise generic figure into a self-portrait of sorts.

An explosion of phallic forms cover Japanese artist Yayoi Kusama's *Phallic Girl* (1967, cat. 60), which on the one hand can be read as a feminist response to the Surrealists' erotic treatment of mannequins; the female mannequin is almost obliterated, conceptually and visually, through the addition of penis-shaped protrusions. On the other hand, the work is an extremely personal act of "self-obliteration," where the body of the artist and the environment become blurred.[33] Here the female mannequin, which appears in a few of her works from this period, acts as a proxy for the artist, consumed by her phobias and neuroses, evident in her work from the 1960s in the proliferation of phallic forms made from stuffed fabric: "I am terrified by just the thought of something long and ugly like a phallus entering me,...that is why I make so many of them."[34] *Phallic Girl*'s protuberant accumulations can seem almost talismanic and are formally even reminiscent of ancient sculptures of goddesses with multiple breasts.[35]

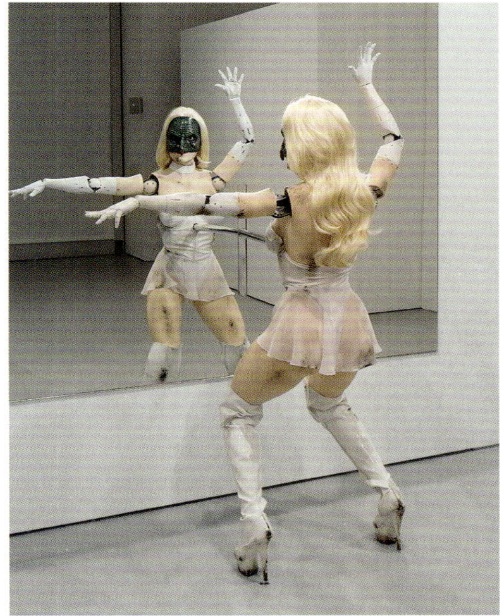

Fig. 69   Jordan Wolfson. *(Female Figure)*, 2014. Mixed media, H. 90 ½ in. (229.9 cm), W. 72 in. (182.9 cm), D. 29 in. (73.7 cm). Broad Art Foundation, Los Angeles

The malleability of the artificial figure with articulate limbs that could be controlled or refigured gave these bodies a metaphoric and kinetic dynamism. The artificial surrogate today can range from the doll or action figure of childhood play to the object of sexual fetish and the robot. Seeming or real autonomous movement of constructed bodies has inspired wonder and horror in equal measure from the historical automata of European courts (cat. 52) to the dangerous fictions of Frankenstein-like monsters. The fantasy of artificial bodies made from inanimate material and brought to life is an ancient one shared across societies, but today as androids are an increasingly visible reality, they represent perhaps the uncanniest approximation of the human body to date. It is therefore unsurprising that much as the Surrealists found the mannequin a compelling form to work with, contemporary artists like the American Jordan Wolfson (fig. 69) and the Polish Goshka Macuga (cat. 51) now incorporate the android into their work.

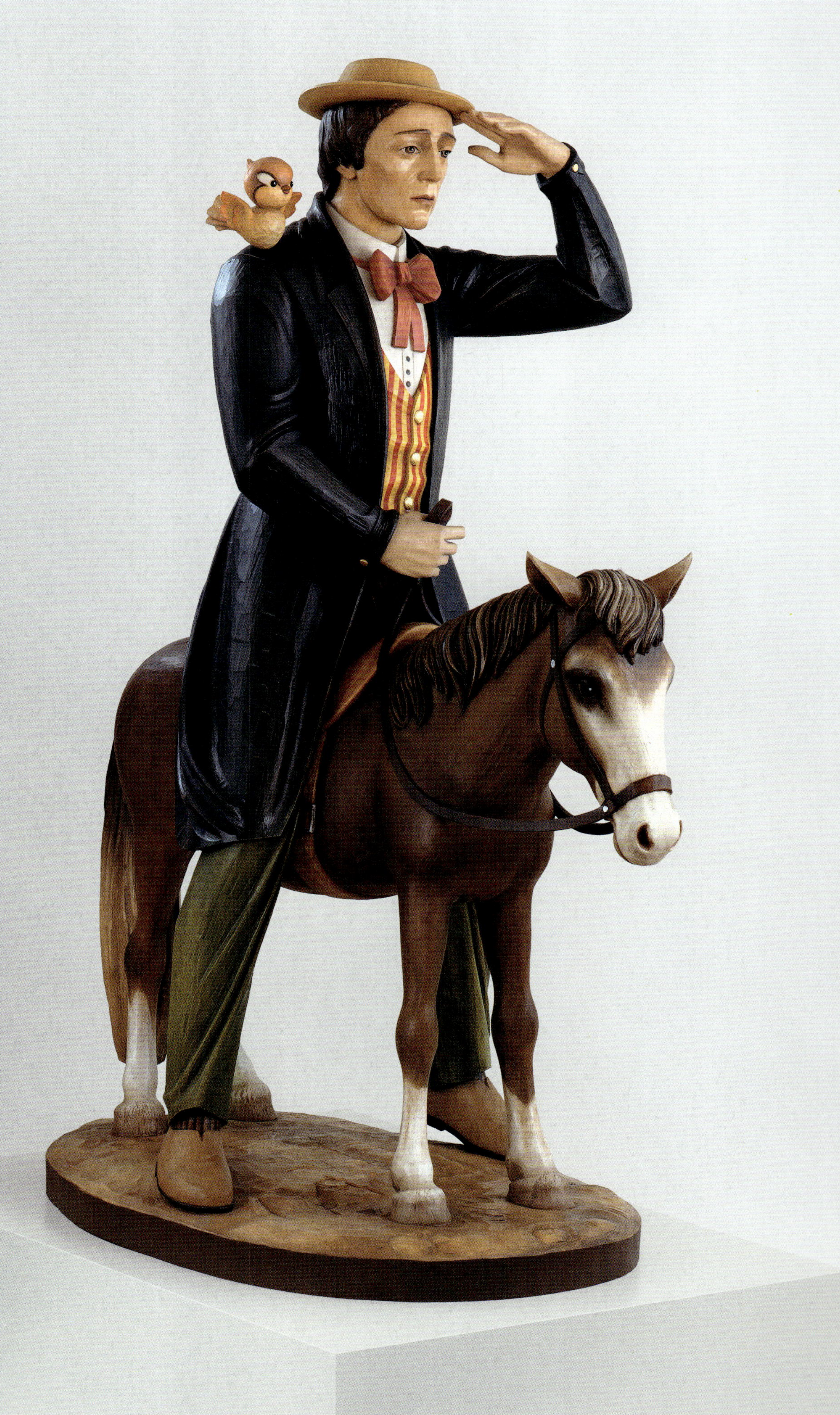

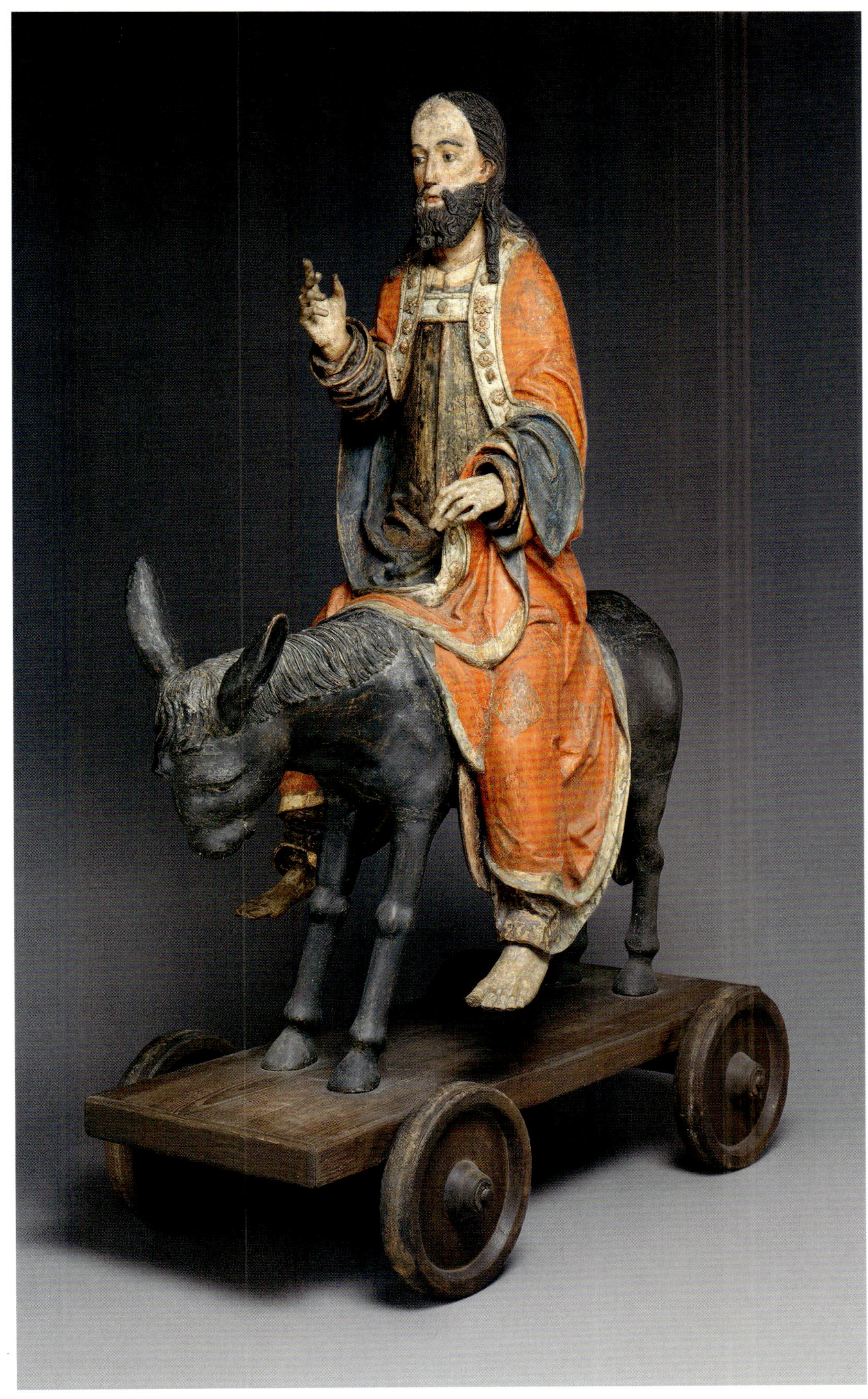

53. Jeff Koons. *Buster Keaton*, 1988. Polychromed wood, H. 66 in. (167.6 cm), W. 47 ⅞ in. (121.6 cm), D. 27 ⅛ in. (68.9 cm). Private collection, courtesy David Zwirner, New York, London, and Hong Kong

54. *Palmesel*, 15th century. Limewood and paint, with base: H. 61 ½ in. (156.2 cm), W. 23 ¾ in. (60.3 cm), D. 54 ½ in. (138.4 cm). German, Lower Franconia. The Metropolitan Museum of Art, New York, The Cloisters Collection, 1955 (55.24)

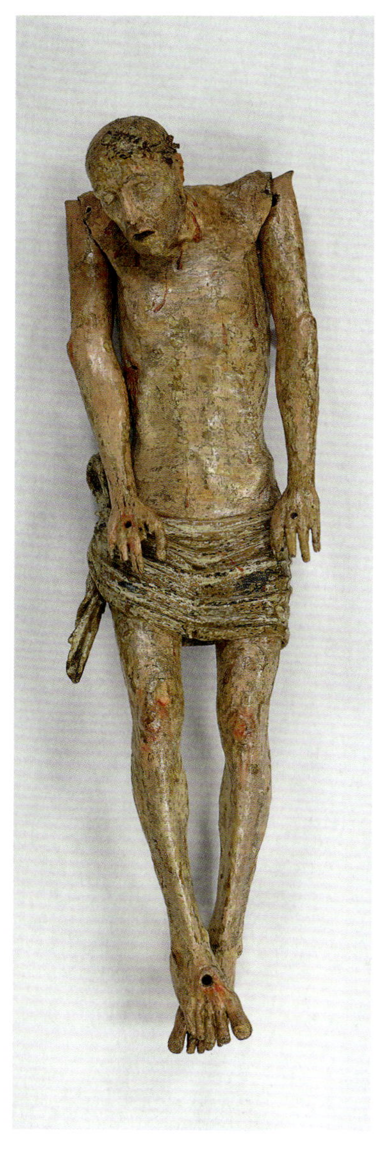

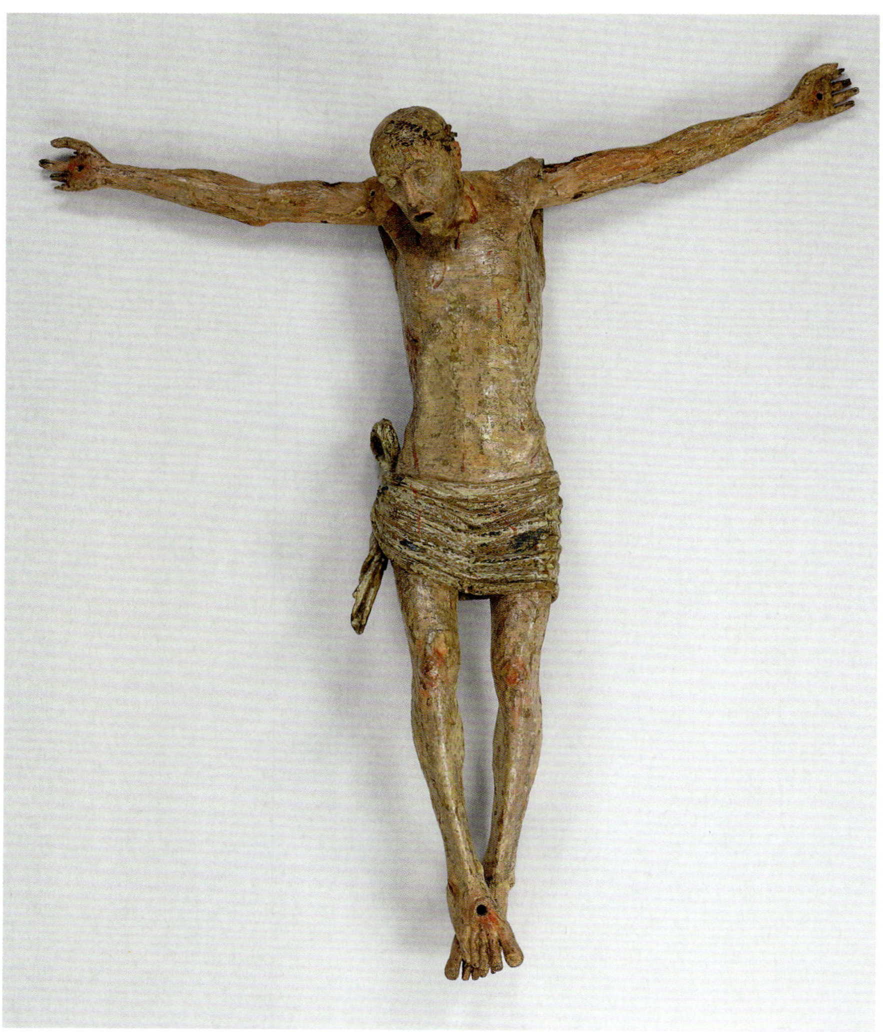

55. *Corpus with Movable Arms,* 1500–1510. Poplar and willow, with arms folded: H. 57⅞ in. (147 cm), W. 17¹¹⁄₁₆ in. (45 cm), D. 11¹⁄₁₆ in. (28 cm). Swiss. Schweizerisches Nationalmuseum, Zurich

56. Bertel Thorvaldsen. *Lay Figure,* before 1806. Wood, metal, and paint, figure: H. 63¾ in. (162 cm); base: H. 6¹¹⁄₁₆ in. (17 cm), W. 23⁷⁄₁₆ in. (59.5 cm), D. 22⁷⁄₁₆ in. (57 cm). Thorvaldsens Museum, Copenhagen

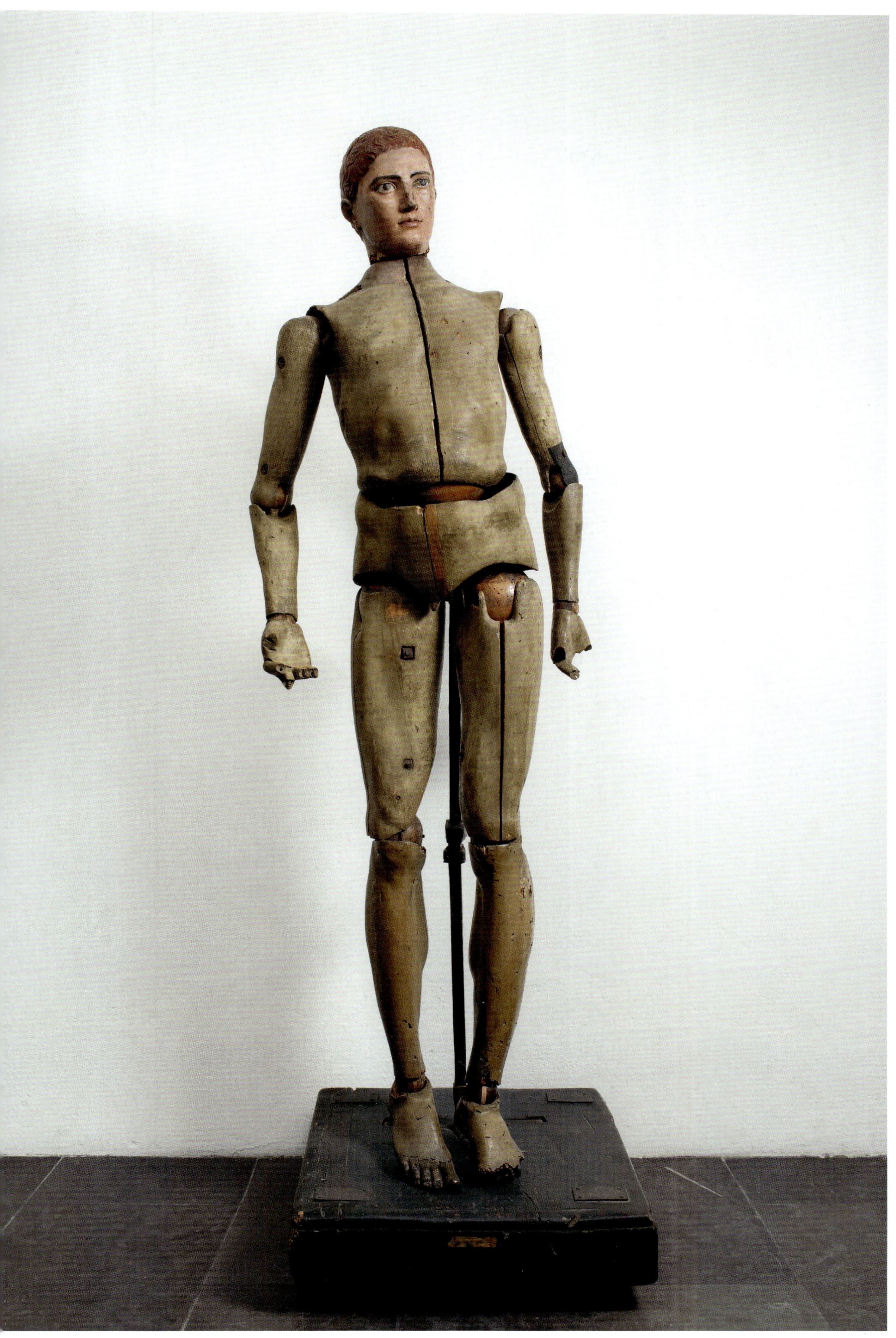

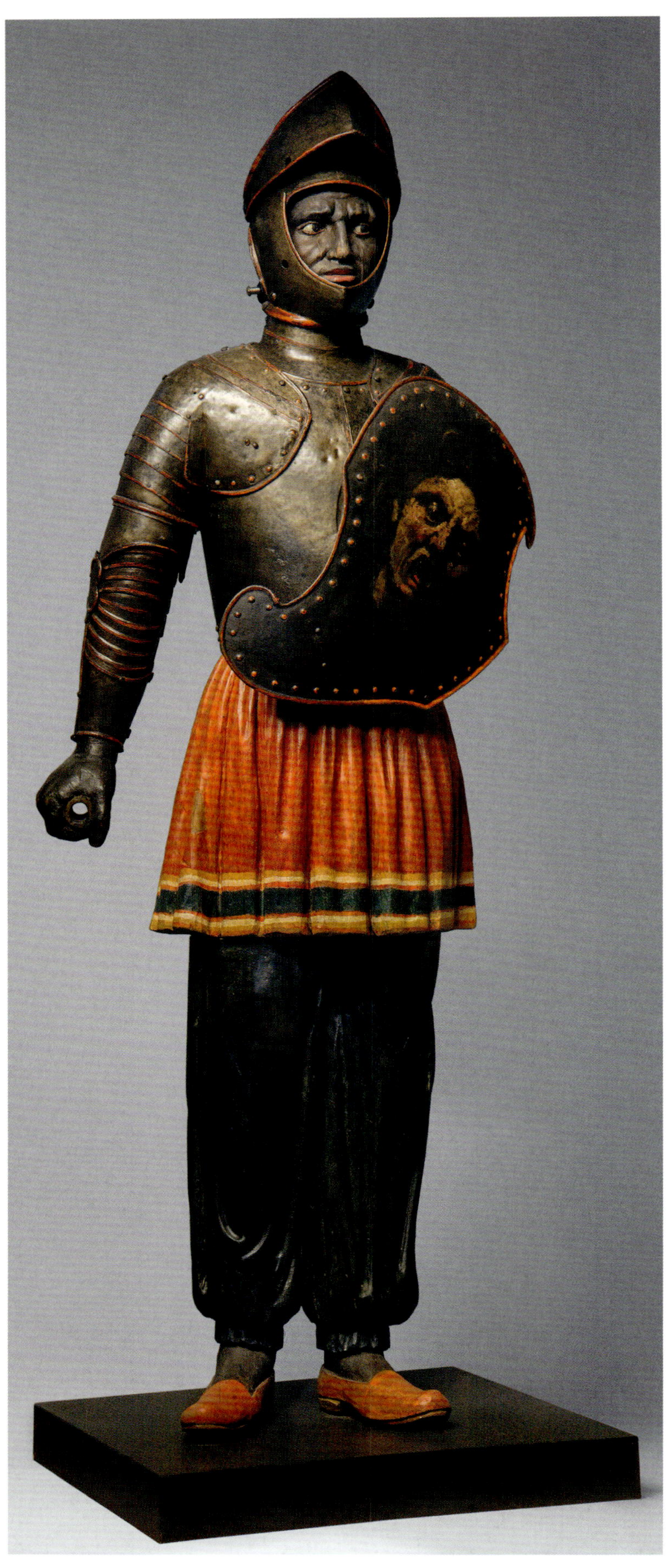

57. *Saracen Jousting Figure*, 1579. Polychromed wood, figure: H. 79 ½ in. (202 cm), W. 31 ½ in. (80 cm), D. 19 ¹¹⁄₁₆ in. (50 cm); base: H. 3 ¹⁵⁄₁₆ in. (10 cm), W. 27 ⁹⁄₁₆ in. (70 cm), D. 27 ⁹⁄₁₆ in. (70 cm). Florentine. Museo Nazionale del Bargello, Florence

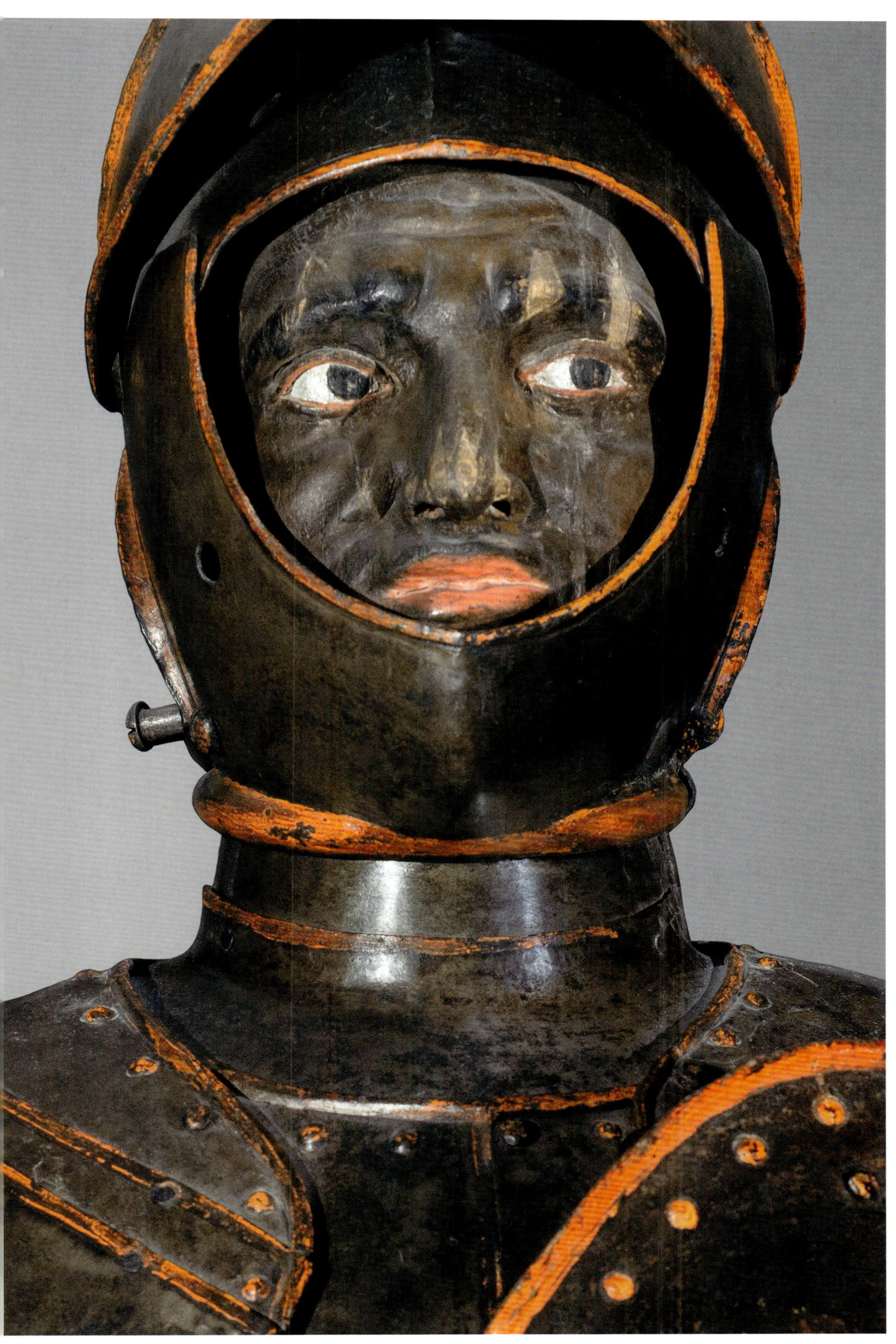

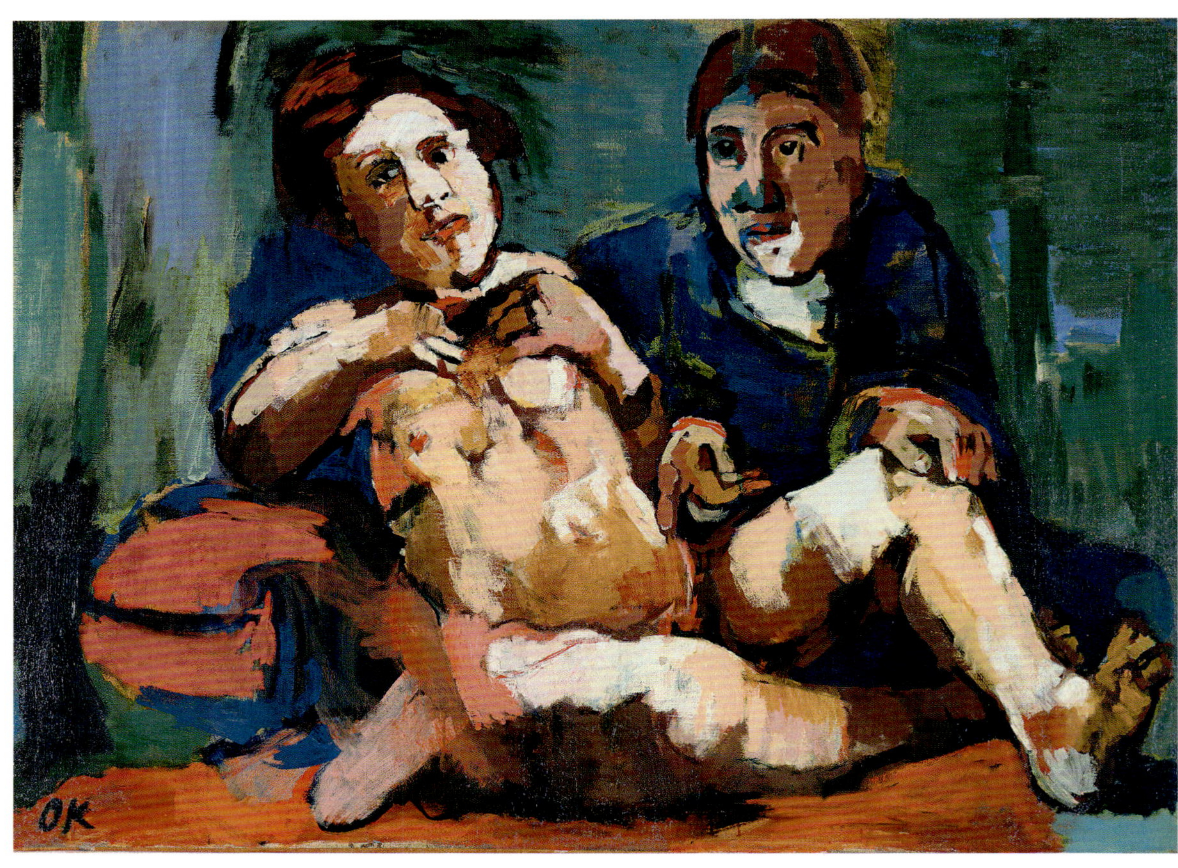

58. Oskar Kokoschka. *Self-Portrait with Doll (Mann mit Puppe)*, ca. 1922. Oil on canvas, 31 ½ × 47 ¼ in. (80 × 120 cm). Neue Nationalgalerie, Staatliche Museen zu Berlin, Nationalgalerie, acquired by the Federal State of Berlin, 1974

59. Paul Huot. *Lay Figure*, ca. 1790. Wood, metal, flax, silk, and painted gesso on papier-mâché, H. 64 in. (162.6 cm); with stand: H. 67 in. (170.2 cm); base: W. 25 ¾ in. (65.4 cm), D. 27 ¼ in. (69.2 cm). The Metropolitan Museum of Art, New York, Paper Conservation Artists' Materials Study Collection, Gift of Ronald N. Sherr, 2015

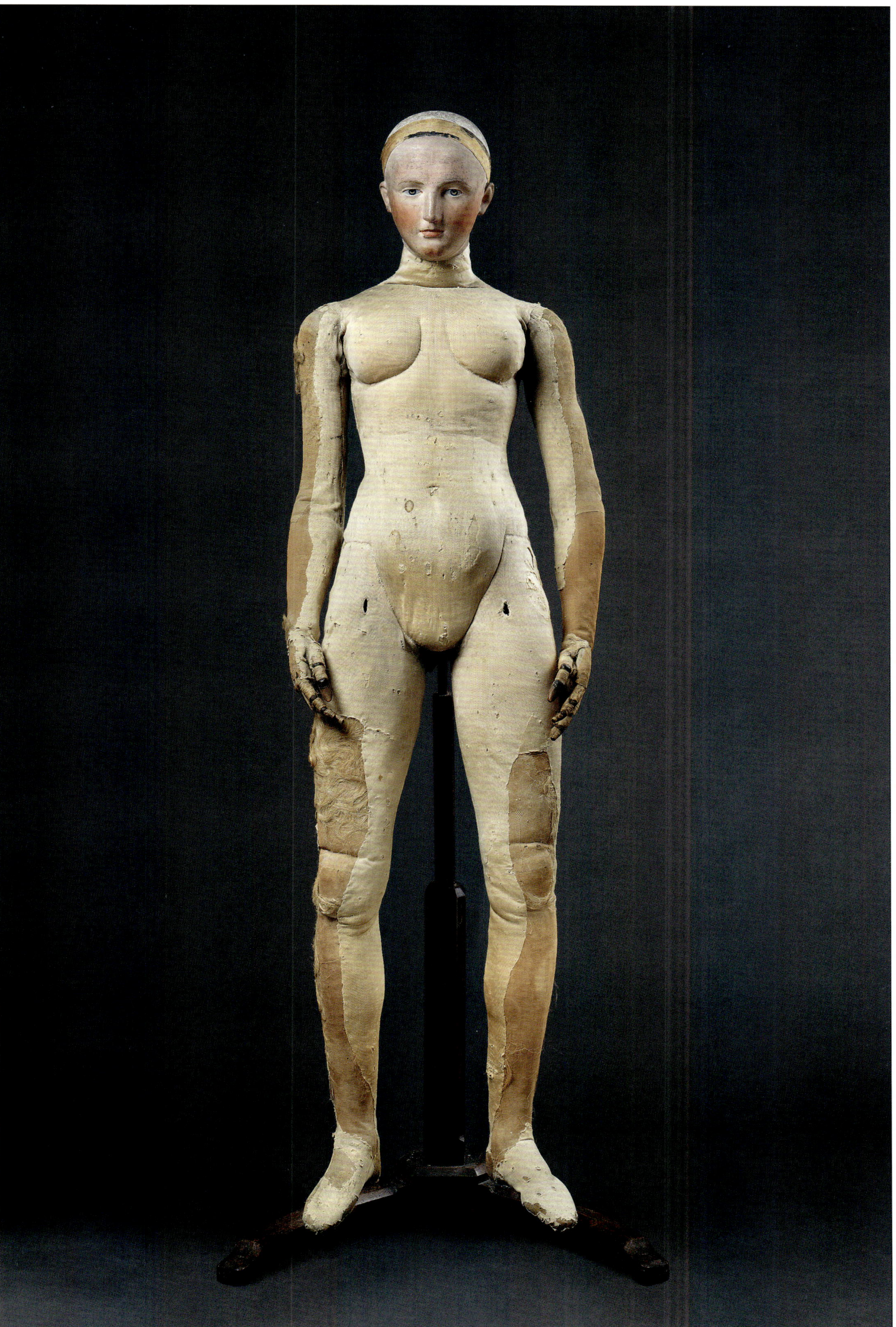

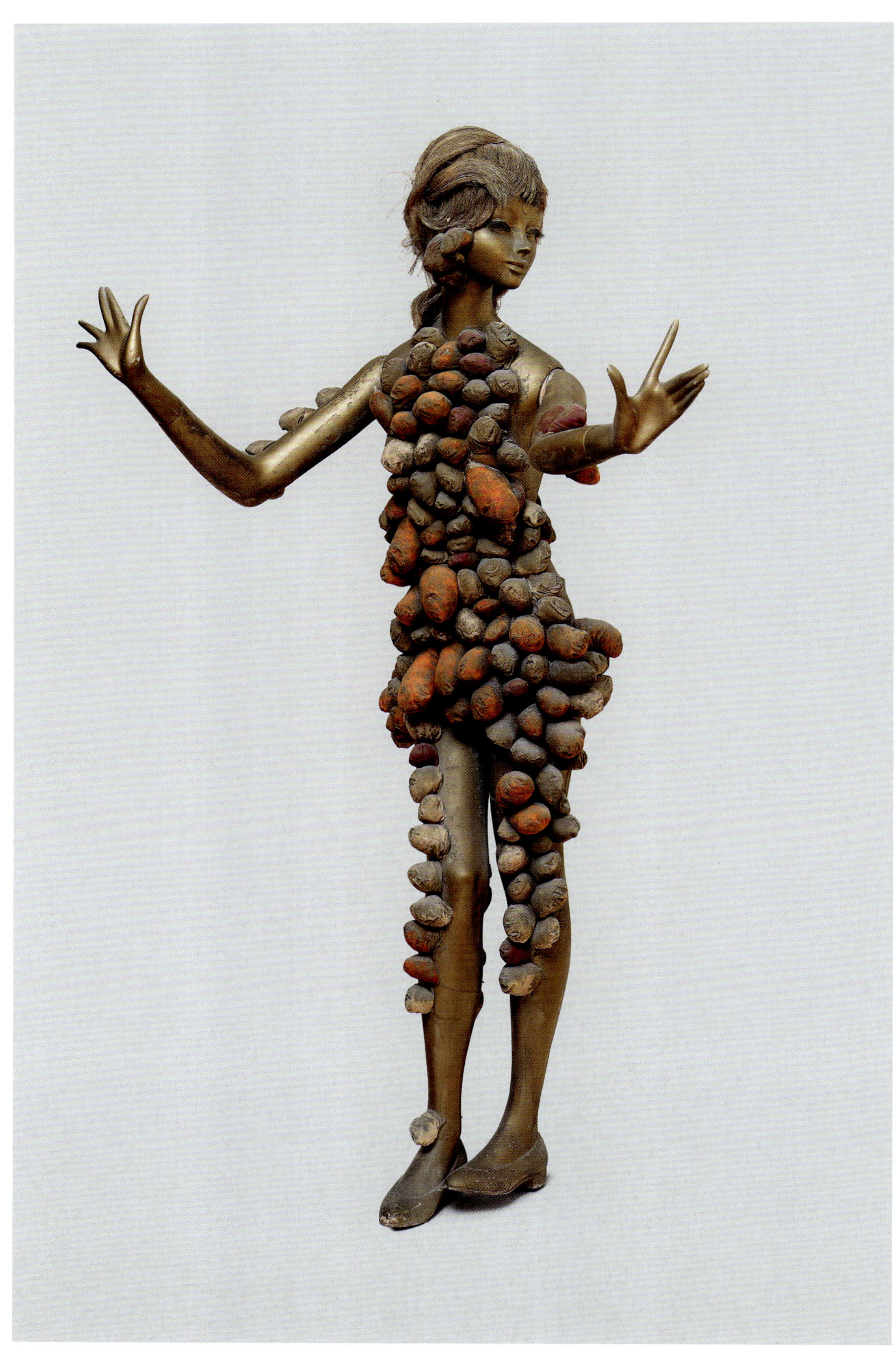

60. Yayoi Kusama. *Phallic Girl*, 1967. Mannequin and mixed media, H. 61 in. (155 cm), W. 34 ¼ in. (87 cm), D. 16 ¹⁵/₁₆ in. (43 cm). Collection of Caroline de Westenholz

61. Charles Ray. *Male Mannequin*, 1990. Mannequin and mixed media, H. 73 ½ in. (186.7 cm), W. 27 ¼ in. (69.2 cm), D. 18 ½ in. (47 cm). Broad Art Foundation, Los Angeles

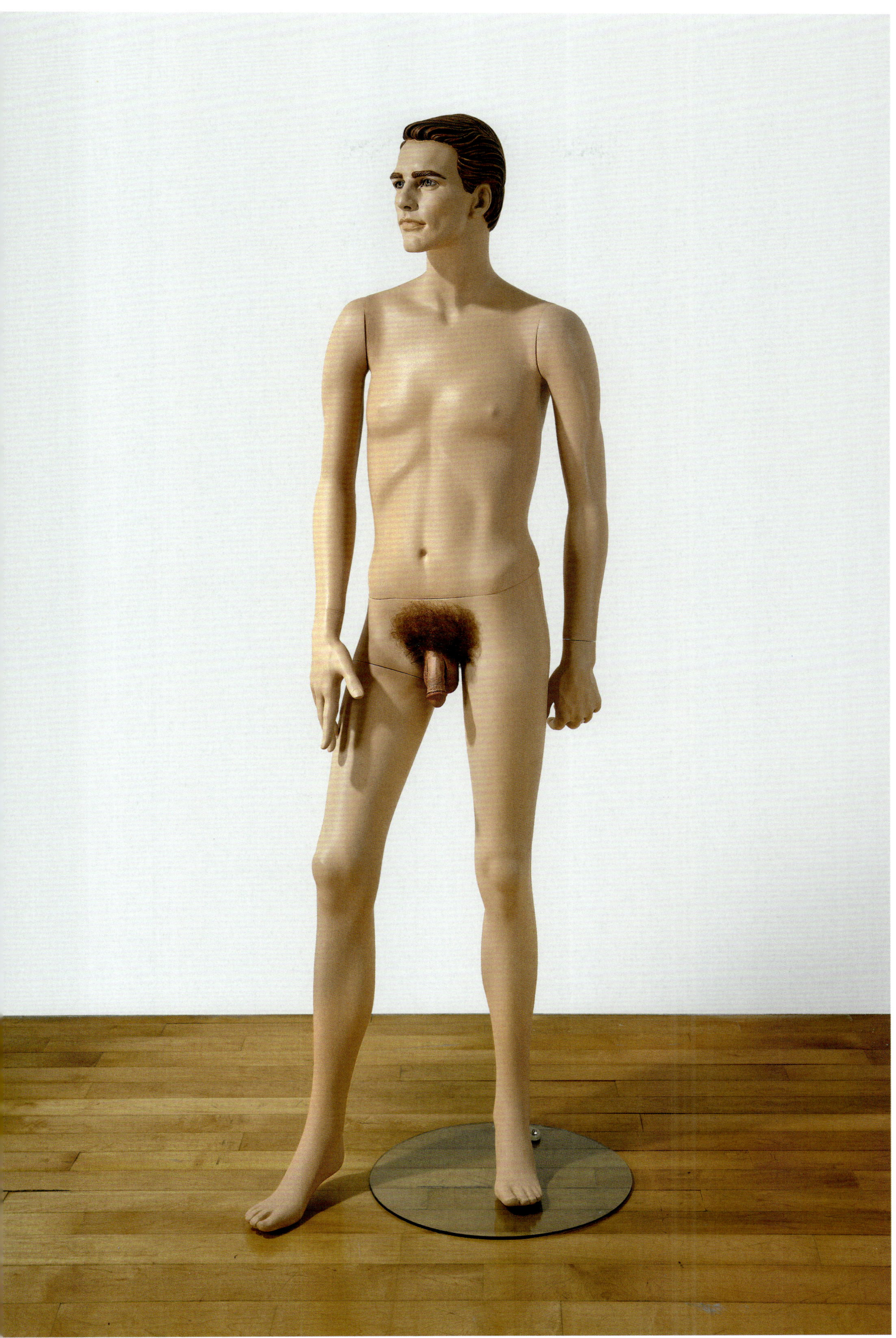

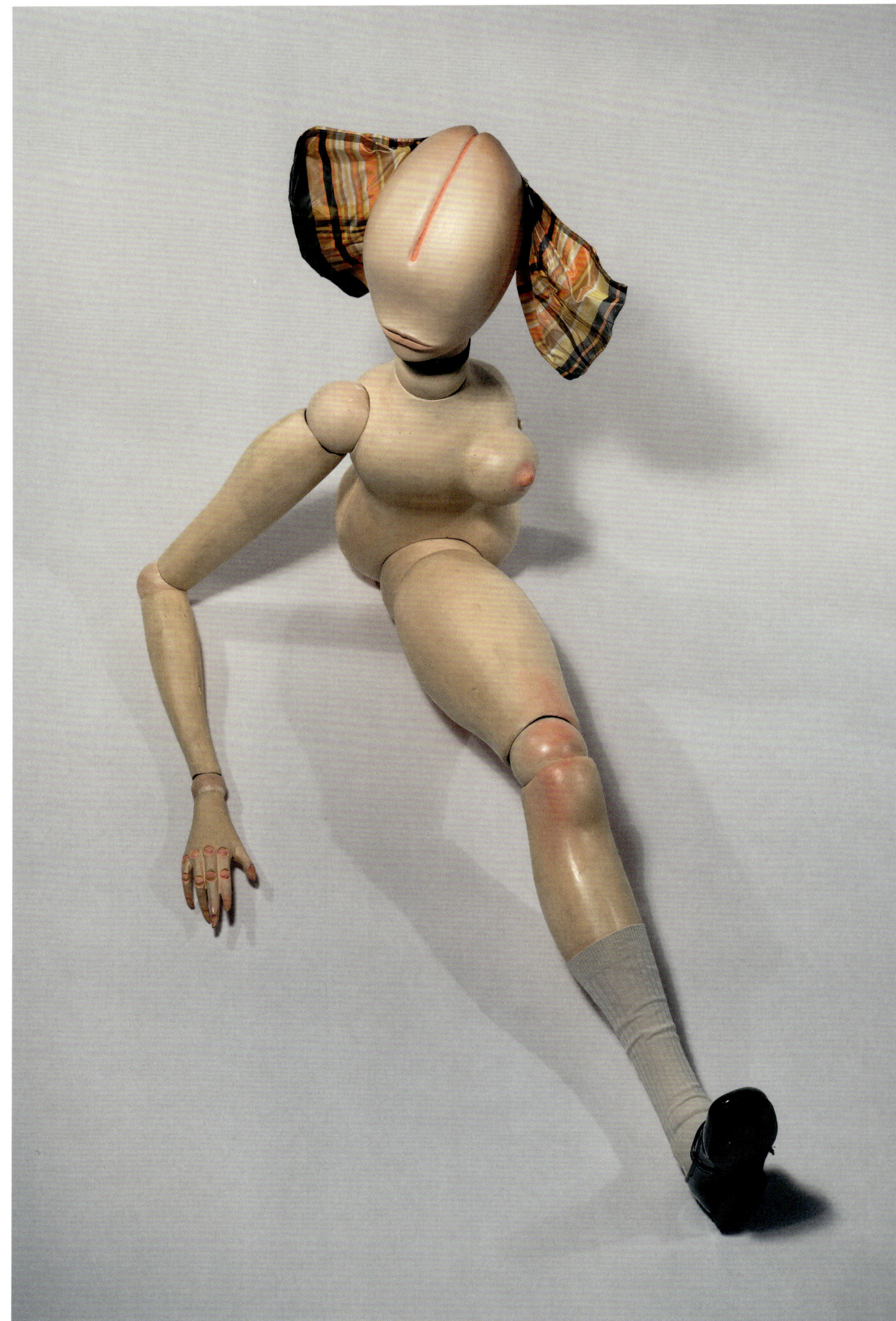

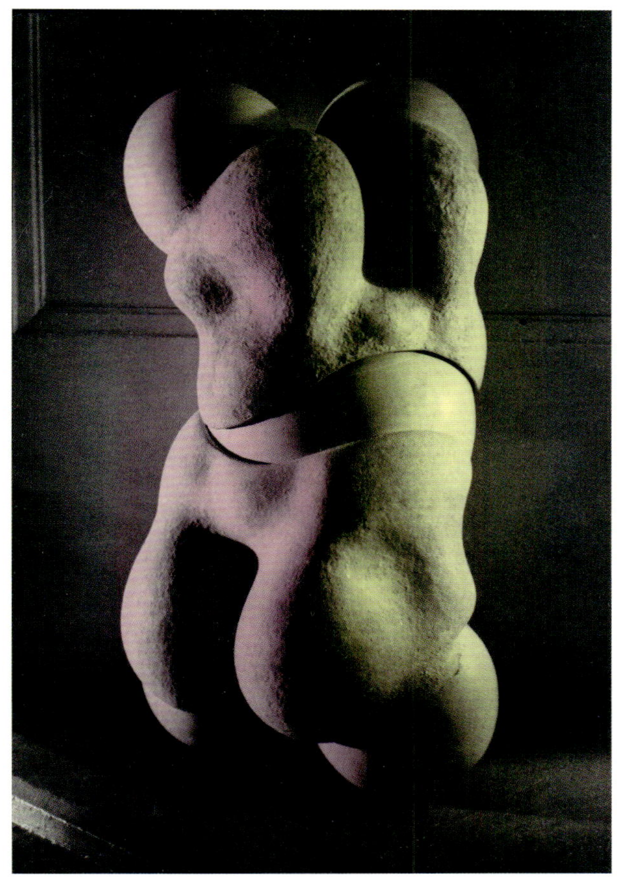

62. Hans Bellmer. *La Demi-Poupée*, 1972. Wood, paint, and fabric, seated: H. 23 ⅝ in. (60 cm), W. 16 ⁹⁄₁₆ in. (42 cm), D. 26 ¾ in. (68 cm). Rachel and Jean-Pierre Lehmann Collection

63. Hans Bellmer. *La Poupeé*, ca. 1936. Gelatin silver print with applied color, 3 ⁹⁄₁₆ × 2 ⅝ in. (9 × 6.7 cm). The Metropolitan Museum of Art, New York, Ford Motor Company Collection, Gift of Ford Motor Company and John C. Waddell, 1987 (1987.1100.333)

64. Hans Bellmer. *La Poupée*, 1936. Gelatin silver print with applied color, 5 ⁵⁄₁₆ × 5 ⁹⁄₁₆ in. (13.5 × 14.1 cm). The Metropolitan Museum of Art, New York, Ford Motor Company Collection, Gift of Ford Motor Company and John C. Waddell, 1987 (1987.1100.444)

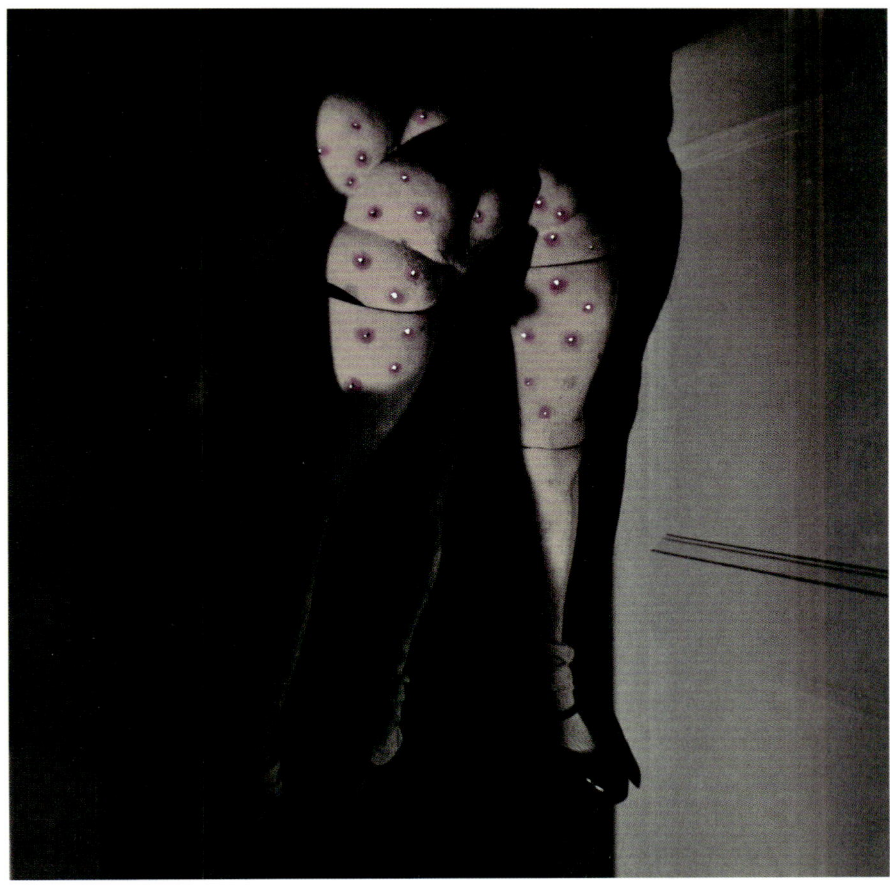

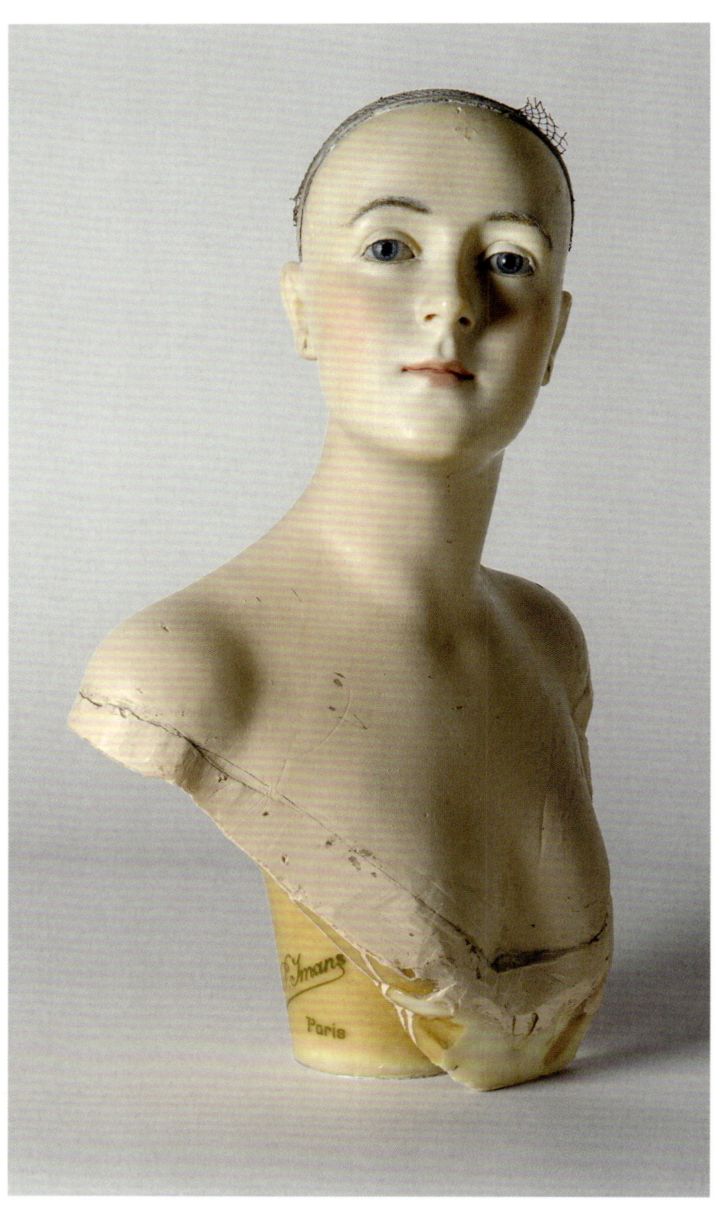
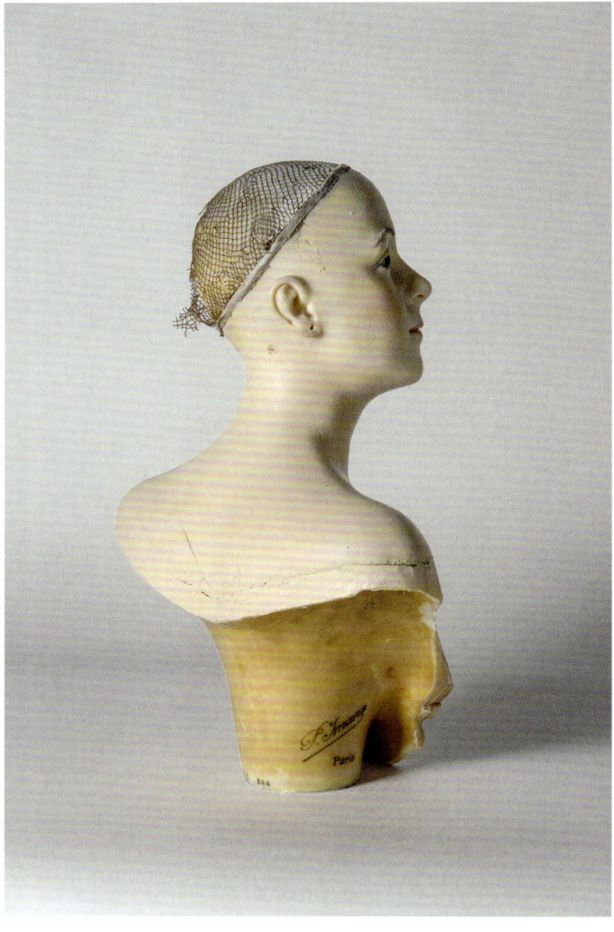
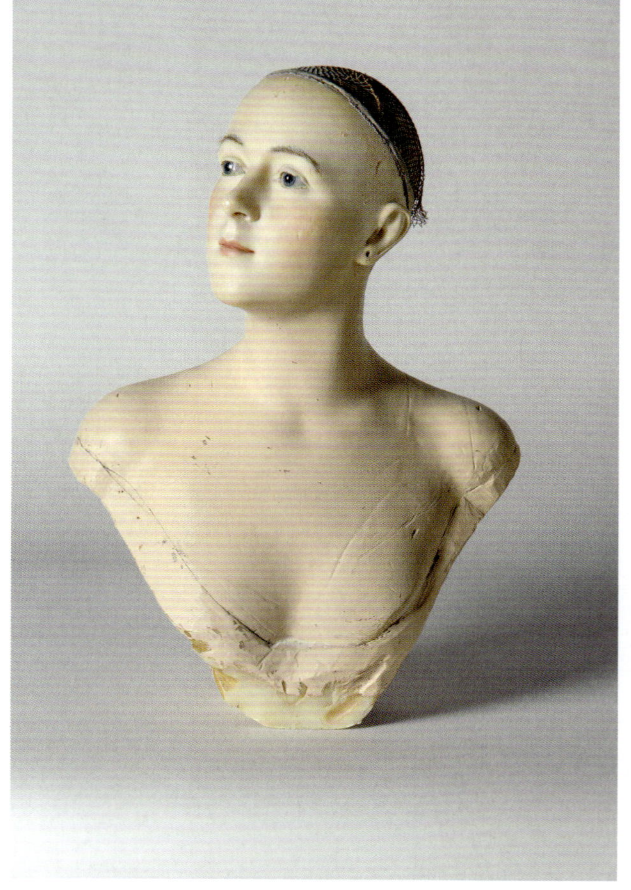

65. Pierre Imans. *Bust*, ca. 1910s. Painted wax, residual hair, silk and cotton net base, and resin, H. $22 \frac{1}{16}$ in. (56 cm), W. $17 \frac{1}{2}$ in. (44.5 cm), D. $8 \frac{1}{4}$ in. (21 cm). Fashion Museum Bath

66. Wilhelm Freddie. *Sex-Paralysappeal*, 1936. Mixed media, H. $30 \frac{11}{16}$ in. (78 cm), W. $13 \frac{3}{8}$ in. (34 cm), D. $13 \frac{3}{8}$ in. (34 cm). Moderna Museet, Stockholm, Purchase 1966

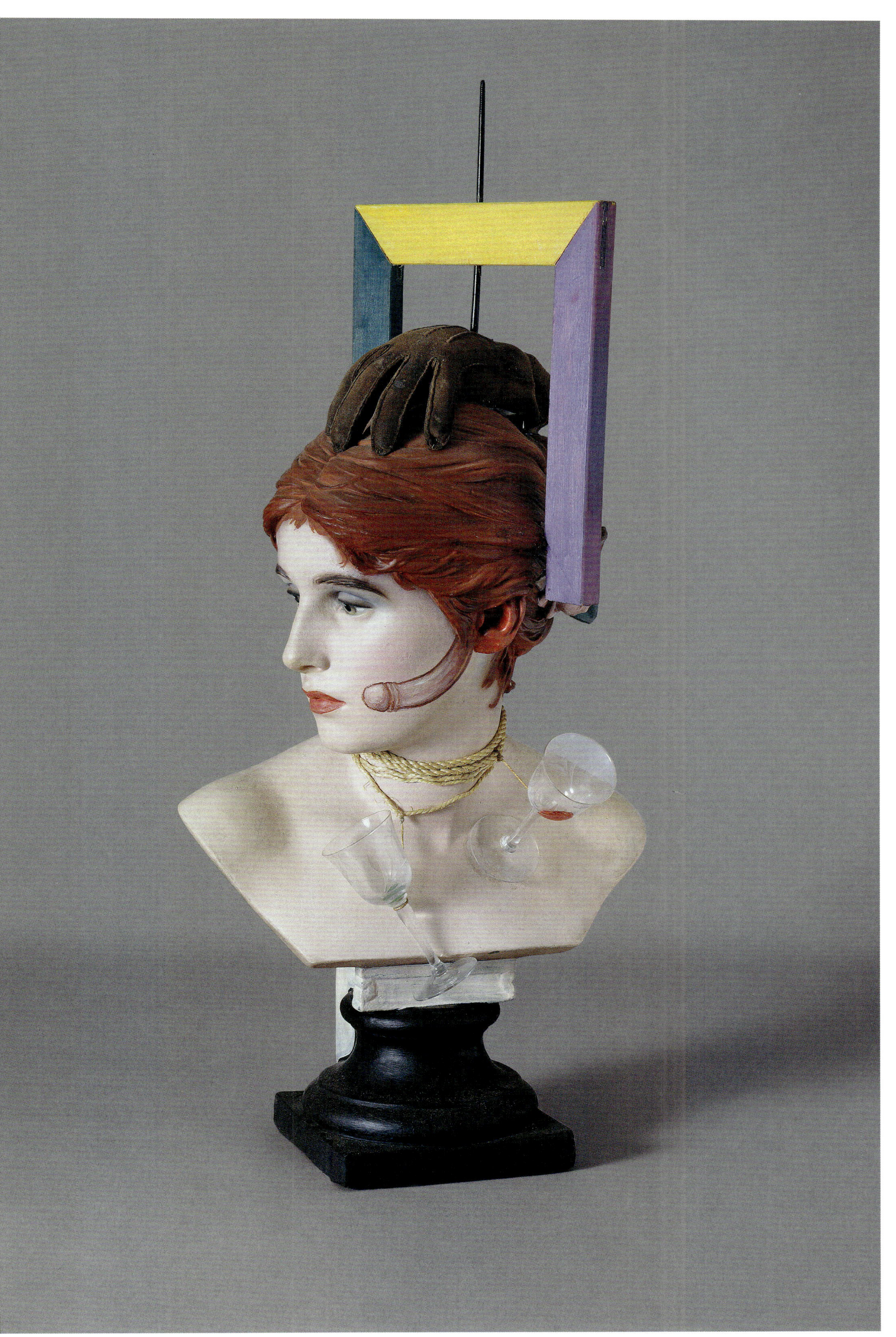

67. Meret Oppenheim. *Evening Dress with Bra-Strap Necklace* (*Abendkleid mit Büstenhalter-Collier*), 1968.
Mannequin torso, skirt, oil paint, glass-bead necklace, and shards of glass, H. 57 ⅟₁₆ in. (145 cm),
W. 16 ⅛ in. (41 cm), D. 11 in. (28 cm). Collection Pictet

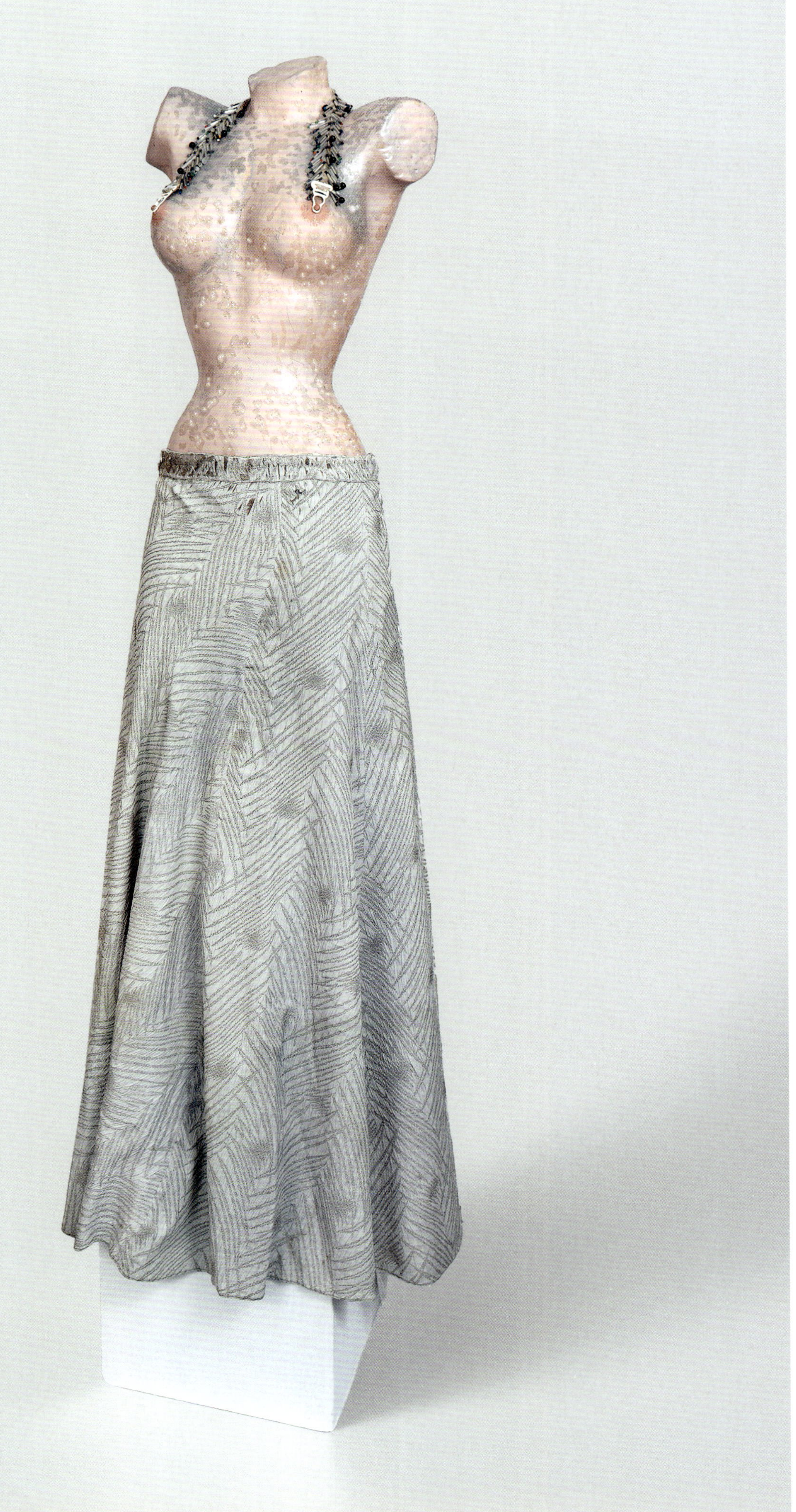

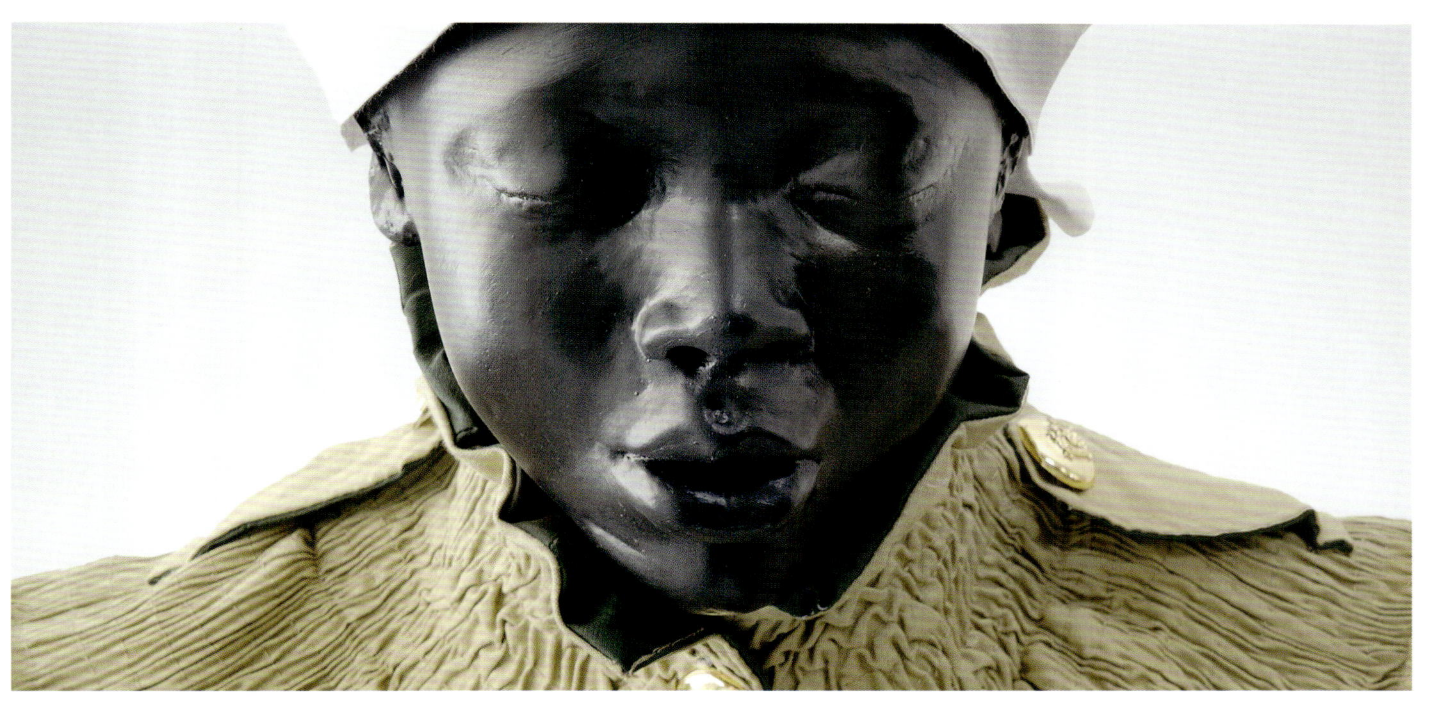
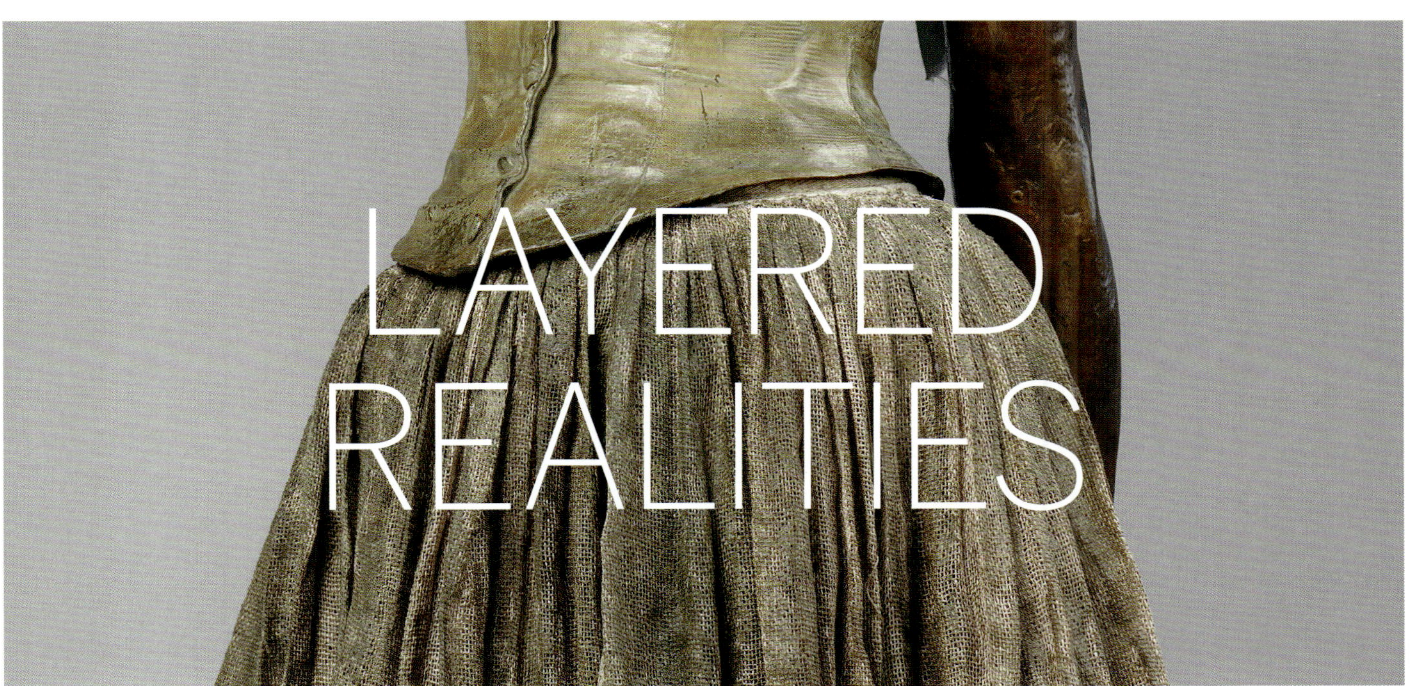
LAYERED
REALITIES
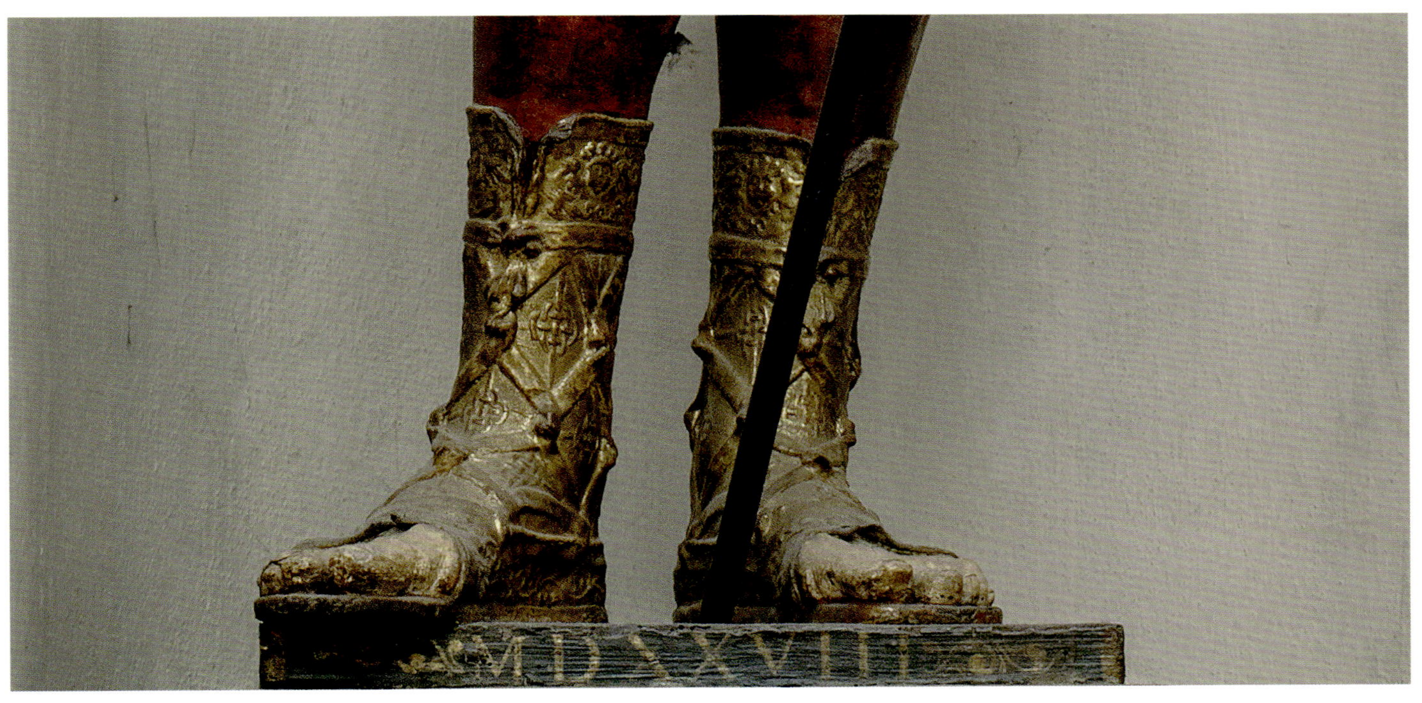

LAYERED REALITIES

BRINDA KUMAR

Long before textiles were developed, pelts and other skins were the first clothing worn by human beings. Since then, clothing has, in essence, worked as a second skin even as it developed increasingly complex social and cultural functions. Clothing conceals and reveals the body in strategic and deliberate ways, and it is in clothing/skin's relationship to the body that it encases that identity is signaled and read (and sometimes misread). Skin and second skin mediate a human being's encounter with the physical, social, and cultural sphere. Art historian and philosopher Veronica Mundi posits, "Skin is a liminal structure, it is in-between, it is the template on which our experience, inner and outer, is inscribed, and our experience, and our inheritance, is there to be read by others. It is where the world confronts the I and where the I meets the world."[1]

In sculpture, skin and clothing are key to articulating the body in three dimensions, and together they are the visible surface that suggests bodily presence. The manner in which it is brought about and the meaning and significance of representing the clothed, adorned, or unclothed body unsurprisingly varies across cultures. In Western aesthetics, beginning with the Renaissance and continuing through Neoclassicism, the epitomized sculptured body was conceived as the youthful figure in the nude, and with drapery, when present, invariably emphasizing the contours of an idealized body intended to reflect an idealized spirit. In this context, as scholar Michel Chaouli has noted, skin functions as a boundary, both real and imagined:

First, it distinguishes between body and world, preventing the former from disintegrating into raw matter and mingling with its environment. And secondly, it distinguishes real bodies, with their creases, wrinkles, hollows and openings, from the ideal male bodies represented in classical sculptures, in which the skin's supple embrace of the body makes its beauty visible. The skin permits the appearance in real bodies of something unreal—of an ideal, a soul, a divinity—but to do that it must render itself invisible. The perfect skin is one that appears perfectly transparent, one that allows us to see right through it, into incorporeality, into transcendence. This, then, is the paradox of skin: it is needed in order to perform the distinction of real from unreal bodies, yet it must appear invisible if this distinction is to be maintained.[2]

In sculpture this meant the articulation of the ideal unblemished body in smooth monochromatic marble or bronze where there was little or no textural or chromatic differentiation between the matter and metaphor of the body and its sheaths. With this paradigm, the representation of the reality of bodies through the mere suggestion of skin color, such as *The Tinted Venus* (ca. 1851–56, cat. 8), could be aesthetically controversial, let alone through the introduction of the materials that simulated or integrated the materiality of skin, flesh, and clothing.

The uproar caused by the presentation of French artist Edgar Degas's *The Little Fourteen-Year-Old Dancer* at the sixth Impressionist exhibition, held in Paris in 1881, is thus not hard to fathom. Based on Degas's studies of young ballet students in practice and at leisure at the Paris Opéra Ballet, this standing portrait of Marie van Goethem was modeled in wax over an armature made of wire, rope, and paintbrushes.

Although Degas had modeled in wax and clay for much of his career, this would be the only sculpture he would ever exhibit. His experimental approach to making sculpture with the integration of a variety of media is evident in this piece, and it can, in addition, be viewed as anticipating the heterogeneity of materials routinely used by artists during the twentieth century. Not only was Degas's presentation of the wax model as the final state of the sculpture (not as an intermediary stage for casting in bronze) to raise eyebrows, but he caused further consternation by dressing the figure in a fabric tutu, ballet slippers, and a wig made of human hair tied in a satin bow. Degas's sculpture was a far cry from idealized Neoclassical nudes and rather a startlingly contemporary figure of a pubescent girl, which replicated the achingly real details of her physiognomy not least because her articulation in tinted wax simulated the texture and appearance of flesh and skin but also through the artist's use of actual clothes, hair, and accessories. At the time, French writer Joris-Karl Huysmans noted, "The terrible realism of this statuette makes the public distinctly uneasy, all its ideas about sculpture, about cold lifeless whiteness, about those memorable formulas copied again and again for centuries are demolished"; nevertheless, the radicalism of Degas's gesture was not overlooked when Huysmans added, "This statuette is the only truly modern attempt I know in sculpture."[3] The shock of the real was thus invigorating as it echoed the changing aesthetics of the late nineteenth century, when modernism was coming into its own. The unembellished immediacy of the figure with her jaunty, almost defiant pose and her slightly upturned head made her strikingly present and grounded, while contemporary critics compared her to a range of (less edifying) figures, such as fourteenth-century Spanish polychromed sculpture, Egyptian mummies, religious relics, kitsch waxworks, and clothes mannequins. The ambivalent response to the figure underscores the tension inherent in the sculpture between its "scrupulously realistic technique and a psychologically disturbing content."[4] Even today, the

voyeurism and power differential between artist and young female subject, which resulted in a work intended to be displayed and optically consumed like a specimen in a glass vitrine, remains unnerving. The figure was never cast in bronze during Degas's lifetime; however, a number were subsequently cast in a limited-edition series by the A. A. Hébrard Foundry, Paris, beginning in 1922 (cat. 68). While the supple sensuality of wax could not be fully replicated in metal, the textural details of the skin and bodice were cast and patinated superbly, and each edition was fitted with her own tutu and ribbon.

Although Degas's *Little Fourteen-Year-Old Dancer* radically departed from prevailing sculpture norms during its time, history has shown how the work prefigured an emerging aesthetic turn. As such, the work has become a touchstone for many artists who have engaged with her iconic status—ranging from feminist approaches to the female body, including British artist Rebecca Warren's *The Twin* (2005, fig. 70) to British artist Damien Hirst's sardonic imagining of her as a pregnant cross-sectioned anatomical figure (*Virgin [exposed]*, 2005, cat. 82). British Nigerian artist Yinka Shonibare MBE's *Girl Ballerina* (2007,

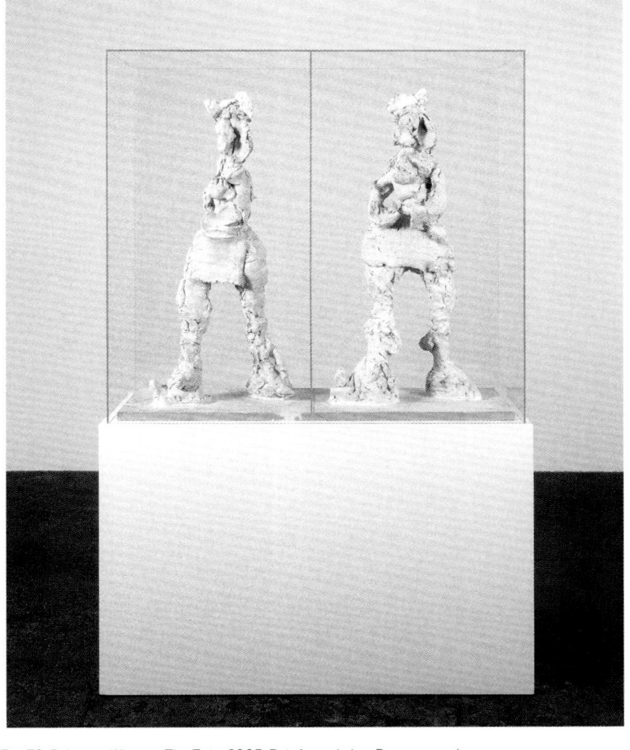

Fig. 70 Rebecca Warren. *The Twin*, 2005. Reinforced clay, Perspex, and paint on medium-density-fiberboard plinth, H. 75 ½ in. (192 cm), W. 51 ½ in. (131 cm), D. 20 in. (51 cm). Private collection

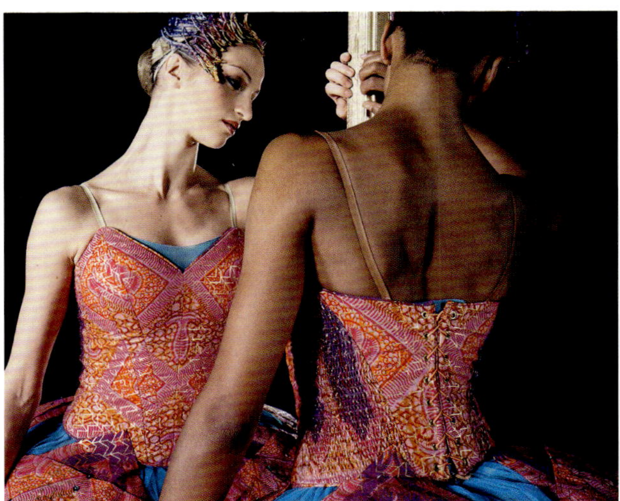

Fig. 71 Yinka Shonibare MBE. *Odile and Odette IV*, 2005–6. Chromogenic print, 49 × 63 ½ in. (124.5 × 161.3 cm). Courtesy of the artist

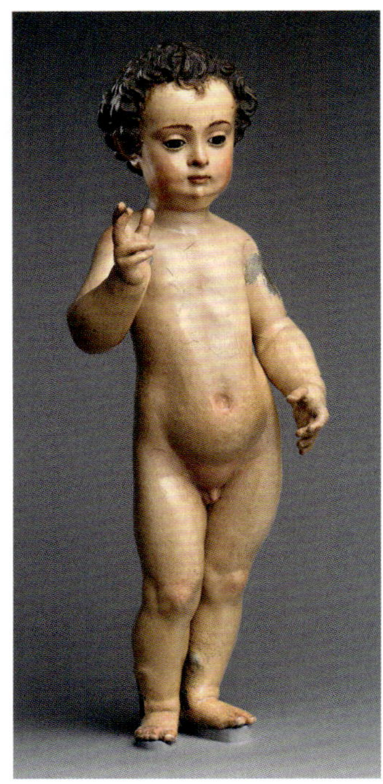

cat. 69) references Degas, but the sculpture stands at the intersection of artistic interests that exceed the formal. Shonibare's investigations into the figure of the ballerina began with a commission from the Royal Opera House, London, which resulted in the film *Odile and Odette* (2005, see fig. 71). It draws on Russian composer Pyotr Tchaikovsky's nineteenth-century ballet *Swan Lake*, a story that centers around the mistaken identity of Odile and Odette. The roles are typically performed by one ballerina with two costumes—one white and one black, representing good and malevolent spirits, respectively. Shonibare interrogates this presumably symbolic use of color by intersecting it with the racially fraught interpretation of chromatic difference. In his film two ballerinas wear the same brightly colored tutus and mirror each other's movements, but one ballerina is white, and the other is black. When he made the film, Shonibare was able to choose from the Royal Ballet corps for the role of the white dancer, but he had to seek an independent dancer for the black performer because the corps did not have a black ballerina at the time.[5] The colonial roots of the politics of race, especially as crystallized in the nineteenth century, run through Shonibare's practice. He creates figures that are recognizably nineteenth-century European by way of their clothes—frock coats, crinolines, bustles—however, their clothing is unexpectedly sewn from brightly colored Dutch wax–print textiles that are associated with West Africa. Shonibare relies on an understanding of form (and formal stereotypes) such that his deliberately discordant sartorial choices create visual and conceptual dissonance, thereby destabilizing the neatness of historical narratives, including colonialism and postcolonial national and cultural identity. His figures, whether single or multiple, are often posed as if engaged in some frivolous or anodyne activity, their luxuriating

amplified by their sensually rich clothes. Yet on closer inspection, there can be a menacing undertone to these scenes, such as a dueling pistol held in the neatly folded hands hidden behind a ballerina whose head has been irreverently (or preemptively?) blown off (cat. 69), which underscores sinister intentions and the consequences of seemingly innocuous people and actions. While a critique of European colonialism inherently exists in this approach, Shonibare also deconstructs the textile as a marker of African authenticity; as scholar Manthia Diawara explains, "In so far as he now uses the material in his art to dress individuals of non-African origin, he reveals the arbitrariness of the meanings given to the fabric in Africa."[6]

Clothing the body in particular ways can confirm or disrupt identity and engender empathy or estrangement from the figure thus presented. It is the former aspect that was shocking with the Degas sculpture and elicited comparisons with Spanish polychrome sculpture of a preceding era. In this interpretation, the realism of sculpture was seen to pander to emotions that may have been acceptable in a religious context but certainly at odds with the aesthetic response expected in the secular context of an exhibition of fine art. The Italian and Spanish polychrome sculptures that were the points of comparison include types such as *Saint Roch* attributed to Italian artist Nero Alberti (1528, cat. 70) and the seventeenth-century *The Child Jesus Triumphant* (ca. 1625, fig. 72) probably by the workshop of the Spanish artist Juan de Mesa. Alberti's figure of the saint, formerly attributed to Maestro di Magione, was originally installed in the Church of San Francesco in what is now Umbertide, Italy, and created around the time of the great plague of 1527. Saint Roch was a pilgrim saint who survived the plague and therefore was frequently invoked as a protector against the disease. Alberti and his workshop specialized in finely carved, highly lifelike polychrome figures for ecclesiastical purposes that were then dressed when installed in churches or on domestic altars. The sculptures were a composite of naturalistically modeled figures with painted skin, attributes, accessories, and real clothes, as depicted in the case of Saint Roch, who stands partially clothed in boots and finely modeled underpants holding a staff. He would have likely been completed by the draping of pilgrim's robes to cover his upper body, even as his left thigh, with his conspicuously rendered infected bubo, would have been deliberately exposed in keeping with the iconography of the saint. The Spanish *Child Jesus* figure demonstrates how a polychrome figure would have appeared when fully clothed (cat. 72). Baby Jesus figures, or *Niños*, were a type of devotional sculpture commonly associated with female patronage: "Widows and nuns used these holy dolls as a way to fulfill their desire for motherhood and to have a more intimate devotional experience with Christ.... There are references to clothing and jewelry to dress the *Niños*... suggesting an active and direct devotional engagement with these figures."[7] The *Child Jesus* was clearly revered in this manner, owing to the fact that his clothes are of a slightly later vintage than the figure itself, which suggests a wardrobe replacement. The gentle contrapposto of the standing figure is not visible when enveloped in a richly embellished, three-piece set of robes (dress, capelet, and bib) made of cream-colored silk brocade. When dressed, only the figure's head with inset glass eyes and right hand raised in benediction peek out.

If the ritual dressing of the figures was necessary for the completion of the reality of their presence, and thus could be spiritually and psychologically efficacious for the devotee or believer, dress can play a key role in the construction and expression of identity as well. In the eighteenth century, Spanish national identity and ideas of masculinity began to take shape around the idea of *majismo* and the figure of the *majo*. As art historian Tara Zanardi explains: "There is a close link between visual representations of majos and toreros, as suggested by the similarities in their clothing, class, and insolent posturing.... Many of the items characteristic of majo dress may be seen in the bullfighter's *traje de luces* (suit of lights), including the short jacket with shoulder embellishments, the hairnet, and the colorful sash around the waist; this outfit underscores the torero's showmanship and stylishness."[8] Bullfights became important national events, and bullfighters were worshiped like heroes. José Delgado Guerra, or Pepe Illo, was one such fighter from Seville who was invited to showcase his talents in a series of bullfights as part of the celebrations to mark Charles IV's accession to the throne in 1789. These inaugural bullfights were commemorated in a series of twenty-seven polychrome wood figures made by Juan Cháez, an artist from Málaga. All the bullfighters (cat. 74) are impeccably costumed in the colorful and richly embellished *traje de luces*, which remains little changed and characteristic of the Spanish bullfight today. The figures were grouped to illustrate stages of the bullfight and specific events that

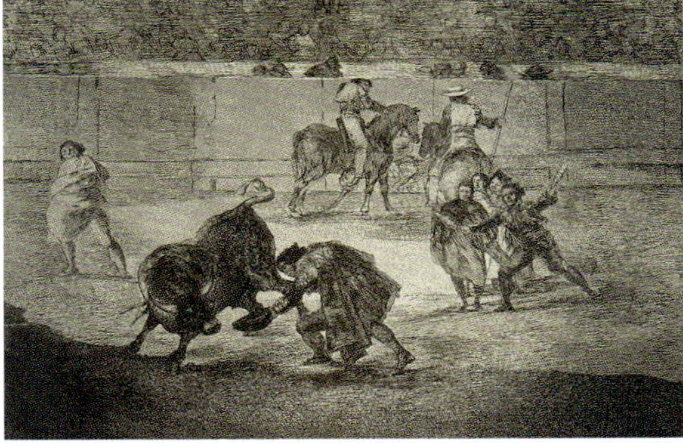

A.

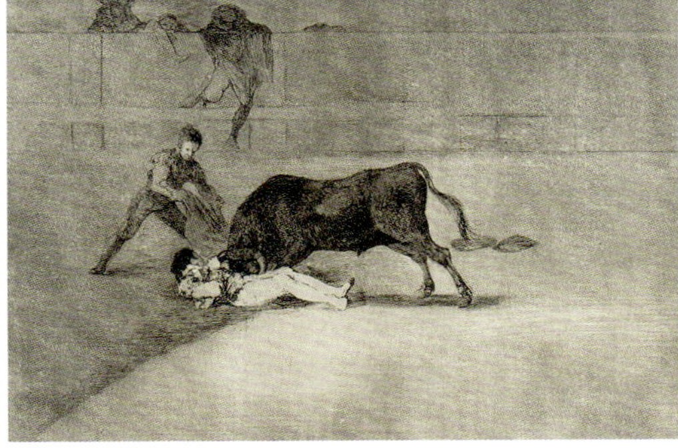

B.

Fig. 73 Goya (Francisco de Goya y Lucientes). A, B: plates 29 and 33 from the series La Tauromaquia: *Pepe Illo Making the Pass of the "Recorte,"* 1816. Etching, burnished aquatint, drypoint, and burin, plate: 9 9/16 × 13 3/4 in. (24.3 × 35 cm); *The Unlucky Death of Pepe Illo in the Ring at Madrid*, 1816. Etching, burnished aquatint, drypoint, and burin, plate: 9 11/16 × 13 3/4 in. (24.6 × 35 cm). The Metropolitan Museum of Art, New York, Rogers Fund, 1921 (21.19.29.33)

occurred. One such event was the goring of Pepe Illo by a bull, in which he was promptly carried from the arena by two fighters. Pepe Illo's celebrity only grew after this occasion, and his bravado was confirmed with his spectacular death by another goring in 1801, an event memorialized by Goya in his Tauromaquia series (fig. 73).

While the deliberate flamboyance of the *traje de luces* and its use in a performative setting suggest "costume" rather than the more quotidian "dress," both senses of clothing are implicated in the projection of identity, and especially in a globalizing context in which the distinction can sometimes blur.[9] In Sokari Douglas Camp's *Material Salsa* (2011, cat. 75), the artist seems to suggest this blending of meaning, identity, and materiality. Made out of hard steel from the oil drums she recycles and uses in her work

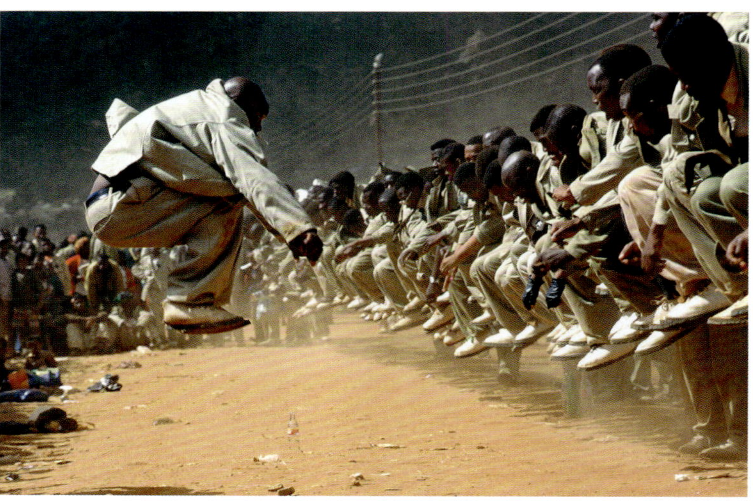

Fig. 74 *Mokhukhu* at the Easter Meeting of the Zion Christian Church, Polokwane, South Africa, 1996

(the politics of oil in Nigeria is a pervasive theme in Douglas Camp's work), yet suggesting the softness and malleability of textiles, her figures address the ambivalence and challenges of changing economies, migration, and the evolving cultures of dress. The two almost-linked figures of mother and son (are they caught midstep in a dance?) represent the connections and polarities of their relationship to each other and to their African heritage. The female figure wears a floor-length African robe with a stole over her shoulder and a wrap around her head, while the male figure is dressed in unremarkable trousers and a white T-shirt but sports a jacket conspicuously emblazoned with Formula One racing car logos, gesturing toward the nexus between these companies and oil profiteering that has overtaken the Kalabari culture of the Nigerian delta region where Douglas

Camp grew up. The contrast between their outfits underscores the complexity in reading identity (Which figure is wearing a dress, and which one is wearing a costume? Or are they wearing both at the same time?) and the political overtones of the symbols that depend so much on the context in which one encounters the figures. The slippage is playfully addressed in Isa Genzken's series Actors (Schauspieler, 2013, cat. 76), in which the German artist used a number of commercially made mannequins and dressed them in a range of eclectic materials and items of clothing. Some of the latter were drawn from the artist's own wardrobe so that the figures are at once generic if eccentric urban types (she named some of the characters variously "urban cowboy," "alien," and "Death") and "in an ultimate act of self-identification and self-inscription," they are her alter egos.[10]

The alter ego, as articulated through costume, is key to Mary Sibande's practice. In her photographs and sculptures she casts herself in the role of the domestic maid Sophie, who wears a cross between a Victorian gown and a uniform. The hybrid dress straddles the eras from the colonial past of servitude experienced by her mother and grandmother to the postcolonial present identity the artist experiences as a South African woman—the move suggests a space of fantasy and time travel where gender and the role of women can be reimagined through empowering characters seemingly from the past or by conjuring future selves. The characters are nonetheless linked to extant traditions, such as the Zion Christian Church (ZCC) in South Africa, which is addressed in Sibande's *Rubber Soul, Monument of Aspiration* (2011, cat. 79).[11] In this sculpture, Sophie is dressed in a voluminous khaki-colored gown-uniform with a white apron and cap and viewed in a midair jump onto a pedestal. The figure is rich with signifiers: the khaki uniform; the distinctive white, handmade canvas shoes with rubber soles; and the act of jumping are all associated with the exclusively male activities of the ZCC, especially the *Mokhukhu* dance (fig. 74).[12] By visualizing Sophie in this subversive role, Sibande challenges gender inequity and demands recognition. In leaping onto the pedestal she powerfully claims visibility in (social and sculptural) settings where women of color are infrequently figured.

The imagining of feminist utopias is germane to Swiss artist Mai-Thu Perret's work as well. In her series Les Guérillères (2016–present, cat. 78), she combines this interest with real-world examples by focusing on the Yekîneyên Parastina Jin (Women's Protection Units [YPJ]), the all-female group of Kurdish militia who are based in Rojava in northern Syria. After watching hours of YouTube videos of the women in action and going about their activities, she settled on representing them at moments of repose. The figures in the series are made from glazed ceramic, wicker, silicone, or papier-mâché; most hold weapons cast in colorful resin; and all wear camouflage fatigues marking their militant roles.[13] The clothes and accessories also underscore the transcendence of traditional gender roles in their sociocultural setting. While the figures cannot be confused for actual YPJ fighters by Perret's conscious referencing of the mannequin form, nevertheless, when clothed, they become proxies for real identities, however utopian or dystopian the contexts of their existence might be.[14]

That clothes can enable the individual to assume or imagine alternative identities is borne out in Elmgreen & Dragset's *The Experiment* (2012, cat. 71), in which a young boy clad in white underpants solemnly gazes at himself in a mirror. As the title suggests, he is probing the prescriptions of gender by standing in (his mother's?) oversize high-heeled shoes and trying on some (of her?) lipstick. The white underpants appear as an erotic accessory in another work by the artists titled *Jason (Briefs)* (2009, fig. 75). Invited to engage with the Neoclassical sculptures of Bertel Thorvaldsen, the artists dressed this Danish sculptor's version of the Greek hero Jason in the titular briefs. Paradoxically the presence of this real "second skin" highlights the eroticism of the nude whose apparent nakedness is brought to the fore by the suggestion of undressing, even as Thorvaldsen's nude figure of Jason carries the golden fleece in one hand while his own robes are draped artfully behind him. In *The Experiment*, however, the white briefs on the boyish frame are a more liminal sheath, as an apparent Lacanian moment of self-formation coupled with the artist duo's interests in exploring queer temporality, gay subjectivity, and gender identity in their collaborative practice.[15]

Another sort of diminutive figure gazes upon herself in a mirror in Spanish sculptor Juan Muñoz's *Sarah with Blue Dress* (1996, cat. 73). Muñoz frequently created mise-en-scènes that interrogate the act of looking, confound the assumptions of the gaze, and challenge representation. The figure of the dwarf

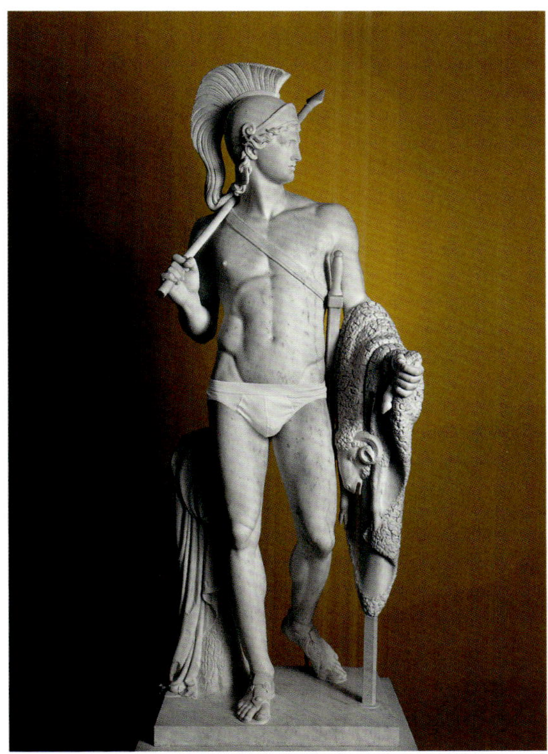

Fig. 75 Elmgreen & Dragset. *Jason (Briefs)*, 2009. Laserchrome color print, mounted on aluminum, 78 ¾ × 59 in. (200 × 150 cm), aluminum D. ⅛ in. (0.4 cm). Courtesy of the artists

allowed him to propose a shifted perspective of the world and the realities perceived and constructed through sight.[16] Recalling Diego Velázquez and his paintings of dwarfs in the Baroque court of Philip IV, King of Spain, Muñoz noted that "the dwarf was the only person that could criticise the court. Because of his physical distortion, he was allowed to distort or exaggerate reality."[17] Foregrounding the "otherness" of their form, Sarah and George, another model, were two such figures whom Muñoz would regularly cast in his works to force viewers to confront and question their own ways of looking and of identifying with the figures and themselves. The mirror as device pushes this intention even further: "Muñoz's works create an encounter, similar to a confrontation with a mirror that constantly alternates between self-recognition and a reflection of the Other."[18] In *Sarah with Blue Dress*, Muñoz connects the act of looking and becoming by painting Sarah's eyes and her dress in the same blue hue, but at the same time, as if to underscore the artifice of the gaze and identity, he leaves her back unpainted to further the illusion of the figure as fully "dressed," which is only brought into focus when seen in the mirror.

Creating mise-en-scènes as a conceptual strategy by Muñoz and other artists is predicated on what art historian Alex Potts describes as

the affective immediacy of theatrical staging and the clear psychological separation it establishes between viewer and work. While the stance and gestures and pro-portions of the figures…are realistic, the figures present themselves as insistently "other" through striking dispar-ities of scale,…or highly artificial, often monochrome colouring,…or associations with mannequins and replicants….There is a double take, in that the figures look very like living persons and yet also feel categori-cally different from them. They are posed in such a way that they seem staged for the viewer, while at the same time refusing any possibility of reciprocal interaction. The effect is rather different from that created by tradi-tional classicising figurative sculpture. The theatricality annuls the centredness and suggested composure or self-absorption of the classical figure, and also disrupts the smooth interplay posited by traditional sculptural aesthetics between the viewer's gazing at a sculpture as an object and identifying or empathising with it as a "being" or "presence."[19]

It is this disjuncture that distinguishes the figures in historic sculptural tableaux from the works of American artists Edward and Nancy Reddin Kien-holz. In *Woman Washing with Scrutator with Parrot Affixed Also* (1983, cat. 80), an installation "drawing" for their larger iconic work *The Hoerengracht* (1983–88), confronting the act of voyeurism is thrust upon the viewer.[20] The two-panel tableau details a seedy domestic interior in which the titular woman—a life-size cast figure dressed in a maroon robe and wearing a wig—is turned away and seemingly absorbed in a private act of washing by a basin. With the figure wedged between a window frame and a mirror, the viewer is forced into the position of a "peeping Tom," a position that is implicated in the title itself—a "scru-tator" is not a thing, but rather someone who scru-tinizes. The Kienholzes' tableaux with their dressed figures recall the Catholic saints discussed earlier, or diorama figures, yet the figures resist complete illusionism, not least because their surface is often

coated with a gray paint or gelatinous resin. As cura-tor Hans-Werner Schmidt explains, "Perceiving one-self facing the familiar, one feels integrated; however, the mind no sooner prepares to 'settle in'…than one finds oneself cast out again and distant."[21]

It is this sense of *Unheimlich*, or the uncanny, that is especially educed and palpable when encounter-ing the sculptured body. It is sufficiently familiar to engender recognition and even identification but nev-ertheless remains estranged, spectral, or eerie. Artists Janine Antoni and Oliver Herring consciously engage this effect in their works that evoke the body, specif-ically through its surface, but whose presence seems fugitive. In *Saddle* (2000, cat. 104), a cast of Antoni's body made from uncured rawhide, the once-present figure of the artist is registered by its residue, a shell in the shape of a kneeling figure on its hands and knees. Yet even with the sensual recognition of the mamma-lian materiality of hide, itself a second skin, the evac-uated space beneath the membrane does not indicate whether it was once a protective covering or a con-strictive sheath. Herring, too, engages with skin, but less with its materiality and more with the idea of skin as image, as the visible surface on which the body is read. A composite portrait of the eponymous *Patrick* (2004, cat. 95), the sculpture was modeled on Auguste Rodin's *The Thinker* (1881). Herring first photographed his subject from every angle, capturing details of his skin, hair, and clothes. A foam core substructure was then carefully overlaid with spliced photographic details of the very sections of skin that corresponded to the section of the body being rendered. The resul-tant figure draws on the indexicality of photography yet presents an undeniable simulacrum:

> It achieved the near perfect coincidence of materials and subject matter—more precisely, of representation with its

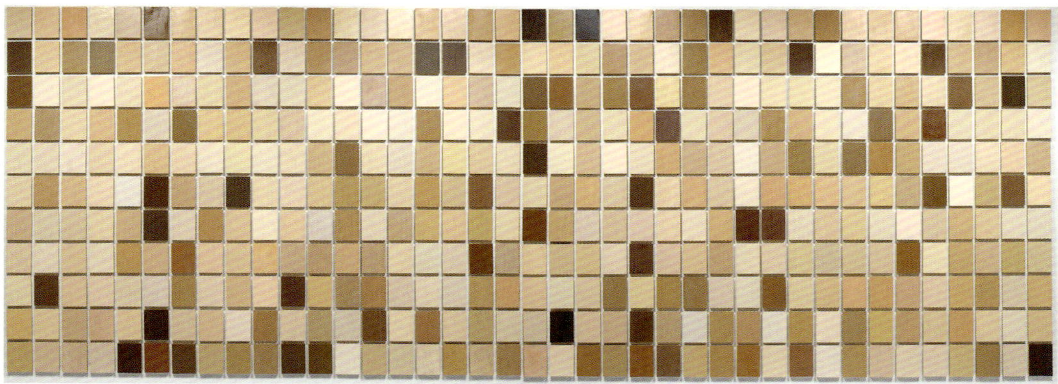

Fig. 76 Byron Kim. *Synecdoche*, 1991–present. Oil and wax on lauan plywood, birch plywood, and plywood; each panel: 10 × 8 in. (25.4 × 20.3 cm), overall: H. 10 ft. ¼ in. × 29 ft. 2 ¼ in. (305.4 × 889.6 cm). National Gallery of Art, Washington, D.C., Richard S. Zeisler Fund

The synecdochic use of skin and surface in Herring's sculpture bears comparison with the work of American artist Byron Kim. In Kim's iconic work *Synecdoche* (1991–present, fig. 76), he creates a seemingly Minimalist grid of oil and wax painted panels, with each color corresponding to the exact skin tone of a specific individual. In doing so, he expands the aesthetics of abstraction by inserting and marking the form with identity politics.[23]

Skin as a composite surface in form and meaning is a subject also addressed in Alison Saar's work. Her (mostly female) figures are carved in wood but are often covered in paint or a range of found organic and inorganic materials from straw and fiber to wire and metal, creating richly layered surfaces. Skin as a marker of race has a particularly fraught history for African Americans, and Saar probes the complexities of black female identity in her work: "The construction and identification of corporeal forms is mediated by the crucial work of skin—as both biological tissue and discursive schema overdetermined by colonialism's obsession with racial and species categorizations. As skin molds itself around bodily contours, it both covers over and yet also throws into relief the real and imagined anatomies beneath the surface."[24] Provocatively titling her work *Strange Fruit* (1995, cat. 110) after the song about lynching immortalized by Billie Holiday, Saar presents a black female figure who is suspended upside down from her feet and hovers eerily above the ground. The abdomen is stuffed in a gesture reminiscent of Nkisi power figures (fig. 45). The surface is clad with discarded

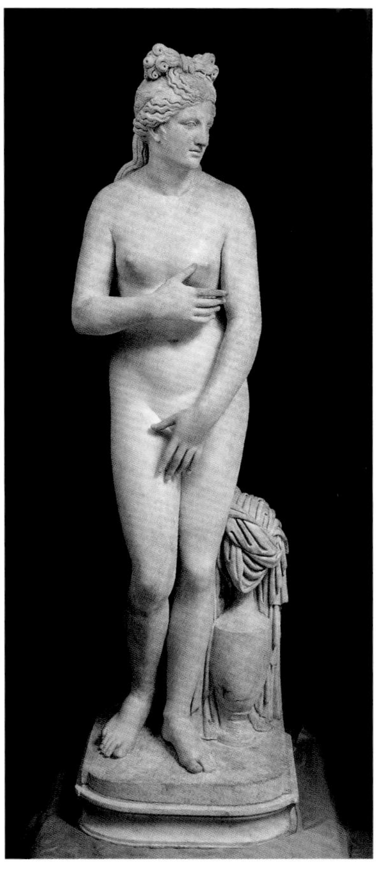

Fig. 77 *Marble Statue of Aphrodite at Her Bath*,
A.D. ca. 100–150. Possibly Thasian marble,
H. 88 in. (223.5 cm). Greek. British Museum,
London

metal ceiling plates with embossed baroque patterns, which become "a form of scarification or keloiding, again looking back to African culture and customs. But it also becomes a form of armor," to use the artist's words.[25] The figure is posed in the upturned stance of the Venus Pudica (fig. 77), even as her thick red lips consciously recall racist caricatures. Saar thus presents the black female body as capable of (literally) upending white, Western, patriarchal narratives of culture, and, as her inversion and liberation from a pedestal suggests, of (classical) sculpture.

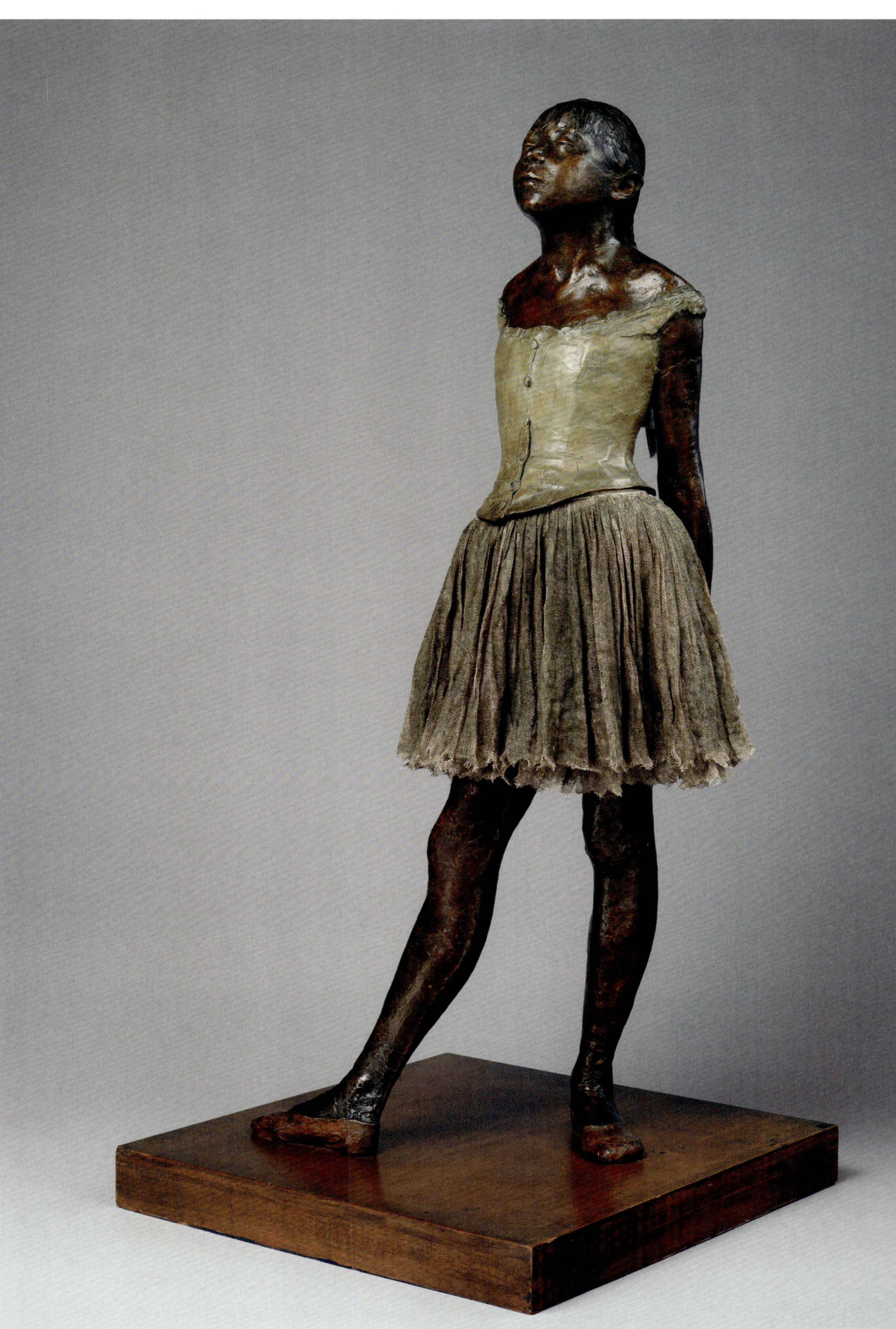

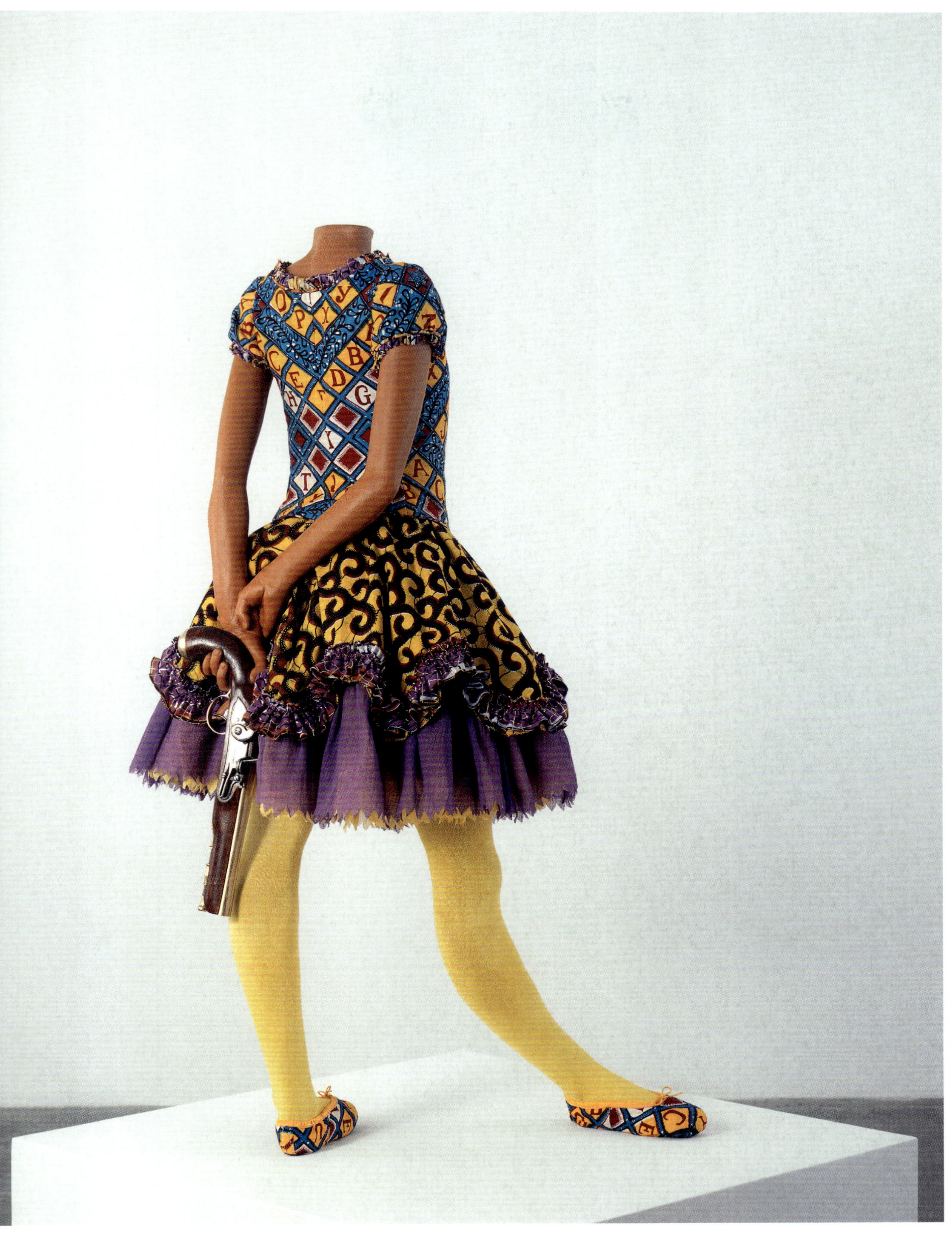

68. Edgar Degas, cast by A. A. Hébrard Foundry, Paris. *The Little Fourteen-Year-Old Dancer*, ca. 1880, cast 1922. Partially tinted bronze, cotton fabric, satin, and wood, H. 38 ½ in. (97.8 cm), W. 17 ¼ in. (43.8 cm), D. 14 ⅜ in. (36.5 cm). The Metropolitan Museum of Art, New York, H. O. Havemeyer Collection, Bequest of Mrs. H. O. Havemeyer, 1929 (29.100.370)

69. Yinka Shonibare MBE. *Girl Ballerina*, 2007. Mannequin, Dutch wax–printed cotton textile, and antique flintlock pistol, H. 47 ¼ in. (120 cm), W. 19 ¹¹⁄₁₆ in. (50 cm), D. 23 ⅝ in. (60 cm). Collection of John and Amy Phelan

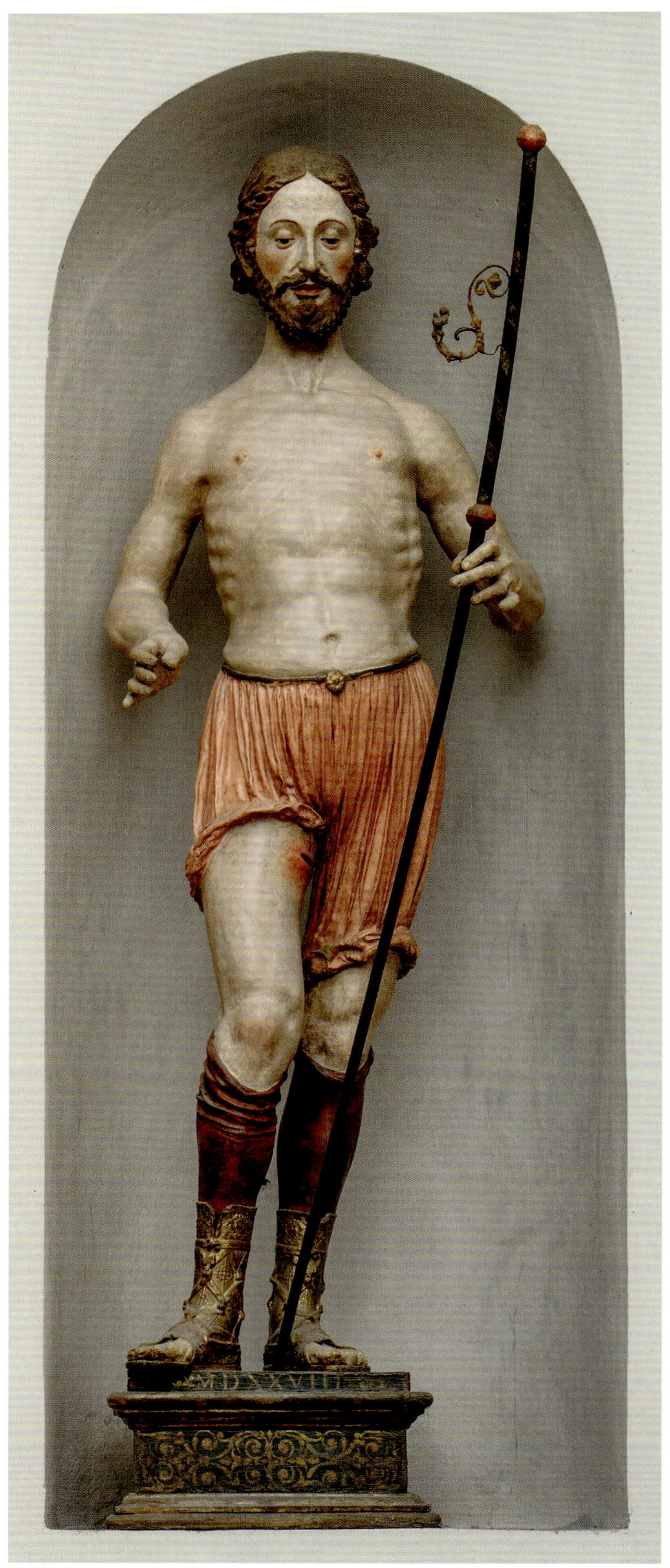

70. Nero Alberti (Romano Alberti). *Saint Roch*, 1528. Polychromed wood, H. 69 ⁵⁄₁₆ in. (176 cm). Chiesa di Santa Croce, Umbertide

71. Elmgreen & Dragset. *The Experiment*, 2012. Polyester resin, glass fiber, acrylic paint, glass, human hair, wood, lacquer, mirror, metal parts, and leather; figure: H. 50 ⅜ in. (128 cm), W. 15 ¾ in. (40 cm), D. 9 ⁷⁄₁₆ in. (24 cm); mirror: H. 74 ⁹⁄₁₆ in. (189.5 cm), W. 31 ³⁄₁₆ in. (79.2 cm), D. 24 ¹³⁄₁₆ in. (63 cm), overall dimensions variable. Krawiecki Gazes Family Collection

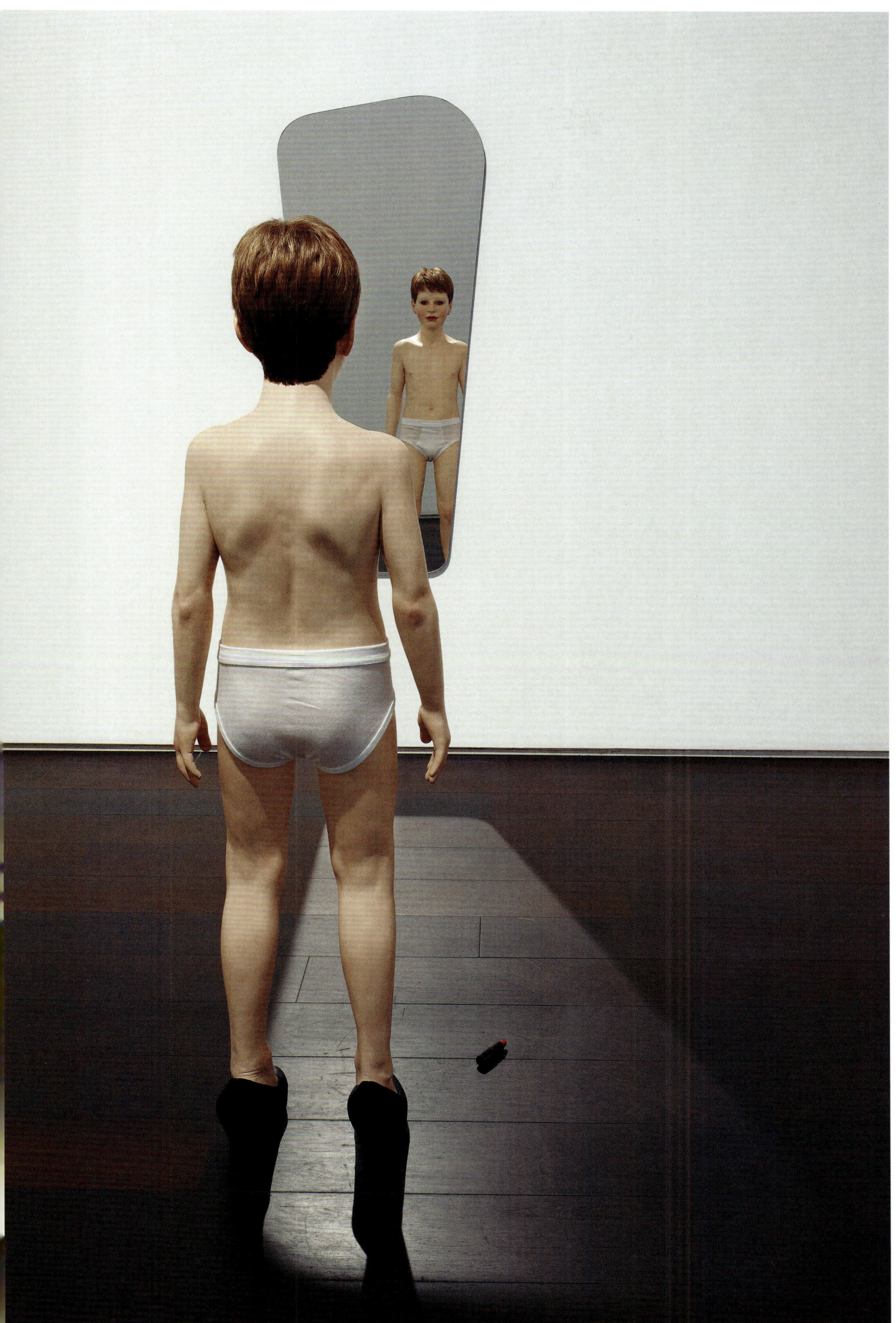

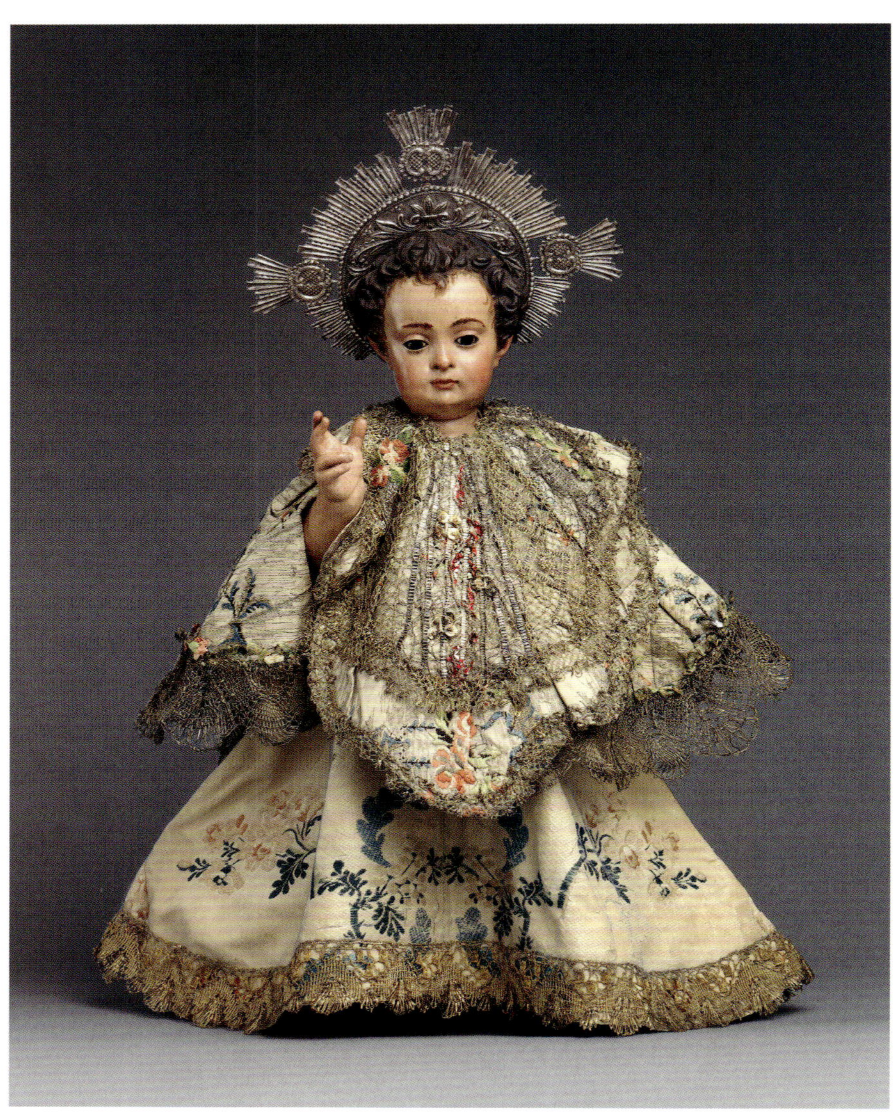

72. *The Child Jesus Triumphant*, ca. 1625 with later costume. Polychromed lead, glass, silver, silk, and silver-gilt lace dress, with halo: H. 19 in. (48.3 cm), W. 6 ⅛ in. (15.6 cm), D. 6 in. (15.2 cm). Spanish or Mexican. The Metropolitan Museum of Art, New York, Gift of Loretta Hines Howard, 1964 (64.164.244a, b)

73. Juan Muñoz. *Sarah with Blue Dress*, 1996. Acrylic on polyester resin and mirror, H. 76 ¾ in. (195 cm), W. 43 ⁵⁄₁₆ in. (110 cm), D. 39 ⅜ in. (100 cm). Juan Varez Collection, Madrid

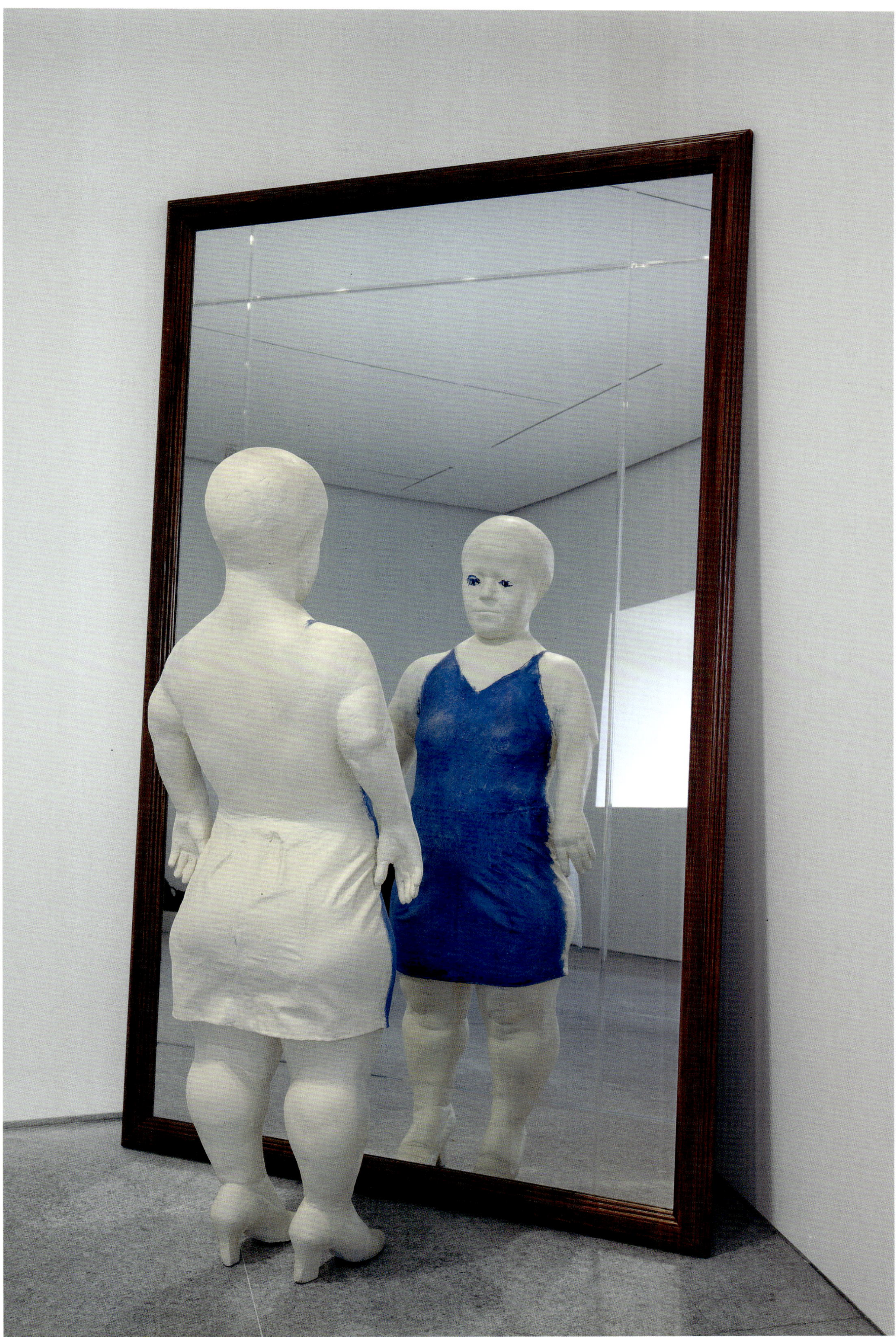

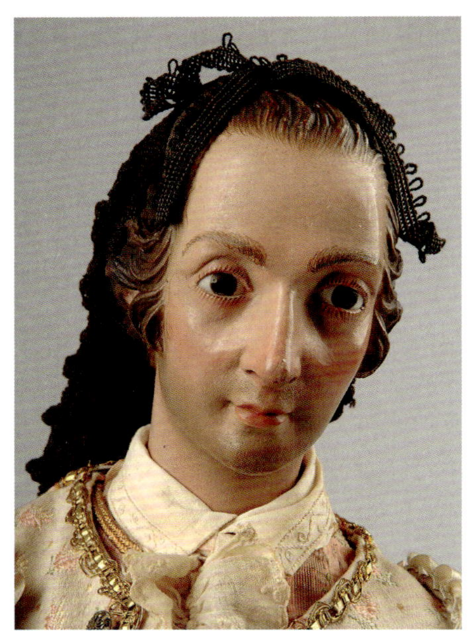

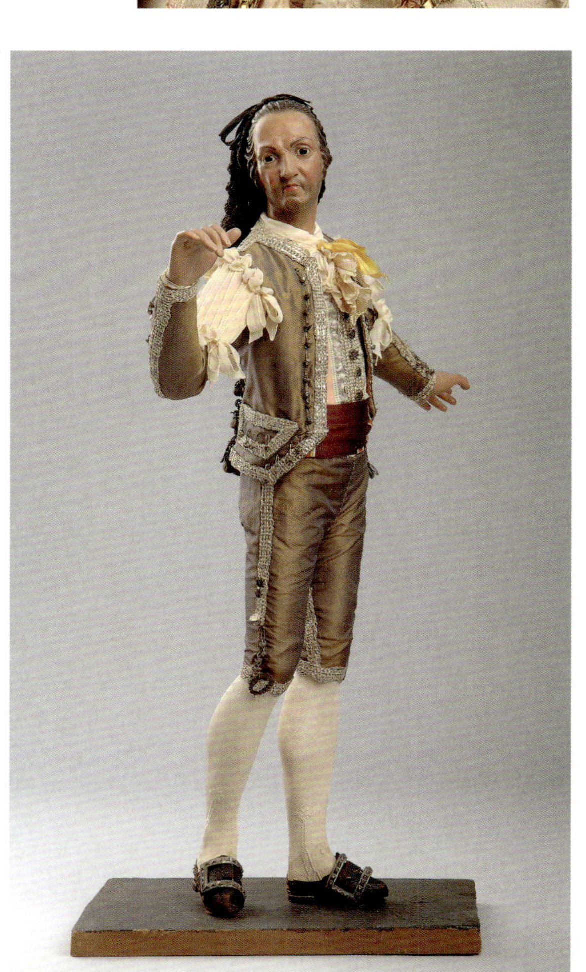

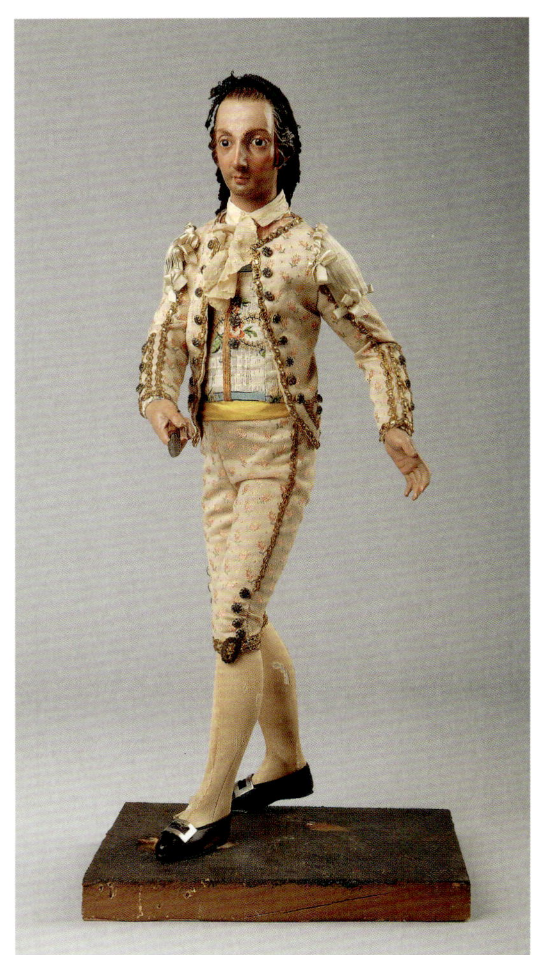

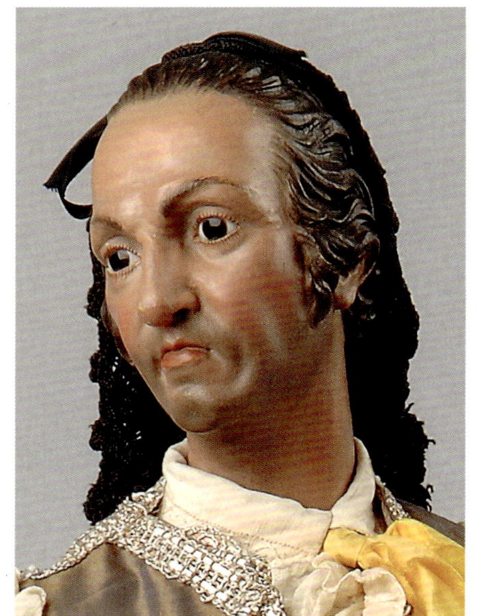

B.

A.

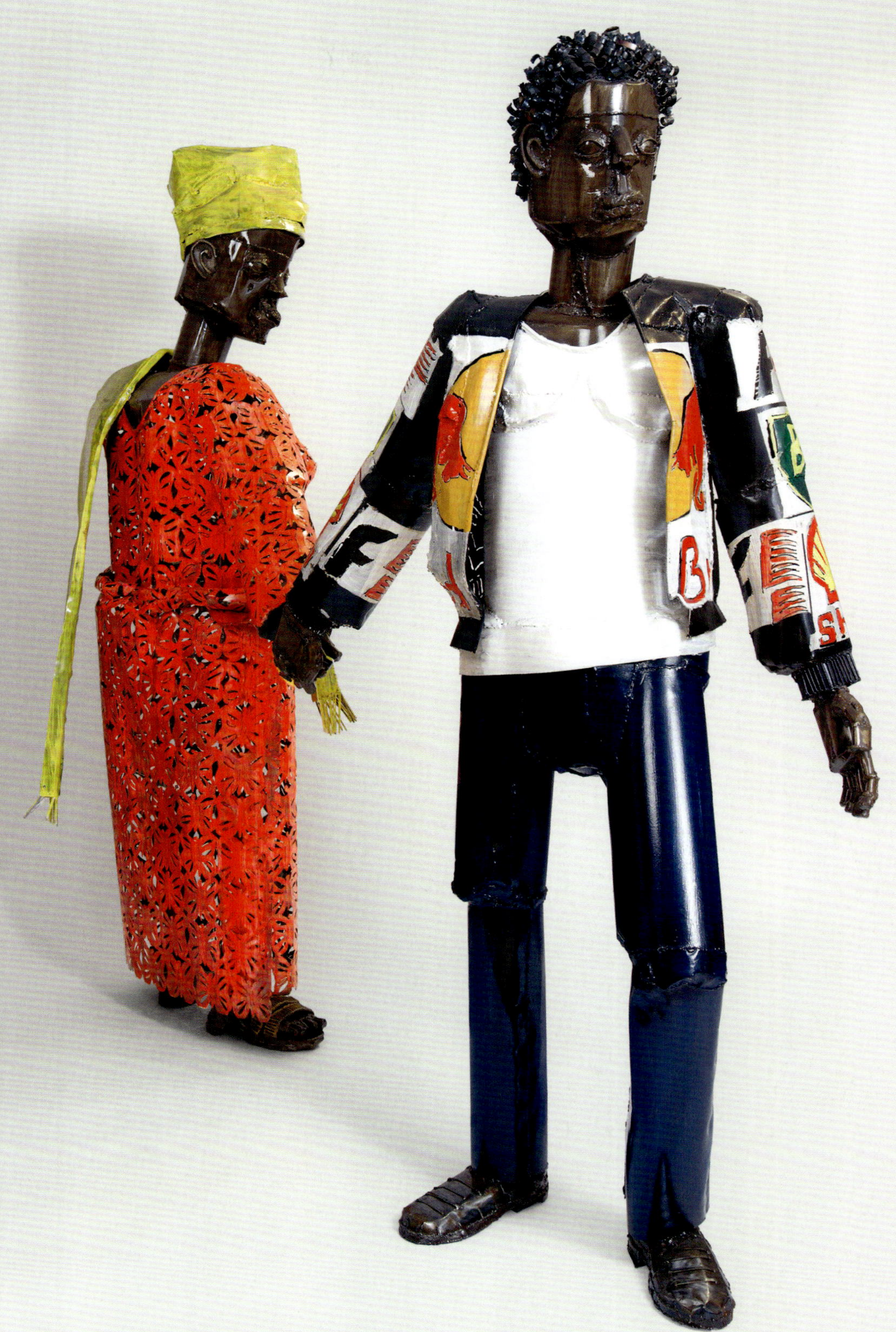

74. Juan Cháez. A. *Bullfighter* and B. *Costillares*, late 18th century. Polychromed wood and textiles, *Bullfighter*: H. 24 ⅝ in. (62.5 cm), W. 9 ¼ in. (23.5 cm), D. 18 ⁷⁄₁₆ in. (46.8 cm), base: H. ¹³⁄₁₆ in. (2.1 cm), W. 12 ¹⁄₁₆ in. (30.7 cm), D. 8 ⅜ in. (21.3 cm); *Costillares*: H. 24 ¹³⁄₁₆ in. (63 cm), W. 10 in. (25.4 cm), D. 10 ⁷⁄₁₆ in. (26.5 cm), base: H. 1 ⁵⁄₁₆ in. (3.3 cm), W. 9 ³⁄₁₆ in. (23.4 cm), D. 11 ⅞ in. (30.1 cm). Museo Nacional de Escultura, Valladolid

75. Sokari Douglas Camp. *Material Salsa*, 2011. Steel and acrylic paint, man: H. 78 in. (198.1 cm), W. 48 in. (121.9 cm), D. 20 in. (50.8 cm); woman: H. 75 in. (190.5 cm), W. 48 in. (121.9 cm), D. 31 in. (78.7 cm), overall dimensions variable. Courtesy of the artist and Stux Gallery, New York

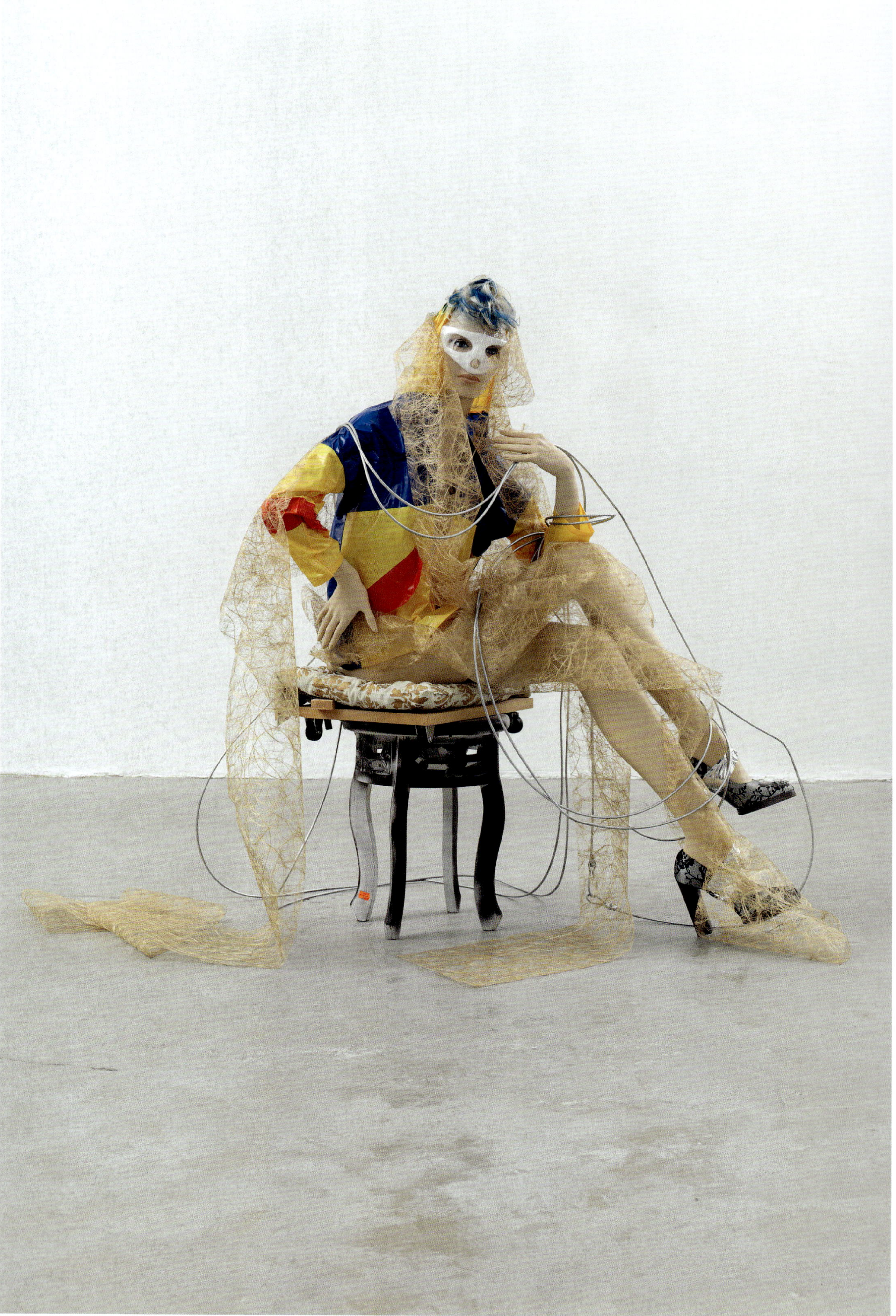

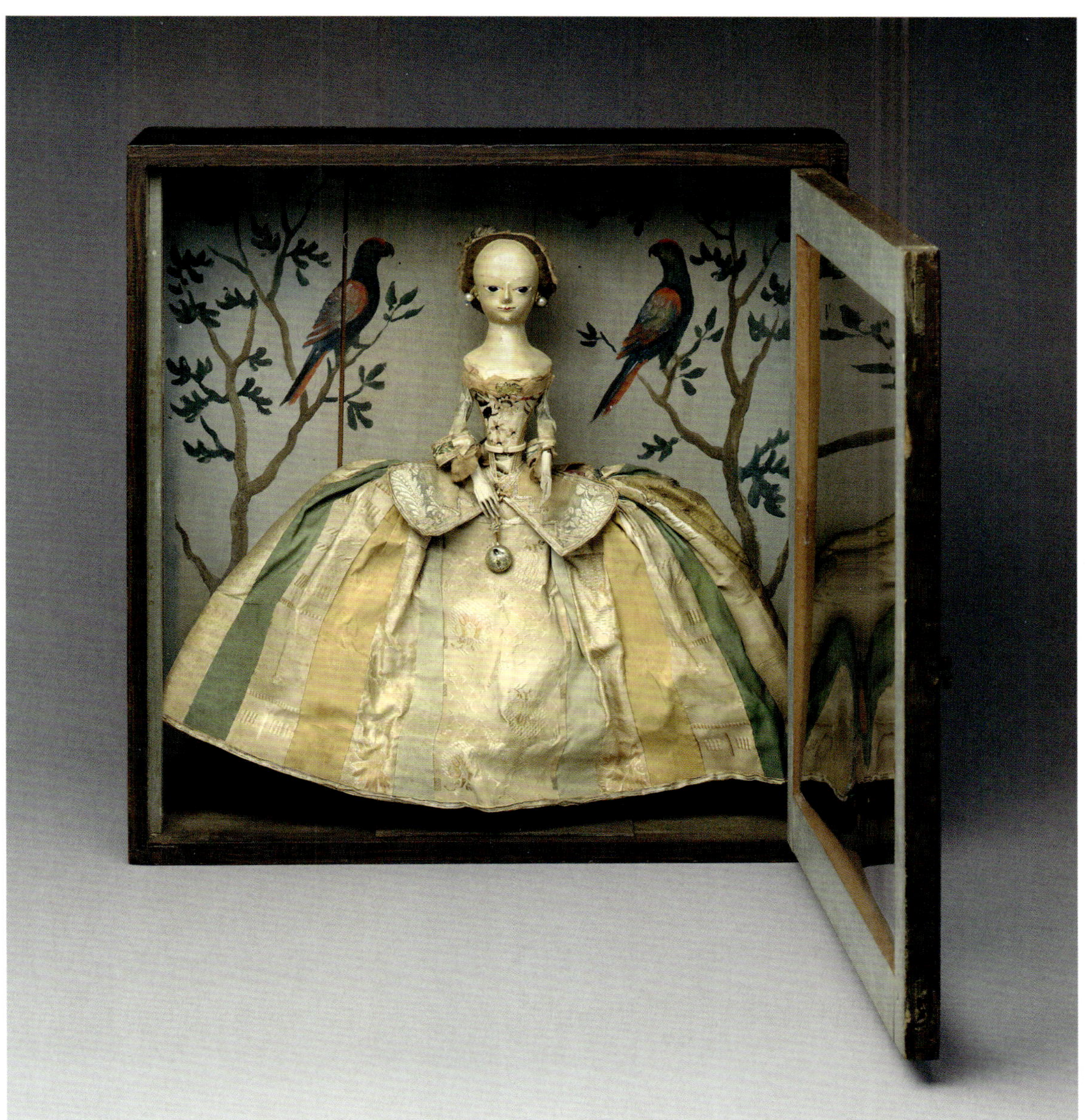

76. Isa Genzken. *Actors (Schauspieler)*, 2013. Mannequin, clothes, shoes, fabric, and paper, approx. H. 59 ¹⁄₁₆ in. (150 cm), W. 59 ¹⁄₁₆ in. (150 cm), D. 59 ¹⁄₁₆ in. (150 cm). SYZ Collection, Switzerland

77. *Doll in a Box*, ca. 1748. Box (American): white pine, crown glass, and paint; doll (British): wood, paint, glass, silk dress with woven linen and metal trim, silk gauze cap and cuffs, human hair with silk floss and gilded metal foil ribbons, glass-bead earrings with metal foil and faux pearls, metal foil watch and brooch, silk stockings, and silk faille embellished shoes, H. 25 in. (63.5 cm), W. 24 in. (61 cm), D. 7 in. (17.8 cm). The Metropolitan Museum of Art, New York, Gift of Mrs. Screven Lorillard, 1953 (53.179.12)

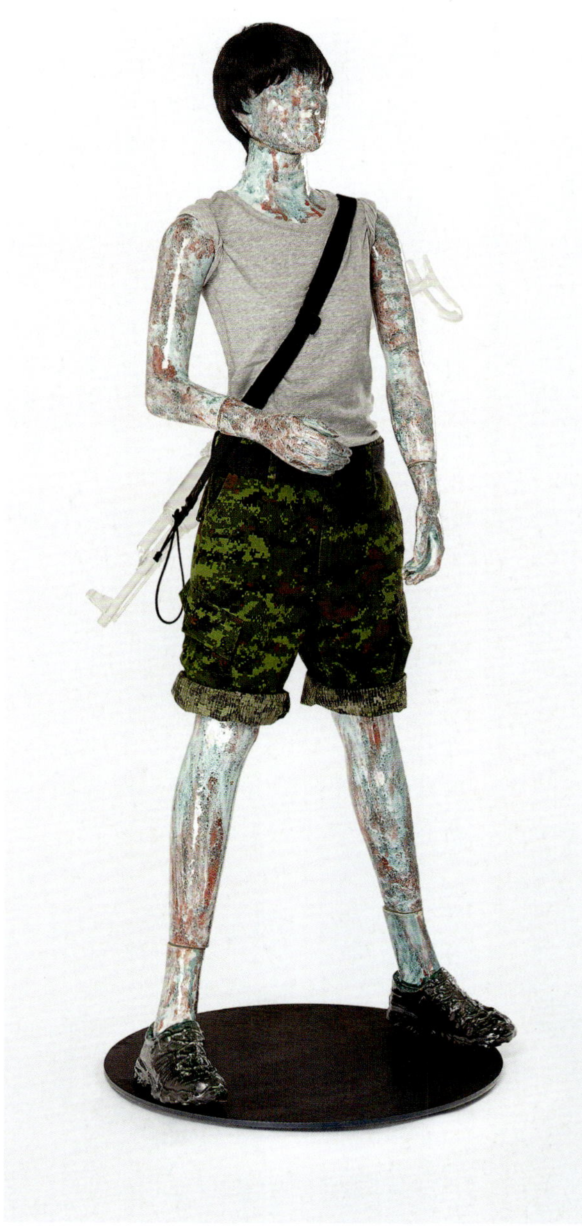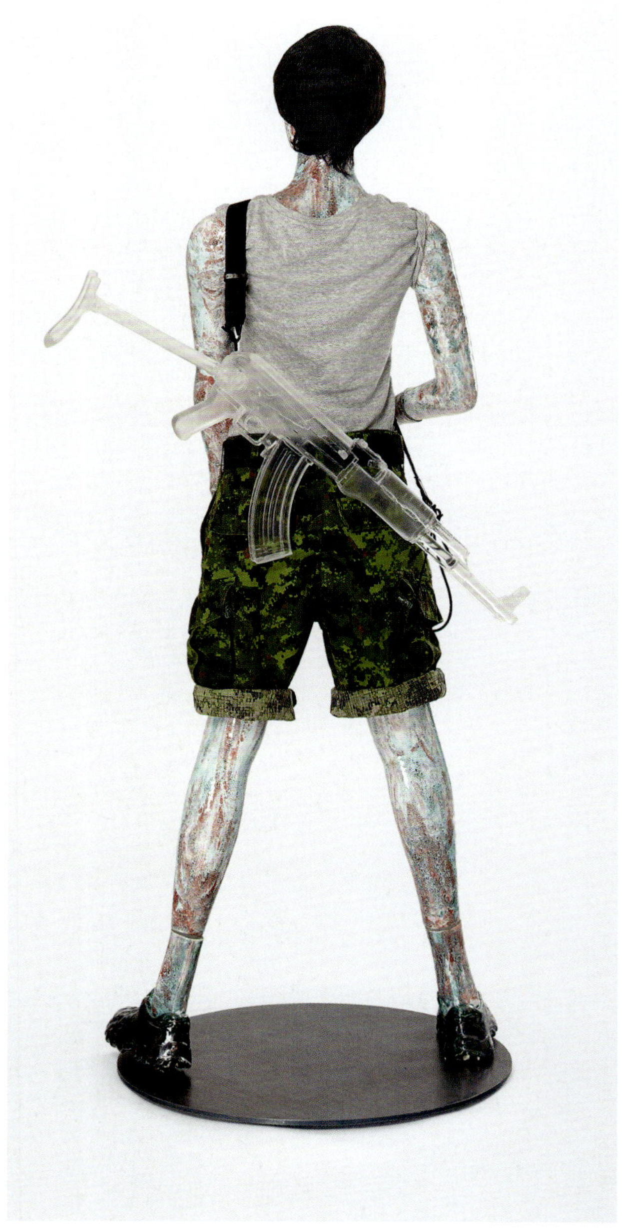

78. Mai-Thu Perret. *Les Guérillères X*, 2016. Glazed ceramic, steel, epoxy, synthetic hair, cotton and polyester fabric, polyester resin, and steel, H. 69 in. (175.3 cm), W. 27 in. (68.6 cm), D. 14 in. (35.6 cm). Green Family Collection

79. Mary Sibande. *Rubber Soul, Monument of Aspiration*, 2011. Cast resin, fiberglass, cotton fabric, tulle, and rubber, H. 101 ½ in. (257.8 cm), W. 57 in. (144.8 cm), D. 64 ½ in. (163.8 cm). Toledo Museum of Art, Ohio, Gift of the Georgia Welles Apollo Society, 2013

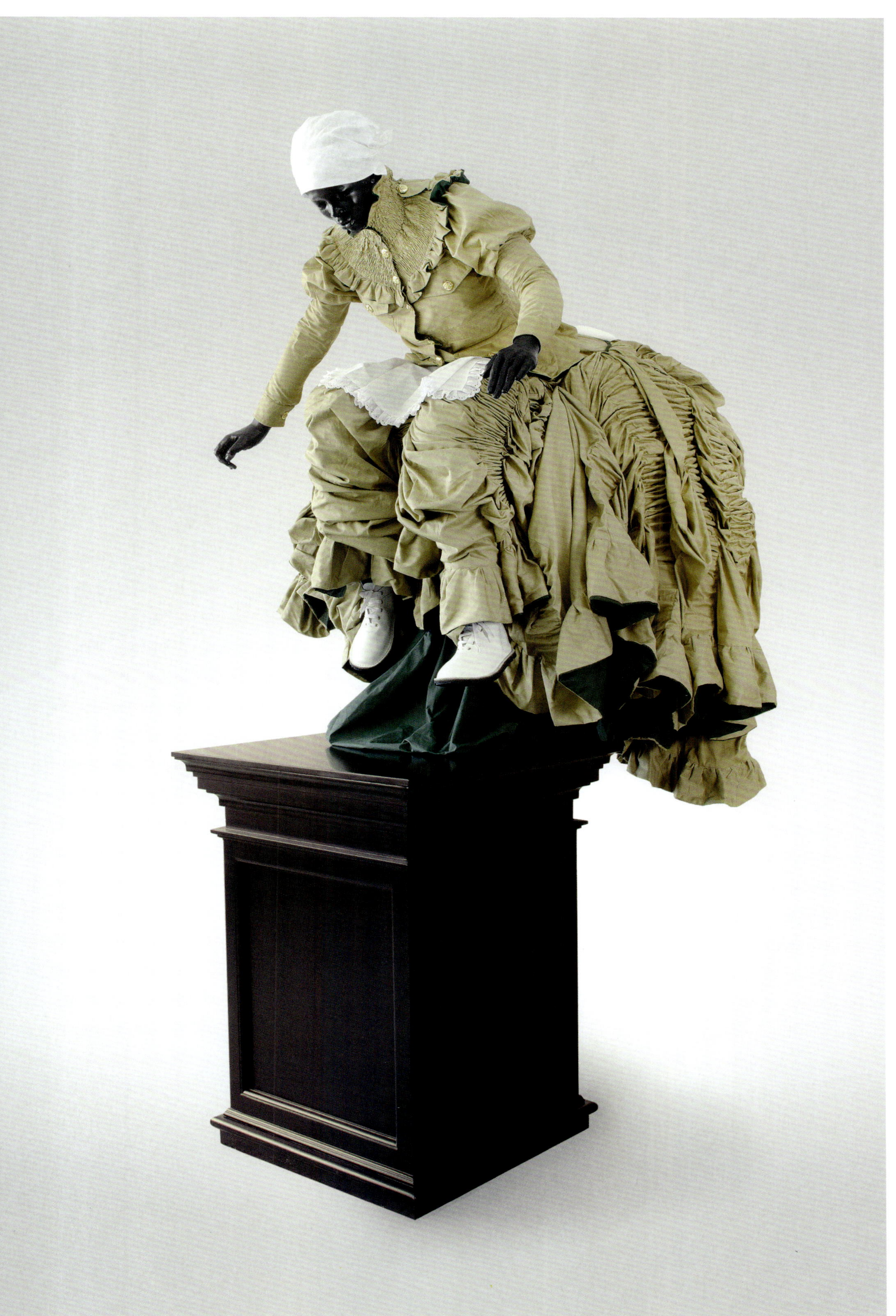

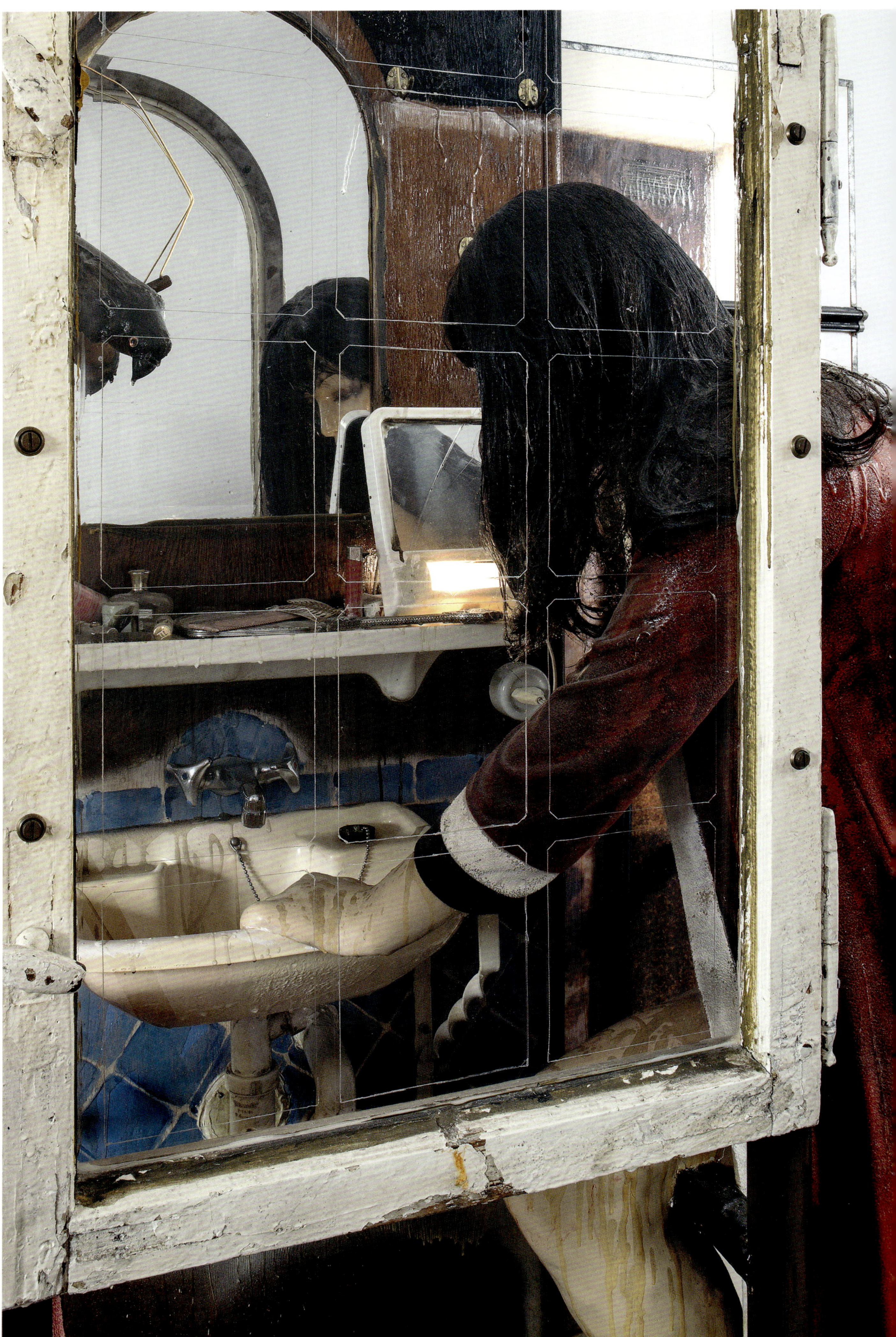

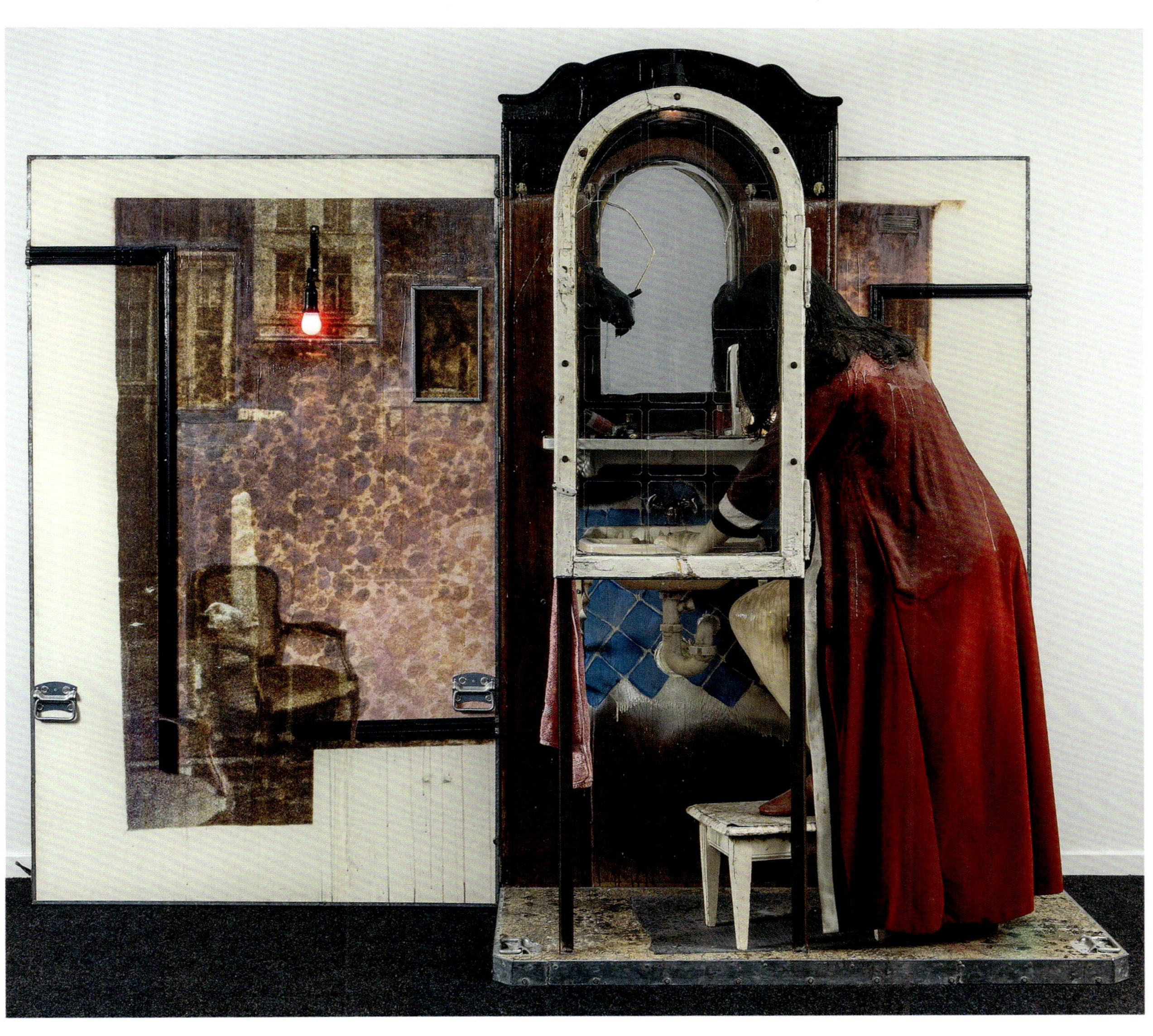

80. Edward Kienholz and Nancy Reddin Kienholz. *Woman Washing with Scrutator with Parrot Affixed Also*, Berlin, 1983. Mixed media, H. 81 in. (205.7 cm), W. 98 in. (248.9 cm), D. 27 in. (68.6 cm). Stefan T. Edlis Collection

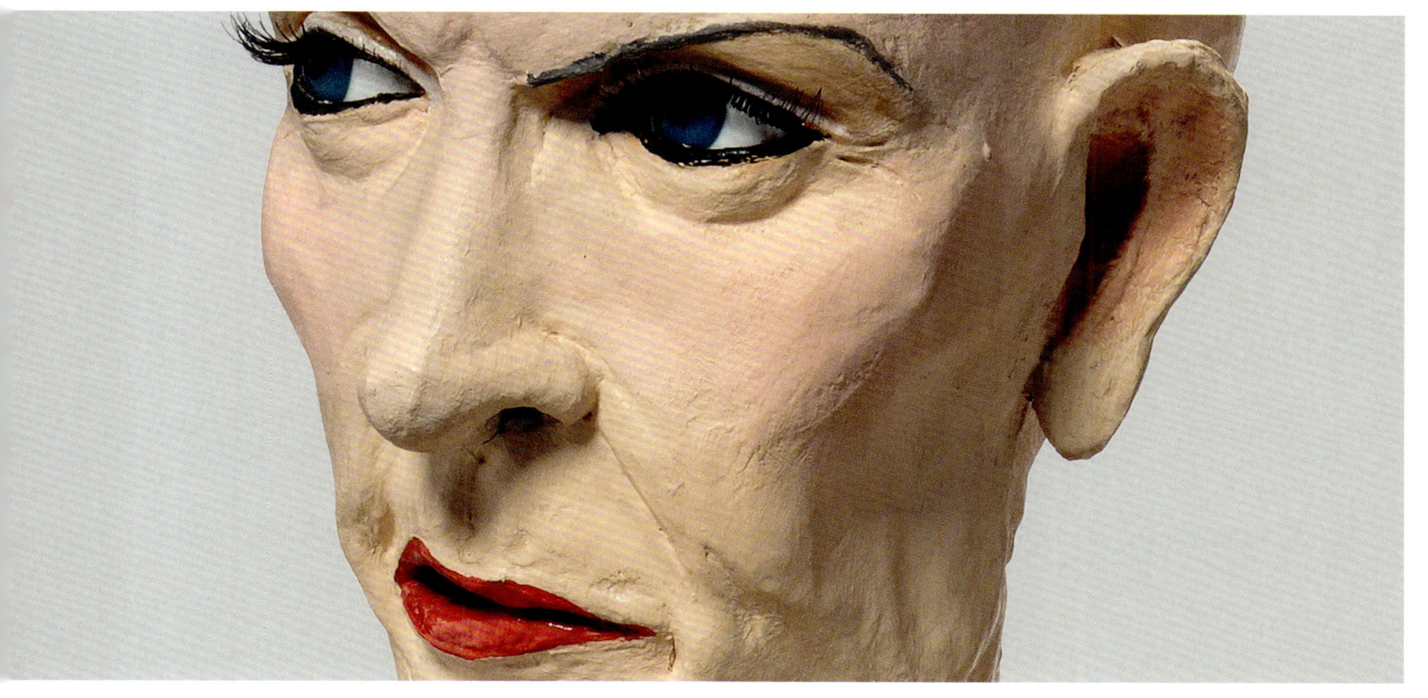

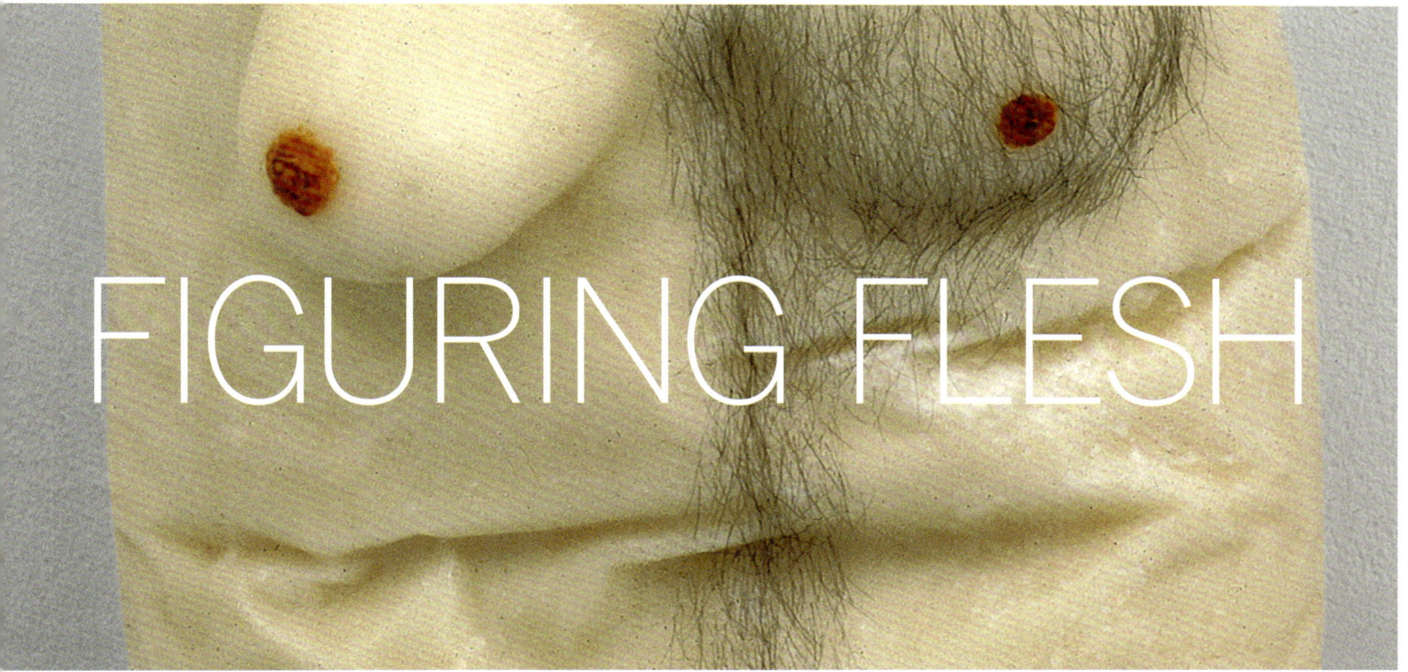
FIGURING FLESH

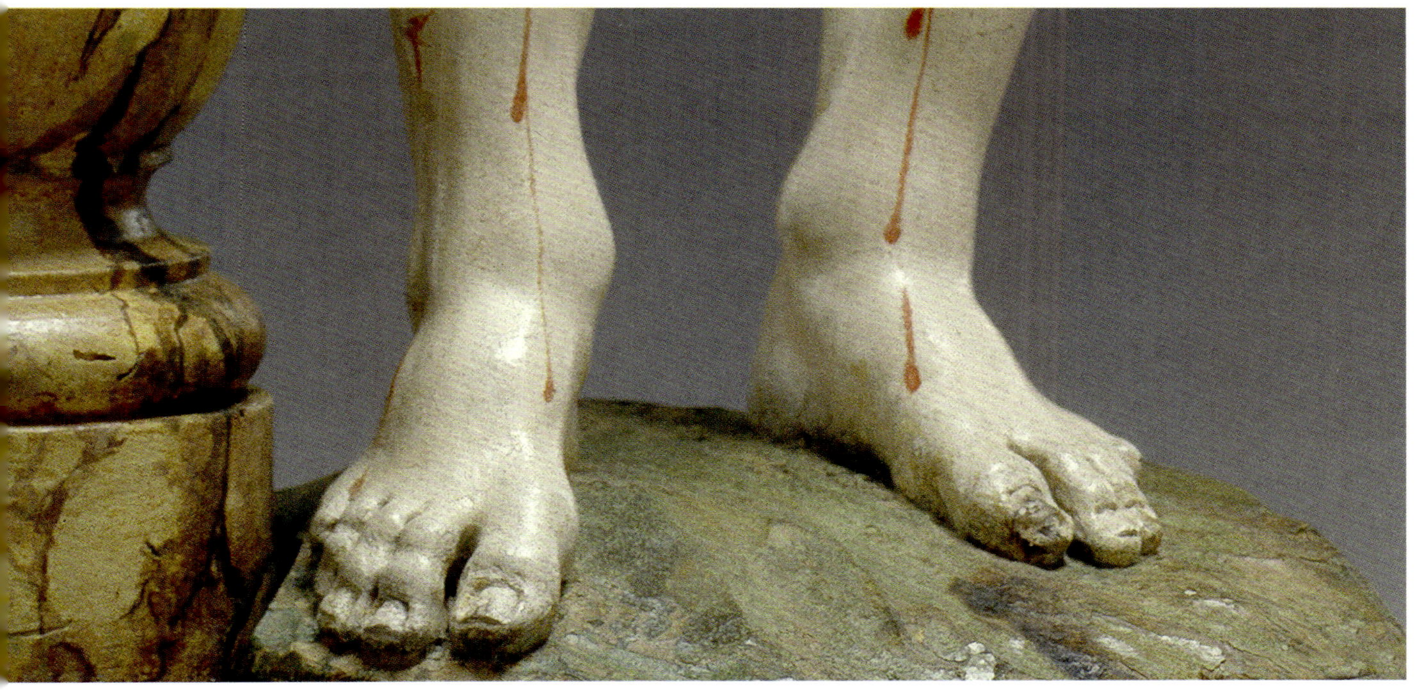

FIGURING FLESH

EMERSON BOWYER

A vague term, "flesh" broadly indicates the living substance of the body. How can sculpture capture the shifting, multicolored hues of human tissue? How can it present the peculiar tactile qualities of a body's interior and exterior? Sculptors have confronted this dilemma with novel approaches to color, material, and form.

The problem of representing flesh in art emerged acutely with the advent of Christianity, for which the Incarnation is the central doctrine. Derived from the Latin *caro* (flesh), the term designates the belief that God became human in the form of Christ. This concept is simply and eloquently expressed in John 1:14, "And the Word was made flesh, and dwelt among us."[1] From the late Middle Ages, artists and theologians increasingly emphasized the humanity of Christ, for it was the act of becoming mortal, of living and dying, that brought forth the Resurrection and the promise of salvation. Worshippers fixated on Christ's material, tangible, and biological reality: his suffering body, one that was beaten and bruised, that bled and died. What better evidence of the humanity of an otherwise immaterial and unknowable God? Take, for example, the southern German *Nellingen Crucifix* (1430–35, cat. 90). Attached to a heavy cross is the lifesize body of Christ, whose half-open eyes suggest continuing agony. The figure is dense but vulnerable, pierced by nails and bearing a gaping side wound. The application of polychromy enhances the depiction of the human organism's mutability: raised blue veins writhe beneath pink skin, representing an internal system of bodily fluids, and a gruesome blue bruise surrounds the exposed wound. Crimson blood spurts from that wound and seemingly streaks down Christ's belly. In other places, blood drips from smaller piercings of the skin. The explicit abjection of the *Nellingen Crucifix* is thrown into harsh relief when compared to Italian artist Lucio Fontana's ceramic *Crocifisso* (see cat. 91). This abstracted crucifixion evokes the malleability of flesh through the

plasticity of clay. The representational body disintegrates in the pressings and moldings made by the artist's fingers, and its materiality is countered by the shifting, shimmering colors of reflective enameled surfaces. Fontana's ecstatic figure hovers ambiguously between palpable flesh and ethereal light—an expression, perhaps, of the irresolution of Christ's dual nature as God and man.

Spanish sculptors of the seventeenth century specialized in hyperreal representations of the suffering Christ. One of the greatest practitioners was Pedro de Mena, who held the uncommon distinction of both carving and painting his figures. His *Ecce Homo* (ca. 1674–85, cat. 96) is a lifesize, bust-length depiction of Christ as he was presented to the Israelites following his flagellation. Carved, subtly painted, and fully in the round, this arresting wood sculpture invites close inspection. The eye follows thin trails of blood as they travel across a body marked by sharp welts and purple bruising. According to Francisco Pacheco, a slightly earlier Spanish painter, "Colour reveals the passions and concerns of the soul with greater vividness. The figure of marble and wood requires the painter's hand to come to life."[2] Indeed, the process of painting skin tones, like the mystery of Christ's humanity, was called *encarnación* (making flesh).

German sculptors, too, imagined unusual ways of emphasizing Christ's fleshiness. A late seventeenth-century *Christ at the Column* (1697, cat. 100), for example, portrays the son of God with a carved patchwork of broken, peeling skin, beneath which is suggested a molten, visceral core of human tissue. German artist Balthasar Permoser's version of the subject is carved from stone that features vibrant red veins (1728, fig. 78). Without applying paint, the sculptor dramatically expressed the coloration and appearance of a body soaked in blood. These two sculptures sit at the furthest extreme from such works as Ignaz Günther's *Christ at the Column* (1754, cat. 99), which, despite the rivulets of blood that run down the legs

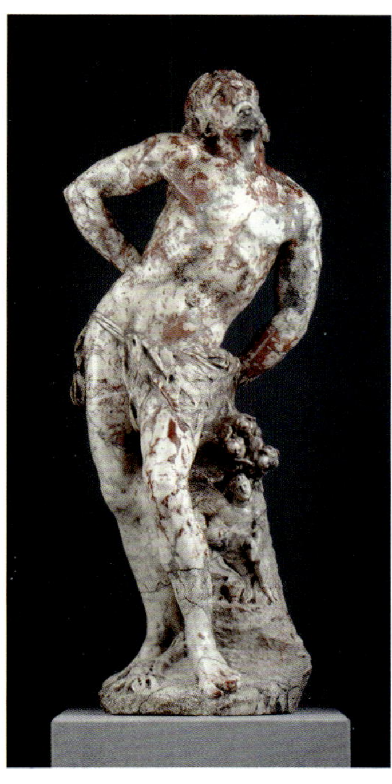

Fig. 78 Balthazar Permoser. *Christ at the Column*, 1728. Colored marble and other material, H. 31 ⅞ in. (81 cm), W. 10 ⅝ in. (27 cm), D. 9 ¹³⁄₁₆ in. (25 cm). Staatliche Kunstsammlungen Dresden, Sculpture Collection

Fig. 79 Pablo Picasso. *Pregnant Woman*, Vallauris, 1950. Plaster, metal armature, wood, ceramic vessel, and pottery jars, H. 43 ¼ in. (110 cm), W. 8 ⅝ in. (22 cm), D. 12 ½ in. (32 cm). Museum of Modern Art, New York, Gift of Louise Reinhardt Smith and gift of Jacqueline Picasso (both by exchange)

interior chamber originally populated by sculpted figurines of God the Father, the dove of the Holy Spirit, and the crucified Christ (in this version, only the God figurine survives). Appropriately, this illustration of the Incarnation takes place within the womblike cavity of the Virgin's body.

In addition to visualizing religious doctrine, the Shrine Madonnas speak to a fascination with the female body and the internal mysteries of its reproductive apparatus. They conceive of it as a container, much as Pablo Picasso did with his *Pregnant Woman* (1950, fig. 79), in which the figure's breasts and enlarged womb are composed of ceramic vessels. Whereas the opaque flesh of Picasso's sculpted woman hides her interior from view, the Shrine Madonnas enact a complex visual and tactile interplay between concealment and revelation. A similar oscillation between visible and invisible, open and closed, is the hallmark of a famous series of anatomical wax models produced in the eighteenth century by Italian sculptor Clemente Susini. The so-called Anatomical Venuses are hyperreal sculptural representations of the idealized female body.[5] These are bodies designed for disassembly and for the exploration of supposedly hidden and mysterious internal chambers. As art historian Roberta Panzanelli describes them, they sit "halfway between artwork and artifact, between scientific tool and horrid simulacrum."[6] Each figure lies passively on

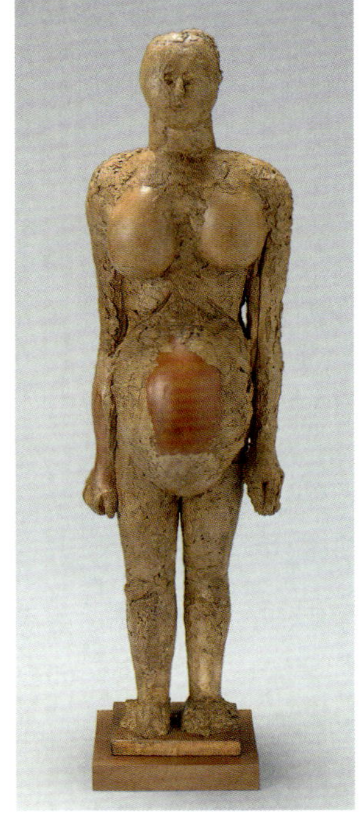

a silken bed, her real human hair falling onto soft pillows, and sometimes she wears a string of pearls around her neck. By removing the external surface of the torso, the anatomist could successively take apart the various strata of the body's interior: the musculature, mammary glands, lungs, heart, intestines, and uterus containing a miniature fetus. The use of wax in the making of these sculptures partly

and chest, depicts an idealized, cream-colored figure with a porcelain-like finish. Even in the aftermath of violence, this Christ retains something of the inviolability of the sacred body. More recently, Belgian artist Berlinde De Bruyckere has produced a series of haunting sculptures depicting nude bodies with tinted wax surfaces, including *Piëta* (2008, cat. 98). The work's title refers to images of the dead Christ supported by the mourning Virgin. In contrast to that tradition, here there is no distinction between the living and the dead. Headless and seemingly mutilated, the two fragmented bodies are reduced to biological matter. In a disconcerting image of the Incarnation, the grisly processes of decay and decomposition unfold before our eyes.

Conventionally, statues rarely reveal the body below the epidermis. For all the illusion of pliant, pulsing flesh in a sculpture by Gian Lorenzo Bernini, there is, ultimately, nothing but uncarved, undifferentiated marble under the polished skin. Sculpted representations of the wounded and tortured Christ, like those discussed in this essay, are an exception. In these works the body is porous, marked by literal openings on to innards highlighted by polychromy. They make tangible the belief of clerics such as Bernard of Clairvaux that through the clefts in Christ's body "the secret of his heart is laid open."[3] Worshippers were also encouraged to enter into the body of the Virgin Mary through devotion to a peculiar genre of sculpture that flourished in Europe from about 1300 to 1500. The Shrine Madonnas, or *Vierges ouvrantes*, depict the enthroned mother with her infant child.[4] In a German example held by The Met (ca. 1300, cat. 81), a vertical slit runs from the figure's neck to her feet, marking the meeting point of two hinged doors. Opening the Virgin's body reveals an

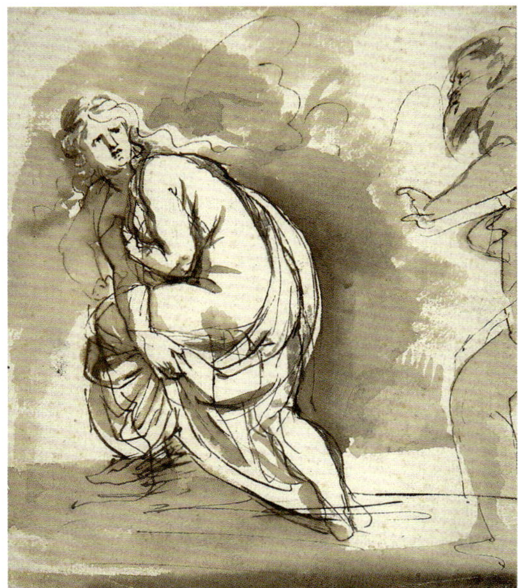

accounts for their uncanny realism. "There probably exists no other substance," philosopher and art historian Georges Didi-Huberman has explained, "that can imitate with such polyvalence both the *external flesh*, the skin, and all the *internal flesh*, the muscles and viscera which are also our flesh, but which in general are felt, seen, and touched as though they were violently heterogeneous to the integuments or the more civilized surfaces of our bodies."[7] Wax also has an inherent eroticism, a quality that is compounded by Susini's supine subject matter. For wax invites touch, it warms in the intimate grasp of the hand and becomes malleable under pressure. Ultimately, Susini's Venuses are endlessly violated bodies, their integrity repeatedly compromised by the excavations of hand and gaze. This is perhaps acknowledged in French artist and anatomist André Pierre Pinson's exquisite anatomical statuette (1784–93, cat. 83), produced at the same moment as Susini's creations. In contrast to those works, Pinson's wax woman is strikingly animated. Seemingly aware of her exposure, she recoils from the viewer in a pose reminiscent of the biblical Susanna surprised at her bath by lecherous old men (fig. 80).

Unlike the Shrine Madonnas, the Anatomical Venuses, and Pinson's little wax bather, British artist Damien Hirst's *Virgin (exposed)* (2005, cat. 82) does not offer the frisson of revelation and concealment. Instead, the partially flayed skin of his pregnant figure opens her body permanently to view.[8] In the case of *Virgin Mother* (2005), Hirst's monumental bronze version of the composition, the female interior is exposed in an outdoor, public space. Crudely colored, like anatomical models and illustrations in physicians' offices, *Virgin (exposed)* deliberately references another controversial sculpture: Edgar Degas's *The Little Fourteen-Year-Old Dancer* of about 1880 (cat. 68), a work that one alarmed critic thought

best suited to a museum of zoology, anthropology, or physiology.[9]

"Body" and "flesh" are not necessarily interchangeable terms. The former can connote the containment and order of form, while the latter can suggest the unruly formlessness of pure matter. Historically, with perhaps the crucial exception of the suffering Christ, flesh and the fleshly have typically been gendered feminine. One immediately pictures the eroticized suppleness of Flemish artist Peter Paul Rubens's ample roseate women or that of French artist Jean-Léon Gérôme's polychrome *Seated Woman* (ca. 1898–1902, cat. 106), whose pigmented wax coating seems to give pliability to carved stone. In recent decades, women artists have played with and critiqued the fleshly connotations of the female body. American artist Kiki Smith's *Untitled a.k.a. The Sitter* (1992, cat. 89) presents the female form as sticky, dense, and disturbingly visceral. Wax, cheesecloth, wood, and dye evoke the thick and messy corporeal reality of a living body that ages, sweats, and bleeds. This distinctly nonerotic and unclassical body is also the subject of horrific violence, as is apparent from the deep, open wounds carved into the figure's back.[10]

"Morbidezza," a term deployed in art theory from the Renaissance onward to denote the illusion of soft flesh in painting and sculpture, is surprisingly well suited to American artist Dorothea Tanning's *Emma* (1970, cat. 108). This pink blob, laid within a nest of dresslike lace, is made of stitched fabric filled with wool. Part stuffed toy, part odalisque, it belongs to a series of soft sculptures constructed by the artist between 1969 and 1973. Named for the unhappy bourgeois protagonist of French novelist Gustave Flaubert's *Madame Bovary* (1856), Tanning's *Emma* is reduced to a pile of swelling bumps and half-formed appendages that orbit a deep, navel-like indentation. As a representation of the female body, this fleshly mound verges on the parodic. British artist Sarah Lucas's *NUD CYCLADIC 9* (2010, cat. 107) similarly seems to present soft flesh, although in a form completely divorced from the context of an external bodily shape. Made from nylon hosiery filled to bursting with fluff, the work bulges with biomorphic tentacles that have the appearance of intestines or meat squeezing forth from an out-of-control sausage maker. While playfully referencing the highly stylized, generally female forms of ancient Cycladic figurines, the writhing mass equally resembles an abstracted version of the canonical Hellenistic Greek statuary group known as *Laocoön and His Sons* (1st century B.C.).

Whereas Lucas's *NUD CYCLADIC 9* suggests a monstrously fecund biological organism, American artist John Outterbridge's *Broken Dance, Ethnic Heritage Series* (ca. 1978–82, cat. 92) is a self-consciously constructed body. This anthropomorphic form is a meticulously crafted assemblage of recycled refuse. As an accretion of materials with individual histories that have been sewn, hammered, and welded together, Outterbridge's seated figure is a body that speaks more of personal and cultural memory than organic matter.

It might be argued that the very vagueness of the term "flesh" has enabled sculptors to think and work imaginatively, seriously, and playfully when representing the human figure. The organic and non-organic, wholes and fragments, interiors and exteriors are all implicated in the notion of flesh, and its physical and theoretical density continues to engage both artists and viewers.

American artist Robert Gober's *Untitled* (1990, cat. 87) focuses not on ethnicity but on sexual difference. This creepily alluring object consists of male and female breasts seemingly grafted on to an organic, torsolike mass that took its form from a bag of plaster found on the floor of the artist's studio. Here, Gober pays witty homage to the notion of the pound of flesh. Incorporating wax, real hair, and pigmented nipples, this weighty, hermaphroditic sack attains an uncanny resemblance to human flesh. It calls to mind the long tradition of sculptural ex-votos (cat. 86), three-dimensional renditions of human body parts that were deposited in churches in gratitude for divine intercession.[11] These talismanic offerings served as proxies for the worshipper's body and signified the completion of a contract with God. Often made from wax, they were imbued with a mimetic realism that strengthened their connection to the body of the votary. The ex-voto is also humorously referenced in Polish artist Alina Szapocznikow's *Dessert II* (1970–71, cat. 85), which presents a tinted polyester resin cast of the artist's breast melting atop a glass dessert bowl, like an overly generous scoop of ice cream. Battling breast cancer, Szapocznikow turned to her own body as a site both familiar and alien. In *Dessert II*, the breast is not offered up to the divine, as an ex-voto, but rather presented as a commodity, a delicacy for consumption. One wonders if Szapocznikow had ever seen the *jattes-tétons*, or "breast bowls," produced in the late 1780s as vessels for drinking milk at Marie Antoinette's dairy in Rambouillet (cat. 84). These bowls are a visual pun on the conceptual relationship between form and function. Although taking their cue from ancient Greek bowls shaped like female breasts (fig. 81), unlike their precursors these delicate porcelain cups emphasize mimetic likeness with their colored bodies and pink nipples. In fact, beginning in the nineteenth century, it was rumored that the bowls were cast from the queen's own body.[12]

The Rambouillet breast bowl also functioned as a kind of body-part reliquary, in which the sculpted container signified or indicated the substance it held.[13] Beginning in the Middle Ages, reliquaries were constructed as vessels to house holy objects, often the body parts of saints. A South Netherlandish reliquary arm at The Met, for example, probably

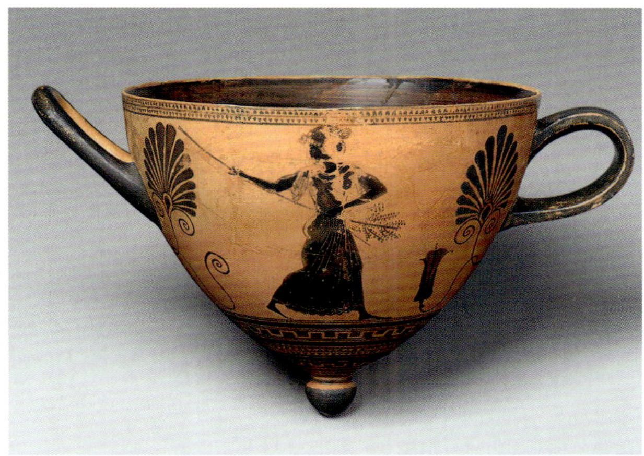

Fig. 81   Attributed to Psiax. *Terracotta Mastos (Drinking Cup in the Form of a Breast)*, ca. 520 B.C. Terracotta, H. 5 ¼ (13.4 cm), W. 8 ⅛ in. (20.6 cm), Diam. 5 ⁹⁄₁₆ in. (14.1 cm). The Metropolitan Museum of Art, New York, Purchase, The Abraham Foundation Inc. Gift, 1975 (1975.11.6)

held fragments of a saint's arm, the bones once visible through small crystal and glass windows. Such reliquaries, either made of precious materials or painted to achieve heightened realism, symbolically re-created the flesh of the desiccated relics within. This tradition is directly referenced in Paul Thek's series of Technological Reliquaries (1964–67), wax effigies of meat and body parts displayed within Plexiglas vitrines. *Untitled* (ca. 1966–67, cat. 94) is a sculpted arm, dismembered at the elbow but joined, bizarrely, to a length of hair. It is entirely unclear if the arm itself is reliquary or relic, container or contained. Coated in silver paint, this arm suggests the armorlike form of the reliquary arm. Yet pink flesh emerges at the fingers, and the entire appendage has the wrinkled surface of real skin. Like a cyborg in its metallic appearance, the arm suggests a disturbing fusion of biological and mechanical bodies—a nightmarish vision, perhaps, of the future of flesh.

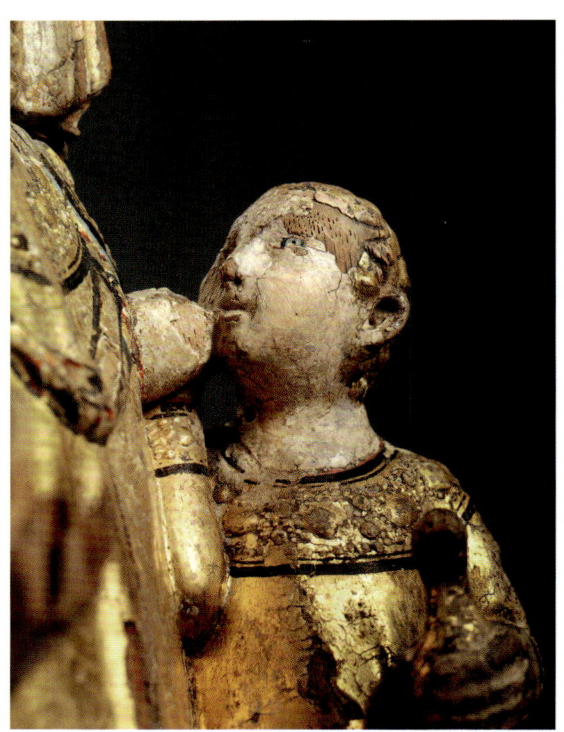

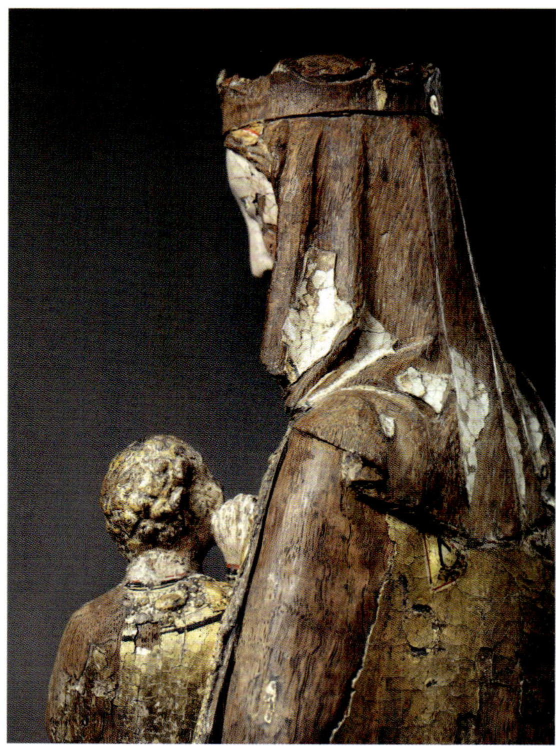

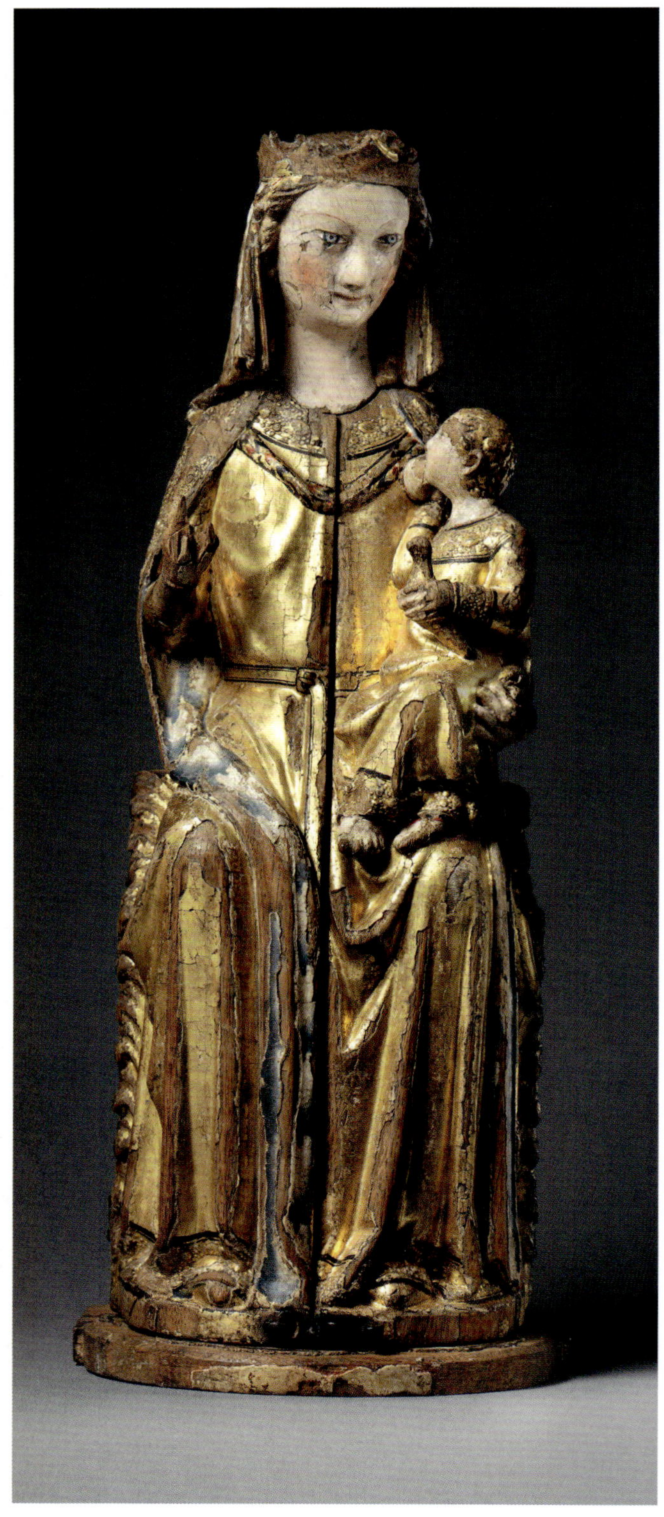

81. *Shrine of the Virgin*, ca. 1300. Oak, linen, polychromy, gilding, and gesso, open: H. 14 ½ in. (36.8 cm), W. 13 ⅝ in. (34.6 cm), D. 5 ⅛ in. (13 cm); closed: H. 14 ½ in. (36.8 cm), W. 13 ⅝ in. (34.6 cm), D. 5 in. (12.7 cm). German, Rhine Valley. The Metropolitan Museum of Art, New York, Gift of J. Pierpont Morgan, 1917 (17.190.185a, b)

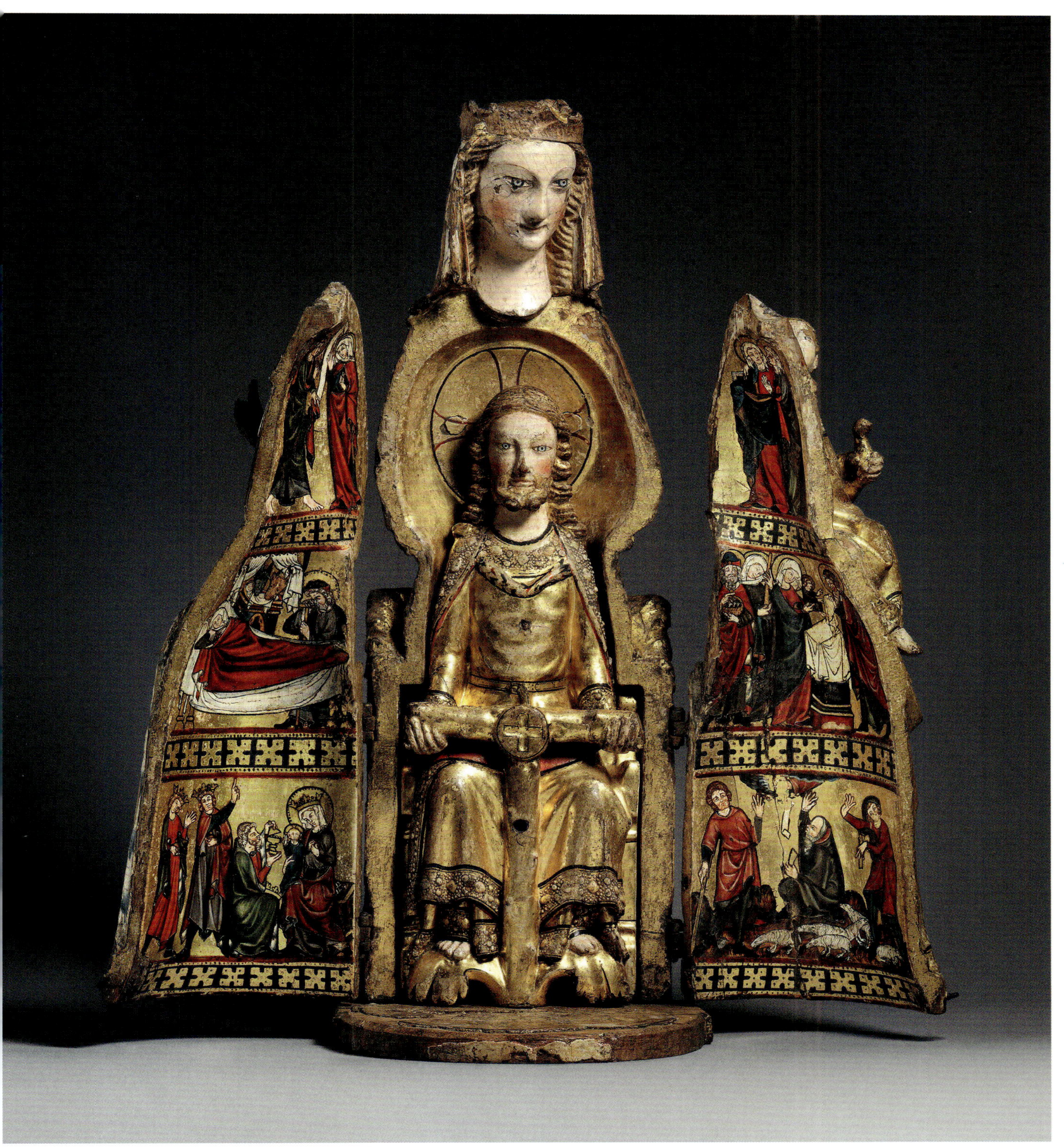

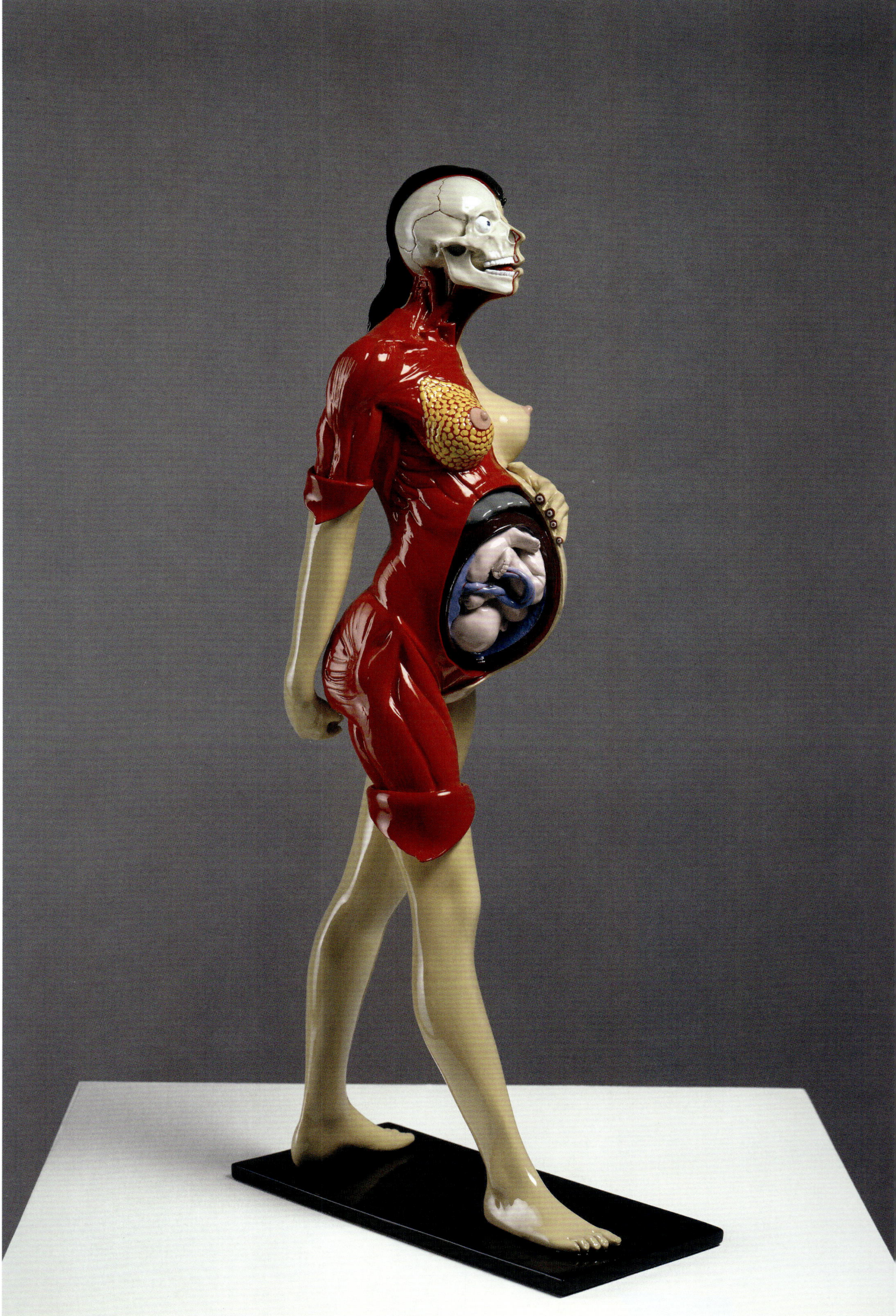

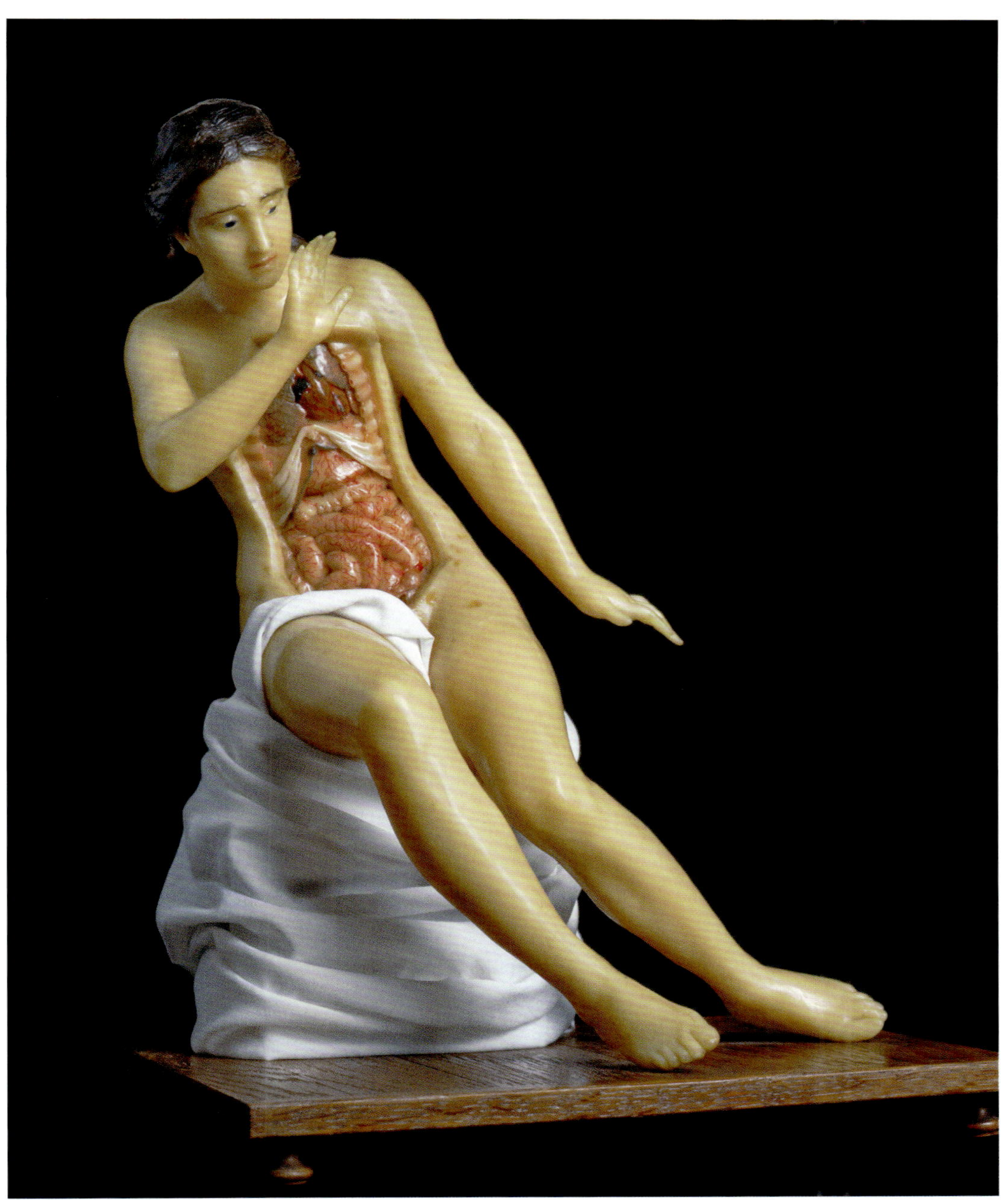

82. Damien Hirst. *Virgin (exposed)*, 2005. Acrylic paint on resin, H. 24 ⁷⁄₁₆ in. (62 cm), W. 6 ⁵⁄₈ in. (16.8 cm), D. 11 ⁵⁄₁₆ in. (28.7 cm). Mugrabi Collection

83. André Pierre Pinson. *Anatomical Seated Woman*, 1784–93. Pigmented wax, H. 16 ⅛ in. (41 cm), W. 9 ¹³⁄₁₆ in. (25 cm), D. 11 ¹³⁄₁₆ in. (30 cm). Musée National d'Histoire Naturelle, Paris

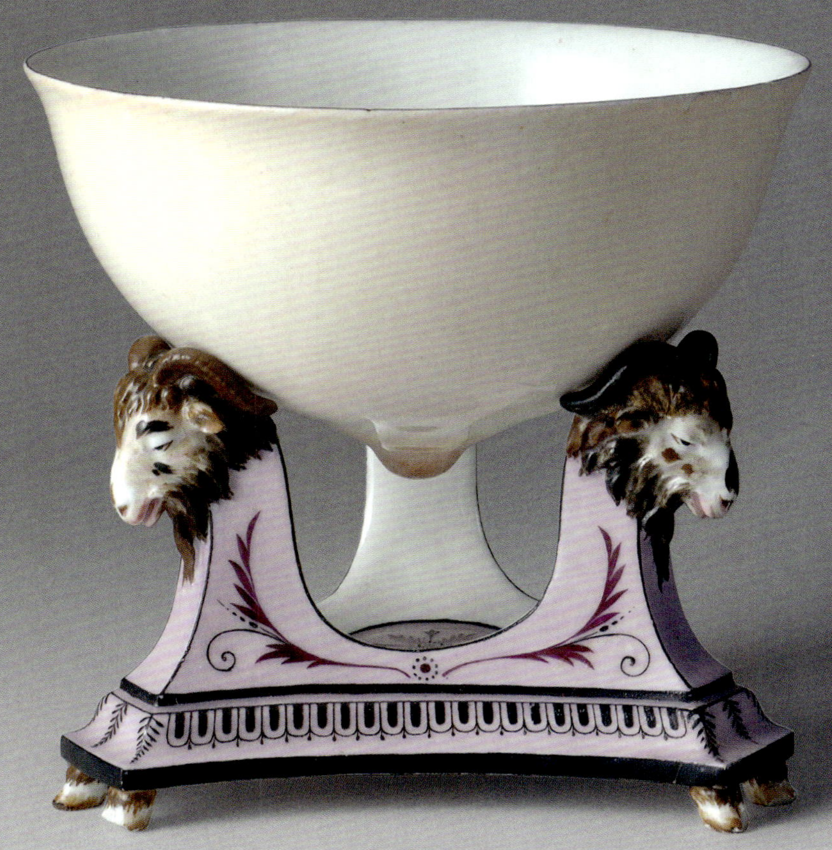

84. Sèvres Manufactory, design attributed to Jean Jacques Lagrenée. *Breast Bowl, Service for the Rambouillet Dairy*, 1787–88. Soft-paste porcelain bowl and hard-paste porcelain support, H. 4 ¹⁵⁄₁₆ in. (12.5 cm), W. 4 ¹³⁄₁₆ in. (12.2 cm), D. 5 ¼ in. (13.3 cm). Cité de la Céramique, Sèvres and Limoges

85. Alina Szapocznikow. *Dessert II*, 1970–71. Polyester resin, glass, and photographs, H. 7 ½ in. (19 cm), W. 5 ⅛ in. (13 cm), D. 5 ⅛ in. (13 cm). Private collection

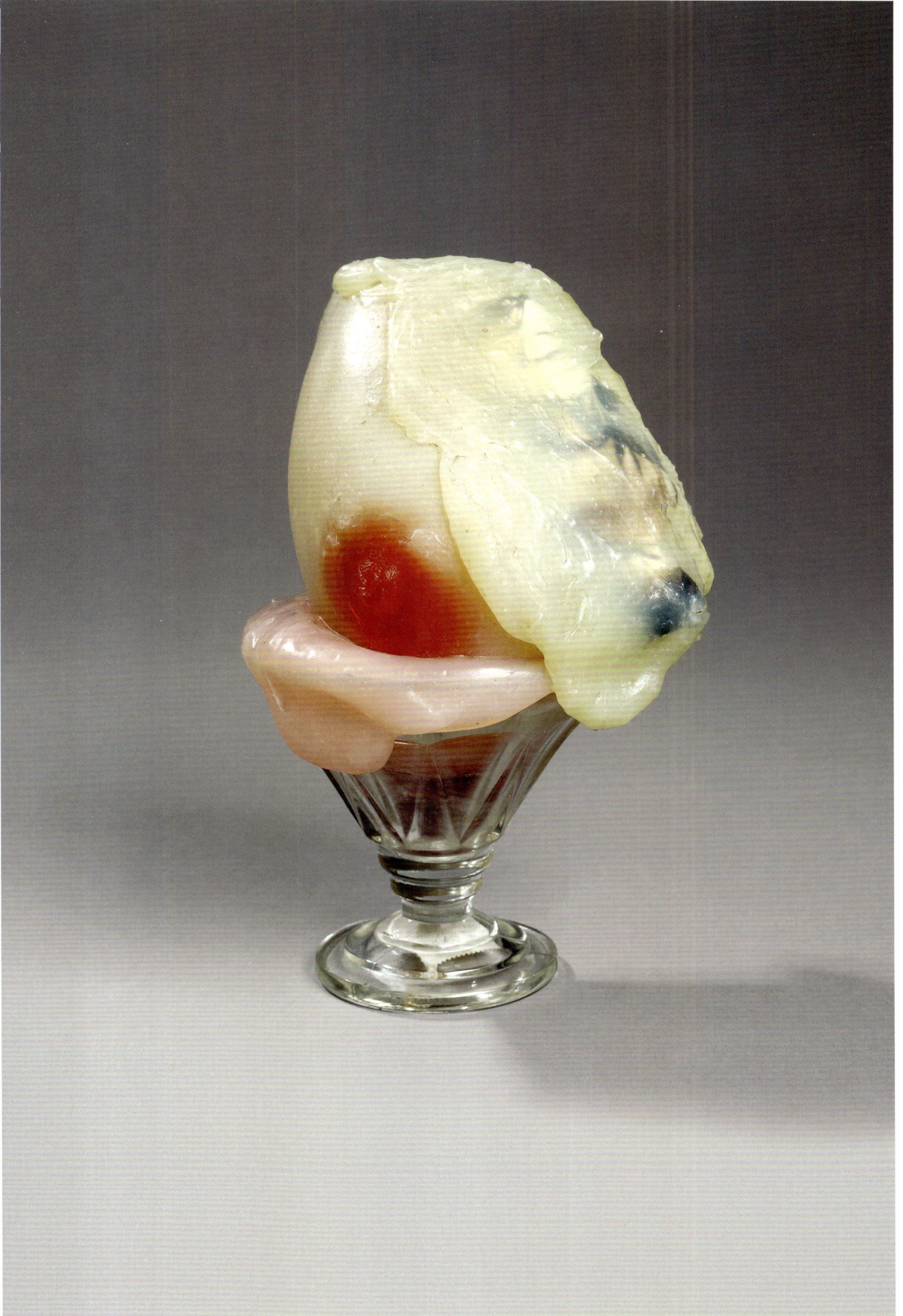

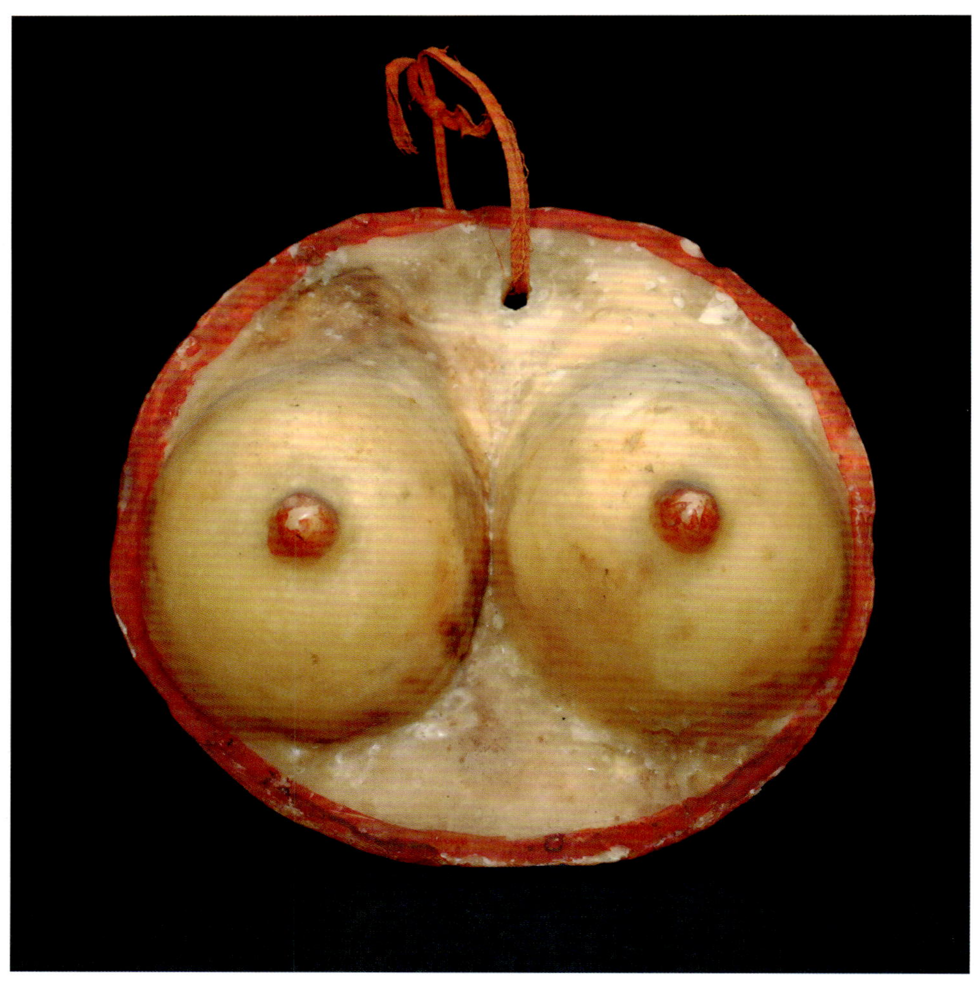

86. *Ex-Voto Breasts*, late 19th–early 20th century. Wax, H. 9 ¹⁄₁₆ in. (23 cm), W. 9 ¼ in. (23.5 cm), D. 3 ⅜ in. (8.5 cm). Italian. Museo Storico Nazionale dell'Arte Sanitaria, Rome

87. Robert Gober. *Untitled*, 1990. Beeswax, human hair, and pigment, H. 24 ¼ in. (61.6 cm), W. 17 in. (43.2 cm), D. 11 in. (27.9 cm). Courtesy of the artist and Matthew Marks Gallery, New York and Los Angeles

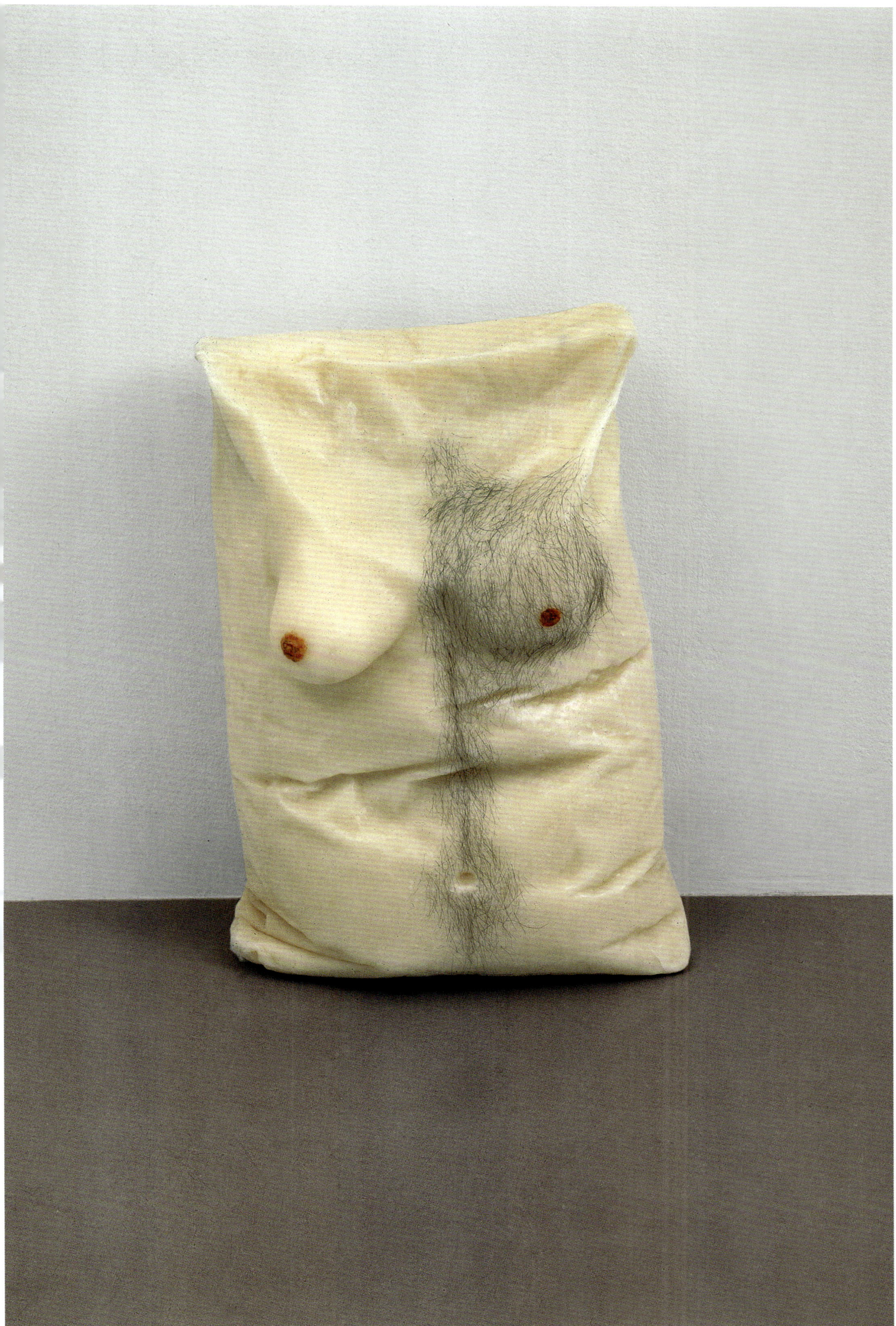

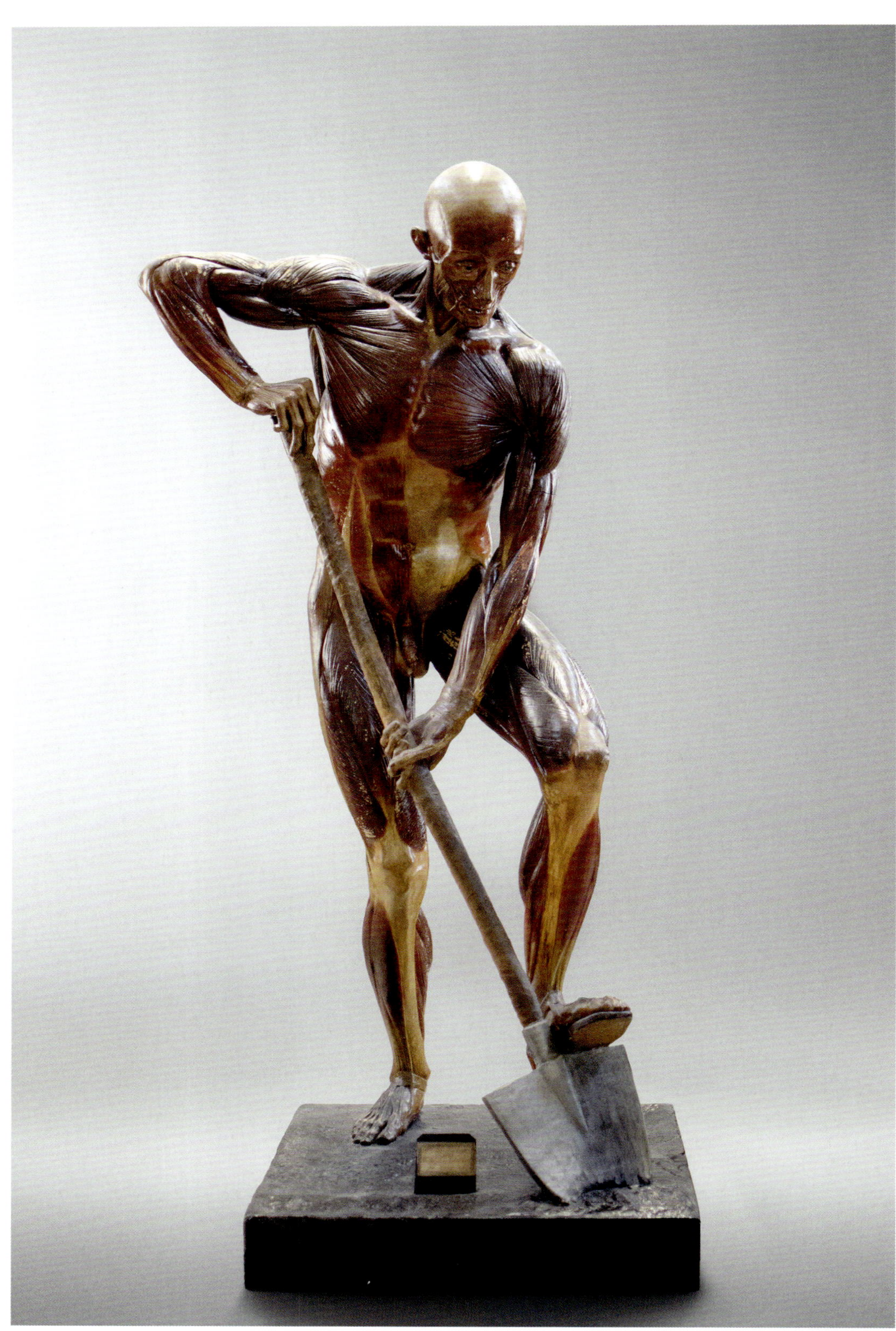

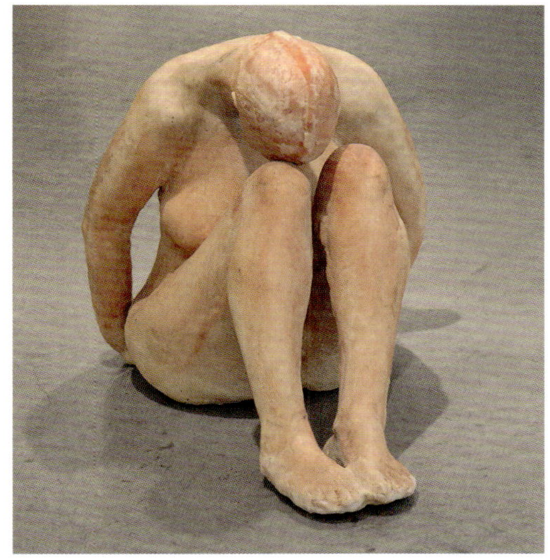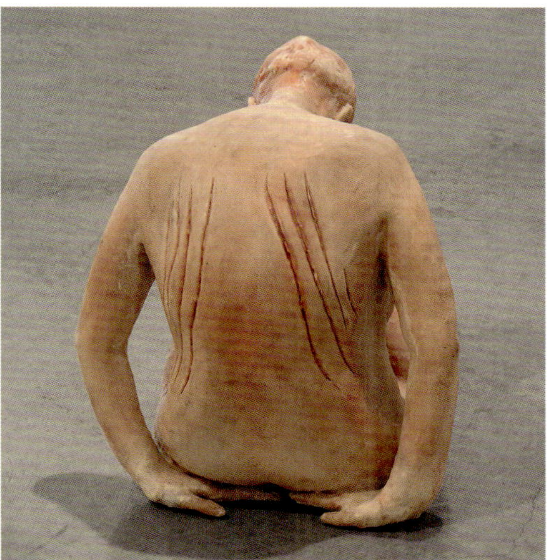

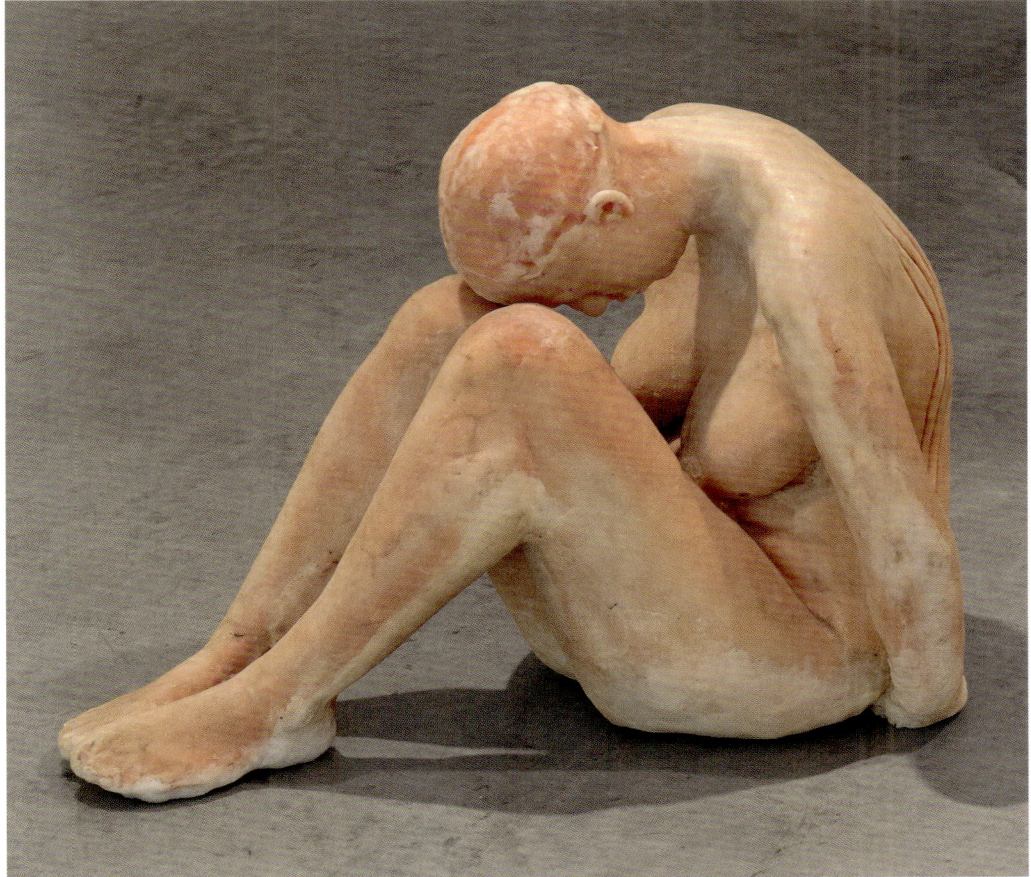

88. Alphonse Lami. *Le Bêcheur*, 1857. Plaster and paint, H. 86 ¼ in. (219 cm), W. 39 in. (99 cm), D. 35 ¼ in. (89.5 cm). Bâtiment Historique de la Faculté de Médecine, Université de Montpellier

89. Kiki Smith. *Untitled a.k.a. The Sitter*, 1992. Wax, cheesecloth, wood, and dye, H. 28 in. (71.1 cm), W. 24 in. (61 cm), D. 36 in. (91.4 cm). Emily Fisher Landau, AMART LLC

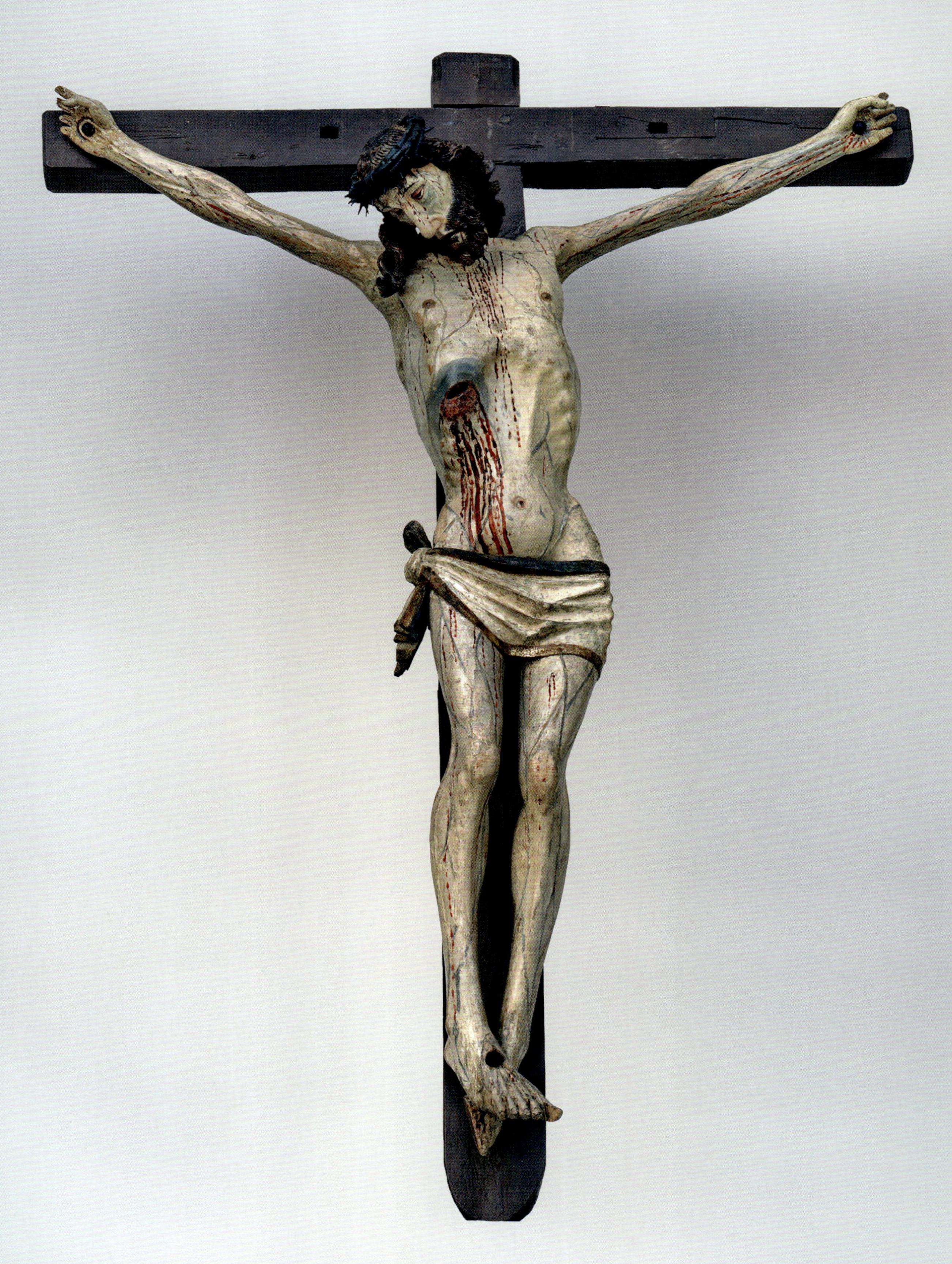

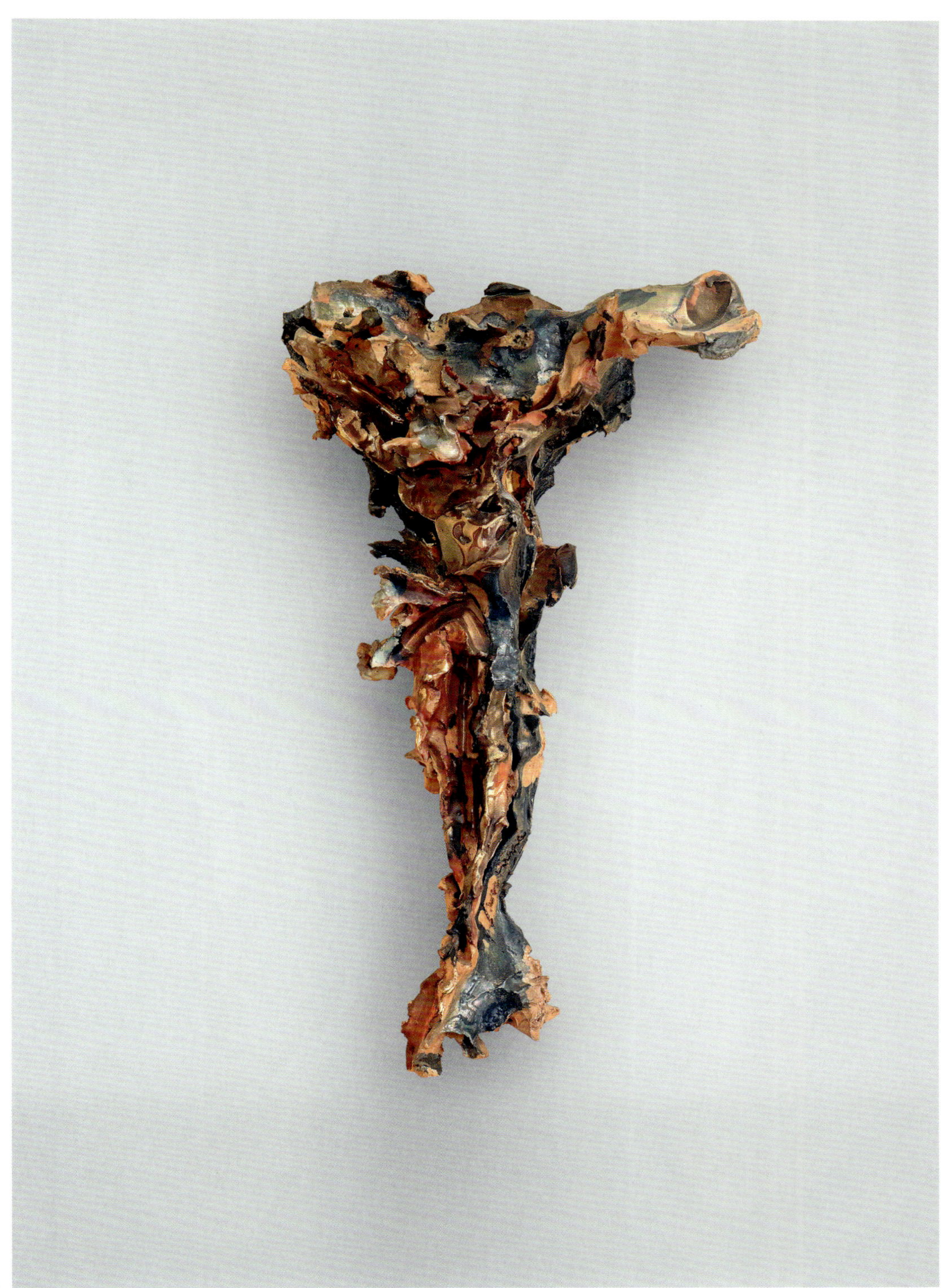

A.

90. *Nellingen Crucifix*, 1430–35. Polychromed limewood, H. 93 ⁵⁄₁₆ in. (237 cm), W. 70 ½ in. (179 cm), D. 17 ¹¹⁄₁₆ in. (45 cm). German, probably Ulm. Landesmuseum Württemberg, Stuttgart

91. Lucio Fontana

A. *Crocifisso* (*Christ on the Cross*), 1950–52. Glazed terracotta. H. 19 ⅝ in. (49.8 cm), W. 12 ⅜ in. (31.4 cm), D. 5 in. (12.7 cm). Collection of Mr. and Mrs. J. Tomilson Hill

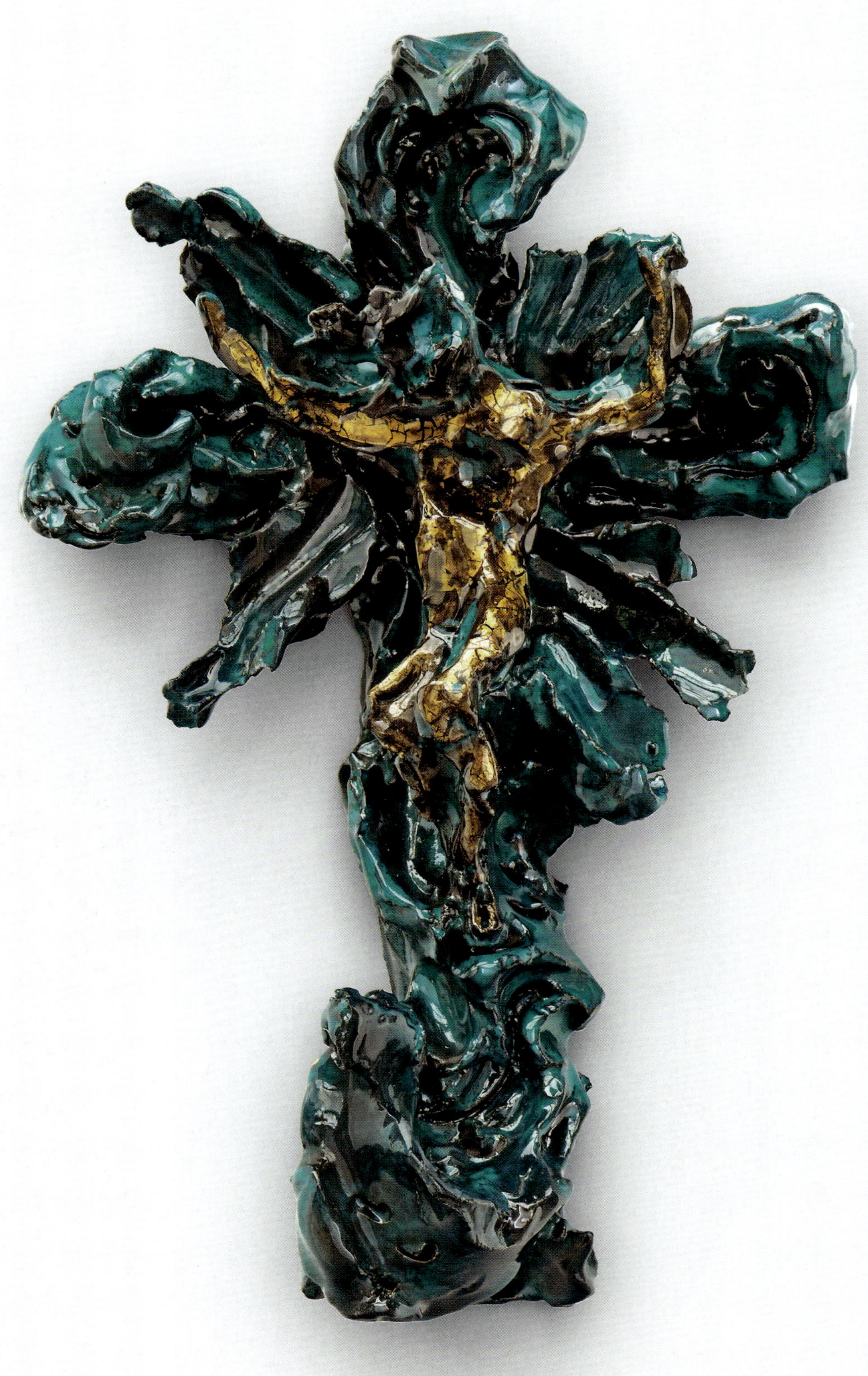

B.

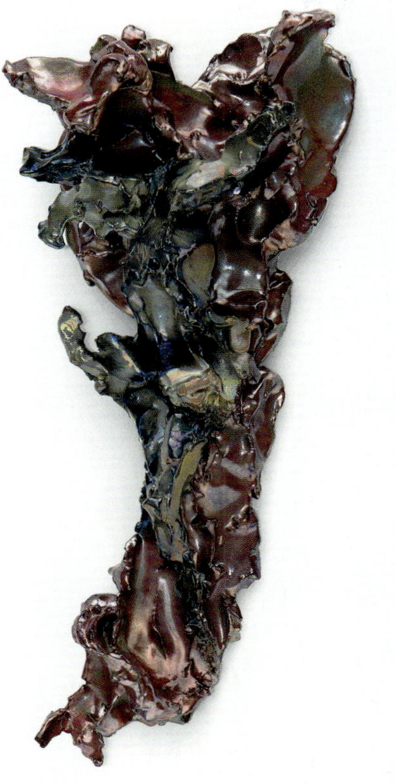

C.

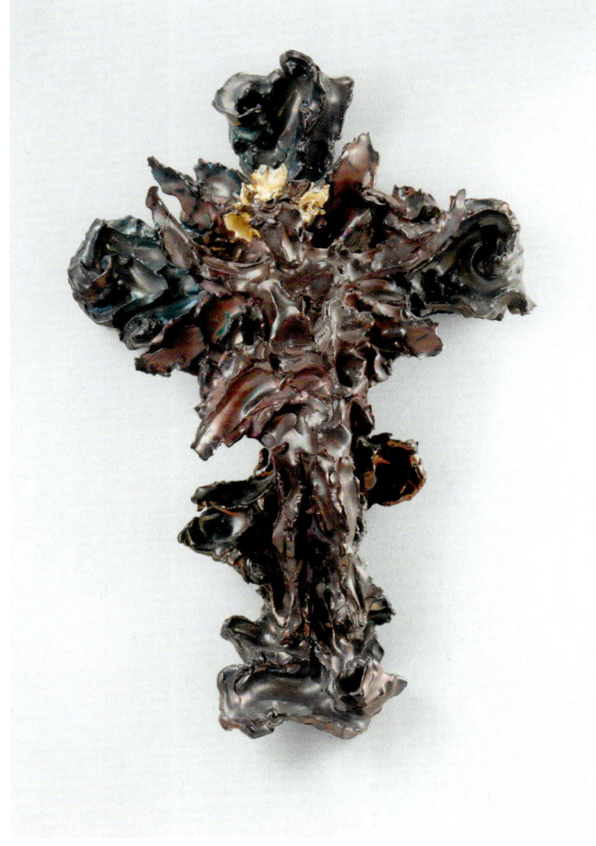

D.

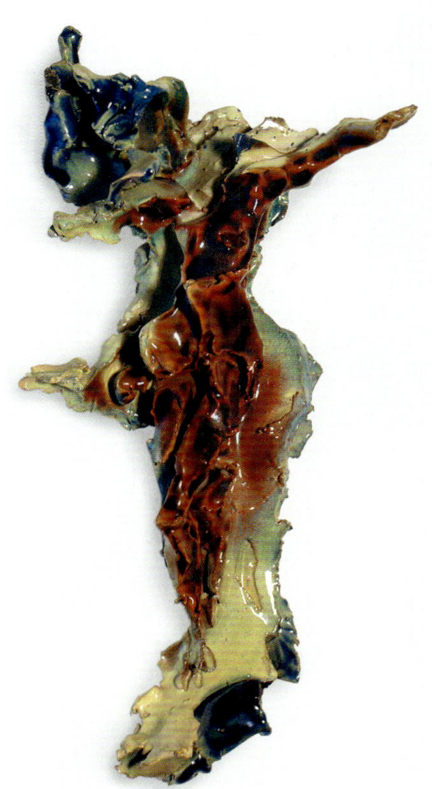

E.

91. Lucio Fontana

B. *Crocifisso*, 1951. Polychromed ceramic, H. 15 ¾ in. (40 cm), W. 10 ⅝ in. (27 cm), D. 4 ¾ in. (12 cm). Courtesy of Galerie Karsten Greve, St. Moritz

C. *Crocifisso*, 1953. Glazed terracotta, H. 16 ¾ in. (42.5 cm), W. 7 ¹¹⁄₁₆ in. (19.5 cm), D. 5 ⁵⁄₁₆ in. (13.5 cm). Courtesy of Galerie Karsten Greve, St. Moritz

D. *Crocifisso*, 1948. Polychromed ceramic, H. 16 ⁹⁄₁₆ in. (42 cm), W. 10 ⅝ in. (27 cm), D. 4 ½ in. (11.5 cm). Courtesy of Galerie Karsten Greve, St. Moritz

E. *Cristo*, 1955. Glazed terracotta, H. 14 ¹⁵⁄₁₆ in. (38 cm), W. 7 ⅞ in. (20 cm), D. 3 ⁹⁄₁₆ in. (9 cm). Courtesy of Galerie Karsten Greve, St. Moritz

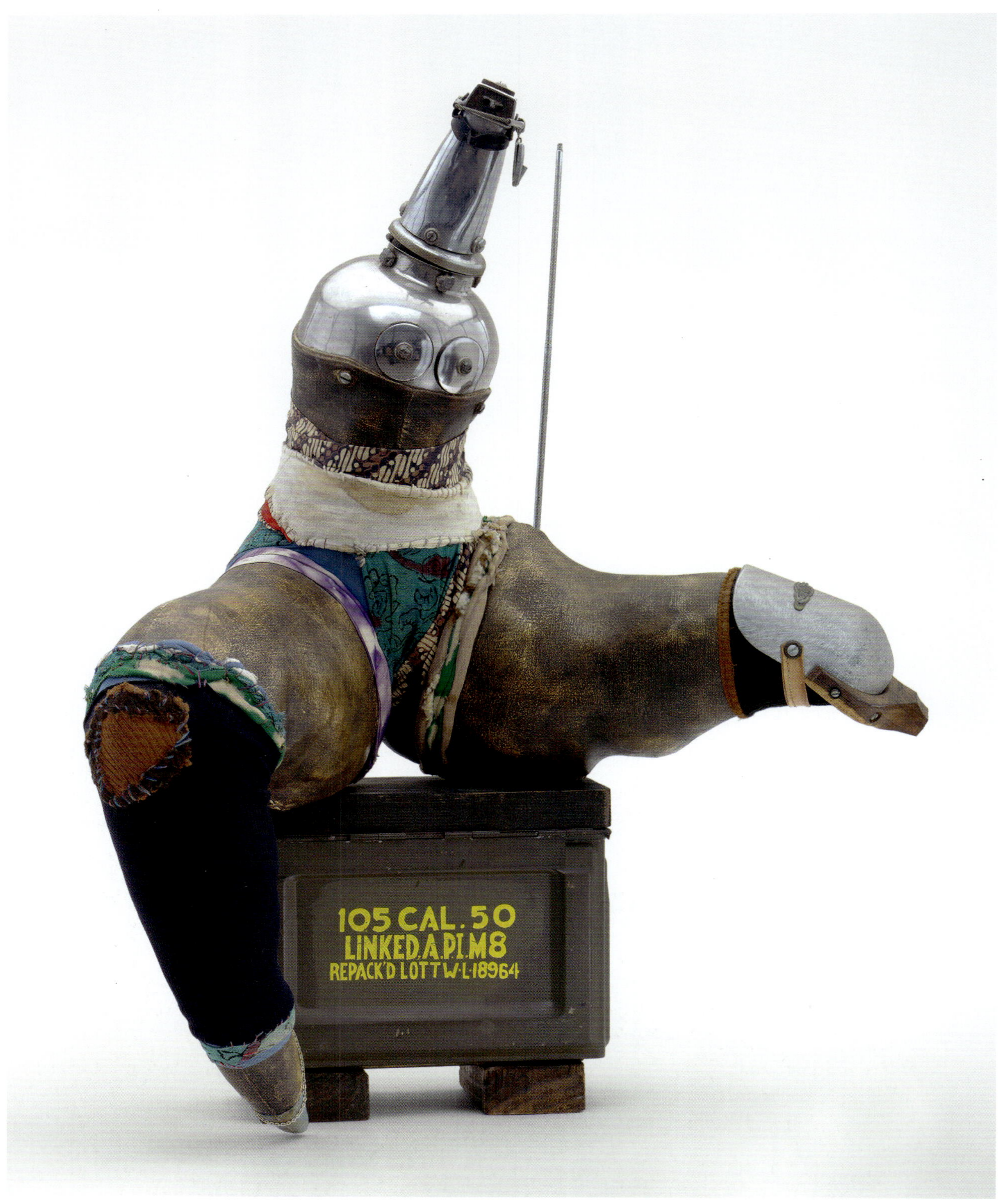

92. John Outterbridge. *Broken Dance, Ethnic Heritage Series*, ca. 1978–82. Stainless steel, wood, leather, sewn cloth, and ammunition box, H. 34 in. (86.4 cm), W. 29 ¼ in. (74.3 cm), D. 33 in. (83.8 cm). Museum of Modern Art, New York, Gift of Marlene Hess and James D. Zirin, 2013

93. Urs Fischer. *The Grass Munchers*, 2007. Cast aluminum and patinated wax, H. 22 ¹⁄₁₆ in. (56 cm), W. 24 ⁷⁄₁₆ in. (62 cm), D. 17 ⁵⁄₁₆ in. (44 cm). Burger Collection, Hong Kong

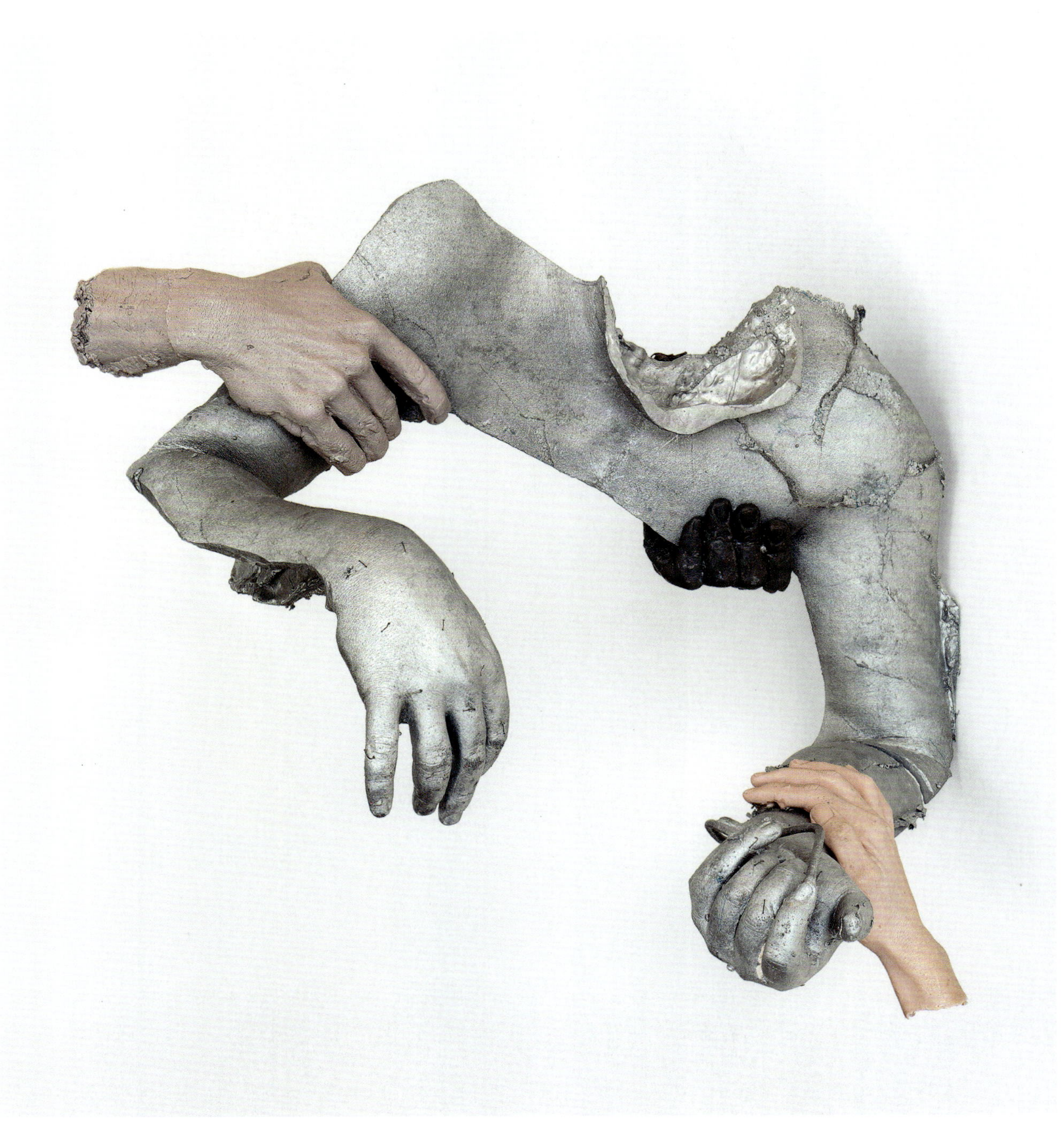

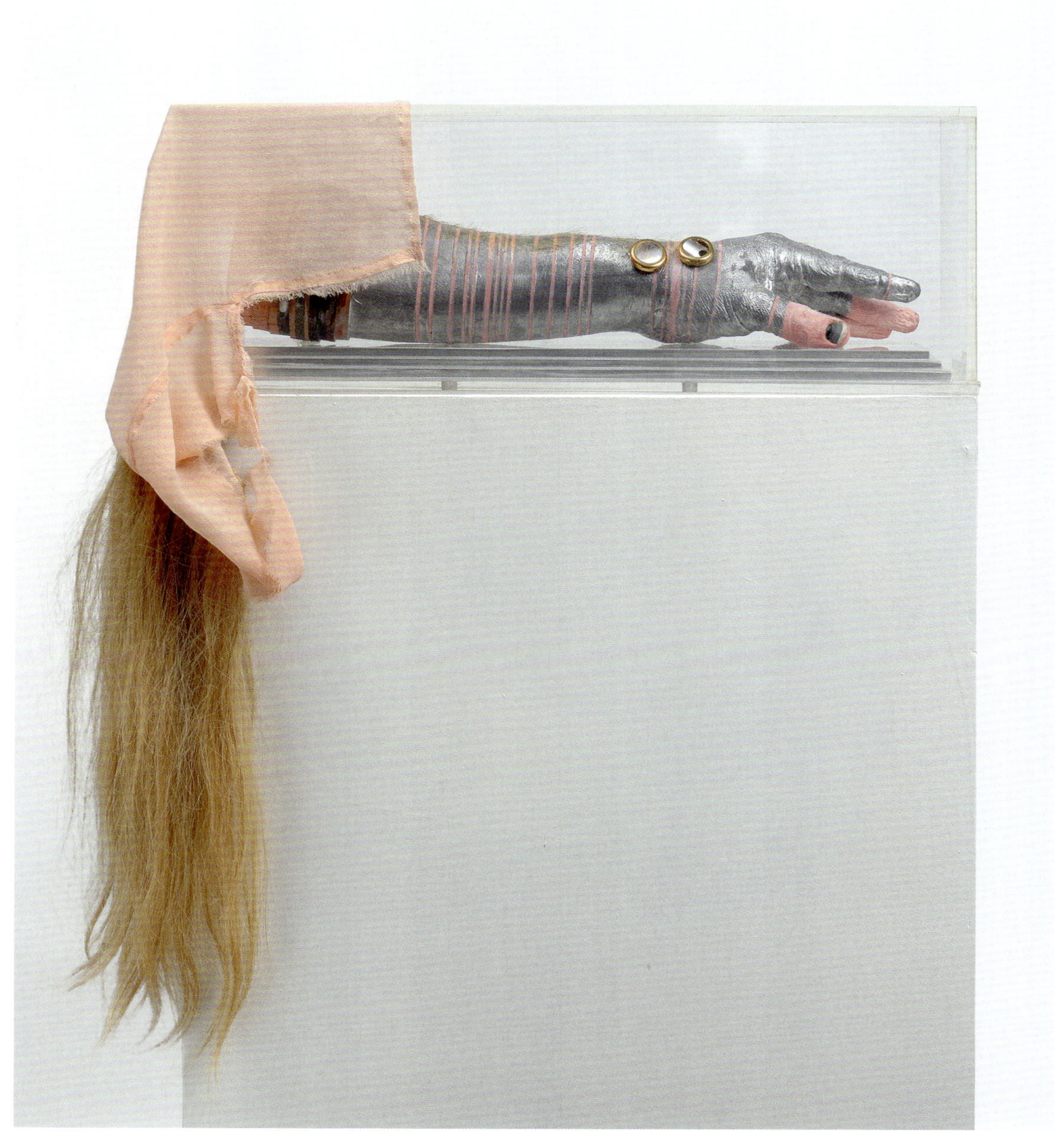

94. Paul Thek. *Untitled* from the series Technological Reliquaries, ca. 1966–67, lost elements re-created 2006. Wax, wood, metal, hair, plaster, paint, and Plexiglas with wig and fabric, H. 6 ½ in. (16.5 cm), W. 20 ¼ in. (51.4 cm), D. 6 ¾ in. (17.1 cm). Watermill Center Collection, Water Mill, New York

95. Oliver Herring. *Patrick*, 2004. Foam core, mat board, digital chromogenic prints, and polystyrene, H. 42 in. (106.7 cm), W. 18 in. (45.7 cm), D. 27 ½ in. (69.9 cm). Blanton Museum of Art, University of Texas at Austin, Partial and pledged gift of Jeanne and Michael Klein, 2005

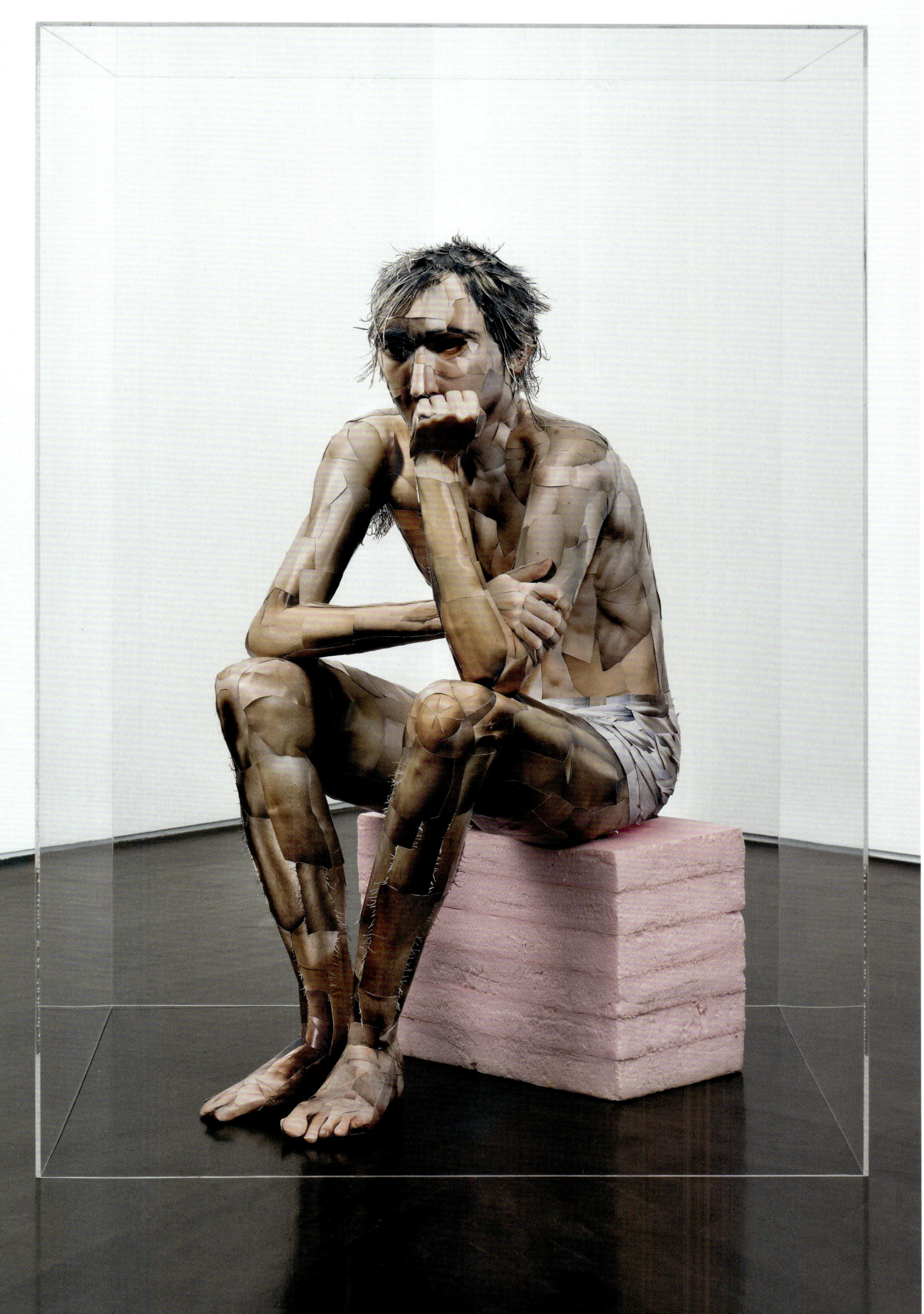

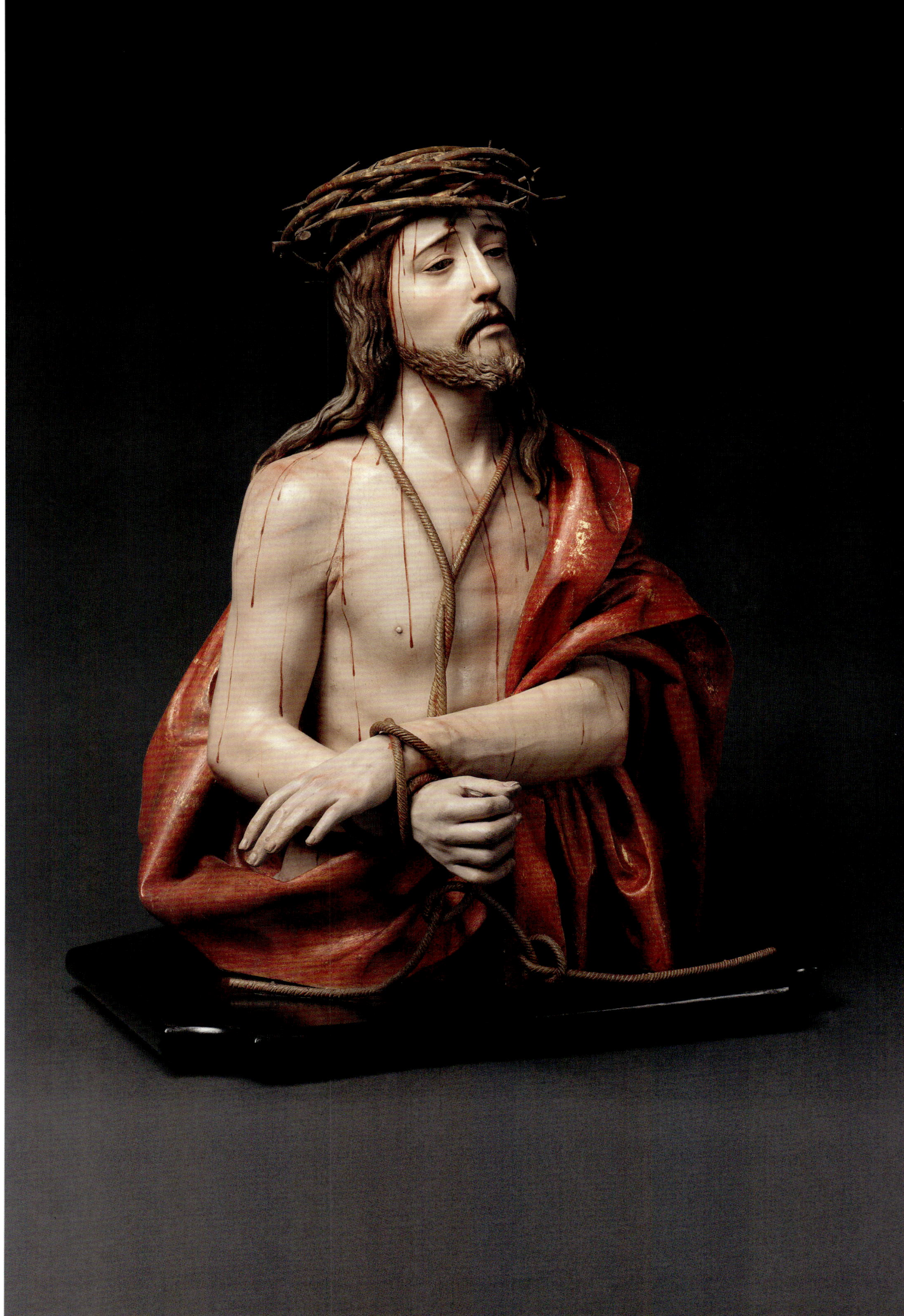

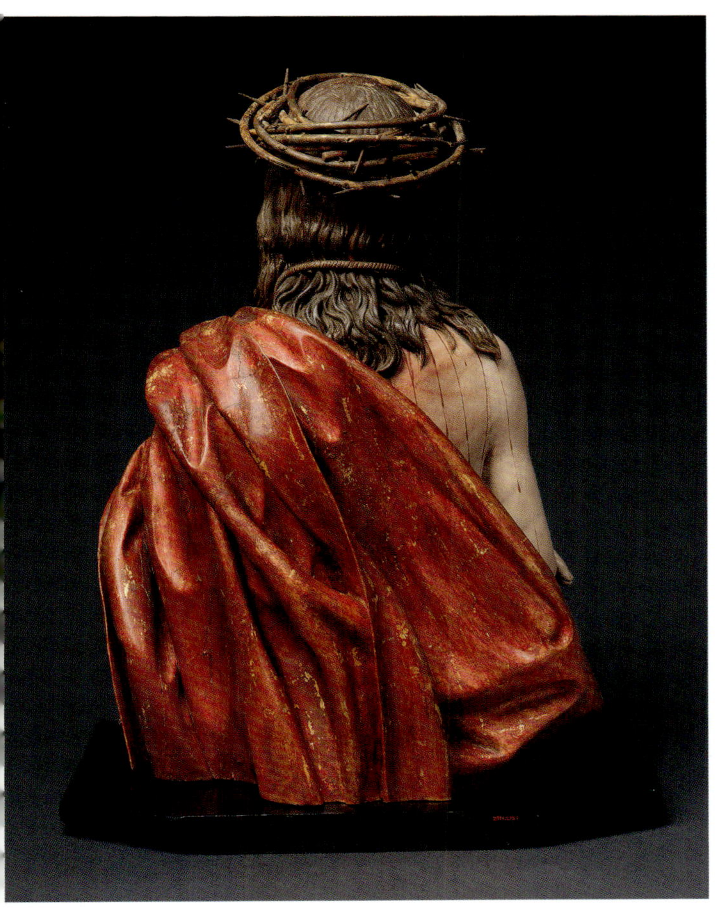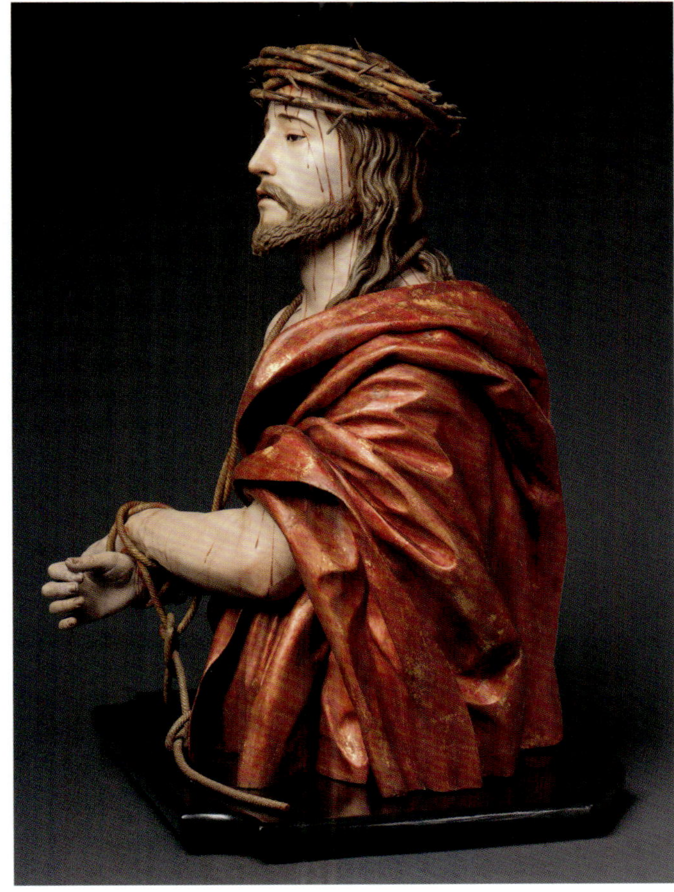

96. Pedro de Mena. *Ecce Homo*, ca. 1674–85. Polychromed wood and gilding, figure: H. 24 ¾ in. (62.9 cm), W. 17 ¾ in. (45.1 cm), D. 18 ⅜ in. (46.7 cm); base: H. 1 ½ in. (3.8 cm), W. 21 in. (53.3 cm), D. 16 ⅛ in. (41 cm). The Metropolitan Museum of Art, New York, Purchase, Lila Acheson Wallace Gift, Mary Trumbell Adams Fund, and Gift of Dr. Mortimer D. Sackler, Theresa Sackler and Family, 2014 (2014.275.1)

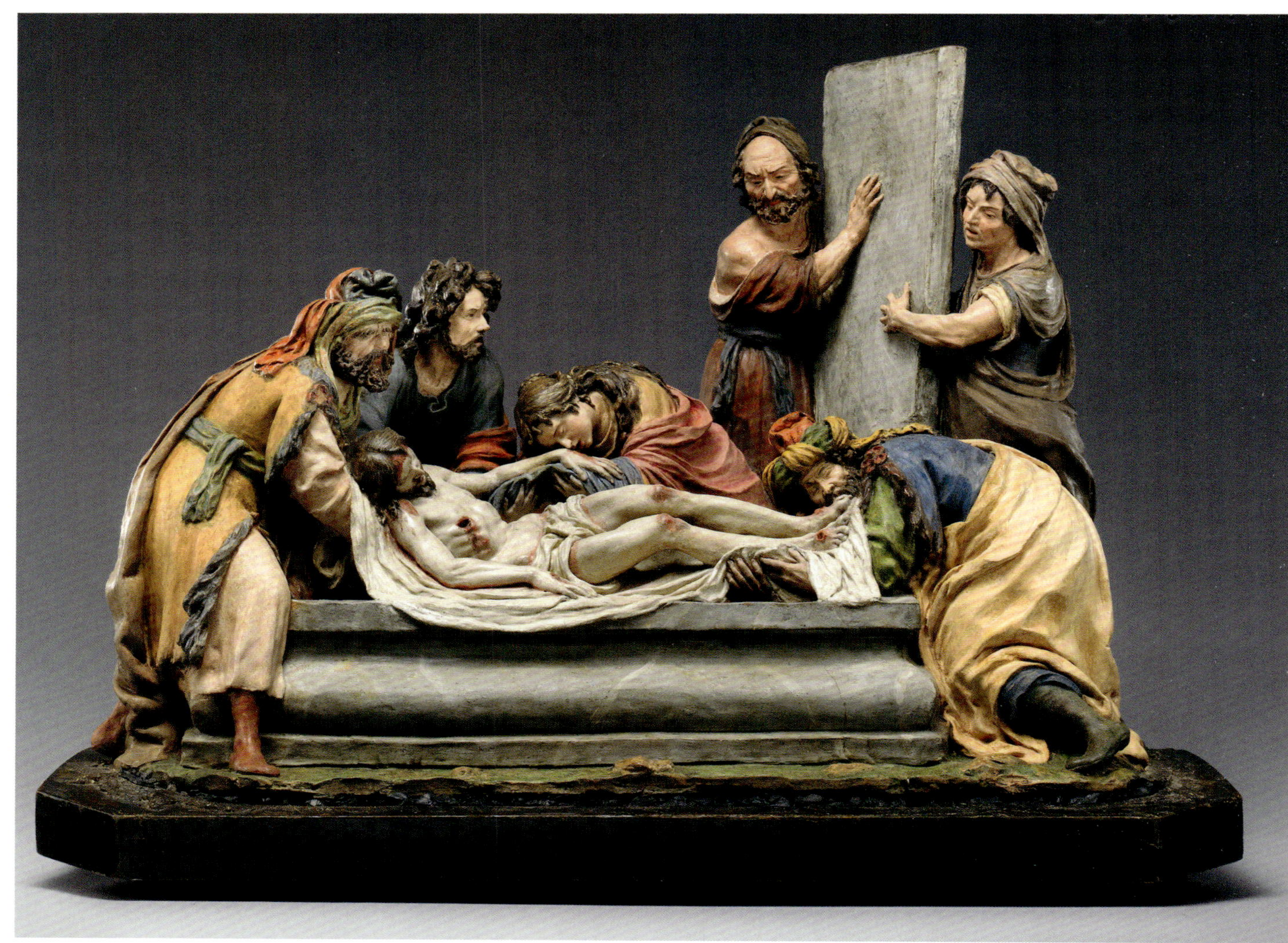

97. La Roldana (Luisa Roldán). *The Entombment of Christ*, 1700–1701. Polychrome terracotta and wood base:
H. 19 ½ in. (49.5 cm), W. 26 in. (66 cm), D. 17 in. (43.2 cm). The Metropolitan Museum of Art, New York, Purchase,
several members of The Chairman's Council Gifts, Walter and Leonore Annenberg Acquisitions Endowment
Fund, Álvaro Saieh Bendeck and Alejandro Santo Domingo Gifts, and Mary Trumbull Adams Fund; Edward J.
Gallagher Jr. Bequest, in memory of his father, Edward Joseph Gallagher, his mother, Ann Hay Gallagher, and
his son, Edward Joseph Gallagher III; The Bernard and Audrey Aronson Charitable Trust Gift, in memory of her
beloved husband, Bernard Aronson; Anonymous Gift and Louis V. Bell Fund, 2016 (2016.482)

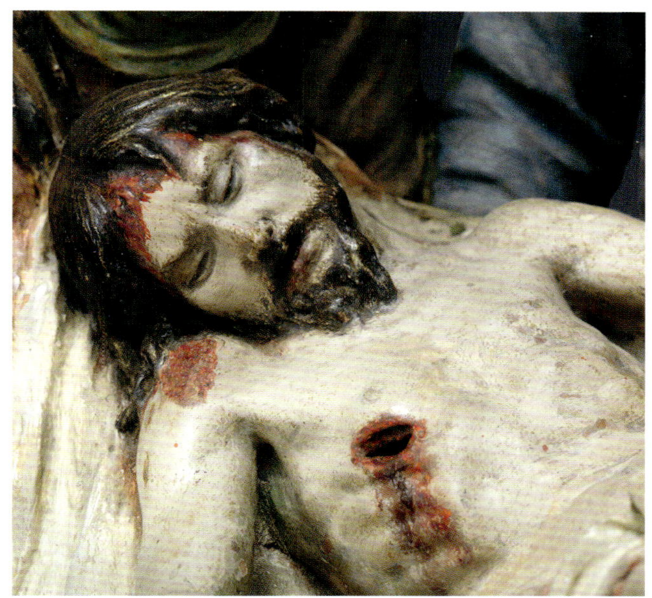

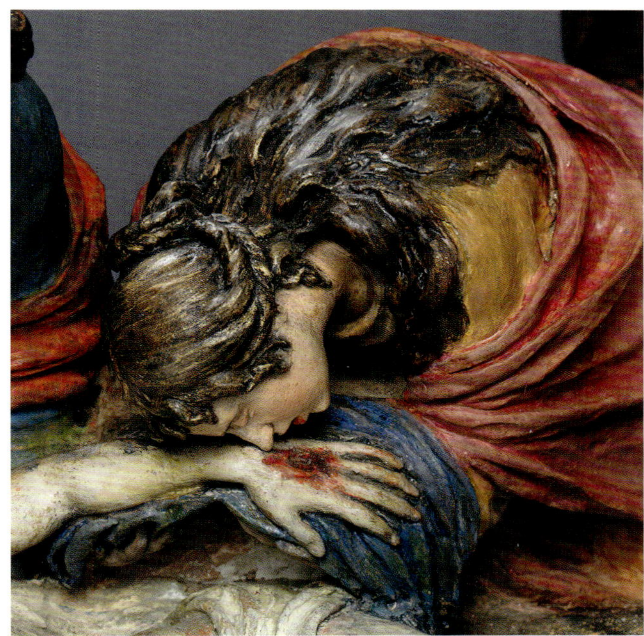

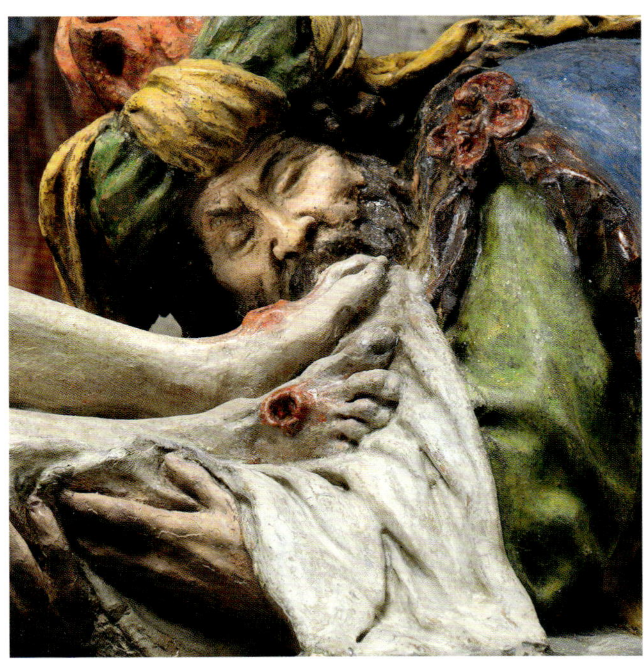

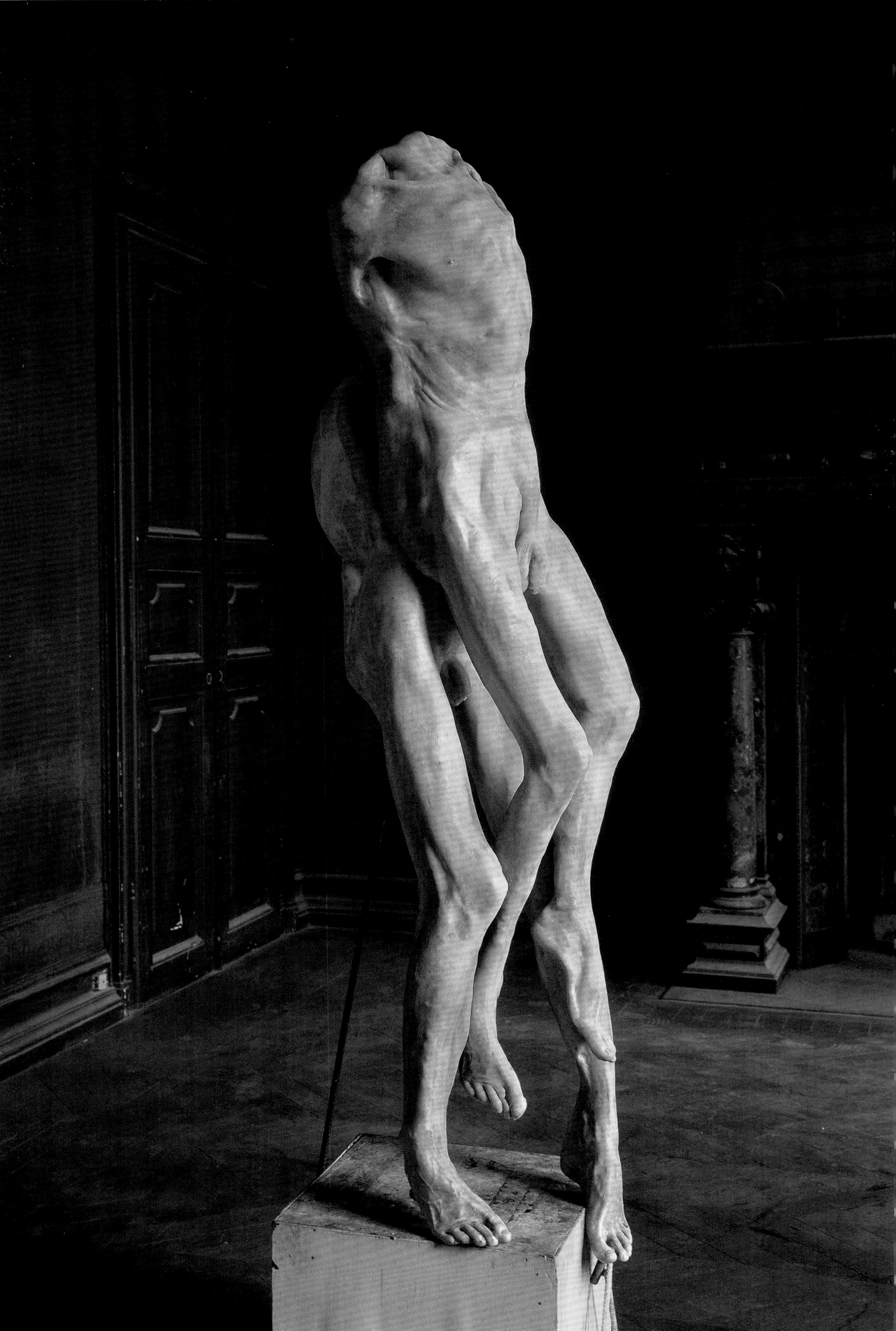

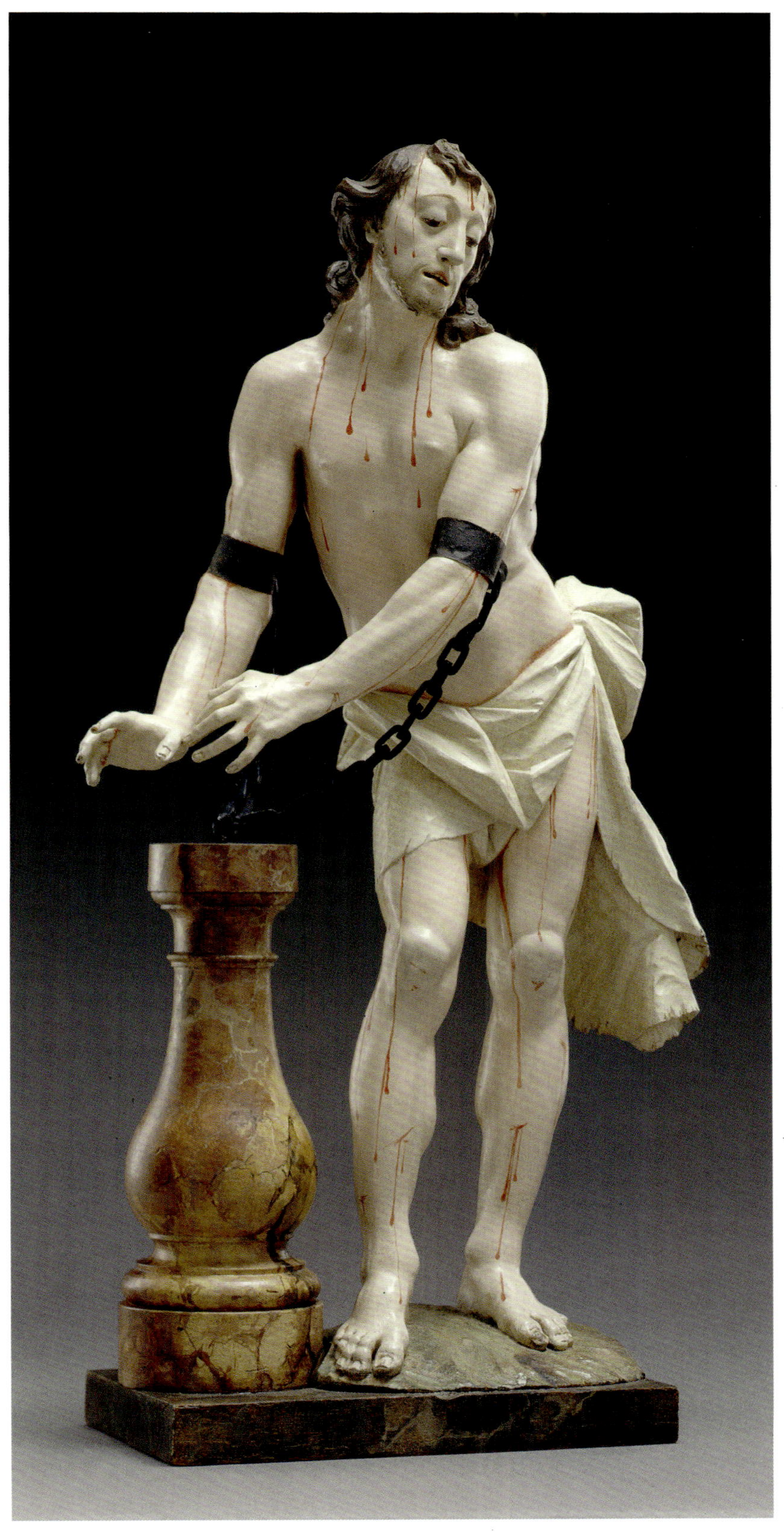

98. Berlinde De Bruyckere. *Piëta*, 2008. Wax, epoxy, metal, and wood, H. 93 ¼ in. (236.9 cm),
    W. 22 ¾ in. (57.8 cm), D. 21 ¼ in. (54 cm). Tony Podesta Collection, Washington, D.C., courtesy
    Galleria Continua

99. Ignaz Günther. *Christ at the Column*, 1754. Polychromed lindenwood and fir, figure:
    H. 29 ¼ in. (74.5 cm), W. 17 ¼ in. (44 cm), D. 7 ½ in. (19.1 cm); base: H. 1 ¼ in. (3.2 cm),
    W. 12 in. (30.5 cm), D. 8 in. (20.3 cm). Detroit Institute of Arts, Founders Society Purchase,
    Acquisitions Fund

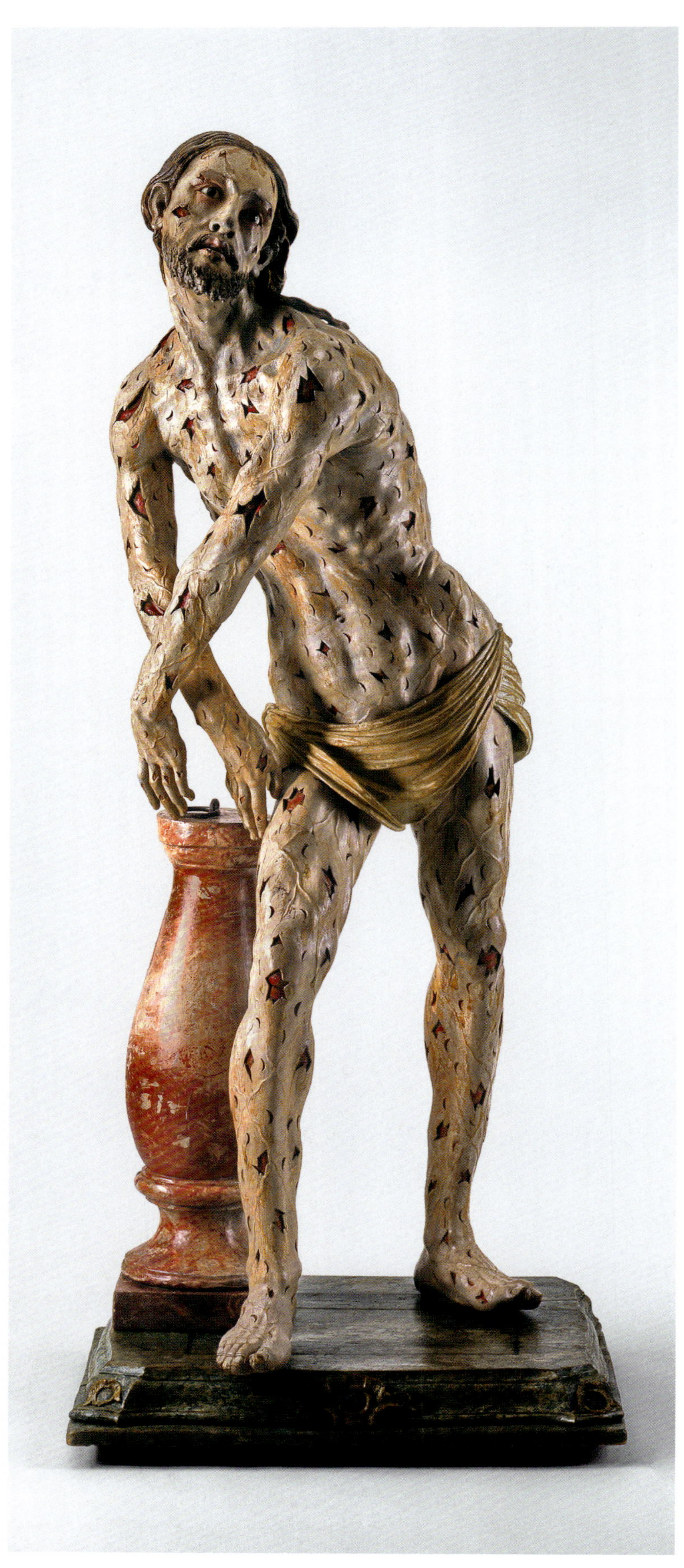

100. Master IPS. *Christ at the Column*, 1697. Polychromed lindenwood, H. 63 $\frac{3}{4}$ in. (162 cm), W. 28 $\frac{3}{4}$ in. (73 cm), D. 26 $\frac{3}{8}$ in. (67 cm); base: H. 4 $\frac{5}{16}$ in. (11 cm). Landesmuseum Württemberg, Stuttgart

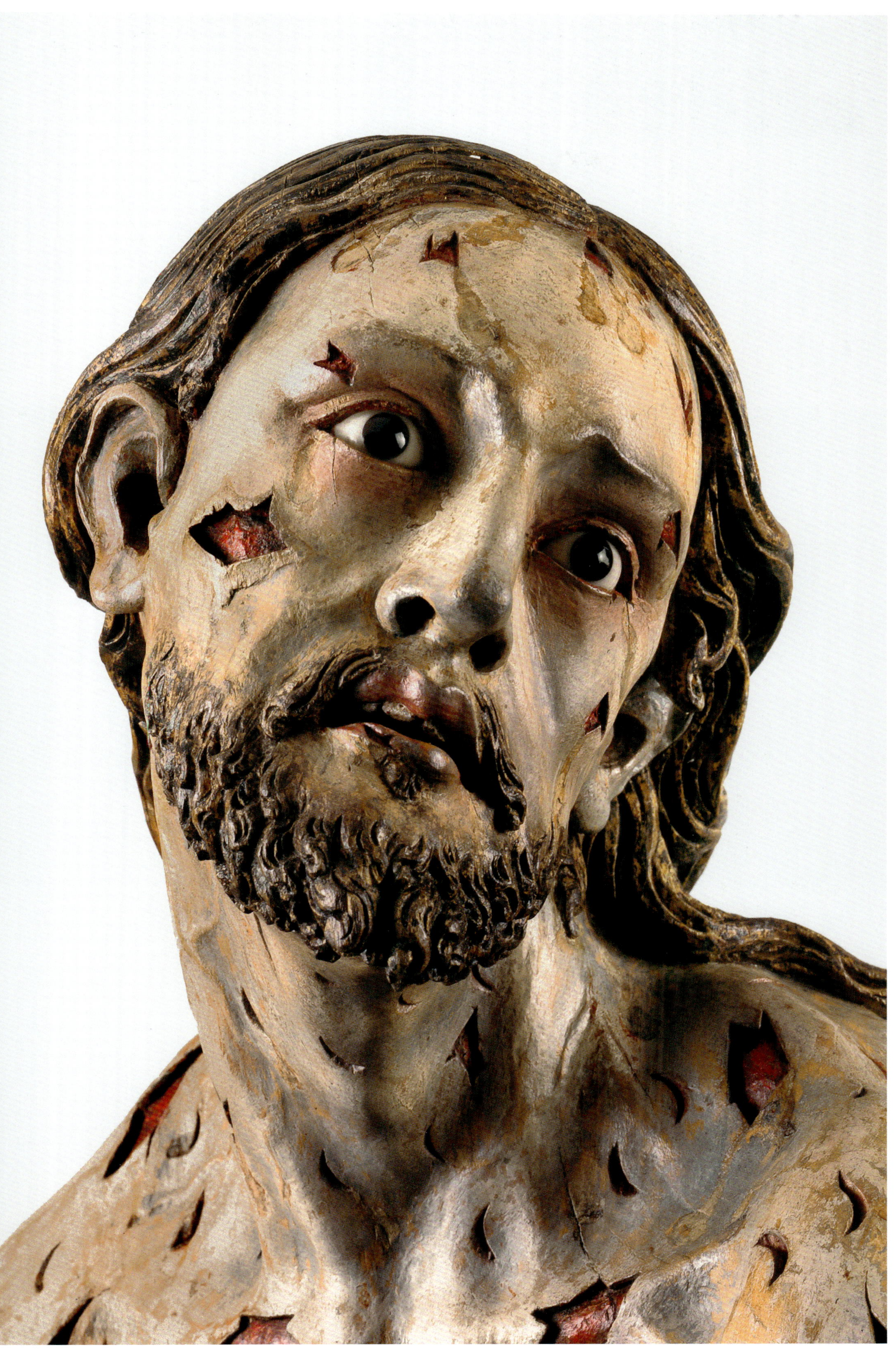

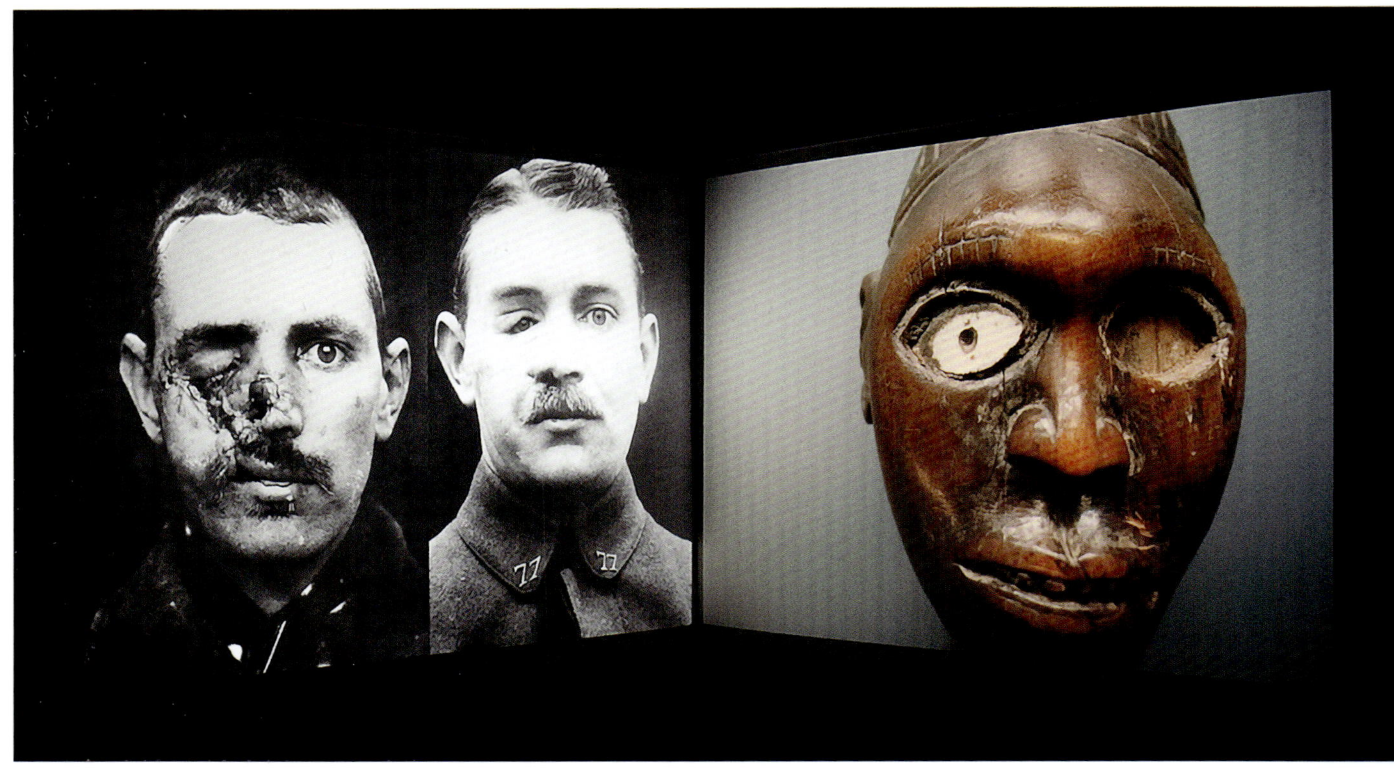

101. Kader Attia. *Open Your Eyes*, 2010. Dual projection of two sets of eighty 35 mm black-and-white and color slides, projection: 63 in. × 8 ft. 6 ⅜ in. (160 × 260 cm), duration: 13 min. (digitized version). Courtesy of the artist and Lehmann Maupin, New York and Hong Kong

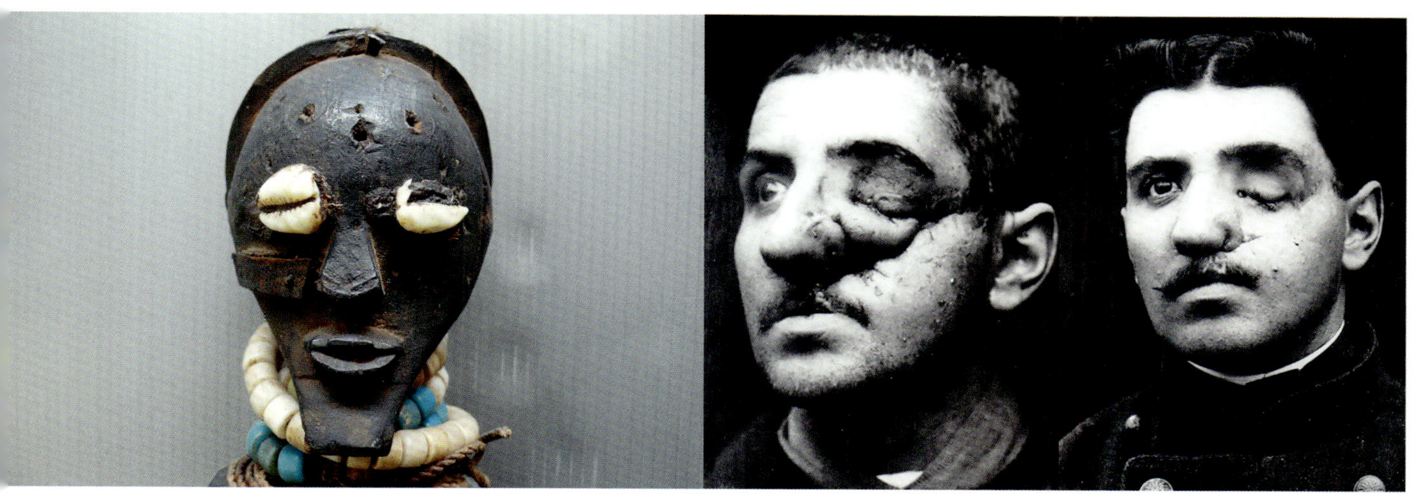

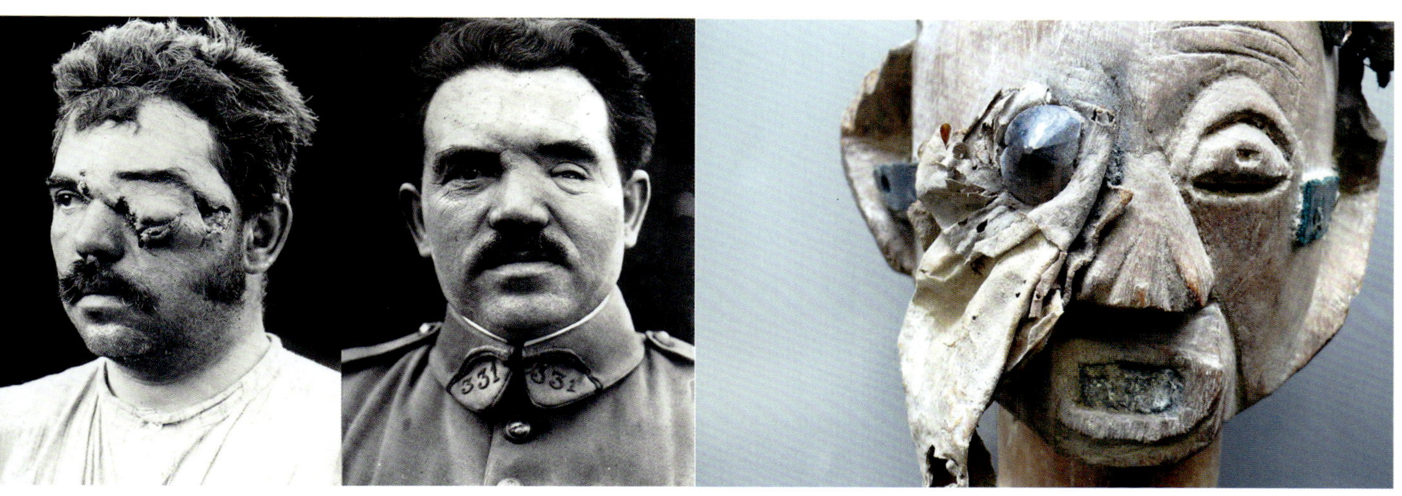

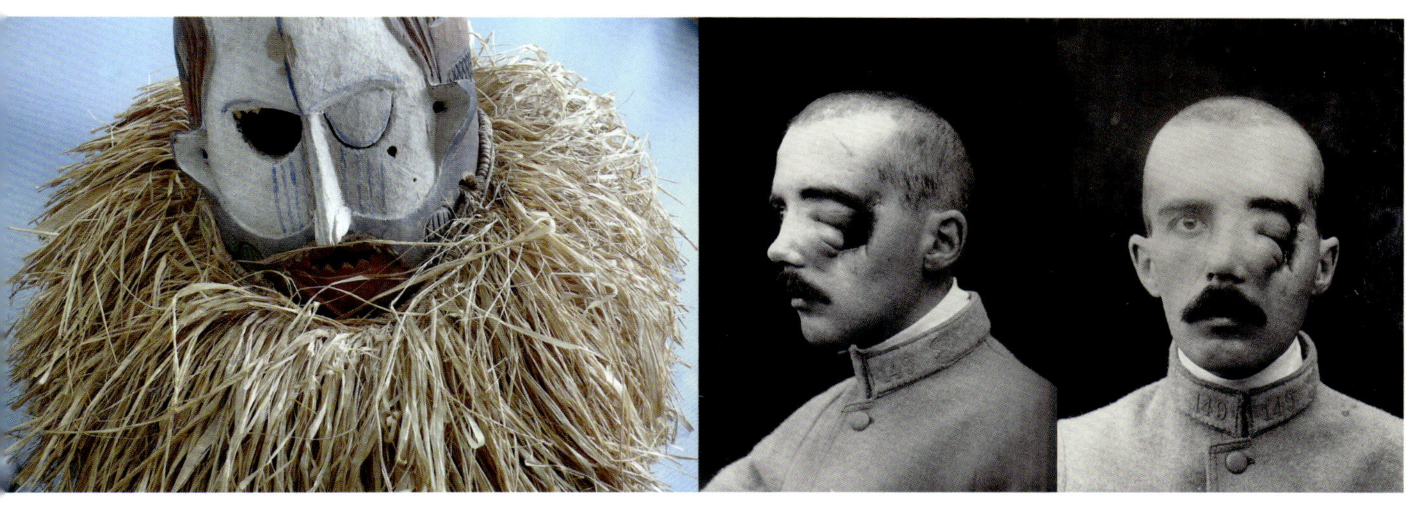

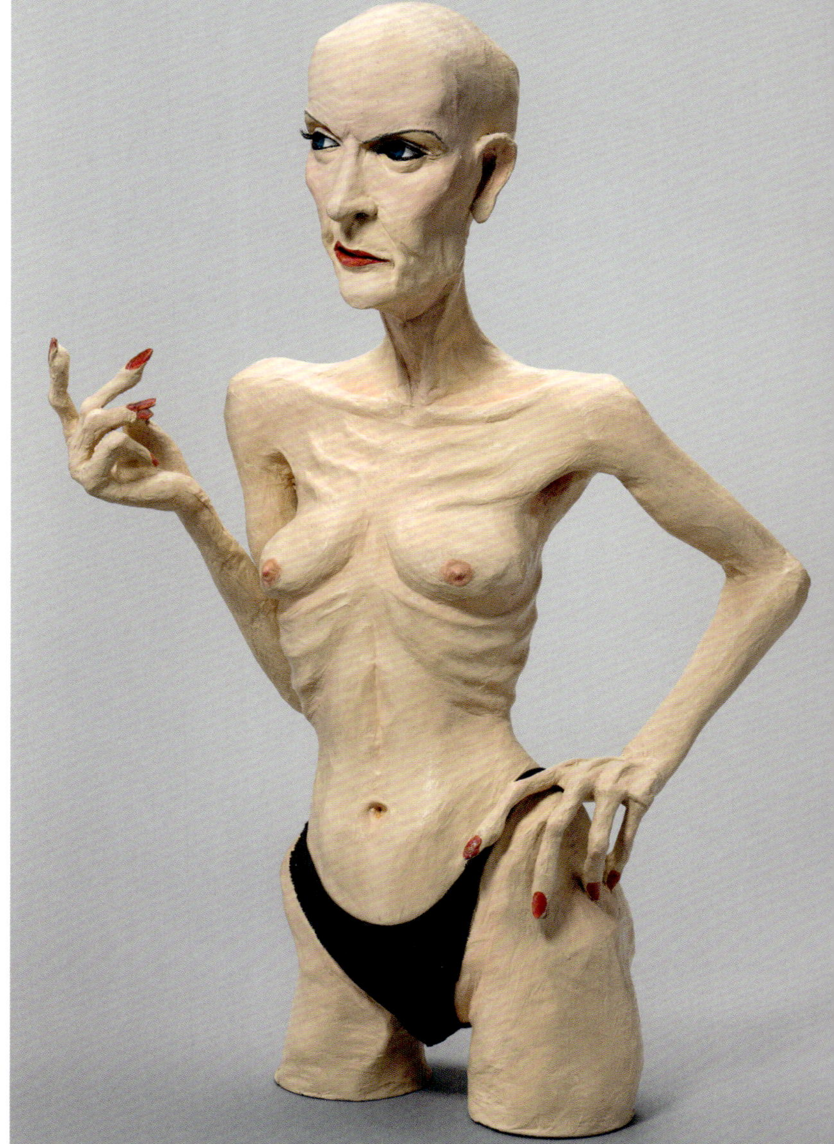

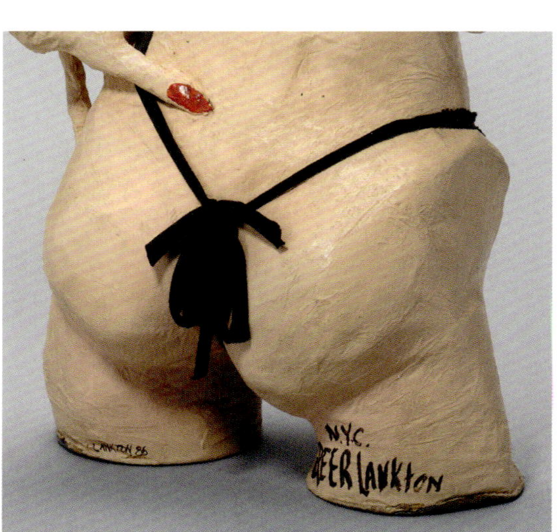

102. Greer Lankton. *Rachel*, 1986. Papier-mâché, metal plates, wire, acrylic paint, and matte medium, H. 28 in. (71.1 cm), W. 21 in. (53.3 cm), D. 11 in. (27.9 cm). Collection of Eric Ceputis and David W. Williams, promised gift to the Art Institute of Chicago

103. Juan Alonso Villabrille y Ron. *Saint Paul the Hermit*, ca. 1715. Polychromed terracotta and reverse-painted glass, H. 24 in. (61 cm), W. 30 in. (76.2 cm), D. 18 ½ in. (47 cm). Meadows Museum, Southern Methodist University, Dallas, Museum Purchase Thanks to a Gift from Jo Ann Geurin Thetford in Honor of Dr. Luis Martín

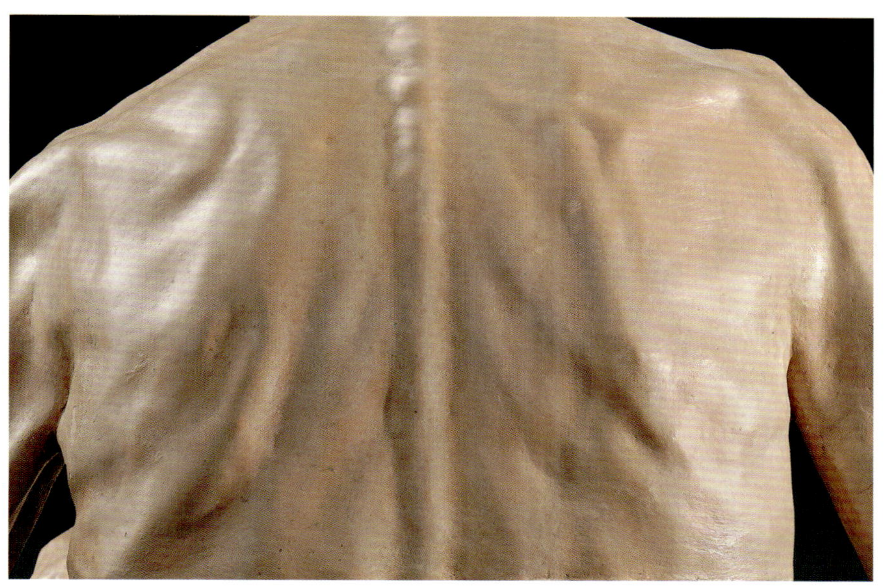

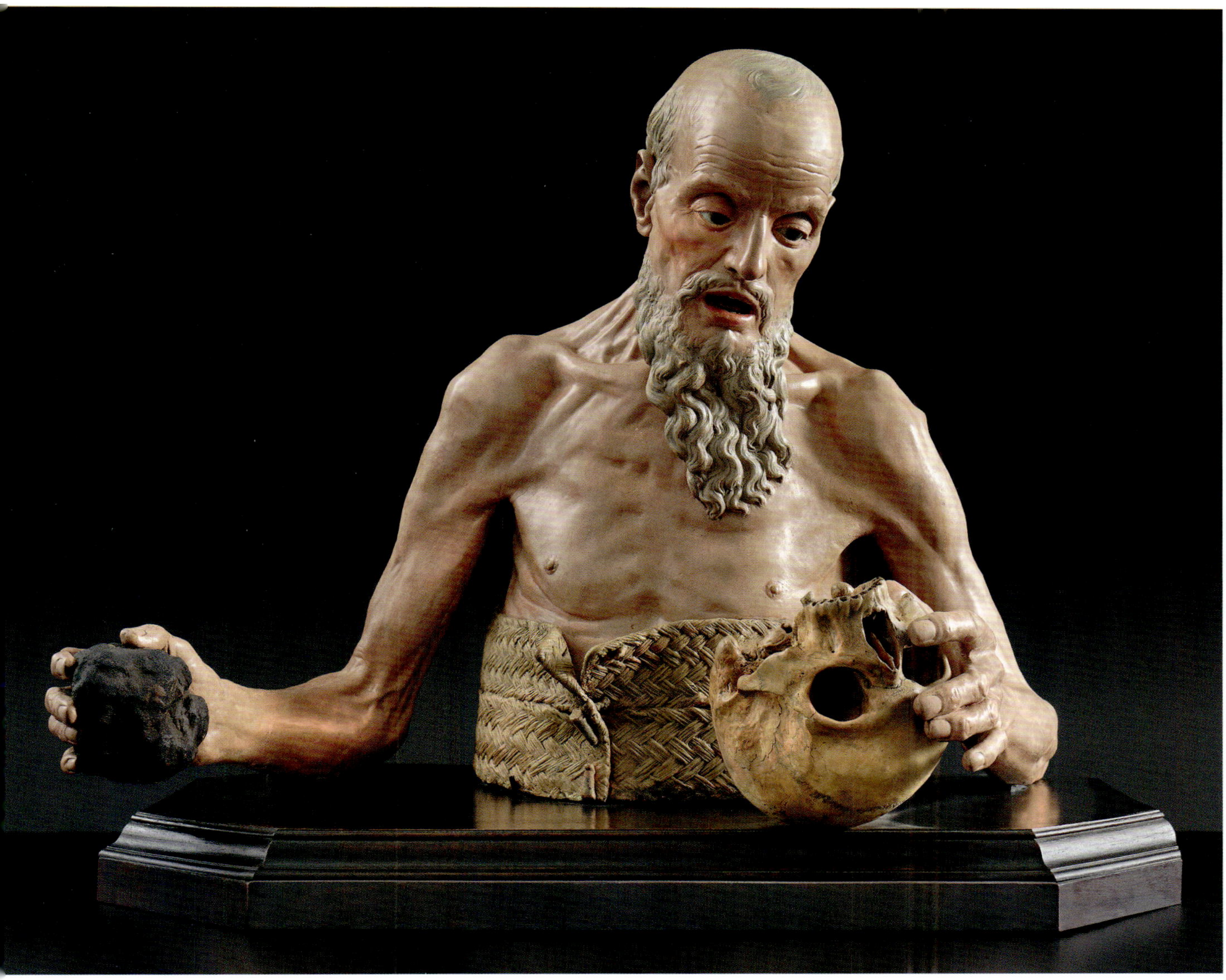

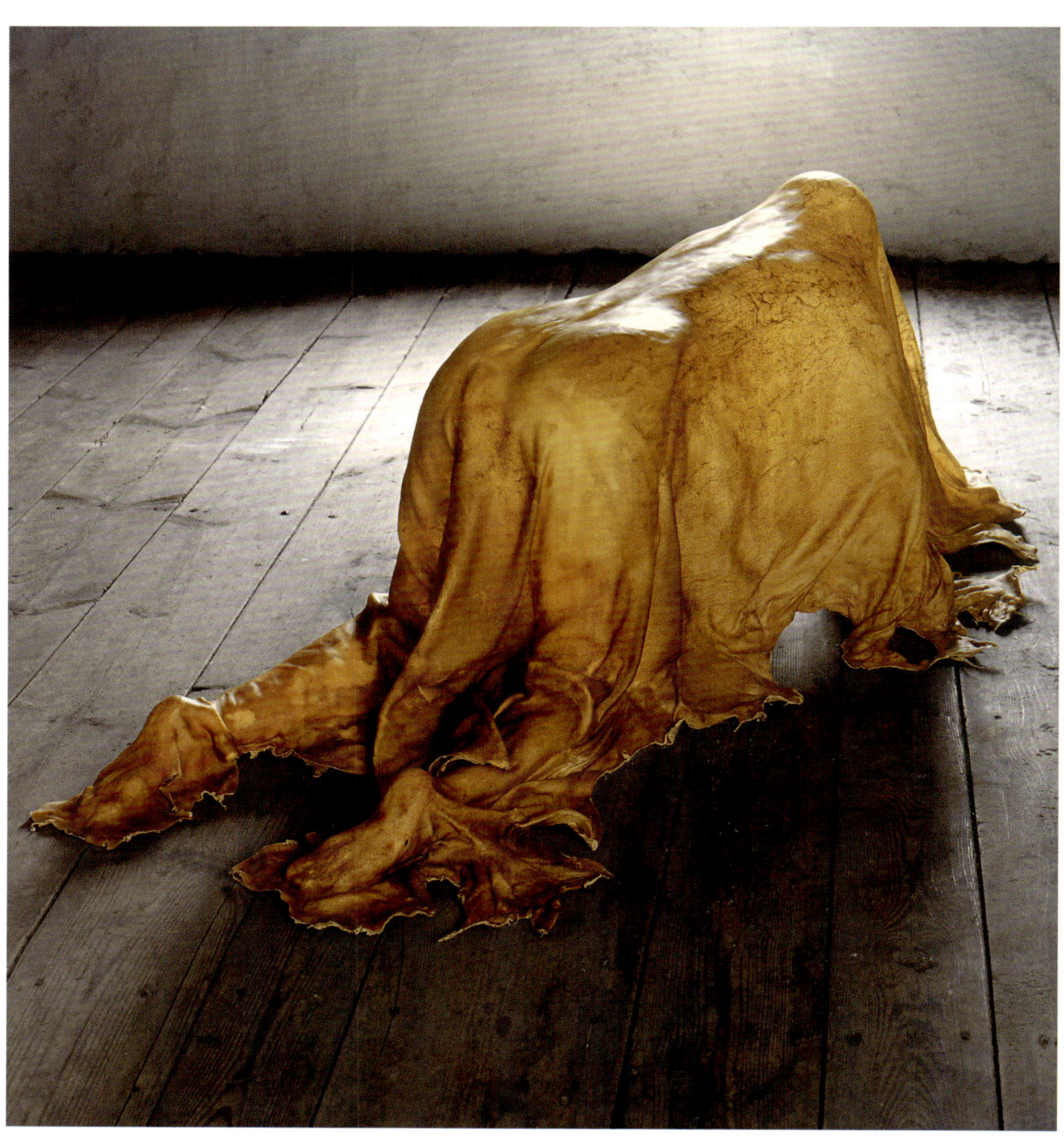

104. Janine Antoni. *Saddle*, 2000. Full rawhide, H. 26 in. (66 cm), W. 33 in. (83.8 cm), D. 79 in. (200.7 cm). Astrup Fearnley Collection, Oslo

105. Anton Maria Maragliano. *Saint Sebastian*, 1700. Polychromed wood and gilding, H. 74 ¹³/₁₆ in. (190 cm), W. 31 ½ in. (80 cm), D. 37 ⅜ in. (95 cm). Oratorio della Santissima Trinità, Rapallo

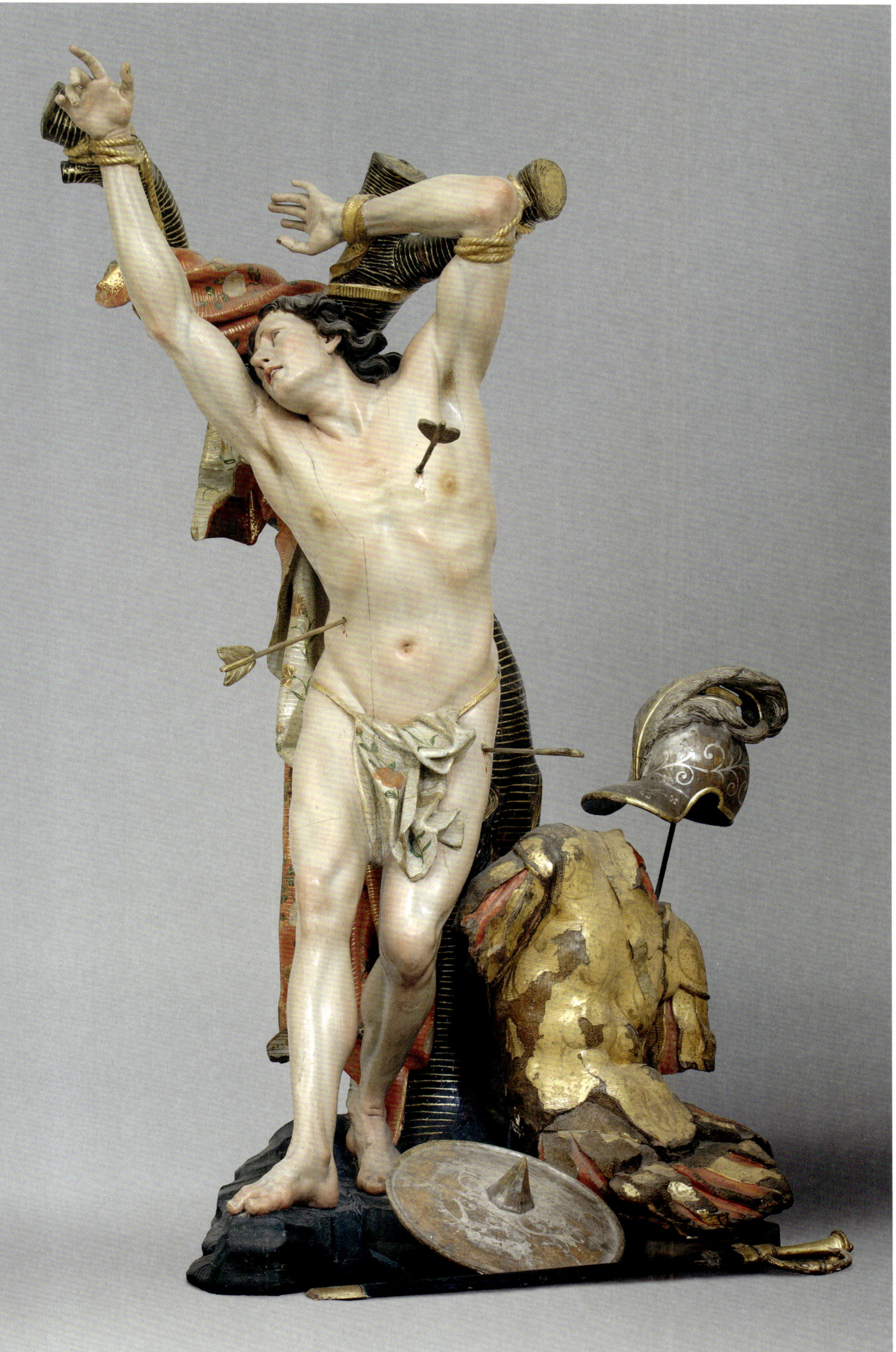

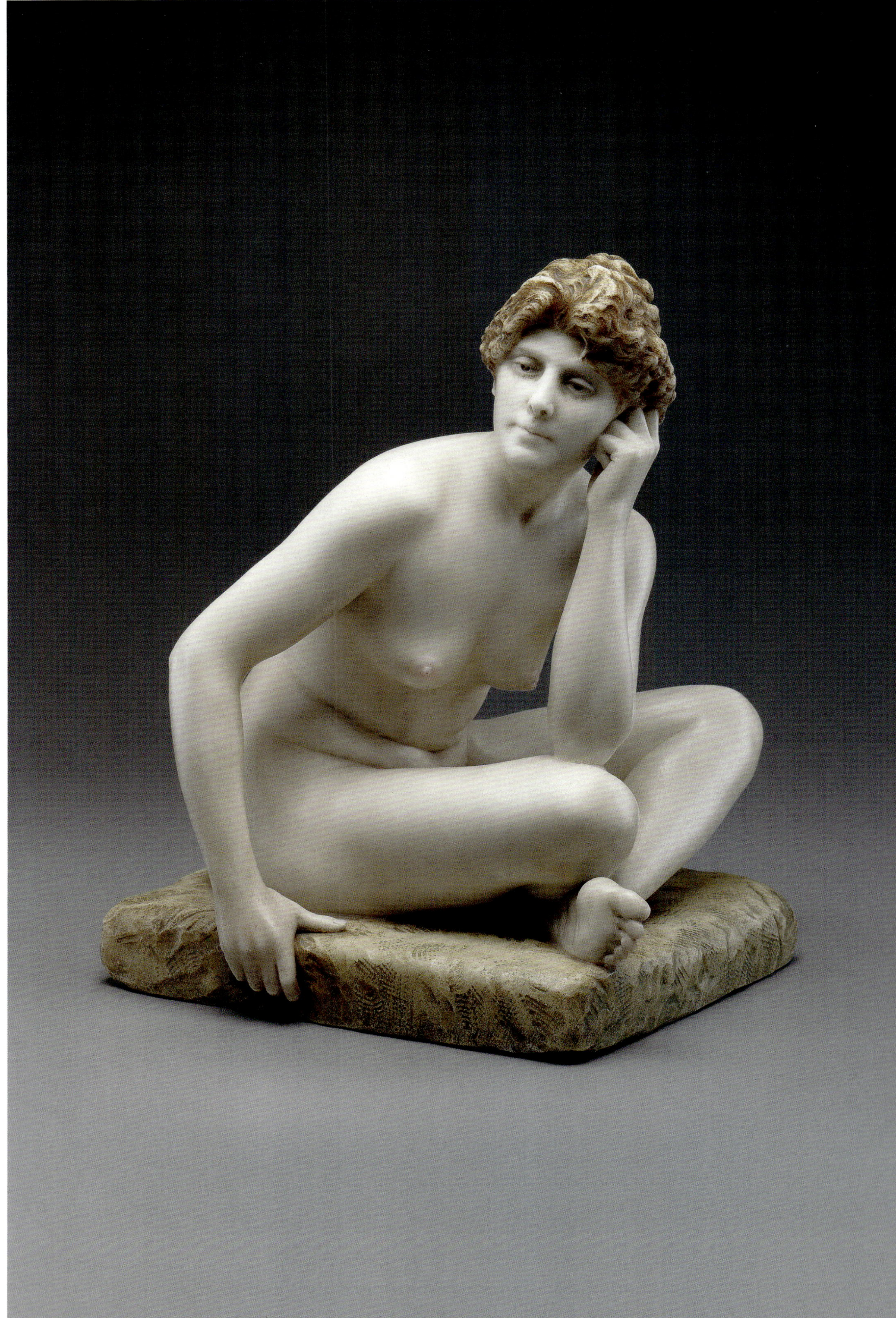

106. Jean-Léon Gérôme. *Seated Woman*, ca. 1898–1902. Marble, pigment, and wax, H. 16 ¹⁵⁄₁₆ in. (43 cm), W. 13 ¾ in. (35 cm), D. 13 ¾ in. (35 cm). Detroit Institute of Arts, Founders Society Purchase, Robert H. Tannahill Foundation Fund

107. Sarah Lucas. *NUD CYCLADIC 9*, 2010. Nylon, synthetic fiber, concrete, and steel wire, H. 21 in. (53.3 cm), W. 24 ½ in. (62.2 cm), D. 24 in. (61 cm). The Metropolitan Museum of Art, New York, Purchase, Lila Acheson Wallace Gift, 2015 (2015.305a–c)

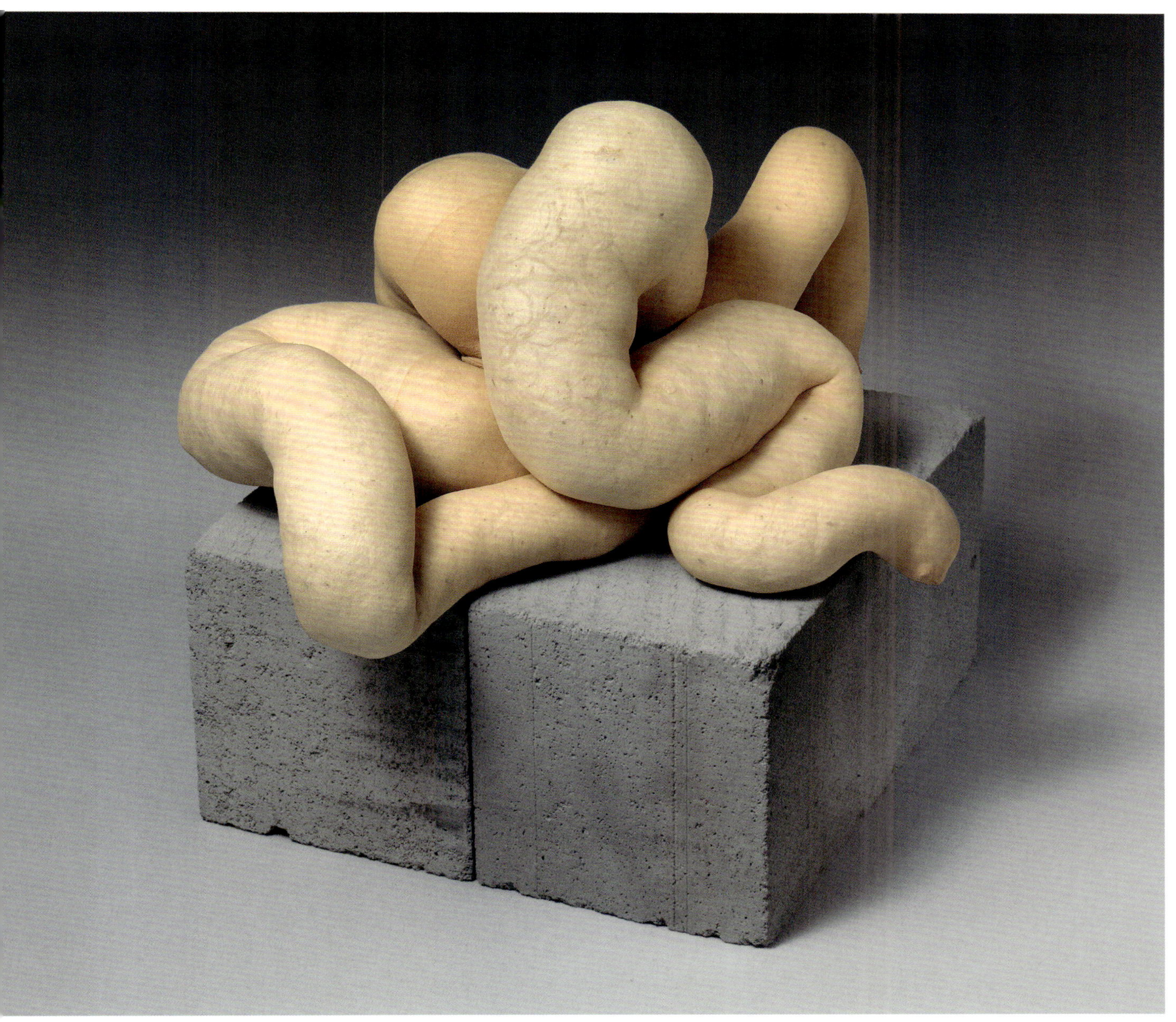

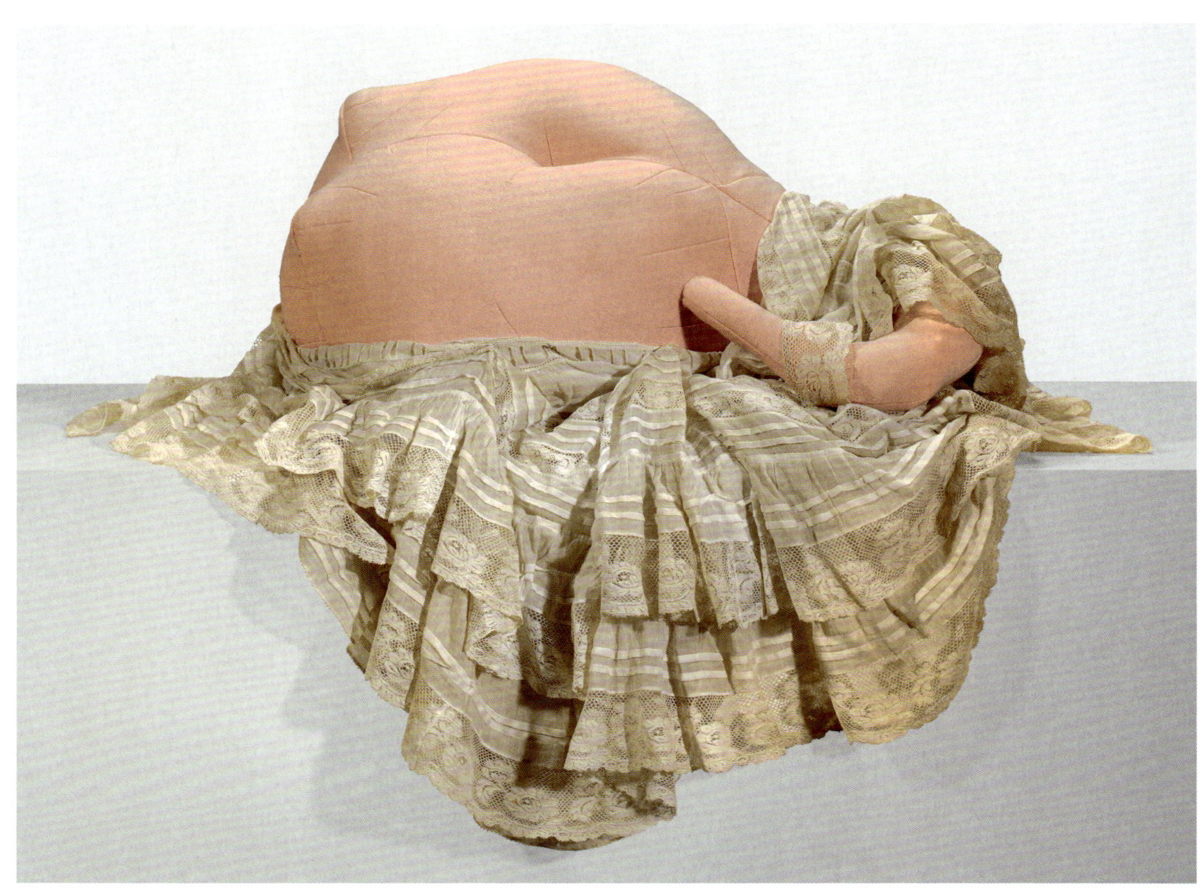

108. Dorothea Tanning. *Emma*, 1970. Fabric, wool, and lace, H. 24 in. (61 cm),
     W. 32 in. (81.3 cm), D. 22 in. (55.9 cm). Nelson-Atkins Museum of Art, Kansas City,
     Missouri, Purchase: acquired through the generosity of the William T. Kemper
     Foundation—Commerce Bank, Trustee

109. Louise Bourgeois. *Three Horizontals*, 1998. Fabric and steel, H. 53 in. (134.6 cm),
     W. 72 in. (182.9 cm), D. 36 in. (91.4 cm). ISelf Collection

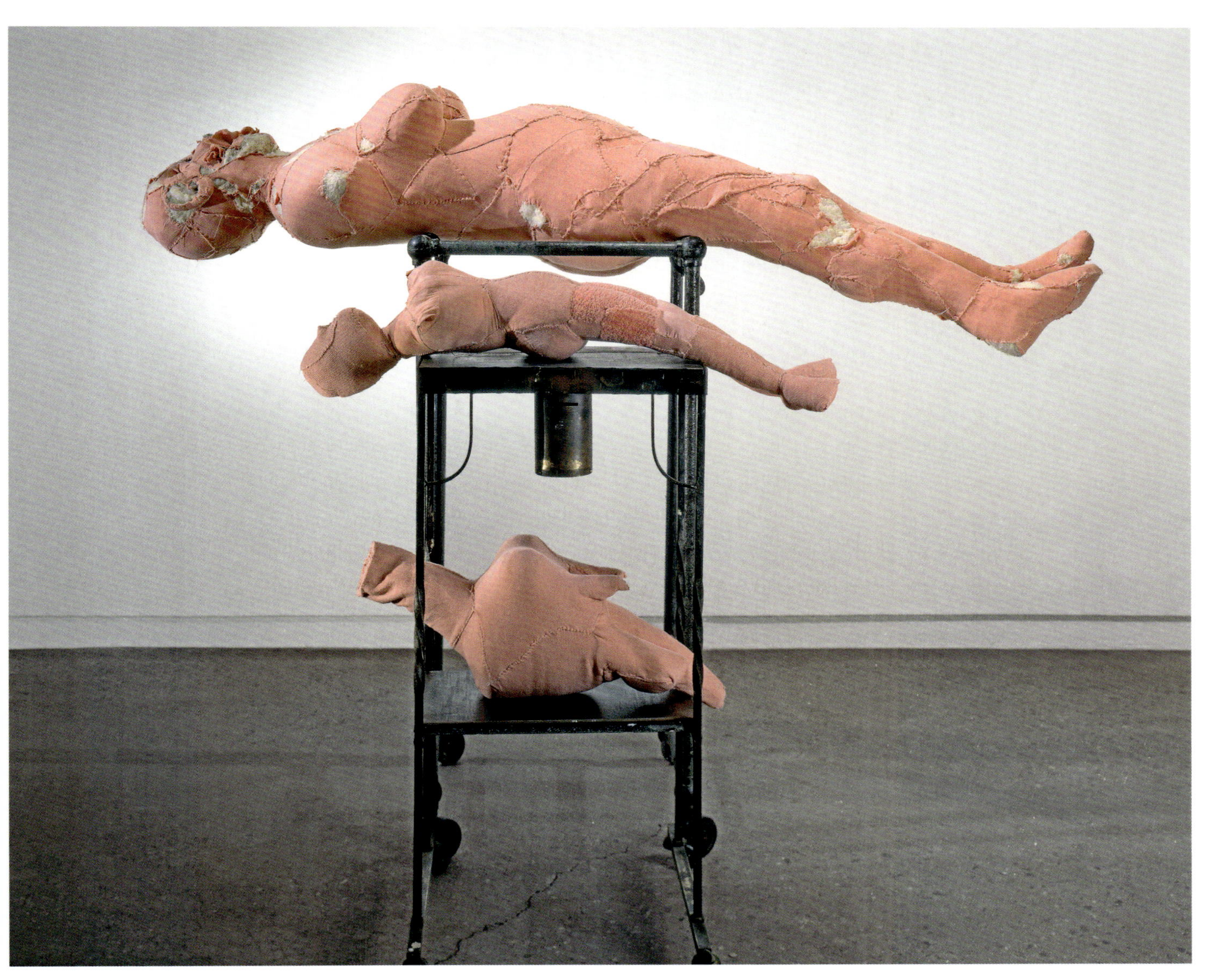

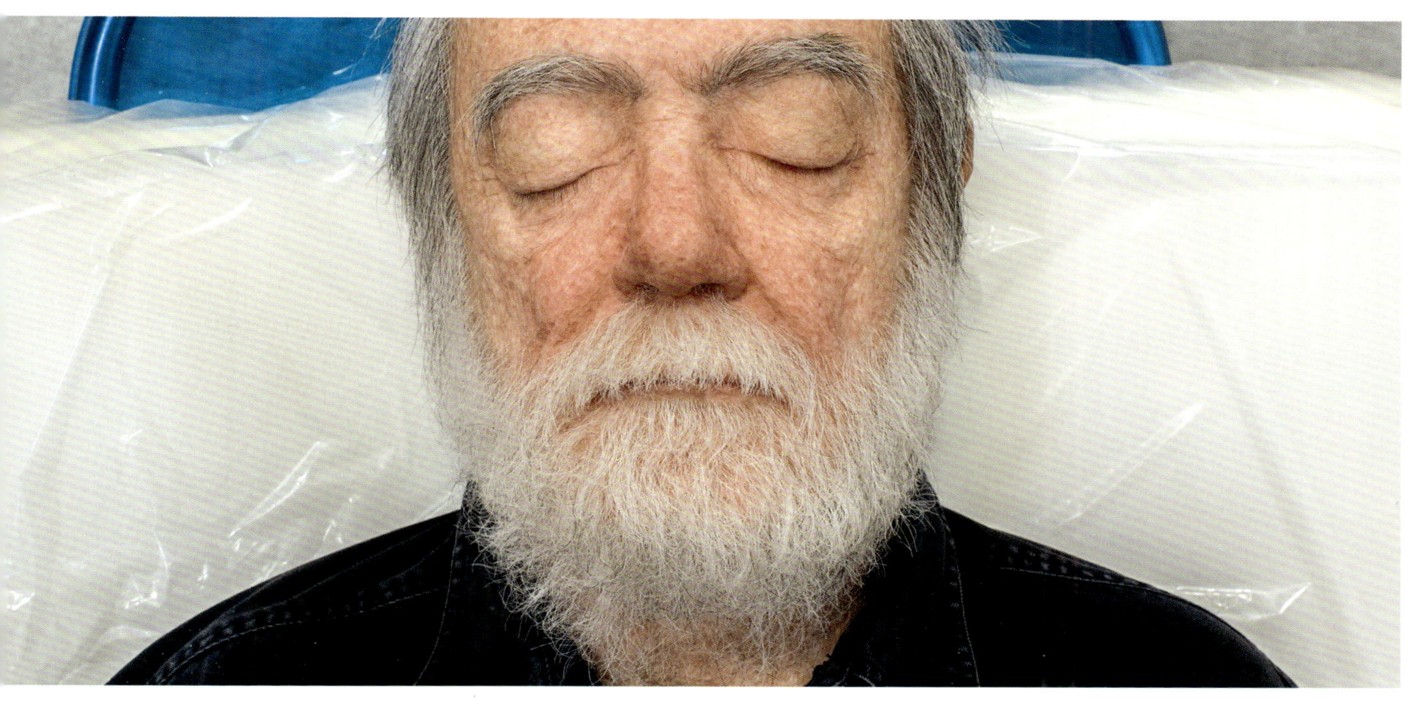

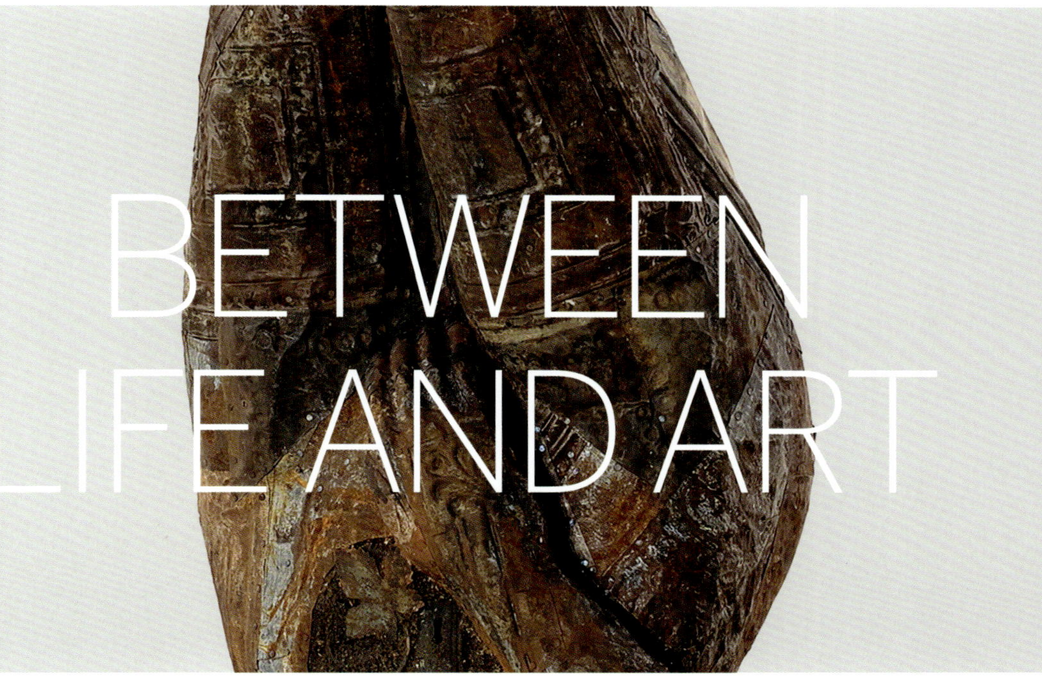
BETWEEN
LIFE AND ART

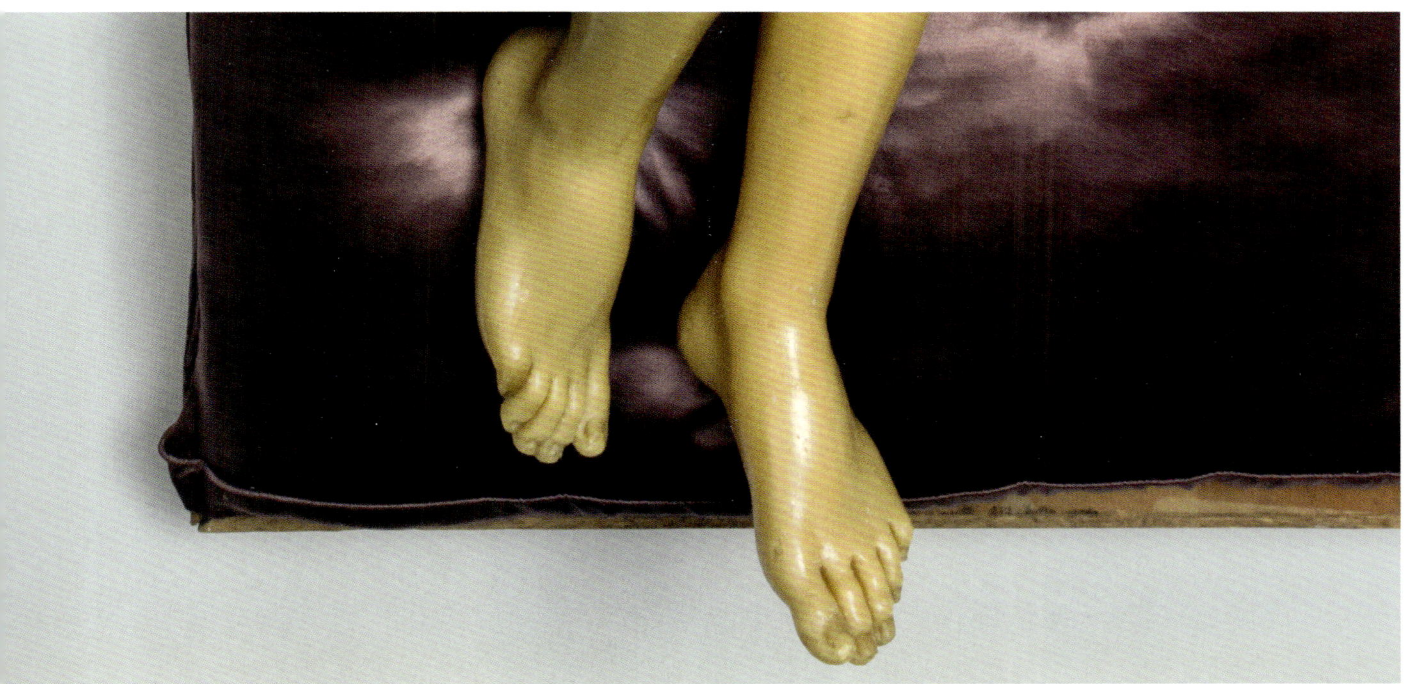

BETWEEN LIFE AND ART

BRINDA KUMAR

To die, to sleep—
No more—and by a sleep to say we end
The heartache and the thousand natural shocks
That flesh is heir to—'tis a consummation
Devoutly to be wished. To die, to sleep—
To sleep, perchance to dream. Ay, there's the rub,
For in that sleep of death what dreams may come
WILLIAM SHAKESPEARE

Figurative sculpture and mortality are inevitably intertwined even as their conceptual bond is often in a form of tension. While the figure rendered in three dimensions represents a form of stilled life—the literal petrification of form—it can also, particularly when made of durable materials such as stone and bronze, be linked to the human desire to transcend the temporal limits of life. Unlike the austere, white marble statuary of the classical tradition, many sculptures in this book wrestle with replicating the literal, living presence of the body, in which life seems to inhere; yet, their patent fabrication paradoxically makes them undeniably unreal, if still uncanny, likenesses.

The various thematic groupings in this volume outline the different tactics and strategies that artists use to simulate real bodies apparently suffused with life color. "The Presumption of White" reveals how classically white figures, when enlivened through coloration, locate the people or ideas they depict in a specific time, space, and personal or cultural experience. In "Likeness," the creation of verisimilitude in portraits is complicated through the potential misrecognition between the individual and the type. "Desire for Life" explores the myths of Pygmalion, the pleasures and perils of the worshipful

gaze, and the endeavors to literally animate figures through mechanical means. The creation of deliberately artificial proxy bodies or those with articulated limbs, including mannequins, is the focus of "Proxy Figures." In "Layered Realities," clothing is considered an extension of the body—a second skin—and a means to engender intimacy and convey identity in the creation of sculpture. From the epidermis to the dissolution of the body into fleshly matter and fragments, the visceral works of "Figuring Flesh" highlight the mutability and ephemerality of the human body. All of these themes bring sculpture as "an art of stable embodiment" into question, and the liminality of the genre is underscored in a series of supine works that gesture, enigmatically and poignantly, toward the slippage between the states of temporary and permanent rest.[1]

Whether in literature or the plastic arts, for religious or secular ends, the creative possibilities of the nearness of the two states has tantalized artists. In *Sleep and His Half-brother Death* (1874, fig. 82) by the Victorian artist John William Waterhouse, the brothers from Greek mythology Hypnos (sleep) and Thanatos (death) are pictured as twins lying side by side on a bed. The young boys are identical but present subtle contrasts: whereas Sleep is rosy lipped and his exposed limbs are warmly hued, Death is in the recessed background, shrouded under the bedclothes, limp and ashen faced. Their different coloring makes the identity of the titular figures instantly distinguishable.

Beyond the literal depiction of sleep and death, a recumbent figure in three dimensions offers additional ambiguities, no better seen than in the famous

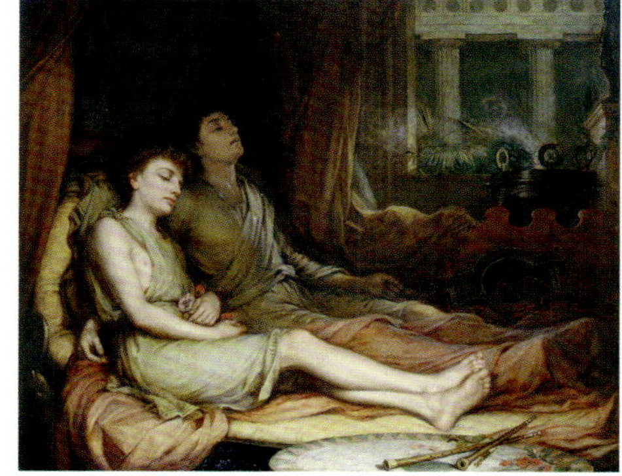

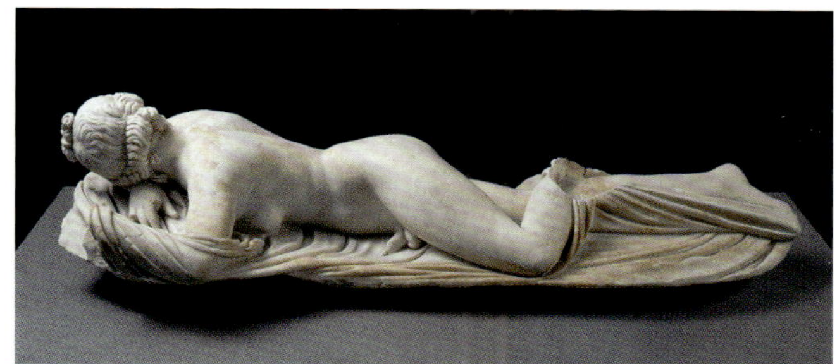

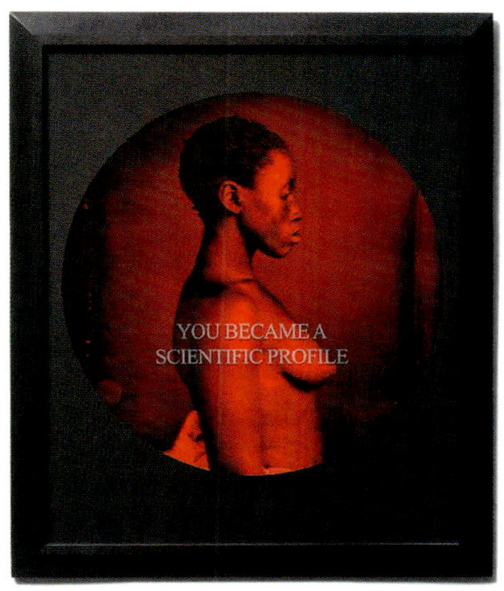

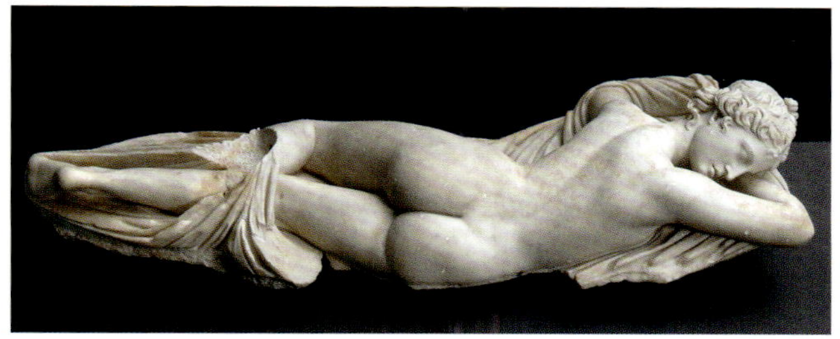

Clockwise from top left

Fig. 82 John William Waterhouse. *Sleep and His Half-brother Death*, 1874. Oil on canvas, 27 ½ × 35 ¹³/₁₆ in. (70 × 91 cm). Private collection

Fig. 83 *Sleeping Hermaphrodite*, A.D. mid-2nd century (two views). Marble, H. 22 ¹/₁₆ in. (56 cm), W. 59 ¹/₁₆ in. (150 cm), D. 14 ⁹/₁₆ in. (37 cm). Roman. Museo Nazionale Romano—Palazzo Massimo alla Terme, Rome

Fig. 84 Carrie Mae Weems. *You Became a Scientific Profile*. Chromogenic print with sandblasted text on glass, 26 ½ × 22 ¾ in. (67.3 × 57.8 cm). Courtesy of the artist and Jack Shainman Gallery, New York

Sleeping Hermaphrodite (A.D. mid-2nd-century, fig. 83). An ancient nude composite of the classical Greek deities Hermes and Aphrodite, the prone body tricks the viewer into misidentification by its rounded feminine limbs and buttocks and a curved waist from one side and the unexpected presentation of male genitalia from the opposite. The work presumes the (male) spectator's view of the sleeping woman as unaware and vulnerable, alluring and seemingly available, a figure of titillation, even as historically the acceptability of this prurience necessitated the couching of such figures in mythological or narrative contexts, from Italian Renaissance painter Giorgione's *Sleeping Venus* (1508–10) to Swiss wax modeler Philippe Curtius's *Sleeping Beauty* (1765, cat. 113). As cultural historian Marina Warner has observed, the latter "conveys a seductive vision of erotic, feminine catalepsy, which the peculiar translucence and slight sweatiness of the wax medium suit so creepily."[2] *Sleeping Beauty*'s uncanniness is heightened through subtle mechanization such that "her breast rises and falls to her breathing. She looks alive. She looks real. She looks as if she has overcome time and death; she creates an illusion of life to strike wonder in the beholder."[3] If the mystery of her seemingly eternal presence was literally hidden beneath her luxurious robes (the original clockwork mechanism that controlled the figure's breathing was replaced by electrical circuitry in the early twentieth century),

in the context of the wax museum of popular entertainment, a more invasive approach to the reclining female figure was that of the *Anatomical Venus* (cat. 115), which could be found in eighteenth-century medical and scientific academies. Both figures share a kinship in form, languorously stretched out on soft cushions, and material articulation in wax. But where the *Beauty* remains an untouchable object of fantasy, the *Venus* is meant to be excavated and examined. Created in an era before the preservation of bodies for scientific study was possible, such figures have detachable torsos that open up to reveal the insides (also rendered in wax) in fine detail and often focus extensively on the reproductive organs and fetuses. Although completely nude, save at times for a few pieces of jewelry, these Venuses are a far cry from cadavers, but rather present beautiful young women whose anatomical manipulability seems incidental to their states of perpetual sleep or languidness. Although the figures are surrogates, their passive demeanor means that the potential for the infliction of sexual violence always lurks.

The black female body as the object of medical experimentation and sexual violence in antebellum America and during Jim Crow has been addressed by a number of African American artists including Lorna Simpson, Renee Cox, Carrie Mae Weems (fig. 84), Kara Walker, and Alison Saar. A shared tactic has been to reconfigure "conventional tropes of the nude to emphasize the historical importance of the visual arts in manipulating the female body to construct racist ideology and justify racist practice."[4] In Alison Saar's sculptural works, the black female nude often appears as a means "to make visible black women's historical struggle to reclaim their own bodies, turning themselves from exoticized objects into critical subjects."[5] In *Strange Fruit* (1995, cat. 110), a work that pointedly takes inspiration from the haunting visualization of lynching in Billie Holiday's song of the same name—"Black bodies swinging in the southern breeze / Strange fruit hanging from the poplar trees"—Saar imagines a black Venus Pudica, an exotic figure not unlike French painter Paul Gauguin's Tahitian women (cat. 49) but whose appearance as ripe and desirable is undercut by the violent trussing-up by her ankles. Yet, this is not a traditional hanging, and the figure in *Strange Fruit* seemingly defies the stillness (and horizontality) of death by eerily swaying, staying in motion, swinging, resisting. She is after all a power figure, made to recall the Minkisi (sing., Nkisi) figures from Central Africa (fig. 45), and her abdominal cavity is no longer a receptacle for anatomical parts, but rather the source of her vital and resilient spirit.

In a series of works cast from real bodies, American artist Paul McCarthy explores the seeming vitality of an upright (grounded) body in contrast to the ambiguity of a horizontal one. Cast from the

scene was transformed from that of a dead body in a morgue to one imaginable in a backyard setting, where the self-described "buffoon" may be sleeping or dreaming.[6] The work can be seen in the context of McCarthy's long-standing interest in the surrogate figure's transgressive potential. As curator Paul Schimmel notes,

[Paul McCarthy] became interested in creating a replacement, or surrogate, for himself. Among the earliest such surrogates was *Human Object* (1981), a crude figure made of rubber, foam, and other materials, consisting of a head with a mouth and a box-like body with both a penis and vagina. One could take this performative sculpture into a private room and interact with it—abusively and sexually. People fed it, burned it with cigarettes, had sex with it. It was an inanimate object that took on "human characteristics" by being acted upon....Some thirty years later, McCarthy created yet another surrogate: *Horizontal* [2012, fig. 85], an uncompromising sculpture of the artist himself, naked and dead.[7]

Related to *Paul Dreaming, Vertical, Horizontal* yet less ambiguous in presentation, the body in *Horizontal* is laid out on a wood plank, and in rendering himself in this way, the artist pictures and confronts his ultimate death.

Every religion has its own manner of reckoning with death, often resulting in a range of horizontal sculptures in sepulchral contexts, from Egyptian mummies and Chinese jade burial suits to Christian tomb effigies. But in terms of the divine figure, the picturing of the death of the body has spiritual significance and can become iconic, whether the *parinirvana* of the Buddha (fig. 86) or the *Dead Christ*. While the former signifies the final moments before the Buddha's

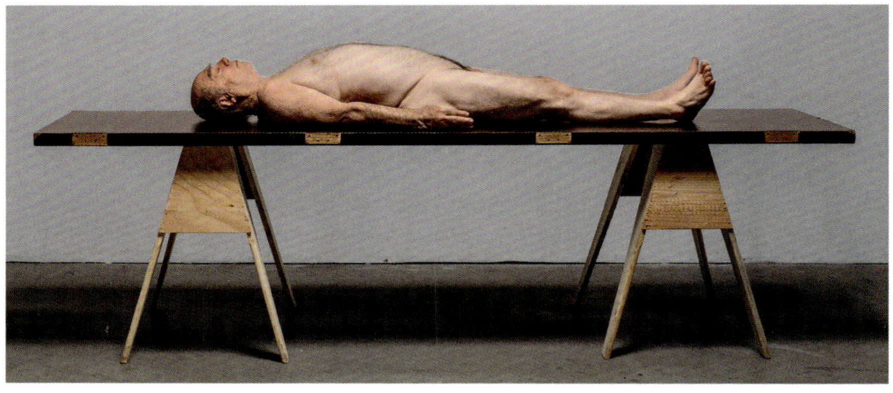

Fig. 85 Paul McCarthy. *Horizontal*, 2012. Platinum silicone, fiberglass, aluminum, stainless steel, natural hair, pigment, paint, wood door with laminate, and wood sawhorses, H. 40 ½ in. (102.9 cm), W. 105 ½ in. (268 cm), D. 35 ⅝ in. (90.5 cm). Courtesy of the artist and Hauser & Wirth

artist's standing body (as evidenced by the figure's flat feet and straight back) in 2005 and intended as a prop for one of his films, the figure for *Paul Dreaming, Vertical, Horizontal* (2005/12, cat. 114) went unused until 2012, when the artist decided to partially clothe and recline it on a padded lawn chair. The

transcendence and release from the cycle of constant rebirth, for the latter, death is the precursor to the Resurrection and signifies the possibility of eternal life in heaven. The pathos of the divine death had an enduring impact on the followers of each, from the sorrow of the Buddha's companion figures to

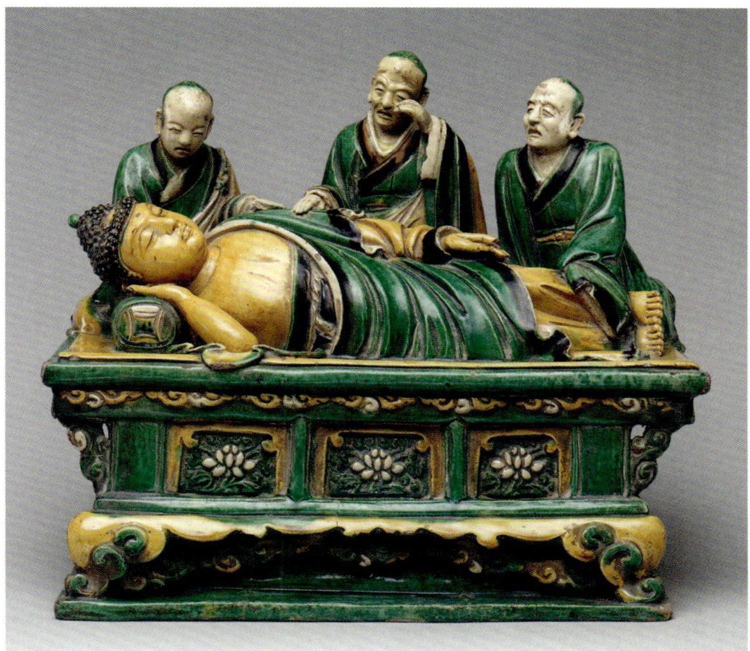

Fig. 86 Qiao Bin. *Final Transcendence*
(Parinirvana) of the Buddha, 1503.
Glazed stoneware, H. 14 in. (35.6 cm),
W. 17 ⅛ in. (43.5 cm), D. 9 in. (22.9 cm).
The Metropolitan Museum of Art, New York,
Fletcher Fund, 1925 (25.227.1)

the grief of worshippers responding to the tragedy of Christ's violent death, as depicted in agonizing detail by Spanish artist Gregorio Fernández (cat. 111). The extreme verism of Fernández's sculpture can be understood not only as a result of the artist's own piety and familiarity with the agony of the flesh (he is said to have practiced extreme penitence before commencing work on a religious sculpture) but also as a means to make the horrific death intensely present.[8] The image of the divine figure in death could thus be a potent symbol for worship: "A sculpture could never grant you a parole from limbo; only the divinity it showed could do you that favor."[9]

The death of secular icons can differ symbolically. For Italian artist Maurizio Cattelan's lifesize effigy of American president John F. Kennedy lying in a coffin, the spectacular violence of his assassination and the endless conspiracy theories it spawned were sources of frustration and disillusionment. Cattelan, who once worked in a morgue, considers sculpture as "dead, distant, deaf," even though he chooses to create hyperrealistic sculpture. Presenting Kennedy in *Now* (2004, cat. 112) "meant making him die once and for all, interrupting this cycle of hypotheses, eternal reincarnations in the news."[10] Yet, ironically JFK's death as enshrined in art, and its reproduction and repeated presentation in exhibitions, create new cycles of visibility and contestation. Cattelan's work seems self-consciously engaged in these inconsistencies, and his practice can be understood as that of the trickster who thwarts expectations of real presence through artificial facsimiles, revels in the uncertainty of belief, and thus always reminds us of the body as a composite—of physical form, cultural imagination, social construction, and personal identity.

110. Alison Saar. *Strange Fruit*, 1995. Tin alloy, wood, dirt, found objects, rope, and paint, H. 76 in. (193.1 cm), W. 21 in. (53.4 cm), D. 14 in. (35.6 cm). Baltimore Museum of Art, Contemporary Art Endowment Fund

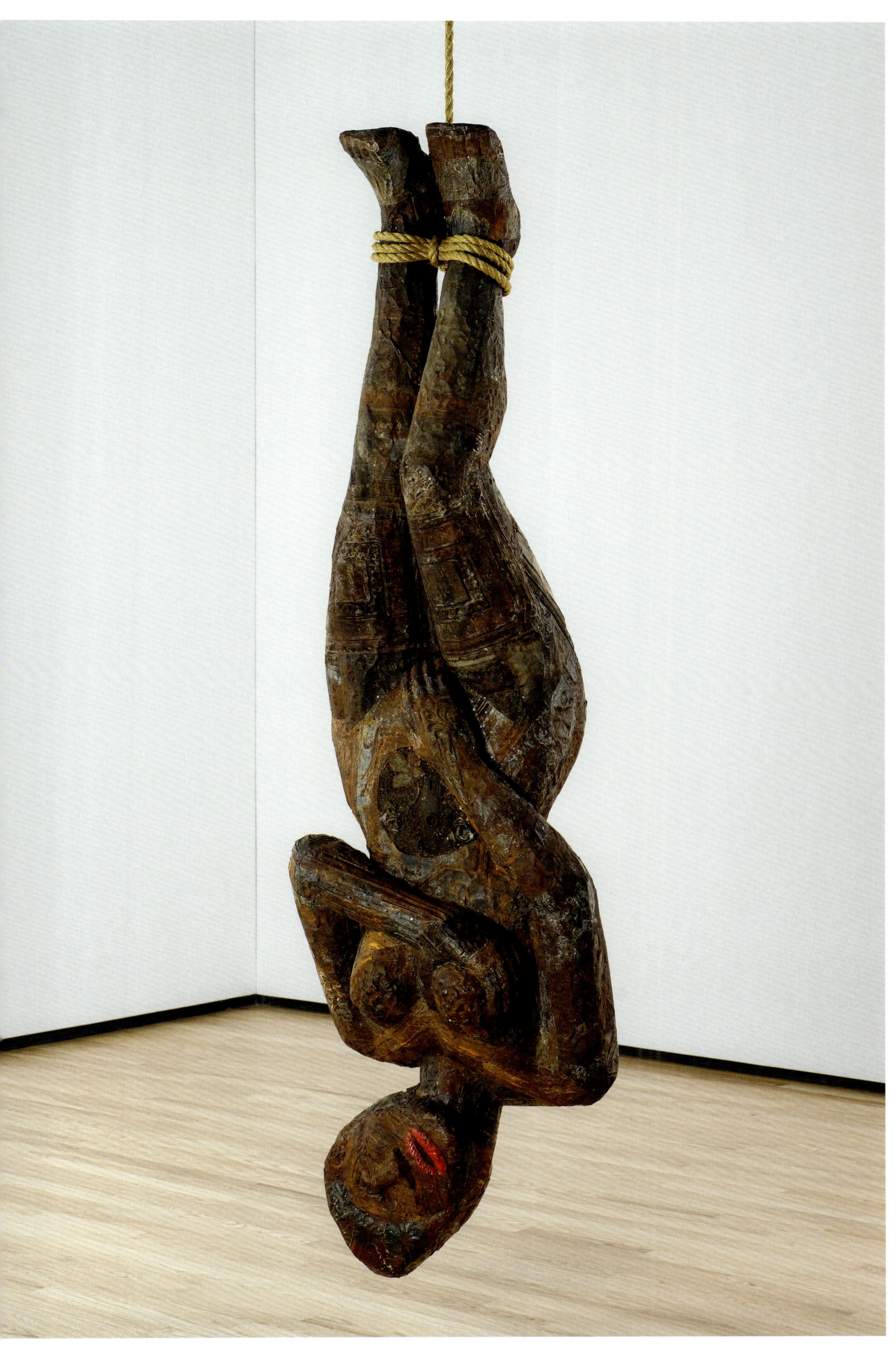

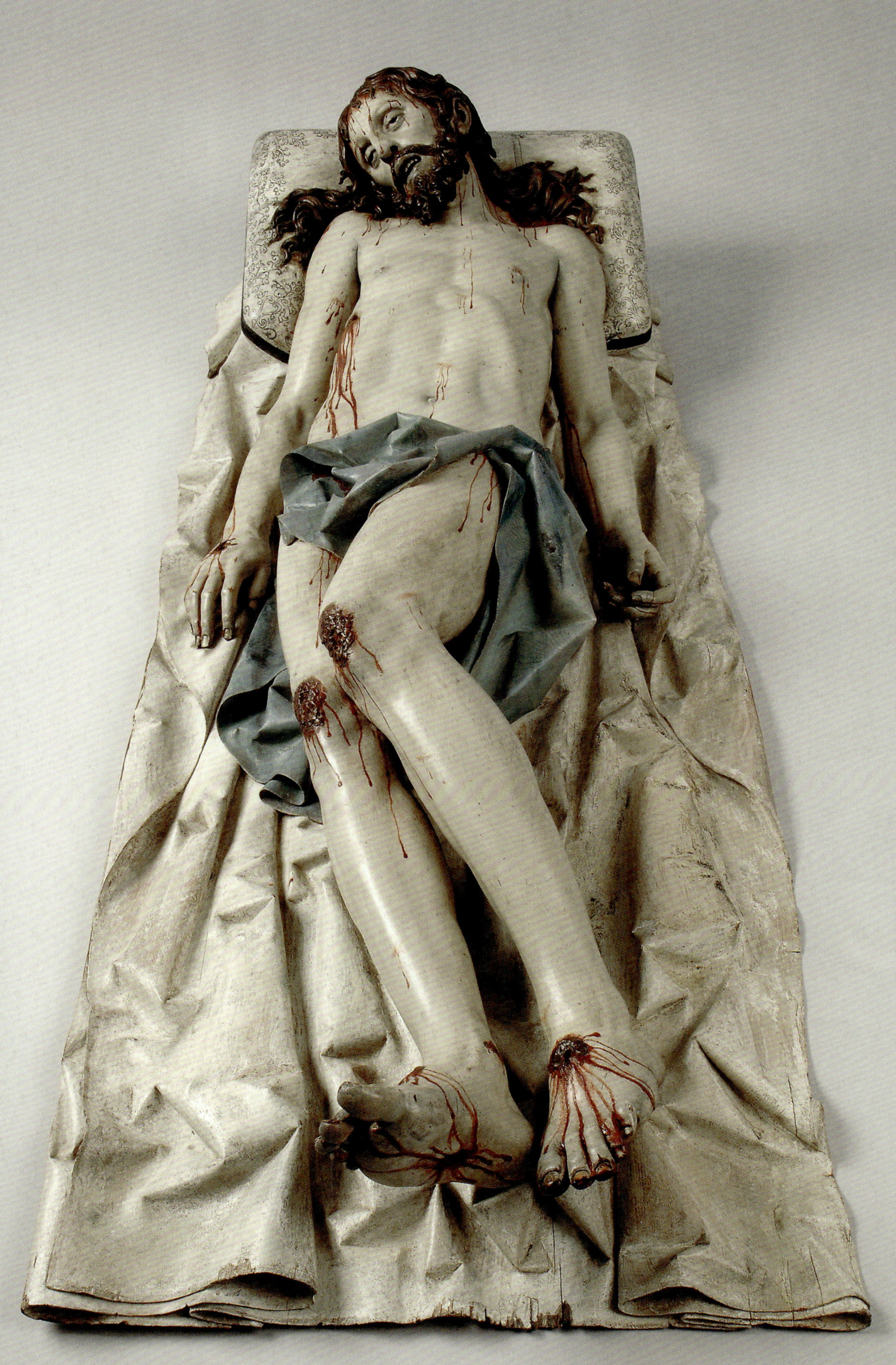

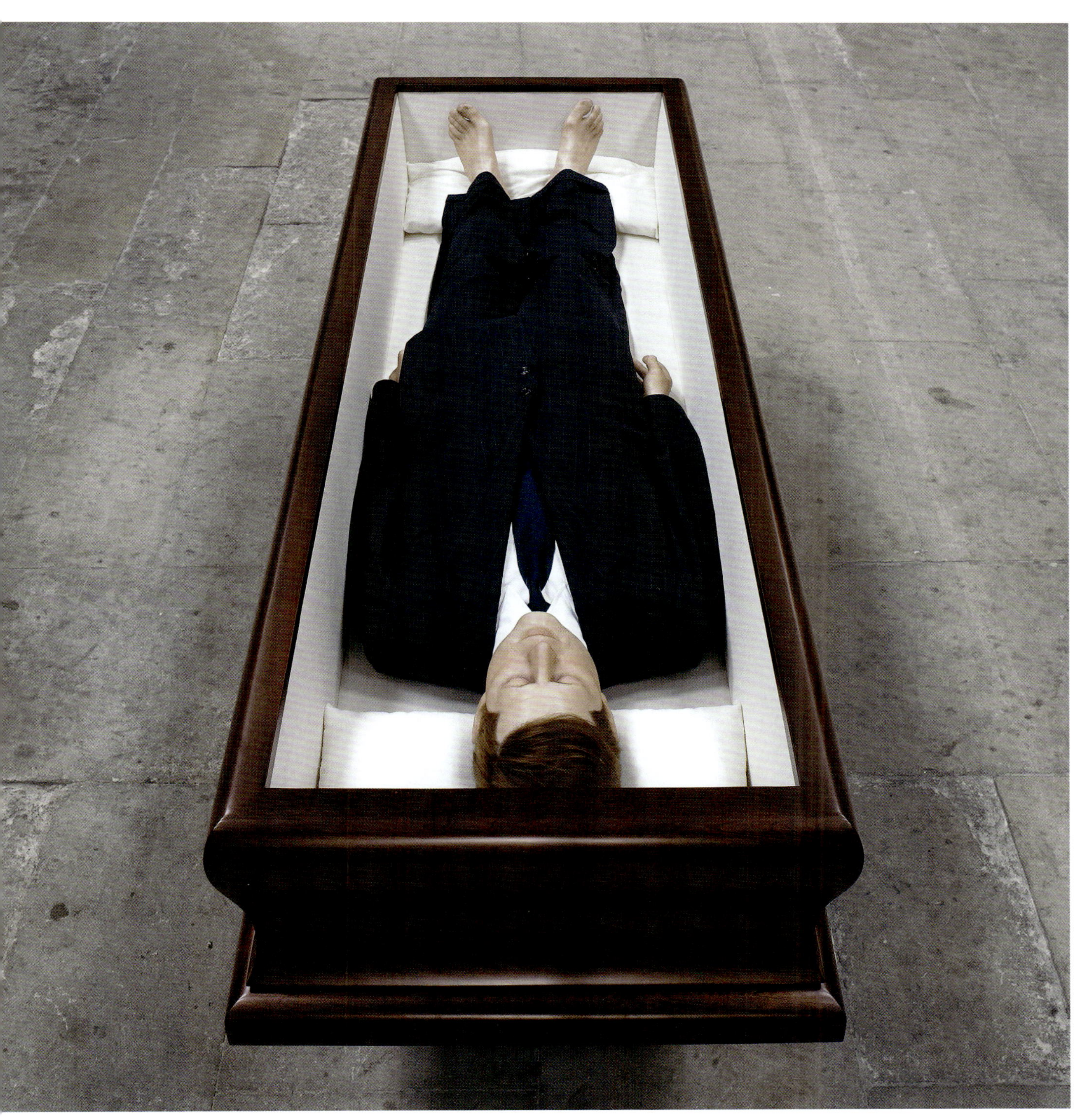

111. Gregorio Fernández. *Dead Christ*, 1625–30. Polychromed wood, horn, glass, and cork, H. 18 ⅛ in. (46 cm), W. 75 ³⁄₁₆ in. (191 cm), D. 29 ⅛ in. (74 cm). Museo Nacional del Prado, Madrid

112. Maurizio Cattelan. *Now*, 2004. Polyester, resin, wax, pigment, human hair, clothing, and coffin, H. 33 ⁷⁄₁₆ in. (85 cm), W. 88 ⁹⁄₁₆ in. (225 cm), D. 30 ¹¹⁄₁₆ in. (78 cm). Astrup Fearnley Collection, Oslo

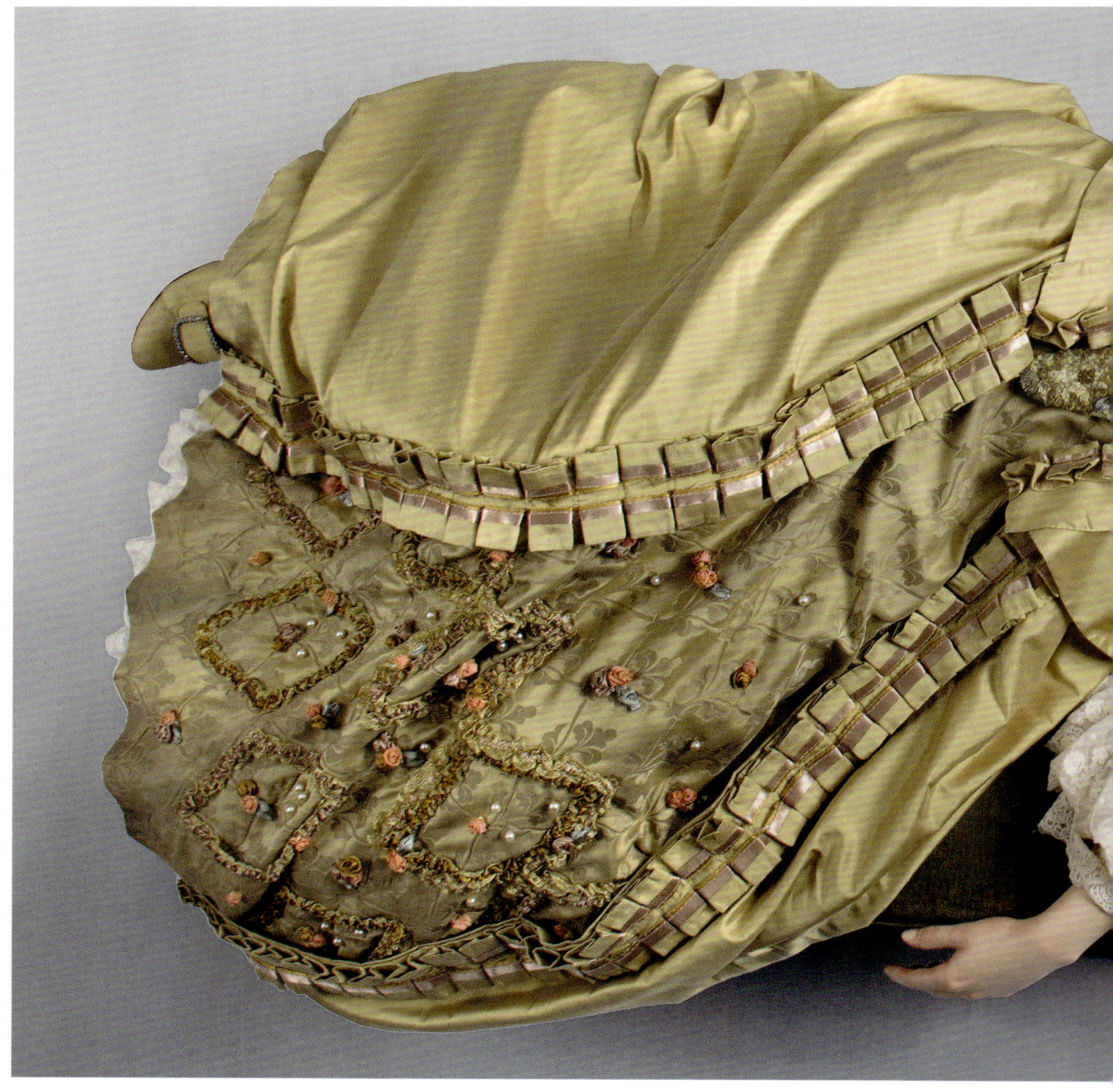

113. Philippe Curtius. *Sleeping Beauty*, 1765, remade 1989. Gold leaf, carved wood, velvet upholstery, beeswax, human hair, laminated fiberglass, alloy and steel servo, tinted slush wax, silk, and cotton lace, H. 32 ¹¹⁄₁₆ in. (83 cm), W. 65 ⅜ in. (166 cm), D. 29 ⅛ in. (74 cm). Madame Tussauds, London

114. Paul McCarthy. *Paul Dreaming, Vertical, Horizontal*, 2005/12. Platinum silicone, clothing, plastic, foam, lawn chair, H. 24 ⅜ in. (61.9 cm), W. 70 ⅞ in. (180 cm), D. 28 in. (71.1 cm). Glenstone Museum, Potomac, Maryland

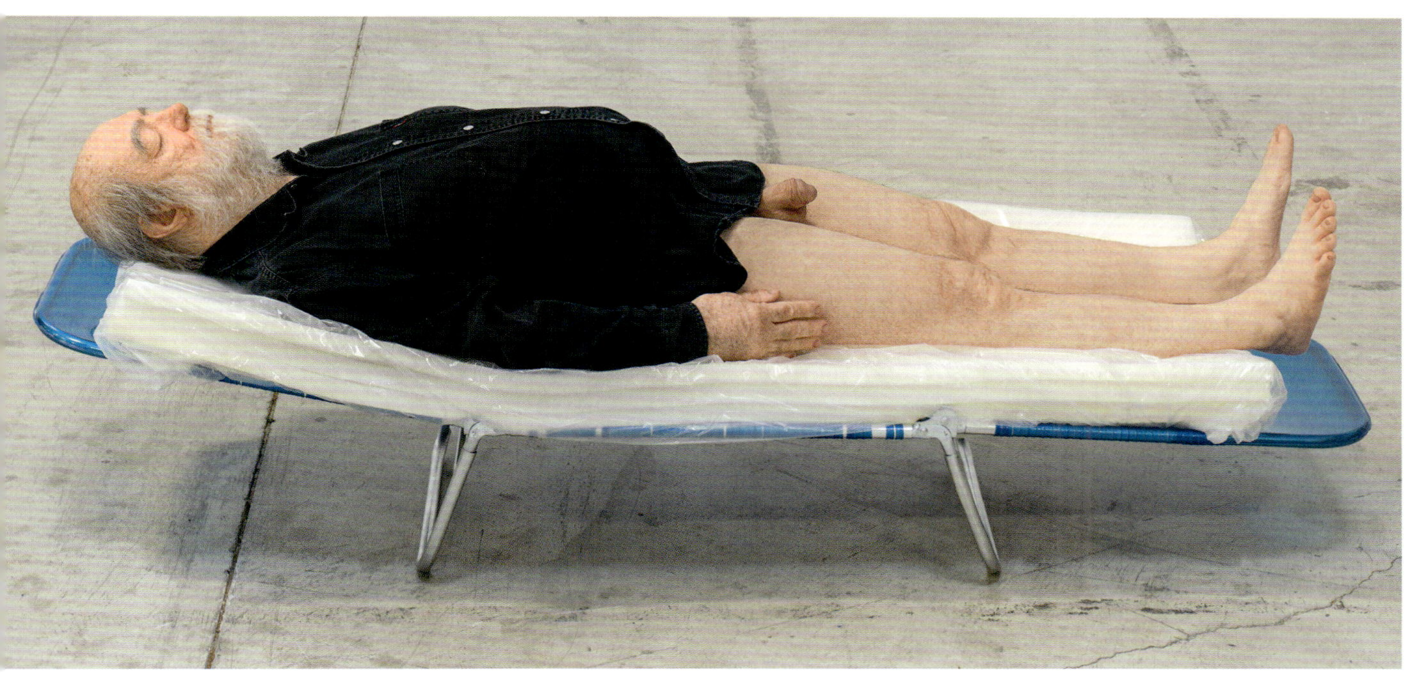

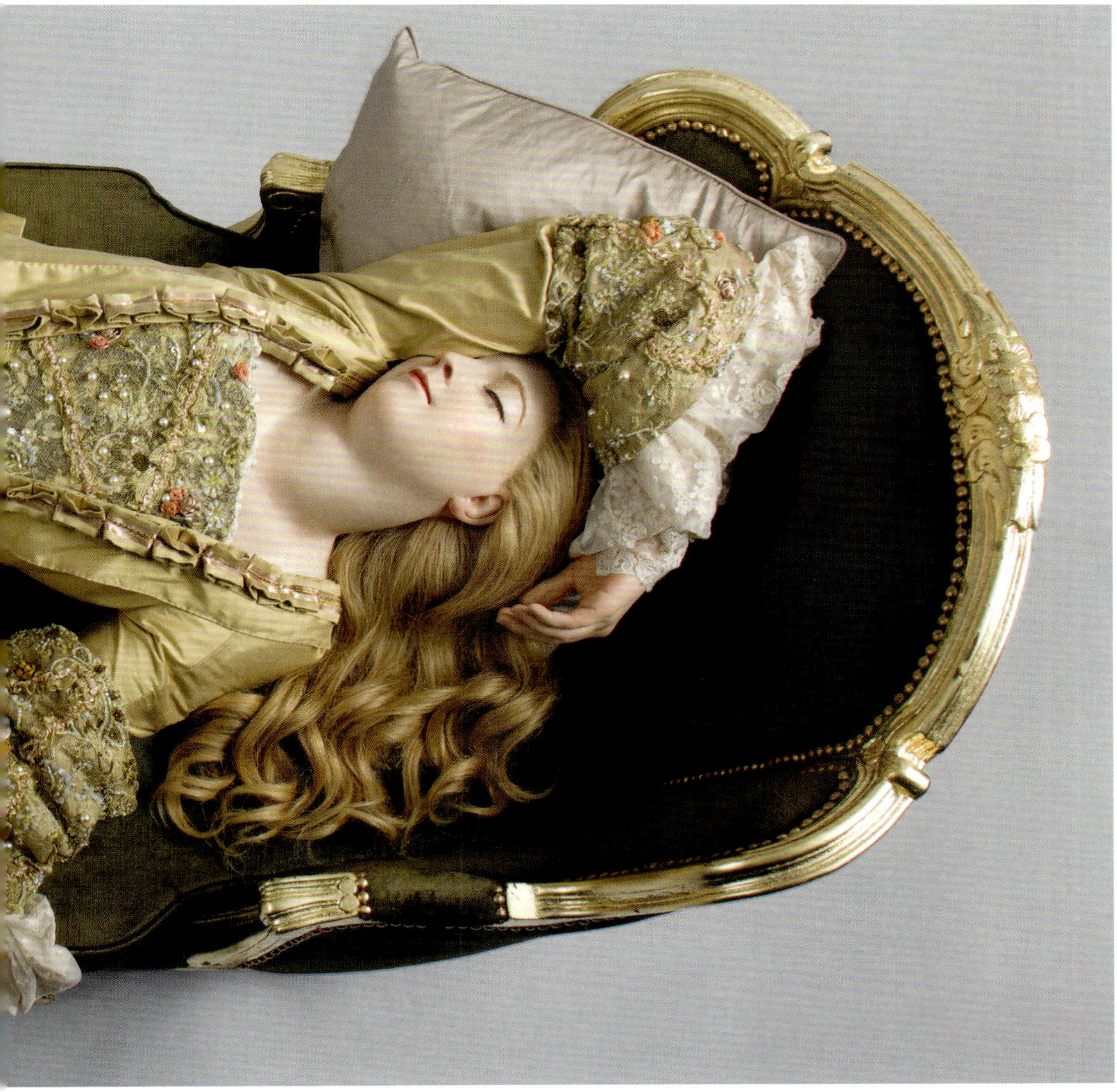

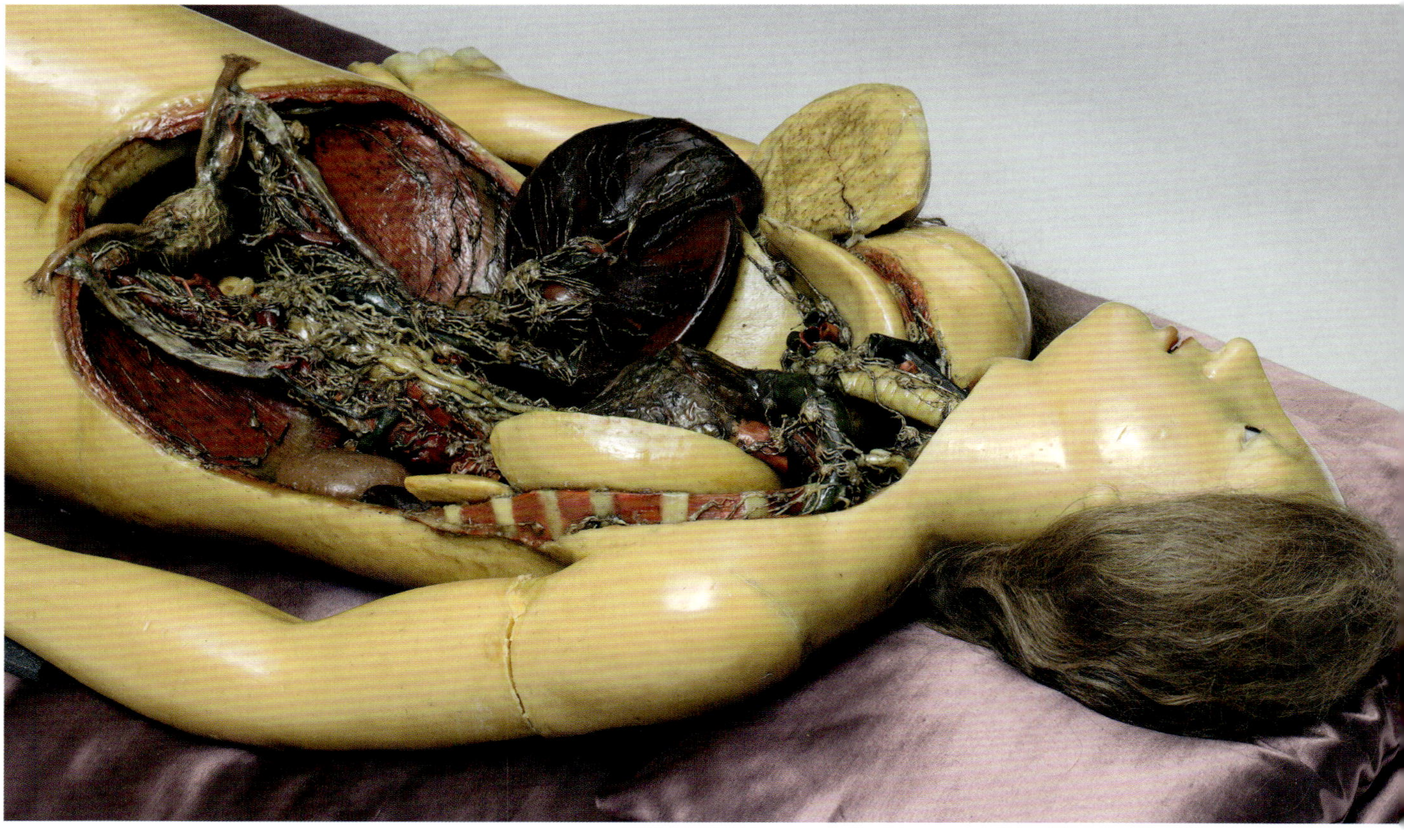

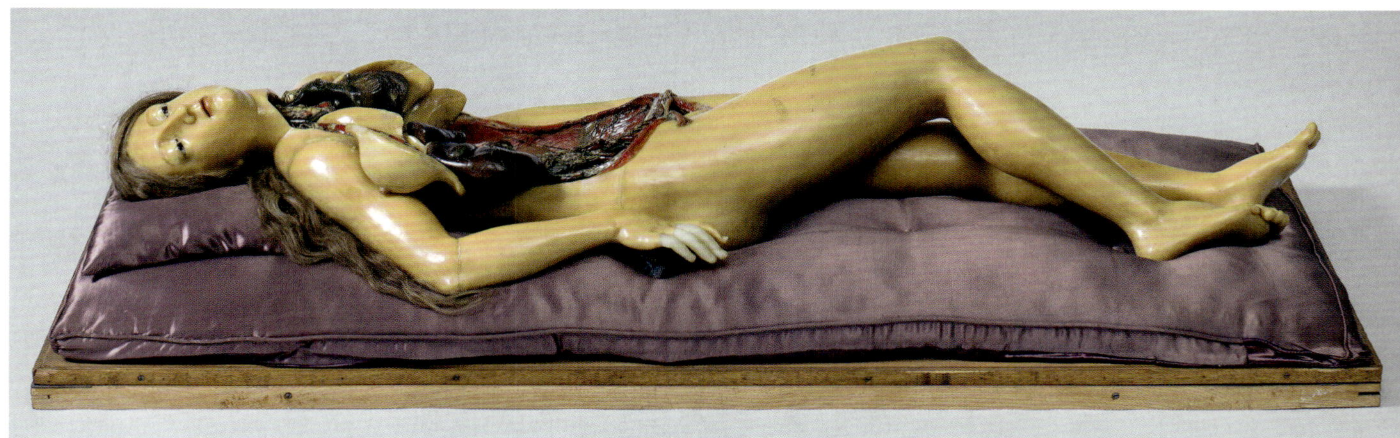

115. Fontana Workshop. *Anatomical Venus*, 1780–85. Wood skeleton, transparent wax, pigmented wax, and hair, W. 68 ½ in. (174 cm), D. 29 ¾ in. (75.5 cm). Semmelweis Orvostörténeti Múzeum, Budapest

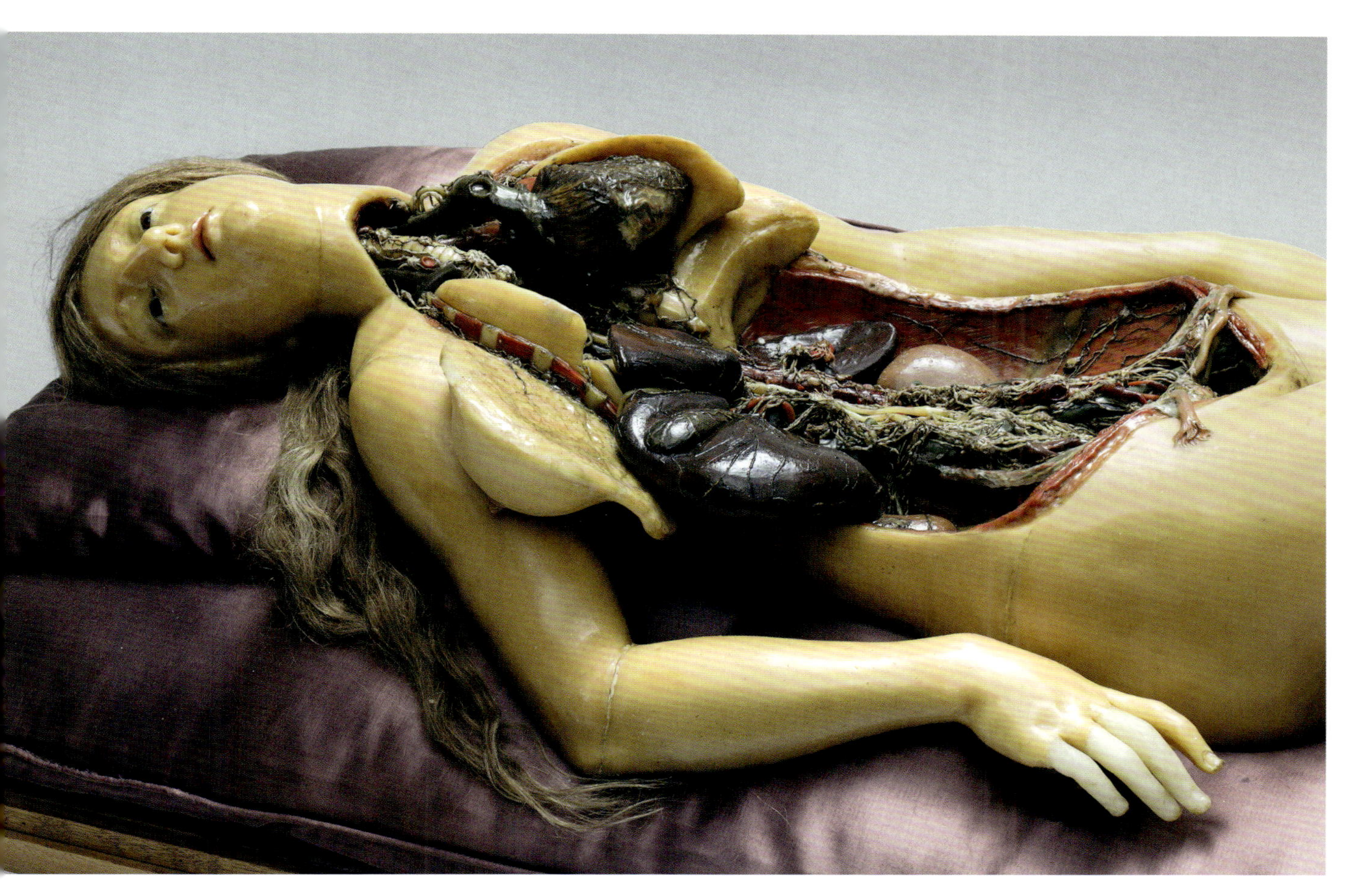

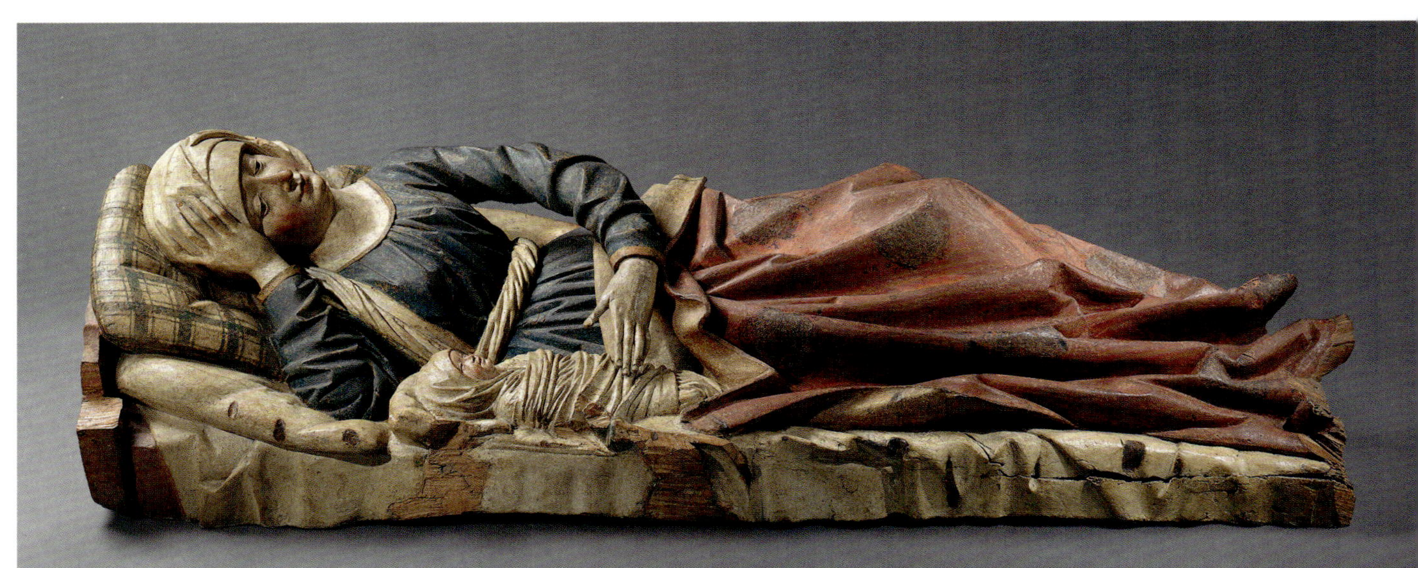

116. *Nativity of the Virgin*, ca. 1480. Limewood and paint, H. 14 ¼ in. (36.2 cm), W. 54 in. (137.2 cm), D. 17 in. (43.2 cm). German, Lower Franconia. The Metropolitan Museum of Art, New York, The Cloisters Collection, 1956 (56.211)

117. Ron Mueck. *Old Woman In Bed*, 2000. Silicone rubber, polyester resin, cotton fabric, polyurethane foam, polyester, and oil paint, H. 9 ⁷⁄₁₆ in. (24 cm), W. 37 ³⁄₁₆ in. (94.5 cm), D. 22 ¹⁄₁₆ in. (56 cm); pedestal: H. 39 ½ in. (100.3 cm), W. 37 ³⁄₁₆ in. (94.5 cm), D. 22 ¹⁄₁₆ in. (56 cm). National Gallery of Canada, Ottawa, Purchased 2001

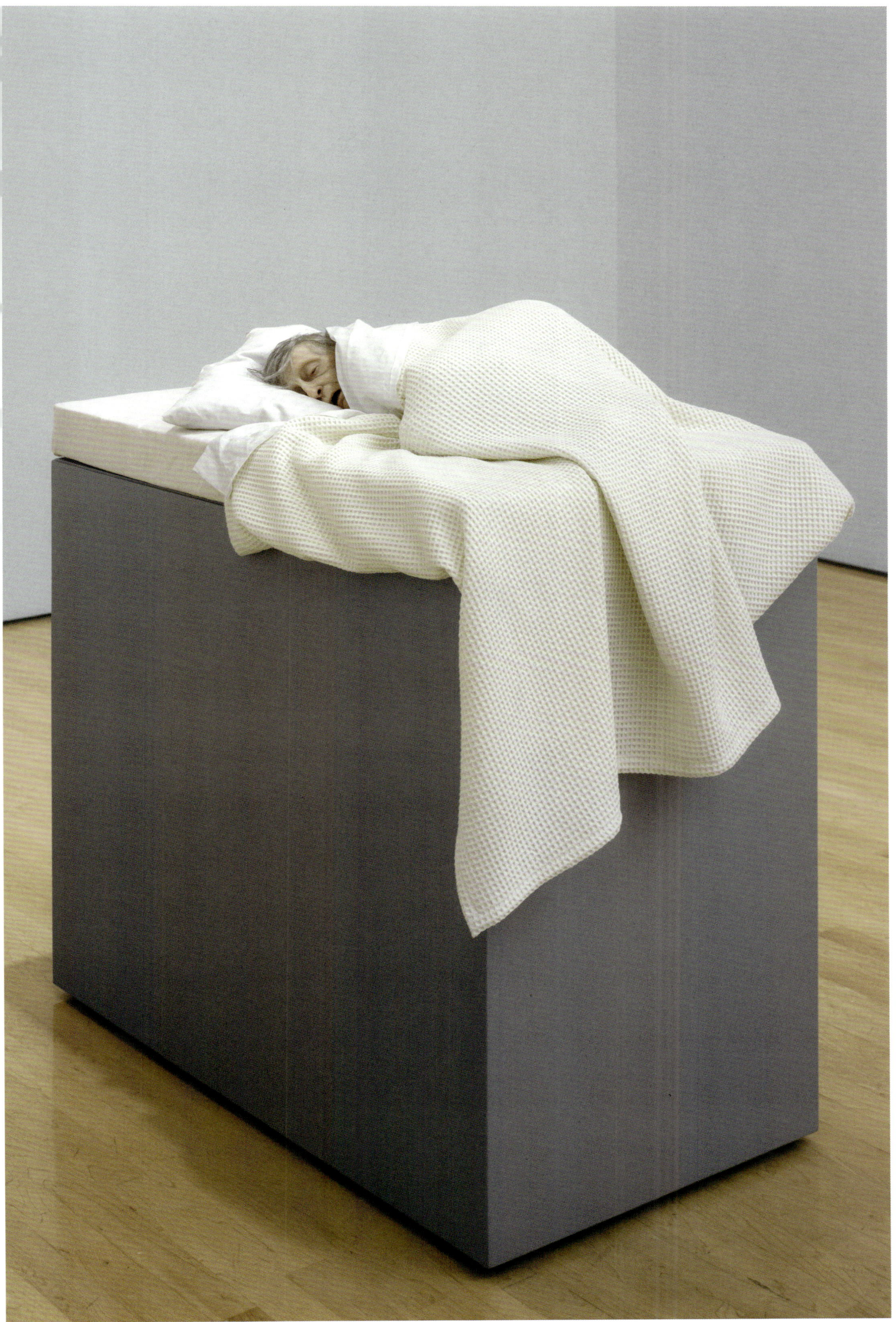

NOTES

Embodied Histories

In exploring such a broad sculptural terrain for this exhibition and book, I honor Alex Potts and Briony Fer, whose extensive pioneering work on the sculpture of our era has not only infused our thinking and writing, but who are also among my earliest teachers and inspirations. For their fierce compact with the human form and the generosity of many conversations puzzling through the topic, I owe much gratitude to Charley Ray, Jeff Wall, and Jeff Koons. This essay has benefited from the keen insight and invaluable input of Brinda Kumar, whose friendship and extraordinary support has been my mainstay for this voyage together. Closer to home, my deep affection and gratitude as ever to Mark Francis, to whom this essay is dedicated, as a labor of love.

The epigraphs are from Giorgio Vasari, *The Lives of the Artists: A Selection*, trans. George Bull (Harmondsworth, Middlesex: Penguin Books, 1965), p. 25; and Jeff Wall, quoted in Gary Dufour, "Against the Reality/Fiction of History," in *Jeff Wall 1990*, by Gary Dufour et al., exh. cat. (Vancouver: Vancouver Art Gallery, 1990), p. 60.

1. Jacob Burckhardt, *The Civilisation of the Renaissance in Italy*, trans. S. G. C. Middlemore (1878; London: Swan Sonnenschein & Co., 1892), p. 4.
2. Michael Hatt, "Transparent Forms: Tinting, Whiteness and John Gibson's *Venus*," *Sculpture Journal* 23, no. 2 (2014), p. 194.
3. The set of objects amassed by Sir Hans Sloane, a founding collection of the British Museum, London, during his visit to Jamaica and the expansion of the Egyptian collections of the Musée du Louvre, Paris, during Napoleon's reign are legendary and directly linked to Britain's and France's colonial projects, respectively.
4. Wilson's show is itself indebted to Andy Warhol's "Raid the Icebox" (1969–70) at the Institute for the Arts, Rice University, Houston; Isaac Delgado Museum, New Orleans; and the Rhode Island School of Design Museum, Providence. "Raid the Icebox 1 with Andy Warhol," in *RISD Museum* (Providence, R.I.: Museum of Art, Rhode Island School of Design, n.d.); https://risdmuseum.org/art_design/exhibitions/103_raid_the_icebox_1_with_andy_warhol.
5. Jennifer González, "Against the Grain: The Artist as Conceptual Materialist," in *Fred Wilson: Objects and Installations, 1979–2000*, by Maurice Berger et al., Issues in Cultural Theory, 4, exh. cat. (Baltimore: Center of Art and Visual Culture, University of Maryland Baltimore County, 2001), p. 29.
6. Having begun his career teaching at The Metropolitan Museum of Art, Wilson learned early about the histories of exclusion that underpin many cultural institutions: "[I]t made me look at history—to see why is it this way and why there are things they're not talking about.... How could this happen ... anthropology and art museums continuing subtle and often unsubtle demeaning, misleading interpretations and rationalizations for the public to absorb?" His practice also relates to a shocking moment as he was leaving art school in New York in 1976, where he was the only black student. His dean asked him, "Are you going to be part of the black art world or the white art world?" Andria Derstine, "A Conversation with Fred Wilson," in *Fred Wilson at Oberlin*, by Denise Birkhofer et al., exh. cat. (Oberlin, Ohio: Allen Memorial Art Museum, Oberlin College, 2017), pp. 68, 66.
7. Wilson cast his figures from copies of copies of original works; his bronzes were made from plaster-cast versions that he had bought at an antique shop and plaster-cast studio in New York. Denise Birkhofer, "Fred Wilson at Oberlin: *Wildfire Test Pit* and *Black to the Powers of Ten*," in *Fred Wilson at Oberlin*, by Birkhofer et al., p. 26.
8. Among other contemporary commentators, the German philosopher Georg Wilhelm Friedrich Hegel considered this taxonomy. "The third stage in the development of 'pre-art' is that of genuinely *symbolic* art in which shapes and images are deliberately designed and created to point to a determinate and quite *separate* sphere of 'interiority' (*Innerlichkeit*) (PKÄ [*Philosophie der Kunst oder Ästhetik, nach Hegel*], 86). This is the province of ancient Egyptian art.... Hegel does not deny the magnificence or elegance of pre-art, but he maintains that it falls short of art proper. The latter is found in *classical* art, or the art of the ancient Greeks." Emphasis in original. Stephen Houlgate, "Hegel's Aesthetics," in *Stanford Encyclopedia of Philosophy Archive*, ed. Edward N. Zalta (2009; [Stanford, Calif.]: Stanford Center for the Study of Language and Information, 2016); https://plato.stanford.edu/archives/spr2016/entries/hegel-aesthetics/.
9. Fred Wilson, typescript artist's statement, Pace Gallery, New York, April 25, 2017; "Like Life" exhibition file, Modern and Contemporary Art, The Metropolitan Museum of Art, New York.
10. Ibid.
11. "Europe appears different when seen from within the experiences of colonization or inferiorization in specific parts of the world. Postcolonial scholars, speaking from their different geographies of colonialism, have spoken of different Europes. The recent critical scholarship of Latin Americanists or Afro-Caribbeanists and others points to the imperialism of Spain and Portugal—triumphant at the time of the Renaissance and in decline as political powers by the end of the Enlightenment.... Yet, however multiple the loci of Europe and however varied colonialisms are, the problem of getting beyond Eurocentric histories remains a shared problem across geographical boundaries." Dipesh Chakrabarty, *Provincializing Europe: Postcolonial Thought and Historical Difference* (Princeton, N.J.: Princeton University Press, 2000), pp. 16–17.
12. "How important is it for the viewer to know that the six women are sex workers and that the other woman who's here, who sits in the middle of them—which is not even the same work—is my mother." Bharti Kher, "The Sensuality of Impermanence," in this volume, p. 67.
13. "When I put *Mother* in the Freud, as well, it was also my way of saying, this is my mother. Do not tell me who my mother is. I know who my mother is. My mother is a woman. And I will not be told by anybody else—politicians and male people in power who have political—You know, they're looking for political polarization in the country. And it's also a very insidious way of now also taking the voice, women's voices again. And we're not just seeing it in India; we're seeing it almost everywhere across the world now again. And so yeah, I mean, all works are political, in many ways." Bharti Kher, interviewed by Emerson Bowyer, Brinda Kumar, Luke Syson, and Sheena Wagstaff, transcript, "Like Life" exhibition file, Modern and Contemporary Art.
14. Ray continues, "I struggled to bring the specificity of the subject's identity back into the work, to bring the stylization I initially employed to move beyond portraiture back into the task of representing the figure. As I negotiated this balance, it slowly became clear that the surface of a figurative sculpture could become a manifold where sculptural events reacted and interrelated." Charles Ray, "Aluminum Girl," in *Charles Ray: Sculpture 1997–2014*, by Bernhard Mendes Bürgi et al., exh. cat. (Ostfildern: Hatje Cantz Verlag, 2014), p. 108, no. 2.
15. "In Greek, the word for 'breath' is *pneuma* and it can mean 'life' and 'spirit,' too. Ray ... refers to it when he discusses particular parts of ancient sculptures that not only look inflated but can breathe life into the future, such as the testicles of the kouros in the Metropolitan Museum of Art in New York, which he describes as having a 'balloon-like quality.'" Mark Godfrey, "Another Kind of Time," in *Charles Ray*, by Charles Ray et al. exh. cat. (Athens: The George Economou Collection, 2017), p. 26.
16. Ray, quoted in Richard Neer, "Tumbling into Time," in *Charles Ray: Sculpture 1997–2014*, by Bürgi et al., p. 69.
17. Ibid., p. 74.

18. "This uncanny is in reality nothing new or foreign, but something familiar and old-established in the mind that has been estranged only by the process of repression." Sigmund Freud, "The 'Uncanny [1919],'" in *Sigmund Freud: Collected Papers*, ed. Joan Riviere, 5 vols. (New York: Basic Books, 1959), vol. 4, p. 394.

19. René Magritte, quoted in David Sylvester, Sarah Whitfield, and Michael Raeburn, *René Magritte: Catalogue Raisonné*, 6 vols. (Houston: Menil Foundation, 1992–97), vol. 2, p. 427.

20. Ibid.

21. Connie H. Choi, "John Outterbridge," in *Now Dig This!: Art & Black Los Angeles, 1960–1980*, by Kellie Jones and Hazel V. Carby (Los Angeles: Hammer Museum; Munich: DelMonico Books/Prestel Verlag, 2011), p. 211.

22. Ibid.

23. Mike Kelley, "Playing with Dead Things," in *The Uncanny*, by Mike Kelley, exh. cat. (Arnhem: Gemeentemuseum Arnhem; Los Angeles: Fred Hoffman, 1993), p. 10.

24. Ibid.

25. Ralph Rugoff, "The Human Factor," in *The Human Factor: The Figure in Contemporary Sculpture*, by Ralph Rugoff et al., exh. cat. (London: Hayward Gallery, 2014), p. 18.

26. Jeff Wall, "An Outline of a Context for Stephan Balkenhol's Work, 1988," in *Jeff Wall: The Complete Edition*, by Thierry de Duve et al. (London: Phaidon Press, 2009), p. 222.

27. Rugoff, "The Human Factor," p. 11.

28. Rosalind Krauss, "Sculpture in the Expanded Field," *October*, no. 8 (Spring 1979), pp. 30–44.

Polychrome and Its Discontents: A History

One of the pleasures of working on an essay and exhibition about sculpture in color is that so many friends and colleagues have fascinating objects, texts, or ideas to spark conversations. I am grateful to them all. I owe special thanks to Domitilla Harding and Hannah Rothschild, whose always stimulating company and unstinting hospitality ensured that this piece got written at all. Linda Wolk-Simon, David Leiber, and Janina Quint provided insightful commentary on the text at different stages. Elyse Nelson did the same and much, much more. Philip Attwood and Sarah Lawrence, on either side of the Atlantic, provided sterling support over many months. This essay is dedicated to Mercedes Bass, with a little trepidation and much love.

1. Nancy Spector, *Maurizio Cattelan: All*, rev. ed., exh. cat. (2011; New York: Guggenheim Museum Publications, 2016), p. 65.

2. *Oxford English Dictionary*, s.v. "Polychrome;" http://www.oed.com/view/Entry/147095?rskey=P05300&result=1&isAdvanced=false#eid.

3. Roberta Panzanelli, "Compelling Presence: Wax Effigies in Renaissance Florence," in *Ephemeral Bodies: Wax Sculpture and the Human Figure*, by Roberta Panzanelli et al. (Los Angeles: Getty Research Institute, 2008), pp. 21–23; Jane Schuyler, *Florentine Busts: Sculpted Portraiture in the Fifteenth Century* (1972; New York and London: Garland Publishing, 1976), pp. 114–45; Peter Dent, "Chellini's Ears and the Diagnosis of Technique," in *"Una insalata di più erbe": A Festschrift for Patricia Lee Rubin*, ed. Jim Harris et al. (London: The Courtauld Institute of Art, 2011), p. 148; Georges Didi-Huberman, "Ressemblance mythifiée et ressemblance oubliée chez Vasari: La légende du portrait 'sur le vif,'" *Mélanges de l'École française de Rome, Italie et Méditerranée* 106, no. 2 (1994), pp. 424–26.

4. Giorgio Vasari, *Le vite de' più eccellenti pittori, scultori ed architettori*, annot. Gaetano Milanesi, 2nd ed., 9 vols. (1568; 1878–85; Florence: G. C. Sansoni, 1906), vol. 3, p. 374. See Julius von Schlosser, "History of Portraiture in Wax," in *Ephemeral Bodies*, by Panzanelli et al., p. 231.

5. Francesco Caglioti, "Niccolò da Uzzano," in *The Renaissance Portrait from Donatello to Bellini*, by Keith Christiansen et al., exh. cat. (New York: The Metropolitan Museum of Art, 2011), pp. 126–27, no. 22.

6. Ibid., p. 128, no. 22.

7. Vincenzo Borghini, "Selva di notizie" (Florence, 1584), cited in Rosalba D'Amico, "Vincenzo Onofri tra pittura e scultura: Un'indagine sulla policromia in terracotte bolognesi," in *Niccolò dell'Arca: Seminario di studi; Atti del convegno 26–27 maggio 1987*, ed. Grazia Agostini and Luisa Ciammitti (Bologna: Nuova Alfa Editoriale, 1989), p. 122; translation by the author.

8. For the term, see David Batchelor, *Chromophobia* (London: Reaktion Books, 2000).

9. Alex Potts, "Colors of Sculpture," in *The Color of Life: Polychromy in Sculpture from Antiquity to the Present*, by Roberta Panzanelli et al., exh. cat. (Los Angeles: J. Paul Getty Museum; Getty Research Institute, 2008), pp. 84–85.

10. See Batchelor, *Chromophobia*, passim.

11. Walter Pater, *Studies in the History of the Renaissance* (London: Macmillan and Co., 1873), p. 185.

12. Ruba Katrib, "Surface Identity," in *Duane Hanson*, ed. Rebecca Lewin, exh. cat. (London: Serpentine Galleries; Koenig Books, 2015), p. 128.

13. Thayer Tolles, "Augustus Saint-Gaudens in The Metropolitan Museum of Art," *The Metropolitan Museum of Art Bulletin* 66, no. 4 (Spring 2009), p. 72, no. 41; Thayer Tolles, "'In a Class by Themselves': Polychrome Portraits by Herbert Adams," in *Perspectives on American Sculpture before 1925*, ed. Thayer Tolles, The Metropolitan Museum of Art Symposia (New York: The Metropolitan Museum of Art, 2003), p. 79.

14. In his critique of Minimalism, Michael Fried decries sculptural theatricality as the negation of art. Michael Fried, "Art and Objecthood," *Artforum* 5, no. 10 (June 1967), pp. 12–23.

15. Timothy Verdon, "'Si tu non piangi quando questo vedi…': Penitenza e spiritualità laica nel Quattrocento," in *Niccolò dell'Arca: Seminario di studi*, ed. Agostini and Ciammitti, p. 152.

16. Janine Chasseguet-Smirgel, *Creativity and Perversion* (New York: W. W. Norton & Company, 1985), p. 100, quoted in Mike Kelley, "Playing with Dead Things: On the Uncanny [1993]," in *The Uncanny by Mike Kelley, Artist*, ed. Cristoph Grunenberg, exh. cat. (Cologne: Verlag der Buchhandlung Walther König, 2004), p. 30.

17. See Assaf Pinkus, *Sculpting Simulacra in Medieval Germany, 1250–1380* (Farnham, Surrey: Ashgate Publishing, 2014), pp. 8–9.

18. Francisco Pacheco, *Arte de la pintura: su antiguedad y grandezas* (Seville: Simon Faxardo, 1649), p. 350. See Xavier Bray, "The Sacred Made Real: Spanish Painting and Sculpture 1600–1700," in *The Sacred Made Real: Spanish Painting and Sculpture 1600–1700*, by Xavier Bray et al., exh. cat. (London: National Gallery Company, 2009), pp. 19–21.

19. Claudia Kryza-Gersch, "Pompeo Leoni's Portrait of Philip II in the Kunsthistorisches Museum in Vienna," in *Leone and Pompeo Leoni*, by Stephan F. Schröder et al., exh. cat. (Madrid: Museo Nacional del Prado, 2012), pp. 104–5.

20. Tom Flynn, *The Body in Three Dimensions* (New York: Harry N. Abrams, 1998), pp. 87–89.

21. See Jeffrey Chipps Smith, *German Sculpture of the Later Renaissance, c. 1520–1580: Art in an Age of Uncertainty* (Princeton, N.J.: Princeton University Press, 1994), p. 31. See also David Freedberg, *The Power of Images: Studies in the History and Theory of Response* (Chicago: The University of Chicago Press, 1989), p. 163.

22. Flynn, *The Body in Three Dimensions*, p. 51.

23. Joanna E. Ziegler, *Sculpture of Compassion: The Pietà and the Beguines in the Southern Low Countries, c. 1300–c. 1600* (Brussels: Brepols Publishers, 1992), pp. 33–34.

24. Ibid., pp. 39–40.

25. Giorgio Bonsanti et al., *Emozioni in terracotta: Guido Mazzoni, Antonio Begarelli; Sculture del Rinascimento emiliano*, exh. cat. (Modena: Franco Cosimo Panini, 2009), pp. 113–37, 208–13.

26. Ziegler, *Sculpture of Compassion*, pp. 127–28.

27. [Desiderius] Erasmus, *The Praise of Folly*, trans. John Wilson, ed. P. S. Allen (1668; Oxford: Clarendon Press, 1913), p. 97; Smith, *German Sculpture of the Later Renaissance*, p. 32.

28. Article 20 of *Documenta Mag. Joannis Hus vitam etc.…illustrantia*, translated in Michael Baxandall, *The Limewood Sculptors of Renaissance Germany* (New Haven, Conn.: Yale University Press, 1980), p. 92.

29. Baxandall, *Limewood Sculptors of Renaissance Germany*, p. 42.

30. Ibid., p. 48.

31. Ibid.

32. Angelo Meli, "Cappella Colleoni: I tre santi dell'ancona," *Bergomum: Bollettino della Civica Biblioteca* 59, no. 1 (1965), pp. 24–27.

33. Charles Wriothesley, *A Chronicle of England during the Reigns of the Tudors, from A.D. 1485 to 1559*, ed. William Douglas Hamilton, 2 vols. ([Westminster]: Camden Society, 1875–77), vol. 1, p. 74.

34. Jane Garnett and Gervase Rosser, *Spectacular Miracles: Transforming Images in Italy, from the Renaissance to the Present* (London: Reaktion Books, 2013), pp. 73–80.

35. Ibid., pp. 77–79.

36. The Council of Trent, Session XXV (December 3, 1563), on the Invocation of Saints, quoted in Alfonso Rodríguez G. de Ceballos, "Image and Counter-Reformation in Spain and Spanish America," in *Sacred Spain: Art and Belief in the Spanish World*, by Ronda Kasl et al., exh. cat. (Indianapolis: Indianapolis Museum of Art, 2009), p. 20.

37. Ibid.

38. Patrick Lenaghan, "Luisa Roldán's Career in Madrid: Intimate Masterpieces in Terracotta," in *Luisa Roldán: Court Sculptor to the Kings of Spain*, by Xavier Bray et al., exh. cat. ([Madrid]: Coll & Cortés, 2016), p. 22.

39. Jorge Coll and Nicolás Cortés, *X Years of Coll & Cortés* (Madrid: Coll & Cortés, 2014), p. 70.

40. Rodríguez G. de Ceballos, "Image and Counter-Reformation in Spain and Spanish America," p. 27. See also Marjorie Trusted, "Exotic Devotion: Sculpture in Viceregal America and Brazil, 1520–1820," in *The Arts in Latin America, 1492–1820*, by Joseph J. Rischel et al., exh. cat. (Philadelphia: Philadelphia Museum of Art, 2006), p. 255.

41. Rodríguez G. de Ceballos, "Image and Counter-Reformation in Spain and Spanish America," p. 25.

42. Elizabeth Wilder Weismann, *Mexico in Sculpture, 1521–1821* (Cambridge, Mass.: Harvard University Press, 1950), p. 178; referenced in Trusted, "Exotic Devotion," p. 255.

43. Rodríguez G. de Ceballos, "Image and Counter-Reformation in Spain and Spanish America," p. 28.

44. Ian Wardropper, *European Sculpture, 1400–1900, in The Metropolitan Museum of Art* (New York: The Metropolitan Museum of Art, 2011), pp. 117–18.

45. Daniele Sanguineti, *Anton Maria Maragliano, 1664–1739, "Insignis sculptor Genue"* (Genoa: Sagep Editori, 2012), p. 236.

46. Ibid., p. 237.

47. Romuald Díaz i Carbonell, *El Sant Crist d'Igualada* (Monserrat: Impremta de l'Abadia, 1965), translated in William A. Christian Jr., *Divine Presence in Spain and Western Europe, 1500–1960: Visions, Religious Images and Photographs* (Budapest and New York: Central European University Press, 2011), p. 53.

48. As described in Christiane Hertel, *Pygmalion in Bavaria: The Sculptor Ignaz Günther and Eighteenth-Century Aesthetic Art Theory* (University Park, Pa.: The Pennsylvania State University Press, 2011), pp. 121–22.

49. Quoted in Hertel, *Pygmalion in Bavaria*, p. 122.

50. John Evelyn's diary quoted in Pamela Pilbeam, *Madame Tussaud and the History of Waxworks* (London and New York: Hambledon and London, 2003), p. 9.

51. John Webster, *The Duchess of Malfi* (1613; London: Ernest Benn, 1964), p. 111. See David M. Bergeron, "The Wax Figures in *The Duchess of Malfi*," *Studies in English Literature, 1500–1900* 18, no. 2 [*Elizabethan and Jacobean Drama*] (Spring 1978), pp. 331–39.

52. Roberta Ballestriero, "The History of Ceroplastics," in *Flesh & Wax: The Clemente Susini's Anatomical Models in the University of Cagliari*, by Alessandro Riva et al. (Nuoro: Ilisso Edizioni, 2007), p. 31.

53. Giorgio Vasari, *Le vite de' più eccellenti pittori scultori ed architettori* (1568; Vicenza, 1963), vol. 3, pp. 229–32, translated in Ballestriero, "The History of Ceroplastics," p. 21; Schlosser, "History of Portraiture in Wax," p. 235.

54. Ballestriero, "The History of Ceroplastics," p. 20. See also Megan Holmes, "Ex-votos: Materiality, Memory and Cult," in *The Idol in the Age of Art: Objects, Devotions and the Early Modern World*, ed. Michael W. Cole and Rebecca E. Zorach (Farnham, Surrey: Ashgate Publishing, 2009), p. 172.

55. Julian Litten, "The Funeral Effigy: Its Function and Purpose," in *The Funeral Effigies of Westminster Abbey*, by Richard Mortimer et al., rev. ed. (1994; Woodbridge, Suffolk: The Boydell Press, 2003), p. 14.

56. *Lettere di Giambattista Busini a Benedetto Varchi sopra l'assedio di Firenze*, ed. Gaetano Milanesi (Florence: Felice Le Monnier, 1861), pp. 32–33.

57. James Boswell, *Boswell's London Journal, 1762–1763*, ed. Frederick A. Pottle (New Haven, Conn.: Yale University Press, 1950),

p. 157. See also Mario Praz, "Le figure di cera in letteratura," in *La ceroplastica nella scienza e nell'arte: Atti del I congresso internazionale, Firenze, 3–7 giugno 1975*, ed. Cristina Piacenti (Florence: Leo S. Olschki Editore, 1977), vol. 3, p. 558.

58. Edward V. Gatacre and Laura Dru, "Portraiture in Le Cabinet de Cire de Curtius and Its Successor Madame Tussaud's Exhibition," in *La ceroplastica nella scienza e nell'arte*, ed. Piacenti, vol. 3, p. 619; translation by the author.

59. A. M. Benoist, "Peintre ordinaire du Roy, & son premier sculpteur en cire," in *Poesies diverses … by* M[artin de] Baraton (Paris: Jean-Baptiste Delespine, 1705), pp. 281–82, translated in Robert Wellington, "Antoine Benoist's Wax Portraits of Louis XIV," *Journal 18: A Journal of Eighteenth-Century Art and Culture*, no. 3 [*Lifelike*] (Spring 2017); http://www.journal18.org/1421.

60. Vasari, *Le vite* (Vicenza, 1963), vol. 3, p. 232, translated in Ballestriero, "The History of Ceroplastics," p. 21.

61. Filippo Baldinucci, *Delle notizie de' professori del disegno da Cimabue in qua: Opera*, ed. Domenico Maria Manni (Florence: Gio Batista Stecchi & Anton Giuseppe Pagani, 1767–74), vol. 12, p. 179, quoted in Praz, "Le figure di cera in letteratura," pp. 557–58; translation by the author.

62. Baldinucci, *Delle notizie*, in Praz, "Le figure di cera in letteratura," pp. 557–58; translation by the author.

63. *Le cere anatomiche bolognesi del settecento: Università degli studi di Bologna, Accademia delle Scienze* (1981; Bologna: Clueb, 1995), p. 35, translated in Ballestriero, "The History of Ceroplastics," p. 26.

64. Mortimer et al., *Funeral Effigies of Westminster Abbey*, pp. 179–81.

65. Ballestriero, "The History of Ceroplastics," p. 31.

66. Quoted in Adeline Gargam, "Savoir mondains, savoirs savants: Les femmes et leurs cabinets de curiosités au siècle des Lumières," *Mnémosyne: Revue genre et histoire* 5 (Autumn 2009), p. 10; translation by the author. For more on Bihéron, see Adeline Gargam, "Between Scientific Investigation and Vanity Fair: A Few Reflections on the Culture of Curiosity in Enlightenment France," in *Women and Curiosity in Early Modern England and France*, ed. Line Cottegnies, Sandrine Parageau, and John J. Thompson (Leiden and Boston: Brill, 2016), pp. 211–13.

67. Pilbeam, *Madame Tussaud*, pp. 11–14.

68. Boswell, *Boswell's London Journal*, July 3, 1763, p. 289.

69. Whitney Davis, "Wax Tokens of Libido: William Hamilton, Richard Payne Knight, and the Phalli of Isernia," in *Ephemeral Bodies*, by Panzanelli et al., pp. 107–29.

70. Franco Sacchetti, *Il Trecentonovelle*, ed. Valerio Marucci (1399; Rome: Salerno Editrice, 1996), Novella CIX, pp. 329–31, translated in Holmes, "Ex-votos: Materiality, Memory and Cult," p. 159.

71. Holmes, "Ex-votos: Materiality, Memory and Cult," p. 173.

72. Francesco Bocchi, *Della imagine miracolosa della SS. Nunziata di Firenze* (1592; Florence: Tommaso Baracchi, 1852), pp. 94–95, translated in Holmes, "Ex-votos: Materiality, Memory and Cult," p. 176.

73. Schlosser, "History of Portraiture in Wax," p. 265.

74. Benedetto Lanza et al., *Le cere anatomiche della specola* (Florence: Arnaud Editore, 1979), pp. 79–80, translated in Ballestriero, "The History of Ceroplastics," p. 25; emphasis by the author.

75. Ballestriero, "The History of Ceroplastics," p. 27.

76. See Maria Luisa Azzaroli, "La Specola: The Zoological Museum of Florence University," in *La ceroplastica nella scienza e nell'arte*, ed. Piacenti, vol. 1, pp. 1–22.

77. Pilbeam, *Madame Tussaud*, p. 5.

78. "Sketches of Society," December 31, 1825, *The London Literary Gazette and Journal of Belles Lettres, Arts, Sciences, &c. for the Year 1825* (London: Whiting and Branston, 1825), p. 843, quoted in Richard D. Altick, *The Shows of London* (Cambridge, Mass.: Belknap Press, Harvard University Press, 1978), p. 339.

79. *Illustrated London News*, June 4, 1853, p. 447.

80. Champfleury, "L'homme aux figures de cire," in *Les Excentriques* (Paris: Michel Lévy Frères, 1852), translated in Ballestriero, "The History of Ceroplastics," p. 32. For Champfleury's text, see Sara Pappas, "The Lessons of Champfleury," *Nineteenth-Century French Studies* 42, nos. 1–2 (Fall–Winter 2013–14), pp. 55–56.

81. Champfleury, "L'homme aux figures de cire," in Ballestriero, "The History of Ceroplastics," p. 32.

82. Ibid.

83. Massimo De Grassi, "Andrea Brustolon: Gli esordi," in *Andrea Brustolon, 1662–1732: "Il Michelangelo del legno,"* by Anna Maria

Spiazza et al., exh. cat. (Milan: Skira Editore, 2009), pp. 16–27, pl. 25.

84. Kelley, "Playing with Dead Things," pp. 30–31.

85. See examples in Julia E. Poole, *Italian Maiolica and Incised Slipware in the Fitzwilliam Museum, Cambridge* (1976–; Cambridge and New York: Cambridge University Press, 1995), pp. 241–42, no. 323, pl. 26; Paul H. D. Kaplan, "Italy, 1490–1700" in *The Image of the Black in Western Art*, vol. 3, *From the "Age of Discovery" to the Age of Abolition*, pt. 1, *Artists of the Renaissance and Baroque*, ed. David Bindman and Henry Louis Gates Jr., new ed. (1976– ; Cambridge, Mass: Belknap Press, Harvard University Press, 2010), pp. 151–52, fig. 75.

86. See Maureen Cassidy-Geiger et al., *The Arnhold Collection of Meissen Porcelain, 1710–50* (New York: The Frick Collection; London: D. Giles, 2008), pp. 257–66; Ulrich Pietsch, "Master of Porcelain Sculpture: Johann Joachim Kändler," and Gerhard Röbbig, "Sculpture and Painting: Johann Joachim Kändler— Johann Gregorius Höroldt," in *Cabinet Pieces: The Meissen Porcelain Birds of Johann Joachim Kändler, 1706–1775*, by Gerhard Röbbig et al. (Munich: Hirmer Verlag, 2008), pp. 12–29; Angela Caròla-Perrotti, *Le porcellane dei Borbone di Napoli: Capodimonte e Real Fabbrica Ferdinandea, 1743–1806* (Naples: Guida Editori, 1986), pp. 149–232, pls. XXXI–XLV; Renate Eikelmann, Katharina Hantschmann, and Alfred Ziffer, *Franz Anton Bustelli: Nymphenburger porzellanfiguren des Rokoko* (Munich: C. H. Beck, 2004); Elizabeth Adams, *Chelsea Porcelain* (London: The British Museum Press, 2001), pp. 93–95, 120–30.

87. See Reginald G. Haggar, "Earthenware, Image Toys," and "Victorian Chimney Ornaments," in *Staffordshire Chimney Ornaments* (New York: Pitman Publishing Corporation, 1955), pp. 18–25, 101–13.

88. Marilyn G. Karmason and Joan B. Stacke, *Majolica: A Complete History and Illustrated Survey*, enl. ed. (1989; New York: Harry N. Abrams, 2002).

89. Christian Bailly, *Automata: The Golden Age, 1848–1914* (London: Sotheby's Publications; Philip Wilson Publishers, 1987), p. 13.

90. Voltaire, "Sur la nature de l'homme," (1734), translated in Bailly, *Automata*, p. 14.

91. William Wordsworth, "The Prelude, Book Seventh: Residence in London," in *The Poetical Works of William Wordsworth*, new ed. (London: Edward Moxon, Son, and Co., 1869), p. 489.

92. Amédée Achard, "Les jouets et les poupées," in *L'Exposition Universelle de 1867 illustrée* (Paris, 1867), pp. 210–11, translated in Bailly, *Automata*, p. 15.

93. Ibid., p. 34.

94. J. T. Smith, in *Streets of London*, quoted in Rupert Gunnis, *Dictionary of British Sculptors, 1660–1851*, rev. ed. (1953; London: The Abbey Library, 1968), p. 99.

95. From Robert Lloyd's 1757 poem, "The Cit's Country Box," quoted in Malcolm Baker, *Figured in Marble: The Making and Viewing of Eighteenth-Century Sculpture* (Los Angeles: J. Paul Getty Museum, 2000), p. 120.

96. [Richard Cumberland], *The Observer: Being a Collection of Moral, Literary and Familiar Essays*, vol. 1 (London: C. Dilly, 1786), pp. 32–33.

97. As quoted in Nicola Spinosa, "The Presepio as Art Work," in *The Art of the Presepio: The Neapolitan Crib of the Banco di Napoli Collection*, by Marisa Piccoli Catello et al. (Naples: Banco di Napoli, 1987), p. 9.

98. As quoted in Raffaello Causa, "The Golden Age of the Neapolitan Presepio," in *Art of the Presepio*, by Piccoli Catello et al., p. 31.

99. Ibid., p. 26.

100. Laure de Margerie, "'The most beautiful Negro is not the one who looks most like us.'—Cordier, 1862," in *Facing the Other: Charles Cordier (1827–1905), Ethnographic Sculptor*, by Laure de Margerie et al., exh. cat. (Paris: Musée d'Orsay; New York: Harry N. Abrams, 2004), p. 28.

101. *Illustrated London News*, June 4, 1853, p. 447.

102. De Margerie, "'The most beautiful Negro,'" p. 20.

103. Claude Vignon, *Le Salon de 1852* (Paris: Dentu, 1852), translated in de Margerie, "The most beautiful Negro," pp. 28–29.

104. Hector de Callias, "Le Salon de 1863: La sculpture," *L'Artiste* 1 (1863), p. 4, translated in Édouard Papet, "'To Have the Courage of His Polychromy': Charles Cordier and the Sculpture of the Second Empire," in *Facing the Other*, by de Margerie et al., p. 63.

105. Papet, "To Have the Courage of His Polychromy," p. 77.

106. George Scharf, "On the Polychromy of Sculpture: Being Recollections of Remarks on this Subject by Professor C. O. Müller," in *The Museum of Classical Antiquities: A Quarterly Journal of Architecture and the Sister Branches of Classic Art*, vol. 1, [ed. Edward Falkener] (London: John W. Parker and Son, 1851), p. 250.

107. Charles Garnier, *Le nouvel opéra de Paris* (Paris, 1878), translated in Papet, "To Have the Courage of His Polychromy," p. 54.

108. See Meredith Shedd, "Phidias at the Universal Exposition of 1855: The Duc de Luynes and the *Athéna Parthenos*," *Gazette des Beaux-Arts*, ser. 6, 107–8 (October 1986), p. 131.

109. Lady [Elizabeth Rigby] Eastlake, ed., *Life of John Gibson, R.A., Sculptor* (London: Longmans, Green, and Co., 1870), p. 211.

110. Ibid., pp. 211–12.

111. "John Gibson, RA," *Athenaeum*, February 3, 1866, p. 172.

112. Richard Kendall et al., *Degas and the Little Dancer*, exh. cat. (New Haven, Conn.: Yale University Press; Omaha: Joslyn Art Museum, 1998), pp. 45–75.

113. Marquis de Sade, *Juliette or Vice Amply Rewarded*, trans. Pieralessandro Casavini (London: Goldstar Publications, 1966), pp. 238–39.

114. Sigmund Freud, "The 'Uncanny' [1919]," in *Sigmund Freud: Collected Papers*, ed. Joan Rivière, 5 vols. (New York: Basic Books, 1959), vol. 4, p. 399.

115. Andreas Blühm, "In Living Colour: A Short History of Colour in Sculpture in the 19th Century," in *The Colour of Sculpture, 1840–1910*, by Andreas Blühm et al., exh. cat. (Zwolle: Waanders Uitgevers, 1996), pp. 40–49.

116. Valerie J. Fletcher, *Marvelous Objects: Surrealist Sculpture from Paris to New York*, exh. cat. (Washington, D.C.: Hirshhorn Museum and Sculpture Garden, 2015), pp. 80–104.

117. Hans Bellmer, *L'anatomie de l'image*, translated in Peter Webb and Robert Short, *Hans Bellmer* (London: Quartet Books, 1985), p. 103.

118. Umberto Eco, *Travels in Hyperreality*, trans. William Weaver (1975; San Diego: Harcourt Brace Jovanovich, 1986), p. 10.

119. Douglas Coupland, "Duane Hanson: Realness, not Realism," in *Duane Hanson*, ed. Lewin, p. 133.

120. Sean O'Hagan, "Ron Mueck: From Muppets to Motherhood," *The Observer*, August 6, 2006, p. 35.

121. David Hurlston, *Ron Mueck*, exh. cat. (Melbourne: National Gallery of Victoria, 2010), p. 65.

122. Norman Rosenthal, *Allen Jones: A Retrospective*, exh. cat. (New York: Michael Werner, 2016), n.p.

123. Jed Perl, "The Cult of Jeff Koons," review of *Jeff Koons: A Retrospective*, by Scott Rothkopf et al., *The New York Review of Books*, September 25, 2014; http://www.nybooks.com/articles/2014/09/25/cult-jeff-koons.

124. Walter Hopps, "A Note from the Underworld," in *Kienholz, A Retrospective: Edward and Nancy Reddin Kienholz*, by Walter Hopps et al., exh. cat. (New York: Whitney Museum of American Art, 1996), p. 33.

125. Ibid., p. 34.

126. Hal Foster et al., *Art Since 1900: Modernism, Antimodernism, Postmodernism*, 2nd ed. (2004; London: Thames & Hudson, 2011), pp. 456–58.

127. Rosetta Brooks, "The Art Show, 1963–77," in *Kienholz, A Retrospective*, by Hopps et al., p. 169, no. 45.

128. Marcel Duchamp, quoted in Hopps, "A Note from the Underworld," p. 33.

129. Calvin Tomkins, *Marcel Duchamp: The Afternoon Interviews* (Brooklyn: Badlands Unlimited, 2013), pp. 56–57.

130. Foster et al., *Art Since 1900*, pp. 540–43.

131. Ibid.; Hopps, "A Note from the Underworld," p. 33; Jeff Wall, "Étant donnés," in *Marcel Duchamp: Étant donnés*, by Jeff Wall et al. (Nuremberg: Verlag für Moderne Kunst, 2009), pp. 18–41.

132. Scott Rothkopf, "No Limits," in *Jeff Koons: A Retrospective*, by Rothkopf et al., exh. cat. (New York: Whitney Museum of American Art, 2014), p. 22, pl. 54.

133. Spector, *Maurizio Cattelan: All*, p. 70.

No Dead Matter

The epigraphs are from William Shakespeare, *The Winter's Tale* (Act 5, Scene 3), ed. Stephen Orgel (Oxford: Oxford University Press, 1996), p. 228; and Bruno Schulz, "From 'Tailors' Dummies,'" in *On Dolls*, ed. Kenneth Gross (London: Notting Hill Editions, 2012), p. 67.

1. Isaiah 64:8; King James Version.
2. Genesis 1:27, 2:7; King James Version. The notorious scene of the "spare rib" taken from Adam's side to create Eve follows later, offering an alternative story with woman secondary in accord with her decreed subordination.
3. Shihab al-Din al-Nuwayri, *The Ultimate Ambition in the Arts of Erudition: A Compendium of Knowledge from the Classical Islamic World*, ed. and trans. Elias Muharna (London: Penguin Books, 2016), pp. 237–39.
4. Hesiod, *Theogony*, in Hesiod, *Theogony—Works and Days*; Theognis, *Elegies*, trans. Dorothea Wender (Harmondsworth, Middlesex: Penguin Books, 1973), p. 40, l. 514. See also Froma I. Zeitlin, "Travesties of Gender and Genre in Aristophanes' *Thesmophoriazousae*," in *Reflections of Women in Antiquity*, ed. Helene B. Foley (New York and London: Gordon and Breach Science Publishers, 1981), pp. 169–217; Froma I. Zeitlin, "Signifying Difference: The Case of Hesiod's Pandora," in *Playing the Other: Gender and Society in Classical Greek Literature*, by Froma I. Zeitlin (Chicago: The University of Chicago Press, 1996), pp. 53–86; Marina Warner, "The Making of Pandora," in *Monuments & Maidens: The Allegory of the Female Form*, by Marina Warner (London: Weidenfeld and Nicolson, 1985), pp. 213–40, 360–61.
5. Hesiod, *Works and Days*, p. 61, ll. 80–82.
6. Hesiod, *Theogony*, p. 42, l. 572.
7. Ibid., l. 573.
8. Hesiod, *Works and Days*, p. 61, ll. 76–77.
9. Hesiod, *Theogony*, in *Hesiod; Homeric Hymns: Epic Cycle; Homerica*, trans. Hugh G. Evelyn-White, rev. ed., The Loeb Classical Library (1914; Cambridge, Mass.: Harvard University Press, 1936), pp. 122–23, l. 589.
10. Hesiod, *Works and Days*, trans. Wender, p. 61, l. 70.
11. Ibid., l. 83.
12. Homer, *The Odyssey*, trans. Robert Fagles (New York: Viking Penguin, 1996), p. 200, bk. 8, ll. 309–22.
13. Ibid., p. 207, bk. 8, ll. 552–55.
14. Froma I. Zeitlin, "Travesties of Gender and Genre in Aristophanes' *Thesmophoriazousae*," *Critical Inquiry* 8, no. 2 (Winter 1981), p. 324.
15. See Caroline van Eck, *Art, Agency and Living Presence: From the Animated Image to the Excessive Object* (Boston and Berlin: Walter De Gruyter; Leiden: Leiden University Press, 2015). See also Philippe-Alain Michaud, *Aby Warburg and the Image in Motion* (1998; New York: Zone Books, 2003); Marina Warner, "Incantesimi e legami," in *Il mondo magico: Padiglione Italia, Biennale Arte 2017*, ed. Cecilia Alemani, exh. cat. (Venice: Marsilio Editori, 2017), pp. 94–115.
16. Alfred Gell, *Art and Agency: An Anthropological Theory* (Oxford: Oxford University Press, 1998). See also Alfred Gell, "The Technology of Enchantment and the Enchantment of Technology," in *The Object Reader*, ed. Fiona Candlin and Raiford Guins (London and New York: Routledge, 2009), pp. 208–28.
17. Van Eck, *Art, Agency and Living Presence*, esp. on Gian Lorenzo Bernini's *Medusa*, pp. 63–65. See also Marjorie Garber and Nancy J. Vickers, eds., *The Medusa Reader* (London and New York: Routledge, 2003), and David Leeming, *Medusa in the Mirror of Time* (London: Reaktion Books, 2013).
18. See also Luca Giordano's painting of the same theme in the National Gallery, London.
19. Ovid, *Metamorphoses*, trans. Frank Justus Miller, rev. G. P. Goold, 3rd ed., The Loeb Classical Library (1916; Cambridge, Mass.: Harvard University Press, 1977), vol. 1, pp. 154–55, bk. 3, l. 419, and pp. 226–27, bk. 4, l. 675.
20. Euripides, *Hecuba*, trans. Peter D. Arnott, in Euripides, *Plays: Two* (London: Methuen Drama, 1991), pp. 19–20, ll. 558–60.
21. For now-classic interventions in this ongoing discussion, see Neil Hertz, "Medusa's Head: Male Hysteria under Political Pressure," *Representations*, no. 4 (Fall 1983), pp. 27–54; and Catherine Gallagher, Joel Fineman, and Neil Hertz, "More about 'Medusa's Head,'" *Representations*, no. 4 (Fall 1983), pp. 55–72.
22. Gell, "Technology of Enchantment," pp. 209–28. See also van Eck, *Art, Agency and Living Presence*, passim.
23. Alfred Gell, quoted in van Eck, *Art, Agency and Living Presence*, p. 21.
24. "The Tale of the City of Brass," Nights 566–78, in *The Arabian Nights*, trans. Malcolm Lyons, 3 vols. (London: Penguin Books, 2009), vol. 2, pp. 518–45; Marina Warner, *Stranger Magic: Charmed States and the Arabian Nights* (Cambridge, Mass.: Belknap Press, Harvard University Press, 2011), pp. 54–62.
25. *The Arabian Nights*, trans. Lyons, vol. 2, p. 540.
26. Ibid., p. 543.
27. Ovid, *Metamorphoses*, trans. Rolfe Humphries (Bloomington and London: Indiana University Press, 1955), pp. 241–43.
28. Laure de Margerie and Édouard Papet, *Charles Cordier: Les Nubiens 1848–1851*, exh. cat. (Le Havre: Musée Malraux; Paris: Somogy, 2011).
29. Ovid, *Metamorphoses*, trans. Humphries, p. 242.
30. Ibid., p. 243.
31. Ibid. Ovid, *Metamorphoses: A New Verse Translation*, trans. David Raeburn (London: Penguin Books, 2004), p. 396.
32. Ovid, *Metamorphoses*, trans. Raeburn, p. 396.
33. The comedy was adapted into the much loved musical *My Fair Lady*, filmed in 1964 with Audrey Hepburn in the role.
34. Shakespeare, *The Winter's Tale* (Act 5, Scene 2), pp. 221–22.
35. Ibid.
36. Ibid. (Act 5, Scene 3), p. 225.
37. See Kenneth Gross, *The Dream of the Moving Statue* (Ithaca, N.Y.: Cornell University Press, 1992); Laura Bossi, *De l'agalmatophilie ou l'amour des statues* (Paris: L'Echoppe, 2012); Marina Warner, *Alone of All Her Sex: The Myth and the Cult of the Virgin Mary* (New York: Alfred A. Knopf, 1976), pp. 158–60; Warner, "The Making of Pandora," p. 237. The rather ponderous term *agalmatophilia* also exists in English to describe the love of statues, and is used in psychiatric as well as literary and aesthetic contexts.
38. Shakespeare, *The Winter's Tale* (Act 5, Scene 3), pp. 226, 228.
39. Ibid., p. 228.
40. Ibid., pp. 225, 226.
41. Ibid., pp. 228, 229.
42. Van Eck, *Art, Agency and Living Presence*, pp. 19, 31–33.
43. Homer, *The Iliad*, trans. Robert Fagles ([New York]: Viking Penguin, 1991), pp. 483–87, bk. 18, ll. 558–709.
44. Maurice Merleau-Ponty, *Phenomenology of Perception*, trans. Colin Smith (1945; London and New York: Routledge, 2002).
45. *The Greek Anthology*, trans. W. R. Paton, 5 vols. (London: William Heinemann; New York: G. P. Putnam's Sons, 1916–18), vol. 3, pp. 392–403, epigrams 713–42.
46. Pliny, *Natural History*, trans. H. Rackham, The Loeb Classical Library (Cambridge, Mass.: Harvard University Press, 1952), vol. 9, pp. 308–11, bk. 35, ll. 65–66.
47. David Freedberg, *The Power of Images: Studies in the History and Theory of Response* (Chicago: The University of Chicago Press, 1989), pp. 13, 16–21, 121–24.
48. William A. Christian Jr., *The Stranger, the Tears, the Photograph, the Touch: Divine Presence in Spain and Europe since 1500* (Budapest: Central European University, 2017), esp. chap. 2, "Images as Beings: Blood, Sweat and Tears," pp. 29–64.
49. William Shakespeare, *Macbeth* (Act 1, Scene 4), ll. 12–15.
50. Giorgio Agamben, "L'Immagine immemoriale," in *La potenza del pensiero: Saggi e conferenze* (Vicenza: Neri Pozza, 2005). See also Leland de la Durantaye, *Giorgio Agamben: A Critical Introduction* (Stanford, Calif.: Stanford University Press, 2009).
51. Bruno Latour, "What is iconoclash? Or is there a world beyond the image wars?" in *Iconoclash: Beyond the Image-Wars in Science, Religion and Art*, ed. Peter Weibel and Bruno Latour (Karlsruhe: ZKM; Cambridge, Mass.: MIT Press, 2002), pp. 16–38.
52. Charles Baudelaire, "Morale du joujou," in *Baudelaire: Oeuvres complètes*, ed. Marcel A. Ruff (Paris: Éditions du Seuil, 1968), p. 358; translated as "The Philosophy of Toys," trans. Paul Keegan, in *On Dolls*, ed. Gross, pp. 11–21.
53. Baudelaire, "The Philosophy of Toys," p. 20.
54. Rainer Maria Rilke, "Some Reflections on Dolls (Occasioned by the Wax Dolls of Lotte Pritzel)," in Rainer Maria Rilke, *Rodin and Other Prose Pieces*, trans. G[ertrude] Craig Houston

(London: Quartet Books, 1986), pp. 119–26; *On Dolls*, ed. Gross, includes a slightly different translation by Idris Parry, "Dolls: On the Wax Dolls of Lotte Pritzel," pp. 51–62.

55. Rilke, "Some Reflections on Dolls," p. 120.

56. E. T. A. Hoffmann, "The Sand-Man," in *The Best Tales of Hoffmann*, ed. E. F. Bleiler, trans. J. T. Bealby (New York: Dover Publications, 1967), pp. 183–214; Sigmund Freud, *The Uncanny*, trans. David McLintock (London: Penguin Books, 2003), excerpted in *On Dolls*, ed. Gross, pp. 22–50. See also Marina Warner, *Phantasmagoria: Spirit Visions, Metaphors, and Media into the Twenty-First Century* (Oxford and New York: Oxford University Press, 2006), pp. 53–54.

57. D. W. Winnicott, *Playing and Reality* (1971; Hove: Brunner-Routledge, 2001), pp. 38–64; Marion Milner, *The Hands of the Living God: An Account of a Psycho-analytic Treatment* (London: Routledge, 2011). See Marina Warner, "Self-Portrait in a Rearview Mirror," and Mary Jacobus, "Magical Arts: From Play-Technique to Transitional Object," in *Only Make-Believe*, by Marina Warner et al., exh. cat. (Compton Verney, Warwickshire: Compton Verney House Trust, 2005), pp. 4–19, 20–32; the latter reprinted slightly differently as "Magical Arts: The Poetics of Play," in *The Poetics of Psychoanalysis in the Wake of Klein*, by Mary Jacobus (Oxford and New York: Oxford University Press, 2005), pp. 91–118.

58. Oskar Kokoschka, quoted in Marquard Smith, *The Erotic Doll: A Modern Fetish* (New Haven, Conn.: Yale University Press, 2013), p. 114.

59. Carol Mavor, *Aurelia: Art and Literature through the Mouth of the Fairy Tale* (London: Reaktion Books, 2017), p. 225.

60. Caroline van Eck discussed this perpetual phenomenon in "'At Rome the Love of Marble Possesses Most People like a New Sense': The Material Turn, 1770–1820," the last of her Slade lectures, Oxford, March 8, 2017.

Double or Nothing

This essay is in memory of my father, an organic-coatings chemist who knew his hues.

1. Species that have passed the "mirror self-recognition test" developed by Gordon G. Gallup Jr. in 1970 include gorillas, orangutans, chimpanzees, bonobos, bottlenose dolphins, orcas, Eurasian magpies, Asian elephants and (controversially) rhesus monkeys, gibbons, pigs, and ants. We humans fail the test until we reach eighteen months of age; before that, we find playmates in mirrors. See Amanda Pachniewska, "List of Animals That Have Passed the Mirror Test," *Animal Cognition*; www.animalcognition.org/2015/04/15/list-of-animals-that-have -passed-the-mirror-test. For the surprising ants, see Marie-Claire Cammaerts and Roger Cammaerts, "Are Ants (Hymenoptera, Formicidae) Capable of Self Recognition?" *Journal of Science* 5, no. 7 (2015), pp. 521–32. As for mirrors themselves, see Jay M. Enoch, "History of Mirrors Dating back 8000 Years," *Optometry and Vision Science* 83, no. 10 (October 2006), pp. 775–81; Marc N. Levine and David M. Carballo, eds., *Obsidian Reflections: Symbolic Dimensions of Obsidian in Mesoamerica* (Boulder: University Press of Colorado, 2014).

2. Waldemar Januszczak et al., "Chimpanzees as Artists," *Artists Ezine* 1, no. 6 (Spring–Summer 2006); www.artistsezine.com /WhyChimp.htm; Jared Diamond, "Animal Art: Variations in Bower Decorating Style among Male Bowerbirds *Amblyornis inornatus*," *Proceedings of the National Academy of Sciences of the United States of America* 83, no. 9 (May 1, 1986), pp. 3042–46.

3. See esp. Natasha Eaton, *Colour, Art and Empire: Visual Culture and the Nomadism of Representation* (London: I. B. Tauris, 2013).

4. See Carol Collier, *Recovering the Body: A Philosophical Story* (Ottawa: University of Ottawa Press, 2013). For the historical context of current philosophical takes on color and color perception, see Barbara Saunders and Jaap van Brakel, eds., *Theories, Technologies, Instrumentalities of Color: Anthropological and Historiographic Perspectives* (Lanham, Md.: University Press of America, 2002).

5. Molly Harbour Bassett and Jeannette Favrot Peterson, "Coloring the Sacred in Sixteenth-Century Central Mexico," in *The Materiality of Color: The Production, Circulation, and Application of Dyes and Pigments, 1400–1800*, ed. Andrea Feeser et al., The Histories of Material Culture and Collecting, 1700–1950 (Farnham, Surrey: Ashgate Publishing, 2012), pp. 45–64; Diana Young, "Mutable Things: Colours as Material Practice in the Northwest of South Australia," *Journal of the Royal Anthropological Institute*, n.s., 17, no. 2 (June 2011), pp. 356–76.

6. Two important exceptions, from the field of urban design and architecture: Lois Swirnoff, *Dimensional Color* (New York: Van Nostrand Reinhold, 1986); Johannes Itten, *The Art of Color: The Subjective Experience and Objective Rationale of Color* (New York: Reinhold Pub. Corp., 1961), arguing that without color there is no form.

7. Roberta Panzanelli et al., *The Color of Life: Polychromy in Sculpture from Antiquity to the Present*, exh. cat. (Los Angeles: J. Paul Getty Museum; Getty Research Institute, 2008); Una Roman D'Elia, "How the Quattrocento Saw Ancient Sculpture in Color," *Source: Notes in the History of Art* 35, no. 3 (Spring 2016), pp. 216–26.

8. Charles Blanc, *Grammaire des arts du dessein* (Paris: Jules Renouard, Libraire-Éditeur, 1867), p. 23, widely quoted, but I am using the translation by Rebecca Zorach in her review of *The Materiality of Color*, ed. Andrea Feeser et al., and *Prismatic Ecology: Ecotheory beyond Green*, ed. Jeffrey Jerome Cohen, *The Art Bulletin* 96, no. 4 (December 2014), pp. 489–91, quotation on p. 489.

9. Lorado Taft, "Introductory," in *Emergency Catalogue of the Exhibition of the National Sculpture Society under the Auspices of the Municipal Art Society of Baltimore, Fifth Regiment Armory, April 4th to April 25th Inclusive, Nineteen Eight* ([Baltimore: National Sculpture Society, 1908]), p. 20.

10. See, for example, Jonathan Cohen and Mohan Matthen, eds., *Color Ontology and Color Science* (Cambridge, Mass.: MIT Press, 2010); and Alex Byrne and David R. Hilbert, "Color Realism and Color Science," *Behavioral and Brain Sciences* 26, no. 1 (February 2003), pp. 3–21, a minority opinion.

11. David Batchelor, *Chromophobia* (London: Reaktion Books, 2000); Natasha Eaton, "Chromophobic Activism: The Politics and Materiality of Art and Colour in India, circa 1917–circa 1966," *Third Text* 28, no. 6 (December 2014), pp. 475–88. Michael Taussig, *What Color Is the Sacred?* (Chicago: The University of Chicago Press, 2009), puts chromophobia in the context of colonialism and racism. There have also been Western chromophiles; see Michel Pastoureau, *Blue: The History of a Color* (Princeton, N.J.: Princeton University Press, 2001), pp. 42–46, on the debate over color among Latin Christian theologians between A.D. 800 and 1200.

12. On physiological optics, see Denis Baylor, "Colour Mechanisms of the Eye," in *Colour: Art & Science*, ed. Trevor Lamb and Janine Bourriau (Cambridge and New York: Cambridge University Press, 1995), pp. 103–26. Reputable authorities debate the exact range of the visible spectrum as well as the number of discriminable colors. For the latter, see Victoria Finlay, *Color: A Natural History of the Palette* (New York: Random House, 2004), pp. 4–7; Joseph W. Lovibond, "The Tintometer—A New Instrument for the Analysis, Synthesis, Matching, and Measurement of Colour," *Journal of the Society of Dyers & Colourists* 3, no. 12 (December 26, 1887), pp. 186–93; Asim Kumar Roy Choudhury, *Principles of Colour and Appearance Measurement*, vol. 1, *Object Appearance, Colour Perception and Instrumental Measurement*, Woodhead Publishing Series in Textiles, 159 ([Amsterdam]: The Textile Institute; Cambridge: Woodhead Publishing, Elsevier, 2014), p. 228, on the nine million permutations; Kenichiro Masaoka et al., "Number of Discernible Object Colors Is a Conundrum," *Journal of the Optical Society of America* A 30, no. 2 (February 2013), pp. 264–77; Rolf G. Kuehni, "How Many Object Colors Can We Distinguish?" *Color Research and Application* 41, no. 5 (October 2016), pp. 439–44.

13. See Ian Paterson, *A Dictionary of Colour: A Lexicon of the Language of Colour* (London: Thorogood Publishing, 2003), p. 1; F. M. Rowf, review of *A Dictionary of Colour*, by Aloys J. Maerz and M. Rea Paul, *Journal of the Society of Chemical Industry* 50, no. 29 (July 17, 1931), p. 626, noting the 7,056 colors presented in the dictionary's color plates and the oddness of many color names.

14. Meyer Schapiro, "From Mozarabic to Romanesque in Silos," *The Art Bulletin* 21, no. 4 (December 1939), pp. 312–74. On cultural

metaphors and color lexicons, see Umberto Eco, "How Culture Conditions the Colours We See," in *On Signs*, ed. Marshall Blonsky (Baltimore: Johns Hopkins University Press, 1985), pp. 157–75; Brent Berlin and Paul Kay, *Basic Color Terms: Their Universality and Evolution* (Berkeley and Los Angeles: University of California Press, 1969), most intriguingly critiqued by Sandra Busatta, "The Perception of Color and the Meaning of Brilliance among Archaic and Ancient Populations and Its Reflections on Language," *Antrocom: Online Journal of Anthropology* 10, no. 2 (2014), pp. 309–47; http://www.antrocom.net/upload/sub/antrocom/100214/09-Antrocom.pdf.

15. On populations of colors, see Sidney R. Lehky and Terrence J. Sejnowski, "Seeing White: Qualia in the Context of Decoding Population Codes," *Neural Computation* 11 (1999), pp. 1261–80. See Christine A. Curcio et al., "Human Photoreceptor Topography," *Journal of Comparative Neurology*, no. 292 (1990), pp. 497–523, for the average numbers of cones and rods, ordinarily reported as 120,000,000 rods and 6,000,000 cones, as in the otherwise trustworthy compendium, Helen Varley, ed., *Colour* (1980; London: Marshall Editions, 1991), p. 32.

16. On metamerism and its implications, see George A. Agoston, *Color Theory and Its Application in Art and Design*, 2nd rev. ed., Springer Series in Optical Sciences, 19 (1970; Berlin: Springer-Verlag, 1987), pp. 40–41; David R. Hilbert, *Color and Color Perception: A Study in Anthropocentric Realism*, CSLI Lecture Notes, 9 (Stanford, Calif.: Center for the Study of Language and Information, 1987), chap. 5, pp. 81–100. Art historians, like dentists inserting implants, must also take into account "observer metamerism," in which different observers perceive color matches differently. See Michael A. Webster and Donald I. A. MacLeod, "Factors Underlying Individual Differences in the Color Matches of Normal Observers," *Journal of the Optical Society of America* A 5, no. 10 (October 1988), pp. 1722–35; Mark D. Fairchild and Rodney L. Heckaman, "Measuring Observer Metamerism: The Nimeroff Approach," *Color Research and Application* 41, no. 2 (April 2016), pp. 115–24. I am indebted here to a series of conversations with two color scientists, Harold Boll and Robert Poe, and to Poe's detailed responses to queries, by email March 11, 2017, and in conversation March 30, 2017.

17. This point is nicely made by Michael Tye, "On Some Alleged Problems for Objectivism about Color," in his *Consciousness, Color, and Content* (Cambridge, Mass.: MIT Press, 2000), pp. 145–70. On the history of negotiating color in the West, see John Gage, *Colour and Meaning: Art, Science, and Symbolism* (Berkeley and Los Angeles: University of California Press, 1999); John Gage, *Colour and Culture: Practice and Meaning from Antiquity to Abstraction* (Boston: Little, Brown, 1981). For a deft comparison of East and West, see Shigehisa Kuriyama, "The Expressiveness of Colors," in his *The Expressiveness of the Body and the Divergence of Greek and Chinese Medicine*, rev. ed. (1999; New York: Zone Books, 2002), pp. 153–92. I cannot address the political, religious, social, and medical meanings of any color or schema of colors. Gage does some of this work, as do Varley, ed., *Colour*, pp. 186–223; Herman Pleij, *Colors Demonic and Divine: Shades of Meaning in the Middle Ages and After* (2002; New York: Columbia University Press, 2004); Faber Birren, *Color: A Survey in Words and Pictures, from Ancient Mysticism to Modern Science* (Secaucus, N.J.: Citadel Press, 1963).

18. See esp. Jacqueline Lichtenstein, *The Eloquence of Color: Rhetoric and Painting in the French Classical Age* (1989; Berkeley and Los Angeles: University of California Press, 1993), which traces historical linkages between theories of the value and effect of bodily gestures in rhetoric and the value and effect of color in art.

19. On light and night throughout this paragraph and the next, see David Park, *The Fire within the Eye: A Historical Essay on the Nature and Meaning of Light* (Princeton, N.J.: Princeton University Press, 1997); Arthur Zajonc, *Catching the Light: The Entwined History of Light and Mind* (New York: Oxford University Press, 1993); A. Roger Ekirch, *At Day's Close: A History of Nighttime* (New York: W. W. Norton & Company, 2005); Wolfgang Schivelbusch, *Disenchanted Night: The Industrialization of Light in the Nineteenth Century* (1983; Berkeley and Los Angeles: University of California Press, 1988); Terry McGowan, "Light Pollution," in *Encyclopedia of Color Science and Technology*, ed. Ming Ronnier Luo (New York: Springer Reference, 2016), pp. 837–42. On

mirrors, see Mark Pendergrast, *Mirror Mirror: A History of the Human Love Affair with Reflection* (New York: Basic Books, 2003); Jurgis Baltrušaitis, *Le miroir: Essai sur une légende scientifique; Révélations, science-fiction et fallacies* (Paris: Elmayan, 1978). On glare (and mirrors, and gas lamps), see Edgar A[llan] Poe, "The Philosophy of Furniture," *Burton's Gentleman's Magazine* 6, no. 5 (May 1840), pp. 243–45, quotation on p. 244.

20. On climate change, art, and light, see Brian Fagan, *The Little Ice Age: How Climate Made History, 1300–1850* (New York: Basic Books, 2000); Wolfgang Behringer, Hartmut Lehmann, and Christian Pfister, eds., *Kulturelle Konsequenzen der "Kleinen Eiszeit"/Cultural Consequences of the "Little Ice Age,"* Veröffentlichungen des Max-Planck-Instituts für Geschichte, 212 (Göttingen: Vandenhoeck & Ruprecht, 2005); John A. Matthews and Keith R. Briffa, "The 'Little Ice Age': Re-evaluation of an Evolving Concept," *Geografiska Annaler* 87A, no. 1 (2005), pp. 17–36, noting different opening and closing years; Franz Ossing, "Der unvollständige Himmel: Zu Wolkendarstellung der holländischen Meister des 17. Jahrhunderts," in *Die "Kleine Eiszeit": Holländische Landschaftsmalerei im 17. Jahrhundert*, by Michael Budde et al., exh. cat. (Berlin: Gemäldegalerie, Staatlichen Museen zu Berlin Preußischer Kulturbesitz, 2001), pp. 41–54, and a typescript translation at http://bib.gfz-potsdam.de/pub/wegezurkunst/uncomplete_sky.pdf.

21. Mariana Figueiro, "Non-Visual Lighting Effects and Their Impact on Health and Well-Being," in *Encyclopedia of Color Science and Technology*, ed. Ronnier Luo, pp. 972–81, noting that the human circadian system is highly sensitive to long exposures to short-wavelength (blue) light.

22. The preeminence of the sense of sight, as well as many of the challenges to it, can be tracked through the essays in Constance Classen et al., *A Cultural History of the Senses*, 6 vols. (London: Bloomsbury Academic, 2014). For historical analysis of modern ambivalences toward vision, see Jonathan Crary, *Techniques of the Observer: On Vision and Modernity in the Nineteenth Century* (Cambridge, Mass.: MIT Press, 1990); Martin Jay, *Downcast Eyes: The Denigration of Vision in Twentieth-Century French Thought* (Berkeley and Los Angeles: University of California Press, 1993).

23. On aging and sight in general, see John S. Werner, David H. Peterzell, and A. J. Scheetz, "Light, Vision, and Aging," *Optometry and Vision Science* 67, no. 3 (March 1990), pp. 214–29; Jun Xu, Joel Pokorny, and Vivianne C. Smith, "Optical Density of the Human Lens," *Journal of the Optical Society of America* A 14, no. 5 (May 1997), pp. 953–60. On night vision, see Pamela A. Sample et al., "The Aging Lens: In Vivo Assessment of Light Absorption in 84 Human Eyes," *Investigative Ophthalmology & Visual Science* 29, no. 8 (August 1988), pp. 1306–11; Gregory R. Jackson, Cynthia Owsley, and Gerald McGwin Jr., "Aging and Dark Adaptation," *Vision Research* 39 (1999), pp. 3975–82. On color vision, see K. H. Ruddock, "The Effect of Age upon Colour Vision: I. Response in the Receptoral System of the Human Eye; II. Changes with Age in Light Transmission of the Ocular Media," *Vision Research* 5 (1965), pp. 37–45, 47–58.

24. Stanley Coren and Joan Stern Girgus, *Seeing Is Deceiving: The Psychology of Visual Illusions* (Hillsdale, N.J.: Lawrence Erlbaum Associates, 1978)—most of which illusions are presented in black-and-white or gray-scale; Harold Boll, "There Is More to Color than Meets the Eye," PowerPoint lecture, New Hampshire Institute of Art, Manchester, N.H., February 28, 2017, furnished by the author, with subsequent conversations.

25. On cochineal, see Carmella Padilla et al., *A Red Like No Other: How Cochineal Colored the World; An Epic Story of Art, Culture, Science, and Trade*, exh. cat. (New York: Skira Rizzoli; Santa Fe, N.Mex.: Museum of International Folk Art, 2015); Elena Phipps, "Cochineal Red: The Art History of a Color," *The Metropolitan Museum of Art Bulletin* 67, no. 3 (Winter 2010), pp. 1–48, cover illus. On indigo, see Eaton, *Colour, Art and Empire*; Taussig, *What Color Is the Sacred?*, pp. 141–63; Boris Wiseman, "The Materiality of Color," *The Senses and Society* 8, no. 2 (July 2013), pp. 223–31. On malachite, see Rock H. Currier, "Into the Heart of Darkness: Searching for Minerals in the Democratic Republic of the Congo," *Mineralogical Record* 33, no. 6 (2002), pp. 473–87.

26. Broadly, see Philip Ball, *Bright Earth: The Invention of Colour* (London and New York: Viking Press, 2001); David Bomford and Ashok Roy, *A Closer Look: Colour*, rev. ed. (2000; London: National

Gallery, 2009); Manlio Brusatin, *A History of Colors* (1983; Boston: Shambhala, 1991); Feeser et al., eds., *The Materiality of Color*. On the Renaissance efflorescence of colors, see Marcia B. Hall, *Color and Meaning: Practice and Theory in Renaissance Painting* (Cambridge and New York: Cambridge University Press, 1992). On Schweinfurt green, see Michel Pastoureau, *Green: The History of a Color* (Princeton, N.J.: Princeton University Press, 2014), pp. 183–85. On coal-tar derivative (aniline) colors, see Simon Garfield, *Mauve: How One Man Invented a Colour That Changed the World* (London: Faber & Faber, 2000); Robert Hunt, "Mauve and Magenta," *The St. James's Magazine* 1 (April–July 1861), pp. 43–46; Mrs. [Mary Philadelphia] Merrifield, "The Use and Abuse of Colours in Dress," *The St. James's Magazine* 1 (April–July 1861), pp. 289–95. On the socioeconomic consequences of the synthesis and industrial production of colors, see Iona Singh, "Color, Facture, Art, and Design," *Capitalism Nature Socialism* 18 (March 2007), pp. 64–80.

27. Tomoko Hashida, Yasuaki Kakehi, and Takeshi Naemura, "Photochromic Sculpture: Volumetric Color-Forming Pixels," in *Proceeding* SIGGRAPH *'11* ACM SIGGRAPH *2011 Studio Talks, Vancouver, British Columbia, Canada—August 07–11, 2011* (New York: ACM, 2011), article no. 11; http://dl.acm.org/citation.cfm?id=2037714.

28. Mary Lisa Gavenas, *Color Stories: Behind the Scenes of America's Billion-Dollar Beauty Industry* (New York: Simon & Schuster, 2002).

29. See, for example, Roderick Floud et al., *The Changing Body: Health, Nutrition, and Human Development in the Western World since 1700*, NBER Series on Long-Term Factors in Economic Development (Cambridge and New York: Cambridge University Press, 2011). A proviso: little in this paragraph applies to the bodies of the most impoverished, abused, and unprotected. Indeed, a counter-history may be called for, as also a counter-exhibition.

30. One of the few histories of sculpture that takes color consistently into account is Tom Flynn, *The Body in Three Dimensions* (New York: Harry N. Abrams, 1998). For a perceptive account of figural sculpture as it took on color since the late 1700s, see Alex Potts, "Colors of Sculpture," in *The Color of Life*, by Panzanelli et al., pp. 78–97.

31. For the quotation, see Jacob Epstein, *Let There Be Sculpture* (New York: G. P. Putnam's Sons, [1940]). I thank the painter Shelley Mackenzie for discussing her own color work with me as well as putting me in touch with Bruce Wood and with another sculptor, Glenn W. Szegedy, whose email responses (February 22 and March 8, 2017) to my queries helped shape the questions I have been asking of historical materials.

32. Lynn Meskell et al., "Figurines," in *Çatalhöyük 2016 Archive Report*, ed. Scott D. Haddow ([Çatalhöyük, Turkey, 2017]), pp. 137–64; http://www.catalhoyuk.com/archive_reports/2016.

33. Susan Stewart, *On Longing: Narratives of the Miniature, the Gigantic, the Souvenir, the Collection* (Baltimore and London: Johns Hopkins University Press, 1984).

34. Irwin M. Braverman, "Anatomy and Physiology of the Cutaneous Microcirculation," in *Bioengineering of the Skin: Cutaneous Blood Flow and Erythema*, ed. Enzo Berardesca, Peter Elsner, and Howard I. Maibach (Boca Raton, Fla.: CRC Press, 1995), pp. 3–22.

35. Hillel Schwartz, *The Culture of the Copy: Striking Likenesses, Unreasonable Facsimiles*, rev. ed. (1996; New York: Zone Books, 2014); and compare, of course, Walter Benjamin, "The Work of Art in the Age of Mechanical Reproduction [1936]," in *Illuminations*, ed. Hannah Arendt (New York: Schocken Books, 1968), pp. 217–51; Jean Baudrillard, *Simulacra and Simulation* (Ann Arbor: University of Michigan Press, 1994).

36. Varley, ed., *Colour*, pp. 52–55.

37. See esp. Elizabeth Harper, "Photographing the Real Bodies of Incorrupt Saints," in *Atlas Obscura* (June 30, 2015); http://www.atlasobscura.com/articles/photographing-the-real-bodies-of-incorrupt-saints.

38. Julia R. R. Drell, "Neanderthals: A History of Interpretation," *Oxford Journal of Archaeology* 19, no. 1 (February 2000), pp. 1–24; "What Happened to the Caveman Dioramas?" in *The Field Museum* [Chicago]; http://www.fieldmuseum.org/node/5036; Anne Hamilton, "Popular Depictions of Neanderthals," *Totem: The University of Western Ontario Journal of Anthropology* 13, no. 1 (2005), pp. 85–92; Alan E. Mann, "Imagining Prehistory: Pictorial Reconstructions of the Way We Were," *American Anthropologist* 105, no. 1 [*Biological Anthropology*] (March 2003), pp. 139–43; Stephanie Moser, *Ancestral Images: The Iconography of Human Origins* (Ithaca, N.Y.: Cornell University Press, 1998), esp. pp. 146–67.

39. Rachel Fulton, *From Judgment to Passion: Devotion to Christ and the Virgin Mary, 800–1200* (New York: Columbia University Press, 2002); Caroline Walker Bynum, *Jesus as Mother: Studies in the Spirituality of the High Middle Ages* (Berkeley and Los Angeles: University of California Press, 1982).

40. For simulation dummies, see "Manikins for Training," including hazmat manikins and firefighters' manikins, at the supplier website *Alternate Force* (Cato, N.Y.); http://www.alternateforce.net/madu.html; and Lore Croghan, "NY Disaster Simulation Center Awash in Fake Blood," *Daily News* (New York), September 7, 2011; http://www.nydailynews.com/life-style/health/bellevue-hospital-disaster-simulation-center-mannequins-shed-fake-blood-give-fake-birth-article-1.952672.

The Presumption of White

1. G[eorg] W[ilhelm] F[riedrich] Hegel, *Aesthetics: Lectures on Fine Art*, trans. T. M. Knox, 2 vols. (Oxford: Clarendon Press, 1975), vol. 2, p. 734.

2. On the late eighteenth-century rise of embodied or subjective vision, see Jonathan Crary, *Techniques of the Observer: On Vision and Modernity in the Nineteenth Century* (Cambridge, Mass.: MIT Press, 1990).

3. Hegel, *Aesthetics*, vol. 2, p. 732.

4. Ibid., p. 726.

5. Joshua Reynolds, *The Discourses of Sir Joshua Reynolds*, annot. John Burnet (London: James Carpenter, 1842), p. 171.

6. Hiram Powers, quoted in Charles Colbert, "Spiritual Currents and Manifest Destiny in the Art of Hiram Powers," *The Art Bulletin* 82, no. 3 (September 2000), p. 533.

7. Felicia H. Sternfeld, *Georg Scholz (1890–1945): Monographie und Werkverzeichnis* (Frankfurt: Peter Lang, 2004), p. 208.

8. Benvenuto Cellini, quoted in Jacqueline Lichtenstein, *The Blind Spot: An Essay on the Relations between Painting and Sculpture in the Modern Age* (Los Angeles: Getty Research Institute, 2008), p. 4.

9. Hegel, *Aesthetics*, vol. 2, p. 706.

10. Ibid., p. 776. In reality, of course, the "whiteness" of marble was more rhetorical than actual. It was well known that marbles extracted from different geographical locations had varying hues.

11. [Johann Wolfgang von Goethe], *Goethe's Theory of Colours*, trans. and annot. Charles Lock Eastlake (London: John Murray, 1840), p. 204.

12. See esp. Daniel Purdy, "The Whiteness of Beauty: Weimar Neo-Classicism and the Sculptural Transcendence of Color," in *Colors 1800/1900/2000: Signs of Ethnic Difference*, ed. Birgit Tautz, pp. 83–99, Amsterdamer Beiträge zur neueren Germanistik, 56 (Amsterdam and New York: Brill, Rodopi, 2004).

13. Johann Joachim Winckelmann, *History of the Art of Antiquity*, trans. Harry Francis Mallgrave (Los Angeles: Getty Research Institute, 2006), p. 195.

14. Powers, quoted in "Fine Art Gossip," *The Literary World*, no. 216 (March 22, 1851), p. 237.

15. Donald M. Reynolds, "The 'Unveiled Soul': Hiram Powers's Embodiment of the Ideal," *The Art Bulletin* 59, no. 3 (September 1977), p. 402 n. 47.

16. Hegel, *Aesthetics*, vol. 2, p. 731.

17. Étienne Maurice Falconet, "Sculpture," in *The Encyclopedia of Diderot & d'Alembert Collaborative Translation Project*, trans. Nelly S. Hoyt and Thomas Cassirer (1765; Ann Arbor: Michigan Publishing, University of Michigan Library, 2003); https://quod.lib.umich.edu/d/did/did2222.0000.166/--sculpture?rgn=main;view=fulltext.

18. [Louis-Antoine de Caraccioli], *Dictionnaire critique, pittoresque et sentencieux, propre à faire connoître les usages du siècle, ainsi que ses bizarreries*, 3 vols. (Lyon: Benoît Duplain, Libraire, 1768), vol. 2, s.v. "Peindre," quoted in Melissa Hyde, "The 'Makeup' of the Marquise: Boucher's Portrait of Pompadour at Her Toilette," *The Art Bulletin* 82, no. 3 (September 2000), p. 462.

19. "Salon de 1808.—No. XVIII. Sculpture.—M. Canova," *Journal de l'Empire*, January 4, 1809, pp. 3–4. On this review and more generally on Canova's coloration of *Hebe*, see David Bindman, "Lost Surfaces: Canova and Color," *Oxford Art Journal* 39, no. 2 (August 2016), pp. 238–40.

20. Lady [Elizabeth Rigby] Eastlake, ed., *Life of John Gibson, R.A., Sculptor* (London: Longmans, Green, and Co., 1870), p. 212.

21. Ibid., p. 211.

22. "John Gibson, R.A.," *The Athenaeum* (London), no. 1997 (February 3, 1866), p. 172.

23. Paul Mantz, "Exposition de Londres: Peinture et Sculpture, III," *Gazette des Beaux-Arts* 3 (1862), p. 374; translation by the author.

24. Richard Westmacott, *On Colouring Statues: Some Observations on Ancient and Modern Polychromy in Sculpture* (London: The Archaeological Institute, 1859), p. 28.

25. [David d'Angers], *Les Carnets de David d'Angers*, ed. André Bruel, 2 vols. (Paris: Librairie Plon, 1958), vol. 1, pp. 182–83; translation by the author.

Likeness

1. "By 'naturalistic portraiture,' I mean physiognomic likeness which is seen to refer to the identity of the living or once-living person depicted. The genre existed in antiquity and the early Christian world, in the form of statues, busts and herms, coins, sarcophagi, wall-paintings. . . . The 'rebirth' of portraiture is considered a definitive feature of the Renaissance." Joanna Woodall, "Introduction: Facing the Subject," in *Portraiture: Facing the Subject*, ed. Joanna Woodall (Manchester and New York: Manchester University Press, 1997), p. 1.

2. Whether outside the West or in medieval Europe, the absence of realism was historically seen as a mark of inferior aesthetics and culture. Realism was also considered in contrast to the religious, symbolic, and abstract. Non-Western art historians have pushed back against such colonialist readings of areas outside the West, occasionally swinging the narrative pendulum to the opposite extreme and glossing over periods of non-Western realism in order to forcefully stake a claim for the values of the symbolic and nonrealistic. For Western assumptions regarding non-Western art and some artistic and scholarly strategies to disrupt such narratives, see Catherine King and Gill Perry with Nicola Durbridge, "Introduction," in *Views of Difference: Different Views of Art*, ed. Catherine King (New Haven, Conn.: Yale University Press, 1999), pp. 7–22.

3. Francesco Caglioti, "Niccolò da Uzzano," in *The Renaissance Portrait from Donatello to Bellini*, by Keith Christiansen et al., exh. cat. (New York: The Metropolitan Museum of Art, 2011), p. 126, no. 22. For the attribution to Donatello, see Luke Syson, "Polychrome and Its Discontents," in this volume, p. 16.

4. "The 1985 cleaning of the bust revealed that it is pieced together from separate casts and is not based solely on one cast of the face, frontal neck, and shoulders, as so many of us once thought. One cast circumscribes the cranium and continues to the nape of the neck, another includes a facial mask, while a third includes the frontal chest and neck area. The ears are modeled separately." Jane Schuyler, "Death Masks in Quattrocento Florence," *Source: Notes in the History of Art* 5, no. 4 (Summer 1986), pp. 3–4.

5. While many early Renaissance terracotta busts were likely painted, the paint was either stripped off or overpainted during the intervening centuries.

6. James David Draper et al., *Playing with Fire: European Terracotta Models, 1740–1840*, exh. cat. (New York: The Metropolitan Museum of Art, 2003), p. 20.

7. The work emerged out of a confluence of factors, including the evolving close relationship between patrons and artists in Nuremberg, a greater emphasis on the oeuvre and individuality of the artist, Van der Schardt's active participation in Kunstkammer collecting, his understanding of the medieval precedent of polychromed sculptural self-portraits in architecture, his exposure to the ideals of antiquity in Italy, and his desire to participate in the prevailing *paragone* debates. Frits Scholten, "Johan Gregor van der Schardt and the Moment of Self-Portraiture in Sculpture," *Simiolus: Netherlands Quarterly for the History of Art* 33, no. 4 (2007/2008), pp. 201–3.

8. Ibid., p. 216.

9. When the Rijksmuseum, Amsterdam, acquired the Van der Schardt self-portrait in 2000, one journalist rightly noted, "Not even modernism is more naturalistic and more radical" ("Naturalistischer, ja radikaler ist auch die Moderne nicht"). See "Feuilleton," *Frankfurter Allgemeine Zeitung für Deutschland*, no. 260 (November 8, 2000), p. 65.

10. Rebecca Messbarger, "As Who Dare Gaze the Sun: Anna Morandi Manzolini's Wax Anatomies of the Male Reproductive System and Genitalia," in *Italy's Eighteenth Century: Gender and Culture in the Age of the Grand Tour*, by Paula Findlen et al. (Stanford, Calif.: Stanford University Press, 2009), p. 256.

11. Anna Morandi Manzolini made a companion portrait bust of her husband, Giovanni Manzolini, who similarly is elegantly dressed and holds the tools of his trade, with an anatomical sample before him.

12. Giovanni Ricci, "Masks of Power: Funeral Effigies in Early Modern Europe," in *Waxing Eloquent: Italian Portraits in Wax*, by Andrea Daninos et al., exh. cat. (Venice: Palazzo Fortuny; Milan: Officina Libraria, 2012), p. 61.

13. Ibid., p. 64.

14. For devotional waxworks including Piò's most well-known wax sculpture *The Holy Family* in the Church of Santi Vitale e Agricola, Bologna, see Andrea Daninos, "Wax Figures in Italy: Outline for a Story Yet to Be Written," in *Waxing Eloquent*, by Daninos et al., pp. 40–41.

15. In 1786 the artist and engraver Thomas Daniel arrived in Calcutta with his nephew William. Their first prints of the colonial capital, titled *Views of Calcutta*, were completed by 1788 and printed and hand colored by Indian assistants. A few years earlier Lady Mary Impey, wife of Sir Elijah Impey, Chief Justice of Bengal, commissioned the well-known artist Bhawani Das, who was trained in Mughal miniature painting, to make extensive natural-history studies at the Impey estate in Calcutta. Other East India Company officers sought a visual record of their own households, including animals, possessions, and servants. Vidya Dehejia, *Indian Art* (London: Phaidon Press, 1997), p. 396.

16. Susan S. Bean, *Yankee India: American Commercial and Cultural Encounters with India in the Age of Sail, 1784–1860* (Salem, Mass.: Peabody Essex Museum; Chidambaram, Ahmedabad: Mapin Publishing, 2001), p. 216.

17. According to Briggs's records, the models were "copied from nature," and there is a no-longer-extant seventh model "executed by the same hand, of a Greek antique statue of the boy extracting a thorn." Ibid., p. 184. The latter refers to the famous *Spinario*, widely circulated through replicas and prints; no doubt, through this means it had become known to the Bengali artist who chose to reproduce it.

18. For the sculptures, see ibid., pp. 184–85, 215, 221. For relations between the East India merchants in Boston and their trading partners, the *banians* of Calcutta, see ibid., pp. 213–17.

19. Ibid., p. 216.

20. These ethnographic models became a regular feature of British displays from their Indian colony. "Krishnanagar sculptors garnered awards at fairs, including Paris 1855 and 1867, Melbourne 1881, Amsterdam 1883, Boston 1883, London 1886, and Glasgow 1888." Susan S. Bean, "The Unfired Clay Sculpture of Bengal in the Artscape of Modern South Asia," in *A Companion to Asian Art and Architecture*, ed. Rebecca M. Brown and Deborah S. Hutton (Chichester, West Sussex, and Malden, Mass.: Wiley-Blackwell, 2011), p. 622.

21. Dennis Adrian, *The Real and Ideal in Figurative Sculpture: John De Andrea, Duane Hanson*, exh. cat. (Chicago: Museum of Contemporary Art, 1974), p. [6].

22. Duane Hanson, "Unpublished. Written in Davie, Florida, 12 November 1973," in *Duane Hanson*, ed. Rebecca Lewin, exh. cat. (London: Serpentine Galleries; Koenig Books, 2015), p. 51.

23. "Hanson was going for realness, a term used by drag queens in competitions when portraying archetypes. . . . The word 'archetype' is important here because Hanson was often dismissed as someone who worked in stereotypes—ontologically similar but wrong. Archetypes depict universal modes of being that reconfigure themselves over and over again across time, geography and culture. Stereotypes are exaggerated characteristics temporarily tainted with conscious or subconscious contempt." Douglas Coupland, "Duane Hanson: Realness, not Realism," in *Duane Hanson*, ed. Lewin, p. 133.

24. Marianne Kinkel, *Races of Mankind: The Sculptures of Malvina Hoffman* (Urbana, Chicago, and Springfield: University of Illinois Press, 2011), p. 6.

25. "I first examine and compare a great number of individuals, I study the form of their head, the traits of their visage, the expression of their physiognomy; I apply myself to seize the characters common to the race that I desire to represent, I appreciate them in their ensemble as well as in their details, I embrace for each one of them the range of individual variations, I come to conceive the ideal or rather, the type of each one of these characters, then grouping all those partial types, I constitute in my mind an ensemble type where I find reunited all the special beauty of that race which I study.... After having thus conceived the ideal type of a race (I do not relate to reproduce it from my mere memories), I seek among the individuals that I have studied and compared those who present in the highest degree the reunion of the special beauties of his race, and that is the one that I choose to execute in an exact and characteristic sculpture." Cordier, quoted in ibid., p. 8.

26. Charmaine A. Nelson, *Representing the Black Female Subject in Western Art* (New York and London: Routledge, Taylor & Francis Group, 2010), p. 165.

27. The pairing of The Metropolitan Museum of Art's busts was the result of a special order. *The Jewish Woman of Algiers* (1862, cat. 30) is normally associated with the *Cheik Arabe* and *La Capresse des Colonies* (1861, RF 2996) with the *Nègre du Soudan* (1856–57, RF 2997), according to the Musée d'Orsay, Paris, website catalogue records.

28. Nelson, *Representing the Black Female Subject*, pp. 165, 168.

29. Édouard Papet, "Ethnographic Life Casts in the Nineteenth Century," in *Facing the Other: Charles Cordier (1827–1905), Ethnographic Sculptor*, by Laure de Margerie et al., exh. cat. (Paris: Musée d'Orsay; New York: Harry N. Abrams, 2004), p. 127.

30. Nelson, *Representing the Black Female Subject*, p. 168.

31. "The 1933 exhibition promoted scientific racism, which defined a set of racial categories based on physical appearance. Having concluded that people belong to fundamentally different racial categories, it was only a short step to decide that they should be treated differently." The Field Museum, [Chicago], "Rethinking the Sculptures of Malvina Hoffman" (N.p.: Google Arts and Culture, [2016]); https://www.google.com/culturalinstitute/beta/u/o/exhibit/bQIyoCOTLheZKA.

32. Ibid.

33. Malvina Hoffman, *Yesterday Is Tomorrow: A Personal History* (New York: Crown Publishers, 1965), p. 150.

34. Janis Connor, "The Ethereal Icon: Malvina Hoffman's Worshipful Imagery of Anna Pavlova," in *Perspectives on American Sculpture before 1925*, ed. Thayer Tolles, The Metropolitan Museum of Art Symposia (New York: The Metropolitan Museum of Art, 2003), p. 148.

35. Yoko Kawaguchi, "Hara-Kiri!: Sadayakko and Madame Hanako on the Western Stage," in *Butterfly's Sisters: The Geisha in Western Culture* (New Haven, Conn.: Yale University Press, 2010), p. 199.

36. Barbara Drake Boehm, "Reliquary Busts: 'A Certain Aristocratic Eminence,'" in *Set in Stone: The Face in Medieval Sculpture*, by Charles T. Little et al., exh. cat. (New York: The Metropolitan Museum of Art, 2006), p. 168.

37. Ibid., p. 170.

38. Ibid., p. 171.

39. "My body I give to my dear friend Doctor Southwood Smith to be disposed of in a manner hereinafter mentioned, and I direct...he will take my body under his charge and take the requisite and appropriate measures for the disposal and preservation of the several parts of my bodily frame in the manner expressed in the paper annexed to this my will and at the top of which I have written Auto Icon. The skeleton he will cause to be put together in such a manner as that the whole figure may be seated in a chair usually occupied by me when living, in the attitude in which I am sitting when engaged in thought in the course of time employed in writing. I direct that the body thus prepared shall be transferred to my executor. He will cause the skeleton to be clad in one of the suits of black occasionally worn by me. The body so clothed, together with the chair and the staff in the my later years bourne by me." Extract from Jeremy Bentham's will, Queens Square Place, Westminster, Wednesday, May 30, 1832.

"Auto-Icon," in *University College London*; http://www.ucl.ac.uk/bentham-project/who/autoicon.

40. Tip Toland, quoted in Emily Donahoe, "Same Tree," *Helena Independent Record*, November 10, 2005.

41. Glenn R. Brown, *Tip Toland: Cycle of Life*, exh. cat. (New York: Nancy Margolis Gallery, 2005), n.p.

42. Marina Pacini, "Marisol: A Biographical Sketch," in *Marisol: Sculptures and Works on Paper*, by Marina Pacini et al., exh. cat. (Memphis: Memphis Brooks Museum of Art; New Haven, Conn.: Yale University Press, 2014), p. 44.

43. Meyer Schapiro, in *The Artist's Studio: Meyer Schapiro Visits George Segal*, film produced and directed by Michael Blackwood (New York: Michael Blackwood Productions, 1979), 28 mins.

44. Lisa M. Messinger, "Twentieth Century Art," in *Notable Acquisitions, 1981–1982* (New York: The Metropolitan Museum of Art, 1982), p. 61.

45. The delicacy of the painting was noted by its donor Paul Jenkins, who wrote in a letter to William Lieberman, then-director of twentieth-century art at the Metropolitan Museum, that "it can be viewed as one of his [Segal's] first polychrome or fresco painted sculptures. It is so sensitively painted that it makes you think not of a Della Robbia but of an Odilon Redon, delicately done in pastels." Paul Jenkins, letter to William L[ie]berman, January 13, 1981, Object Files, Modern and Contemporary Art, The Metropolitan Museum of Art, New York.

46. Schapiro, in *The Artist's Studio: Meyer Schapiro Visits George Segal*.

47. In response to being asked why it was important that he worked outside, Ahearn responded: "That has to do with circulating the activity and keeping it public. People are a lot more natural and trusting outside than they would be in a private studio setting. It also allows me to display some of the completed casts which relate to the sculpture that I am doing at the moment. I hang the other casts on nails on the outside of the building. It makes it an event and I like the feedback that I get from the audience." *John Ahearn: Horizons*, exh. cat. (Kansas City, Mo.: The Nelson-Atkins Museum of Art, 1990), n.p.

48. Ibid.

49. Megan Murray, "Casting Director: A Sculptor Who Makes His Living Preserving the Neighborhood," *Daily News* (New York), *Sunday News Magazine*, July 3, 1983, pp. 12–13.

50. "The neoclassicist's privileging of uncoloured sculpture was ironically later reinforced by modernist sculpture's insistence on 'truth to materials,' which, for different reasons, insisted that sculpture reveal rather than disguise its material." Alexander Sturgis, *Presence: The Art of Portrait Sculpture*, exh. cat. (Woodbridge, Suffolk: Antique Collectors' Club, 2012), p. 49. Although the practice of casting was known in the ancient world, artists after the Renaissance used it as an aid but distanced themselves from mechanical reproduction, finding in its technique a lack of artistry and spirit. Rodin even observed, "A cast from life is the most exact copy that one can obtain, but it is without life, that is to say that it has neither movement nor eloquence, and it says very little." Auguste Rodin, quoted in Édouard Papet, "Historical Life Casting," in *Second Skin: Historical Life Casting and Contemporary Sculpture*, by Stephen Feeke et al., exh. cat. (Leeds: Henry Moore Institute, 2002), p. [8].

Desire for Life

1. Lucian, "A Literary Prometheus," in *The Works of Lucian of Samosata*, trans. H. W. Fowler and F. G. Fowler, 4 vols. (Oxford: Clarendon Press, 1905), vol. 1, p. 8.

2. On representations of Prometheus, see Olga Raggio, "The Myth of Prometheus: Its Survival and Metamorphoses up to the Eighteenth Century," *Journal of the Warburg and Courtauld Institutes* 21, nos. 1–2 (January–June 1958), pp. 44–62, pls. 4–10.

3. Genesis 2:7; Douay-Rheims Bible. On Prometheus, see, for example, Lactantius, "The Epitome of the Divine Institutes," in *The Ante-Nicene Fathers: Translations of the Writings of the Fathers down to A.D. 325*, ed. Alexander Roberts and James Donaldson, vol. 7 (Buffalo, N.Y.: The Christian Literature Company, 1886), pp. 230–31.

4. Lactantius, "The Epitome of the Divine Institutes," pp. 230–31.

5. For a discussion of these issues, see, for example Jacqueline E. Jung, "The Tactile and the Visionary: Notes on the Place of

Sculpture in the Medieval Religious Imagination," in *Looking Beyond: Visions, Dreams, and Insights in Medieval Art & History*, ed. Colum Hourihane, Index of Christian Art Occasional Papers, 11 (Princeton, N.J.: Department of Art and Archaeology, Princeton University, 2010), pp. 202–40.

6.   Rupert of Deutz, *De gloria et honore Filii hominis super Mattheum*, ed. Rhabanus Haacke, CCCM, 29 (Turnhout: Brepols Publishers, 1979), pp. 382–83, quoted in Sara Lipton, "'The Sweet Lean of His Head': Writing about Looking at the Crucifix in the High Middle Ages," *Speculum: A Journal of Medieval Studies* 80, no. 4 (October 2005), pp. 1175–76.

7.   Ovid, *Metamorphoses*, trans. Charles Martin (New York and London: W. W. Norton & Company, 2004), p. 350, bk. 10, ll. 313–19.

8.   Ibid., ll. 324–26.

9.   Ibid., p. 351, bk. 10, ll. 353–63.

10. See, for example, Paul Barolsky, "As in Ovid, So in Renaissance Art," *Renaissance Quarterly* 51, no. 2 (Summer 1998), pp. 451–74; Victor I. Stoichita, *The Pygmalion Effect from Ovid to Hitchcock* (2006; Chicago: The University of Chicago Press, 2008).

11. Oil on canvas, 50.2 x 69.2 cm, Art Gallery of Ontario, Toronto.

12. John De Andrea, quoted in Jane Fudge, "Galatea and Company," in *John De Andrea: Painted Bronze*, exh. cat. (New York: Bernarducci Meisel Gallery, 2011), n.p.

13. Marina Warner, *Phantasmagoria: Spirit Visions, Metaphors, and Media into the Twenty-First Century* (Oxford and New York: Oxford University Press, 2006), p. 49.

14. There is a vast literature on automata. See, in particular, Jessica Riskin, "The Defecating Duck, or, the Ambiguous Origins of Artificial Life," *Critical Inquiry* 29, no. 4 (Summer 2003), pp. 599–633; Adelheid Voskuhl, *Androids in the Enlightenment: Mechanics, Artisans, and Cultures of the Self* (Chicago: The University of Chicago Press, 2013).

15. René Descartes, *The Philosophical Writings of Descartes*, ed. and trans. John Cottingham, Robert Stoothoff, and Dugald Murdoch, 3 vols. (Cambridge and New York: Cambridge University Press, 1984–91), vol. 1, p. 99.

16. Julien Offray de la Mettrie, *Machine Man and Other Writings*, trans. and ed. Ann Thomson (Cambridge and New York: Cambridge University Press, 1996), p. 39.

17. David M. Fryer and John C. Marshall, "The Motives of Jacques de Vaucanson," *Technology and Culture* 20, no. 2 (April 1979), pp. 258–59.

18. Auguste de Villiers de l'Isle-Adam, *L'Ève future* (Paris, 1886), translated by Robert Martin Adams as *The Future Eve*, in *The Decadent Reader: Fiction, Fantasy, and Perversion from Fin-de-siècle France*, ed. Asti Hustvedt (New York: Zone Books, 1998), pp. 497–750.

19. Émile Pierre, "L'Ève future par Villiers de l'Isle-Adam," *Le Chat noir*, May 29, 1886, p. 712.

Proxy Figures

1.   Adam Geczy, ed., *The Artificial Body in Fashion and Art: Marionettes, Models, and Mannequins* (London: Bloomsbury Academic, 2017), p. 2.

2.   Amy Knight Powell, *Depositions: Scenes from the Late Medieval Church and the Modern Museum* (New York: Zone Books, 2012), pp. 85–86.

3.   Dione Flühler-Kreis, Peter Wyer, and Donat Stuppan, *Die Holzskulpturen des Mittelalters: Katalog der Sammlung des Schweizerischen Landesmuseums Zürich* (Zurich: Schweizerisches Landesmuseum, 2007), p. 199.

4.   Powell, *Depositions*, p. 89.

5.   Jane Munro et al., *Silent Partners: Artist and Mannequin from Function to Fetish*, exh. cat. (Cambridge: Fitzwilliam Museum; New Haven, Conn.: Yale University Press, 2014), p. 32.

6.   D. Medina Lasansky, *The Renaissance Perfected: Architecture, Spectacle, and Tourism in Fascist Italy* (University Park, Pa.: The Pennsylvania State University Press, 2004), pp. 149–50.

7.   Ibid., pp. 145–46.

8.   "In their wider usage, both words have acquired additional meanings: 'lay figure,' for example, is also used to signify 'a person lacking in individuality, a nonentity, an unrealistic character in a novel etc.'; while 'layman' now more commonly designates a non-specialist, or member of the laity. In English, both 'mannequin' and 'manikin' exist, the former being more commonly applied to describe a model used by artists, dressmakers and couturiers (again, the French origins of the term are likely to be important), while the latter is applied more often to figures used in scientific research and training, medical especially, and to ornithologists denotes a particularly extrovert species of bird." Munro et al., *Silent Partners*, p. 4.

9.   Marjorie Shelley, "Mannequins: A Tool of the Artist's Workshop," in *Now at the Met* (New York: The Metropolitan Museum of Art, 2016); http://www.metmuseum.org/blogs/now-at-the-met/2016/mannequins-as-tool-of-the-artist-workshop.

10. Munro et al., *Silent Partners*, p. 39.

11. Bjarne Jørnaes, *The Sculptor Bertel Thorvaldsen* (1993; Copenhagen: Thorvaldsens Museum, 2011), p. 20.

12. Munro et al., *Silent Partners*, p. 48.

13. "Once we claim that artworks are able to do something, we have presupposed that they are alive. So is there no way around a certain degree of animism? I am quite aware of the fact that we need to believe that artworks can or even do change something, otherwise we wouldn't be interested in them. But it is also necessary to remember that they don't have the capacities of a subject, they only occasionally present themselves as objects that turn into quasi-subjects, thereby pushing their flirtation with subjecthood to the extreme." Isabelle Graw, "Introduction: When Objecthood Turns into Subjecthood," in *Art and Subjecthood: The Return of the Human Figure in Semiocapitalism*, ed. Isabelle Graw et al. (Berlin: Sternberg Press, 2011), p. 14.

14. Oskar Kokoschka, letter to Hermione Moos, December 10, 1918, quoted in Nathan J. Timpano, *Constructing the Viennese Modern Body: Art, Hysteria, and the Puppet*, Studies in Art Historiography (New York and London: Routledge; Taylor and Francis, 2017), p. 165.

15. Kokoschka's frustration with his lover's desertion of him and of the figure's apparent insufficiency as a true substitute led him to behead and destroy the Alma doll, which is now known only through a series of photographs and the paintings he made. Christiane Hertel, *Pygmalion in Bavaria: The Sculptor Ignaz Günther and Eighteenth-Century Aesthetic Art Theory* (University Park, Pa: The Pennsylvania State University Press, 2011), p. 194.

16. Keith Hartley et al., *Otto Dix, 1891–1969*, exh. cat. (London: Tate Gallery, 1992), p. 124.

17. Hal Foster, "Philosophical Toys and Psychoanalytic Travesties: Anthropomorphic Avatars in Dada and at the Bauhaus," in *Art and Subjecthood*, ed. Graw et al., p. 23.

18. Roxana Marcoci, Geoffrey Batchen, and Tobia Bezzola, *The Original Copy: Photography of Sculpture, 1839 to Today*, exh. cat. (New York: The Museum of Modern Art, 2010), p. 186.

19. Brooks Johnson, [ed. and annot.], *Photography Speaks: 150 Photographers on Their Art* (New York: Aperture Foundation, 2004), p. 156.

20. Sue Taylor, "Hans Bellmer in The Art Institute of Chicago: The Wandering Libido and the Hysterical Body," in *The Art Institute of Chicago—Ryerson and Burnham Libraries* (Chicago: The Art Institute of Chicago, 2001); http://www.artic.edu/reynolds/essays/taylor.php.

21. Agnès [Angliviel] de La Beaumelle et al., *Hans Bellmer: Anatomie du désir*, exh. cat. (Paris: Centre Pompidou, Musée National d'Art Moderne; Éditions Gallimard, 2006), p. 255.

22. In December 1934 the Surrealist journal *Minotaure* published a two-page spread with eighteen photographs by Bellmer of his first *poupée* under the title "Poupée: Variations sur le montage d'une mineure articulée."

23. The Exposition Internationale du Surréalisme took place at the Galérie Beaux-Arts at 140 Rue du Fauberg Saint-Honoré in Paris in 1938. Mannequins appeared in several places in the exhibition, from Salvador Dalí's figures in his *Rainy Taxi* (1938) outside the venue to the entranceway, which was lined with sixteen mannequins each decorated by a member of the group, and finally to the integration of mannequin limbs and heads in other installations, especially furniture, throughout the show. Lewis Kachur, *Displaying the Marvelous: Marcel Duchamp, Salvador Dalí, and Surrealist Exhibition Installations* (Cambridge, Mass.: MIT Press, 2001), pp. 20–101.

24. Acacia Rachelle Warwick, "Prefabricated Desire: Surrealism, Mannequins, and the Fashioning of Modernity" (Ph.D. diss., University of California, Los Angeles, 2006), p. vii.

25. Marianne Thesander, *The Feminine Ideal* (1994; London: Reaktion Books, 1997), p. 74.

26. Warwick, "Prefabricated Desire," p. 27.

27. Adel Rootstein, quoted in Hillel Schwartz, *The Culture of the Copy: Striking Likenesses, Unreasonable Facsimiles*, rev. ed. (1996; New York: Zone Books, 2014), p. 97.

28. "The Surrealists, in particular, developed a special fascination with the display mannequin—a 'phantom object being,' as Dalí called it—that was poised at the interface between fashion, the body and sexual desire." Munro et al., *Silent Partners*, p. 10.

29. Kachur, *Displaying the Marvelous*, p. 41.

30. Keith Aspley, *Historical Dictionary of Surrealism* (Lanham, Md.: The Scarecrow Press, 2010), p. 205. Wilhelm Freddie had sent works to the Surrealists' London exhibition, but some of his paintings were seized by customs officials for being too pornographic and were returned to Denmark. Silvano Levy, *The Scandalous Eye: The Surrealism of Conroy Maddox* (Liverpool: Liverpool University Press, 2003), p. 45. Works from "Træk Gaflen Ud af Øjet på Sommerfuglen" were confiscated by the police. Bruun Rasmussen Kunstauktioner, *Modern Art: International Auction 854*, sale cat. (Copenhagen, 2015), pp. 116–17, no. 592.

31. Meret Oppenheim created *Fur Gloves with Wooden Fingers* in 1936. For more on Oppenheim and Elsa Schiaparelli's use of materials to create uncanny gloves and Surrealist objects, see Victoria R. Pass, "Schiaparelli's Convulsive Gloves," in *Extravagances: Habits of Being 4*, ed. Cristina Giorcelli and Paula Rabinowitz ([Minneapolis]: University of Minnesota Press, 2015), pp. 127–46.

32. Munro et al., *Silent Partners*, p. 4.

33. "In one of [Kusama's photographs in her studio], Kusama combs her hair in front of a phallus-covered dresser. She is confronted by a macaroni-covered female mannequin who holds a brush in its left hand. Kusama and the mannequin's faces are reflected in the mirror of the dresser. By equating herself with the mannequin and by wearing a heavily textured shirt whose pattern matched that of the macaroni and the nets in her paintings, Kusama tried to integrate her presence in her environment." Midori Yoshimoto, *Into Performance: Japanese Women Artists in New York* (New Brunswick, N.J.: Rutgers University Press, 2005), p. 60.

34. Yayoi Kusama, quoted in Massimiliano Gioni et al., *The Great Mother: Women, Maternity, and Power in Art and Visual Culture, 1900–2015*, exh. cat. (Milan: Fondazione Nicola Trussardi; Skira Editore, 2015), p. 349.

35. Ibid.

Layered Realities

1. Veronica Mundi, "The Image Made Flesh," in *Skin*, ed. Heide Hatry (Heidelberg: Kehrer Verlag, 2005), p. 22.

2. Michael [sic] Chaouli, "*Laocoön* and the Hottentots," in *The German Invention of Race*, ed. Sara Eigen and Mark Larrimore (Albany, N.Y.: State University of New York Press, 2006), p. 28.

3. Joris-Karl Huysmans, quoted in Fronia E. Wissman, "Realists among the Impressionists," in *The New Painting: Impressionism 1874–1886*, by Charles S. Moffett et al., exh. cat. (San Francisco: The Fine Arts Museums of San Francisco, 1986), pp. 341, 342.

4. Theodore Reff, *Degas: The Artist's Mind* (New York: The Metropolitan Museum of Art, 1976), p. 244.

5. [Rachel Kent], *Yinka Shonibare MBE*, exh. website (Washington, D.C.: National Museum of African Art, Smithsonian Institution, 2009); https://africa.si.edu/exhibits/shonibare/odette.html.

6. Manthia Diawara, "Independence Cha Cha: The Art of Yinka Shonibare," in *Yinka Shonibare: Double Dutch*, ed. Jaap Guldemond et al., exh. cat. (Rotterdam: Museum Boijmans Van Beuningen, 2004), p. 20.

7. Kelley Helmstutler Di Dio and Rosario Coppel, *Sculpture Collections in Early Modern Spain* (Farnham, Surrey: Ashgate Publishing, 2013), p. 18.

8. Tara Zanardi, *Framing Majismo: Art and Royal Identity in Eighteenth-Century Spain* (University Park, Pa.: The Pennsylvania State University Press, 2016), p. 42.

9. "The chief difference between costume and dress lies in the ability of garments to differently project identity. Costume is usually set apart from dress in its rarity, cost, and elaborate materials, trims, and embellishments, and in its pronounced silhouette or exaggerated proportions. It is not meant to be ordinary, but, rather, evocative, urging the daily further along an artistic trajectory that leads to heightened communication and often culminates in a spectacle for public consumption." Pravina Shukla, *Costume: Performing Identities through Dress* (Bloomington and Indianapolis: Indiana University Press, 2015), p. 4.

10. Jeffrey Grove, "Isa Genzken's Homage to Herself," in *Isa Genzken: Retrospective*, by Sabine Breitwieser et al., exh. cat. (New York: The Museum of Modern Art, 2013), p. 300.

11. The figure was produced in collaboration with Pirelli and the figure's dress is made from Pirelli P Zero fabric, while the soles of the shoes are made from rubber car tires.

12. "When they dance Mokhukhu, members frequently leap into the air and then come down stamping their feet on the ground with their huge white boots, called *manyanyatha*, in order symbolically to subjugate evil. The heavy stamps have a musical function as well in that they give each dance a particular rhythmic pattern. The leaps are also symbolic of each member's desire to fly on the wings of faith—wings which help the faithful to remain buoyant even in adversity. Thus the leaps are a self-energizing act for the believer; they are a way of replenishing spiritual resources and of expressing spiritual vitality physically. Mokhukhu gives male members of the Church a strong sense of identity and a forum for social interaction. Their khaki uniforms and white boots provide a visible sign of oneness for members and emphasize their role as *mash ole a thapelo* (an army of prayer)." Marcus Ramogale and Sello Galane, "Faith in Action: Mokhukhu of the Zion Christian Church," in *Festival of American Folklife 1997* ([Washington, D.C.: Smithsonian Institution; National Park Service], 1997), p. 64.

13. "When you watch these videos…these Rojava videos, these women are fighting against ISIS…when you watch them clean their guns and when they say 'I didn't know that, as a woman, I could touch a gun. I didn't know how it worked. I was so afraid of it. I couldn't touch it.' All these taboos and everything. And in fact, there is a sort of gun fetishism that is very strong…. These images are potent because you see these accessories….It was obvious to me that I wasn't going to have real guns. That was quite obvious, and I didn't want it to look like real in any way. I mean, I didn't want to have any possible confusion on that level and I thought this candy color and the sort of regressive—because it is very regressive—quality…that was what I was looking for. So in the same way that when you're a little child and you see a toy gun and, you know, it's brightly colored, you run for it and you want it. I wanted to sort of appeal to that drive. You know, guns are very….People get very fetishistic about them." "Artist Mai-Thu Perret in Conversation with Artist John Armleder Presented March 12, 2016 at Nasher Sculpture Center," in *360 Speaker Series* (Dallas: Nasher Sculpture Center, 2016); http://www.nashersculpturecenter.org/Portals/0/Documents/Learn/360%20Transcripts/360-Transcript-Mai-Thu-Perret.pdf.

14. "Perret's figures, inspired by soldiers in the YPJ, a female-only Kurdish militia currently fighting in the Syrian civil war, also nod to the presence of what could be construed as a real-world dystopia, one in which brutal conditions have forced women to band together to combat the violence that threatens their communities and their lives." *Mai-Thu Perret: Frieze New York, May 05–08, 2016, Booth B3* (Los Angeles: David Kordansky Gallery, 2016), n.p.

15. A deliberate mirroring of movements is evident in the description of a collaborative performance as well. As Ingar Dragset explains, "In the second version of that work, rather than knitting, we wore these two skirts that we'd made, held up with black braces, which added a more masculine detail. Then we unravelled the skirts from each other's bodies until we basically stood there in our underpants at the end. It became a beautiful ritualized act. You had to be very aware of each other's movements all the time, because otherwise everything gets tangled." Ellen Mara De Wachter, *Co-Art: Artists on Creative Collaboration* (London: Phaidon Press, 2017), p. 105.

16. "When I made a dwarf, I was not so interested in the physical presence of the dwarf. It was more a reference to the question of strangeness than a problem of size. . . . It's also the sense of being uncomfortable. When I meet a dwarf I feel uncomfortable. It is not my fault. But I feel strange." Muñoz, quoted in Manuela Mena, "Juan Muñoz: Insights and Interpretations," in *Juan Muñoz: A Retrospective*, by Sheena Wagstaff et al., exh. cat. (London: Tate Publishing, 2008), p. 124.

17. Muñoz, quoted in Sheena Wagstaff, "A Mirror of Consciousness," in *Juan Muñoz: A Retrospective*, p. 100.

18. Ibid., pp. 102–3.

19. Alex Potts, "Muñoz's Sculptural Theatre: 'The gap in-between is the territory of Meaning,'" in *Juan Muñoz: A Retrospective*, by Wagstaff et al., pp. 112–13.

20. "The whores' canal" puns on the title of Amsterdam's Herengracht—"the gentlemen's canal." Marco Livingstone, "Today's Whoroscope," in *Kienholz, The Hoerengracht: Ed and Nancy Reddin Kienholz*, exh. cat. (New York: PaceWildenstein, 2002), p. 7.

21. Hans-Werner Schmidt, "Edward and Nancy Kienholz from the 80's," in *Edward and Nancy Kienholz: 1980's*, by Jürgen Harten et al., exh. cat. (Düsseldorf: Kunsthalle Düsseldorf, 1989), pp. 22–23.

22. Kelly Baum, "Oliver Herring," in *Blanton Museum of Art: American Art since 1900*, ed. Annette DiMeo Carlozzi and Kelly Baum (Austin: Blanton Museum of Art, The University of Texas at Austin, 2006), p. 132.

23. "As his title describes, every panel stands in for the larger whole—an individual within an interrelated group for which Kim serves as the connecting tissue—but the uniqueness of each skin tone is never overshadowed by the whole. What is made particularly evident in this work is how our language for skin color—white, black, yellow, red—is so alarmingly inadequate. Indeed, not one of these commonplace color designations adequately describes a single person's skin tone; and the perceptible nuances and shades of pinks and browns found in the *Synecdoche* show us that each panel (and by extension, each person's skin color) is, in fact, unique. Kim's insertion of questions of identity into the realm of abstract painting is a deliberate challenge to the formalist argument for stripping away content and reference from the medium to arrive at its so-called essence, one concerned strictly with the flatness of the picture plane and the materiality of the paint on the canvas." Anne Ellegood, "Nadia Myre: Scarscapes," in *Hide: Skin as Material and Metaphor*, by Kathleen Ash-Milby et al., exh. cat. (Washington, D.C., and New York: NMAI Editions, National Museum of the American Indian, Smithsonian Institution, 2010), p. 57.

24. Pauline Wakeham, *Taxidermic Signs: Reconstructing Aboriginality* (Minneapolis and London: University of Minnesota Press, 2008), p. 25.

25. "When I start covering them with the tin, it kind of harkens back to my sewing skills as a kid, making little dresses. So it's very much like cutting darts in all of these sort of pieces that kind of then can form to the body, and nailing them together. So she's solid wood underneath, except for the hole, where I then pack the mud and stuff inside of her belly." Alison Saar, interviewed by Emerson Bowyer, Brinda Kumar, and Sheena Wagstaff, transcript, "Like Life" exhibition file, Modern and Contemporary Art, The Metropolitan Museum of Art, New York.

Figuring Flesh

1. John 1:14; Douay-Rheims Bible.

2. Francisco Pacheco, quoted in Xavier Bray et al., *The Sacred Made Real: Spanish Painting and Sculpture 1600–1700*, exh. cat. (London: National Gallery Company, 2009), p. 194.

3. Bernard of Clairvaux, *On the Song of Songs*, trans. Kilian Walsh and Irene M. Edmonds, 4 vols. (Kalamazoo, Mich.: Cistercian Publications, 1971–80), vol. 3, p. 144.

4. On these sculptures more generally, see Elina Gertsman, *Worlds Within: Opening the Medieval Shrine Madonna* (University Park, Pa.: The Pennsylvania State University Press, [2015]).

5. See, for example, Ludmilla Jordanova, *Sexual Visions: Images of Gender in Science and Medicine between the Eighteenth and Twentieth Centuries* (New York: Harvester Wheatsheaf, 1989); Lyle

Massey, "On Waxes and Wombs: Eighteenth-Century Representations of the Gravid Uterus," in *Ephemeral Bodies: Wax Sculpture and the Human Figure*, by Roberta Panzanelli et al. (Los Angeles: Getty Research Institute, 2008), pp. 83–105; Roberta Ballestriero, "Anatomical Models and Wax Venuses: Art Masterpieces or Scientific Craft Works?" *Journal of Anatomy*, no. 216 (2010), pp. 223–34.

6. Roberta Panzanelli, "Introduction: The Body in Wax, the Body of Wax," in *Ephemeral Bodies*, by Panzanelli et al., p. 5.

7. Georges Didi-Huberman, "Wax Flesh, Vicious Circles," in *Encyclopaedia Anatomica: A Complete Collection of Anatomical Waxes/ Vollständige Sammlung anatomischer Wachse/Collection complète des cires anatomiques*, by Monika v[on] Düring, Georges Didi-Huberman, and Marta Poggesi (Cologne: Benedikt Taschen Verlag, 1999), p. 66.

8. See Caroline Rupprecht, *Womb Fantasies: Subjective Architectures in Postmodern Literature, Cinema, and Art* (Evanston, Ill.: Northwestern University Press, 2013), pp. 97–106.

9. Henri Trianon, "Sixième exposition de peinture par un groupe d'artistes, 35, boulevard des Capucines," *Le Constitutionnel*, April 24, 1881, p. 2. On the "scientific" discourses invoked by Degas and viewers of his sculpture, see Anthea Callen, *The Spectacular Body: Science, Method, and Meaning in the Work of Degas* (New Haven, Conn.: Yale University Press, 1995).

10. See also Linda Nochlin, "Unholy Postures: Kiki Smith and the Body," in *Kiki Smith: A Gathering, 1980–2005*, by Siri Engberg et al., exh. cat. (Minneapolis: Walker Art Center, 2006), pp. 30–37.

11. See, for example, Megan Holmes, "Ex-Votos: Materiality, Memory, and Cult," in *The Idol in the Age of Art: Objects, Devotions and the Early Modern World*, ed. Michael W. Cole and Rebecca E. Zorach (Farnham, Surrey: Ashgate Publishing, 2009), pp. 159–81. On votives and contemporary art practice, see Irene V. Small, "Believing in Art: The Votive Structures of Conceptual Art," *RES: Anthropology and Aesthetics*, nos. 55–56 (Spring–Autumn 2009), pp. 294–307.

12. Meredith Martin, *Dairy Queens: The Politics of Pastoral Architecture from Catherine de' Medici to Marie-Antoinette* (Cambridge, Mass.: Harvard University Press, 2011), pp. 239–40.

13. On the use of "body-part reliquary" as a historical and religious category of object, see Caroline Walker Bynum and Paula Gerson, "Body-Part Reliquaries and Body-Parts in the Middle Ages," *Gesta* 36, no. 1 (1997), pp. 3–7.

Between Life and Art

The epigraph is from William Shakespeare, *Hamlet* (Act 3, Scene 1), ll. 68–74.

1. Alex Potts, *The Sculptural Imagination: Figurative, Modernist, Minimalist* (New Haven, Conn.: Yale University Press, 2000), p. 23.

2. Marina Warner, *Phantasmagoria: Spirit Visions, Metaphors, and Media into the Twenty-First Century* (Oxford and New York: Oxford University Press, 2006), p. 49.

3. Ibid., p. 47.

4. Jessica Dallow, "Reclaiming Histories: Betye and Alison Saar, Feminism, and the Representation of Black Womanhood," *Feminist Studies* 30, no. 1 (Spring 2004), p. 93.

5. Ibid.

6. "'One day I put a shirt on it, no pants, and I could . . . deal with it more because it became a buffoon. And seeing it in a lawn chair, made it not about death but about sleeping. . . . It was all of a sudden sleeping or dreaming, and the piece could be dealt with.'" Paul McCarthy, quoted in Paul Schimmel, "Capturing Time/Cheating Life," in *Inbetween: Baselitz, McCarthy*, by Paul Schimmel and Carla Schulz-Hoffmann, exh. cat. (Athens: The George Economou Collection, 2015), p. 20.

7. Ibid., p. 18.

8. Xavier Bray et al., *The Sacred Made Real: Spanish Painting and Sculpture, 1600–1700*, exh. cat. (London: National Gallery Company, 2009), p. 33.

9. Blake Gopnik, "Divine Inspirations: 'Sacred Made Real' Examines the Balance between Sculpture and Painting in 17th-Century Spain," *Washington Post*, February 28, 2010, p. E7.

10. Ralph Rugoff et al., *The Human Factor: The Figure in Contemporary Sculpture*, exh. cat. (London: Hayward Gallery, 2014), p. 70.

WORKS IN THE EXHIBITION

The Presumption of White

1.
Copy of work attributed to
Polykleitos (mid-5th century B.C.)
Hermes, A.D. 1st or 2nd century
Pentelic marble, H. 71 ¼ in.
(181 cm), W. 29 ½ in. (74.9 cm),
D. 23 ½ in. (59.7 cm)
Roman
The Metropolitan Museum of Art,
New York, Gift of the Hearst
Foundation, 1956 (56.234.15)
Page 82

2.
Domenico Poggini
(Italian, Florence 1520–1590 Rome)
Bacchus, 1554
Marble, H. 54 in. (137.2 cm),
W. 21 in. (53.3 cm), D. 18 in.
(45.7 cm)
The Metropolitan Museum of Art,
New York, Bequest of George
Blumenthal, 1941 (41.190.269)
Page 83

3
Fred Wilson (American, born
Bronx, New York, 1954)
The Mete of the Muse, 2006
Bronze, black patina, and white
paint, African figure: H. 65 in.
(165.1 cm), W. 26 in. (66 cm),
D. 14 in. (35.6 cm); European fig-
ure: H. 61 in. (154.9 cm), W. 18 in.
(45.7 cm), D. 20 in. (50.8 cm)
Edition 5 of 5 + 2 A.P.
Courtesy of the artist and Pace
Gallery
Page 85

4.
Hiram Powers (American,
Woodstock, Vermont, 1805–1873
Florence)
California, 1850–55, carved 1858
Marble, H. 71 in. (180.3 cm),
W. 18 ¼ in. (46.4 cm), D. 24 ¾ in.
(62.9 cm)
The Metropolitan Museum of Art,
New York, Gift of William
Backhouse Astor, 1872 (72.3)
Page 86

5.
Charles Ray
(American, born Chicago 1953)
Aluminum Girl, 2003
Aluminum and paint, H. 62 ⅝ in.
(159 cm), W. 18 ½ in. (47 cm),
D. 11 ⁷⁄₁₆ in. (29 cm)
Astrup Fearnley Collection, Oslo
Page 87

6.
Bharti Kher
(British, born London 1969)
Mother, 2016
Plaster of Paris and wood,
H. 55 ⅛ in. (140 cm), W. 24 ¹³⁄₁₆ in.
(63 cm), D. 37 ¹³⁄₁₆ in. (96 cm)
Courtesy of the artist and
Hauser & Wirth
Pages 88–89

7.
René Magritte (Belgian, Lessines
1898–1967 Brussels)
Les Menottes de Cuivre
(*The Copper Handcuffs*), 1936
Oil on plaster miniature of the
Venus de Milo, H. 14 ⁹⁄₁₆ in. (37 cm),
W. 4 ⁹⁄₁₆ in. (11.5 cm), D. 4 ⁵⁄₁₆ in.
(11 cm)
Private collection
Page 90

8.
John Gibson (British, Gwynedd,
Wales, 1790–1866 Rome)
The Tinted Venus, ca. 1851–56
Tinted marble, H. 69 ⁵⁄₁₆ in.
(176 cm), W. 25 ⁹⁄₁₆ in. (65 cm),
D. 17 ¹¹⁄₁₆ in. (45 cm); base:
W. 20 ¹⁄₁₆ in. (51 cm), D. 17 ⁵⁄₁₆ in.
(44 cm)
Walker Art Gallery, National
Museums Liverpool
Page 91

Signed in Greek on the turtle:
ΓΙΒΣΩΝ ΕΠ ΡΩΜΗΙ
(Gibson made me in Rome)
Inscribed in Greek on the apple:
Η ΚΑΛΗ ΛΑΒΕΤΩ
(The beautiful one must take this)

9.
Frank Benson (American,
born Norfolk, Virginia, 1976)
Human Statue, 2005
Fiberglass, medium-density fiber-
board, acrylic, and oil paint,
H. 68 ⅛ in. (173 cm), W. 19 ¹¹⁄₁₆ in.
(50 cm), D. 11 ¹³⁄₁₆ in. (30 cm)
Edition of 3 + A.P.
Astrup Fearnley Collection, Oslo
Page 92

10.
El Greco (Doménikos
Theotokópoulos, Greek, Iráklion,
Crete, 1541–1614 Toledo)
*Epimetheus** and *Pandora*,
1600–1610
Polychromed wood, *Epimetheus*:
H. 17 ⁵⁄₁₆ in. (44 cm); *Pandora*:
H. 16 ¹⁵⁄₁₆ in. (43 cm)
Museo Nacional del Prado, Madrid
Page 93

11.
Antonio Canova
(Italian, Possagno 1757–1822 Venice)
Creugas, 1795–96
Plaster and paint, H. 32 ⁵⁄₁₆ in.
(82 cm), W. 18 ⅞ in. (48 cm),
D. 7 ½ in. (19 cm)
Fondazione Canova, Gipsoteca e
Museo Antonio Canova, Possagno
Page 94

12.
Willem Danielsz van Tetrode
(Netherlandish, Delft ca. 1525–1580
Westphalia)
Hercules, ca. 1545–60
Terracotta and paint, H. 18 ½ in.
(47 cm), W. 8 ¹¹⁄₁₆ in. (22 cm),
D. 5 ⅞ in. (15 cm)
Quentin Foundation, London
Page 95

13.
Meissen Manufactory (German,
1710–present), design attributed to
Johann Joachim Kändler (German,
Fischbach 1706–1775 Meissen)
The Judgment of Paris, ca. 1762
Hard-paste porcelain, H. 23 ¹⁄₁₆ in.
(58.5 cm), W. 26 in. (66.1 cm),
D. 33 ¹⁄₁₆ in. (83.9 cm)
Wadsworth Atheneum Museum of
Art, Hartford, Connecticut,
Gift of J. Pierpont Morgan
Page 96

14.
Jeff Koons (American,
born York, Pennsylvania, 1955)
Michael Jackson and Bubbles, 1988
Ceramic, glaze, and paint, H. 42 in.
(106.7 cm), W. 70 ½ in. (179.1 cm),
D. 32 ½ in. (82.6 cm)
Astrup Fearnley Collection, Oslo
Page 97

30.
Charles-Henri-Joseph Cordier
(French, Cambrai 1827–1905
Algiers)
The Jewish Woman of Algiers, 1862
Algerian onyx-marble, bronze,
gilt bronze, enamel, amethyst,
and white marble, with socle:
H. 35 ½ in. (90.2 cm), W. 25 ¼ in.
(64.1 cm), D. 13 ¾ in. (34.9 cm)
The Metropolitan Museum of Art,
New York, European Sculpture
and Decorative Arts Fund, 2006
(2006.113a–c)
Page 126

31.
Rigoberto Torres (American, born
Aguadilla, Puerto Rico, 1960)
*Shorty Working in the C & R
Statuary Corp.*, 1985
Acrylic on plaster, H. 29 in.
(73.7 cm), W. 24 in. (61 cm),
D. 11 ½ in. (29.2 cm)
El Museo del Barrio, New York,
Gift of John Ahearn, 2014
Page 127

32.
Rigoberto Torres (American, born
Aguadilla, Puerto Rico, 1960)
Raúl with Bust of Ruth Fernández,
1998
Acrylic on plaster, H. 28 in.
(71.1 cm), W. 28 in. (71.1 cm),
D. 12 in. (30.5 cm)
El Museo del Barrio, New York,
Gift of John Ahearn, 2014
Page 128

33.
Charles-Henri-Joseph Cordier
(French, Cambrai 1827–1905
Algiers)
La Capresse des Colonies, 1861
Algerian onyx-marble, bronze, gilt
bronze, enamel, and white marble,
with socle: H. 37 ¾ in. (95.9 cm),
W. 23 ¼ in. (59.1 cm), D. 12 ¼ in.
(31.1 cm)
The Metropolitan Museum of Art,
New York, European Sculpture
and Decorative Arts Fund, 2006
(2006.112a–c)
Page 129

34.
Attributed to Sri Ram Pal (Indian,
flourished mid-19th century)
Raj Kissen Mitter, ca. 1840
Unfired clay, pigments, cotton
over bamboo, and straw, H. 48 in.
(121.9 cm), W. 18 in. (45.7 cm),
D. 29 in. (73.7 cm)
Peabody Essex Museum, Salem,
Massachusetts, Gift of John A.
Parker, 1840
Pages 130–31

35.
Duane Hanson (American,
Alexandria, Minnesota, 1925–1996
Boca Raton, Florida)
Housewife, 1969–70
Polyester, resin, fiberglass, oil,
mixed media, and accessories,
H. 44 in. (111.7 cm), W. 35 in.
(88.9 cm), D. 61 in. (155 cm)
Astrup Fearnley Collection, Oslo
Pages 132–33

Desire for Life

36.
Jean-Léon Gérôme
(French, Vesoul 1824–1904 Paris)
Pygmalion and Galatea, ca. 1890
Oil on canvas, 35 × 27 in.
(88.9 × 68.6 cm)
The Metropolitan Museum of Art,
New York, Gift of Louis C.
Raegner, 1927 (27.200)
Page 142

37.
John De Andrea
(American, born Denver 1941)
Self-Portrait with Sculpture, 1980
Polyvinyl and oil paint, H. 62 in.
(157.5 cm), W. 32 in. (81.3 cm),
D. 62 in. (157.5 cm)
Collection of Foster Goldstrom
Page 143

38.
*Jean-Léon Gérôme
(French, Vesoul 1824–1904 Paris)
The Ball Player, 1901
Polychromed marble, H. 65 ¾ in.
(167 cm), W. 25 ½ in. (64.8 cm),
D. 21 ½ in. (54.6 cm)
Collection of David H. Koch
Page 144

39.
Pablo Picasso (Spanish, Málaga
1881–1973 Mougins, France)
Plates from the *Vollard Suite*
Etchings
Private collection

A. *Reclining Sculptor and Model
with Mask (Le Repos du Sculpteur et
le Modèle au Masque)*, plate 50,
March 27, 1933
10 ½ × 7 ⅝ in. (26.7 × 19.4 cm)
Page 145

B. *Sculptor and Standing Model
(Sculpteur et Modèle Debout)*,
plate 68, April 7, 1933
14 ⁷⁄₁₆ × 11 ¹¹⁄₁₆ in. (36.7 × 29.7 cm)

C. *Sculptor and His Model Before a
Window (Sculpteur et Son Modèle
Devant une Fenêtre)*, plate 59,
March 31, 1933

7 ¾ × 10 ⁹⁄₁₆ in. (19.7 × 26.8 cm)
Page 146

D. *Sculptor, Reclining Model, and
Sculpture (Sculpteur, Modèle Couché
et Sculpture)*, plate 37, March 17, 1933
10 ⁷⁄₁₆ × 7 ⅝ in. (26.5 × 19.4 cm)

E. *Sculptors, Models, and Sculpture
(Sculpteurs, Modèles et Sculpture)*,
plate 41, March 20, 1933
7 ⅝ × 10 ⁷⁄₁₆ in. (19.4 × 26.5 cm)

F. *Sculptor and Kneeling Model
(Sculpteur et Modèle Agenouillé)*,
plate 69, April 8, 1933
14 ⅜ × 11 ⅝ in. (36.5 × 29.5 cm)
Page 147

40.
Augustus Saint-Gaudens
(American, Dublin 1848–1907
Cornish, New Hampshire)
Louise Adele Gould, modeled 1894,
carved 1895
Marble, H. 22 in. (55.9 cm),
W. 15 ½ in. (39.4 cm), D. 10 in.
(25.4 cm)
The Metropolitan Museum of Art,
New York, Gift of Charles W.
Gould, 1915 (15.105.2)
Page 148

41.
Augustus Saint-Gaudens
(American, Dublin 1848–1907
Cornish, New Hampshire)
Louise Adele Gould, after 1894
Pigmented wax, H. 14 ½ in.
(36.8 cm), W. 17 in. (43.1 cm), D. 9 in.
(22.8 cm)
Collection of Jonathan and
Ute Kagan
Page 149

42.
Lucas Cranach the Younger
(German, Wittenberg 1515–1586
Wittenberg)
The Idolatry of Solomon, ca. 1537
Oil on limewood, 47 ¹³⁄₁₆ × 29 ⅛ in.
(121.5 × 74 cm)
Gemäldegalerie Alte Meister,
Staatliche Kunstsammlungen
Dresden
Page 150

43.
Saint Barbara, ca. 1490
Limewood and paint, H. 50 ¼ in.
(127.6 cm), W. 17 in. (43.2 cm),
D. 13 ¼ in. (33.7 cm)
Alsacian, probably Strasbourg
The Metropolitan Museum of Art,
New York, The Cloisters
Collection, 1955 (55.166)
Page 151

44.
Alonso Berruguete (Spanish,
Paredes de Nava ca. 1489–1561
Toledo)
Saint Sebastian, mid-16th century
Polychromed wood and parcel gilt,
H. 64 9/16 in. (164 cm), W. 16 1/8 in.
(41 cm), D. 20 1/16 in. (51 cm)
Fondation Palatine, courtesy
Colnaghi, London
Page 152

45.
Reza Aramesh (British, born
Ahvaz, Iran, 1970)
*Action 105: An Israeli soldier points
his gun at the Palestinian youth
asked to strip down as he stands at
a military checkpoint along the
separation barrier at the entrance of
Bethlehem, March 2006*, 2017. Hand-
carved polychromed limewood,
glass eyes, and concrete plinth,
H. 37 3/16 in. (94.5 cm), W. 8 1/4 in.
(21 cm), D. 10 1/4 in. (26 cm);
plinth: 39 3/8 in. (100 cm), W. 21 5/8 in.
(55 cm), D. 21 5/8 in. (55 cm)
A.P.
Courtesy of the artist and Leila
Heller Gallery, New York and
Dubai
Page 153

46.
Ángel Zárraga y Argüelles
(Mexican, Durango 1886–1946
Mexico City)
Votive Offering (Saint Sebastian),
ca. 1910–12
Oil on canvas, 72 13/16 × 52 15/16 in.
(185 × 134.5 cm)
Museo Nacional de Arte,
Instituto Nacional de Bellas Artes,
Mexico City
Page 153

47.
Max Klinger (German,
Leipzig 1857–1920 Großjena)
New Salome, 1893–1903
Marble and paint, H. 34 5/8 in.
(88 cm), W. 21 7/8 in. (55.5 cm),
D. 17 1/8 in. (43.5 cm)
Museum der Bildenden Künste,
Leipzig
Page 154

48.
Juan Martínez Montañés (Spanish,
Alcalá la Real 1568–1649 Seville)
Saint John the Baptist, ca. 1620–30
Polychromed wood and gilding,
H. 60 5/8 in. (154 cm), W. 29 5/8 in.
(75.2 cm), D. 27 5/8 in. (70.2 cm)
The Metropolitan Museum of Art,
New York, Purchase, Joseph
Pulitzer Bequest, 1963 (63.40)
Page 155

49.
Paul Gauguin (French, Paris
1848–1903 Atuona, Marquesas
Islands)
Eve, 1890
Ceramic and glaze, H. 23 7/8 in.
(60.6 cm), W. 11 in. (27.9 cm),
D. 10 3/4 in. (27.3 cm)
National Gallery of Art,
Washington, D.C., Ailsa Mellon
Bruce Fund
Page 156

50.
Nancy Grossman
(American, born New York 1940)
Male Figure, 1971
Leather and zippers on wood,
H. 66 15/16 in. (170 cm), W. 27 9/16 in.
(70 cm), D. 23 5/8 in. (60 cm)
Israel Museum, Jerusalem,
Gift of Joseph H. Hazen, New York,
to the American Friends of the
Israel Museum
Page 157

51.
Goshka Macuga
(Polish, born Warsaw 1967)
*To the Son of Man Who Ate the
Scroll*, 2016
Android, plastic coat, expandable
foam shoe, and cardboard and
linen shoe, seated: H. 55 1/8 in.
(140 cm), W. 19 11/16 in. (50 cm),
D. 33 1/16 in. (84 cm), overall
dimensions variable
Fondazione Prada, Milan and
Venice
Page 158

52.
Alexandre-Nicolas Théroude
(French, Saint-Pierre-en-Val
1807–ca. 1885 Paris)
Flute Player, ca. 1869–77,
costume 1970s
Textiles, European oak and
pine, steel, iron, brass, papier-
mâché, leather, glass, mohair,
and oil paint, H. 60 in. (152.4 cm),
W. 19 1/2 in. (49.5 cm), D. 15 in.
(38.1 cm)
Murtogh D. Guinness Collection
of Mechanical Musical
Instruments and Automata,
Morris Museum, Morristown,
New Jersey
Page 159

Proxy Figures

53.
Jeff Koons (American, born York,
Pennsylvania, 1955)
Buster Keaton, 1988
Polychromed wood, H. 66 in.
(167.6 cm), W. 47 7/8 in. (121.6 cm),
D. 27 1/8 in. (68.9 cm)
Private collection, courtesy David
Zwirner, New York, London, and
Hong Kong
Page 170

54.
Palmesel, 15th century
Limewood and paint, with base:
H. 61 1/2 in. (156.2 cm), W. 23 3/4 in.
(60.3 cm), D. 54 1/2 in. (138.4 cm)
German, Lower Franconia
The Metropolitan Museum of Art,
New York, The Cloisters
Collection, 1955 (55.24)
Page 171

55.
Corpus with Movable Arms,
1500–1510
Poplar and willow, with arms
folded: H. 57 7/8 in. (147 cm),
W. 17 11/16 in. (45 cm), D. 11 1/16 in.
(28 cm)
Swiss
Schweizerisches Nationalmuseum,
Zurich
Page 172

56.
Bertel Thorvaldsen (Danish,
Copenhagen 1770–1844
Copenhagen)
Lay Figure, before 1806
Wood, metal, and paint, figure:
H. 63 3/4 in. (162 cm); base:
H. 6 11/16 in. (17 cm), W. 23 7/16 in.
(59.5 cm), D. 22 7/16 in. (57 cm)
Thorvaldsens Museum,
Copenhagen
Page 173

57.
Saracen Jousting Figure, 1579
Polychromed wood, figure:
H. 79 1/2 in. (202 cm), W. 31 1/2 in.
(80 cm), D. 19 11/16 in. (50 cm);
base: H. 3 15/16 in. (10 cm),
W. 27 9/16 in. (70 cm), D. 27 9/16 in.
(70 cm)
Florentine
Museo Nazionale del Bargello,
Florence
Pages 174–75

58.
Oskar Kokoschka (Austrian,
Pöchlarn 1886–1980 Montreux,
Switzerland)
*Self-Portrait with Doll
(Mann mit Puppe)*, ca. 1922
Oil on canvas, 31 1/2 × 47 1/4 in.
(80 × 120 cm)
Neue Nationalgalerie, Staatliche
Museen zu Berlin, Nationalgalerie,
acquired by the Federal State of
Berlin, 1974
Page 176

59.
Paul Huot
(French, flourished 1790s–1820s)
Lay Figure, ca. 1790
Wood, metal, flax, silk, and
painted gesso on papier-mâché,
H. 64 in. (162.6 cm); with stand:
H. 67 in. (170.2 cm); base:
W. 25 ¾ in. (65.4 cm), D. 27 ¼ in.
(69.2 cm)
The Metropolitan Museum of Art,
New York, Paper Conservation
Artists' Materials Study Collection,
Gift of Ronald N. Sherr, 2015
Page 177

60.
Yayoi Kusama (Japanese,
born Matsumoto 1929)
Phallic Girl, 1967
Mannequin and mixed media,
H. 61 in. (155 cm), W. 34 ¼ in.
(87 cm), D. 16 ¹⁵⁄₁₆ in. (43 cm)
Collection of Caroline de
Westenholz
Page 178

61.
Charles Ray
(American, born Chicago 1953)
Male Mannequin, 1990
Mannequin and mixed media,
H. 73 ½ in. (186.7 cm), W. 27 ¼ in.
(69.2 cm), D. 18 ½ in. (47 cm)
Broad Art Foundation,
Los Angeles
Page 179

62.
Hans Bellmer (German, born
Katowice, Poland, 1902–1975 Paris)
La Demi-Poupée, 1972
Wood, paint, and fabric, seated:
H. 23 ⅝ in. (60 cm), W. 16 ⁹⁄₁₆ in.
(42 cm), D. 26 ¾ in. (68 cm)
Edition 4 of 9
Rachel and Jean-Pierre Lehmann
Collection
Page 180

63.
Hans Bellmer (German, born
Katowice, Poland, 1902–1975 Paris)
La Poupeé, ca. 1936
Gelatin silver print with applied
color, 3 ⁹⁄₁₆ × 2 ⅝ in. (9 × 6.7 cm)
The Metropolitan Museum of Art,
New York, Ford Motor Company
Collection, Gift of Ford Motor
Company and John C. Waddell,
1987 (1987.1100.333)
Page 181

64.
Hans Bellmer (German, born
Katowice, Poland, 1902–1975 Paris)
La Poupée, 1936
Gelatin silver print with applied
color, 5 ⁵⁄₁₆ × 5 ⁹⁄₁₆ in. (13.5 × 14.1 cm)
The Metropolitan Museum of Art,

New York, Ford Motor Company
Collection, Gift of Ford Motor
Company and John C. Waddell,
1987 (1987.1100.444)
Page 181

65.
Pierre Imans (French)
Bust, ca. 1910s
Painted wax, residual hair, silk and
cotton net base, and resin,
H. 22 ¹⁄₁₆ in. (56 cm), W. 17 ½ in.
(44.5 cm), D. 8 ¼ in. (21 cm)
Fashion Museum Bath
Page 182

66.
Wilhelm Freddie (Danish,
Copenhagen 1909–1995
Copenhagen)
Sex-Paralysappeal, 1936
Mixed media, H. 30 ¹¹⁄₁₆ in. (78 cm),
W. 13 ⅜ in. (34 cm), D. 13 ⅜ in.
(34 cm)
Moderna Museet, Stockholm,
Purchase 1966
Page 183

67.
Meret Oppenheim
(Swiss, Berlin 1913–1985 Basel)
*Evening Dress with Bra-Strap
Necklace (Abendkleid mit
Büstenhalter-Collier)*, 1968
Mannequin torso, skirt, oil paint,
glass-bead necklace, and shards of
glass, H. 57 ¹⁄₁₆ in. (145 cm),
W. 16 ⅛ in. (41 cm), D. 11 in. (28 cm)
Collection Pictet
Page 185

Layered Realities

68.
Edgar Degas
(French, Paris 1834–1917 Paris),
cast by A. A. Hébrard Foundry,
Paris
The Little Fourteen-Year-Old Dancer,
ca. 1880, cast 1922, tutu 2018
Partially tinted bronze, cotton
fabric, satin, and wood, H. 38 ½ in.
(97.8 cm), W. 17 ¼ in. (43.8 cm),
D. 14 ⅜ in. (36.5 cm)
The Metropolitan Museum of Art,
New York, H. O. Havemeyer
Collection, Bequest of Mrs. H. O.
Havemeyer, 1929 (29.100.370)
Page 196

69.
Yinka Shonibare MBE
(British, born London 1962)
Girl Ballerina, 2007
Mannequin, Dutch wax–printed
cotton textile, and antique flint-
lock pistol, H. 47 ¼ in. (120 cm),
W. 19 ¹¹⁄₁₆ in. (50 cm), D. 23 ⅝ in.
(60 cm)

Collection of John and Amy
Phelan
Page 197

70.
Nero Alberti (Romano Alberti,
Italian, Sansepolcro 1502–1568
Sansepolcro)
Saint Roch, 1528
Polychromed wood, H. 69 ⁵⁄₁₆ in.
(176 cm)
Chiesa di Santa Croce, Umbertide
Page 198

71.
Elmgreen & Dragset
The Experiment, 2012
Polyester resin, glass fiber, acrylic
paint, glass, human hair, wood,
lacquer, mirror, metal parts, and
leather; figure: H. 50 ⅜ in. (128 cm),
W. 15 ¾ in. (40 cm), D. 9 ⁷⁄₁₆ in.
(24 cm); mirror: H. 74 ⁹⁄₁₆ in.
(189.5 cm), W. 31 ³⁄₁₆ in. (79.2 cm),
D. 24 ¹³⁄₁₆ in. (63 cm), overall
dimensions variable
Krawiecki Gazes Family
Collection
Page 199

72.
The Child Jesus Triumphant,
ca. 1625, with later costume
Polychromed lead, glass, silver,
silk, and silver-gilt lace dress,
with halo: H. 19 in. (48.3 cm),
W. 6 ⅛ in. (15.6 cm), D. 6 in. (15.2 cm)
Spanish or Mexican
The Metropolitan Museum of Art,
New York, Gift of Loretta Hines
Howard, 1964 (64.164.244a, b)
Page 200

73.
Juan Muñoz (Spanish,
Madrid 1953–2001 Ibiza)
Sarah with Blue Dress, 1996
Acrylic on polyester resin and
mirror, H. 76 ¾ in. (195 cm),
W. 43 ⁵⁄₁₆ in. (110 cm), D. 39 ⅜ in.
(100 cm)
Juan Varez Collection, Madrid
Page 201

74.
Juan Cháez (Spanish,
Málaga ca. 1750–ca. 1809)

A. *Bullfighter*, late 18th century
Polychromed wood and textiles,
H. 24 ⅝ in. (62.5 cm), W. 9 ¼ in.
(23.5 cm), D. 18 ⁷⁄₁₆ in. (46.8 cm),
base: H. 1³⁄₁₆ in. (2.1 cm),
W. 12 ¹⁄₁₆ in. (30.7 cm), D. 8 ⅜ in.
(21.3 cm)
Museo Nacional de Escultura,
Valladolid

B. *Costillares*, late 18th century
Polychromed wood and textiles,

H. 24 ¹³⁄₁₆ in. (63 cm), W. 10 in.
(25.4 cm), D. 10 ⁷⁄₁₆ in. (26.5 cm),
base: H. 1 ⁵⁄₁₆ in. (3.3 cm),
W. 9 ³⁄₁₆ in. (23.4 cm), D. 11 ⁷⁄₈ in.
(30.1 cm)
Museo Nacional de Escultura,
Valladolid
Page 202

75.
Sokari Douglas Camp
(Nigerian, born Buguma 1958)
Material Salsa, 2011
Steel and acrylic paint, man:
H. 78 in. (198.1 cm), W. 48 in.
(121.9 cm), D. 20 in. (50.8 cm);
woman: H. 75 in. (190.5 cm),
W. 48 in. (121.9 cm), D. 31 in.
(78.7 cm), overall dimensions
variable
Courtesy of the artist and
Stux Gallery, New York
Page 203

76.
Isa Genzken (German,
born Bad Oldesloe 1948)
Actors (Schauspieler), 2013
Mannequin, clothes, shoes, fabric,
and paper, approx. H. 59 ¹⁄₁₆ in.
(150 cm), W. 59 ¹⁄₁₆ in. (150 cm),
D. 59 ¹⁄₁₆ in. (150 cm)
SYZ Collection, Switzerland
Page 204

77.
Doll in a Box, ca. 1748
Box (American): white pine, crown
glass, and paint; doll (British):
wood, paint, glass, silk dress with
woven linen and metal trim, silk
gauze cap and cuffs, human hair
with silk floss and gilded metal foil
ribbons, glass-bead earrings with
metal foil and faux pearls, metal
foil watch and brooch, silk stockings, and silk faille embellished
shoes, H. 25 in. (63.5 cm), W. 24 in.
(61 cm), D. 7 in. (17.8 cm)
The Metropolitan Museum of Art,
New York, Gift of Mrs. Screven
Lorillard, 1953 (53.179.12)
Page 205

78.
Mai-Thu Perret (Swiss, born
Geneva 1976)
Les Guérillères X, 2016
Glazed ceramic, steel, epoxy, syn-
thetic hair, cotton and polyester
fabric, polyester resin, and steel,
H. 69 in. (175.3 cm), W. 27 in.
(68.6 cm), D. 14 in. (35.6 cm)
Green Family Collection
Page 206

79.
Mary Sibande (South African,
born Barberton 1982)

*Rubber Soul, Monument of
Aspiration*, 2011
Cast resin, fiberglass, cotton fabric,
tulle, and rubber, H. 101 ½ in.
(257.8 cm), W. 57 in. (144.8 cm),
D. 64 ½ in. (163.8 cm)
Toledo Museum of Art, Ohio,
Gift of the Georgia Welles Apollo
Society, 2013
Page 207

80.
Edward Kienholz (American,
Fairfield, Washington, 1927–1994,
Sandpoint, Idaho) and Nancy
Reddin Kienholz (American,
born Los Angeles 1943)
*Woman Washing with Scrutator
with Parrot Affixed Also*, Berlin,
1983
Mixed media, H. 81 in. (205.7 cm),
W. 98 in. (248.9 cm), D. 27 in.
(68.6 cm)
Stefan T. Edlis Collection
Pages 208–9

Figuring Flesh

81.
Shrine of the Virgin, ca. 1300
Oak, linen, polychromy, gilding,
and gesso, open: H. 14 ½ in.
(36.8 cm), W. 13 ⅝ in. (34.6 cm),
D. 5 ⅛ in. (13 cm); closed:
H. 14 ½ in. (36.8 cm), W. 13 ⅝ in.
(34.6 cm), D. 5 in. (12.7 cm)
German, Rhine Valley
The Metropolitan Museum of Art,
New York, Gift of J. Pierpont
Morgan, 1917 (17.190.185a, b)
Pages 216–17

82.
Damien Hirst
(British, born Bristol 1965)
Virgin (exposed), 2005
Acrylic paint on resin,
H. 24 ⁷⁄₁₆ in. (62 cm), W. 6 ⅝ in.
(16.8 cm), D. 11 ⁵⁄₁₆ in. (28.7 cm)
Edition 9 of 15
Mugrabi Collection
Page 218

83.
*André Pierre Pinson
(French, 1746–1828)
Anatomical Seated Woman, 1784–93
Pigmented wax, H. 16 ⅛ in. (41 cm),
W. 9 ¹³⁄₁₆ in. (25 cm),
D. 11 ¹³⁄₁₆ in. (30 cm)
Musée National d'Histoire
Naturelle, Paris
Page 219

84.
Sèvres Manufactory (French, 1740–
present), design attributed to Jean
Jacques Lagrenée (French, Paris

1739–1821 Paris)
*Breast Bowl, Service for the
Rambouillet Dairy*, 1787–88
Soft-paste porcelain bowl and
hard-paste porcelain support,
H. 4 ¹⁵⁄₁₆ in. (12.5 cm), W. 4 ¹³⁄₁₆ in.
(12.2 cm), D. 5 ¼ in. (13.3 cm)
Cité de la Céramique, Sèvres
and Limoges
Page 220

85.
*Alina Szapocznikow (Polish,
Kalisz 1926–1973 Passy, France)
Dessert II, 1970–71
Polyester resin, glass, and photo-
graphs, H. 7 ½ in. (19 cm),
W. 5 ⅛ in. (13 cm), D. 5 ⅛ in. (13 cm)
Private collection
Page 221

86.
Ex-Voto Breasts, late 19th–early
20th century
Wax, H. 9 ¹⁄₁₆ in. (23 cm), W. 9 ¼ in.
(23.5 cm), D. 3 ⅜ in. (8.5 cm)
Italian
Museo Storico Nazionale dell'Arte
Sanitaria, Rome
Page 222

87.
Robert Gober (American, born
Wallingford, Connecticut, 1954)
Untitled, 1990
Beeswax, human hair, and
pigment, H. 24 ¼ in. (61.6 cm),
W. 17 in. (43.2 cm), D. 11 in. (27.9 cm)
Courtesy of the artist and Matthew
Marks Gallery, New York and
Los Angeles
Page 223

88.
Alphonse Lami (French, Paris
1822–1867 Alexandria, Egypt)
Le Bêcheur, 1857
Plaster and paint, H. 86 ¼ in.
(219 cm), W. 39 in. (99 cm),
D. 35 ¼ in. (89.5 cm)
Bâtiment Historique de
la Faculté de Médecine,
Université de Montpellier
Page 224

89.
Kiki Smith (American, born
Nuremberg, Germany, 1954)
Untitled a.k.a. The Sitter, 1992
Wax, cheesecloth, wood, and dye,
H. 28 in. (71.1 cm), W. 24 in. (61 cm),
D. 36 in. (91.4 cm)
Emily Fisher Landau, AMART LLC
Page 225

90.
Nellingen Crucifix, 1430–35
Polychromed limewood,
H. 93 ⁵⁄₁₆ in. (237 cm), W. 70 ½ in.

(179 cm), D. 17 ¹¹⁄₁₆ in. (45 cm)
German, probably Ulm
Landesmuseum Württemberg,
Stuttgart
Page 226

91.
Lucio Fontana (Italian, Rosario
de Sante Fé, Argentina, 1899–1968
Varese)

A. *Crocifisso (Christ on the Cross)*,
1950–52
Glazed terracotta, H. 19 ⅝ in.
(49.8 cm), W. 12 ⅜ in. (31.4 cm),
D. 5 in. (12.7 cm)
Collection of Mr. and
Mrs. J. Tomilson Hill
Page 227

B. *Crocifisso*, 1951
Polychromed ceramic, H. 15 ¾ in.
(40 cm), W. 10 ⅝ in. (27 cm),
D. 4 ¾ in. (12 cm)
Courtesy of Galerie Karsten Greve,
St. Moritz
Page 228

C. *Crocifisso*, 1953
Glazed terracotta, H. 16 ¾ in.
(42.5 cm), W. 7 ¹¹⁄₁₆ in. (19.5 cm),
D. 5 ⁵⁄₁₆ in. (13.5 cm)
Courtesy of Galerie Karsten Greve,
St. Moritz

D. *Crocifisso*, 1948
Polychromed ceramic, H. 16 ⁹⁄₁₆ in.
(42 cm), W. 10 ⅝ in. (27 cm),
D. 4 ½ in. (11.5 cm)
Courtesy of Galerie Karsten Greve,
St. Moritz

E. *Cristo*, 1955
Glazed terracotta, H. 14 ¹⁵⁄₁₆ in.
(38 cm), W. 7 ⅞ in. (20 cm),
D. 3 ⁹⁄₁₆ in. (9 cm)
Courtesy of Galerie Karsten Greve,
St. Moritz
Page 229

92.
John Outterbridge (American,
born Greenville, North Carolina,
1933)
*Broken Dance, Ethnic Heritage
Series*, ca. 1978–82
Stainless steel, wood, leather, sewn
cloth, and ammunition box,
H. 34 in. (86.4 cm), W. 29 ¼ in.
(74.3 cm), D. 33 in. (83.8 cm)
Museum of Modern Art,
New York, Gift of Marlene Hess
and James D. Zirin, 2013
Page 230

93.
Urs Fischer
(Swiss, born Zurich 1973)
The Grass Munchers, 2007
Cast aluminum and patinated wax,
H. 22 ¹⁄₁₆ in. (56 cm), W. 24 ⁷⁄₁₆ in.

(62 cm), D. 17 ⁵⁄₁₆ in. (44 cm)
Burger Collection, Hong Kong
Page 231

94.
Paul Thek (American, Brooklyn
1933–1988 New York)
Untitled from the series
Technological Reliquaries,
ca. 1966–67,
lost elements re-created 2006
Wax, wood, metal, hair, plaster,
paint, and Plexiglas with wig
and fabric, H. 6 ½ in. (16.5 cm),
W. 20 ¼ in. (51.4 cm), D. 6 ¾ in.
(17.1 cm)
Watermill Center Collection,
Water Mill, New York
Page 232

95.
Oliver Herring
(German, born Heidelberg 1964)
Patrick, 2004
Foam core, mat board, digital
chromogenic prints, and polysty-
rene, H. 42 in. (106.7 cm), W. 18 in.
(45.7 cm), D. 27 ½ in. (69.9 cm)
Blanton Museum of Art, University
of Texas at Austin, Partial and
pledged gift of Jeanne and Michael
Klein, 2005
Page 233

96.
Pedro de Mena (Spanish, Granada
1628–1688 Málaga)
Ecce Homo, ca. 1674–85
Polychromed wood and gilding,
figure: H. 24 ¾ in. (62.9 cm),
W. 17 ¾ in. (45.1 cm), D. 18 ⅜ in.
(46.7 cm); base: H. 1 ½ in. (3.8 cm),
W. 21 in. (53.3 cm), D. 16 ⅛ in.
(41 cm)
The Metropolitan Museum of Art,
New York, Purchase, Lila Acheson
Wallace Gift, Mary Trumbell
Adams Fund, and Gift of Dr.
Mortimer D. Sackler, Theresa
Sackler and Family, 2014
(2014.275.1)
Pages 234–35

97.
La Roldana (Luisa Roldán,
Spanish, Seville 1652–1706 Madrid)
The Entombment of Christ,
1700–1701
Polychrome terracotta and wood
base: H. 19 ½ in. (49.5 cm), W. 26 in.
(66 cm), D. 17 in. (43.2 cm)
The Metropolitan Museum of Art,
New York, Purchase, several
members of The Chairman's
Council Gifts, Walter and Leonore
Annenberg Acquisitions Endow-
ment Fund, Álvaro Saieh Bendeck
and Alejandro Santo Domingo
Gifts, and Mary Trumbull Adams

Fund; Edward J. Gallagher Jr.
Bequest, in memory of his father,
Edward Joseph Gallagher, his
mother, Ann Hay Gallagher,
and his son, Edward Joseph
Gallagher III; The Bernard and
Audrey Aronson Charitable Trust
Gift, in memory of her beloved
husband, Bernard Aronson;
Anonymous Gift and Louis V. Bell
Fund, 2016 (2016.482)
Pages 236–37

98.
Berlinde De Bruyckere
(Belgian, born Ghent 1964)
Piëta, 2008
Wax, epoxy, metal, and wood,
H. 93 ¼ in. (236.9 cm), W. 22 ¾ in.
(57.8 cm), D. 21 ¼ in. (54 cm)
Tony Podesta Collection,
Washington, D.C., courtesy
Galleria Continua
Page 238

99.
Ignaz Günther (German,
Altmannstein 1725–1775 Munich)
Christ at the Column, 1754
Polychromed lindenwood and fir,
figure: H. 29 ¼ in. (74.5 cm),
W. 17 ¼ in. (44 cm), D. 7 ½ in.
(19.1 cm); base: H. 1 ¼ in. (3.2 cm),
W. 12 in. (30.5 cm), D. 8 in. (20.3 cm)
Detroit Institute of Arts, Founders
Society Purchase, Acquisitions
Fund
Page 239

100.
Master IPS (German)
Christ at the Column, 1697
Polychromed lindenwood,
H. 63 ¾ in. (162 cm), W. 28 ¾ in.
(73 cm), D. 26 ⅜ in. (67 cm);
base: H. 4 ⁵⁄₁₆ in. (11 cm)
Landesmuseum Württemberg,
Stuttgart
Pages 240–41

101.
Kader Attia
(French, born Dugny 1970)
Open Your Eyes, 2010
Dual projection of two sets of
eighty 35 mm black-and-white and
color slides, projection:
63 in. × 8 ft. 6 ⅜ in. (160 × 260 cm),
duration: 13 min. (digitized
version)
Courtesy of the artist and
Lehmann Maupin, New York
and Hong Kong
Pages 242–43

102.
Greer Lankton (American, Flint,
Michigan, 1958–1996 Chicago)
Rachel, 1986
Papier-mâché, metal plates, wire,
acrylic paint, and matte medium,
H. 28 in. (71.1 cm), W. 21 in.
(53.3 cm), D. 11 in. (27.9 cm)
Collection of Eric Ceputis and
David W. Williams, promised gift
to the Art Institute of Chicago
Page 244

103.
Juan Alonso Villabrille y Ron
(Spanish, Argul ca. 1663–ca. 1732
Madrid)
Saint Paul the Hermit, ca. 1715
Polychromed terracotta and
reverse-painted glass, H. 24 in.
(61 cm), W. 30 in. (76.2 cm),
D. 18 ½ in. (47 cm)
Meadows Museum, Southern
Methodist University, Dallas,
Museum Purchase Thanks to a
Gift from Jo Ann Geurin
Thetford in Honor of Dr. Luis
Martín
Page 245

104.
Janine Antoni (American,
born Freeport, Bahamas, 1964)
Saddle, 2000
Full rawhide, H. 26 in. (66 cm),
W. 33 in. (83.8 cm), D. 79 in.
(200.7 cm)
Astrup Fearnley Collection, Oslo
Page 246

105.
Anton Maria Maragliano
(Italian, Genoa 1664–1739 Genoa)
Saint Sebastian, 1700
Polychromed wood and gilding,
H. 74 ¹³⁄₁₆ in. (190 cm), W. 31 ½ in.
(80 cm), D. 37 ⅜ in. (95 cm)
Oratorio della Santissima Trinità,
Rapallo
Page 247

106.
Jean-Léon Gérôme
(French, Vesoul 1824–1904 Paris)
Seated Woman, ca. 1898–1902
Marble, pigment, and wax,
H. 16 ¹⁵⁄₁₆ in. (43 cm), W. 13 ¾ in.
(35 cm), D. 13 ¾ in. (35 cm)
Detroit Institute of Arts, Founders
Society Purchase, Robert H.
Tannahill Foundation Fund
Page 248

107.
Sarah Lucas
(British, born London 1962)
NUD CYCLADIC 9, 2010
Nylon, synthetic fiber, concrete,

and steel wire, H. 21 in. (53.3 cm),
W. 24 ½ in. (62.2 cm), D. 24 in.
(61 cm)
The Metropolitan Museum of Art,
New York, Purchase, Lila Acheson
Wallace Gift, 2015 (2015.305a–c)
Page 249

108.
Dorothea Tanning (American,
Galesburg, Illinois, 1910–2012
New York)
Emma, 1970
Fabric, wool, and lace,
H. 24 in. (61 cm), W. 32 in. (81.3 cm),
D. 22 in. (55.9 cm)
Nelson-Atkins Museum of Art,
Kansas City, Missouri, Purchase:
acquired through the generosity
of the William T. Kemper
Foundation—Commerce Bank,
Trustee
Page 250

109.
Louise Bourgeois
(American, Paris 1911–2010
New York)
Three Horizontals, 1998
Fabric and steel, H. 53 in. (134.6 cm),
W. 72 in. (182.9 cm), D. 36 in.
(91.4 cm)
ISelf Collection
Page 251

Between Life and Art

110.
Alison Saar
(American, born Los Angeles 1956)
Strange Fruit, 1995
Tin alloy, wood, dirt, found
objects, rope, and paint, H. 76 in.
(193.1 cm), W. 21 in. (53.4 cm),
D. 14 in. (35.6 cm)
Baltimore Museum of Art,
Contemporary Art Endowment
Fund
Page 259

111.
Gregorio Fernández (Spanish,
Sarria, Lugo, 1576–1635 Valladolid)
Dead Christ, 1625–30
Polychromed wood, horn, glass,
and cork, H. 18 ⅛ in. (46 cm),
W. 75 ³⁄₁₆ in. (191 cm), D. 29 ⅛ in.
(74 cm)
Museo Nacional del Prado, Madrid
Page 260

112.
Maurizio Cattelan (Italian, born
Padua 1960)
Now, 2004
Polyester, resin, wax, pigment,
human hair, clothing, and coffin,

H. 33 ⁷⁄₁₆ in. (85 cm), W. 88 ⁹⁄₁₆ in.
(225 cm), D. 30 ¹¹⁄₁₆ in. (78 cm)
Astrup Fearnley Collection, Oslo
Page 261

113.
Philippe Curtius (Swiss,
Stockach, Germany, 1737–1794
Ivry-sur-Seine, France)
Sleeping Beauty, 1765, remade 1989
Gold leaf, carved wood, velvet
upholstery, beeswax, human hair,
laminated fiberglass, alloy and
steel servo, tinted slush wax, silk,
and cotton lace, H. 32 ¹¹⁄₁₆ in.
(83 cm), W. 65 ⅜ in. (166 cm),
D. 29 ⅛ in. (74 cm)
Madame Tussauds, London
Pages 262–63

114.
Paul McCarthy (American,
born Salt Lake City 1945)
Paul Dreaming, Vertical, Horizontal,
2005/12
Platinum silicone, clothing, plastic,
foam, lawn chair, H. 24 ⅜ in.
(61.9 cm), W. 70 ⅞ in. (180 cm),
D. 28 in. (71.1 cm)
Glenstone Museum, Potomac,
Maryland
Page 263

115.
Fontana Workshop
(Florentine)
Anatomical Venus, 1780–85
Wood skeleton, transparent wax,
pigmented wax, and hair
W. 68 ½ in. (174 cm), D. 29 ¾ in.
(75.5 cm)
Semmelweis Orvostörténeti
Múzeum, Budapest
Pages 264–65

116.
Nativity of the Virgin, ca. 1480
Limewood and paint, H. 14 ¼ in.
(36.2 cm), W. 54 in. (137.2 cm),
D. 17 in. (43.2 cm)
German, Lower Franconia
The Metropolitan Museum of Art,
New York, The Cloisters
Collection, 1956 (56.211)

117.
Ron Mueck (Australian,
born Melbourne 1958)
Old Woman in Bed, 2000
Silicone rubber, polyester resin,
cotton fabric, polyurethane foam,
polyester, and oil paint, H. 9 ⁷⁄₁₆ in.
(24 cm), W. 37 ³⁄₁₆ in. (94.5 cm),
D. 22 ¹⁄₁₆ in. (56 cm); pedestal:
H. 39 ½ in. (100.3 cm), W. 37 ³⁄₁₆ in.
(94.5 cm), D. 22 ¹⁄₁₆ in. (56 cm)
National Gallery of Canada,
Ottawa, Purchased 2001

SELECTED BIBLIOGRAPHY

Adrian, Dennis. *The Real and Ideal in Figurative Sculpture: John De Andrea, Duane Hanson*. Exh. cat. Chicago: Museum of Contemporary Art, 1974.

Agamben, Giorgio. "L'Immagine immemoriale." In *La potenza del pensiero: Saggi e conferenze*. Vicenza: Neri Pozza, 2005.

Agostini, Grazia, and Luisa Ciammitti, eds. *Niccolò dell'Arca: Seminario di studi; Atti del convegno 26–27 maggio 1987*. Bologna: Nuova Alfa Editoriale, 1989.

[Angliviel] de La Beaumelle, Agnès, et al. *Hans Bellmer: Anatomie du désir*. Exh. cat. Paris: Centre Pompidou, Musée National d'Art Moderne; Éditions Gallimard, 2006.

Armaroli, Maurizio, and Raffaele A. Bernabeo. *Le cere anatomiche bolognesi del Settecento: Università degli studi di Bologna, Accademia delle scienze*. Musei e archivi dello studio bolognese, 2. Bologna: Clueb, 1981.

Ash-Milby, Kathleen, et al. *Hide: Skin as Material and Metaphor*. Exh. cat. Washington, D.C., and New York: NMAI Editions, National Museum of the American Indian, Smithsonian Institution, 2010.

Aspley, Keith. *Historical Dictionary of Surrealism*. Lanham, Md.: The Scarecrow Press, 2010.

Attia, Kader, et al. *The Repair: From Occident to Extra-Occidental Cultures*. Berlin: Green Box, 2014.

Augaitis, Daina, and Diana Freundl. *Bharti Kher: Matter*. Exh. cat. London: Black Dog Publishing; Vancouver: Vancouver Art Gallery, 2016.

Bailly, Christian. *Automata: The Golden Age, 1848–1914*. London: Sotheby's Publications; Philip Wilson Publishers, 1987.

Baker, Malcolm. *Figured in Marble: The Making and Viewing of Eighteenth-Century Sculpture*. Los Angeles: J. Paul Getty Museum, 2000.

Barolsky, Paul. "As in Ovid, So in Renaissance Art." *Renaissance Quarterly* 51, no. 2 (Summer 1998), pp. 451–74.

Bassett, Molly Harbour, and Jeannette Favrot Peterson. "Coloring the Sacred in Sixteenth-Century Central Mexico." In *The Materiality of Color: The Production, Circulation, and Application of Dyes and Pigments, 1400–1800*, ed. Andrea Feeser et al., pp. 45–64. The Histories of Material Culture and Collecting, 1700–1950. Farnham, Surrey: Ashgate Publishing, 2012.

Batchelor, David. *Chromophobia*. London: Reaktion Books, 2000.

———, ed. *Colour*. Cambridge, Mass.: MIT Press, 2008.

Baudrillard, Jean. *Simulacra and Simulation*. Ann Arbor: University of Michigan Press, 1994.

Baum, Kelly. "Oliver Herring." In *Blanton Museum of Art: American Art since 1900*, ed. Annette DiMeo Carlozzi and Kelly Baum, pp. 132–33. Austin: Blanton Museum of Art, The University of Texas at Austin, 2006.

Baxandall, Michael. *The Limewood Sculptors of Renaissance Germany*. New Haven, Conn.: Yale University Press, 1980.

Bean, Susan S. "The Unfired Clay Sculpture of Bengal in the Artscape of Modern South Asia." In *A Companion to Asian Art and Architecture*, ed. Rebecca M. Brown and Deborah S. Hutton, pp. 604–28. Chichester, West Sussex, and Malden, Mass.: Wiley-Blackwell, 2011.

———. *Yankee India: American Commercial and Cultural Encounters with India in the Age of Sail, 1784–1860*. Salem, Mass.: Peabody Essex Museum; Chidambaram, Ahmedabad: Mapin Publishing, 2001.

Bellandi, Alfredo, et al. *"Fece di scoltura di legname e colori": Scultura del Quattrocento in legno dipinto a Firenze*. Exh. cat. Florence: Giunti; Galleria degli Uffizi, 2016.

Benjamin, Walter. "The Work of Art in the Age of Mechanical Reproduction [1936]." In *Illuminations*, ed. Hannah Arendt, pp. 217–51. New York: Schocken Books, 1968.

Berger, Maurice, et al. *White: Whiteness and Race in Contemporary Art*. Exh. cat. Baltimore: Center for Art and Visual Culture, 2004.

Berry, Ian, et al. *Nancy Grossman: Tough Life Diary*. Exh. cat. Saratoga Springs, N.Y.: Frances Young Tang Teaching Museum and Art Gallery, Skidmore College; Munich and New York: Prestel Verlag, 2012.

Bhattacharya-Stettler, Therese, et al. *Meret Oppenheim Retrospective: "An Enormously Tiny Bit of a Lot."* Exh. cat. Ostfildern: Hatje Cantz Verlag, 2007.

Bindman, David. "Lost Surfaces: Canova and Color." *Oxford Art Journal* 39, no. 2 (August 2016), pp. 229–41.

Bindman, David, and Henry Louis Gates Jr., eds. *The Image of the Black in Western Art*. New ed. 10 vols. 1976– . Cambridge, Mass: Belknap Press, Harvard University Press, 2010–14.

Birren, Faber. *Color: A Survey in Words and Pictures, from Ancient Mysticism to Modern Science*. Secaucus, N.J.: Citadel Press, 1963.

Bloom, Michelle E. *Waxworks: A Cultural Obsession*. Minneapolis: University of Minnesota Press, 2003.

Blühm, Andreas, et al. *The Colour of Sculpture, 1840–1910*. Exh. cat. Zwolle: Waanders Uitgeverij, 1996.

Bondil, Nathalie, et al. *Metamorphoses in Rodin's Studio*. Exh. cat. Montreal: Montreal Museum of Fine Arts; Milan: 5 Continents Editions, 2015.

Bonsanti, Giorgio, et al. *Emozioni in terracotta: Guido Mazzoni, Antonio Begarelli; Sculture del Rinascimento emiliano*. Modena: Franco Cosimo Panini, 2009.

Bossi, Laura. *De l'agalmatophilie ou l'amour des statues*. Paris: L'Echoppe, 2012.

Bray, Xavier, et al. *Luisa Roldán: Court Sculptor to the Kings of Spain*. Exh. cat. [Madrid]: Coll & Cortés, 2016.

———, et al. *The Sacred Made Real: Spanish Painting and Sculpture 1600–1700*. Exh. cat. London: National Gallery Company, 2009.

Breitweiser, Sabine, et al. *Isa Genzken: Retrospective*. Exh. cat. New York: The Museum of Modern Art, 2013.

Buchsteiner, Thomas, and Otto Letze. *Duane Hanson: Sculptures of the American Dream*. New ed. Ostfildern: Hatje Cantz Verlag, 2007.

Bürgi, Bernhard Mendes, et al. *Charles Ray: Sculpture 1997–2014*. Exh. cat. Ostfildern: Hatje Cantz Verlag, 2014.

Burnham, Jack. *Beyond Modern Sculpture: The Effects of Science and Technology on the Sculpture of This Century*. New York: George Braziller, 1968.

Bynum, Caroline Walker. *Jesus as Mother: Studies in the Spirituality of the High Middle Ages*. Berkeley and Los Angeles: University of California Press, 1982.

Bynum, Caroline Walker, and Paula Gerson. "Body-Part Reliquaries and Body-Parts in the Middle Ages." *Gesta* 36, no. 1 (1997), pp. 3–7.

Callen, Anthea. *The Spectacular Body: Science, Method, and Meaning in the Work of Degas*. New Haven, Conn.: Yale University Press, 1995.

Camille, Michael. *The Medieval Art of Love: Objects and Subjects of Desire*. New York: Harry N. Abrams, 1998.

[Caraccioli, Louis-Antoine de]. *Dictionnaire critique, pittoresque et sentencieux, propre à faire connoître les usages du siècle, ainsi que ses bizarreries*. 3 vols. Lyon: Benoît Duplain, Libraire, 1768.

Celant, Germano. *Louise Bourgeois: The Fabric Works*. Exh. cat. Milan: Skira Editore; Venice: Fondazione Emilio e Annabianca Vedova, 2010.

Chaouli, Michael [*sic*]. "Laocoön and the Hottentots." In *The German Invention of Race*, ed. Sara Eigen and Mark Larrimore, pp. 23–31. Albany, N.Y.: State University of New York Press, 2006.

Christian, William A., Jr. *The Stranger, the Tears, the Photograph, the Touch: Divine Presence in Spain and Europe since 1500*. Budapest: Central European University, 2017.

Christiansen, Keith, et al. *The Renaissance Portrait from Donatello to Bellini*. Exh. cat. New York: The Metropolitan Museum of Art, 2011.

Classen, Constance, et al. *A Cultural History of the Senses.* 6 vols. London: Bloomsbury Academic, 2014.

Cole, Michael W., and Rebecca E. Zorach, eds. *The Idol in the Age of Art: Objects, Devotions and the Early Modern World.* Farnham, Surrey: Ashgate Publishing, 2009.

Colón Mendoza, Ilenia. *The Cristos yacentes of Gregorio Fernández/ Polychrome Sculptures of the Supine Christ in Seventeenth-Century Spain.* Burlington, Vt.: Ashgate Publishing, 2015.

Connor, Janis. "The Ethereal Icon: Malvina Hoffman's Worshipful Imagery of Anna Pavlova." In *Perspectives on American Sculpture before 1925,* ed. Thayer Tolles, pp. 130–49. The Metropolitan Museum of Art Symposia. New York: The Metropolitan Museum of Art, 2003.

Coppel, Stephen. *Picasso Prints: The Vollard Suite.* Exh. cat. London: British Museum Press, 2012.

Coren, Stanley, and Joan Stern Girgus. *Seeing Is Deceiving: The Psychology of Visual Illusions.* Hillsdale, N.J.: Lawrence Erlbaum Associates, 1978.

Crary, Jonathan. *Techniques of the Observer: On Vision and Modernity in the Nineteenth Century.* Cambridge, Mass.: MIT Press, 1990.

Curtis, Penelope. *Sculpture 1900–1945: After Rodin.* Oxford and New York: Oxford University Press, 1999.

Dallow, Jessica. "Reclaiming Histories: Betye and Alison Saar, Feminism, and the Representation of Black Womanhood." *Feminist Studies* 30, no. 1 (Spring 2004), pp. 74–113.

Dallow, Jessica, Barbara C. Matilsky, and Tracye Saar-Cavanaugh. *Family Legacies: The Art of Betye, Lezley, and Alison Saar.* Exh. cat. Chapel Hill: Ackland Art Museum, the University of North Carolina at Chapel Hill; Seattle and London: University of Washington Press, 2005.

Daninos, Andrea, et al. *Waxing Eloquent: Italian Portraits in Wax.* Exh. cat. Venice: Palazzo Fortuny; Milan: Officina Libraria, 2012.

Davies, David, et al. *El Greco.* Exh. cat. London: National Gallery Company, 2003.

Des Cars, Laurence, et al. *The Spectacular Art of Jean-Léon Gérôme, 1824–1904.* Exh. cat. Los Angeles: J. Paul Getty Museum; Milan: Skira Editore, 2010.

De Wachter, Ellen Mara. *Co-Art: Artists on Creative Collaboration.* London and New York: Phaidon Press, 2017.

Di Dio, Kelley Helmstutler, and Rosario Coppel. *Sculpture Collections in Early Modern Spain.* Farnham, Surrey: Ashgate Publishing, 2013.

Diederen, Roger, et al. *Mit Leib und Seele: Münchner Rokoko von Asam bis Günther.* Exh. cat. Munich: Sieveking, 2014.

Draper, James David, et al. *Playing with Fire: European Terracotta Models, 1740–1840.* Exh. cat. New York: The Metropolitan Museum of Art, 2003.

Droth, Martina, et al. *Sculpture Victorious: Art in an Age of Invention, 1837–1901.* Exh. cat. New Haven, Conn.: Yale Center for British Art, 2014.

Dufour, Gary, et al. *Jeff Wall 1990.* Exh. cat. Vancouver: Vancouver Art Gallery, 1990.

Durantaye, Leland de la. *Giorgio Agamben: A Critical Introduction.* Stanford, Calif.: Stanford University Press, 2009.

Düring, Monika v[on], Georges Didi-Huberman, and Marta Poggesi. *Encyclopaedia Anatomica: A Complete Collection of Anatomical Waxes/Vollständige Sammlung anatomischer Wachse/Collection complète des cires anatomiques.* Cologne: Benedikt Taschen Verlag, 1999.

Eastlake, Lady [Elizabeth Rigby], ed. *Life of John Gibson, R.A., Sculptor.* London: Longmans, Green, and Co., 1870.

Eaton, Natasha. "Chromophobic Activism: The Politics and Materiality of Art and Colour in India, circa 1917–circa 1966." *Third Text* 28, no. 6 (December 2014), pp. 475–88.

———. *Colour, Art and Empire: Visual Culture and the Nomadism of Representation.* London: I. B. Tauris, 2013.

Ebenstein, Joanna. *The Anatomical Venus: Wax, God, Death & the Ecstatic.* New York: D.A.P./Distributed Art Publishers, 2016.

Eck, Caroline van. *Art, Agency and Living Presence: From the Animated Image to the Excessive Object.* Boston and Berlin: Walter De Gruyter; Leiden: Leiden University Press, 2015.

Falconet, Étienne Maurice. "Sculpture." In *The Encyclopedia of Diderot & d'Alembert Collaborative Translation Project,* trans. Nelly S. Hoyt and Thomas Cassirer. 1765. Ann Arbor: Michigan Publishing, University of Michigan Library, 2003; https://quod.lib.umich.edu/d/did/did2222.0000.166/--sculpture?rgn=main;view=fulltext.

Feeke, Stephen, et al. *Second Skin: Historical Life Casting and Contemporary Sculpture.* Exh. cat. Leeds: Henry Moore Institute, 2002.

Fletcher, Valerie J. *Marvelous Objects: Surrealist Sculpture from Paris to New York.* Exh. cat. Washington, D.C.: Hirshhorn Museum and Sculpture Garden, 2015.

Flühler-Kreis, Dione, Peter Wyer, and Donat Stuppan. *Die Holzskulpturen des Mittelalters: Katalog der Sammlung des Schweizerischen Landesmuseums Zürich.* Zurich: Schweizerisches Landesmuseum, 2007.

Flynn, Tom. *The Body in Three Dimensions.* New York: Harry N. Abrams, 1998.

Fore, Devin. *Realism after Modernism: The Rehumanization of Art and Literature.* Cambridge, Mass.: MIT Press, 2012.

Foster, Hal, et al. *Art Since 1900: Modernism, Antimodernism, Postmodernism.* 2nd ed. 2004. London: Thames & Hudson, 2011.

Freedberg, David. *The Power of Images: Studies in the History and Theory of Response.* Chicago: The University of Chicago Press, 1989.

Freud, Sigmund. *The Uncanny.* Trans. Hugh Haughton and David McLintock. 1919. London: Penguin Books, 2003.

Fulton, Rachel. *From Judgment to Passion: Devotion to Christ and the Virgin Mary, 800–1200.* New York: Columbia University Press, 2002.

Gage, John. *Colour and Culture: Practice and Meaning from Antiquity to Abstraction.* Boston: Little, Brown, 1981.

———. *Colour and Meaning: Art, Science, and Symbolism.* Berkeley and Los Angeles: University of California Press, 1999.

Galassi, Cristina. *Sculture 'da vestire': Nero Alberti da Sansepolcro e la produzione di manichini lignei in una bottega del Cinquecento.* Exh. cat. Milan: Electa Editrice, 2005.

Gallagher, Catherine, Joel Fineman, and Neil Hertz. "More about 'Medusa's Head.'" *Representations,* no. 4 (Fall 1983), pp. 55–72.

Garber, Marjorie, and Nancy J. Vickers, eds. *The Medusa Reader.* London and New York: Routledge, 2003.

Garnett, Jane, and Gervase Rosser. *Spectacular Miracles: Transforming Images in Italy, from the Renaissance to the Present.* London: Reaktion Books, 2013.

Gatacre, Edward V., and Laura Dru. "Portraiture in Le Cabinet de Cire de Curtius and Its Successor Madame Tussaud's Exhibition." In *La ceroplastica nella scienza e nell'arte: Atti del I congresso internazionale, Firenze, 3–7 giugno 1975,* ed. Cristina Piacenti, vol. 3, pp. 617–38. Florence: Leo S. Olschki Editore, 1977.

Gavenas, Mary Lisa. *Color Stories: Behind the Scenes of America's Billion-Dollar Beauty Industry.* New York: Simon & Schuster, 2002.

Geczy, Adam, ed. *The Artificial Body in Fashion and Art: Marionettes, Models, and Mannequins.* London: Bloomsbury Academic, 2017.

Gell, Alfred. *Art and Agency: An Anthropological Theory.* Oxford: Oxford University Press, 1998.

———. "The Technology of Enchantment and the Enchantment of Technology." In *The Object Reader,* ed. Fiona Candlin and Raiford Guins, pp. 208–28. London and New York: Routledge, 2009.

Gertsman, Elina. *Worlds Within: Opening the Medieval Shrine Madonna.* University Park, Pa.: The Pennsylvania State University Press, [2015].

Giannini, Claudia, ed. *Installations, Mattress Factory, 1990–1999.* Pittsburgh, Pa.: Mattress Factory; University of Pittsburgh Press, 2001.

Gioni, Massimiliano, et al. *The Great Mother: Women, Maternity, and Power in Art and Visual Culture, 1900–2015.* Exh. cat. Milan: Fondazione Nicola Trussardi; Skira Editore, 2015.

Globus, Doro, ed. *Fred Wilson: A Critical Reader.* London: Ridinghouse, 2011.

[Goethe, Johann Wolfgang von]. *Goethe's Theory of Colours.* Trans. and annot. Charles Lock Eastlake. London: John Murray, 1840.

Graw, Isabelle, et al., eds. *Art and Subjecthood: The Return of the Human Figure in Semiocapitalism*. Berlin: Sternberg Press, 2011.

Gray, Christopher. *Sculpture and Ceramics of Paul Gauguin*. Baltimore: Johns Hopkins Press, 1963.

Gross, Kenneth. *The Dream of the Moving Statue*. Ithaca, N.Y.: Cornell University Press, 1992.

———, ed. *On Dolls*. London: Knotting Hill Editions, 2012.

Guldemond, Jaap, et al., eds. *Yinka Shonibare: Double Dutch*. Exh. cat. Rotterdam: Museum Boijmans Van Beuningen, 2004.

Guratzsch, Herwig, et al. *Max Klinger: Bestandskatalog der Bildwerke, Gemälde und Zeichnungen im Museum der bildenden Künste Leipzig*. Leipzig: E. A. Seemann, 1995.

Harari, Yuval Noah. *Homo Deus: A Brief History of Tomorrow*. 2015. New York: HarperCollins 2017.

Harper, Elizabeth. "Photographing the Real Bodies of Incorrupt Saints." In *Atlas Obscura* (June 30, 2015); www.atlasobscura.com/articles/photographing-the-real-bodies-of-incorrupt-saints.

Harper, Glenn, and Twylene Moyer, eds. *A Sculpture Reader: Contemporary Sculpture Since 1980*. Hamilton, N.J.: ISC Press, 2006.

Harten, Jürgen, et al. *Edward and Nancy Kienholz: 1980's*. Exh. cat. Düsseldorf: Kunsthalle Düsseldorf, 1989.

Heartney, Eleanor, et al. *After the Revolution: Women Who Transformed Contemporary Art*. Munich and London: Prestel Verlag, 2013.

Hegel, G[eorg] W[ilhelm] F[riedrich]. *Aesthetics: Lectures on Fine Art*. Trans. T. M. Knox. 2 vols. Oxford: Clarendon Press, 1975.

Hersey, George L. *Falling in Love with Statues: Artificial Humans from Pygmalion to the Present*. Chicago: The University of Chicago Press, 2009.

Hertel, Christiane. *Pygmalion in Bavaria: The Sculptor Ignaz Günther and Eighteenth-Century Aesthetic Art Theory*. University Park, Pa: The Pennsylvania State University Press, 2011.

Hertz, Neil. "Medusa's Head: Male Hysteria under Political Pressure." *Representations*, no. 4 (Fall 1983), pp. 27–54.

Hiller, Susan, ed. *The Myth of Primitivism: Perspectives on Art*. London and New York: Routledge, 1991.

Hoffer, Andreas, and Christine Klinger. *Figur Skulptur: Katalog zur Ausstellung mit einem Bildverzeichnis sämtlicher weiterer Skulpturen der Sammlung Essl/Figure Sculpture: Catalogue of the Exhibition with Colourplates of All Further Sculptures from the Essl Collection*. Exh. cat. Klosterneuburg: Edition Sammlung Essl, 2005.

Hoffman, Malvina. *Yesterday Is Tomorrow: A Personal History*. New York: Crown Publishers, 1965.

Hoffmann, E. T. A. "The Sand-Man." In *The Best Tales of Hoffmann*, ed. E. F. Bleiler; trans. J. T. Bealby, pp. 183–214. New York: Dover Publications, 1967.

Holmes, Brooke, and Karen Marta, eds. *Liquid Antiquity*. Geneva and Athens: The DESTE Foundation for Contemporary Art, 2017.

Holmes, Megan. "Ex-Votos: Materiality, Memory, and Cult." In *The Idol in the Age of Art: Objects, Devotions and the Early Modern World*, ed. Michael W. Cole and Rebecca E. Zorach, pp. 159–81. Farnham, Surrey: Ashgate Publishing, 2009.

Hopps, Walter, et al. *Kienholz, A Retrospective: Edward and Nancy Reddin Kienholz*. Exh. cat. New York: Whitney Museum of American Art, 1996.

Hurlston, David, et al. *Ron Mueck*. Exh. cat. Melbourne: National Gallery of Victoria, 2010.

Itten, Johannes. *The Art of Color: The Subjective Experience and Objective Rationale of Color*. New York: Reinhold Pub. Corp., 1961.

Jones, Amelia. *Self/Image: Technology, Representation, and the Contemporary Subject*. London and New York: Routledge, 2006.

Jones, Caroline A., et al. *Sensorium: Embodied Experience, Technology, and Contemporary Art*. Cambridge, Mass.: MIT Press; The MIT List Visual Arts Center, 2006.

Jones, Kellie, and Hazel V. Carby. *Now Dig This!: Art & Black Los Angeles, 1960–1980*. Exh. cat. Los Angeles: Hammer Museum; Munich: DelMonico Books/Prestel Verlag, 2011.

Jordanova, Ludmilla. *Sexual Visions: Images of Gender in Science and Medicine between the Eighteenth and Twentieth Centuries*. New York: Harvester Wheatsheaf, 1989.

Jørnaes, Bjarne. *The Sculptor Bertel Thorvaldsen*. 1993. Copenhagen: Thorvaldsens Museum, 2011.

Jung, Jacqueline E. "The Tactile and the Visionary: Notes on the Place of Sculpture in the Medieval Religious Imagination." In *Looking Beyond: Visions, Dreams, and Insights in Medieval Art & History*, ed. Colum Hourihane, pp. 202–40. Index of Christian Art Occasional Papers, 11. Princeton, N.J.: Department of Art & Archaeology, Princeton University, 2010.

Kachur, Lewis. *Displaying the Marvelous: Marcel Duchamp, Salvador Dali, and Surrealist Exhibition Installations*. Cambridge, Mass.: MIT Press, 2001.

Kasl, Ronda, et al. *Sacred Spain: Art and Belief in the Spanish World*. Exh. cat. Indianapolis: Indianapolis Museum of Art, 2009.

Kelley, Mike. *The Uncanny*. Exh. cat. Arnhem: Gemeentemuseum Arnhem; Los Angeles: Fred Hoffman, 1993.

———, et al. *The Uncanny by Mike Kelley, Artist*. Edited by Christoph Grunenberg. Exh. cat. Liverpool: Tate Liverpool; Cologne: Verlag der Buchhandlung Walther König, 2004.

Kendall, Richard, et al. *Degas and the Little Dancer*. Exh. cat. New Haven, Conn.: Yale University Press; Omaha: Joslyn Art Museum, 1998.

Kent, Rachel, et al. *Yinka Shonibare MBE*. Rev. ed. 2008. Munich and New York: Prestel Verlag, 2014.

King, Catherine, ed. *Views of Difference: Different Views of Art*. New Haven, Conn.: Yale University Press, 1999.

Kinkel, Marianne. *Races of Mankind: The Sculptures of Malvina Hoffman*. Urbana, Chicago, and Springfield: University of Illinois Press, 2011.

Krauss, Rosalind E. *Passages in Modern Sculpture*. New York: Viking Press, 1977.

Kuriyama, Shigehisa. "The Expressiveness of Colors." In *The Expressiveness of the Body and the Divergence of Greek and Chinese Medicine*, pp. 153–92. Rev. ed. 1999. New York: Zone Books, 2002.

Lasansky, D. Medina. *The Renaissance Perfected: Architecture, Spectacle, and Tourism in Fascist Italy*. University Park, Pa.: The Pennsylvania State University Press, 2004.

Latour, Bruno. "What is iconoclash? Or is there a world beyond the image wars?" In *Iconoclash: Beyond the Image-Wars in Science, Religion and Art*, ed. Peter Weibel and Bruno Latour, pp. 16–38. Karlsruhe: ZKM; Cambridge, Mass.: MIT Press, 2002.

Leeming, David. *Medusa in the Mirror of Time*. London: Reaktion Books, 2013.

Leithe-Jasper, Manfred, and Patricia Wengraf. *European Bronzes from the Quentin Collection*. Exh. cat. New York: The Frick Collection, 2004.

Letze, Otto, et al. *Escultura hiperrealista 1973–2016*. Exh. cat. Bilbao: BBK, 2016.

Levine, Marc N., and David M. Carballo, eds. *Obsidian Reflections: Symbolic Dimensions of Obsidian in Mesoamerica*. Boulder: University Press of Colorado, 2014.

Lewin, Rebecca, ed. *Duane Hanson*. Exh. cat. London: Serpentine Galleries; Koenig Books, 2015.

Lichtenstein, Jacqueline. *The Blind Spot: An Essay on the Relations between Painting and Sculpture in the Modern Age*. Los Angeles: Getty Research Institute, 2008.

———. *The Eloquence of Color: Rhetoric and Painting in the French Classical Age*. 1989. Berkeley and Los Angeles: University of California Press, 1993.

Little, Charles T., et al. *Set in Stone: The Face in Medieval Sculpture*. Exh. cat. New York: The Metropolitan Museum of Art, 2006.

Livingstone, Marco. *Kienholz, The Hoerengracht: Ed and Nancy Reddin Kienholz*. Exh. cat. New York: PaceWildenstein, 2002.

Mann, Alan E. "Imagining Prehistory: Pictorial Reconstructions of the Way We Were." *American Anthropologist* 105, no. 1 [*Biological Anthropology*] (March 2003), pp. 139–43.

Marcoci, Roxana, Geoffrey Batchen, and Tobia Bezzola. *The Original Copy: Photography of Sculpture, 1839 to Today*. Exh. cat. New York: The Museum of Modern Art, 2010.

Margerie, Laure de, et al. *Facing the Other: Charles Cordier (1827–1905), Ethnographic Sculptor*. Exh. cat. Paris: Musée d'Orsay; New York: Harry N. Abrams, 2004.

Martin, Meredith. *Dairy Queens: The Politics of Pastoral Architecture from Catherine de' Medici to Marie-Antoinette*. Cambridge, Mass.: Harvard University Press, 2011.

Mavor, Carol. *Aurelia: Art and Literature through the Mouth of the Fairy Tale*. London: Reaktion Books, 2017.

Messbarger, Rebecca. "As Who Dare Gaze the Sun: Anna Morandi Manzolini's Wax Anatomies of the Male Reproductive System and Genitalia." In *Italy's Eighteenth Century: Gender and Culture in the Age of the Grand Tour*, by Paula Findlen et al., pp. 251–74. Stanford, Calif.: Stanford University Press, 2009.

———. *The Lady Anatomist: The Life and Work of Anna Morandi Manzolini*. Chicago: The University of Chicago Press, 2010.

Michaud, Philippe-Alain. *Aby Warburg and the Image in Motion*. 1998. New York: Zone Books, 2003.

Mortimer, Richard, et al. *The Funeral Effigies of Westminster Abbey*. Rev. ed. 1994. Woodbridge, Suffolk: The Boydell Press, 2003.

Moser, Stephanie. *Ancestral Images: The Iconography of Human Origins*. Ithaca, N.Y.: Cornell University Press, 1998.

Mundi, Veronica. "The Image Made Flesh." In *Skin*, ed. Heide Hatry, pp. 21–28. Heidelberg: Kehrer Verlag, 2005.

Munro, Jane, et al. *Silent Partners: Artist and Mannequin from Function to Fetish*. Exh. cat. Cambridge: Fitzwilliam Museum; New Haven, Conn.: Yale University Press, 2014.

Nelson, Charmaine A. *The Color of Stone: Sculpting the Black Female Subject in Nineteenth-Century America*. Minneapolis: University of Minnesota Press, 2007.

———. *Representing the Black Female Subject in Western Art*. New York and London: Routledge, Taylor & Francis Group, 2010.

Nochlin, Linda. *Realism*. Harmondsworth, Middlesex: Penguin Books, 1971.

———. "Unholy Postures: Kiki Smith and the Body." In *Kiki Smith: A Gathering, 1980–2005*, by Siri Engberg et al., pp. 30–37. Exh. cat. Minneapolis: Walker Art Center, 2006.

Nordgren, Sune, et al. *Dorothea Tanning*. Exh. cat. Malmö, Sweden: Malmö Konsthall, 1993.

Østergaard, Jan Stubbe, et al. *Transformations: Classical Sculpture in Colour*. Meddelelser fra Ny Carlsberg Glyptotek, 16. Exh. cat. Copenhagen: Ny Carlsberg Glyptotek, 2014.

Pacini, Marina, et al. *Marisol: Sculptures and Works on Paper*. Exh. cat. Memphis: Memphis Brooks Museum of Art; New Haven, Conn.: Yale University Press, 2014.

Panzanelli, Roberta, et al. *The Color of Life: Polychromy in Sculpture from Antiquity to the Present*. Exh. cat. Los Angeles: J. Paul Getty Museum; Getty Research Institute, 2008.

———. *Ephemeral Bodies: Wax Sculpture and the Human Figure*. Los Angeles: Getty Research Institute, 2008.

Pass, Victoria R. "Schiaparelli's Convulsive Gloves." In *Extravagances: Habits of Being 4*, ed. Cristina Giorcelli and Paula Rabinowitz, pp. 127–46. [Minneapolis]: University of Minnesota Press, 2015.

Pastoureau, Michel. *Black: The History of a Color*. Princeton, N.J.: Princeton University Press, 2009.

———. *Blue: The History of a Color*. Princeton, N.J.: Princeton University Press, 2001.

Penny, Nicholas. *The Materials of Sculpture*. New Haven, Conn.: Yale University Press, 1993.

Piccoli Catello, Marisa, et al. *The Art of the Presepio: The Neapolitan Crib of the Banco di Napoli Collection*. Naples: Banco di Napoli, 1987.

Pilbeam, Pamela. *Madame Tussaud and the History of Waxworks*. London and New York: Hambledon and London, 2003.

Pinkus, Assaf. *Sculpting Simulacra in Medieval Germany, 1250–1380*. Farnham, Surrey: Ashgate Publishing, 2014.

Pleij, Herman. *Colors Demonic and Divine: Shades of Meaning in the Middle Ages and After*. 2002. New York: Columbia University Press, 2004.

Potts, Alex. *The Sculptural Imagination: Figurative, Modernist, Minimalist*. New Haven, Conn.: Yale University Press, 2000.

Powell, Amy Knight. *Depositions: Scenes from the Late Medieval Church and the Modern Museum*. New York: Zone Books, 2012.

Praz, Mario. "Le figure di cera in letteratura." In *La ceroplastica nella scienza e nell'arte: Atti del I congresso internazionale, Firenze, 3–7 giugno 1975*, ed. Cristina Piacenti, vol. 3, pp. 549–68. Florence: Leo S. Olschki Editore, 1977.

Purdy, Daniel. "The Whiteness of Beauty: Weimar Neo-Classicism and the Sculptural Transcendence of Color." In *Colors 1800/1900/2000: Signs of Ethnic Difference*, ed. Birgit Tautz, pp. 83–99. Amsterdamer Beiträge zur neueren Germanistik, 56. Amsterdam and New York: Brill, Rodopi, 2004.

Quinn, Marc. *Marc Quinn: Selfs*. Exh. cat. London: Space; Basel: Fondation Beyeler, 2009.

Raggio, Olga. "The Myth of Prometheus: Its Survival and Metamorphoses up to the Eighteenth Century." *Journal of the Warburg and Courtauld Institutes* 21, nos. 1–2 (January–June 1958), pp. 44–62, pls. 4–10.

Ray, Charles. *A four dimensional being writes poetry on a field with sculptures*. Exh. cat. New York: Matthew Marks Gallery; Göttingen: Steidl Publishers, 2006.

Reff, Theodore. *Degas: The Artist's Mind*. New York: The Metropolitan Museum of Art, 1976.

Reilly, Maura, et al. *Global Feminisms: New Directions in Contemporary Art*. Exh. cat. New York: Merrell; Brooklyn Museum, 2007.

Reynolds, Donald M. "The 'Unveiled Soul': Hiram Powers's Embodiment of the Ideal." *The Art Bulletin* 59, no. 3 (September 1977), pp. 394–414.

Reynolds, Joshua. *The Discourses of Sir Joshua Reynolds*, annot. John Burnet. London: James Carpenter, 1842.

Rilke, Rainer Maria. "Some Reflections on Dolls (Occasioned by the Wax Dolls of Lotte Pritzel)." In Rainer Maria Rilke, *Rodin and Other Prose Pieces*, trans. G[ertrude] Craig Houston, pp. 119–26. London: Quartet Books, 1986.

Rishel, Joseph J. *The Arts in Latin America, 1492–1820*. Exh. cat. Philadelphia: Philadelphia Museum of Art, 2006.

Riskin, Jessica. "The Defecating Duck, or, the Ambiguous Origins of Artificial Life." *Critical Inquiry* 29, no. 4 (Summer 2003), pp. 599–633.

Riva, Alessandro, et al. *Flesh & Wax: The Clemente Susini's Anatomical Models in the University of Cagliari*. Nuoro: Ilisso Edizioni, 2007.

Roller, Stefan, et al. *Die grosse Illusion: Veristische Skulpturen und ihre Techniken*. Exh. cat. Frankfurt: Liebieghaus Skulpturensammlung; Munich: Hirmer Verlag, 2014.

Romano, Giovanni, et al. *Maestri della scultura in legno nel Ducato degli Sforza*. Exh. cat. Milan: Silvana Editoriale, 2005.

Rosenthal, Norman. *Allen Jones: A Retrospective*. Exh. cat. New York: Michael Werner, 2016.

Rothkopf, Scott, et al. *Jeff Koons: A Retrospective*. Exh. cat. New York: Whitney Museum of American Art, 2014.

Rugoff, Ralph, et al. *The Human Factor: The Figure in Contemporary Sculpture*. Exh. cat. London: Hayward Gallery, 2014.

Rupprecht, Caroline. *Womb Fantasies: Subjective Architectures in Postmodern Literature, Cinema, and Art*. Evanston, Ill.: Northwestern University Press, 2013.

"Salon de 1808.—No. XVIII. Sculpture.—M. Canova." *Journal de l'Empire*, January 4, 1809, pp. 3–4.

Sanguineti, Daniele. *Anton Maria Maragliano, 1664–1739, "Insignis sculptor Genue."* Genoa: Sagep Editori, 2012.

———. *Scultura genovese in legno policromo dal secondo Cinquecento al Settecento*. Turin: Umberto Allemandi & Cie, 2013.

Satz, Aura, et al. *Articulate Objects: Voice, Sculpture and Performance*. Oxford: Peter Lang, 2009.

Saunders, Barbara, and Jaap van Brakel, eds. *Theories, Technologies, Instrumentalities of Color: Anthropological and Historiographic Perspectives*. Lanham, Md.: University Press of America, 2002.

Schapiro, Meyer. "From Mozarabic to Romanesque in Silos." *The Art Bulletin* 21, no. 4 (December 1939), pp. 312–74.

Schimmel, Paul, and Carla Schulz-Hoffmann. *Inbetween: Baselitz, McCarthy*. Exh. cat. Athens: The George Economou Collection, 2015.

Scholten, Frits. *The Image of a Sculptor: Johan Gregor van der Schardt, c. 1573*. Amsterdam: Rijksmuseum, 2015.

———. "Johan Gregor van der Schardt and the Moment of Self-Portraiture in Sculpture." *Simiolus: Netherlands Quarterly for the History of Art* 33, no. 4 (2007/2008), pp. 195–220.

Schuyler, Jane. "Death Masks in Quattrocento Florence." *Source: Notes in the History of Art* 5, no. 4 (Summer 1986), pp. 1–6.

———. *Florentine Busts: Sculpted Portraiture in the Fifteenth Century*. 1972. New York and London: Garland Publishing, 1976.

Schwartz, Hillel. *The Culture of the Copy: Striking Likenesses, Unreasonable Facsimiles*. Rev. ed. 1996. New York: Zone Books, 2014.

Schweizer, Nicole, et al. *Kader Attia*. Exh. cat. Lausanne: Musée Cantonal des Beaux-Arts: Zurich: JRP Ringier, 2015.

Shukla, Pravina. *Costume: Performing Identities through Dress*. Bloomington and Indianapolis: Indiana University Press, 2015.

Silver, Kenneth E., et al. *Chaos & Classicism: Art in France, Italy, and Germany, 1918–1936*. Exh. cat. New York: Guggenheim Museum, 2010.

Smith, Jeffrey Chipps. *German Sculpture of the Later Renaissance, c. 1520–1580: Art in an Age of Uncertainty*. Princeton, N.J.: Princeton University Press, 1994.

Smith, Marquard. *The Erotic Doll: A Modern Fetish*. New Haven, Conn.: Yale University Press, 2013.

Spector, Nancy. *Maurizio Cattelan: All*. Rev. ed. Exh. cat. 2011. New York: Guggenheim Museum Publications, 2016.

Spiazza, Anna Maria, et al. *Andrea Brustolon, 1662–1732: "Il Michelangelo del legno."* Exh. cat. Milan: Skira Editore, 2009.

Stewart, Susan. *On Longing: Narratives of the Miniature, the Gigantic, the Souvenir, the Collection*. Baltimore and London: Johns Hopkins University Press, 1984.

Stoichita, Victor I. *The Pygmalion Effect from Ovid to Hitchcock*. 2006. Chicago: The University of Chicago Press, 2008.

Stratton, Suzanne L., et al. *Spanish Polychrome Sculpture 1500–1800 in Unites States Collections*. Exh. cat. New York: The Spanish Institute, 1993.

Sturgis, Alexander. *Presence: The Art of Portrait Sculpture*. Exh. cat. Woodbridge, Suffolk: Antique Collectors' Club, 2012.

Sussman, Elisabeth, et al. *Paul Thek: Diver, A Retrospective*. Exh. cat. New York: Whitney Museum of American Art, 2010.

Taubert, Johannes, et al. *Polychrome Sculpture: Meaning, Form, Conservation*. Los Angeles: Getty Conservation Institute, 2015.

Taussig, Michael. *What Color Is the Sacred?* Chicago: The University of Chicago Press, 2009.

Taylor, Sue. "Hans Bellmer in The Art Institute of Chicago: The Wandering Libido and the Hysterical Body." In *The Art Institute of Chicago-Ryerson and Burnham Libraries*. Chicago: The Art Institute of Chicago, 2001); http://www.artic.edu/reynolds/essays/taylor.php.

Temkin, Ann, et al. *Robert Gober: The Heart Is Not a Metaphor*. Exh. cat. New York: The Museum of Modern Art, 2014.

Timpano, Nathan J. *Constructing the Viennese Modern Body: Art, Hysteria, and the Puppet*. Studies in Art Historiography. New York and London: Routledge; Taylor and Francis, 2017.

Tripps, Johannes. *Das Handelnde Bildwek in der Gotik: Forschungen zu den Bedeutungsschichten und der Funktion des Kirchengebäudes und seiner Ausstattung in der Hoch- und Spätgotik*. Berlin: Gebr. Mann Verlag, 1998.

Trusted, Marjorie. *Spanish Sculpture: Catalogue of the Post-Medieval Spanish Sculpture in Wood, Terracotta, Alabaster, Marble, Stone, Lead and Jet in the Victoria and Albert Museum*. London: Victoria and Albert Museum, 1996.

Tye, Michael. "On Some Alleged Problems for Objectivism about Color." In *Consciousness, Color, and Content*, by Michael Tye, pp. 145–70. Cambridge, Mass.: MIT Press, 2000.

Villiers de l'Isle-Adam, Auguste de. "The Future Eve [1886]," trans. Robert Martin Adams. In *The Decadent Reader: Fiction, Fantasy, and Perversion from Fin-de-siècle France*, ed. Asti Hustvedt, pp. 497–750. New York: Zone Books, 1998.

Vischer, Theodora, et al. *Robert Gober: Sculptures and Installations, 1979–2007*. Exh. cat. Basel: Schaulager Basel; Göttingen: Steidl, 2007.

Voskuhl, Adelheid. *Androids in the Enlightenment: Mechanics, Artisans, and Cultures of the Self*. Chicago: The University of Chicago Press, 2013.

Wagstaff, Sheena, et al. *Juan Muñoz: A Retrospective*. Exh. cat. London: Tate Publishing, 2008.

Wakeham, Pauline. *Taxidermic Signs: Reconstructing Aboriginality*. Minneapolis and London: University of Minnesota Press, 2008.

Wallace, Isabelle Loring, et al. *Contemporary Art and Classical Myth*. Farnham, Surrey: Ashgate Publishing, 2011.

Wardropper, Ian. *European Sculpture, 1400–1900, in The Metropolitan Museum of Art*. New York: The Metropolitan Museum of Art, 2011.

Warner, Marina. *Alone of All Her Sex: The Myth and the Cult of the Virgin Mary*. New York: Alfred A. Knopf, 1976.

———. "Incantesimi e legami." In *Il mondo magico: Padiglione Italia, Biennale Arte 2017*, ed. Cecilia Alemani, pp. 94–115. Exh. cat. Venice: Marsilio Editori, 2017.

———. *Monuments & Maidens: The Allegory of the Female Form*. London: Weidenfeld and Nicolson, 1985.

———. *Phantasmagoria: Spirit Visions, Metaphors, and Media into the Twenty-First Century*. Oxford and New York: Oxford University Press, 2006.

———. *Stranger Magic: Charmed States and the Arabian Nights*. Cambridge, Mass.: Belknap Press, Harvard University Press, 2011.

Warwick, Acacia Rachelle. "Prefabricated Desire: Surrealism, Mannequins, and the Fashioning of Modernity." Ph.D. diss., University of California, Los Angeles, 2006.

Webb, Peter, and Robert Short. *Hans Bellmer*. London: Quartet Books, 1985.

Webster, Susan Verdi. *Art and Ritual in Golden-Age Spain: Sevillian Confraternities and the Processional Sculpture of Holy Week*. Princeton, N.J.: Princeton University Press, 1998.

Weismann, Elizabeth Wilder. *Mexico in Sculpture, 1521–1821*. Cambridge, Mass.: Harvard University Press, 1950.

Westmacott, Richard. *On Colouring Statues: Some Observations on Ancient and Modern Polychromy in Sculpture*. London: The Archaeological Institute, 1859.

Wiethege, Katrin, et al. *Berlinde de Bruyckere: The Embalmer*. Exh. cat. Cologne: Buchhandlung Walther König, 2015.

Willis, Deborah, et al. *Black Venus 2010: They Called Her "Hottentot."* Philadelphia: Temple University Press, 2010.

Winckelmann, Johann Joachim. *History of the Art of Antiquity*. Trans. Harry Francis Mallgrave. Los Angeles: Getty Research Institute, 2006.

Winnicott, D. W. *Playing and Reality*. 1971. Hove: Brunner-Routledge, 2001.

Wissman, Fronia E. "Realists among the Impressionists." In *The New Painting: Impressionism 1874–1886*, by Charles S. Moffett et al., pp. 341, 342. Exh. cat. San Francisco: The Fine Arts Museums of San Francisco, 1986.

Wood, Jon, David Hulks, and Alex Potts, eds. *Modern Sculpture Reader*. Leeds: Henry Moore Institute, 2007.

Woodall, Joanna, ed. *Portraiture: Facing the Subject*. Manchester and New York: Manchester University Press, 1997.

Yoshimoto, Midori. *Into Performance: Japanese Women Artists in New York*. New Brunswick, N.J.: Rutgers University Press, 2005.

Zanardi, Tara. *Framing Majismo: Art and Royal Identity in Eighteenth-Century Spain*. University Park, Pa.: The Pennsylvania State University Press, 2016.

Zeitlin, Froma I. "Signifying Difference: The Case of Hesiod's Pandora." In *Playing the Other: Gender and Society in Classical Greek Literature*, by Froma I. Zeitlin, pp. 53–86. Chicago: The University of Chicago Press, 1996.

Ziegler, Joanna E. *Sculpture of Compassion: The Pietà and the Beguines in the Southern Low Countries, c. 1300–c. 1600*. Brussels: Brepols Publishers, 1992.

INDEX

Page references to illustrations are in *italics*.

A

Acquate, Paolo di, 22
Adam and Eve, 42, 43, *43*
Adam and Eve in Paradise, Adam on a Dragon, Eve on a Peacock, *43*
Africa
  clothing, 190, 192
  culture, 70, 195
  ethnographic sculptures, 103
  Nkisi power figures, 69, *69*, 195, 256
  sculptors, 11, 192
  see also colonialism
African Americans
  female bodies, 255–56
  female identity, 195
  invisibility, 71–72
  lynchings, 70, 195, 256
  women, 195, 255
Africans, *see* blackamoor images
Agamben, Giorgio, 54
Ahearn, John, 11, 106–7, *106*, 277n47
  Bernice (cat. 28), 57, 106, *124*, 282
Alberti, Nero (Romano Alberti), *Saint Roch* (cat. 70), *187*, 190–91, *198*, 285
anatomical models
  colors, 65
  female bodies, 30, 213–14, 255
  makers, 52, 101
  museums, 30, 34
  wax, 29–30, 52–53, 65, 101, 213–14, 255
Anatomical Venuses, 30, 52, 65, 101, 213–14, *219*, 255, *264–65*
Andras, Catherine, 28
androids, 64, 141, 169
Anisfeld, Boris, 103
anthropology, 34–35, 45
Antoni, Janine, *Saddle* (cat. 104), 194, *246*, 288
Arabian Nights, 43, 47
Aramesh, Reza, 138
  Action 105 (cat. 45), *99*, 138, *139*, *153*, 284
Arce, Raúl, 107
Arezzo, Italy, Joust of the Saracen, 163, *163*
Athena, 6, 35, 42, 44, 45, 136
Attia, Kader, *Open Your Eyes* (cat. 101), *242–43*, 287
Austen, Jane, *Northanger Abbey*, 52–53
automata, 32–33, 41, 140–41, 165, 169

B

Baldinucci, Filippo, 28
Baraton, Martin, 27–28
Bartlett, Morton, 56
Bartolo, Giovanni di, circle of, *Reliquary Bust of Saint Juliana* (cat. 20), 5, 64, 104, *114*, 282
Baudelaire, Charles, 55, 57
Beguines, 21
Bellmer, Hans, 36, 63, 165
  La Demi-Poupée (cat. 62), 5, 55, 165, *180*, 285
  La Poupée (cat. 63), 5, 55, *181*, 285
  La Poupée (cat. 64), 5, 55, *181*, 285
Benedict IV, Pope, 28
Benintendi, Filippo, 26
Benintendi, Orsino, 26, 28
Benoist, Antoine, 27–28
  Louis XIV, 27, *27*
Benson, Frank, *Human Statue* (cat. 9), 81, *92*, 281
Bentham, Jeremy, 51, 105, *116–17*, 277n39
Bergamo, Cappella Colleoni, 22

Bernard of Clairvaux, 213
Bernini, Gian Lorenzo, 213
Berruguete, Alonso, *Saint Sebastian* (cat. 44), 22, *135*, 137, 138, *152*, 284
Bible, 42, 43
Bihéron, Marie Marguerite, 28
blackamoor images, 31, *31*, 32, 33, 72
Blade Runner, 141
Blanc, Charles, 58
Bocchi, Francesco, 29
body parts
  ex-votos, 29, 215, *222*
  relics of saints, 20, *53*, 54, 64, 65, *114*, 215
  see also anatomical models; human body; reliquaries
Bologna
  anatomical model makers, 101
  mummified effigy of Saint Catherine of Bologna, Church of Corpus Domini, 53, *53*
Bontempi, Gabriella, 104
Borghini, Vincenzo, 16
Boswell, James, 29
Bourdelle, Antoine-Emile, *Irene Millett*, 104, *104*
Bourdin, Michel, 29
Bourgeois, Louise, 55
  Three Horizontals (cat. 109), *251*, 288
Bowie, David, 73
Breton, André, 9, 54
Briggs, James B., 101–2, 276n17
Britain
  anatomical wax models, 30
  automata, 32
  Catholic religious sculpture, 26
  lead garden sculpture, 33
  porcelain figurines, 31–32, 73
  waxworks, 26, 27, 28–29, 52
  see also London
British East India Company, 101, 102, 276n15
Bronx, New York, portrait sculptures, 106–7, *106*
Brustolon, Andrea
  furniture carvings, 31
  Pedestal with figure of an "Ethiopian," *31*
Buddha, 256
Burckhardt, Jacob, *The Civilization of the Renaissance in Italy*, 3
Bustelli, Franz Anton, 31

C

Caglioti, Francesco, 16
Callias, Hector de, 35
Calyx Krater Featuring the Creation of Pandora, *44*
Canova, Antonio
  Creugas (cat. 11), *79*, 94, 281
  Hebe, 79, *79*
  Ideal Head (Erato?), *76*
Caraccioli, Louis-Antoine de, *Dictionnaire critique*, 79
Carlo, King of Naples, 34
Carobbi, Giuseppe, 30
Caterina de Julianis, 28
Catholic Church
  altarpieces, 22
  in Britain, 26
  Council of Trent, 23, 24
  Counter-Reformation, 22–23
  processions, 23–24, 25, 45, 162–63
  reliquaries, 20, 39, *53*, 64, *64*, 104, *114*, 215
  Synod of Saint Wenceslas, 22
  see also Christian church; saints

Cattelan, Maurizio
  Daddy, Daddy, 14–15, *15*
  hyperrealism, 100, 137
  Now (cat. 112), 64, 137, 257, *261*, 288
  Untitled, 41, *41*
Cellini, Benvenuto, 45, 77
ceramics, *see* porcelain
Cézanne, Paul, 106
Cháez, Juan, *Bullfighter* and *Costillares* (cat. 74), 191, *202*, 285–86
Chakrabarty, Dipesh, 7
Champfleury, 30–31
Chaouli, Michael, 188
Chapman brothers, 38, 55
Charles I, King of England, 26
Charles IV, King of Spain, 191
Chasseguet-Smirgel, Janine, 18
Cheere, John, 33
Chelsea Porcelain Manufactory, *The Music Lesson*, 73, *73*
The Child Jesus Triumphant (cat. 72), 190–91, *190*, *200*, 285
Christ figures
  crucifixes, 5, 21, 22, 25, 52, 138, 162–63, 212
  dead, 256–57
  depictions of flesh, 212–13
  emotional reactions, 18, 20–21, 25
  infants (*Niños*), 190–91
  with movable arms, 162–63
  openings, 213
  realism, 18, 137, 212
  worship of, 22, 52
Christian church
  imitatio Christi, 21
  incarnation doctrine, 212, 213
  view of sculpture, 23, 136
  see also Catholic Church; Protestant churches
Christine of Lorraine, 28
Cicero, 100
classicism, 3, 9, 78
  see also Neoclassicism
clothing
  African, 190, 192
  of bullfighters, 191–92
  colors, 61
  costumes, 192, 279n9
  fashion, 61
  functions, 188
  identity construction and, 5, 190, 191–92
  of mannequins, 5, 192
  on religious sculpture, 24, 34, 51, 191
  social status and, 11
  on wax sculptures, 27, 189
  of women, 11, 193
color
  perception of, 59, 60, 77–78
  significance, 58, 59, 64
  synthetic pigments, 61
  in Western art, 58–59, 61
  see also polychrome sculpture
Congreve, William, 27
Connor, Janis, 104
Cordier, Charles-Henri-Joseph, 34–35, 103, 277n25
  La Capresse des Colonies (cat. 33), 5, 34, 48, 103, *129*, 283
  The Jewish Woman of Algiers (cat. 30), 5, 34,